Clockwise beginning below:

- *Mata Hari*
- *Nuclear Bomb Testing*
- *Martin Luther King, Jr.*
- *Charles and Diana*
- Challenger *Explosion*
- *Vietnam Veterans Memorial*
- *Integrated Circuit*
- *Americans in Vietnam*
- *Winston Churchill*

Primary illustrations sources
for this volume:

Archive Photos
Corbis
FPG International
Hulton Getty/Tony Stone Images
The Gamma Liaison Network

National Geographic Society
Washington, D.C.

National Geographic
Eyewitness to the
'20th Century

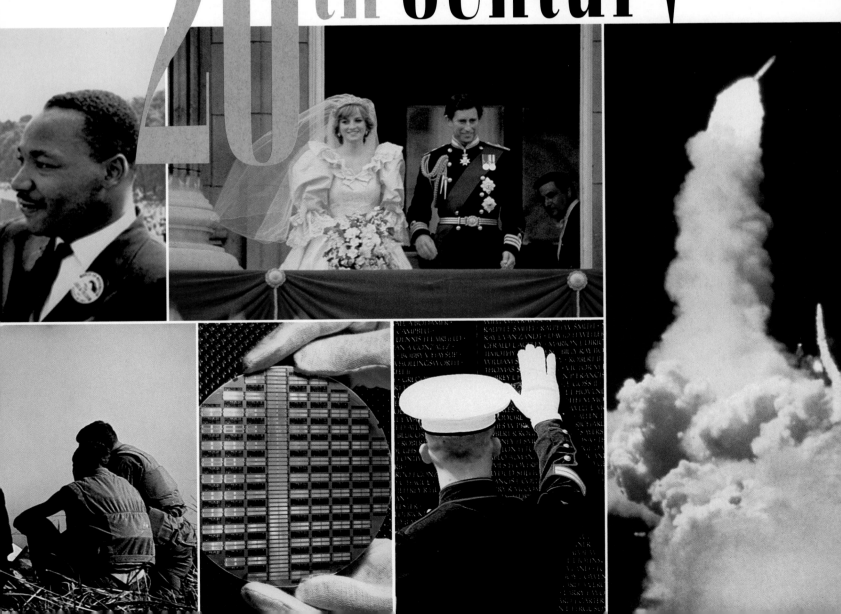

Contents

INTRODUCING THE CENTURY

As I look back over the ten long decades of the 20th century—decades that nearly parallel the existence of the National Geographic Society, which was founded in 1888—I think of something my great-grandfather, Alexander Graham Bell, said at the beginning of the century, when he was President of the Society. In setting the course for the then fledgling organization, Bell was expansive; the purview of the Society, he declared, should be "the world and all that is in it."

Indeed, the history of the 20th century is firmly entwined with that of the Society; we have reported on the world to our millions upon millions of members, bringing incredible visual images, interpretive text, and distinctive cartography directly into their homes. Our portfolio has been broad: Geography, of course, is the critical foundation of virtually every science, and it underpins much of human activity—travel, exploration, the search for food and natural resources.

The Society, though, has not just reported; we have explored and pioneered. In the early years of the century, we sponsored Adm. Robert E. Peary in his quest to reach the North Pole; Hiram Bingham in his discovery of the lost Inca city of Machu Picchu in Peru; William Beebe in his probing of the ocean depths in a fragile bathysphere. Later, we worked with Louis Leakey and his incredible family in pioneering research into mankind's earliest ancestors; with Jane Goodall, Dian Fossey, and Birute Galdikas in their definitive studies of primates; and with Jacques-Yves Cousteau as he began—unfettered by heavy equipment—to explore the underwater realm. Today is no different—explorer Will Steger mounts expeditions to both Poles; Paul Sereno unearths startling new dinosaur finds; Lee Berger pushes back the fossil record of early man even further with his discoveries in South Africa; Bob Ballard finds the *Titanic*—and startling new realms of life at the bottom of the ocean.

We have covered in-depth such monumental efforts as the space program, the development of nuclear energy, the expansion of the national park system, and the impact of the automobile on our lives. We have closely tracked the growth—and eventual collapse—of the

Soviet Union and the rebirth of a new Russia, and we have reported on the emergence of new nations in Africa and Asia; our maps even served Franklin D. Roosevelt, Winston Churchill, and Gen. Dwight D. Eisenhower during World War II—and the military leaders of Desert Storm earlier in this decade.

What strikes me most as I look at the 20th century through the special lens of the National Geographic Society is the continuity of coverage over time of key Society subjects—archaeology; exploration of land, sea, and space; animal studies; the environment; paleontology; history; cultures; and others—in all our media: magazines, books, television, electronic. By far, the foremost among these key subjects is our coverage of changing planet Earth. We have documented powerful volcanoes, destructive hurricanes, rampaging floods—and explained the science behind plate tectonics and weather phenomena. Our first issue of NATIONAL GEOGRAPHIC magazine, in fact, carried a story examining the effects of a devastating storm that decimated the eastern United States. But more, we have taken an activist role in presenting and discussing such environmental issues as acid rain, declining water quality, desertification, and the depletion of natural resources. In our position as an educational organization we believe we must provide objective, broad-based information that will help assure the responsible stewardship of our planet at the international level.

In the pages of this book, you will find all this and more—a vivid and living record of the 20th century that explores both the monumental events of history and the more subtle happenings and trends that have affected our daily lives. Through remarkable photographs and compelling text, you learn about the forces that have touched us all—and helped formulate the lives we now lead.

I am proud of the important role the National Geographic Society has played in bringing the story of this century to our readers and in summarizing it so well in the pages of this book; clearly, the focus of presenting "the world and everything that is in it" will not waver as we enter a new millennium.

Gilbert M. Grosvenor
Chairman, Board of Trustees
National Geographic Society

1900-

The Age of Big Business

by Robert D. Johnston
ASSISTANT PROFESSOR OF HISTORY, YALE UNIVERSITY

HAVING SURVIVED THE MANY HARDSHIPS of the 19th century—including a
wrenching Civil War at mid-century and, in the last decade, economic
depression and labor unrest in both city and countryside—Americans breathed
a sigh of relief in the new century. For the most part, the first 10 years of the
20th century were a time of prosperity. The Cake Walk was the fashionable
dance, prepared foods such as dressed beef and tinned ham were making their
appearance in markets, and, three years into the new century, Henry Ford
founded the Ford Motor Company. As the decade progressed, the automobile
began to reach a mass audience, as did electricity, radio, and the telephone—
all of them inventions and discoveries that would simultaneously shrink
distance and transform society. Yet even as the American people gazed in
wonder at the various technological achievements they associated with the
rise of Big Business, they found themselves uneasy at what scholar Alan
Trachtenberg has characterized as the rapid "Incorporation of America."

Indeed, the ascendancy of large corporations to economic, political, and
even cultural dominance would be one of the defining themes of the century
itself. Corporations were vigorously swallowing up not only their smaller
competitors but each other as well. Between 1897 and 1904, the so-called

*Opposite: Theodore Roosevelt was an energetic President who led the charge for changes in the American way of life.
Preceding pages: The invention of the airplane in 1903 got the 20th century off to a flying start.*

Great Merger Movement created companies of almost undreamed of size and scale. In the early 1890s, for example, it was rare for a corporation to be worth more than ten million dollars. A decade later, almost 200 corporations were capitalized at that value. The top one percent of companies employed more than a quarter of all workers in the country. If Americans hadn't known it before, they knew it now: This was the age of Big Business.

Perhaps not surprisingly, the symbol of power for the age was not an industrialist, but the financier J. P. Morgan. Huge financial resources were needed to fund huge companies, and often those in charge of the banks became rulers over the new empires. Morgan had twice been instrumental in national efforts to recover from or avert financial panics, first in 1893 and again in 1907. Moreover, "the House of Morgan," as the banking firm of J. P. Morgan and Company was known, played a crucial role in the reorganization of the nation's railroads. Morgan himself became the effective head of the most gargantuan of the new "trusts"—U.S. Steel Corporation, which controlled more than 60 percent of all American production of that critical metal.

The Jungle's *descriptions of the meat industry spurred enactment of food inspection laws.*

Faced with this concentration of power, Americans grew increasingly ambivalent about the cost of the prosperity and efficiency that big corporations promised. Often suspicious of "Wall Street," many ordinary citizens feared that the new corporate structure rested on a system of manipulated financial transactions whose bubble would surely burst. Would the so-called trusts, such as those organized by Morgan specifically to limit if not stamp out competition among railroads, spell the demise of the common dream of owning one's own business? Could consumers be confident that national conglomerates, operating without effective local oversight, would offer fair prices and safe products? And finally, what about the workers employed by these huge corporations? Was wage labor on such a massive scale truly compatible with American institutions? A number of early 20th-century reformers were horrified at the conditions workers endured. Hazen Pingree, powerful reform mayor of Detroit and a former businessman, spoke for many when he said that the employees of great corporations "become a part of a vast industrial army. Their personal identity is lost.... There is no real advance for them. They may perhaps become larger cogs or larger wheels in the great complicated machine, but they can never look forward to a life of business freedom."

One person who undertook the workers' cause during this period was the relatively unknown 26-year-old writer Upton Sinclair. In 1904 Sinclair arrived in Chicago with a simple goal: "I have come to write the *Uncle Tom's Cabin* of the labor movement." His novel, *The Jungle,* became one of the landmarks of 20th-century American social criticism. First published in serial form in 1905 by the socialist newspaper *Appeal to Reason,* the 1906 book was read by millions and eventually translated into 17 languages. It was a peculiar work to gain mass attention, however, for readers overwhelmingly considered *The Jungle* a disgusting tale. Yet the story, as well as the reactions to it, reveal much about the issues Americans wrestled with during a period of tremendous change.

Sinclair's novel tells the story of Jurgis Rudkus, a Lithuanian immigrant who comes to the New World full of hope, wanting only a job to support his family and prove his manhood. Yet Jurgis finds little of the American Dream. Instead, while working in one of Chicago's many meatpacking houses, he goes from one tragedy to another. He is injured on the job and is thrown out of work. He becomes a drunk, and his wife Ona is forced to become her boss's mistress. Ona dies in childbirth, and their baby son then drowns. Jurgis becomes a tramp and a criminal, and his dear cousin Marija becomes a prostitute. Such were the lives, according to Sinclair, of the "wage slaves of the Beef Trust"—the great group of companies such as Armour and Swift that dominated meatpacking.

Having dedicated the book "To the Workingmen of America," Sinclair hoped that his readers would all become ardent socialists, as did Jurgis by the end of the novel. Instead, Americans reacted most strongly—and with nausea—to Sinclair's relatively brief descriptions of rats being swept up into sausage; tubercular pork making its way past the bribed eyes of government inspectors; and workers slipping and falling into great scalding vats, their remains becoming part of "Durham's Pure Leaf Lard." As one of the characters jokes early in the novel, "They use everything about the hog except the squeal." After learning the many ways that rotten, poisoned meat made its way into Packingtown's products—and from there, into neighborhood stores—Sinclair's readers were not laughing.

Popular disgust and outrage fueled a renewed push for governmental regulation not only of meat processing but of food production generally, something reformers had long been advocating, to little avail—until President Theodore Roosevelt read *The Jungle*. Although put off by Sinclair's political radicalism, Roosevelt was incensed by the book's revelations, as summed up by a popular fictional political commentator, "Mr. Dooley": "Tiddy was toyin' with a light breakfast an' idly turnin' over th' pages iv th' new book with both hands. Suddenly he rose fr'm th' table, and cryin': 'I'm pizened,' began throwin' sausages out iv th' window... Since thin th' Prisidint, like th' rest iv us, has become a viggytaryan."

Roosevelt threw himself into the reform cause, sending investigators to Chicago's stockyards. Their report, although written by bureaucrats, was as sickening as Sinclair's novel. Not long thereafter, Roosevelt signed into law the Pure Food and Drug Act and the Meat Inspection Act, which forbade the sale of adulterated and mislabeled food either at home or abroad and also mandated the federal inspection and grading of meat. Although the public benefited from these much needed reforms, Sinclair himself bitterly regretted that his book had led only to a healthier sausage link and not to the glorious proletarian revolution. "I aimed at the public's heart," Sinclair famously observed, "and by accident I hit it in the stomach."

As his reaction to *The Jungle* suggests, one who would feature prominently in the country's love-hate relationship with Big Business was Theodore Roosevelt. Although he became President by accident, taking over as chief executive when anarchist Leon Czolgosz assassinated President William McKinley in September 1901, TR would prove to be the defining political figure of the decade.

Roosevelt's own ambivalence toward Big Business could not necessarily have been forecast from his social background. Like his much younger cousin Franklin Delano Roosevelt, TR belonged to the nearest thing the United States had to an aristocracy. Descended from some of New York's earliest Dutch settlers, TR was born in 1858. He traveled extensively in Europe and Africa and had the finest of private tutors before enrolling at Harvard. Although physically weak and often in poor health as a youth, he cultivated his body and mind through vigorous exercise and a belief in the virtues of the rugged outdoors. In the first McKinley administration, Roosevelt was Secretary of the Navy. While in office he volunteered to fight in the Spanish-American War, raising a regiment that mixed Ivy Leaguers and cowboys, with whom he had become acquainted during a stint ranching in the Dakota Badlands. The charge of the "Rough Riders" up San Juan Hill turned Roosevelt into an instant national hero, directly leading to his election to the New York governorship and then to his nomination as Vice President in 1900.

Upon assuming the Presidency, Roosevelt the activist used his "bully pulpit" to help guide the country though a decade of change. Although he continued, and took credit for, many of McKinley's policies, Roosevelt was the first President to deliberately move away from a doctrine of laissez-faire (minimal government involvement in the economy). Instead, he insisted that government had a critical role to play if the United States was to maintain its democratic institutions in the face of the burgeoning influence of Big Business. In his inaugural address, for example, he used language that would be quite rare in political debates nearly a century later. "The great corporations which we have grown to speak of rather loosely as trusts," he declared, "are creatures of the State, and the State not only has the right to control them, but it is in duty bound to control them wherever the need of such control is shown."

Roosevelt was not in principle antibusiness, or even antitrust. He believed that the consolidation and centralization of the economy would provide cheaper and more abundant goods. However, he was convinced that he could distinguish between "good trusts" and "bad trusts," depending on their moral behavior. TR thus gained a somewhat undeserved reputation as a "trust buster." Early in his Presidency, he ordered the Justice Department to use the Sherman Antitrust Act to dissolve the Northern Securities Company, a gigantic railroad holding company. To the surprise of many, the Supreme Court upheld the government. Except for a 1902 action against the beef trust, however, Roosevelt did not order any further antitrust prosecutions until his second term, and even then he assured citizens that he did not support the more radical antimonopoly policies of figures such as the popular Wisconsin Senator "Fighting Bob" LaFollette. Only later, in the dramatic campaign of 1912—where he ran, and lost, as the Progressive Party candidate against three others: William Howard Taft, the incumbent and Roosevelt's handpicked successor; Democrat Woodrow Wilson; and Socialist Eugene V. Debs—did Roosevelt move significantly away from the moderate centrism he espoused during his political prime from 1901 to 1909.

A curious combination of aristocratic elegance and quasi-populist rough-and-tumble, Theodore Roosevelt is an intriguing historical figure. On the one hand, he has retained his place in the popular memory as one of our most revered Presidents. One historian has written that "no chief executive has better caught, exemplified, and gloried in the spirit of modern America than Theodore Roosevelt." In 1979 *Time* magazine declared that Roosevelt simply "was America." At the same time, his reputation among scholars has generally fallen in recent decades. Much of this decline comes as historians reexamine his ideology in light of more critical views on issues crucial to our own times.

Most significantly, it is hard to deny that Theodore Roosevelt was a confirmed racist who used his belief in the inferiority of nonwhites to support American imperial intervention abroad. For example, he believed that Negroes were the most primitive of human groups—in his words, "a perfectly stupid race." He also supported restrictions on Japanese immigration, fearing that an unfettered influx would lead to "race suicide," with whites being overrun, first numerically by a high Japanese birthrate and then by political and cultural conquest. Indeed, Roosevelt considered "race suicide" and "the conflict between race and race" to be "infinitely more important than any other question in this country." It was in that spirit that he called on his fellow white Americans to "gird up our loins as a nation, with the stern purpose to play our part manfully in winning the ultimate triumph" abroad as well as at home.

In the early 1900s, many American businesses thrived by employing child laborers. States began regulating this practice in 1903.

It was no accident that the Spanish-American War (more accurately, the Spanish-Filipino-Cuban-Puerto Rican-American War) played such a critical role in vaulting both Roosevelt and the United States to world power. Although the country had a vigorous anti-imperialist movement, most Americans considered the military action in 1898, by which the United States annexed the Philippines and Puerto Rico and formally liberated Cuba from Spanish rule, to be a "splendid little war."

The costs of the new empire were enormous, however. In the short-term, the revolt of Filipinos against the United States from 1899 to 1913 ultimately would lead to 4,200 American and 200,000 Filipino deaths. In the long run, Cuban governments would rarely adhere to American visions of proper behavior when left to their own devices.

Faced with strong anticolonial resistance in countries where the United States was trying to catch up with Europe in the imperial game, Roosevelt foreswore formal territorial expansion. Nonetheless, he made it clear that he would back up United States interests with force whenever he deemed it useful.

The most spectacular example of this style of gunboat diplomacy came with the creation of the Panama Canal. Americans on either coast had long dreamed of a Central American shortcut from the Atlantic to the Pacific that would eliminate the long trip around the tip of South America. In 1901 Britain, the strongest European power in the region, agreed to let the United States construct and fortify such a canal on its own. Deciding where to locate it was problematic, however. When a volcanic eruption took Nicaragua out of the running, Panama became the likeliest site, in large part as a result of effective lobbying by a group with special interests in the area. However, Panama was a province of Colombia, which was in no mood to let the United States dictate terms. When Roosevelt made it known that he would not be displeased if Panama staged a revolution—after all, nationalist movements had been active there since the 1880s—the Panamanians declared their independence in November 1903. As U.S. warships protected the rebels, the Roosevelt administration quickly recognized the new government. Panama and the U.S. soon thereafter signed a treaty that gave Panama 10 million dollars plus 250 thousand dollars annually in exchange for a ten-mile-wide canal zone that split the new nation in two and that would effectively become U.S. territory. Despite opposition from the *New York Times* and other major newspapers, most Americans were pleased at the acquisition, marveling as the canal became the largest construction project ever. Begun in 1904, it took a decade to complete. But when it finally opened in 1914, the distance between New York City and San Francisco was cut by nearly two-thirds, from 13,615 miles to 5,300.

TR's actions in Panama were part of what has been called the "Roosevelt Corollary" to the Monroe Doctrine, formulated 80 years earlier. The United States under the Monroe Doctrine had long warned European powers to stay out of the affairs of Latin America. Teddy Roosevelt insisted that it was the right of the United States to intervene in any country in the Western Hemisphere that was not meeting its obligations to Americans or to other foreigners. In practice, this self-proclaimed "right" meant that, for reasons ranging from collection of debts to fighting revolutions, U.S. troops would invade Latin American countries 20 times between 1898 and 1920. Thus, the 20th century opened with a President whose policies would set the tone for U.S.-Latin American relations for the next 80 years, through the end of the Cold War.

Perhaps the greatest irony of Theodore Roosevelt's brand of diplomacy is that so much of the imperial expansion he sanctioned was, in the end, performed not for the glory of the country or even for racial supremacy, but rather in the interest of opening up global markets. In this, the concerns and workings of Big Business not only dominated the early decades of the century but also foreshadowed the globalization that would characterize the century's end. ∎

Linking the Pacific and Atlantic Oceans, the Panama Canal was one of the century's most ambitious engineering projects.

NATIONAL GEOGRAPHIC

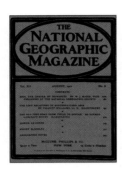

With the turn of the century, NATIONAL GEOGRAPHIC was 12 years old but still finding its way. It began to find its own distinctive voice with the arrival of Gilbert H. Grosvenor, who was hired as assistant editor in 1899. Looking for ways to increase the circulation—and therefore the revenue—of the magazine, he pored over geography-rich books like Charles Darwin's *Voyage of the Beagle* and Richard Henry Dana, Jr.'s *Two Years Before the Mast.* Grosvenor realized that the appeal of these books lay in the fact that "each was an accurate, eyewitness, firsthand account. Each contained simple, straightforward writing—writing that sought to make pictures in the reader's mind." This became the model for GEOGRAPHIC articles.

From the Atlantic to the Pacific

"A canal connecting the Atlantic and Pacific Oceans has occupied public attention for upward of four centuries.... It was not until the nineteenth century, however, that any definite action was taken looking toward its accomplishment." So wrote Lt.

INDIAN DUGOUTS CARRY BANANAS, THE CHIEF EXPORT OF PANAMA, TO GATUN

Col. George Goethals to President William Howard Taft, as reported by NATIONAL GEOGRAPHIC in 1909. As chief engineer of the Panama Canal project, Goethals knew all too well the political and logistical nightmares that befell earlier attempts.

Frenchman Ferdinand de Lesseps, builder of the Suez Canal, made the first serious attempt in 1878. But he found it impossible to build the sea-level canal he had planned. Furthermore, he lost some 20,000 men to malaria and yellow fever before giving up 11 years later. The United States bought the concession from its French owners, and promptly found itself unable to forge a treaty for the canal zone with Colombia—of which Panama was then a part. The stalemate broke in 1903 when the Panamanians revolted; Roosevelt immediately recognized the new government, placed the U.S. Navy between it and Colombia, and struck a deal that gave America the canal zone in perpetuity. Construction began in 1904, and for the next ten years as many as 40,000 workers—eventually relieved of the threat of disease by the Army Medical Corps—labored to dig the trench and locks for the 51-mile-long canal.

The Boxers

In July 1900, NATIONAL GEOGRAPHIC readers learned of the Boxer Rebellion in China shortly after it erupted, in "The Chinese Boxers" by Llewellyn James Davies. Davies had followed the Boxer movement for years and offered the following description of their spread:

"Whatever may have been its past history, the society has now collected its forces against the foreigners within the Chinese Empire. It has been preparing for this present outbreak for several years.... Its anti-foreign purpose was known distinctly at that time [three and a half years before]. It was said to be spreading from the south toward the north.... Chinese Christians were told, 'Well, you will soon have a chance to enjoy the heaven of which you talk,' and 'Soon, soon; your time is coming soon.' Shortly before the outbreak it was frequently and plainly said that at no very distant date all foreigners and foreign sympathizers would be killed."

The goal of the Boxers was summed up in their motto: "Death and destruction to the foreigner and all his works." In the province of Manchuria, this meant disrupting construction of Russia's Trans-Siberian Railway, which was taking a shortcut through Chinese soil. Farther south, the residence of the British minister was burned down. Among the besieged was 25-year-old mining consultant Herbert Hoover, who, with his wife and 200 foreigners, held out in the city of Tientsin for a month.

The San Francisco Earthquake

Though the Richter scale was not invented until 1935, seismologists estimate that the earthquake that struck San Francisco in the predawn hours of April 18, 1906, would have measured about an 8.3—making it much stronger than the one that would rock the city in 1989. As reported in the May 1906 issue, initially only the brick and stone structures collapsed, with the more flexible wooden structures holding. But then fires broke out, and the wooden architecture provided kindling for a blaze that lasted three days. By the time the last flames were doused, 514 city blocks burned to the ground, and over 28,000 buildings were destroyed. About 2,500 people were killed, and 300,000—roughly two-thirds of the population—were homeless.

After only nine years, San Francisco had recovered so

completely that it hosted the 1915 Panama-Pacific International Exposition. To create new space for the Exposition, engineers extended the city's marina by filling in part of San Francisco Bay with rubble from the quake. When the 1989 earthquake hit, older buildings in the marina district crumbled under the unstable landfill, causing history to repeat itself as a raging fire damaged the area.

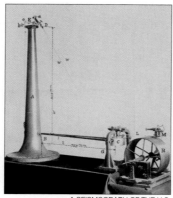

A SEISMOGRAPH OF THE U.S. WEATHER BUREAU

The Dawn of Species Conservation

"The fact that the wild animals of the world are in danger of extermination is being forcibly driven home to the minds of all who are interested in natural history," wrote NATIONAL GEOGRAPHIC in 1900. "This condition is the result of the ruthless persistence with which game of every kind is hunted, and it may be laid at the door mainly of the rapacious gatherers of hides and ivory." Though the author was referring to Africa—"the largest game preserve in the world"—it was becoming clear all around the globe that many species of animals were in danger. In 1900 America passed its first endangered species legislation, the Lacey Act, which made it illegal to move unlawfully killed wildlife across state lines. Other domestic and international legislation followed, culminating 69 years later with the passage of the Endangered Species Conservation Act and ratification of the Convention on International Trade in Endangered Species in 1973.

Fire, Brimstone, and Snakes in Paradise

"Not in history has such a favorable opportunity occurred for an investigation of the causes of volcanic and seismic action," noted the GEOGRAPHIC, which sent an expedition to the Caribbean island of Martinique in 1902. On May 8 of that year, Mount Pelée erupted for just the third time in recorded history, killing some 36,000 people. Most were burned to death by blasts of 1,500°F steam and volcanic ash; others fell to sulfurous lava. Another 50 had been killed a few days earlier by an invasion of 6-foot-long fer-de-lance snakes, which were driven from the mountainside by pre-eruption conditions. There were only three known survivors in the town of Saint Pierre, one of whom was a prisoner protected by the thick walls of his underground jail cell. Those "hidden forces...smothered in the bowels of the earth," as the article described them, would reappear more than 90 years later, as a series of eruptions on nearby Montserrat forced the evacuation of nearly the entire island.

Reaching the Pole

Few stories have captivated NATIONAL GEOGRAPHIC readers as did the tale of Robert E. Peary's assault on the North Pole. After three failed attempts, the 52-year-old naval commander finally reached 90 degrees north on April 6, 1909. "The pole at last!!!" he wrote in his journal that day. "The prize of three centuries. My dream and goal for 20 years! Mine at last. I cannot bring myself to realize it." A sponsor of Peary's expeditions, the National Geographic Society published his account in the magazine in 1909, along with that of Dr. Frederick Cook, who claimed to have reached the Pole the previous year.

Cook's claim was quickly dismissed and Peary was hailed as conqueror of the North, earning the thanks of Congress and a promotion to rear admiral. But in 1988 a new study of his records, which had been kept under seal at the National Archives, found that Peary may have miscalculated. The results of the study, published by the Society in 1988, indicate that Peary may have missed the mark by up to 60 miles; he may not have compensated for the drifting of polar ice, and his chronometer, crucial for navigation, was ten minutes fast. Also troubling was Peary's journal. There were no entries for April 7 and 9, and his jubilant April 6 entry was written not in the journal itself but on a loose sheet

ROBERT EDWIN PEARY

of paper. These mysteries notwithstanding, yet another review in 1990 offered vindication. An analysis of the shadows in expedition photographs helped triangulate the explorer's position at various places along the route, showing that Peary reached the Pole "within the limits of his instruments," which were about five miles.

Coming to America

"The subject of our immigration is perhaps the most discussed and least understood public question now before the people." So began an address to the Society by former Assistant Commissioner of Immigration Z. F. McSweeny, the text of which appeared in the January 1905 issue of the magazine. "On one side we find a portion of our citizens claiming that all kinds of economic and social evils are to be attributed to immigration. The supporters of the other side are equally positive that the nation's growth and progress are due to these alien races.... On one thing both will agree, that for the poor of Europe, America spells 'opportunity.' " Though McSweeny shared the notion, common to the day, that many of the immigrants were incapable of assimilating, his opinion of immigration was clearly positive. "There is only one Ellis Island in the world; no other country has its mate, because none offers the inducements to the poor of the world that we do. Let us thank God that this is so and pray that we may be able to keep it so.... "

A later issue published some statistics on the newcomers in 1905, the first year in which total immigration topped one million people. That year there were more than 221,000 new arrivals from Italy. In second place was Russia, with nearly 170,000, followed by Hungary with 163,000 and Great Britain with 134,000. In all, nearly 975,000 immigrants came from Europe, with most of the rest coming from Asia.

The Remarkable Dr. Bell

The Wright brothers were not the only Americans trying to solve the riddle of flight in the early 20th century. Among the competition was Alexander Graham Bell, educator of the deaf, inventor of the telephone, and second president of the National Geographic Society. Following the example of the Wrights, who began their work by studying gliders, Bell experimented with kites. From his summer home in Nova Scotia, Bell flew massive kites of various shapes—among them boxes, tetrahedrons, and stacked rings—to test their lift and strength. He even built kites capable of carrying a man aloft.

KITE "SIAMESE TWINS," SEEN FROM THE REAR, LOOKING INSIDE KITE

Given the years of work Bell put into his kite studies, he was understandably dismayed when observers dismissed his creations as mere toys. "The word 'kite,' " he wrote in the January 1907 issue, "unfortunately is suggestive to most minds of a toy—just as the telephone at first was thought to be a toy; so that the word does not at all adequately express the nature of the enormous flying structures employed in some of my experiments. These structures were really aërial vehicles rather than kites, for they were capable of lifting men and heavy weights into the air... They could not be held...in a heavy breeze, but had to be anchored to the ground by several turns of the ropes around stout cleats, like those employed on steamships and men-of-war." Over the course of Bell's career, NATIONAL GEOGRAPHIC would publish a number of stories on the gifted inventor. Yet for all his research, the inventor of the telephone took the greatest joy in his original profession: a teacher of the deaf.

Photographing Wildlife

Former U.S. Congressman George Shiras III had been an avid hunter, but eventually he decided to trade his rifle for a camera. Starting in 1906, the GEOGRAPHIC published a series of picture essays by Shiras that displayed his ingenious techniques for photographing wildlife. Realizing the futility of trying to sneak up on creatures, he hid cameras in the woods with trip wires strung around them; when an animal tripped the wire, it snapped its own picture. For taking photos at night, Shiras equipped his cameras with powerful flashes.

Though the publication of Shiras's first article, along with 74 of his photographs, caused two members of the Society's board to resign—they felt that "wandering off into nature is not geography"—the magazine went on to publish "Wild Animals that Took Their Own Pictures by Night" in the July 1919 issue.

FLASHLIGHT. "INNOCENTS ABROAD." DOE AND TWIN FAWNS AT A MICHIGAN LAKE

Counting Americans

Following the census of 1900, Dr. F. H. Wines, assistant director of the Census Bureau, took the opportunity to demystify the process for NATIONAL GEOGRAPHIC readers. "The census impresses the imagination of the American people as something vast and mysterious," he wrote, "simply because of the magnitude of the numbers with which it deals and the extent of territory which it covers." But the truly remarkable aspect of the 1900 census was the way in which the information was tabulated. In the 1890s, a young Census Bureau employee named Herman Hollerith devised an electronic machine that used punched cards to count the responses. Each person surveyed was represented by a card, and the card was punched with holes in a unique pattern for each response. The counting machine "is so contrived that needles passing through the punched holes on each card form electrical connections which operate clock-faced dials, showing numbers corresponding to each individual fact, or combination of facts," explained Wines.

Hollerith was so certain that his punched card system could become a financial success that he left the Bureau, and in 1896 founded the Tabulating Machine Company in New York City. The company would later become IBM.

The New Empire

Around the turn of the century, the United States came into possession of a large number of new territories. As a result of the victory over Spain in 1898, the U.S. took possession of the Philippines, Puerto Rico, and Guam, and although the original declaration of war forbade the direct acquisition of Cuba, that nation became a de facto protectorate of the United States. The other great territorial gain was Hawaii. A group of American businessmen, most prominently plantation owner Sanford Dole, had engineered the overthrow of Queen Liliuokalini in 1893. Five years after that, America officially annexed the islands, and on June 14, 1900, Hawaii became a U.S. territory with Dole as its governor.

ADULT NEGRITO WOMAN OF THE PHILIPPINES, SHOWING RELATIVE SIZE

In "Our New Possessions and the Interest They are Exciting," published in the January 1900 magazine, much was made of the economic potential of America's new islands. Information from the Bureau of Statistics claimed that "their present consuming power is, in round terms, one hundred million dollars—about equally divided between agricultural products and manufactures, but that this can and will be greatly increased by the introduction of modern methods of production and by the creation of roads and railways by which the uncultivated area can be opened...."

Teaching Geography

Given that the National Geographic Society was founded "for the increase and diffusion of geographical knowledge," it is no surprise that the magazine took an active interest in geography education. This philosophy is evident in "The Teaching of Geography," written by Cornell geography professor Ralph Tarr in 1902. "Geography has an important position as a fundamental branch of instruction in the schools.... " wrote Tarr. "Yet one is frequently hearing the statement made that geography instruction is woefully barren of educational results."

Tarr presented a number of solutions to this problem. The first was to get better geography teachers (though he hastened

to add that this "is in no sense intended as a criticism of the teachers.") Another was to create a coherent plan for the study of geography in public schools; still another called for the creation of more university courses in the subject. And, in a lament that still applies, he felt that geography needed to be made more interesting to students. "It was only yesterday," he related regretfully, "that a young girl said to me, 'I hate geography. I passed the regents' examination in it and now I am going to forget it just as fast as I can.' This view is far too common...."

North to the Future

"Alaska has been maligned, abused, and totally misunderstood," wrote C. C. Georgeson in the March 1902 NATIONAL GEOGRAPHIC. "It has been regarded as a frozen, worthless waste, whose only value consisted in its seal fisheries, and totally incapable of furnishing homes for a civilized people." Maj. Gen. A. W. Greeley echoed those sentiments in the July 1909 issue, ruefully relating a story of how a prominent writer referred to Alaska as being "inhabited by a few savages, and...not likely ever to support a population large enough to make its government a matter of practical consequence."

In Alaska, which the United States purchased from Russia in 1867 for two cents an acre, Georgeson and Greeley saw opportunity where others saw nothing but snow. The 1890 population of the territory was estimated at a mere 4,000 people, but the discovery of gold in the Yukon, Nome, and Fairbanks, among other locales, helped boost the population to 340,400 in 1900. In that year the capital moved from Sitka to Juneau, and the territory elected its first (nonvoting) delegate to Congress. Ten years later, the population had grown by another 6,400. The vast wealth of natural resources to be found in Alaska— most important its oil reserves—helped turn what was once called "Seward's Folly," after the Secretary of State who engineered the purchase, into a booming territory. On January 3, 1959, it became America's 49th state.

NATURALIST RETURNS FROM GLACIER MOUNTAIN, ALASKA, WITH CARIBOU SKULLS AND HORNS

THE BOXER REBELLION

They called themselves I-ho ch'uan, the "Righteous and Harmonious Fists." To Westerners they were known as the Boxers, for the boxing skills they ritually practiced. Deeply resentful of the Westerners that had been pouring into the country since the late 19th century, the society—secretly supported by the ruling Qing (Manchu) Dynasty—began killing foreigners and destroying foreign-owned buildings in May of 1900. They also targeted Chinese who had converted to Christianity.

In June a force of Americans, Europeans, and Japanese sailed to China to quell the Boxer Rebellion and protect their interests. But the

DEFENDERS AGAINST BOXERS

force was initially rebuffed, and the furious Empress Dowager ordered the death of every foreigner on Chinese soil. When the expeditionary forces finally succeeded in capturing Beijing, they looted the city and forced the country to accept peace terms favorable to Western interests.

The humiliating defeat helped foster a nationalist spirit in China that would lead to the overthrow of China's last dynasty in 1911.

▶ THE MYSTERIES OF BLOOD

Physicians and surgeons had long wondered why some patients responded well to blood transfusions, while others quickly died. In 1900 Austrian immunologist Karl Landsteiner discovered that blood cells can contain two different types of proteins, called antigens, which he dubbed types A and B. The presence of both antigens created type AB blood, and the absence of all antigens resulted in type O blood. Furthermore, type A contains antibodies that attack type B, and vice versa. The usefulness of this system became apparent during World War I, when blood banks were formed to provide wounded soldiers with blood of the proper type.

Landsteiner's work won him the Nobel Prize in 1930. Ten years later, he made yet another discovery—the Rh factor. Named for the Rhesus monkey, the animal used in the experiments, the Rh factor is a protein that is either present or absent, resulting in Rh positive or Rh negative blood. This discovery solved the riddle of why some babies are attacked in the womb by the mother's immune system, and led to a treatment.

▶ THE WORLD OF DREAMS

"The poets and philosophers before me discovered the unconscious," Sigmund Freud (above, right) once said. "What I discovered was the scientific method by which the unconscious can be studied." One method, according to Freud, was through dreams, a theory he put forth in his book *The Interpretation of Dreams*. Victorian sensibilities were offended by the book's frank discussion of sexuality. But in laying bare the structure of the unconscious, Freud established not only the science of psychoanalysis but also the

modern field of psychology. Though Freud revised the book repeatedly throughout his life, he had no doubt that *The Interpretation of Dreams* was his greatest accomplishment. "I had completed my life work," he would write to his colleague Carl Jung. "There was nothing more for me to do... I might just as well lie down and die." In the years since his death some of his work has been discredited. But many of his theories about personality endure to this day, and take their place alongside those of Charles Darwin and Karl Marx as cornerstones of modern thought.

▶ THE QUANTUM WORLD

Until 1900 it was believed that any object that contained energy radiated it—whether in the form of light, heat, or x-rays—in a continuous manner. But in that year German physicist Max Planck proposed a revolutionary idea: All energy emitted by any object is *not* continuous, but rather composed of discrete packets of energy called quanta. He came to this conclusion by considering the radiation emitted by a "black body," a theoretical object that absorbs and emits all forms of energy. His calculations implied that a black body must emit energy in multiples of an infinitesimally small figure now known as Planck's constant.

Planck's discovery set the stage for the development of physics in the 20th century. Niels Bohr used the notion of quanta to determine how atoms are structured, with electrons buzzing about the nucleus

---

- **JANUARY 31**
Death of the Marquess of Queensberry, creator of the rules of modern boxing.

- **FEBRUARY 6**
Theodore Roosevelt vows that he will never accept the nomination for Vice President.

- **MARCH 31**
The French National Assembly restricts the workday for women and children to 11 hours.

- **APRIL 16**
The U.S. Postal Service begins selling stamps in books.

- **MAY 14**
The U.S. Supreme Court rules that inheritance taxes are constitutional.

- **MAY 14**
Olympic Games open in Paris.

- **JUNE 14**
Haiti becomes an official U.S. Territory.

- **JUNE 5**
Writer Stephen Crane dies.

in orbits whose energies are multiples of Planck's constant. And in 1905 Albert Einstein built his explanation of the photoelectric effect on quantum theory; it would later influence his work on the relationship between matter and energy.

▶ TAMING THE MOSQUITO

In early 1900 the surgeon general of the United States Army dispatched Maj. Walter Reed and a team of physicians to Cuba to find the agent responsible for the spread of yellow fever. Reed quickly turned his attention to the theories of a Cuban physician named Carlos Finlay, who believed that the disease was carried by a species of mosquito, *Aëdes aegypti.* Under controlled conditions, the researchers then subjected volunteers, including themselves, to bites from mosquitoes that had been exposed to infected people; some of them became sick. One of the doctors, Jesse Lazear, died after deliberately subjecting himself to a bite. Though the cost was dear, Reed had his answer. The next year a widespread mosquito extermination program reduced the number of deaths in Havana to just 18.

CONQUERORS OF YELLOW FEVER INOCULATE A VOLUNTEER

▶ THE ILGWU

Samuel Gompers, who founded the American Federation of Labor in 1886, was steadfastly opposed to admitting women to his union, which left much of the garment industry without a voice. In 1900 members of local garment unions in four cities joined to form the International Ladies Garment Workers Union. The members fought against their inhumane working conditions, which included 70-hour workweeks and wages averaging about 30 cents a day. They gained some concessions and much public sympathy in 1909 during a violent, three-month strike.

POINT AND SHOOT

Before George Eastman, photography was a difficult, time-consuming process. The equipment was large and clumsy, the long exposure times limited what could be captured, and the cumbersome wet plates used as film had to be developed on the spot. But the innovations of Eastman and the company he founded in 1887, Kodak, changed all that. Eastman's first great invention was the dry plate, which could be developed at leisure. Then came roll film, and smaller cameras. And in 1900 Kodak introduced the Brownie, providing the masses with a camera that was simple and, at a dollar apiece, relatively inexpensive.

Living up to its motto—"you press the button, we do the rest"—the Brownie came preloaded with a roll of 15 exposures. After shooting the pictures, the user would send the whole camera off to Kodak for developing. The camera was a phenomenal success, selling 250,000 in its first year alone. It stayed on the market in various incarnations for some 80 years.

■ TRENDS & TRIVIA

Davis Cup tennis tournament between U.S. and England is founded.

Folk hero Casey Jones dies at the throttle trying to slow his train in Mississippi, saving the lives of his passengers.

Sir Arthur Evans discovers the ruins of the Minoan civilization on the Greek island of Crete.

L. Frank Baum's *The Wonderful Wizard of Oz* is published.

Baseball introduces the five-sided home plate.

Joseph Conrad's *Lord Jim* is published.

Baseball's American League forms with teams from Boston, Detroit, Milwaukee, Baltimore, Chicago, and St. Louis.

World Exposition opens in Paris, the largest world's fair to date in Europe.

America adopts the gold standard with President McKinley signing the Currency Act.

German chemist Friedrich Dorn discovers the element that in 1923 will be named radon.

The U.S. College Entrance Exam (the Scholastic Aptitude Test) is introduced.

Finnish composer Jean Sibelius publishes his tone poem "Finlandia."

The *Daily Express* becomes Britain's first newspaper to hit one million in circulation.

The *Guide Michelin,* the first guide to European restaurants, is published.

First international automobile race, from Paris to Lyons, is held.

23

• JUNE 14
Hawaii becomes an official U.S. Territory two years after it was annexed.

• JULY 19
The Paris Metro opens.

• JULY 20
First flight of a zeppelin.

• JULY 29
Italy's King Umberto I is assassinated by an anarchist.

• AUGUST 25
German philosopher Friedrich Nietzsche dies.

• SEPTEMBER 18
The first direct primary in the United States is held, in Minnesota.

◀ NOVEMBER
The McKinley-Roosevelt team is elected.

• NOVEMBER 30
Writer Oscar Wilde dies.

END OF AN ERA

For Great Britain, the 19th century ended on January 22, 1901, with the death of Queen Victoria, the longest reigning monarch in British history. A granddaughter of George III, who lost the American Colonies, Victoria ascended the throne in 1837 at the age of 18. She presided over a vast expansion of the British Empire, which grew to encompass India and much of Africa, and ushered in a long period of prosperity. Among her 44 grandchildren were several European heads of state, including Kaiser Wilhelm II of Germany and the wife of Nicholas II of Russia. But most importantly, she redefined the British monarchy. In the wake of her three predecessors—Kings George III, George IV, and William IV, famously described as "an imbecile, a profligate, and a buffoon"—she brought wisdom and propriety to the throne. In place of thundering royal authority she made the monarchy an institution of quiet influence that endured as Parliaments came and went. Her long, dignified rule so endeared her to her subjects that upon her death, it is said, even the prostitutes dressed in black.

▶ A CONTRIBUTION TO BENEFIT MANKIND

His 355 patents, for things like the blasting cap, dynamite, and smokeless gunpowder, changed the world and made him a fortune. He spoke six languages and moved comfortably all over the world; Victor Hugo called him "the millionaire vagabond." Yet Swedish chemist Alfred Nobel found little joy in these accomplishments, once declaring that "his miserable existence should have been terminated at birth by a humane doctor." He never married, and his life was marked by a profound loneliness and a deep distrust of human nature. When he died in 1896 at the age of 66, he was surrounded only by servants who could not understand his Swedish, the only language a stroke left him able to speak.

Nobel left his $9,000,000 estate for the creation of prizes to honor "those persons who shall have contributed most materially to benefit mankind" every year. The prizes would be awarded for medicine, chemistry, physics, literature—he was an amateur poet—and peace. (The economics prize was not created until 1969.) The first prizes, worth $42,000, were awarded on December 10, 1901, the fifth anniversary of Nobel's death. The recipients included French poet Sully-Prudhomme and German physicist Wilhelm Roentgen for his discovery of x-rays.

▶ BLUE PERIOD

By the turn of the century, Pablo Picasso had begun to establish himself as a painter. The 19-year-old Spaniard had his own studio in Barcelona and was finding a small measure of success in Paris, which he first visited in 1900. But in 1901 he inexplicably took his art in a new direction, beginning a three-year span known as his "blue period." The term comes from both his palette—he worked predominantly in shades of blue—and the mood of these paintings, which is unfailingly melancholy. Among the great works produced during the "blue period" are the "Old Guitarist," the "Absinthe Drinker," and "La Vie."

"FAMILY GROUP" BY PICASSO

Scholars have failed to provide a compelling reason why Picasso rejected his budding commercial success to begin his "blue period." But the master may have supplied his own explanation when he cited "the constant flight forward of the spirit" as a driving force in his career. Rather than repeat past successes, he chose to blaze new trails, which resulted in his giving up the blues for his "rose period" in 1905. After that he experimented with Cubism and abstract painting, as well as sculpture, engraving, and pottery. By the time of his death in 1973 his work, in all its styles, had come to dominate 20th-century art.

▶ A RAILROAD BOONDOGGLE

Among the holdings of the British Empire at the turn of the century was Uganda, a remote African outpost that bordered Lake Victoria, the source of the Nile. Spurred by visions of profits, the Imperial British East Africa Company lobbied mercilessly for the construction of a railroad from the eastern coast of Kenya through Uganda to the lake, planting in the heads of members of Parliament the notion that without a railway, the entire region lay vulnerable to foreign powers. Though the threat was wholly manufactured by company officials, enough London lawmakers bought into it to charter the Mombasa-Victoria-Uganda Railway.

• JANUARY 1
The Commonwealth of Australia is established.

• JANUARY 7
Trading on the New York Stock Exchange exceeds two million shares in a single day.

• JANUARY 23
French hospitals accept their first female interns.

• FEBRUARY 21
Physicist Albert Einstein becomes a Swiss citizen, renouncing his German citizenship.

• MARCH 11
America's tentative plans to build a canal through Nicaragua fall through.

• JUNE 12
French physicist Antoine-Henri Becquerel discovers a phenomenon later named radioactivity.

• JULY 4
William Howard Taft becomes governor of the Philippines.

The railroad was quickly to become known as the "lunatic express." Cost overruns more than doubled the budget, to more than £5,000,000, all for laying just 582 miles of rail. The backbreaking work was carried out by 32,000 imported Indian laborers, of whom 2,500 died and 6,000 were permanently disabled. On December 20, 1901, the final spike was driven home in what is now Kisumu, Kenya.

The British discouraged the Indians from staying after the railway's completion. And with much of the area cleared of natives—with the help of smallpox, brought by the British—white settlers poured in and, with the aid of cheap local labor, built fortunes in coffee and sisal. As the only outlet for the exports, the East Africa Company more than recouped its immense costs.

▶ "SMASH, SMASH, SMASH"

Carry Nation knew firsthand the evils of drink. Her first husband was an alcoholic who showed up drunk to their wedding. Her second husband, David Nation, was a ne'er-do-well lawyer, farmer, journalist, and preacher who took her to Medicine Lodge, Kansas. There she became appalled at the drunkenness she saw in what was, at least according to the law, a dry state.

Peaceful efforts to get the state's prohibition laws enforced met with ridicule. Then in 1899 she had a vision in which God told her to travel to Kiowa, Kansas, where, He promised, "I'll stand by you." So with brickbats in hand, she walked into a Kiowa saloon and laid waste to the bottles and glassware. After building a small following called the "Home Defenders' Army," in 1901 she took her fight to the "joints" of Topeka, many of which felt the wrath of her new weapon of choice, the hatchet. After numerous fights and arrests she spent the next few years, until her death in 1911, traveling, lecturing, and exhorting women to "smash, smash, smash."

WITHOUT A WIRE

Italian physicist Guglielmo Marconi (below) was only 22 years old when he patented a system for wireless communication in 1896. The Italian government had refused his gift of the rights to his "wireless telegraph," most likely due to its limited range at the time. But radio, as it later came to be known, found increasing use as Marconi improved its range.

On December 12, 1901, the "wireless" sounded the telegraph's death knell when Marconi, stationed in Newfoundland, received a Morse code radio signal sent from Cornwall, England. By 1918 he had succeeded in sending radio signals from England to Australia, and a few years later inventions like the vacuum tube and the Audion made it possible to send voice signals through the airwaves. By the time of Marconi's death in 1937, his invention had completely changed the way the world communicated.

▶ THE MAESTRO SILENCED

With the death of Giuseppe Verdi on January 27, 1901, Italy lost a national hero and the world lost the last of perhaps the three greatest operatic composers—with Mozart and Wagner—who ever lived. Born in 1813, Verdi sealed his reputation with a "trinity" of operas written between 1851 and 1853—*Rigoletto*, *Il Trovatore*, and *La Traviata*—works so popular that one prominent musician commented, "the youthful, vigorous singers of today have only one name on their lips, and that is Verdi. Upon his operas rests the whole art of music."

■ TRENDS & TRIVIA

J. P. Morgan buys Carnegie Steel from Andrew Carnegie for 492 million dollars. The resulting company, U.S. Steel, is the world's first billion-dollar company.

Andrew Carnegie announces his intention to give away his personal fortune of over 300 million dollars.

Electric hearing aid is developed.

First driving school is founded, in England.

The Platt Amendment makes Cuba a *de facto* U.S. colony.

Rudyard Kipling publishes *Kim.*

Booker T. Washington's *Up from Slavery* is published.

German writer Thomas Mann makes his literary debut with *Buddenbrooks.*

The first practical electric vacuum cleaner is patented, in England.

English composer Edward Elgar writes "Pomp and Circumstance."

Discovery of oil at Spindletop, Texas, ushers in an oil boom.

Ransom Olds markets the first commercially successful automobile.

Instant coffee is invented.

The electric typewriter is new.

Modern paper clips are patented in the U.S.

Some Georgia planters are found to be still using slaves.

A lottery grants more than two million acres of Oklahoma Territory to 6,500 homesteaders.

Playwright Anton Chekhov's *Three Sisters* premieres.

25

• **AUGUST 22**
The Cadillac automobile company is founded.

▶ **SEPTEMBER 6**
U.S. President William McKinley is shot; he dies on September 14.

• **SEPTEMBER 7**
Boxer Rebellion officially ends in China.

• **SEPTEMBER 9**
French painter Henri de Toulouse-Lautrec dies.

• **OCTOBER 4**
The U.S. defeats Great Britain in the America's Cup yachting race.

• **OCTOBER 23**
Yale University celebrates its bicentennial.

• **NOVEMBER 28**
Alabama's new constitution requires literacy tests for voting and a "grandfather clause" that disenfranchises blacks.

The gold and diamond riches in what is now South Africa were the source of a long-simmering dispute. On one side were the Boers, descendants of 17th-century Dutch settlers, who controlled two autonomous regions: the South African Republic and the Orange Free State. On the other were the British, who held the nearby Cape Colony and wanted control of the entire area. The British provoked the Boers into starting a war in 1899.

The Boers initially laid siege to British positions, but as England sent reinforcements, they resorted to guerrilla tactics. Lord Horatio Kitchener then interned the wives and children of Boer soldiers, as well as

ENVOYS MEET TO NEGOTIATE PEACE

the Africans who worked their farms, in horrific concentration camps where thousands died.

Finally, on May 31, 1902, the Boers surrendered and were forced to pledge their allegiance to King Edward VII. In 1910 the Boer states were absorbed into the British Union of South Africa, which proclaimed that there would be "no equality between coloured people and the white inhabitants either in church or state."

▶ A LITERARY JOURNEY INTO DARKNESS
British author Joseph Conrad drew on his vast experience at sea to provide the background for most of his novels and stories. Born to Polish parents in present-day Ukraine in 1857, Józef Teodor Konrad Korzeniowski first emigrated to France, where he spent four years on a French merchant vessel. He then switched to the British merchant fleet, spending the next 16 years sailing around the world. After settling briefly in London and trying his hand at writing, he took off again, this time captaining a steamboat down the Congo River in Africa.

This journey provided the material for his most famous work, *Heart of Darkness*, published in 1902. The novella tells the tale of an Englishman who travels to Africa in search of the mysterious Mr. Kurtz, a trader who, having established a murderous rule in the jungles of the Belgian Congo, had descended into madness. The work was also a social commentary on the nature of power and an indictment of European colonialism, made more palatable to the English by setting it in a Belgian colony. This was in direct opposition to his adopted countryman Rudyard Kipling, who advocated the "white man's burden" of bringing civilization to the savages of Africa and India. As a literary work *Heart of Darkness* also broke ground, taking the familiar story of a dangerous journey into uncharted territory and retelling it in a modernist vein, casting the mission as a journey into the human soul.

▶ THE ASWAN DAM
"The great Nile dam at Assuan..." proclaimed *Harpers* in September 1902, "fastens the British mortgage on Egypt so firmly that it can never be lifted." In true

CONSTRUCTION OF THE ASWAN DAM ACROSS THE NILE

colonial fashion, the cornerstone to the Aswan Dam was laid in 1899 by British nobility—His Royal Highness the Duke of Connaught—but much of the manpower needed for the vast excavation was provided by Africans. The "primitive methods of labor" for the excavation required that "all debris, except the large stones, [be] carried up inclines upon the heads of Nubian workmen." In all, the 176-foot-high dam stretched over a mile across the Nile and held back a billion tons of water.

With a dependable system of irrigation and protection from disastrous Nile floods, Egypt was able to produce up to three crops a year, instead of just one. Furthermore, the dam gave the country 40 percent more arable land. In the bargain, however, some treasures of ancient Egypt, like the Philae Temple, were flooded. When the nearby Aswan High Dam was completed in 1970, it was capable of generating more than 2,100 megawatts of hydroelectric power, and its reservoir was capable of irrigating seven million more acres. Though the High Dam also imperiled archaeological wonders, the two dams have saved Egypt from the periodic droughts and famines that have cursed its African neighbors.

▶ BIRTH OF A COWBOY HERO
America's perception of the cowboy as the strong, silent hero who tamed the West stems in large part from a novel written a dozen years after the federal government

- **JANUARY 1**
The first Rose Bowl is held—Michigan defeats Stanford.

- **JANUARY 4**
The Carnegie Institute is founded.

- **FEBRUARY 15**
The Berlin subway opens in Germany.

- **FEBRUARY 18**
Charles Lewis Tiffany dies.

- **MARCH 4**
The American Automobile Association is founded.

- **MARCH 6**
The U.S. Bureau of the Census is established.

- **APRIL 28**
A revolution takes place in the Dominican Republic.

- **MAY 5**
American writer Bret Harte dies.

- **MAY 8**
A volcanic eruption destroys St. Pierre, Martinique.

officially declared the frontier "closed." In 1902 a Harvard graduate from Philadelphia named Owen Wister, who spent some time out west recovering from a nervous breakdown, published *The Virginian*, which created an enduring archetype that has been copied in books and movies ever since.

The tale tells of "a slim young giant, more beautiful than pictures," who has come to Wyoming from his native Virginia. There he meets a beautiful, spunky schoolmarm, with whom he finds love after a series of adventures. But before they can ride into the sunset, he must face down a villain named Trampas. In the book's most famous scene, during a hand of poker Trampas calls the Virginian a "son of a b----," to which the laconic hero responds by laying his revolver on the table and delivering the classic line, "When you call me that, *smile!*" Eastern audiences found the story irresistible; the book was turned into a play in 1904, a silent movie in 1914, and then a "talkie" in 1929, which launched the career of a little-known actor named Gary Cooper.

▶ THE DISCOVERY OF HORMONES

Based on the work of Russian physiologist Ivan Pavlov, prevailing medical wisdom held that digestion was a process controlled by the nervous system. But in 1902 British researchers and brothers-in-law William Maddock Bayliss and Ernest Starling discovered a new route. When they stimulated the small intestine of a dog whose intestinal nerves were severed, they found that the dog's pancreas continued to secrete digestive juices.

Bayliss and Starling concluded that the only possible explanation was that the intestine was releasing some sort of signalling chemical into the bloodstream; it eventually traveled to the pancreas, where it triggered the release of digestive juices.

HOLMES RETURNS

Readers thought they had heard the last of Sherlock Holmes in 1893's *The Adventure of the Final Problem,* which found Holmes and his archrival Professor Moriarty facing certain death. After six years of spinning tales about the world's most famous detective, Arthur Conan Doyle (below) had had enough: "I feel towards him as I do towards pâté-de-fois-gras, of which I once ate too much...." But the public's appetite was still keen, and in 1902 Doyle relented with *The Hound of the Baskervilles*, which he cast as a "reminiscence" to sidestep the matter of the hero's apparent death. So great was the demand for the story that Doyle considered a resurrection. Holmes may not have actually died, he teased in a 1901 interview.

In *The Adventure of the Empty House,* Holmes reveals himself to Dr. Watson, who faints from the shock upon learning that Holmes hadn't actually fallen over a cliff. Settling back into his rooms at 221 Baker Street, Holmes was once again "free to devote his life to examining those interesting little problems which the complex life of London so plentifully presents."

They called the chemical "secretin," and coined a new term for the class of substances it represented: hormones, from the Greek word *horman*, meaning to set in motion. Since this 1902 discovery, scientists have identified more than 100 hormones, which play countless vital roles in the body in addition to digestion.

■ TRENDS & TRIVIA

The Teddy bear is named after Theodore Roosevelt, who refused to shoot a bear captured on a hunting trip.

An air conditioner prototype is invented by Willis Carrier.

The premiere of Claude Debussy's opera *Pelléas et Mélisande* creates a stir with its unorthodox composition.

J. C. Penney opens its first store, in Wyoming.

Gasoline-powered lawn mowers are introduced.

The first automat opens, in Philadelphia.

Pepsi-Cola Company is founded.

Nabisco introduces animal crackers.

The electric hair dryer is invented.

Scott Joplin, prime mover behind the growing popularity of ragtime, publishes "The Entertainer."

William James's *The Varieties of Religious Experience* promotes his philosophy of pragmatism.

"In the Good Old Summertime" is a popular song.

Art Nouveau peaks in popularity.

Beatrix Potter's children's classic *The Tale of Peter Rabbit* is published. ▶

Phonograph records of tenor Enrico Caruso help make the Italian singer a star, and popularize the phonograph.

Martha Washington becomes the first woman pictured on a postage stamp.

• JUNE 9
Woodrow Wilson assumes the presidency of Princeton University.

• JUNE 9
The U.S. Military Academy at West Point, New York, celebrates its centennial.

• JUNE 17
The Newlands Act authorizes the building of dams across the U.S. Southwest.

• AUGUST 3
Oliver Wendell Holmes, Jr. is appointed to the U.S. Supreme Court.

• SEPTEMBER 29
French writer Émile Zola dies.

• OCTOBER 26
Suffragist Elizabeth Cady Stanton dies.

• DECEMBER 7
British cartoonist Thomas Nast dies.

"My brother Orville and myself lived together, played together, worked together, and in fact thought together," Wilbur Wright (top) once wrote. Starting in 1896, the bicycle shop owners turned their joint thoughts to building a flying machine. They first tackled the theoretical aspects, devising ailerons and rudders to maintain an even ride in shifting winds. They then meticulously tested their theories with gliders, which they took every autumn to Kitty Hawk, North Carolina, where the winds were constant and powerful.

The brothers then turned to the problem of adding an engine. Finding none light and powerful enough for their use, they built their own. Their first successful test came on December 17, 1903, with Orville at the controls. The history-making flight spanned 852 feet in 59 seconds.

Not until 1909, after adding a more powerful engine, sophisticated controls, and a passenger seat, were they able to establish a commercial demand for their invention. When governments realized how useful a flying machine might be in combat, the orders began to pour in.

▶ A SCIENTIFIC DYNASTY

In 1896 French physicist Antoine-Henri Becquerel discovered a mysterious form of energy dubbed "radiation." Shortly afterward, a 30-year-old woman named Marie Curie (below) took up the study of radiation for her doctoral thesis. Curie's husband Pierre was supervisor of the School of Physics and Industrial Chemistry in Paris, and there the couple made an unusual discovery: Certain compounds of uranium emitted more radiation than could be accounted for by the uranium alone. After careful examination they proposed the existence of another radioactive element, which they fittingly named radium. Along the way they also found evidence for the radioactive element polonium, named in honor of Marie's native country of Poland. Their discoveries won the Curies, along with Becquerel, the 1903 Nobel Prize in physics, the first Nobel to be awarded to a woman.

Devastated by the death of her husband just two years later, Madame Curie threw herself into her work and finally managed to isolate an appreciable amount of radium. Though this feat won her the 1911 Nobel Prize for chemistry, it likely also cost her her life. Her 1934 death from leukemia was almost certainly the result of prolonged exposure to radiation. The year after her death a Nobel Prize went to her daughter and son-in-law, Irene and Frederic Joliot-Curie, for their own work in the synthesis of new radioactive elements.

▶ A CLOSER SHAVE

In 1895 an American named King Gillette had a brainstorm. Frustrated with his dull shaving razor, he decided he would invent one that used disposable blades that never needed sharpening. "As I stood there with the razor in my hand," he recalled, "my eyes resting on it as lightly as a bird settling down on its nest, the Gillette razor and disposable blade were born."

Getting the product to market, however, was another task entirely. Gillette spent six years searching for someone who could manufacture the thin, sharp blades he needed. Finally, MIT professor William Nickerson joined forces with Gillette to produce the blades, and by 1903 their product went on sale at a cost of five dollars apiece. Their initial batch of only 51 razors sold rapidly. In 1906 they sold 300,000 razors and more than 500,000 replacement blades. But what really made Gillette's fortune was World War I. The U.S. government placed an order for 3.5 million razors and 36 million blades to send with its soldiers overseas. And when foreign soldiers saw the razors, they too had to have them. By the time of his retirement in 1931, the onetime socialist was an immensely wealthy man.

▶ THE FIRST MOVIES

Although Thomas Edison invented a camera for recording moving pictures, called the kinetograph, he never bothered to secure foreign patent rights for it. So it was Louis and Auguste Lumière, two Frenchmen who built a camera very

---

- **JANUARY 19**
The first Tour de France bicycle race is announced.

- **FEBRUARY 1**
The first American student receives a Rhodes scholarship.

- **MARCH 29**
Regular radio news service between New York and London is established.

- **MAY 8**
French painter Paul Gauguin dies.

- **JUNE 11**
King Alexander and Queen Draga of Serbia are assassinated.

- **JULY 23**
The Ford Motor Company sells its first automobile.

- **AUGUST 1**
Frontierswoman Martha "Calamity Jane" Canary dies.

- **MAY 23**
Telephone service links Paris and Rome.

similar to Edison's, who screened the first motion pictures for paying audiences in 1895. These films were short, single-shot scenes—usually a minute or less—of everyday life, such as parades and men at work.

Back at the Edison Company, a man named Edwin Porter was working on more substantial movies that would incorporate filmmaking techniques still in use today. In 1903 he produced *The Life of an American Fireman*, which featured one of the first close-ups. Also in 1903, he made *The Great Train Robbery* (below), considered by many to be America's first Western. The 12-minute

movie had a plot—bandits rob a train and are chased by a posse—and was made by editing together scenes to create a coherent narrative. It also included one of the most famous scenes in the early history of movies: a man firing a gun straight into the camera.

▶ PROTECTING WILDLIFE

"It is hereby ordered that Pelican Island in Indian River in section nine, township thirty-one south, range thirty-nine east, State of Florida, be…reserved and set apart for the use of the Department of Agriculture as a preserve and breeding ground for native birds." With this 1903 directive, Theodore Roosevelt created the Pelican Island National Wildlife Refuge, the first such sanctuary in the country.

Conservationists had been pressing for federal protection of wildlife for years, and when Roosevelt became President, they

A NEW BALL GAME

As the 1903 baseball season wound down, the Pittsburgh Pirates were running away with the National League title and the Boston Pilgrims—later the Red Sox—were doing the same in the new American League. Looking to drum up some interest in an anticlimactic season, Pirates owner Barney Dreyfuss wrote to Pilgrims owner Henry Killilea with a proposition: "The time has come for the National League and the American League to organize a World Series.... We would create great interest in baseball, in our leagues, and in our players. I also believe it would be a financial success." There was exceptionally bad blood between the National League and the upstart American League, which had raided the senior league for talent when it formed in 1900. Still, the two owners set aside any differences for their sport—and for the profit, splitting the gate receipts 50-50.

Pittsburgh was heavily favored in the best-of-nine series. But the Pilgrims and their pitching staff—including the legendary Cy Young—were too much for the Pirates, and they took the contest five games to three.

finally found a kindred soul in the White House. By issuing the executive order, the President skirted Congress but was unable to secure federal funding to administer the refuge. To the rescue came insurance magnate Albert Willcox, who gave a substantial part of his fortune for the creation of the National Audubon Society, which would then manage the refuge. By 1909 Roosevelt had set aside 53 wildlife sanctuaries in 20 states and territories. In 1956 they were folded into the Fish and Wildlife Service.

■ TRENDS & TRIVIA

British suffragist Emmeline Pankhurst founds the Women's Social and Political Union.

The first Crayola crayons are produced. One box contains the six primary and secondary colors, plus black and brown.

First automobile license plates are issued, in Massachusetts.

Sanka decaffeinated coffee is introduced.

A December fire at Chicago's Iroquois Theater kills 600 people, prompting new fire codes.

The Harley-Davidson motorcycle company is founded.

Milton S. Hershey begins construction of a chocolate factory in Derry Church, Pennsylvania, which will eventually be renamed Hershey, Pennsylvania.

Russian scientist Konstantin Tsiolkovsky publishes *The Exploration of Cosmic Space by Means of Reaction Devices,* which predicts the use of liquid-fueled rockets to reach outer space.

Dutch physiologist Willem Einthoven invents the electrocardiogram.

The operetta *Babes in Toyland*, by Victor Herbert, debuts in Chicago.

The Souls of Black Folk by W. E. B. Du Bois is published.

The successful use of porcelain fillings in dentistry is announced.

Joseph Pulitzer donates two million dollars to Columbia University to found a school of journalism.

Jack London's *The Call of the Wild* is published.

Rebecca of Sunnybrook Farm by Kate Douglas Wiggin is published.

29

• AUGUST 4
Giuseppe Sarto becomes Pope Pius X.

• AUGUST 21
The first coast-to-coast automobile trip is completed.

• SEPTEMBER 23
Columbia University celebrates its 150th anniversary.

• SEPTEMBER 26
Women are granted the vote in the state of Connecticut.

• OCTOBER 16
The boundary between Alaska and Canada is settled.

▶ DECEMBER 17
The Wright brothers achieve the first controlled, powered flight in an airplane at Kitty Hawk, North Carolina.

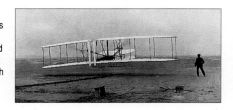

"A glance at the occupational statistics of any country of mixed religious composition brings to light with remarkable frequency a situation which has several times provoked discussion...namely, the fact that business leaders and owners of capital...are overwhelmingly Protestant." So begins *The Protestant Ethic and the Spirit of Capitalism* published in 1904 by German social scientist Max Weber (below). In his book Weber cast aside the fashionable Marxist belief that economics helps define a country's social structure. Instead he contended the opposite, that social structures and beliefs—especially religion—influence economics.

And the belief system most conducive to capitalist economies was Calvinism, which places a premium on hard work and moral rectitude. In tying capitalist behavior to religious and moral behavior, Weber gave the pursuit of wealth a spiritual seal of approval. By the time of his death he had also incorporated many of these ideas into his groundbreaking studies of how bureaucracies function.

UNDER THE SIDEWALKS OF NEW YORK

Ever since the London Underground opened in 1863, the government of New York City had considered building a rapid transit system to alleviate the tangle of pedestrians, carriages, wagons, and automobiles that snarled every major street. Various schemes were tested in the 19th century, but the city did not implement a serious plan until an 1894 referendum allocated city funds for construction. The first stretch was opened on October 27, 1904, as a group of dignitaries boarded a car at the ornate City Hall station for the first ride. Mayor George McClellan manned the controls; he was only supposed to take the train a short way, but in his enthusiasm drove it nearly five miles, up to 103rd Street. The original fare was a nickel, where it stayed until a 1948 increase pushed it up to a dime.

The original plan simply called for subway trains to run from City Hall north into the Bronx, tunneling under the Harlem River, and south into Brooklyn, under the East River. But the trains were so successful that the system was expanded almost immediately. Lines through densely populated parts of the city eased congestion, while lines in sparsely populated areas promoted growth. By 1990 the New York subway system was the largest in the world, with more than 700 miles of track and 469 stations, served by 20 different lines.

A VOICE FOR THE DISABLED

Helen Keller's 1904 graduation from Radcliffe College was just one of many achievements in a remarkable life. Born in 1880 in Alabama, she lost her sight and hearing to disease when just 19 months old. Her parents sought the advice of Alexander Graham Bell who, in addition to inventing the telephone, was a renowned educator of the deaf. Bell's

HELEN KELLER FEELS THE VIBRATIONS OF HER TEACHER'S LIPS

references led them to Anne Sullivan, a teacher who was herself visually impaired. "Thus I came up out of Egypt and stood before Sinai," Keller wrote of her partnership with Sullivan, "and a power divine touched my spirit and gave it sight, so that I beheld many wonders."

Until her death in 1936, Sullivan was Keller's near-constant companion, helping her learn Braille and the manual alphabet, as well as how to "hear" others speak by feeling their lips and throats. Of her decision to attend Radcliffe, Keller wrote that "a potent force within me...stronger even than the pleadings of my heart, had impelled me to try my strength by the standards of those who see and hear."

Keller and Sullivan attended classes together, with Sullivan spelling out the lectures into Keller's hands. The brilliant pupil mastered French, Latin, and Greek, and earned her degree *cum laude*. Along the way she wrote her autobiography, *The Story of My Life*, published in 1903 and dedicated to Bell.

REVOLUTIONIZING THE AIRWAVES

In 1904 a British engineer named John Ambrose Fleming invented what he termed the "missing link" of radio communications. An employee of Guglielmo Marconi's Wireless Telegraphy Company Ltd., Fleming was looking for a way to

• **FEBRUARY 5**
The American occupation of Cuba, which began in 1899, ends.

▶ **FEBRUARY 10**
Japan declares war on Russia, start of Russo-Japanese War (Japanese woodcut, right).

•**MARCH 22**
The first color newspaper photograph is published, in London's *Daily Illustrated Mirror*.

• **MARCH 31**
Japan destroys the Russian fleet at Vladivostok.

• **APRIL 26**
The Workers Party is founded in Australia.

boost the power of radio detectors; at the time, the poor sensitivity of detectors was a major problem with radio technology.

He found his solution in discoveries made by Thomas Edison. While working as a consultant to the Edison Electric Light Company years earlier, he noticed that Edison had discovered an unusual property of light bulbs, dubbed the "Edison effect." Fleming exploited the Edison effect to "rectify" radio signals, or convert the oscillating, two-directional waves into unidirectional waves. Fleming rigged a light bulb with a metal plate in between the terminals that rectified incoming radio signals, making them detectable by ordinary telephone receivers. Fleming's valve, which became known as the diode, also made it possible to transmit voices by radio. Two years later an eccentric American engineer named Lee DeForest improved on the diode by inventing the Audion. More than any other invention, the Fleming valve and the Audion made possible the transformation of the world by radio.

▶ FROM MOSCOW TO VLADIVOSTOK
The Trans-Siberian Railway remains the longest continual rail line on earth. Work began in 1891 under Tsar Alexander III, and took 250 million dollars to lay the 5,500 miles of track. Construction proceeded in six places simultaneously. By July 1904 all the segments were completed. Derailments, heavy rains, and spring thaws frequently caused the tracks to shift. There was also the problem of Lake Baikal, which lay in the railway's path. Until the rails stretched around the southern end of the lake, ferries linked the eastern and western banks. In winter, tracks were placed directly over the frozen water.

Russia had obtained permission from China to build a 945-mile shortcut through Manchuria. But the bypass generated conflict between Russia and Japan and helped spark the Russo-Japanese War, during which Moscow used the railroad to send supplies to the front. When Russia lost the war in 1905 it had to reconfigure the railway entirely within its borders, a task it did not complete until 1916.

WORLD'S FAIR

To commemorate the centennial of the 1803 Louisiana Purchase, the city of St. Louis hosted the World's Fair of 1904. The fair lasted seven months, and drew 187,798 visitors on the first day alone. One of the many attractions at the fair was the third Olympic Games—a decidedly American affair, since 432 of the 554 athletes came from the United States. Many countries did not send teams at all, believing the American Midwest to be a lawless wilderness. Despite the lack of international competition several records were set, including world records for the 1,500 meters and long jump, and Olympic records in the 200- and 400-meter hurdles. All told, American athletes won 238 of the 300 medals awarded.

But perhaps the most lasting contribution of the fair came from Ernest Hamwi and Arnold Fornachou, whose side-by-side concession stands sold baked goods and ice cream. Legend has it that when Fornachou ran out of paper dishes for his ice cream, Hamwi provided rolled-up pastries called "zalabias." These "World's Fair Cornucopias" were the world's first ice cream cones.

EXHIBITS FROM THE 1904 WORLD'S FAIR

■ TRENDS & TRIVIA

A woman is arrested on New York City's Fifth Avenue for smoking a cigarette.

Offset printing is developed.

Archaeologists discover much of the Maya city of Chichen Itza in Mexico.

English Author J. M. Barrie writes *Peter Pan.*

Englishmen Charles Rolls and Henry Royce team up to found what will become Rolls-Royce, Ltd.

The National Child Labor Committee forms in the United States.

The Northern Securities railroad holding company is broken up as a monopoly by the Supreme Court.

Sheherazade by Maurice Ravel premieres in Paris.

Novocain is introduced.

Tea bags are a new convenience.

The area of New York City known as Times Square gets its name as the *New York Times* moves to the location.

George Bernard Shaw's *John Bull's Other Island* becomes the Irish writer's first hit.

The International Professional Hockey League is founded.

Theodore Roosevelt advances the "Roosevelt Corollary" of the Monroe Doctrine, stating that the U.S. has a responsibility to protect any country within America's "sphere of influence."

New York State adopts speed limits: 10 mph for cities; 15 in small towns; and 20 in the country.

Anton Chekhov's *The Cherry Orchard* opens.

31

• APRIL 30
President Roosevelt opens the St. Louis World's Fair.

• MAY 1
Composer Anton Dvorak dies at 63.

• MAY 4
Work begins on the Panama Canal.

• MAY 5
Cy Young pitches the first perfect game in major league baseball history.

• JULY 15
Russian playwright Anton Chekhov dies.

• NOVEMBER 8
Theodore Roosevelt wins the Presidential election.

• DECEMBER 10
Russian physiologist Ivan Pavlov wins the Nobel Prize for his work on the nature of digestion.

Albert Einstein made 1905 one of the most productive years in the history of science. While employed as an examiner in a Swiss patent office, the 27-year-old physicist (below) turned out three seminal papers in his spare time. One offered a comprehensive explanation of the photoelectric effect, in which light striking certain metals causes the metals to release electrons. Another explained a phenomenon first noted in 1827 by English botanist Robert Brown, who observed the random motion of microscopic particles suspended in fluid. According to Einstein, this "Brownian motion" arose from the particles being buffeted about by molecules of the suspending fluid.

In the third paper, titled "On the Electrodynamics of Moving Bodies," Einstein introduced the special theory of relativity. One of the theory's wilder predictions was that at speeds near that of light objects become longer and heavier. Furthermore, he stated, time slows at extreme speeds, rendering both space and time completely malleable. In 1916 he would publish his general theory of relativity.

▶ BLOODY SUNDAY

Added to the troubles of Tsar Nicholas II, whose troops were losing the Russo-Japanese War, was growing civil unrest. The catalyst was the firing of four workers from the Putilov armaments factory in St. Petersburg in December 1904. A protest strike among the factory workers snowballed to other industries, and by early January 1905 some 80,000 workers were on strike in the Russian capital. The next day a priest organized a march to demand better wages and other social reforms. When the crowd approached the Winter Palace, Cossack troops opened fire, killing some 200 demonstrators. This confrontation, known as Bloody Sunday, triggered a round of strikes and skirmishes between civilians and tsarist troops all over the vast country.

After months of near anarchy, Nicholas realized that he was facing a genuine revolution. To mollify the citizens he agreed to the creation of an elective body called the Duma, from the Russian word for "thought." Peasants and landowners alike would be represented, and their recommendations would be "submitted to the supreme autocratic authority" for consideration. But this did little to quell the violence. A semblance of order eventually came to the country, and the first Duma convened in 1906, but the social issues that led to Bloody Sunday still simmered.

▶ THE "LIGHT OF DAY" DEBUTS

In 1902 a 26-year-old Dutch woman named Margaretha Zelle left an unhappy marriage in the Dutch East Indies and moved to Paris to begin a new life. Failing to make a career as an artist's model, in 1905 she hit upon another one—exotic

dancing. Combining elements from native dances she had seen in the East Indies with striptease, she reinvented herself as Mata Hari (right), taking her stage name from an Indonesian term for "the light of day."

Mata Hari's renown as a dancer was enhanced by her reputation as a noted courtesan. She lived well through the wealth of her many lovers until the outbreak of World War I, which found her in Berlin. The Germans seized her money and jewels, and the 38-year-old Zelle was destitute. Journeying to Paris, she was contacted by French intelligence officials and asked to spy for France. She agreed, making it clear that she was driven by money, not patriotism. But as a spy she was a naive amateur and quickly found herself a pawn in various plots and counterplots between the French, Germans, and British. The French eventually arrested her for espionage and executed her by firing squad in 1917. She maintained her innocence throughout, insisting she had lived only "for love and pleasure."

▶ THE MEASURE OF INTELLIGENCE

Alfred Binet was a French psychologist who had spent his entire career studying the workings of intelligence. In 1905, at the request of the Ministry of Public Instruction, which sought a way to weed out children who needed special

---

- **JANUARY 2**
The Russians surrender Port Arthur to the Japanese.

- **FEBRUARY 27**
Russian writer Maksim Gorky is exiled to Latvia.

- **MARCH 18**
Eleanor and Franklin Roosevelt are married.

- **MARCH 22**
Great Britain limits child miners to an eight-hour workday.

- **MARCH 24**
French writer Jules Verne dies.

- **APRIL 1**
Telephone service links Paris and Berlin.

- **JUNE 4**
Property at Broadway and Wall Street in New York City sells for four dollars per square inch.

education, he and colleague Theodore Simon devised a system for rating students. A series of tests that measured aptitudes, like the ability to remember information and reach logical conclusions, yielded a "mental age" for a child, which might be higher or lower than the child's chronological age. In 1912 a German colleague hit upon the idea of generating an "intelligence quotient" by dividing the mental age by the chronological age and multiplying by 100. In this way, an average person—one whose mental and chronological ages coincided—would have an IQ of 100. In 1916, Stanford University psychologist Lewis Terman set about improving Binet's work, giving rise to the now-common Stanford-Binet IQ test.

Binet's original test sought only to identify children who might need extra attention in school, and Binet himself felt the test did not truly measure intelligence. He was also keenly aware that IQ tests had the potential to label a person, potentially for life, and he feared—correctly, in many cases—that children who scored poorly would fall into a "self-fulfilling prophecy" of low expectations and low achievement. Furthermore, some researchers have taken his work to imply that intelligence is inherited, something Binet never believed.

▶ AN AWARD FOR GERMS

The 1905 Nobel Prize awarded to German physician Robert Koch honored a milestone in the study of disease. Over 30 years earlier, as a country doctor working with a microscope that his wife had given him as a birthday gift, Koch started examining infectious diseases. His labors paid off in 1876 when he isolated the bacterium responsible for anthrax; it was the first time a germ was linked to a specific illness. He then turned his attention to tuberculosis, a disease that was the leading cause of death at that time. Though medicine abounded with theories as to what caused TB, Koch ended all

debate with his discovery of *Mycobacterium tuberculosis*, which he proved in an exhaustive series of experiments to be the causative agent of tuberculosis.

In 1890 Koch created a substance he called tuberculin, a sterilized solution of extracts from the bacterium, which he believed would cure the disease. He was mistaken, but tuberculin turned out to be useful in diagnosing the disease and helped French researchers develop a vaccine in 1921. And the advent of antibiotics in the 1940s finally offered a cure.

NICKEL MOVIES

In 1905 a Pittsburgh showman named Harry Davis began screening movies for the public in a small storefront theater. He christened it the "nickelodeon," a name coined from the admission price—five cents—and *odea*, the Greek word for theater. It was an instant success, showing two short films repeatedly from morning until night and drawing an average of 7,000 people each day. Nickelodeons—the name quickly became generic—soon sprouted up all over the country, in storefronts, on rooftops, in tents, and anywhere else a person could set up a screen, projector, and some benches. By 1908 there were an estimated 10,000 nickelodeons in America.

Nickelodeons gave immigrants a window into the culture of their new country and provided most Americans with their first exposure to movies. The demand they created was the driving force behind the nascent motion picture industry. In fact, virtually all of Hollywood's early moguls, including Louis B. Mayer, the Warner brothers, and Adolph Zukor, got their starts running nickelodeons.

■ TRENDS & TRIVIA

Philosopher George Santayana publishes the first volume of *The Life of Reason*.

Ty Cobb begins his baseball career with the Detroit Tigers.

The chemical fire extinguisher is invented.

The first pizzeria in the United States opens in New York City.

Zane Grey's *The Spirit of the Border*, the first of his more than 80 Western novels, is published.

The Fauve (Wild Beast) movement in art becomes popular.

The Qing (Manchu) Dynasty in China abolishes the civil service exam required for government employment for 2,000 years.

France establishes a separation between the Catholic Church and the State.

Norwegian explorer Roald Amundsen discovers that the north magnetic pole has shifted from the location at which it was detected 60 years earlier.

Irish group Sinn Fein is formed.

The newspaper *Variety* is founded.

The Rotary Club is founded.

The Spiegel mail-order catalog is introduced.

The ballet *The Dying Swan* is created for Russian dancer Anna Pavlova. ▼

33

• **JUNE 27**
The crew aboard the Russian battleship *Potemkin* mutinies.

• **JULY 2**
France limits miners to a nine-hour workday.

• **JULY 16**
Commander Robert Peary begins an unsuccessful expedition to the North Pole.

• **AUGUST 8**
President Roosevelt brings Russian and Japanese negotiators to Portsmouth, New Hampshire, in an attempt to end the Russo-Japanese War.

• **SEPTEMBER 5**
Treaty of Portsmouth ends the Russo-Japanese War.

• **OCTOBER 4**
First 30-minute airplane flight, by Orville Wright.

• **NOVEMBER 8**
The first electric lights are used on trains.

34

In 1894, French intelligence came across a letter implying that a member of the General Staff was selling information and weapon specifications to the Germans. Suspicion fell on Capt. Alfred Dreyfus, even though his handwriting matched that of the letter only vaguely, and his wealth discounted the obvious motive of greed. But his family was from Alsace—a region long suspected of German sympathies—and, more significantly, he was Jewish. A court-martial convicted Dreyfus and sentenced him to life in the hellish prison on Devil's Island off French Guiana.

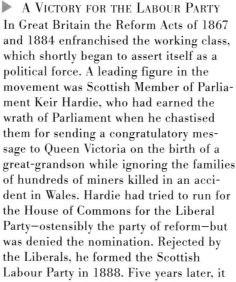

DEGRADATION OF DREYFUS

Even when the identity of the real traitor, Maj. Ferdinand Esterhazy, was discovered, the evidence was suppressed. But writer Émile Zola refused to let the matter die, publishing a blistering attack on the army entitled *J'Accuse* ("I accuse"). This prompted another investigation, in which the main evidence against Dreyfus was proven to be forged. He was inexcusably reconvicted, but freed by a presidential pardon. True vindication did not come until 1906, when a civilian court declared him innocent and restored him to the army.

▶ A VICTORY FOR THE LABOUR PARTY

In Great Britain the Reform Acts of 1867 and 1884 enfranchised the working class, which shortly began to assert itself as a political force. A leading figure in the movement was Scottish Member of Parliament Keir Hardie, who had earned the wrath of Parliament when he chastised them for sending a congratulatory message to Queen Victoria on the birth of a great-grandson while ignoring the families of hundreds of miners killed in an accident in Wales. Hardie had tried to run for the House of Commons for the Liberal Party—ostensibly the party of reform—but was denied the nomination. Rejected by the Liberals, he formed the Scottish Labour Party in 1888. Five years later, it merged with other worker-friendly groups to form the Independent Labour Party, and, in 1900, became the Labour Representations Committee (LRC). Their resolve grew in the face of a 1901 ruling by the House of Lords that held labor unions liable for any money lost by companies during strikes.

As the 1906 elections drew near, the LRC struck a deal with the Liberal Party whereby the LRC would run unopposed in 23 districts and support Liberal candidates in the others. As a result 29 seats went to the LRC, which then changed its name to simply the Labour Party. In 1924 Britain would have its first Labour government.

▶ DEATH OF A MODERN MASTER

In the 19th century, French playwright Augustin-Eugène Scribe advanced his theory of "the well-made play," which delineated the elements of good drama. A play should stick to the tried-and-true form of the melodrama, he claimed, with stock characters that stumbled through contrived plot devices, such as mistaken identity, to the inevitable happy ending. Scribe's views held sway through much of the 19th century.

What made Norwegian playwright Henrik Ibsen (right) famous is that he ignored Scribe's advice. His plays were not farcical and had decidedly unhappy endings. His characters were neither good nor bad; they were drawn in shades of gray and faced real problems. In *A Doll's House* (1879), a wife walks out on an unhappy marriage; in *Ghosts* (1881), a widow confronts the unpleasant circumstances surrounding her husband's death and her son's insanity. By writing plays that reflected the moral ambiguities of real life, Ibsen virtually invented modern drama and influenced a host of other writers, including Oscar Wilde and George Bernard Shaw. At the time of Ibsen's death in 1906 at the age of 78, he was celebrated throughout the world for his depictions of lives that, while not always pleasant, resonated with truth.

▶ A VOICE FOR MUSLIMS

The Indian National Congress, formed in 1885, was an attempt to give the citizens of India a greater voice in their own affairs. But the Muslims of India, overwhelmed by the Hindu majority, still felt without a voice. As a result, in 1906 the Aga Khan III and prominent Muslim leaders formed the All-India Muslim League, later known as simply the Muslim League. An early achievement of the League was "communal representation,"

- **FEBRUARY 17**
Theodore Roosevelt's oldest daughter, Alice, marries Speaker of the House Nicholas Longworth.

- **MARCH 7**
Finland becomes the first country to give women the vote.

- **MARCH 13**
American suffragist Susan B. Anthony dies.

- **APRIL 6**
In Naples, Italy, Mount Vesuvius sprays a column of fire.

◀ **APRIL 18**
One of the strongest earthquakes in U.S. history strikes San Francisco.

- **JUNE 30**
The Pure Food and Drug Act and the Meat Inspection Act are passed in the U.S.

which set aside government positions for members of various ethnic and religious groups, including Muslims.

Though the Indian National Congress became increasingly militant in its desire to achieve Indian independence, the Muslim League remained content with the status quo in order to protect Muslim interests. When independence seemed inevitable, the League pressed for the creation of a separate country. They got their wish in 1947, when the Muslim-dominated nation of Pakistan was carved from the newly independent India. The territory was originally known as West Pakistan, to distinguish it from the Indian region of East Pakistan, which became Bangladesh in 1971.

▶ MASTER OF MODERN ART
Though his work influenced most of 20th-century art—Picasso referred to him as "the father of us all"—Paul Cézanne found little success before his death in 1906 at the age of 67. Until he inherited his family's wealth in 1886, he had to rely on support from both his father and his childhood friend, writer Émile Zola. The first major showing of his work did not occur until 1895, and it was not until a 1904 exhibition that the art world began to recognize his importance.

Cézanne's early work was similar to that of the Impressionists, and he was particularly influenced by Camille Pissarro and

STUDIO OF PAINTER PAUL CÉZANNE

TYPHOID MARY

In the summer of 1906, six people who were staying in George Thompson's Long Island house came down with typhoid fever. Worried that potential renters would be scared away unless he could track down the cause, Thompson hired sanitary engineer George Soper to help him. Soper soon became suspicious of a cook named Mary Mallon, who had come to work at the house three weeks before the outbreak—the standard incubation period for typhoid. Tracing her job history, Soper found that wherever Mallon went, typhoid followed.

Mallon turned out to be the first known carrier of typhoid fever in the U.S., spreading the disease to others but immune to it herself. Her doctors released her on the condition that she never again work with food, but she quickly broke her word and spent the next five years spreading disease as a cook. Before she was found and confined to a hospital, where she spent the last 23 years of her life, "Typhoid Mary" gave the disease to at least 53 people, three of whom died.

Édouard Manet. He eventually moved beyond Impressionism, and began, in the late 1870s, a period known as his "constructive" phase, characterized by his technique of building depth on canvases with crosshatching patterns of brushstrokes.

Later in his life he settled in Aix, where he turned his attention to still lifes and landscapes, though the simplicity of his subjects belied the sophisticated techniques he used to portray them. His use of sharp borders, bold colors, and distorted perspectives helped inspire a number of artistic movements, including Cubism.

■ TRENDS & TRIVIA

First animated cartoon is shown.

Freeze-dried food is introduced.

The term "hot dog" is coined.

Permanent wave hairstyles are introduced, in England.

Russian author Maksim Gorky visits America in a futile attempt to rally support for the 1905 Russian revolution.

Ruth St. Denis introduces modern dance in the U.S.

The Victrola debuts. ▶

Britain launches the H.M.S. *Dreadnought*, the most powerful battleship in the world, prompting an arms race with Germany.

The New York City Police Department begins using fingerprints as a means of identification.

China begins a new effort to help its estimated 100 million opium addicts break their habit.

Sonar for submarines is introduced.

President Theodore Roosevelt begins antitrust proceedings against John D. Rockefeller's Standard Oil Co.

Mormon leader Joseph Smith is fined 300 dollars for polygamy after fathering his 43rd child by his 5th wife.

Theodore Roosevelt becomes the first sitting President to leave U.S. soil as he surveys construction of the Panama Canal.

Jukeboxes are new.

The world record for the fastest mile by automobile is set at 28.2 seconds.

35

• JULY 9
Tsar Nicholas II dissolves the first Russian Duma.

• AUGUST 3
Secretary of War William Howard Taft is sent to Cuba as provisional governor to help quell a rebellion.

• AUGUST 11
First patent for talking films issued, in France.

• SEPTEMBER 25
State troopers attempt to quell massive race riots in Atlanta, Georgia.

• OCTOBER 3
S.O.S. is adopted as the international distress signal.

• OCTOBER 17
Telegraph is used to transmit pictures.

• NOVEMBER 2
Russian revolutionary Leon Trotsky is exiled to Siberia.

• DECEMBER 10
Theodore Roosevelt wins the Nobel Prize for peace for his work in ending the Russo-Japanese War.

36

When Cardinal Giuseppe Melchiorre Sarto became pope in 1903 he took the name Pius X, an indication that he intended to reverse the liberal policies of the man he succeeded, Leo XIII, in favor of Leo's predecessor, the conservative Pius IX. Leo's papacy had been marked by diplomatic initiatives and by an increasing social awareness. In an 1891 encyclical titled *Rerum Novarum,* for example, he encouraged employers to provide their workers with reasonable wages and to recognize labor unions. But most troubling to Pius X was Leo's embrace of Modernism, a movement that sought to reconcile Catholic dogma with the realities of the 20th century—including science—and encourage a more critical interpretation of the Bible.

A strict adherent to the concept of papal infallibility—a doctrine created by the First Vatican Council, convened by Pius IX in 1869—Pius X (left) made clear that he would brook no dissent in matters of morals or faith. His 1907 encyclical, *Pascendi Dominici Gregis,* rejected Modernism.

▶ CYLINDER, SPHERE, AND CONE

Taking to heart the advice of Paul Cézanne, who urged artists to "see in nature the cylinder, the sphere, and the cone," Pablo Picasso adopted a technique that combined geometric figures with primitivism, as well as influences from African and Oceanic sculpture. French painter Georges Braque followed the same inspiration, and the style the two founded became known as Cubism, from a critic's derisive comment that Braque had reduced nature to cubes. Picasso introduced Cubism to the world in his 1907 work "Les Demoiselles d'Avignon," a startling depiction of five ladies from Barcelona's notorious Avignon Street. Picasso originally intended to depict the women in a brothel, but the painting's fractured, distorted style sets the scene even without a backdrop. The painting was "a battering ram against the classical conception of beauty," wrote one critic.

Picasso and Braque eventually explored colors and shading in Cubist paintings. Their work attracted a following, and within a few years painters such as Juan Gris and Fernand Léger adopted Cubism. Still others, like Joan Miró and Marcel Duchamp, used elements of Cubism to create their own styles. Though Cubism declined in popularity by the 1920s, it was instrumental in the evolution of abstract art and Surrealism.

▶ ALLIANCES AND ENTENTES

By 1907 the sides that would face off against each other in World War I were already formed. In that year the Anglo-Russian Convention forged a military alliance between Britain and Russia, powers that had previously squared off in the Crimean War and were currently struggling for control of Persia. Britain, more fearful of the military threat from Germany than its colonial rivalry with the French, had already formed the Entente Cordiale with France in 1904. This solidified their military ties and settled a number of nagging colonial disputes in North Africa and Southeast Asia. France—with substantial investments in Russia and a need to bolster defenses against Germany—had no objections. The so-called Triple Entente was born.

The Triple Entente was also a reaction to the Triple Alliance, an 1882 agreement by which Germany, Austria-Hungary, and Italy—which would become the Central Powers in the war—promised to come to each other's aid if any of them were attacked by two or more powers. The motives of the three countries were varied: Germany sought to isolate France, which it had already defeated in the Franco-Prussian War of 1871; Austria-Hungary wanted to shore up its defenses against Russia; and Italy needed assistance in pursuing colonial interests in North Africa (though it would eventually side with the Entente powers in the war).

▶ THE TRIAL OF THE CENTURY

The original "trial of the century" began in New York City on January 23, 1907. Facing a charge of murder was 35-year-old Harry Kendall Thaw, scion of a wealthy Pittsburgh family. The victim was 53-year-old Stanford White, the famous architect whose firm designed the Columbia University campus, Pennsylvania Station, and the original Madison Square Garden. On June 25 of the previous year, Thaw had walked up to White's table at the Garden's rooftop restaurant, pulled out a pistol, and fired three bullets into White's head. The motive was jealousy; the mercurial Thaw was tormented by the fact that his wife, 21-year-old Evelyn Nesbit, had had an affair with White.

- **JANUARY 26**
  U.S. Congress forbids companies from making direct campaign contributions.

- **FEBRUARY 26**
  Theodore Roosevelt declares that the Panama Canal will be built by the U.S. Army instead of private contractors.

- **MARCH 8**
  The British Parliament defeats a measure to give women the vote.

- **APRIL 6**
  The German Roentgen Society declares x-rays dangerous and urges restricted use.

- **MAY 25**
  The Finnish Diet becomes the first national governing body to admit women.

- ▶ **AUGUST 24**
  New York's Singer Tower becomes the tallest building in the world.

- **JUNE 14**
  Norway grants women the vote.

WAVE CRESTS

HARRY K. THAW (RIGHT) WITH CHAPLAIN MCGUIRE AT THE TOMBS

The defense painted the less-than-pure Nesbit, a one-time chorus girl and former lover of actor John Barrymore, as a helpless young victim who fell under White's influence. Local newspapers—even the gray *New York Times*—eagerly published Nesbit's testimony of how White forced her to drink champagne until she passed out, later waking up naked in his bed. When Thaw learned of these and other salacious details, his attorneys argued, he shot White in a fit of temporary insanity. The trial ended with a hung jury, and a subsequent one ended with Thaw being committed to a psychiatric institution. In 1967, the year of her death, Nesbit claimed that White was the only man she ever loved.

▶ BIRTH OF THE FUNNY PAPERS
On November 15, 1907, the *San Francisco Chronicle* ran a cartoon about the adventures of Mr. Augustus Mutt, "a rum working for $10 a week" who was looking to hit it big at the racetrack. A "Low Down Kid" at the track offers him a hot tip, straight from "a guy who knows a bloke who knows a friend of a fellow wot used to go with a sister of a man who is a half cousin to a gazabo who was a stable boy...." The strip ends with the teaser, "see what Mr. Mutt does for himself in tomorrow's *Chronicle*.

"Mr. A. Mutt" was not America's first comic strip but it was the first to appear

By the late 19th century, New York City was home to half as many Italians as lived in Naples, and two-and-one-half times as many Irish as lived in Dublin. The wave of immigrants that was transforming America peaked in 1907, with the arrival of more than 1.2 million people. To help deal with the vast influx, Congress had passed the Naturalization Act the previous year, creating the federal agency that would eventually become the Immigration and Naturalization Service.

Troubling to many Americans was the change in the ethnic makeup of the new arrivals. In the 1880s, more than 80 percent had immigrated from northern and western Europe. But in the 1900s, fully half came from central and eastern Europe, and in the 1910s the proportion of these immigrants rose to more than 70 percent. The predominantly Catholic and Jewish newcomers were not as warmly welcomed as earlier Protestants, and many lawmakers proposed legislation to either slow immigration or at least restrict it to more "desirable" immigrants.

daily instead of just on Sundays. A few months later, creator Bud Fisher gave Mutt a foil—a top-hatted, mustachioed ex-psychiatric patient named Jeff—and renamed the strip "Mutt and Jeff." Soon millions were following the pair's get-rich-quick schemes and scams in papers all over the country.

■ TRENDS & TRIVIA

Italian educator Maria Montessori opens her first nursery schools, in Rome.

New York's Bronx Zoo ships 15 bison to the West to help repopulate the species.

Salaries for congressmen and senators are increased to 7,500 dollars per year, and cabinet members and the vice president to 12,000 dollars.

The U.S. sends Marines to Honduras to protect American interests in the war with Nicaragua.

President Roosevelt sends the "Great White Fleet" of warships on a cruise around the world in a show of American naval power.

Canned tuna fish is introduced.

United Methodist Church is founded.

Photographer Edward S. Curtis publishes the first volume of his 20-volume series *The North American Indian*.

New York's Plaza Hotel opens.

Great Britain gives New Zealand dominion status.

Russian "holy man" Grigory Rasputin establishes his influence at the Russian royal court.

Attorney Mohandas K. Gandhi organizes a civil disobedience movement in South Africa when Asian immigration is restricted.

Frenchmen Auguste and Louis Lumière devise a method for color photography.

Dr. Sun Yat-sen advances his theories for democracy in China.

New York's *Ziegfeld Follies* opens.

Neiman-Marcus opens its first store, in Dallas, Texas.

37

● **SEPTEMBER 6**
The British liner *Lusitania* makes her maiden voyage.

● **OCTOBER 22**
The Ringling brothers buy the Barnum and Bailey Circus.

● **NOVEMBER 4**
J. P. Morgan persuades New York bankers to prop up failing banks and the stock market in order to end a financial panic.

● **NOVEMBER 13**
World's first helicopter flight is made, in France.

● **NOVEMBER 16**
Oklahoma becomes the 46th state.

● **NOVEMBER 28**
The Congo becomes an official territory of Belgium.

● **DECEMBER 10**
British writer Rudyard Kipling wins Nobel Prize.

1908

38

Henry Ford was not the first person to build a practical automobile, but he knew what the public wanted. "I will build a car for the great multitude," he once said, and he made good on his promise with the Model T in 1908.

The Model T became the first car to be mass-produced by assembly-line techniques, which were introduced by Ford in 1913. This resulted in the car's price dropping from $850 in 1908 to $290 in 1925. To make repairs easier, Ford had his dealers stock spare parts. For those not near a dealership, a mail-order catalog offered every one of the car's 4,830 parts. In addition, the automobile "aftermarket" sprang up to provide Model T owners with devices to improve the look and performance of their cars. Along the way, Ford added conveniences: electric lights in 1915, an electric starter in 1919, and balloon tires and manual windshield wipers in 1925.

Throughout the "Tin Lizzie's" 19-year production history, Ford largely stood by his vow to produce "no new models…no new bodies, and no new colors." In the Model T's heyday, it accounted for 60 percent of all cars in America.

FIRST · CAR

▶ INCREASING "NATIONAL EFFICIENCY"

"Conservation…stands for development," stated Gifford Pinchot, who headed the Department of Agriculture's Division of Forestry during Theodore Roosevelt's administration, "for the prevention of waste…the use of foresight, prudence, thrift, and intelligence in dealing with public matters…[for] national efficiency." Roosevelt held a deep love for nature and believed the best course to pursue was a "wise use" policy that combined preservation with Pinchot's vision of carefully measured development. Conservationists, such as the famous naturalist John Muir, wanted huge tracts of wilderness left completely pristine, while western lawmakers wanted no interference in exploiting natural resources in any way they saw fit.

In an attempt to reach common ground, Roosevelt convened a National Conservation Commission in 1908, which was attended by 44 of 46 state governors and hundreds of experts in conservation matters. The commission generated much heat but little light, as many of the environmental reforms Roosevelt proposed were voted down in Washington. But the commission did start the tradition of an annual governors' meeting, and it brought the issue of conservation to the forefront of American politics.

▶ END OF A DYNASTY

The Empress Dowager Cixi, in the words of one historian, made "both Messalina and the Borgias look positively bourgeois." Originally a low-ranking concubine of the Emperor Xianfeng, she won favor by bearing his only son, who became emperor in 1862. Cixi (above, right) became Empress Dowager, dismissed the young emperor's eight regents,

and had their leader executed. Upon her son's death in 1875, she became regent to the new emperor, three-year-old Guangxu. Throughout her tenure as Guangxu's regent, Cixi squandered her country's coffers as China fell apart around her. Britain, France, Germany, and Japan were all making colonial inroads, and she sat helplessly by as Japan and Russia fought a war on Chinese soil for control of Manchuria. Internally, the Qing (Manchu) Dynasty was collapsing as republican revolutionaries gained strength. When Guangxu reached maturity and attempted to stabilize the country with social reforms, Cixi had him exiled. He died on November 14, 1908, possibly from poison administered at her behest. The very next day Cixi herself died at the age of 72, leaving her handpicked successor, three-year-old Puyi, as the new emperor. Puyi's reign lasted barely three years before he and his regents abdicated in the face of republican advances.

▶ A GENTLEMAN'S AGREEMENT

Though America was founded and populated by immigrants, its citizens clearly felt that some immigrants were better than others. The Chinese, for example, were so resented that, in 1882, Congress passed the Chinese Exclusion Act, which prohibited Chinese from entering the country for ten years. Japanese immigrants fared little better; though an 1894

- **JANUARY 20** New York City bans smoking by women in public places.

- **FEBRUARY 1** The King and Crown Prince of Portugal are assassinated in Lisbon.

- **FEBRUARY 25** A rail tunnel under the Hudson River between New York and New Jersey makes the trip three times faster than by ferry.

- **MARCH 4** The New York Board of Education bars whipping in schools.

- **APRIL 27** First International Congress of Psychoanalysis opens, in Austria.

- **MAY 9** Winston Churchill is elected to the British House of Commons.

- **MAY 28** Congress passes a law regulating child labor in the District of Columbia.

treaty promised unrestricted immigration, the influx of Japanese into California was met with increasing hostility. The Japanese government tried to stem the problem by refusing to issue passports to its citizens seeking work in America, but many simply entered through Canada or Mexico. In response, a Japanese and Korean Exclusion League was formed in 1905, and in 1906 San Francisco's school board began segregating Asian children from all other students.

President Theodore Roosevelt sought to smooth over the incident; he brought the mayor of San Francisco and the entire school board to the White House and cajoled them into ending the segregation on the promise that he would take care of the immigration problem personally. His solution, the so-called "gentleman's agreement," allowed the U.S. to deny entry to any Japanese immigrant carrying a passport issued by any country. The agreement was formalized and went into effect on February 18, 1908, and remained in effect until supplanted by the National Origins Act of 1924, an egregiously racist law that was intended to maintain, in the words of one official, the "racial preponderance [of] the basic strain of our people."

▶ OUT OF THE ASHCANS

Mirroring the trend in literature, many American artists of the early 20th century turned to realism. In particular, a group of artists known as the Eight—Arthur B. Davies, Maurice Prendergast, Ernest Lawson, John Sloan, William Glackens, Everett Shinn, George Luks, and Robert Henri—began paying attention to the largely ignored street life of New York City. Their fascination with the noisome back alleys of urban life would later inspire a critic to dub the American Realism movement the "Ashcan School."

The Eight, who first exhibited together in 1908, were agents of their own undoing, when in 1913 they organized the

BE PREPARED

His defense of the British garrison at Mafeking against a 217-day-long siege during the Boer War made Gen. Robert Baden-Powell (below) a national hero. But when he returned home after years abroad, the hardy outdoorsman came to believe that the children of England were, in his words, "without individuality or strength of character, utterly without resourcefulness, initiative, or guts for adventure."

Hoping to strengthen the mettle of the "pale, narrow-chested hunched-up miserable specimens" who would someday rule the empire, Baden-Powell founded the Boy Scouts in 1908. In that year he wrote *Scouting for Boys*, an adaptation of a survival guide he had written for soldiers. It included the Scout's Oath and scouting's official motto, "Be prepared"—a play on Baden-Powell's initials. The scouting movement quickly spread to the United States, where the Boy Scouts of America was founded in 1910. That same year, Baden-Powell and his sister Agnes founded the Girl Guides, which would later become the Girl Scouts.

International Exhibition of Modern Art in New York. The display of art by European Modernists like Paul Cézanne and Vincent van Gogh electrified the American art world, which quickly embraced the Modernist aesthetic. But though the Ashcan School was short-lived, its influence was deeply felt. The emphasis on the mundane was an element that inspired the Pop art movement in Europe and America in the 1950s and '60s.

■ TRENDS & TRIVIA

Skin test for tuberculosis is developed.

Jack Johnson is the first black heavyweight boxing champion.

Dancer Isadora Duncan revolutionizes ballet.

The electric razor is invented.

The paper cup is a new convenience.

The first round-the-world automobile race begins in New York City.

The U.S. Supreme Court rules that laws restricting the number of hours per week a woman can work are constitutional.

The *Christian Science Monitor* debuts.

The first horror film, *Dr. Jekyll and Mr. Hyde*, premieres.

Ex-Lax laxatives are introduced.

General Motors Company is formed.

The first primitive version of the Geiger counter is invented.

Gideon Bibles are placed in hotel rooms for the first time.

Dutch physicist Heike Kammerlingh-Onnes produces liquid helium.

The Bureau of Investigation, forerunner of the FBI, is formed within the U.S. Justice Department.

A Room with a View, by E. M. Forster, is published.

The Census Bureau reports that the U.S. divorce rate is higher than in any other country.

U.S. Postal Service buys automobiles for delivery of Rural Free Delivery mail.

39

• **JUNE 21**
Russian composer Nicolay Rimski-Korsakov dies.

• **JUNE 24**
Former U.S. President Grover Cleveland dies.

• **AUGUST 5**
The Philadelphia subway opens.

• **AUGUST 11**
Britain's King Edward VII meets with Germany's Kaiser Wilhelm II to protest growth of the German navy.

• **SEPTEMBER 9**
Orville Wright becomes the first person to fly a plane for longer than one hour.

• **OCTOBER 1**
The first international soccer tournament is held.

• **NOVEMBER 3**
William Howard Taft is elected President of the U.S.

The quest for empire and the thirst for petroleum met in turn-of-the-century Persia, where an Englishman named William Knox D'Arcy purchased from Shah Muzaffar al-Din the oil rights to three-quarters of the entire country. D'Arcy had made a fortune mining gold in Australia and hoped to make another drilling for the oil the Persians had for centuries used to caulk ships and mortar bricks. The purchase also helped fend off Russian colonial advances in the area.

Within three years, D'Arcy had stretched his personal fortune to its limits without striking oil. Saving him from financial collapse was the British government, which arranged for a syndicate to bankroll the project and keep the oil concession from falling into foreign hands. The "syndicate of patriots" finally struck large amounts of oil in 1908, just as its directors were about to pull the plug on the entire operation. In 1909 the first stock went on sale for the new Anglo-Persian Oil Company, which would later become British Petroleum.

EARLY OIL WELL
IN PERSIA

▶ THE RULES OF INHERITANCE

In 1856 Austrian monk Gregor Mendel established the modern science of genetics with his series of experiments on pea plants. By crossing plants with different traits—tall plants crossed with short ones, or yellow-pod plants crossed with green-pod ones—he discovered that an offspring's appearance was determined by "heritable factors" that came from each parent. Mendel's ideas were largely ignored in his own lifetime, but in the first decade of the 20th century biologists rediscovered them and started to shed light on the biochemical basis behind them.

In 1903 American graduate student Walter Sutton and German biologist Theodor Boveri independently realized that the agents of inheritance must be chromosomes, mysterious cellular structures discovered in the 1870s. However, the number of chromosomes in a cell was woefully inadequate to account for the myriad physical characteristics believed to be inherited. A solution was provided by researchers who postulated that Mendel's heritable factors—dubbed "genes" in 1909 by Danish biologist Wilhelm Johannsen—formed very small segments on the chromosomes. Supported by Thomas Hunt Morgan's discovery the next year of a gene that coded for eye color in fruit flies, the gene theory of inheritance was established.

▶ ART IN ARCHITECTURE

By the end of the 19th century, architecture was freeing itself from the restraints of classicism. Spurred by the availability of high-quality structural steel, American architects like Louis Sullivan were introducing the world to skyscrapers, which consisted of steel skeletons onto which walls, floors, and ceilings were hung. On a smaller scale, Sullivan's protégé Frank Lloyd Wright was perfecting his "prairie houses." Low-slung, with long, horizontal

lines, the houses were designed to fit seamlessly into their environments. Nowhere is Wright's philosophy more evident than in the Chicago house he built for bicycle manufacturer Frederick Robie in 1909. Likened to the architectural equivalent of Cubism, The Robie House (above) contains a series of "space blocks" rather than rooms, which are divided by the light that permeates them from the long horizontal rows of exterior windows. The exaggerated eaves, supported by steel beams, are practical as well as decorative, as they help keep the house cool.

Though no less reliant on steel skeletons as Sullivan, Spanish architect Antonio Gaudi represented a polar opposite in terms of design. Working in the Art Nouveau style, which emphasizes curves instead of straight lines, Gaudi took the concept to extremes with his Casa Milá apartment complex, completed in 1907. There is not a straight wall in the interior or exterior of the entire building; even the chimneys, in the words of one critic, "seem to have been squeezed from a pastry tube."

▶ DOUBLE-EDGED SWORD

In 1909 German chemist Fritz Haber invented a cheap, efficient process for manufacturing ammonia by combining its constituent elements—hydrogen and nitrogen—under high temperature and pressure

---

in the presence of a catalyst. The Haber process, as it came to be known, proved immensely valuable in the manufacture of fertilizers, explosives, and chemical weapons. During World War I Haber headed the German effort to create chemical weapons; the first chemical attack of the war, in 1915 at Ypres, used a gas of Haber's invention to kill 150,000 soldiers.

▶ THE MAGIC BULLET

At the 1906 opening of a new medical research institute in Frankfurt, physician Paul Ehrlich delivered a speech outlining the type of research he hoped to conduct there. He wanted to create antimicrobial compounds that could "exert their full action exclusively on the parasite harbored within the organism and would represent, so to speak, magic bullets which seek their target of their own accord." Having spent much of his career devising stains that would dye certain types of cells but not others, he believed it was possible to create drugs that would act in the same way, targeting invading cells without affecting the rest of the body.

Ehrlich turned his attention to syphilis, a scourge that caused the slow, painful deaths of thousands of people every year. He tested nearly 1,000 compounds on rabbits before discovering that "compound 606" worked well. In 1909 he and a

PAUL EHRLICH IN HIS LABORATORY

PLASTIC

Working in his Yonkers, New York, lab in 1907, a Belgian-born chemist named Leo Baekeland mixed together a series of chemicals to create a "solidified matter yellowish and hard," he wrote in his notebook. "Looks promising…it will be worth while to determine how far this mass is able to make moulded materials…may make a substitute for celluloid and for hard rubber."

Baekeland had invented the world's first synthetic plastic, a remarkable liquid resin that, when heated, turned into a hard, amber-colored solid. It was resistant to heat and cold, and would not melt, burn, or dissolve. Introduced in 1909 as Bakelite, it soon replaced hard rubber as an insulator in electrical appliances. But such utilitarian uses soon yielded to more decorative ones, as the easily dyed Bakelite found its way into vividly colored handbags and jewelry. And in the 1920s the material lent itself to the Art Deco movement, producing stylish radios and telephones.

BAKELITE DRESSING TABLE SET

coworker filed a patent for 606, which would later go by the trade name Salvarsan. Although he wanted to test the drug on at least 10,000 patients before marketing it, so great was the demand from doctors and patients that Ehrlich's institute quickly distributed 65,000 units of the drug, free of charge, throughout the world. Salvarsan remained the treatment of choice until the advent of penicillin in the 1940s, and Ehrlich's work created the modern science of chemotherapy—a term he coined.

■ TRENDS & TRIVIA

Ezra Pound publishes his first volume of poetry.

The *Ballets Russes* debuts in Paris.

Intrauterine device method of birth control is invented.

U.S.Congress passes the 16th Amendment, which creates a federal income tax.

W. C. Handy composes the first blues song to be written down on paper.

Sigmund Freud makes his first—and only—trip to America, to lecture.

Lipton's tea is introduced.

The electric toaster is new.

The Kewpie doll debuts.

The Lincoln penny replaces the Indian-head penny.

Newsreels are introduced.

Italian poet Filippo Tommaso Marinetti ushers in the Futurist movement in art and literature.

President William Howard Taft selects Hawaii's Pearl Harbor as America's main naval base in the Pacific.

The first kibbutz is established, in Palestine.

Clay tennis courts are introduced.

Coca-Cola is exported to Great Britain.

Former President Theodore Roosevelt embarks on a scientific expedition to Africa, sponsored by the Smithsonian Institution and *Scribner's* magazine.

The first commercially produced airplane is built.

Jigsaw puzzles become popular.

41

• JULY 25
French aviator Louis Blériot is first to fly across the English Channel.

• SEPTEMBER 9
100th anniversary of Robert Fulton's steamboat, the *Clermont.*

• OCTOBER 2
Orville Wright sets an airplane altitude record of over 1,600 feet.

• OCTOBER 26
Japanese statesman Prince Ito is assassinated.

• OCTOBER 13
A mob of 100,000 suffragists storms Britain's Parliament.

• DECEMBER 21
A committee declares Robert Peary discoverer of the North Pole.

• DECEMBER 26
American artist Frederic Remington dies.

HUMAN BEGINNINGS

by George E. Stuart

ARCHAEOLOGIST AND CHAIRMAN, NATIONAL GEOGRAPHIC
COMMITTEE FOR RESEARCH AND EXPLORATION

On a warm winter day in early 1939, Smithsonian Institution archaeologist Matthew W. Stirling reached the end of an arduous horseback journey on the jungle trails of southern Veracruz, on the Gulf Coast of Mexico. He had come to the farmstead of Tres Zapotes to see firsthand a unique discovery that had taken place there some 80 years earlier. In the 1860s, farmers chanced upon a huge rounded boulder protruding slightly from the ground. Too regular in form to be natural, and in an area where stone was rare anyway, it attracted their attention, and they began to dig. What they found astonished the entire village—a colossal human head carved in stone. Some 6 feet high and weighing an estimated 12 tons, the mysterious monument portrayed a man in a close-fitting helmet. For some, the scowling countenance

Left: Olmec head, Mexico   Middle: Ramses's coffin, Egypt   Right: Neandertal skull, Israel

recalled American Indian ancestors; for others, the enormous head seemed African. All agreed on one thing: Nothing like it had been seen before.

Matt Stirling had read of the great stone head of Tres Zapotes, and of others nearby, and on a 1935 visit to a museum in Europe he had seen another artifact said to be from the same part of Mexico—a brilliant carving in jade that depicted a snarling feline. The style of the jade carving and of the stone heads was unlike anything else in the known archaeological record. Who had made such unusual things, and when, and why?

With his expedition in 1939, Stirling launched an effort to solve the mystery. During the next eight years, he, his wife Marion Stirling, and photographer Richard H. Stewart uncovered and documented the essential story of an enigmatic people called the Olmec. In so doing, they revealed America's first great civilization, a people who lived in the hot, humid lowlands of Mexico's Gulf Coast around 1200 B.C., thrived for nearly a millennium, and set the stage for the great cultures, from Maya to Aztec, who succeeded them in southern Mexico and Central America.

Sponsored in part by the National Geographic Society, the fieldwork of Matthew Stirling exemplifies the quest for knowledge of the human past that the Society has supported for more than a century as part of its primary mission to promote "the increase and diffusion of geographic knowledge." Of the more than 6,000 grants for scientific research and exploration given since the Society's founding in 1888, an estimated 40 percent has focused on finding and studying the remains of the ancestors of humanity on every habitable continent. The effort has taken archaeologists from the frozen heights of the Andes to the darkest depths of the sea. Plagued by a paucity of surviving evidence, it has never been easy. One colleague has likened the search for human origins to an attempt to reconstruct an epic film from a random sample of relatively few frames.

As a member of the Society's Committee for Research and Exploration, I have been fortunate to have witnessed much of this quest. One of the most exciting moments during my tenure on the committee occurred when the announcements of Louis S. B. and Mary Leakey would come in to the Society from Olduvai Gorge, where the couple labored together on one of the most noteworthy deposits of early human and humanlike fossils on the planet.

In 1959 the Leakeys discovered an Australopithecine skull, dubbed *Zinjanthropus* and later reclassified as *Australopithecus boisei*, that pushed human ancestry back to 1.75 million years. A dozen years later, in 1972, when their son Richard Leakey and his team of specialists were working promising fossil beds beside Lake Rudolf, Kenya, we were thrilled to hear of another remarkable find. The skull, estimated to be 2.8 million years old and designated "1470," represented the earliest known example of the genus *Homo*. Two years later, in northeastern Ethiopia, paleoanthropologist Donald C. Johanson found the most complete early skeleton to date. Nicknamed "Lucy" (after the Beatles song "Lucy in the Sky With Diamonds"), the female designated *Australopithecus afarensis* walked upright some three million years ago. And in 1976 Mary discovered the famed footprints at Laetoli, where two adolescent Australopithecines walked along a muddy river flat during a volcanic ash fall some

3.6 million years ago. Supported by the National Geographic Society and other funding agencies, the accomplishments of the Leakeys and their colleagues in paleoanthropology have just begun to tell us not only of individuals in the deep past of the human epic, but also of their relationships and their lines of evolution.

The Society has played a similar role in supporting underwater archaeology, an endeavor that first had to overcome the considerable mechanical problems involved in deep diving. Beginning in the early 1950s, the innovations of famed diver-explorer Jacques-Yves Cousteau and Society staff member Luis Marden resulted in not only the development and refinement of the "Aqua-Lung" for ever deeper dives but also the equipment indispensable to underwater photography.

My own introduction to the world of underwater archaeology took place under Luis Marden's tutelage in 1958 at Cenote Xlacah, a deep natural well at the heart of the ancient Maya site of Dzibilchaltun, in Yucatán, Mexico. I survived that dive to the bottom of the 160-foot deep underwater cavern and remember it vividly to this day. As the beam of my light played over the rocky slope of limestone rubble that reached from the surface to the deepest, darkest part of the cenote, I saw large fragments of pottery vessels; the occasional symmetry of carefully cut and smoothed stones—evidently architectural wall elements that had fallen from buildings above; animal and human bones, polished and browned by the water; pieces of green stone, probably jade; and white shell carvings. Through and above all this swarmed tropical fish, lit like jewels in the light that had invaded their world.

My single dive deep into the Maya past later allowed me to appreciate the calling of George F. Bass, who virtually invented the field of underwater archaeology. Through Texas A&M University's Institute of Nautical Archaeology, which he founded, Bass imposes rigorous standards on the discipline that have allowed it to make an enormous contribution to our knowledge of the past. The National Geographic Society is proud to have had a part in his long and productive career.

Bass was the first to use a submersible vessel and to employ stereo photography to map ancient shipwreck sites. In 1984 Bass and his team excavated a 3,300-year-old wreck off the southern Turkish coast that contained what has been called the most important collection of Bronze Age artifacts ever found. Since the 1960s Bass has led teams of divers and archaeologists to numerous sites, untouched for thousands of years, whose contents have told us much of ancient Mediterranean trade routes; of the exchange of goods and ideas that took place among those ancient peoples; and of the talents of the artisans, sculptors, and shipbuilders of that distant world. Many of their works, now among the treasures of museums for the edification of the present living, would otherwise have been lost forever.

Helping to find and preserve archaeological sites has been a longstanding challenge and goal of the Society's from the beginning. In 1911 and 1912, backed by a Society research grant of $10,000, Hiram Bingham reached—and mapped—the legendary Inca city of Machu Picchu in a lofty saddle of the Andean ridge above Peru's Urubamba River. Nearly 80 years later, in 1987, in an arid lowland valley between the Andes and the Pacific Ocean, Peruvian archaeologist Walter Alva fought off hostile tomb robbers who had already sacked much of a large adobe mound at the site of Sipán. With the Society's help, he uncovered one of the greatest treasuries of ancient Moche art—tombs containing elite warrior-priests buried some 1,500 years ago in full regalia, including jewelry, ritual weapons, and costume ornaments of gold and turquoise.

In North America, investigations aided by Society support have ranged from Mesa Verde and Chaco Canyon in the Southwest to the ancient mound sites of the Ohio and Mississippi Valleys. Recent developments in the question of the original settlement of the Americas have culminated in the consensus among scholars that Monte Verde, Chile, so meticulously excavated by archaeologist Tom Dillehay and dated to some 30,000 years ago, is the earliest human site of certain date in the Western Hemisphere.

Most recently, on a rather routine afternoon in September 1995, I received a telephone call from Arequipa, Peru. "We have just come down from Mount Ampato," said anthropologist Johan Reinhard. "We have found a frozen Inca corpse about 500 years old, and we need help."

The discovery proved more important than even Reinhard realized at the time. With Society funds wired to Peru that very afternoon, Reinhard was able to secure the body in deep freeze and to return to the discovery site ahead of potential looters. There the anthropologists found the remnants of a series of high mountain shrines set up on the frozen summits five centuries ago. The analysis of artifacts found deposited there—including figurines of gold and silver dressed in cloth much like that of the frozen body—revealed in hitherto unknown detail the Inca devotion to mountains as part of their sacred landscape. Physical analysis of the body itself, undertaken at Johns Hopkins University after the mummy was brought to the United States, revealed that the young Inca woman, who was estimated to have been about 14 years old when she died, had been killed by a blow to the head as she knelt, doubtless sedated, as an honored sacrificial victim.

As the National Geographic Society reaches the turn of the millennium, it can look back with pride at the hundreds of field projects or endeavors related to the study of the human past that were funded either fully or in part by the Society's Committee for Research and Exploration. Today and into the new century, scores of scientific teams will be in the field to continue this work. In one project, for example, Society grantee Ann Cyphers brings our story full circle as she and her colleagues continue the work that Matthew Stirling began at Tres Zapotes some 60 years ago. Cyphers is currently excavating San Lorenzo, a site Matt Stirling discovered in 1946, seeking more clues to the puzzle of the origins and ways of America's first civilization. Like Matthew Stirling, Ann Cyphers realizes—and welcomes—that others will follow, for much remains to be done. True to its traditions, the National Geographic Society will doubtless be on hand to help the quest for knowledge—wherever it may lead.

1910-

1919

The Woman's Decade

1910-1919

by Glenda Gilmore
ASSOCIATE PROFESSOR OF HISTORY, YALE UNIVERSITY

WOODROW WILSON WATCHED ANXIOUSLY as his train pulled into Washington, D.C.'s Union Station on the eve of his inauguration in March 1913. The streets and the station seemed eerily quiet. Where, he asked himself, were the people? Finally someone told him that his constituency was otherwise engaged: Those who could vote—men—rioted on the sidewalks and stumbled over the curbs, shoving, jeering, and blocking the way of the thousands who could not vote—women—who were marching down Pennsylvania Avenue. As Wilson made his way down from the station on Capitol Hill, 5,000 women literally fought their way through the city. Ultimately, the National Guard rode in to clear the streets of rioting spectators.

Most of those in the parade belonged to the National American Woman Suffrage Association (NAWSA), which had been working for more than 20 years, without much success, to implement woman suffrage one state at a time. So far, only nine states allowed women to vote on an equal footing with men. Many women came to believe that it would take a federal constitutional amendment to extend the vote to all U.S. women. Thus it was that in the capital of the United States, American women struggled in the streets to advance block by block, just as they fought to advance woman suffrage state by state. The movement had come of age, using political tactics to demand political rights.

Opposite: Throughout the world during the 1910s, women struggled for the right to vote.
Preceding pages: Weapons introduced in the Great War, or World War I, changed the course of warfare forever.

Woman suffrage was not the only issue that caused politics to spill over its traditional boundaries between 1910 and 1920, but seen through the eyes of the women who marched down Pennsylvania Avenue in 1913, it would be a woman's decade. American men and women who called themselves Progressives believed that ignorance, poverty, violence, public graft, and even disease could be vanquished by extending democracy to an educated and informed public around the world. To that end, they not only engaged in civic work in their hometowns but also sought to make changes on a national level.

US troops, shown here in a children's magazine, suffered fewer deaths in World War I than their European allies.

Only one other decade (the 1860s) saw so many amendments to the U.S. Constitution. The 16th and 17th Amendments both passed in 1913, authorizing a federal income tax that would fund the work of reform, and beginning the election of U.S. senators directly by the people. But the 18th Amendment, which came in 1919, and the 19th, which finally passed in 1920, would most please the suffragists, many of whom had cut their political teeth in the Woman's Christian Temperance Union (WCTU). In this international organization, dedicated to controlling the consumption and sale of alcohol, women in the U.S., Canada, England, and Australia first learned to organize, to lobby, and to share their concerns with each other across national lines. The 18th Amendment to the U.S. Constitution enacted national Prohibition, making the "manufacture, sale, or transportation of intoxicating liquors" illegal in all of the states. The 19th Amendment, also known as the Susan B. Anthony Amendment, would ultimately give U.S. women the right to vote on equal terms with men.

Like temperance, woman suffrage was also an international movement. In June 1910 delegates from Norway, New Zealand, and Australia—the only countries where women then had the vote—had headed a parade of 10,000 women in London who marched to support the woman suffrage bill recently introduced in Parliament. In the wake of this and other suffrage demonstrations, England's jails had teemed with 600 women whom the Liberal British government had arrested for violence. By the time of the march on Washington three years later, women from eight countries had joined the International Alliance for Woman Suffrage: Britain, the United States, Australia, Denmark, Germany, the Netherlands, Norway, and Sweden.

Two of the women who marched down Pennsylvania Avenue in 1913 symbolized struggles within the American suffrage movement itself. Alice Paul had spent several years as a student in England, where she learned the militant tactics of the British suffragists. Just two months prior to the march, Paul had moved to Washington, and the confrontational parade was the product of her organizing efforts. Paul, who believed that NAWSA should concentrate on getting a woman suffrage amendment on the floor of Congress, headed the organization's congressional committee. However, NAWSA's national board felt that the state associations remained a valuable resource and that Paul's plan would undercut their efforts. The board replaced Paul as head of the congressional committee, and she ultimately formed her own organization, the Congressional Union. Paul's experience in the British suffrage movement had convinced her that American suffragists were much too ladylike and apolitical to get results. Under Paul's leadership, the Congressional Union followed the British lead, adopting more militant tactics. They demonstrated in front of the White House, heckled male politicians, and targeted anti-suffrage members of Congress for defeat with door-to-door campaigns.

Some of the American women went to jail for their efforts. Once there, many followed the example of the British women by staging hunger strikes. U.S. prison officials took a lesson from their English counterparts and force-fed the women through tubes inserted down their throats. After a few years, anti-suffrage politicians came to regard NAWSA as the lesser of two evils, as compared with Congressional Union members, who never took no for an answer. As one historian put it, "Here was an army of young Amazons who looked congressmen straight in the eye, who were absolutely informed, who knew their rights, who were not to be frightened by bluster, put off by rudeness, or thwarted either by delay or political trickery. They never lost their tempers and they never gave up."

ANOTHER MARCHER WHO DID NOT SEE EYE TO EYE with NAWSA's policies—but for very different reasons—was Ida B. Wells-Barnett. An African-American woman from Chicago, Wells-Barnett had crusaded against the lynching of southern African Americans since she was a girl. She was also active internationally in the cause of black civil rights. But in 1913, in her own nation's capital, she found herself segregated. When white women suffragists from the southern states objected to her marching with the Chicago delegation, NAWSA relegated all the black women to the rear of the parade. In the U.S. South, a legal system of segregation kept blacks and whites apart in public places, and state constitutions kept African Americans away from the polls. While southern white women wanted the right to vote for themselves, most of them did not want to extend that right to black women. Wells-Barnett wouldn't stand for it. She slipped out of the back of the parade, circled around the block, and met the white Chicago delegation, where she marched in step, shielded by two white supporters.

Many of the suffragists who marched in 1913 were also pacifists, who watched with dismay as war broke out in Europe just over a year later. For three years, each side in the war— the Central Powers (Germany and Austria-Hungary) and the Allies (Great Britain, France, Russia, and Italy after 1915)—sought to convince the United States of the justness of their cause. For three years, the U.S. tried to remain impartial. Many Americans had just emigrated from European nations on both sides, and the U.S. made loans to both sides. But as U.S. ships ran afoul of Germany's submarines, the U.S. affinity for the British meant that trade with the Allies rose dramatically, even as German Americans came under increasing scrutiny in the

United States. During the same period, the United States was sparring with Mexico, where political unrest was jeopardizing American investments. In response, President Wilson sent troops into that country in 1914 and again in 1916.

In the years between the Washington march and America's entry into the Great War in 1917, dissension among American women disrupted the suffrage movement. In 1916, as Alice Paul's Congressional Union continued to push for a constitutional amendment, NAWSA watched suffrage go down to defeat in New Jersey, New York, Pennsylvania, and Massachusetts. NAWSA prevailed upon its former president, Carrie Chapman Catt, a New Yorker and then president of the International Suffrage Alliance, to move to Washington and once again assume leadership of the organization. Determined to work on both the state and national levels, Catt spoke optimistically: "The turn of the road has come," she declared. "I really believe that we might pull off a campaign which would mean the vote within the next six years." She was right.

Campaigns for woman suffrage around the world bolstered U.S. women. In many places, women gained the right to vote incrementally. In Britain, for example, unmarried women who owned property had been able to vote in municipal and school board elections since the mid-19th century, and more British women won the right to vote in 1918, although even then it was limited to "householders, wives of householders, and women of thirty and over." By 1919 women voted in Austria, Canada, Czechoslovakia, Denmark, England, Germany, Hungary, Ireland, Mexico, Norway, Poland, Russia, and Scotland.

What finally helped turn the tide for woman suffrage in the U.S. was Woodrow Wilson's rationale for entering the Great War (now called World War I). Even as Wilson preached to the American people that this would be a war "to guarantee peace and justice throughout the world," his domestic policies did not extend justice and democracy at home, to either the female half of the United States population or to African Americans. Wilson's ideological zeal to "show mankind the way to liberty" rested on an unlikely base: the unprogressive and undemocratic political methods practiced by white supremacists in the southern states whose votes the Democratic Party had needed to win a majority in the election of 1912. White supremacists in the South opposed any federal directive on voting, fearing it would endanger state-mandated disenfranchisement of African Americans by causing the federal judiciary to enforce the 15th Amendment guaranteeing all citizens the right to vote. Reluctant to anger this southern constituency, Wilson had consistently argued that suffrage should be left to the states to decide. To people of color both at home and abroad—as well as to American women and their sisters in countries where women already had the vote—Wilson's pronouncements on America's fitness to teach democracy rang exceedingly false.

In the face of Wilson's war rhetoric, Carrie Chapman Catt quickly made peace a women's issue. Men had led nations into this conflict, she argued. "War falls on the women most heavily, and more so now than ever before. This war should be a good argument for suffrage. It shows that men, as I have always believed, are as hysterical as women, only they show it in a different way. Women weep and men fight." In 1916 Catt capitalized on Wilson's avid interest in the European war and on Alice Paul's work in Washington to convince the President to end his opposition to a federal amendment for woman suffrage. Aware that he would need America's women if he took the country into war, Wilson made a mild statement at a NAWSA convention: "I have come to fight not for you but with you," he said, "and in the end I think we shall not quarrel over the method." In return for Wilson's support for a federal amendment, Catt agreed to refrain from a break that could prove embarrassing to his high-minded war ideology. However, she determined to press forward on both state and federal levels, since state victories would mean more pro-suffrage congressmen in Washington. In January 1918, as the British House of Lords passed its own suffrage amendment, the U.S. House of Representatives sent to the Senate a constitutional amendment to give women the vote. Wilson made public his support for the amendment by arguing that war presented an emergency, that the U.S. could not wait for state-by-state approval of suffrage, and that "the early adoption of this measure is necessary to the successful prosecution of the war."

W. E. B. Du Bois hoped that by supporting America's war efforts abroad blacks would gain equal treatment at home.

By then the United States had been a combatant in the war for nearly a year, Wilson having taken the country into the European fray on April 2, 1917. Shortly thereafter, African Americans took to the streets of New York as the suffragists had in Washington four years earlier. More than 8,000 men, women, and children marched in what became known as the Silent Parade, carrying banners that asked: "MR. PRESIDENT, WHY NOT MAKE AMERICA SAFE FOR DEMOCRACY?"

Despite these sentiments, the National Association for the Advancement of Colored People (NAACP), led by W. E. B. Du Bois, agreed to cooperate in the American war effort. This would be a war, Du Bois argued, in which the American principles would be held up in sharp relief. After such a war, democracy would surely be extended to black soldiers and sailors who died beside their white countrymen. Du Bois led African Americans in an about-face: to quit fighting on the home front for their own rights and to wage war abroad for the rights of others. "Let us, while this war lasts, forget our special grievances," Du Bois urged, "and close our ranks shoulder to shoulder with our white fellow citizens and the allied nations that are fighting for democracy." More than 200,000 African Americans served in France.

Allied soldiers on the Western Front in France welcomed American reinforcements. By the time the Allies declared victory at 11:00 on the morning of November 11, 1918, some 50,000 Americans had been killed in combat. But the toll for European nations was far greater: 615,00 Italians, 947,000 soldiers of Britain and the Empire, 1.3 million Austro-Hungarians, 1.4 million French, 1.7 million Russians, and 1.8 million Germans had died in action.

In the war for democracy at home, Carrie Chapman Catt won her bet, but W. E. B. Du Bois lost his. African Americans returned to a constricting job market, increasingly segregated housing in northern urban cities, and, sometimes, to murder. White violence against blacks broke out in 25 American cities during the summer of 1919. During the same hot summer, however, suffragists had cause to rejoice. On June 4, by a vote of 56 to 25, the Senate passed the Susan B. Anthony Amendment and sent it to the states for ratification as the 19th Amendment to the United States Constitution. The battle for ratification in the states would be close. As suffragists fanned out across the country to win over the 36 state legislatures needed to make the amendment law, they realized that the southern states were crucial to their effort. In August 1920, only one state short of final passage, North Carolina failed to act. But neighboring Tennessee took up the amendment the next day. There the vote came down to one legislator, 24-year-old Harry Burn. The legend is that Burn hesitated, unable to make up his mind, until he received a communication from his mother, ordering him to "help Mrs. Catt." On August 26, 1920, Burn cast the deciding ballot, Tennessee voted for suffrage, and American women gained the right to vote.

ALICE PAUL, WHOSE CONSTITUTIONAL AMENDMENT STRATEGY had been vindicated, quickly founded the National Woman's Party. But would black women share in the franchise? Certainly in Chicago, where Ida B. Wells-Barnett lived, black women voted and became an important force in city and state politics. But just as Wilson had failed to make America safe for democracy for all of its citizens, so had Alice Paul. In October 1920 Anna A. Clemmons, a nurse in Southport, North Carolina, wrote to the National Woman's Party, requesting their help in obtaining an absentee ballot. Clemmons had tried to register, she wrote, but the registrar had refused her, saying she could not read and write to "suit" him. "All persons of colored origin in this whole country have been unable to suit the registrar," Clemmons told the NWP, at the same time urging that they keep her complaint quiet. There is "so much prejudice existing," she wrote, "I am certain I will be a victim of a lawless mob." The National Woman's Party promised to look into her situation, but Anna Clemmons never heard from the party again. Not until 1965 would the federal Voting Rights Act guarantee the right to vote to all black Americans and put voter registration in Anna Clemmons's hometown under federal control.

Thus, as America's women went to the polls in the Presidential election of 1920, they found they were divided by class, race, and religion when they exercised their newly won right. Indeed, Alice Paul would work in vain until she died in 1977 for the passage of the Equal Rights Amendment, facing stiff opposition from women who feared that mandating equal treatment for women would erode certain protections they enjoyed in the workplace. Making America safe for democracy would remain a major unfinished task of the 20th century. ■

President Woodrow Wilson was willing to extend voting rights to women, but not to blacks.

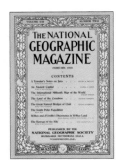

For NATIONAL GEOGRAPHIC, the second decade of the 20th century was rich with exploration, from the race between Robert Falcon Scott and Roald Amundsen to the South Pole, to the discovery of Machu Picchu by Hiram Bingham. It was also in this decade that the magazine's visual elements flourished, from the first hand-tinted color photographs to the vivid maps for which it is famous. "…The NATIONAL GEOGRAPHIC magazine has found a new universal language which requires no deep study…," wrote staff member John Oliver LaGorce in 1915, "the language of the Photograph!"

The Lost City of the Incas

In 1908 NATIONAL GEOGRAPHIC Editor Gilbert H. Grosvenor received a pair of articles by Yale University professor Hiram Bingham, detailing his explorations of South America. Grosvenor was not impressed; he told Bingham that "we have on hand a number of articles on South America, and therefore cannot find room for them." Grosvenor would have a change of heart the following year, after seeing Bingham's book *The Journal of an Expedition Across Venezuela and Colombia*, and

INTIHUATANA HILL AND THE TERRACES WEST OF THE SACRED PLAZA AT MACHU PICCHU

solicited an article from the young professor. This time it was Bingham's turn to sniff at the offer. "I scarcely know what to say…." he responded. "As you did not find those articles desirable…I do not believe that you would find anything that I might write…worth printing or paying for."

In 1911 Bingham made the discovery of a lifetime high in the Peruvian Andes. Guided by a native Indian, Bingham climbed sheer rock faces and braved dense jungle to find the

city of Machu Picchu, the best-preserved example of pre-Columbian civilization ever found. Though the age of Machu Picchu remains a mystery, as does the exact identity of its inhabitants, the city offers a testament to the skill of its builders. Working without mortar, expert masons constructed houses, terraced gardens, mausoleums, and some 3,000 steps linking everything. "No pin could penetrate between these [stone] blocks," marveled Bingham. "It was the work of master craftsmen."

Despite his initial problems with the GEOGRAPHIC's editors, Bingham ultimately contributed a number of articles and photographs detailing his Latin American explorations. And in 1912, 1914, and 1915, he led joint Yale University-National Geographic Society expeditions to the area.

The Last Pole

The turn of the century saw a number of attempts to reach the South Pole. British explorer Capt. Robert Falcon Scott mounted an assault in 1901, but had to turn back two years later as he and his two companions fell sick with scurvy. One of them, Ernest Shackleton, tried again in 1907, and came within 97 miles of the Pole before nearly succumbing to starvation.

Better prepared was Norwegian Roald Amundsen, whose 1906 navigation of the Northwest Passage had already earned him the National Geographic Society's Hubbard Medal. While exploring the Arctic, Amundsen studied the ways of the Eskimos, who taught him about dog handling and how to withstand the cold by wearing layers of loose-fitting garments made of caribou fur. It had been his dream to conquer the North Pole, but when he heard of Robert E. Peary's success he turned south. In August 1910, he set sail with 19 men, 97 sled dogs, and provisions for all.

Amundsen's wise planning made the expedition itself almost anticlimactic. The expedition reached the South Pole on December 14, 1911, planted the Norwegian flag, and then returned the 700 miles to their supply ship exactly on schedule and in excellent health. This was in stark contest to his competitor, Captain Scott, who had departed for the Pole before Amundsen. On January 15, 1912, Scott reached the Pole and found, to his bitter disappointment, the evidence of Amundsen's triumph. Disappointment turned to disaster on the return trip, as Scott and his companions perished from starvation and exposure by the end of March. In November another expedition found Scott's frozen body just 11 miles from his supplies.

Ten Thousand Smokes

The National Geographic Society sent Robert F. Griggs of Ohio State University to Alaska to study the effects of a 1912 eruption of the Novarupta Volcano in the Aleutian mountain range.

ALASKA'S MOUNT KATMAI, WITH ONE BRANCH OF THE KATMAI RIVER IN THE FOREGROUND

The eruption blew nearly five cubic miles of ash into the air, which settled into a foot-deep blanket as far as a hundred miles away. In his account in the January 1917 issue of NATIONAL GEOGRAPHIC, Griggs offered a useful analogy: "The comparative magnitude of the eruption can be better realized if one should imagine a similar eruption of Vesuvius. Such an eruption would bury Naples under 15 feet of ash; Rome would be covered nearly a foot deep; the sound would be heard at Paris; dust from the crater would fall in Brussels and Berlin; and the fumes would be noticeable far beyond Christiana, Norway."

The eruption and ash laid waste a 60-square-mile region Griggs named the Valley of Ten Thousand Smokes. The summit of nearby Mount Katmai volcano collapsed, and a series of fissures opened up on the valley floor, spewing 1,200°F steam. To protect the valley as it recovered, the federal government created the Katmai National Monument in 1918, and in 1980 the area was designated a national park and preserve.

● A Good Map Is Hard to Find

The editors of NATIONAL GEOGRAPHIC recognized early on the importance of maps. Its first—"Theatre of Military Operations in Luzon"—appeared in 1899. And it was ready for the outbreak of World War I with its "Map of the New Balkan States and Central Europe," which came with the August 1914 issue. So good were the GEOGRAPHIC's maps that a number of military leaders and aviators came to rely on them during the war.

Up until 1916, however, all the maps published by the magazine had been commissioned from outside sources. In that year, National Geographic Society President Gilbert H. Grosvenor founded the Society's Cartographic Division, headed by distinguished mathematician Albert H. Bumstead.

Grosvenor's goal was to "organize a highly competent research and cartographic staff to design and produce distinctive maps and to contribute original techniques and projections to the science of cartography." By the outbreak of World War II, the division had fulfilled this mission brilliantly; both Franklin D. Roosevelt and Winston Churchill relied on the Society's maps, and Adm. Chester Nimitz used one to help navigate a B-17 through a storm over the Pacific. On January 15, 1945, the *New York Times* took the opportunity to congratulate the division on its maps. The paper called it "probably the most ambitious cartographical undertaking on record," adding that "its maps not only enable us to follow the war's progress but convince us, as never before, that China, Australia, and Europe are our next-door neighbors."

● A Passage to Asia

Though NATIONAL GEOGRAPHIC had been printing travelogues ever since its founding, the one that appeared in the November 1910 issue, "Glimpses of Korea and China" by William Chapin, was different. For the first time the magazine ran hand-tinted photographs, some 40 in all, to accompany an article. Exactly a year later the magazine duplicated the feat, this time with Chapin's article "Glimpses of Japan."

Chapin traveled through Asia for months at a time, availing himself of virtually every possible mode of transportation, from modern trains to rickshas and basket chairs called *kagos*. And in the conclusion of "Glimpses of Japan," he shared the main lesson he learned: "If we criticize the Japanese in some of their ways, the fact remains that in many directions we could very profitably profit from them; for, all in all, where can be found a more happy or contented people? Two elements which contribute much to this condition appeared to us to be the simple life, which is so much talked of but so seldom realized in our own land, and their love of the beautiful in nature and considerateness for others, as evidenced in their extreme courtesy."

CITIZENS IN FUSAN, KOREA

• Strange Lands, Strange Customs

Early in the century, NATIONAL GEOGRAPHIC was one of the few reliable sources for information on the customs and cultures of exotic locales. Few articles were so exotic as "Head Hunters of Northern Luzon," written for the September 1912 issue by Dean Worcester, Secretary of the Interior for the Philippines. Accompanying the text on the practice of headhunting was a startling photograph of the headless body of a Philippine native on display, with the caption, "An Unlucky Ifugao Head-Hunter Who Lost His Own Head and Thereby Brought Disgrace Upon His Family and Village." In a later issue—and a much lighter vein—the magazine ran an unusual photo of local Philippine chieftains relaxing in the bush around a modern Victrola.

In the December 1913 issue, the spotlight was on the "Religious Penances and Punishments Self-Inflicted by the Holy Men of India." The article, by the Rev. W. M. Zumbro, focused on the practices of Hindu *sadhus*, or ascetics. "The foreigner hurrying through India rarely understands or appreciates these *Sadhus*," writes Zumbro. "He looks upon them as droll fellows...knows little of their subtle philosophy, and sees only the body clothed in white ashes, dirt, and rags, or the self-torture by which they seek to gain release." Accompanying the article were photographs detailing some of the methods of penance, including lying on beds of thorns and placing one's arms behind the back for so long "that they can never again be brought back to a natural attitude."

A PHILIPPINE NATIVE IN FULL REGALIA

• East and West

In the December 1910 NATIONAL GEOGRAPHIC appeared a frank, though sometimes condescending, assessment of relations between Asia and the West by Melville Stone, general manager of the Associated Press. "Although whole libraries have been written concerning Asia and the Asians," he began, "there is widespread belief that, because of the differences in our mentalities, it is not possible for us ever to understand them, or they us." This belief, Stone claimed, helped promote racism, and he responded by offering the view of Cicero, who claimed that a "common bond" unites all men.

According to Stone, the imperialism of America and Great Britain—based on the notion of the "white man's burden"—was fated to end. "How long will the 6,000 soldiers we have in the Philippines [as a result of the Spanish-American War] be able to keep our flag afloat among 8,000,000 of natives? How long will the 75,000 English soldiers in India be able to maintain British sovereignty over 300,000,000 of Asians? Believe me, these are not idle questions.... Upon our ability to make answer will depend the future of what we are pleased to call Western civilization. And I am convinced that there is real danger awaiting us unless we mend our ways. It is not the Asian who needs educating; it is the European. I am not worrying half so much about the heathen in his blindness as I am about the Christian in his blindness."

• On Safari with the Geographic

After retiring from the Presidency, the ever restless Theodore Roosevelt embarked on an African safari with his son Kermit. He published an account of the trip in his 1910 book *African Game Trails: An Account of the African Wanderings of an American Hunter-Naturalist*. In the book, excerpted and reviewed in the GEOGRAPHIC, Roosevelt marveled at the variety of nature:

"The land teems with beasts of the chase, infinite in number and incredible in variety. It holds the fiercest beasts of ravin, and the fleetest and most timid of those beings that live in undying fear of talon and fang. It holds the largest and the smallest of hoofed animals. It holds the mightiest creatures that tread the earth or swim in its rivers; it also holds distant kinfolk of these same creatures, no bigger than woodchucks, which dwell in crannies of the rocks and in the treetops. There are antelope smaller than hares, and antelope larger than oxen. There are creatures which are the embodiments of grace, and others whose huge ungainliness is like that of a shape in a nightmare."

• A Celestial Trial

In the August 1919 issue, with a whimsy uncharacteristic of NATIONAL GEOGRAPHIC, writer William Showalter explained the mysteries of the cosmos in "Exploring the Glories of the Firmament." Playing the role of a celestial attorney, Showalter summoned astronomical objects to testify to the vast distances and incredible speeds that are commonplace in space.

One witness was Halley's Comet, which offered the following testimony: "...Sir Isaac Newton had worked out the fundamental principle of celestial mechanics, namely, the law of gravitation. He had a friend by the name of Halley. This man undertook to see whether or not I was subject to that law.... Applying Isaac Newton's law to me, he said that I was traveling thirty-four miles a second when I was nearest the sun, and that I had turned round and was headed for the regions whence I had come. He said I

A VIEW OF THE GREAT NEBULA IN ORION

would travel out into space some three billion miles, my gait slowing down as I journeyed, and that when I got ready to make the turn to come back I would be loafing along at the celestial snail's pace of a mile a second.... Then he said that if he was right I would come back in about seventy-six years.... I knew that he had fathomed my mystery and solved my secret. But the people of the Earth did not. They said: 'Oh, yes, Halley is a cheap-John notoriety-seeker. He is trying to get fame by a prediction that will attract attention, but he postpones the date of the comet's reappearance to a time when he is dead and his forecast forgotten!... But Halley stood pat.... Sure enough, in the language of the streets, 'he had my number.' With less proportional departure from his schedule than the Congressional Limited makes in its Washington-New York run, I reappeared...."

• A Patriotic Appeal

Like the nation, NATIONAL GEOGRAPHIC remained officially neutral when World War I broke out. But articles like "The World's Debt to France" (November 1915), "Belgium's Plight" (September 1914), and "The Burden France Has Borne" (April 1917) made its sympathies clear. When America entered the war, the magazine published patriotic pieces like "Do Your Bit for America," by President Woodrow Wilson in April 1917, and "Stand by the Soldier," by Gen. John Pershing the next month.

"My Fellow-Countrymen," began Wilson. "The entrance of our own beloved country into the grim and terrible war for democracy and human rights which has shaken the world creates so many problems of national life and action which call for immediate consideration and settlement that I hope you will permit me to address to you a few words of earnest counsel and appeal with regard to them.... There is not a single selfish element, so far as I can see, in the cause we are fighting for. We are fighting for what we believe and wish to be the rights of

mankind and for the future peace and security of the world...."

Wilson exhorted every farmer, miner, manufacturer, and worker to become "more prolific and efficient than ever," and ended with a patriotic flourish: "Let every man and every woman assume the duty of careful, provident use and expenditure as a public duty, as a dictate of patriotism which no one can now expect ever to be excused or forgiven.... The supreme test of the nation has come. We must all speak, act, and serve together!"

• Russia in Transition

For the most part, NATIONAL GEOGRAPHIC steered clear of politics in its early days. But it was not completely blind to the troubles of the world, as evidenced by Gilbert H. Grosvenor's article "Young Russia: The Land of Unlimited Possibilities," which took up the entire November 1914 issue. "Russia is not a state," said Grosvenor, "it is a world." But for all its vast resources and the boundless energy of its people, it had severe problems; one of the most important was its lack of international trade. "Holland could be hidden in the vast reaches of the Russian plain," he wrote, "almost as a needle in a haystack, and yet Amsterdam alone does more international business than all the seaports of Russia together."

Grosvenor noted that most Russians lived in poverty and saw little hope for improvement under the autocratic rule of Tsar Nicholas II. "There are conditions in Russia which a visitor from the land of free schools, free speech, and a free press finds it difficult to understand; the deplorable rarity of good schools, making it a sore trial for a poor man to get his son educated; the arrival of his American newspaper, with often half a page stamped out by the censor in ink so black that it is impossible to decipher a single letter; the timidity, nay fear, of some people of being overheard when talking frankly on political subjects...."

THE HORIZON OF MOSCOW, MARKED BY COUNTLESS GILDED SPIRES AND STARRY DOMES

60

Gen. Porfirio Díaz had ruled Mexico as a dictator since overthrowing the government of President Sebastian Lerdo de Tejada in 1877, maintaining a guise of legitimacy by periodically engineering reelection as president. When wealthy landowner and political neophyte Francisco Madero lost the election to Díaz in 1910 as a result of election fraud, he was arrested, but escaped and fled to Texas. From Texas he organized a revolt that in just six months succeeded in overthrowing the dictatorship.

Madero's success lay in his ability to unify the disparate groups that opposed Díaz. The wealthy resented the dictator's arbitrary and capricious rule, and the lower classes were reduced to destitution as the government seized their land. Champion of the dispossessed in the south was Emiliano Zapata, while bandit and revolutionary Francisco "Pancho" Villa helped lead the fight in the north. But this uneasy coalition fell apart after Madero was elected president in 1911. The poor found his attempts at reform too slow, and business leaders opposed them altogether. Just two years later, Victoriano Huerta unseated Madero in a military coup that plunged the country into years of civil war.

▶ THE ANNEXATION OF KOREA

After Japan's success in the Russo-Japanese War, the Emperor set his sights on Korea, an underdeveloped country that was nonetheless of vital strategic importance. In 1905 Korea was forced to approve an agreement that made it a Japanese "protectorate"—something Theodore Roosevelt tacitly allowed in the Treaty of Portsmouth, which ended the war. Five years later, an agreement between Japan and Russia established strict trade policies that ended the "open door" policies in Manchuria that were favored by the West.

In 1909 Japanese Prince Ito had been assassinated by a Korean student, an act that fueled the already strong martial spirit in Japan. On August 22, 1910, Japan responded by annexing Korea. According to the terms of the annexation agreement, Emperor Kojong would retain the Korean throne, but Japan would assume control of virtually every aspect of Korean government, from the police force to the judiciary to foreign policy. But even as a figurehead Kojong proved too independent, and in 1912 was replaced by his son Sunjong, who was presumed to be more malleable. The Japanese forces that had been in Manchuria were moved to Korea, where they enforced a brutal rule in which all forms of protest were swiftly quashed. Japan was firmly ensconced as the dominant power in Asia.

▶ THE FOLLIES

Much of the credit for establishing musical theater in America belongs to Florenz Ziegfeld, who in 1907 unveiled a musical revue centered around his wife, Polish singer Anna Held. *The Ziegfeld Follies*, as the revue was called, hit its stride in 1910 when Ziegfeld hired performers like vaudevillian Bert Williams—one of a number of black performers to find success on stage—and comedienne Fanny Brice

(right). Not yet 20 years old, Brice had already begun to establish herself with routines like "Sadie Salome," a mock-sultry dance in which she spoke with a Yiddish accent. Irving Berlin had written the music to the dance, and by 1911 he was writing for Ziegfeld. One of his tunes, "A Pretty Girl Is Like a Melody," became the theme song of the *Follies*. Brice and Berlin were soon joined by talents like W. C. Fields (who started out as a juggling comedian), songwriters Jerome Kern and George Gershwin, humorist Will Rogers, and singer Eddie Cantor. In the meantime Ziegfeld also produced dozens of Broadway shows, including *Show Boat* (1927), which established the model for the modern musical.

▶ THE WHITE SLAVERY SCARE

Conservatives in America were worried about what they perceived as a decline in the country's moral fiber. Divorce rates were rising, women were pressing for the vote, and attitudes toward sex were loosening. Furthermore, the vast numbers of immigrants coming into the country fueled paranoia that many women were being brought to America to work as prostitutes. To combat this "threat," in 1910 Congressman James Mann of Illinois sponsored the White Slave Traffic Act, better known as the Mann Act.

The law's wording was as highbrow as its subject matter was lowbrow: Any persons "who shall knowingly transport or

---

- **JANUARY 8**
French aviator Hubert Latham sets an altitude record of 3,300 feet.

- **FEBRUARY 6**
The Boy Scouts of America is founded.

- **MARCH 8**
French Baroness de Laroche becomes the first woman to earn a pilot's license.

- **APRIL 23**
The World's Fair opens in Brussels, Belgium.

- **JUNE 1**
Capt. Robert Falcon Scott sets off for the South Pole.

- **JUNE 2**
Charles Stewart of Great Britain makes the first round-trip flight across the English Channel.

- **JULY 9**
Archaeologists in Egypt discover tablets recording the fall of Jerusalem to the Romans.

cause to be transported, or aide or assist in obtaining transportation for, or in transporting, in interstate or foreign commerce...any women or girls for the purpose of prostitution or debauchery, or for any other immoral purpose...shall be guilty of a felony." Though the act ostensibly focused on prostitution and the forcible transport of women, it was in truth a thinly veiled attempt to legislate personal morality. In a famous Supreme Court challenge to the case, the court ruled in 1917 that the act even applied to two men who had been convicted of driving two female acquaintances across state lines to Reno, Nevada, for what were presumably immoral—though completely private and consensual—acts.

In 1942 the Mann Act would claim its most famous victim, when Charlie Chaplin found himself on trial for allegedly having a young California woman meet him in New York for an extramarital tryst. Though the actor was acquitted, the woman won a paternity suit against Chaplin, and the scandal of the two trials put an end to his Hollywood career.

▶ BATTLE OVER THE FORESTS
Nature-lover and ardent conservationist Theodore Roosevelt found a kindred soul in Gifford Pinchot (below), a wealthy New Yorker who directed the Department of Agriculture's Forestry Division. Appalled at the unchecked destruction of western forests, the two men spent seven years set-

ting aside vast tracts of public land to preserve them from the saws of rapacious loggers. By the time Roosevelt's Presidency ended in 1909, America had 148 million acres of protected forests.

But with William Howard Taft in the White House, Pinchot's policies fell under siege. The first shot came when Taft's Secretary of the Interior, Richard Ballinger, announced his intention to grant coal-mining claims in Alaska that Roosevelt had expressly forbidden. Pinchot fought the decision with his characteristic vigor and passion, but the President sided with Ballinger. Pinchot wrote an open letter to a Senate committee investigating the matter, after Taft prohibited all parties from speaking out. Citing Pinchot's defiance—an act "almost unparalleled in the history of the government"—the President fired him in January 1910.

YEAR OF THE COMET

In 1910 Halley's Comet made its first appearance of the 20th century. And like every other appearance since British physicist Edmond Halley discovered its periodic nature in 1705, it brought out the superstitious in people. Writer Mark Twain, born with the comet's last appearance in 1835, died with its latest on April 21. Two weeks later Edward VII of England fell suddenly to pneumonia.

Superstition turned to hysteria when astronomers announced that the Earth would pass through the comet's gaseous tail. Some people attempted to seal off their homes from the gases, and doctors and priests were swamped with requests for curatives. Those who knew better scoffed; many held skywatching parties on rooftops hoping to catch a once-in-76-year glimpse of the comet.

■ TRENDS & TRIVIA

The ballet *The Firebird*, by Igor Stravinsky and Sergey Diaghilev premieres.

"Let Me Call You Sweetheart" is a popular tune.

Chemotherapy is introduced.

Iodine is used as a disinfectant.

E. M. Forster's *Howards End* is published.

The first volume of Bertrand Russell and Alfred North Whitehead's groundbreaking work *Principia Mathematica* is published.

Father's Day is first celebrated.

First policewoman is hired, in Los Angeles.

The Good Housekeeping Seal of Approval is created.

Neon lights are invented.

Hallmark, Inc., is founded in Kansas City, Missouri.

Women's Wear Daily is founded.

The electric washing machine debuts. ▶

Safety glass is developed.

The NAACP is founded.

The trench coat is introduced by Burberry's of London.

Sickle-cell anemia is identified.

Elizabeth Arden opens her first beauty salon, on New York's Fifth Avenue.

The book *The Fundamentals: A Testimony to the Truth* helps usher in the fundamentalist religious movement.

Vichysoisse is created at the Ritz-Carlton Hotel in New York.

61

• AUGUST 27
Thomas Edison demonstrates the first talking motion pictures.

• SEPTEMBER 19
Gen. Louis Botha becomes premier of the Union of South Africa.

• OCTOBER 4
King Manuel II of Portugal flees to Gibraltar in the wake of a republican revolution.

• NOVEMBER 8
A Democratic-majority U.S. Congress is elected for the first time since 1894.

• NOVEMBER 8
Franklin D. Roosevelt is elected to the New York State Senate, from Dutchess County, New York.

• NOVEMBER 11
Russian writer Leo Tolstoy dies.

• DECEMBER 17
The first parliament of the Union of South Africa convenes.

1911

On March 25, 1911, in New York City, a fire started in a waste bin on the eighth floor of the Asch Building (below) at Washington Place and Green Street, which housed the Triangle Shirtwaist Company's factory. Workers tried fighting it with the building's fire hose but the nozzle was rusted shut and the rotted hose disintegrated. Though some workers escaped by the elevators, the cables quickly burned through, making them inoperable. Workers raced down the three-foot-wide staircase, but the crowd pressing against the exterior doors—which swung inward—kept them from opening. Another exit was locked shut. The flimsy fire escape collapsed under the weight of so many people. In desperation, a number of women jumped out of windows, to their deaths.

After just 18 minutes the fire burned itself out, but not before killing 146 people, mostly young Jewish and Italian women. In an era when sweatshops were rampant, the fire finally brought the issue of workplace safety to national attention, and resulted in the revision of fire codes throughout the country.

▶ THE CENTER OF THE ATOM

In the early years of the 20th century the prevailing theory of atomic structure was the "plum pudding" model of British physicist J. J. Thomson, director of Cambridge University's renowned Cavendish Laboratory. Thomson, who had discovered the electron in 1897, postulated an atom in which positively charged protons formed a loosely packed ball interspersed with negatively charged electrons.

The man who changed that view was Ernest Rutherford, an ebullient New Zealander who had studied under Thomson. Heading the physics department of the University of Manchester, he performed a series of experiments in which he fired so-called alpha particles—a positively charged form of helium—into thin sheets of gold foil. Though most of the particles traveled straight through the gold, to his astonishment he found that a few of the particles ricocheted straight back. It was "almost as incredible as if you fired a 15-inch shell at a piece of tissue paper and it came back and hit you," he later marveled.

Mulling over the results, he proposed a new theory in 1911 to explain everything. The atom must consist of a small, densely packed nucleus of protons around which electrons orbited at relatively great distances. Most of the atom was empty space, explaining why most of the particles passed straight through. But when one struck a nucleus head-on, the mutual repulsion pushed the alpha particle back.

▶ REVOLUTION IN CHINA

As the corrupt Qing (Manchu) Dynasty crumbled in China, revolutionaries seized the opportunity to put the final nail in the imperial coffin. In October 1911, armed soldiers seized the city of Wuhan and from there moved outward, slaughtering any imperial troops that stood in their way.

YOUNG CHINESE MODERNIZE BY RELINQUISHING THEIR PIGTAILS

The frightened child emperor Puyi and his regents offered concessions but they were too little, too late. The rebels soon captured Shanghai, and then established a republican government in the city of Canton.

The elected president of the new republic was Dr. Sun Yat-sen, a physician who had been living in exile for the past 14 years. While in exile he had founded the New China Party, which advocated a wide range of progressive reforms. Amid growing factionalism and civil war, Sun was soon to be replaced by a general.

▶ THE SPIRIT OF PHILANTHROPY

"This, then, is held to be the duty of the wealthy," wrote Andrew Carnegie. "To consider all surplus revenues which come to him simply as trust funds, which he is called upon to administer...in the manner which, in his judgement, is best calculated to produce the most beneficial results for the community." Through his domination of the steel industry, the Scottish-born Carnegie had amassed a fortune. In 1901 he sold his company to J. P. Morgan and devoted his life to giving his money away.

Despite endowing the Carnegie Foun-

• JANUARY 21
The National Progressive Republican League, a forerunner of the Progressive Party in the U.S., is formed by Robert LaFollette.

• FEBRUARY 18
American aviator Eugene Ely accomplishes the first successful takeoff and landing of a plane from a ship.

• MARCH 7
In the wake of the 1910 Mexican Revolution, the U.S. sends 20,000 troops to the Mexican border.

• APRIL 30
Portugal grants women the right to vote.

• MAY 18
Bohemian composer and conductor Gustav Mahler dies.

• MAY 25
The Mexican Revolution forces President Porfirio Díaz to resign and flee to Paris.

• JUNE 9
Temperance agitator Carry Nation dies.

dation for the Advancement of Teaching in 1905 and the Carnegie Endowment for International Peace in 1910, the tycoon discovered to his dismay that the interest on his fortune was accruing faster than he could donate the capital. The solution came from his friend Elihu Root, then Secretary of State, who advised Carnegie to put his money into a charitable trust to be administered by a board of trustees. Thus was born the Carnegie Corporation, founded in 1911 to promote "the advancement and diffusion of knowledge among the people of the United States." The corporation became a model for philanthropy, spreading its largess to worthy institutions—most notably libraries—all over America.

▶ RAGTIME TAKES HOLD

"Syncopation is the soul of every American," Irving Berlin (below, right) once said, "and ragtime is a necessary element of American life." Berlin invented neither, but he helped make them both popular. Born Israel Baline in Russia in 1888, he emigrated to New York with his family a few years later. He wrote his first published song in 1907 while working as a singing waiter in a Chinatown cafe. Four years later he had his first big hit with "Alexander's Ragtime Band." Though not actually written in a ragtime style, it helped popularize the composers who did write rags, such as Scott Joplin. It also made Berlin rich and helped foster an "American sound."

Amazingly, Berlin had no formal musical training and barely even read music. He could only play in the key of F-sharp—the black keys on a piano—and had a number of pianos custom-made with "transposing key boards" that would, at the flip of a lever, play in another key while allowing him to stick with the black keys. He also worked with "musical scribes," who would take the melodies he picked out on his piano and write them down. Despite these difficulties, Berlin wrote more than a thousand songs—including such classics as "White Christmas," "God Bless America," and "Blue Skies"— in a career that spanned more than 50 years.

NO RESISTANCE

Dutch physicist Heike Kamerlingh Onnes had been the first to generate significant amounts of liquid hydrogen, which condenses at -253°C, barely 20 degrees above absolute zero. Then, in 1895, British scientist William Ramsay discovered the element helium—previously known to exist only on the sun—on Earth. It was believed that helium would have a much lower condensation point than hydrogen, and Onnes made liquid helium his quest. In 1908 he finally succeeded in obtaining droplets at the temperature of nearly absolute zero. But not until 1911 was he able to build a device that would store liquid helium. Once he did, his first experiment was to test the effects of extreme cold on electrical current. Running a current through mercury immersed in liquid helium, Onnes found that all resistance disappeared. He termed the phenomenon "superconductivity." It eventually helped make possible inventions like magnetic resonance imaging (MRI) and vast particle accelerators.

■ TRENDS & TRIVIA

For the first time a cancer caused by a virus is discovered.

The first transcontinental airplane flight takes place.

The first Indianapolis 500 automobile race is held.

Harriet Quimby becomes the first female licensed pilot in the U.S.

The electric starter for automobiles is introduced.

The 60-story Woolworth Building in New York City becomes the world's tallest.

Scottish physicist C. T. R. Wilson invents the cloud chamber.

The National Insurance Act provides health and disability insurance for the British working class.

Theodore Dreiser's *Jennie Gerhardt* is published.

The "Mona Lisa" is stolen from the Louvre in August; it is recovered in December 1913.

Louis Chevrolet founds his automobile company.

The debut of John M. Synge's play *The Playboy of the Western World* provokes outrage at its New York premiere.

Children's classic *The Secret Garden,* by Frances Hodgson Burnett, is published.

John D. Rockefeller's Standard Oil Co. is declared a monopoly by the Supreme Court and is broken up.

Edith Wharton's *Ethan Frome* is published.

Crisco vegetable shortening is introduced.

"Goodnight Ladies" and "I Want a Girl (Just Like the Girl that Married Dear Old Dad)" are popular songs.

◀ JUNE 22
George V is crowned King of Great Britain after the death of Edward VII.

● AUGUST 10
The British House of Lords is stripped of its power to veto laws.

● SEPTEMBER 2
An American sets a new record by driving two miles in 1.37:89 minutes.

● OCTOBER 1
Winston Churchill is appointed Britain's First Lord of the Admiralty.

● DECEMBER 10
French physicist Marie Curie wins her second Nobel Prize, for chemistry.

● DECEMBER 14
Norwegian explorer Roald Amundsen reaches the South Pole.

● NOVEMBER 5
Italy officially annexes Tripoli.

THE ELECTION OF 1912

When he was elected President in 1904, Theodore Roosevelt promised it would be his last term. But barely a year out of office in 1909, he began regretting that decision. He missed the spotlight, and felt that President William Howard Taft, his friend and handpicked successor, had strayed from the progressive principles he believed in so dearly. Still enormously popular, he sought the Republican nomination in 1912. At the convention in Chicago, party bosses stuck with Taft, but over 300 Roosevelt supporters walked out. They formed the Progressive Party, better known as the "Bull Moose" Party, six weeks later. The Progressives nominated Roosevelt for President and Columbia University president Nicholas Murray Butler for Vice President.

By splitting their own party, Republicans opened the door for the Democratic nominee, New Jersey governor Woodrow Wilson (above), who received nearly 6.3 million votes, with Roosevelt earning 4.1 million and Taft 3.5 million. The American Socialist Party's perennial candidate Eugene V. Debs collected almost one million votes—six percent of the total.

▶ CONTINENTS ADRIFT

In 1912 German meteorologist and explorer Alfred Wegener (below) advanced a bold theory of how the Earth's continents came into being. Noting how well the land masses seemed to fit together, Wegener theorized that they had been, some 200 million years ago, part of one great land mass—he called it Pangaea, Greek for "all lands"—whose pieces broke off and slowly drifted apart. "It is just as if we were to refit the torn pieces of a newspaper by matching their edges," Wegener claimed.

Virtually the entire geological community scoffed at the notion, however, and at the time of Wegener's death in 1930 his theory of "continental drift" was languishing for want of a solid explanation of how it could possibly work. Not until the 1960s did it find vindication, as geologists discovered that the world's land masses moved around the globe as if on conveyor belts. Not only had the continents moved in the distant past, they were still moving. Some of them crash into each other, forming mountain ranges like the Himalaya and the Andes. Some retreat from each other, creating vast gaps into which molten rock wells  from the planet's depths. Still others slide alongside each other in opposite directions, creating fault lines—like California's San Andreas fault—that generate earthquakes as they move.

▶ THE WORLD'S GREATEST ATHLETE

The star of the 1912 Olympics in Stockholm was a 24-year-old Oklahoman of Native American ancestry named Jim Thorpe (above, right). A football phenomenon at Pennsylvania's Carlisle Indian

School, Thorpe won gold medals in the decathlon—posting a world record—and the pentathlon. He also charmed the crowd with his folksy manner; when King Gustav V said to him, "Sir, you are the greatest athlete in the world," the reticent Thorpe fumbled for a moment, then simply replied, "Thanks, King."

Thorpe returned home to a hero's welcome, but a year later Olympic officials stripped him of his medals and barred him from future competition when they discovered that he had played semi-pro baseball prior to Stockholm. It was not until 1982, 29 years after Thorpe's death, that the International Olympic Committee returned the medals to his family and put his 1912 Olympic records back on the books.

▶ THE AFRICAN NATIONAL CONGRESS

Upon his 1906 graduation from Columbia University, South African-born Pixley ka Izaka Seme delivered a speech detailing his hopes for his homeland. "The giant is awakening," he said. "From the four corners of the earth, Africa's sons are marching up to the future's golden door, bearing the record of deeds of valour done…. The brighter day is rising upon Africa." From Columbia he moved on to Oxford, where he received a law degree, then returned home to South Africa to practice law.

Once there, he learned that the "brighter day" did not apply to him or any other blacks. The South African Act of Union, passed in 1909, restricted their movements—black Africans were required to carry as many as 12 different documents to avoid imprisonment—prohibited them from serving in Parliament, and

---

- **JANUARY 6**
New Mexico becomes the 47th state.

- **JANUARY 15**
Robert Falcon Scott reaches the South Pole.

- **FEBRUARY 14**
Arizona becomes the 48th state.

- **MARCH 12**
In the U.S., Juliette Lowe founds the Girl Guides, forerunner of the Girl Scouts.

- **APRIL 12**
American nurse Clara Barton dies.

- **MAY 17**
Gas is first used for cooking and heating, on a Pennsylvania farm.

- **MAY 30**
American aviator Wilbur Wright dies.

- **JULY 15**
The British National Health Insurance Act goes into effect.

- **AUGUST 24**
The parcel post system is created in the U.S.

restricted their educational opportunities.

In 1912 Seme convened a meeting of black leaders in a shack in Bloemfontein at which he issued a call to action. "We have called you…to this conference so that we can together devise ways and means of forming our national union for the purpose of creating national unity and defending our rights and privileges." He also decried the ethnic divisions between blacks, which he saw as counterproductive to their cause, claiming that "we are one people." The result was the formation of what would become the African National Congress, which over the course of the 20th century would help destroy the political system that so outraged Seme.

▶ STRIKES IN MASSACHUSETTS

In the 1910s the town of Lawrence, Massachusetts, was the site of two influential labor strikes. The first started on January 12, 1912, when some 10,000 employees—many of them women—walked out of the town's textile factories to protest a cut in their hours. Organized by the Industrial Workers of the World (IWW), the strike began peacefully, but the strikers gained sympathy when local police violently interfered with the strikers' attempts to remove their children to safety. Two months later the factory owners conceded defeat, granting

STRIKERS MARCH IN LAWRENCE, MASSACHUSETTS.

UNSINKABLE

"God himself could not sink this ship," a crewmember of the *Titanic* remarked. A series of watertight compartments within the steel hull was supposed to render the luxury liner unsinkable. This belief was tested on her maiden voyage across the Atlantic, when she struck an iceberg. Passengers felt at most a minor bump, but the berg had ruptured the ship's hull beyond the ability of the compartments to compensate. Within three hours she slipped under the waves.

An investigation revealed the arrogance behind the disaster. The ship was steaming far too fast through an ice field and carried only enough lifeboats to save fewer than half those on board. Of the 2,224 passengers and crew, 1,522 perished. The disaster led to new safety regulations.

their workers raises and back wages. Not long afterwards, Massachusetts became the first state to pass a minimum-wage law.

Nearly seven years later, Lawrence's textile workers hit the picket lines again, this time pressing for a 48-hour workweek with pay for 54 hours. Though the IWW had ceased to be a force in organized labor, the Amalgamated Textile Workers picked up the slack and helped organize the workers. This time, however, the factories held fast, bolstered by the refusal of Massachusetts Governor Calvin Coolidge to support the strikers. The strike, which was marred by repeated acts of violence on both sides and at least one death, dragged on until May 21, when the workers returned to their jobs.

■ TRENDS & TRIVIA

Electric heating pad is invented.

Mack Sennett founds the Keystone movie studio, introducing the Keystone Kops.

Zane Grey's *Riders of the Purple Sage* is published.

Universal Pictures is founded.

Nabisco introduces Oreo and Lorna Doone cookies.

First successful parachute jump from an airplane is made.

Hellman's mayonnaise is introduced.

The L. L. Bean Co. is founded in Freeport, Maine.

Vitamins are identified by Polish biochemist Casimir Funk.

American neurosurgeon Harvey Cushing identifies the hormonal disorder known as Cushing's Syndrome.

The size of the football field is standardized at 360 x 160 feet, the touchdown is valued at 6 points, and the 4th down is added.

The basketball net is opened up at the bottom, allowing the ball to fall through.

Italian educator Maria Montessori publishes her theories on teaching children.

The Bolshevik newspaper *Pravda* is founded in Russia.

The Beverly Hills Hotel opens in Los Angeles.

Swiss psychoanalyst C. G. Jung establishes his own theories, breaking from his mentor, Sigmund Freud.

German writer Thomas Mann's novel *Death in Venice* is published.

65

● **SEPTEMBER 7**
French aviator Roland Garros sets new altitude record of 13,200 feet.

● **OCTOBER 4**
Theodore Roosevelt is shot in Milwaukee; the bullet is slowed by the folded-up speech in Roosevelt's pocket.

● **OCTOBER 18**
War between Italy and Turkey ends, with Turkey ceding Libya to the Italians.

● **NOVEMBER 3**
The first all-metal plane is flown, in France.

● **NOVEMBER 5**
Woodrow Wilson is elected president.

● **DECEMBER 5**
Italy, Austria, and Germany renew the Triple Alliance for six more years.

● **DECEMBER 8**
Congress bars illiterate immigrants from entering the U.S.

What made Henry Ford stand out among the early automakers was his adherence to simplicity and scientific principles. Chief among his innovations was the moving assembly line (below), instituted in 1913. By reducing the construction of a Model T to a series of subprocesses—such as engines, transmissions, and dashboards—the time it took to assemble a car dropped to just 2 hours and 40 minutes. Productivity soared from 202,000 cars in 1913 to more than 1.8 million in 1924, during which time the Model T's price dropped from $550 to $355. Ford followed the principles of management authority Frederick Taylor, who stressed the elimination of all nonproductive motions to make "men, machines, and materials...an intricately interconnected mechanical organism." The assembly line became a model of efficiency, but the mind-numbing repetitiveness of the job created a tremendous turnover in workers. To fight this, Ford again revolutionized the industry in 1914. He paid workers the unprecedented sum of five dollars a day—but only if they met productivity standards and had a stable home life.

▶ THE FED

In 1912 and 1913 a Congressional committee revealed to the country how the vast majority of America's wealth lay concentrated in the hands of just a few immensely powerful financiers like J. P. Morgan and John D. Rockefeller. So shocked was the public over the power of the "money trusts" that the Democratic Party platform in 1912 called for revamping the country's banking system.

The solution Congress devised was the Federal Reserve Act, which Woodrow Wilson signed into law on December 23, 1913. The act created a network of 8-12 Federal Reserve banks spread from Boston, Massachusetts to San Francisco, California, with the regional banks under the control of a board of governors in Washington. All privately owned national banks were required to join the network, and state banks were encouraged to join. By having each member bank keep a certain percentage of its assets in federal reserve banks, the government regained a measure of control over the nation's money supply. It could tighten or loosen the supply by increasing or decreasing the contributions required from member banks, as well as by directing the buying and selling of government securities on the open market. Furthermore, "the Fed" has the power to adjust the interest rate at which it loans money to its member banks—the so-called discount rate. By increasing the money supply through the federal reserve system, America was able to pay for World War I without resorting to new taxes. However, the increase resulted in rampant inflation; the consumer price index nearly doubled between 1916 and 1920.

▶ DR. SCHWEITZER GOES TO AFRICA

By the time he was 30, Albert Schweitzer had amassed a lifetime of accomplishments. Born in Germany in 1875,

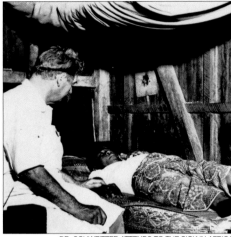

DR. SCHWEITZER ATTENDS TO THE SICK IN AFRICA.

Schweitzer earned doctorates in philosophy and religion, and became a well-known professor of theology at the University of Strasbourg. He was also one of the world's greatest concert organists and had written a definitive biography of Johann Sebastian Bach.

Upon turning 30 he quit his job and entered medical school, vowing to alleviate his "share of the misery which lies upon the world." In 1913 he sailed to French Equatorial Africa (now Gabon) and opened a clinic, which he maintained with income from concerts and writings. His wife, Helene, an accomplished scholar, became a nurse to help out in the clinic. Schweitzer ministered to the sick of Africa until his death in 1965. In 1952 he was awarded the Nobel Peace Prize for his tireless labors.

▶ THE QUANTUM ATOM

In 1913 Danish physicist Niels Bohr helped put the finishing touches on the model of atomic structure advanced by his former teacher, Ernest Rutherford. In Rutherford's atom the electrons orbited around the nucleus, but nobody could figure out what kept the electrons from spiraling inward. The key lay in "forces in

● **JANUARY 7**
The first patent is awarded for a process that turns oil into gasoline.

● **FEBRUARY 15**
The indoor record for the mile run is set at 4:18.2 minutes.

● **FEBRUARY 25**
The 16th Amendment to the Constitution, providing for a federal income tax, is adopted.

● **MARCH 15**
Abolitionist Harriet Tubman dies.

● **MARCH 31**
American financier J. P. Morgan dies.

● **APRIL 8**
President Woodrow Wilson delivers the first in-person State of the Union Address in 112 years.

● **APRIL 19**
In California the Webb Alien Land-Holding Bill prohibits Japanese from owning land.

nature of a kind completely different from the usual mechanical sort," Bohr believed, and he found them in the quantum theory of German physicist Max Planck. Bohr theorized that the orbits of electrons could not decay because they were locked into specific energy levels that could not vary. An electron could jump to a higher level only with an infusion of energy precisely equal to the energy difference between levels; conversely, a drop to a lower level resulted in the emission of a specific amount of energy. This helped explain why each element displays a unique spectrum of energy absorption and emission, as well as why various gases—notably neon—glow in a characteristic color under an electric current.

Support for the "Bohr atom" quickly gained momentum, and when Bohr returned to Denmark after World War I his reputation helped him establish the world-renowned Institute for Theoretical Physics in Copenhagen. In 1922 the modest Dane was rewarded with the Nobel Prize for physics.

▶ ART IN THE ARMORY

On February 17, 1913, the International Exhibition of Modern Art opened at the 69th Regiment Armory in New York City.

ARMORY SHOW MARKS THE BEGINNING OF MODERN ART IN AMERICA.

Dubbed the "Armory Show," it was perhaps the most important American art show of the 20th century. It gave American audiences their first glimpse of what was going on in the European art world. The more than 13,000 works on display represented a vast array of artists and styles, from Impressionists like Pierre-Auguste Renoir and Claude Monet,

THE BRA

Early in the century bras had been built into heavy whalebone corsets, which were tightly laced up to produce the hourglass silhouette then in fashion. They were uncomfortable but, then, as now, fashion often superseded comfort. In 1913 New York society matron Mary Phelps Jacobs discovered that her new evening dress's sheer fabric clearly revealed much of her corset. So Jacobs and her maid fashioned the first modern bra, a jury-rigged device of two handkerchiefs held together with ribbons and cords. It was an immediate success, and she gave a number of her inventions away to friends. Not until a stranger offered to buy one from her, however, did she begin to realize its true potential.

In 1914 Jacobs received a patent for her "contraption," which she eventually sold to the Warner Brothers Corset Company for 1,500 dollars.

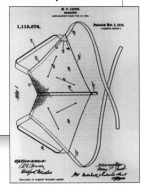
FIRST PATENT FOR THE BRASSIERE

to brash modernists like Pablo Picasso, Wassily Kandinsky, and Henri Matisse. One of the most controversial pieces was Marcel Duchamp's fractured work "Nude Descending a Staircase," likened by one reviewer to "an explosion in a shingle factory."

Most critics liked the show, but one confidently wrote, "I have no fear that this kind of art will prevail, or even that it can long endure." The public thought otherwise, however, and 75,000 people flocked to the Armory in the first month. By the time the show traveled to Chicago and Boston, over 250,000 people had seen it.

■ TRENDS & TRIVIA

An artificial kidney is developed.

The first crossword puzzle is published in a newspaper.

A diphtheria vaccine is created.

Mammography is invented.

Igor Stravinsky's ballet *The Rite of Spring* debuts.

D. H. Lawrence's *Sons and Lovers* is published.

The American Cancer Society is founded.

Grand Central Terminal opens in New York City.

B'nai B'rith Anti-Defamation League is founded.

Camel cigarettes are new.

The Dusenberg automobile is introduced.

Pollyanna, by Eleanor Hodgman Porter, is published.

The U.S. Bureau of Labor Statistics begins compiling the Consumer Price Index.

Peppermint Life Savers are introduced.

Ebbets Field, home of the Brooklyn Dodgers, opens.

The forward pass is introduced in football.

Swann's Way, the first volume of Marcel Proust's *Remembrance of Things Past* is published.

Hollywood becomes the center of the movie industry.

The first home refrigerators become available.

The Erector Set is introduced.

67

• MAY 3
10,000 march in a parade for woman's suffrage in New York.

• JUNE 14
South Africa passes the Immigration Act, which restricts the immigration and movement of Asians.

• JUNE 15
American suffragist Carrie Chapman Catt convenes a Women's Suffrage Congress in Budapest, Hungary.

• JULY 2
The record for the longest airplane flight is set at 3,100 miles.

• AUGUST 26
The Keokuk Dam, the world's largest, opens on the Mississippi River.

• NOVEMBER 5
The Owens Valley Aqueduct opens, bringing water to Los Angeles.

• DECEMBER 23
The Federal Reserve Act, creating the Federal Reserve System, is enacted.

68

On June 28, 1914, Archduke Franz Ferdinand of Austria and his wife paid a state visit to the capital of Bosnia-Herzegovina. Gavrilo Princip, an agent of the Black Hand, a Serbian terrorist group, dashed up to their car and shot the royal couple dead (below). Austria demanded the right to conduct an investigation on Serbian soil. Not knowing that Austria had already received the support of Germany, one of its partners in the Triple Alliance, Serbia refused the demand, whereupon Austria mobilized its army. Hardliners in Russia then convinced Tsar Nicholas II to go to war if Austria were to invade Serbia. This called for a response from England and France, Russia's partners in the Triple Entente of 1907. With the hammers cocked on virtually every gun in Europe, Germany took the first shot on August 1 by declaring war on Russia. Germany then attacked France through Belgium, prompting England and Belgium to declare war on Germany. Finally, Austria declared war on Russia. "The lamps are going out all over Europe," said British Foreign Secretary Sir Edward Grey. "We shall not see them lit again in our lifetime."

▶ THE FIRST BATTLES

The German plan was to keep the Russians at bay while running through France, then turn its army east. The strategy worked at first, as an elite force took the Belgian city of Liege and prepared to sweep through northern France. The Germans would then curl around and attack the French Army from the west. As expected, the French moved into Alsace-Loraine, where in August they fought a series of devastating engagements known as the Battles of the Frontiers that left them retreating in disarray. The British expeditionary force met a similar fate in Belgium, where Gen. Alexander von Kluck's First Army drove it back into France.

Desperate, French commander-in-chief Gen. Joseph Joffre launched a counterattack in early September, led by the newly created Sixth Army from Paris. Kluck spotted the Sixth's advance and counterattacked, but this left a gap in the German line that was exploited by the French and the British. Though the engagement itself, known as the first Battle of the Marne for a nearby tributary of the Seine, was essentially a brutal stalemate—the French and British lost about 250,000 men to some 300,000 German casualties—it was regarded as a victory for the Allies, who finally stemmed the German onslaught.

Meanwhile, the Russian Army advanced on Prussia at the request of the

TRENCHES IN THE STREET OF A FLANDERS TOWN

French. Under the command of Gens. Pavel Rennenkampf and Aleksandr Samsonov, the army initially inflicted heavy losses on the Germans. But once Germany placed Gens. Paul von Hindenburg and Erich Ludendorff in command, the Kaiser's troops routed the Russians at the Battle of Tannenberg August 27-29. The Russians suffered some 125,000—dead, wounded, or captured; the Germans no more than 14,000. The debacle dashed Allied hopes that the Tsar's troops could keep a large portion of the German Army occupied on the eastern front.

▶ THE CANAL COMPLETED

"The greatest liberty man has ever taken with nature," the Panama Canal (opposite, top) opened for business on August 14, 1914 (though it would not be officially dedicated until the following year). Under the capable leadership of engineer George Washington Goethals, the 51-mile-long canal was completed nearly a year ahead of schedule. Some 40,000 workers had labored on the canal for a decade, digging a trench whose volume would fill a channel 10 feet deep and 55 feet wide from Maine to Oregon. Six huge, precisely balanced locks raised ships to 85 feet above sea level; 64 years later inspectors would marvel that the lock mechanisms still worked flawlessly. Because it opened during World War I, traffic through the canal was initially low, but once the war ended, use of the canal skyrocketed.

Theodore Roosevelt, the prime mover behind the canal, was justifiably proud of his achievement. "If I had followed traditional conservative methods," he boasted in a 1911 speech, "[negotiations to begin the Canal] would have been going on yet; but I took the Canal Zone and let Congress debate, and while the debate goes on the Canal does also." When in 1914 President Wilson tried to smooth over

Roosevelt's bragadoccio by expressing his "sincere regret" to Colombia and offering 25 million dollars in reparations, a furious Roosevelt shot back that such a gesture could "only be justified upon the ground that this nation has played the part of a thief or of a receiver of stolen goods." His reaction persuaded Congress to quash the payment, though it was ultimately approved in 1921, two years after Roosevelt's death.

▶ LORD OF THE APES

In 1911, while working as an agent for a company that made pencil sharpeners, Chicagoan Edgar Rice Burroughs started bootlegging company time to write science-fiction stories. "If people were being paid for writing rot," he reasoned, "I could write stories just as rotten." His first effort, "Under the Moons of Mars"—the tale of a Confederate officer who is transported to the red planet—sold for $400. Later that year he went to work on an equally improbable tale of a highborn English child named John Clayton, Lord Greystoke, who is raised in the jungles of Africa by apes. *Tarzan of the Apes*, published in book form in 1914, was an immediate hit and spurred some 20 sequels. Four years later Hollywood made its first Tarzan film, starring strongman Elmo Lincoln, which became one of the first motion pictures to gross more than a million dollars.

THE CASTLE WALK

Through the 1910s Vernon and Irene Castle inspired much of America to take up dancing. The couple met while acting together in a musical in 1910. On their honeymoon in Paris, the two got up to dance the fox-trot, but Irene's constricting dress forced them to do a faster, shorter-stepped version that quickly caught on as the "Castle Walk." Upon returning home, they gave demonstrations of the dance to enthusiastic New York crowds. Popular dancing was considered risqué by many, but the Castles gave it a wholesome image. "We were clean-cut," explained Irene, "we were married, and when we danced there was nothing suggestive about it. We made dancing look like the fun it was."

Since Irene couldn't dance in the restricting corsets and narrow skirts of the day she wore flowing dresses, which became all the rage. And when she cut her hair short, women rushed to copy the "Castle Bob."

By the time of Burroughs's 1950 death, Tarzan had made its creator very wealthy—which was his goal from the start. "I was not writing because of any urge to write," he recalled, "nor for any particular love of writing. I was writing because I had a wife and two babies, a combination which does not work well without money."

He reportedly offered the benefit of this wisdom to a young Ernest Hemingway, who in 1919 had just returned to Chicago from the war. When the young man wondered aloud to Burroughs what he should do with his life, Tarzan's creator advised, "Write a book."

■ TRENDS & TRIVIA

The 35-mm camera is introduced.

The zipper is new.

W. C. Handy composes "St. Louis Blues."

The Perils of Pauline comes to movie screens.

American scientist Robert Goddard takes out patents for the liquid-fueled rocket and the multistage rocket.

Gulf Oil introduces the first road maps.

The *New Republic* magazine debuts.

Wrigley comes out with Doublemint chewing gum.

Tinkertoys are introduced.

Congress passes a resolution establishing Mother's Day.

Director Cecil B. DeMille moves his studio to Hollywood.

Charlie Chaplin appears in his first film, Mack Sennett's *Making a Living*.

Tillie's Punctured Romance, the first full-length comedy, starring Charlie Chaplin, premieres.

The first airplane meal is served.

Margaret Sanger founds magazine on birth control, *The Woman Rebel*.

Self-service shopping is introduced, in California.

The first red and green traffic lights are used, in Cleveland, Ohio.

The American Society of Composers, Authors, and Publishers (ASCAP) is founded in New York.

The teletype machine debuts.

69

• **AUGUST 23**
Japan declares war on Germany.

• **SEPTEMBER 26**
In the U.S., the Federal Trade Commission is created.

• **OCTOBER 4**
The first German zeppelin raids on London are made.

• **OCTOBER 15**
The Clayton Antitrust Act is passed; it exempts labor unions from antitrust laws.

• **OCTOBER 22**
The first federal income tax is levied, on yearly incomes over $3,000.

• **NOVEMBER 2**
Great Britain declares the entire North Sea a military area.

• **DECEMBER 18**
Great Britain declares Egypt a protectorate, to help defend the Suez Canal.

70

By every measure, D. W. Griffith's 1915 film *Birth of a Nation* was groundbreaking. The epic of the Civil War and its aftermath had an unprecedented running time of 2 hours and 40 minutes. The film boasted a cast of 18,000 people and some 3,000 horses. On the other side of the camera, innovations like the fade-out, tracking shots, and the close-up came into their own. Griffith created "the grammar of filmmaking," said star Lillian Gish, and in the process helped turn the movies into a genuine art form.

Though a cinematic tour de force, *Birth of a Nation* was reviled by many for the racism of its second half. Blacks—most of whom were played by whites in blackface—were portrayed as villains, and white-sheeted Klansmen as avenging angels of the South. The NAACP protested and tried to keep the film from being screened in cities across the country. Griffith followed up the next year with *Intolerance*, a depiction of religious persecution throughout history. It had its own historical problems, however, as Jewish groups persuaded Griffith to reshoot a scene that inaccurately portrayed Jews as the killers of Jesus.

▶ THE WAR WIDENS

As the Germans, Austrians, French, and British lay hunkered in trenches on the western front, the military masterminds on both sides felt the only way to break the stalemate was to widen the war. This is exactly what happened in October 1914, when Turkey joined the Central Powers and brought its guns to bear on Russian bases on the Black Sea.

With the Russians pleading for help, in February 1915 the British launched a daring plan devised by Winston Churchill, then First Lord of the Admiralty. Sixteen British and French battleships would force through the Dardanelles, storm Constantinople, and take the Turks out of the war. But mines sank three of the battleships, and the land assault quickly devolved into a miniature of the western front, with Turkish and Allied forces dug into trenches around the Gallipoli peninsula. Casualties on each side exceeded 250,000.

Meanwhile, Italy wriggled out of its obligations under the Triple Alliance—claiming it was only a defensive agreement—and joined the Allies in April. It spent the war fighting a dozen costly campaigns against Austria along the Isonzo River.

▶ TOO PROUD TO FIGHT

Though America was officially neutral at the start of World War I, the line between neutrality and partisanship became blurred when it came to shipping. Both the Allied and Central Powers were happy to receive American goods, but naturally resented anything falling into the hands of the enemy. England blockaded European ports and blacklisted American companies doing business with the Central Powers, while Germany declared the waters around Great Britain a war zone

SINKING OF THE *LUSITANIA* BY A GERMAN SUBMARINE

and claimed the right to sink any vessels it found there. The Germans made good on their threats on May 7, 1915, by torpedoing the Cunard liner *Lusitania*, traveling from America to Great Britain. The ship sank to the bottom of the Celtic Sea in just 18 minutes, taking with it 1,198 of the nearly 2,000 people on board, 128 of whom were Americans.

Germany argued that the *Lusitania* was carrying armaments, a claim supported by the ship's manifest, which listed over 60 tons of ammunition. President Wilson nonetheless demanded "reparation so far as reparation is possible" and extracted a promise from Germany to cease unrestricted submarine warfare. But he remained steadfast in his refusal to get involved militarily, claiming there was such a thing as "too proud to fight."

▶ GENOCIDE IN ARMENIA

The slaughter of Armenians at the hands of the Turks was the first major systematic genocide of the 20th century. Though part of Turkey for two thousand years, Armenia refused to join the Turks in World War I because they were reluctant to turn against the millions of Armenians living across the border in Russia. Outraged, the ultranationalist "Young Turk" rulers turned against their Armenian countrymen.

The Turks made the Armenians

• **JANUARY 9**
Pancho Villa signs a truce with the U.S., promising to halt border raids.

• **JANUARY 15**
Fanny Farmer, cookbook author who revolutionized American cooking, dies.

• **JANUARY 28**
The United States Coast Guard is created.

• **APRIL 30**
President Wilson creates the Naval Petroleum Reserve at Teapot Dome, Wyoming.

• **MAY 3**
Italy renounces its membership in the Triple Alliance.

• **JUNE 1**
German zeppelins bomb London.

• **JULY 27**
Wireless communication is set up between Japan and the U.S.

relinquish their weapons, which were then offered as evidence of insurrection. Armenian leaders were imprisoned, tortured, and summarily executed. With most able-bodied men dead or conscripted into the army, attention then turned to women, children, and the aged, who were sent on long marches to concentration camps. Thousands fell to starvation, dehydration, exhaustion, rape, and beatings. By 1923 between 600,000 and 1.5 million Armenians—out of a population of about 2.5 million—had perished.

▶ A TERRIBLE NEW WEAPON

Early in 1915 Gen. Sir John French sent his British Expeditionary Force on the offensive; under the command of Gen. Douglas Haig it established a deep salient in the German line in Belgium. German Chief of Staff Erich von Falkenhayn responded by launching a massive counteroffensive near the Belgian city of Ypres on April 22, in which he introduced a new weapon to the western front—chlorine gas.

The British had considered using poison gas in battle as early as the mid-19th century, but abandoned the notion as inhumane. That assessment was borne out by the French Algerians who first fell victim

SOLDIERS WITH GAS MASKS

to the greenish-yellow gas at Ypres. Three days later, a second gas attack killed 2,000 Canadian troops. Despite the confusion created by the gas, the Germans were unable to breach the Allied lines, due in large part to the ferocity of the Canadians, who fought to the death despite their seared lungs. "I saw some hundred poor fellows laid out in the open," wrote another witness to the battle, "in the forecourt of a church, to give them all the air they could get, slowly drowning with water in their lungs—the most horrible sight, and the doctors quite powerless." In May the Germans introduced gas to the eastern front battles.

Though the Allies deplored the use of gas, they eventually began using it themselves. Defensive measures like gas masks proliferated, though they simply prompted the invention of more insidious gases that penetrated skin and clothing and caused even more hideous deaths.

FORDSON

In 1915 Henry Ford announced that the Ford Motor Company would go into the tractor business. Two years later he made good on his promise with a versatile, gas-powered machine dubbed the Fordson. Small, simple, and reliable, the Fordson was a godsend during World War I, as it helped American farms increase productivity and meet the wartime demand for food.

After the war, however, the increased productivity became a curse. Crop surpluses drove down prices, and to pay off their loans farmers grew even more, turning increasingly to fertilizers and pesticides. Farms failed at an alarming rate, and agriculture went from a small-scale enterprise to one ruled by big business.

The Model T's immense profits allowed Ford to vastly undersell his competitors for tractors. When in 1922 the price of the Fordson fell to $395, many rivals dropped out of the tractor business. One of the few that remained was International Harvester, which ultimately stole the market from Ford.

■ TRENDS & TRIVIA

Taxicab service is introduced.

Pyrex glass is invented by the Corning Glass Works.

Lipstick comes on the market.

A Spoon River Anthology by Edgar Lee Masters is published.

The U.S. Lawn Tennis Championships, later the U.S. Open, move to Forest Hills, Queens, in New York City.

Kraft introduces processed cheese.

Bayer introduces aspirin tablets.

W. Somerset Maugham's *Of Human Bondage* is published.

The Neighborhood Playhouse and the Washington Square Players in New York City, and the Provincetown Players in Massachusetts are founded.

The State of Delaware loosens its laws to attract corporations.

The Pan-Pacific International Exposition is held in San Francisco.

The preparedness movement in America takes hold as President Wilson orders a 50-percent increase in the regular army and a 300-percent increase in the reserves.

"Vamp" actress Theda Bara is a popular movie attraction.

The first transcontinental telephone line becomes operational.

The Metamorphosis by Franz Kafka is published.

Women's skirts, which have been at ankle length since the 13th century, rise to ten inches from the floor, in Europe.

71

- **AUGUST 10**
Gen. Leonard Wood sets up the country's first military training camp for civilians, in Plattsburgh, New York.

- **SEPTEMBER 8**
Tsar Nicholas II takes direct control of the Russian Army, replacing his cousin, the Grand Duke Nicholas.

- **SEPTEMBER 18**
A new automobile speed record is set at 108 miles per hour.

- **NOVEMBER 14**
Booker T. Washington, author of *Up From Slavery* and founder of the Tuskeegee Institute, dies.

- **NOVEMBER 25**
The Ku Klux Klan, long dormant, is revived in Atlanta, Georgia.

- **DECEMBER 10**
The Ford Motor Company produces its one-millionth automobile.

- **DECEMBER 18**
President Wilson marries Edith Bolling Galt.

72

In 1916 two of history's most horrendous military engagements were fought in France. In February Germany's Gen. Erich von Falkenhayn planned an offensive "to bleed France white," centered on the town of Verdun. French Gen. Joseph Joffre assigned Gen. Henri Petain to mastermind the defense; Petain's rallying cry *"Ils ne passeront pas!"*—"They shall not pass!"—bolstered French morale. The battle raged for six months before the Germans gave up the offensive. By the end the French had suffered 542,000 casualties and the Germans 434,000. Once again, the lines had barely moved.

Meanwhile, the British launched an attack on the German position at the Somme River on July 1. This day went down as the bloodiest in British military history as 60,000 men fell, 19,000 of them killed. They pressed the fight until November, during which time they made their last-ever charge with horse cavalry and their first-ever charge with tank cavalry. By the fall, total casualties for both sides topped one million men. As with Verdun, very little territory ultimately changed hands.

▶ The Mysterious Mr. Lawrence

During World War I, a key figure in the fight to drive the Turks from Syria and western Arabia was Thomas Edward (T. E.) Lawrence (below). A 28-year-old Oxford-trained historian, Lawrence had spent a great deal of time in Arabia on archaeological expeditions and spoke fluent Arabic. When the war broke out, he became a lieutenant in the British Army, where his expertise in Middle Eastern customs and geography was highly valued. But Lawrence never really fit into the regular army and so in 1916 was assigned to turn the various Arab tribes into an effective guerrilla force.

Adopting native dress from head to toe—"If you wear Arab things at all," he once advised, "go all the way"—Lawrence led small raiding parties that destroyed sections of the Hejaz Railway, the main Turkish supply link between Damascus and Medina, and seized the city of Aqaba. In 1918 his forces played a vital role in the successful battle for Syria. At the end of the war Lawrence was hailed as a hero, but he felt that he had failed the Arabs when they failed to achieve true independence. Much of the area fell under French and British colonial rule.

▶ A Final Creative Burst

By the early 1910s, French artist Claude Monet had retired from painting. He was in his 70s, losing his eyesight to cataracts, and despondent over the deaths of his wife and son. But he soon found that he could not turn his back on his life's work, and in 1916 he embarked on a series of murals, based on the water lilies in the pond of his garden at Giverny.

Monet had painted scenes from his garden for decades (right). But in the new murals he focused on fragments, such as an individual lily rather than on a scene as a whole. A fellow artist hailed the vast canvases as "The Sistine Chapel of Impressionism."

▶ The Man Who Wouldn't Die

While unrest among the peasantry was threatening to topple Tsar Nicholas II, the Russian nobility was also dealing with another serious threat: the growing influence of a self-proclaimed holy man and faith healer named Grigory Rasputin. The "mad monk" first gained entry into the inner royal circle in 1907, when he allegedly cured the Tsar's young son Alexis of a serious hemorrhage brought on by hemophilia. He soon became a favorite of the superstitious Tsarina Alexandra, who pressured her weak husband to accept his advice on political matters.

On December 29, 1916, Prince Felix Yussoupov, a nephew by marriage of Nicholas, with the help of a few co-conspirators, lured Rasputin to his home. There the monk ate cakes and wine poisoned with enough cyanide to "kill several men instantly," according to one of the conspirators. Two hours later he remained unaffected. Yussoupov then shot Rasputin in the back, but after a few minutes the victim stirred, lunged at the panicked prince, then fled the house. Another bullet felled him as he reached the front gate, and after beating him savagely, the conspirators wrapped his body in a curtain and threw it into a hole in the frozen Neva River. When the body was found three days later, the cause of death was determined to be drowning.

Less than two weeks earlier the canny Rasputin, sensing he was in danger, had written a letter directed to Nicholas. "I feel that I shall leave life before January 1…," he predicted, "if it was your relations who have wrought my death then no one of your family, that is to say, none of your children or relations will remain alive for more than two years. They will be killed by the Russian people…."

▶ TECHNOLOGY AT THE FRONT

More new weapons were developed in World War I than in any other conflict. In fact, aside from the atomic bomb, World War II was fought almost exclusively with refined versions of the same weaponry that had devastated Europe 20 years earlier.

A major innovation was the tank, developed by the British Admiralty. Germany created the first truly useful submarines, which terrorized Allied shipping through much of the war. Defenses against submarines quickly sprouted up, like the hydrophone—an underwater microphone that detected submarine noise—and the depth charge.

French Marshal Ferdinand Foch felt that

HUGE RAILROAD GUNS USED BY THE FRENCH AT RHEIMS

PARK SERVICE

In 1872 Ulysses S. Grant ordered the creation of Yellowstone National Park "for the benefit and enjoyment of the people." Yellowstone was eventually joined in splendid preservation by the likes of Sequoia, Glacier, Yosemite, and Crater Lake National Parks. The Antiquities Act, signed by Theodore Roosevelt in 1906, allowed for the preservation of "historic landmarks, historic and prehistoric structures, and other objects of scientific interest."

As parks and monuments proliferated, administration became a problem. Those created by acts of Congress received funding, while those instituted by Presidential proclamation did not. And some fell under the jurisdiction of the Agriculture Department, while others were the province of the Interior Department. Secretary of the Interior Franklin Lane hired wealthy businessman and nature lover Stephen Maher as a special assistant in charge of parks. Maher's intense lobbying led Congress to pass the 1916 Organic Act, which created the National Park Service.

airplanes were "interesting toys, but of no military value." While the airplane may have had little effect on the war's outcome, military planners were able to test the tactics that would make planes dominant in future conflicts. The first aerial assaults took place during World War I, carried out by large, bomb-laden planes escorted by smaller planes. One-on-one dogfights between flying aces like America's Eddie Rickenbacker and Germany's Manfred von Richthofen—the famous "Red Baron"—helped establish the romantic image of the fearless fighter pilot.

73

Albert Einstein publishes his general theory of relativity.

Windshield wipers are introduced.

James Joyce's *A Portrait of the Artist as a Young Man* is published.

D. W. Griffith's motion picture *Intolerance* debuts.

Guide dogs for the blind are introduced, in Germany.

Professional Golfers Association (PGA) is founded, and the first PGA tournament is held.

Keds sneakers are introduced.

Lucky Strike cigarettes are new.

Lincoln Logs debut.

American educator John Dewey's theories are published in his *Democracy and Education*.

The first Norman Rockwell painting appears on the cover of the *Saturday Evening Post*.

French actress Sarah Bernhardt makes her last American tour.

Tuning devices for radios are introduced.

The bobby pin is invented.

The Owen-Keating Law prohibits the interstate trade of goods made in factories using child labor; the law is later struck down by the U.S. Supreme Court.

Congress passes a workman's compensation act for U.S. government employees.

Fortune cookies are invented by the Hong Kong Noodle Company of Los Angeles, California.

A submachine gun, known as the Tommy gun, is invented by Brig. Gen. John Taliaferro Thompson.

• **JUNE 15**
American artist Thomas Eakins dies.

• **JULY 17**
The Federal Farm Loan Act, which establishes a U.S. banking system to help farmers, is passed.

• **AUGUST 16**
The U.S. and Canada sign a treaty to protect migratory birds.

• **OCTOBER 24**
Henry Ford offers equal pay—now five dollars per day—to his female employees.

• **OCTOBER**
Margaret Sanger opens America's first birth control clinic, in Brooklyn, New York.

• **NOVEMBER 7**
Jeanette Rankin of Montana becomes the first woman elected to the U.S. House of Representatives.

• **NOVEMBER 12**
The U.S. reports a 100 percent increase in food prices from the previous year.

By early 1917 it had become virtually impossible for America to maintain its neutrality. Unrestricted submarine warfare, which the Germans had sworn off in the wake of the *Lusitania* incident, had resumed. Soon after, England revealed to President Wilson the contents of an intercepted telegram between Germany and Mexico. "We make Mexico a proposal of alliance on the following basis," it read. "Make war together, make peace together, generous financial support and an understanding on our part that Mexico is to reconquer the lost territory in Texas, New Mexico, and Arizona.... Please call the [Mexican] President's attention to the fact that the ruthless employment of our submarines now offers the prospect of compelling England in a few months to make peace." The outrage voiced by the American public was exactly what England had hoped for.

Wilson, whose 1916 reelection slogan was "he kept us out of war," finally gave in. On April 2, he asked Congress for a formal declaration of war against Germany, claiming that "the world must be made safe for democracy."

▶ THE DOUGHBOYS ARRIVE

With great fanfare, Gen. John J. "Black Jack" Pershing led the first contingent of American troops to France in the summer of 1917. On July 4 the commander of the American Expeditionary Force laid a wreath on the grave of the Marquis de Lafayette, the French hero of the American Revolution. An aide made a brief speech—the stolid Pershing was a man of few words—concluding with the exclamation: "Lafayette, we are here!"

GEN. JOHN J. PERSHING WITH MAJ. GEN. C. MENOHEN

Desperate and weary from three years of battles as bloody as they were inconclusive, the French were grateful for the American presence. But they soon discovered that while Pershing was willing to help out, he would only do so on his own terms. The Allies wanted to incorporate American soldiers into their depleted ranks immediately, but Pershing insisted on keeping his men separate. Furthermore, he refused to let them fight at all until they had been fully trained. A consummate soldier, Pershing knew his raw recruits—many of them new conscripts and most untested in battle—would be little more than cannon fodder until he whipped them into shape. So while the Allies spent the rest of 1917 and the spring of 1918 in the trenches, the Americans drilled and practiced their marksmanship.

Not until April 1918 would American units be deployed on a large scale. But when they were, their presence was decisive. They halted a German advance toward Paris at Château-Thierry in June and took control at the second Battle of the Marne in July. From there, the Allies steadily pushed forward until the German defenses finally crumbled in October.

▶ RACIAL UNREST

America's most savage race riot to date began on July 4, 1917, in East St. Louis, Illinois, when a group of white men fired guns into the air as they drove through town. Shortly afterward, 200 armed blacks assembled downtown. When they encountered police, they opened fire, killing two officers. The killings sparked a 36-hour rampage in which whites chased down any blacks they could find, including children and the elderly. Though Illinois Guardsmen were called out to restore order, they stood by while the mob beat, stoned, and lynched 50 blacks.

The East St. Louis riot foreshadowed the "Red Summer" of 1919, in which race riots broke out in 25 cities throughout the country. Mobs of blacks and whites took to the streets of Washington D.C., killing seven people. In Chicago, a deadly riot was precipitated by an incident on Lake Michigan, when a young black swimmer drifted toward a beach used by whites. When the whites began throwing stones at the young man, he was unable to return to shore and drowned. In a three-day riot sparked by the incident, 37 people died, 537 were injured, and nearly 1,000 people were left homeless by fires.

▶ UPHEAVAL IN RUSSIA

In January 1917 Vladimir Lenin, exiled in Switzerland, delivered a speech in commemoration of the 1905 "Bloody Sunday" uprising against the tsarist government. "We must not be deceived by the present grave-like stillness in Europe," he said. "Europe is pregnant with revolution. The monstrous horror of the imperialist war, the suffering caused by the high cost of living everywhere engender a revolutionary mood, and the ruling classes...are more and more moving into a blind alley from which they can never extricate themselves without tremendous upheavals."

Lenin's claim was certainly true for his homeland, which had been living on borrowed time since 1914. The government was self-destructing, both from Nicholas's inability to come to grips with the crises facing his country and from the constant shuffling of officials at the behest of Grigory Rasputin. The war united Russians for a few years, but by 1917 food shortages, rampant inflation, and workers' strikes had brought the country to the breaking point. Faced with near anarchy, Nicholas (right) abdicated on March

15. A provisional government was set up in April 1917, and eventually was headed by Aleksandr Kerensky, who quickly initiated universal suffrage and other liberal reforms. In the meantime, Lenin had returned to Russia, sensing his time had come.

▶ PROVISIONAL GOVERNMENT COLLAPSES
The Russian government led by Aleksandr Kerensky was unable to quell the dissent that led to the abdication of Tsar Nicholas II, and Vladimir Lenin seized upon the discontent. His followers, the Bolsheviks, grew in numbers and support until they engineered a takeover of the government in October 1917. "The Provisional government has been overthrown," wrote Lenin in a declaration to the Russian people. "Long live the workers', soldiers', and peasants'

revolution!" Lenin would preside over the new government, with Leon Trotsky as his second-in-command.

Lenin moved quickly to redistribute land to peasants and nationalize banks and industry. Another priority was to get Russia out of the war at all costs; he did this through the humiliating Treaty of Brest-Litovsk, which ceded huge tracts of land to Germany. With the war over, he soon faced battles from within as right-wing supporters of the tsar took up arms against him. The civil war between the Bolsheviks—the Reds—and the anti-Bolsheviks—the Whites—would tear Russia assunder for another two years and cost millions of lives.

FROZEN FOODS

Clarence Birdseye changed the way the world eats when he discovered how to freeze food in a way that preserved its freshness. The Brooklyn native was working as a naturalist and fur trader in Labrador when he made an interesting observation: once Inuit caught fish through the ice, the combination of low temperatures and Arctic winds froze them almost immediately. When thawed and cooked, they still tasted fresh. Through experimentation, Birdseye discovered that the key was speed. When plant or animal tissue freezes slowly, large ice crystals form and rupture the cells in the tissue. But when freezing is fast, the crystals stay small and the cells remain intact.

Birdseye returned to New York in 1917, and perfected a method of flash-freezing foods. Then, in 1924, he and three partners formed the General Seafoods Company of Gloucester, Massachusetts, which marked the beginning of the frozen food industry.

■ TRENDS & TRIVIA

Violinist Jascha Heifetz makes his debut at New York City's Carnegie Hall.

Prufrock and Other Observations by T. S. Eliot is published.

"The Darktown Strutters' Ball" becomes the first recorded jazz song.

BMW is founded.

First Sunday baseball games are played.

The first Pulitzer Prizes are awarded by Columbia University.

The *World Book* encyclopedia is introduced.

In Toronto, hockey arenas begin using man-made ice.

Union Carbide is founded.

Phillips Petroleum is founded.

Army recruitment posters featuring the now-famous depiction of Uncle Sam saying "I Want You" are introduced.

George M. Cohan's song "Over There" becomes an anthem for American soldiers in World War I.

The Selective Draft Act establishes conscription in the U.S.

Edna St. Vincent Millay's first book of poetry, *Renascence and Other Poems,* is published.

The *stijl* movement in art, epitomized by the geometric paintings of Piet Mondrian, takes hold.

In Britain, the Balfour Declaration promotes the creation of the state of Palestine.

Dodge introduces the first all-steel auto body.

C. J. Jung's *Psychology of the Unconscious* is published.

• AUGUST 14	• SEPTEMBER 27	• OCTOBER 15	• NOVEMBER 6	• DECEMBER 7	• DECEMBER 10	• DECEMBER 10
China declares war on the Central Powers.	French artist Edgar Degas dies.	The French execute Mata Hari as a spy.	New York State gives women the vote.	The U.S. declares war on Austria-Hungary.	Britain takes Jerusalem from the Turks.	The International Red Cross is awarded the Nobel Peace Prize.

"What we demand in this war...," President Wilson told Congress on January 8, "is that the world be made fit and safe to live in; and particularly that it be made safe for every peace-loving nation." Wilson went on to describe his "fourteen points" for stabilizing postwar politics. Most of the points addressed the adjustment of borders and issues of sovereignty. Others called for the abolition of trade barriers and "private international understandings."

The fourteenth was the sticking point: "A general association of nations must be formed under specific covenants for the purpose of affording mutual guarantees of political independence and territorial integrity to great and small states alike." Wilson's proposed League of Nations found many opponents in Europe, whose long history of political machinations and animosities made such a proposal hard to swallow. "President Wilson and his Fourteen Points bore me," scoffed French Prime Minister Georges Clemenceau. "Even God Almighty has only ten!" Domestically, conservative lawmakers dismissed the League because they feared it would diminish American sovereignty. Wilson would face an uphill battle in trying to establish the League at the war's end.

THE END OF THE ROMANOVS

In 1918 Lenin and Trotsky decided to eliminate the Russian royal family, which was under house arrest in the town of Ekaterinburg. "The ex-Tsar Nicholas Romanov," read a government directive, "guilty before the people of innumerable bloody crimes, shall be shot."

On the night of July 16 guards awakened the family and herded Nicholas, Alexandra, Grand Duke Alexis, Grand Duchesses Olga, Marie, Tatiana, and Anastasia, and four attendants into a basement room. They then opened fire. Nicholas and Alexandra died instantly, but Alexis clung to life, grasping his father's coat. Amazed at Alexis's "strange vitality," the guards savagely kicked the boy's head and put two bullets in his ear. The duchesses, protected by jewels sewn into their corsets, survived the first volley but were then set upon with clubs and bayonets. The bodies were dismembered, soaked in acid, burned, and dropped down a nearby mine shaft.

Within a few years, women throughout Europe began presenting themselves

TSAR NICHOLAS II OF RUSSIA AND HIS FAMILY

as Anastasia, each claiming to have miraculously escaped the massacre. The most famous of these pretenders was Anna Anderson, who settled in Charlottesville, Virginia. She died in 1984, but posthumous genetic testing revealed her to be yet another impostor.

THE SIGNING OF THE ARMISTICE

THE ARMISTICE

Depleted of men and matériel, exhausted, and fractured by internal dissension, the Central Powers could wage war no longer. Bulgaria and Turkey were the first to surrender, on October 30. Four days later Austria-Hungary, beaten into submission by the Italians, also sued for peace. This left Germany alone to face the Allies, recently unified under the supreme military command of French Marshal Ferdinand Foch and bolstered by fresh American troops.

Facing a mutiny of his High Seas Fleet and revolts within the country, Kaiser Wilhelm II fled Germany for the Netherlands. The provisional socialist government negotiated an armistice with Foch, which went into effect on the morning of November 11. All that remained was to settle on general peace terms, which turned out to be a battle in itself.

THE NEW BIOGRAPHY

With his 1918 book *Eminent Victorians*, British writer Lytton Strachey at once revolutionized the art of biographical writing and deglorified the Victorian era. The book profiled four icons of the Victorian age—nurse Florence Nightingale, educator Thomas Arnold, Roman Catholic Cardinal Henry Manning, and Gen. Charles "Chinese" Gordon—and stood their reputations on end with a razor-sharp wit that made the book wildly popular. Certain character

---

- **JANUARY 28**
Leon Trotsky forms the Red Army in Russia.

- **FEBRUARY 3**
The *New York Times* begins home delivery.

- **MARCH 3**
Russia signs the Treaty of Brest-Litovsk with Germany.

- **MARCH 5**
The Russian capital is moved from St. Petersburg to Moscow.

- **MARCH 21**
In an attempt to gain ground before American troops become involved, Germany launches its final offensive into France.

- **APRIL 14**
French Marshal Ferdinand Foch is made supreme commander of Allied forces.

- **APRIL 18**
Gavrilo Princip, the Serbian assassin of Austrian Archduke Franz Ferdinand, is executed.

traits were emphasized to the point of caricature, and Strachey liberally sprinkled his work with fictional conversations and distorted time frames—all for the sake of probing the souls of his subjects. His methods prompted one historian to quip that Strachey worked "without fear and without research."

Despite its shortcomings, *Eminent Victorians* was an important milestone in British literature. It swept away the concept of biography as uncritical hagiography, and helped distance postwar England from idealized notions of the Victorian era. It also served to express the attitudes of the so-called Bloomsbury group, a collection of liberal intellectuals who met regularly in the Bloomsbury section of London. Its members—including Strachey, writers E. M. Forster and Virginia Woolf, and economist John Maynard Keynes—formed the core of British letters through much of the early 20th century.

▶ ESPIONAGE AND SEDITION

With ultranationalist feelings running high during the war, Congress passed a draconian law in 1917 to quell public dissent with the federal government. The Espionage Act prohibited conduct that might aid the enemy, promote rebellion in the armed forces, or obstruct military recruitment. In 1918 passage of the Sedition Act made it a federal offense to "utter, print, write, or publish any disloyal or abusive language" about the United States and its policies.

Especially hard hit by the legislation was the American Socialist Party, led by Eugene V. Debs. A former labor leader and Presidential candidate, Debs was sentenced in 1918 to ten years for voicing his contrary views about the war. He was soon joined in prison by Charles Schenck, the party's general secretary, whose appeal went all the way to the Supreme Court. Chief Justice Oliver Wendell Holmes, Jr. upheld the conviction by claiming that Schenck's right to free

SPANISH FLU

In March 1918 a soldier at Fort Riley, Kansas, came down with the flu. With World War I raging, Army doctors had bigger things to worry about. But then the flu began to spread, aided by troop movements, until it had reached every corner of the globe. Hospitals were overwhelmed, governments closed down, and people refused to go outside. It became illegal to spit or even sneeze in public, and police in many cities patrolled the streets wearing face masks.

But nothing stopped the spread of the Spanish Flu, so-called because Spain was mistakenly blamed for its origin. In a year more than 550,000 Americans succumbed. The 1918 influenza outbreak was the world's worst pandemic since the bubonic plague wiped out a quarter of Europe's population in the 14th century.

A year later the flu vanished as mysteriously as it appeared, leaving a host of unanswered questions.

HOSPITAL VISITORS WEAR PROTECTIVE GEAR

speech was not absolute. "The most stringent protection of free speech would not protect a man in falsely shouting fire in a theater and causing a panic...," Holmes wrote in his famous 1919 opinion. "The question in every case is whether the words...create a clear and present danger that they will bring about the substantive evils that Congress has a right to prevent." When calmer heads prevailed after the war, Debs was released by order of President Warren Harding in 1921.

■ TRENDS & TRIVIA

The first school of public health is established in the U.S., at Johns Hopkins University.

The electric mixer debuts.

Willa Cather's *My Ántonia* is published.

Regular airmail service begins.

United Lutheran Church is founded.

First three-color traffic light is introduced, in New York City.

Daylight Savings Time is first instituted.

The military magazine *Stars & Stripes* is founded.

Granulated laundry soap is invented.

Raggedy Ann doll is introduced.

Ripley's Believe It or Not! begins publication.

The pop-up toaster is patented.

Kotex sanitary napkins are introduced.

Sales peak for Liberty Bonds, helping to finance the war effort.

American astronomer Harlow Shapley establishes that the solar system is located far from the center of the Milky Way galaxy.

Knute Rockne becomes coach of the Notre Dame football team.

The Magnificent Ambersons, by Booth Tarkington, is published.

German philosopher Oswald Spengler's pessimistic book *Decline of the West* is published.

The Browning automatic rifle is new.

77

▶ **APRIL 22**
Manfred von Richthofen, the "Red Baron," is killed at the Battle of the Somme.

● **JULY 17**
The Allies halt the German advance in the Second Battle of the Marne.

● **AUGUST 10**
General Pershing is allowed to establish an independent American Army.

● **OCTOBER 9**
Kaiser Wilhelm II abdicates.

● **NOVEMBER 4**
Austria surrenders.

● **NOVEMBER 11**
Germany signs armistice treaty.

At the Paris Peace Conference, convened on January 18, 1919, leaders of the Allied powers met to iron out peace terms and determine the new world order. Debate was dominated by the "Big Four" (below)—British Prime Minister David Lloyd George, French Premier Georges Clemenceau, U.S. President Woodrow Wilson, and Italian Premier Vittorio Orlando—who promptly were at odds with each other. The hawks carried the day, and the Treaty of Versailles called for massive territorial concessions and monetary reparations amounting to tens of billions of dollars. Most unpalatable to the Germans was the "war guilt" clause, which insisted they accept responsibility for "causing all the loss and damage to which the Allied and Associated Governments…have been subjected…."

Germany found the treaty odious but accepted it under pressure from an Allied naval blockade. The French felt it was not harsh enough, and the U.S. Congress, no less impressed, ultimately rejected it. The treaty had satisfied few and its harsh conditions set the stage for the next world war.

▶ RISE OF THE FASCISTS

When World War I erupted Benito Mussolini was the 31-year-old editor of *Avanti!*, the newspaper of the Milan Socialist Party. Initially opposed to Italy entering the war, he eventually supported joining the Allies, a stance for which his party expelled him. He then formed his own newspaper, *Il Popolo d'Italia*, to serve as a mouthpiece for his views. He later joined the Italian Army and was wounded in battle in 1917.

On March 23, 1919, Mussolini and a number of other like minds—veterans, ultranationalists, and general malcontents—met in Milan to form the *Fasci di Combattimento* ("combat bundle"). The name of the group was taken from the term *fasces*, an axe tied together with elm or birch twigs, which had been an emblem of power in the Roman Empire. Some of the attendees wore black shirts, which would become another symbol of the group. Among other things, the fascists called for the establishment of an empire in Africa. "We want our place in the world because it is our right to have it," they proclaimed. Otherwise their beliefs were vague; they detested socialists, communists, and democrats, and proposed a governmental body whose leader, chosen by the populace, would determine what was good for the country. Mussolini wanted to be that leader.

▶ ARTISTS TAKE CHARGE

They were some of Hollywood's leading lights: swashbuckling actor Douglas Fairbanks, Sr.; Mary Pickford, "America's sweetheart" and future wife of Fairbanks; Charlie Chaplin, the actor who made a fortune playing a tramp; and legendary director D. W. Griffith. The four were already drawing some of the largest paychecks in Hollywood, and they were worried that their salaries might scare away producers. So in 1919 the four founded their own studio, United Artists. By producing their own movies, they would never have to worry about pricing themselves out of the business. When Richard

DOUGLAS FAIRBANKS, SR., MARY PICKFORD, AND CHARLIE CHAPLIN

Rowland, the head of Metro Studio, heard of the deal, he said: "The lunatics have taken charge of the asylum." But the four proved to be nearly as skillful behind the camera as they were in front of it—especially Fairbanks, who signed talent like Gloria Swanson, Buster Keaton, and John Barrymore, and eventually recruited producer Darryl Zanuck. By the 1950s, when Chaplin and Pickford, the two surviving founders, sold their interests in United Artists, the studio had turned out some of Hollywood's greatest movies.

▶ THE PRESIDENT FALTERS

On September 3 Woodrow Wilson set out on a train trip across America to drum up support for the Treaty of Versailles and the League of Nations. But by the 25th, suffering from severe headaches and exhaustion, he cancelled the tour. A week later, Wilson suddenly collapsed, the victim of a massive stroke that paralyzed his left side and slurred his speech. He was completely incapacitated for two months, and even after leaving his bed could work no more than an hour or two a day. Compounding the physical difficulties were the mental effects: His cognitive powers were severely diminished, and his behavior was marked by irritability and bouts of crying.

- **JANUARY 6**
Former President Theodore Roosevelt dies.

- **JANUARY 29**
The 18th Amendment, establishing Prohibition, is ratified.

- **FEBRUARY 6**
The Weimar Republic holds its first session.

- **MARCH 12**
Allies reach an agreement to supply Germany with food.

- **APRIL 2**
Finland abolishes its monarchy.

- **APRIL 5**
Eamon De Valera becomes President of Irish political group Sinn Fein.

- **MAY 10**
Douglas MacArthur becomes superintendent of the U.S. Military Academy at West Point, New York.

During Wilson's convalescence, his wife, Edith, ferociously restricted access to her husband. She became the de facto president by controlling what received his attention. One of the matters that still reached Wilson was the debate over ratifying the Treaty of Versailles. Though he had strong support from Senate Democrats and moderate Republicans, conservatives insisted on revisions that would have eviscerated the League of Nations. Unwilling to forge a compromise, his irrational refusal to yield at all led to the treaty's defeat.

▶ THE BAUHAUS

Much of 20th-century architecture owes a debt to Walter Gropius, who in 1919 opened the Bauhaus school in Weimar, Germany. Literally the "house of building," the Bauhaus offered instruction in a variety of visual arts, which students learned to integrate in order to "breathe a soul" into a structure. Among the teachers Gropius brought to the Bauhaus were Paul Klee, Wassily Kandinsky, and Ludwig Mies van der Rohe; among the students were Marcel Breuer and Josef Albers.

Pressures from both the art world and the German government forced Gropius to move the school from Weimar to Dessau in 1925. There, the buildings Gropius designed for the new school became synonymous with the "international style" of architecture—boxy, concrete-and-steel structures with

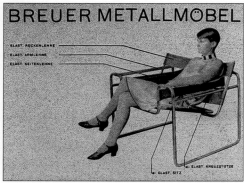

BREUER METALLMÖBEL

BAUHAUS-STYLE CHAIR DESIGNED BY HERBERT BAYER

PROHIBITION

On December 18, 1917, Congress presented to the states what would become the 18th Amendment to the Constitution: "The manufacture, sale, or transportation of intoxicating liquors within, the importation thereof into, or the exportation thereof from the United States...is hereby prohibited." On January 19, 1919, Nebraska pushed the amendment over the top by becoming the 36th state to ratify it. Later that year, the Volstead Act established the legal limit of 0.5 percent alcohol for any beverage.

In one sense, Prohibition was a success in that it did curb drinking. But on the other hand, it created a demimonde of speakeasies and bootleggers that flourished wherever there were people with enough money to buy a drink on the sly. Vast criminal enterprises made millions of dollars importing liquor. Within a decade Prohibition would be widely regarded as a failure.

exterior walls dominated by glass and devoid of ornamentation. Interiors were spare, with furnishings that emphasized functionality and lent themselves to mass production. Many were furnished with the classic metal-framed, S-shaped chairs designed by Marcel Breuer. Though the Nazis shut down the school in 1933—Hitler decried it as "un-German"—the Bauhaus influence spread as Gropius became dean of the architecture school at Harvard and Mies van der Rohe moved to Chicago, where his simple, elegant buildings emphasized his philosophy of "less is more."

■ TRENDS & TRIVIA

Shortwave radio is introduced.

Sherwood Anderson's *Winesburg, Ohio* is published.

British physicist Francis Aston invents the mass spectrograph.

The pogo stick is invented.

Grand Canyon, Zion, and Lafayette (later Acadia) National Parks are established.

The American Legion is founded.

First nonstop transatlantic airplane flight and first commercial airline service occur.

Dial telephones are introduced.

The first Algonquin Round Table convenes, at New York City's Algonquin Hotel.

American John Reed publishes *Ten Days that Shook the World*, his firsthand account of the Russian revolution.

The first gasoline tax is imposed, in Oregon.

Bentley and Citroën automobiles are introduced.

The first greyhound dog races with mechanical rabbits are held.

Experiments performed during a solar eclipse prove key aspects of Einstein's general theory of relativity.

New York City introduces written tests for driver's licenses.

The American Communist Party is founded.

United Parcel Service is incorporated.

Jack Dempsey defeats Jess Willard to win the world heavyweight crown.

79

• JUNE 28
Germany signs the Treaty of Versailles.

• JUNE 29
Sir Barton becomes the first horse to win the Triple Crown.

• SEPTEMBER 3
Italy grants women the vote.

• AUGUST 11
Industrialist and philanthropist Andrew Carnegie dies.

• SEPTEMBER 9
Most of Boston's police force goes on strike; Massachusetts governor Calvin Coolidge fires them.

• NOVEMBER 2
Lady Astor becomes the first woman elected to the British Parliament.

• NOVEMBER 19
The U.S. Senate votes down the Treaty of Versailles.

• DECEMBER 17
French painter Pierre-Auguste Renoir dies.

ADVENTURE AND EXPLORATION

80

by *Will Steger*

INAUGURAL NATIONAL GEOGRAPHIC EXPLORER-IN-RESIDENCE
AND POLAR ADVENTURER

October 17th, 1989 – Day 81

Today is our forty-first day of this blizzard. This wind on the Antarctic Peninsula seems eternal, it never stops blowing and the snow keeps falling. Each morning when we look outside our tents it seems it will be impossible to travel. But somehow one of the six of us always rallies the strength and the optimism to encourage the others back to reality—the reality that if we are to survive we must keep moving. This morning was extremely dark. When I poked my head out of the tent, I first noticed that the winds had changed, now blowing from the south, off the Antarctic Plateau, at 50 miles an hour. The temperature had dropped overnight to minus 55° F. I had hoped this storm would break as we headed up, into the interior of the continent. Instead,

Left: Scott's ship, Antarctica   Middle: Skeleton dancer, China   Right: America's first Everest expedition, Nepal

it's only intensifying. We have no retreat. Our only contact is sparse radio communication. Even if we could call for help, no airplane could land within 1,000 miles of us. Our only hope for survival now lies in finding our food cache, which is about 40 miles ahead of our position. [But] we have only three days of food left, and minimal fuel to heat our tents, to dry our clothing. We are damp and chilled and the gusts that hammer our tent shake loose the frost that clings to the nylon walls, coating our clothing and sleeping bags with a frosty white rime. Dahe is quite sick, from a combination of the cold and exhaustion. Again today it is impossible to travel, and I spend most of my day caring for him. He misses his wife and family in China; sometimes, in our darkest hours, I wonder if he will ever return to them.

—from Will Steger's journal

Hardship is the currency of the explorer, the lure that draws us to the far corners of the planet even in this day of jet travel and global communication. Those distant places have not changed much this past century. The winds of the Antarctic Plateau were as brutal when I crossed it as they were for Roald Amundsen and Robert Falcon Scott. The grinding ice-sea of the Arctic Ocean shifts today as it did under the boots of Robert E. Peary and Fridtjof Nansen. And the isolation, in spite of radios, airplanes, and Gore-tex, is still profound.

The link between the National Geographic Society and exploration dates to the Society's first days, when its President, Alexander Graham Bell, chartered a Potomac River steamer and traveled from Washington, D.C., to Norfolk, Virginia, to photograph a total eclipse of the sun in 1900. Over the years, the Society has encouraged a host of adventurers to report back from the planet's wild places. In 1911 Theodore Roosevelt wrote on his expeditions into the wilds of Africa and game hunting. In 1928, the year after Charles A. Lindbergh became the first to fly solo across the Atlantic, the aviator reported on a trip to South America. Joseph F. Rock took the Society into China and Tibet in the 1920s, Edmund Hillary climbed the world's highest peak in 1953, and Jacques-Yves Cousteau explored the depths of the sea many times. The Society helped finance early efforts to reach the North Pole and the first crossings of Antarctica. It supported re-creations of historic traverses of Asia and the Soviet Union. New geography, above and below sea level, has been discovered by Society explorers. The ancient archaeology of Machu Picchu was uncovered, China's Great Wall detailed, the skies mapped, and the trail of early man discovered—all with the Society's assistance. Despite the widely varying geographies, the expeditions had one thing in common: All carried, often stuffed in some cranny of their various craft, the flag of the National Geographic Society.

I have made a life exploring the frozen regions of the planet. Ever since I began reading NATIONAL GEOGRAPHIC magazine as a boy, I was drawn to walk in the footsteps of my polar predecessors, to gain a firsthand glimpse into their experiences. The explorers of what I call the Golden Age of Polar Exploration—from roughly 1894 to 1911—are most compelling to me. Launched from Norway, England, Australia, and the United States, the expeditions were led by the men who would become the heroes of polar exploration: Nansen, Amundsen, Mawson, Scott, Shackleton, Peary.

Norwegian Fridtjof Nansen, explorer and scientist, was the most profound contributor to this century's understanding of the Arctic Ocean. In the late 1890s he constructed a ship called the *Fram*, whose hull was shaped like a walnut shell, designed to respond to the pressure of the ice in the polar sea by popping up onto the ice rather than being crushed by it. Nansen wanted to test his theory that the ice on the Arctic Ocean drifted from western Siberia across the North Pole and down into the Greenland Sea. In 1893 he sailed the *Fram*, with a crew of 12, into the pack ice off the coast of northern Russia. For three years, the ship was frozen into the ice of the Arctic Ocean, serving as a scientific platform adrift near the top of the world. Nansen hoped that the *Fram* would drift over the North Pole, but—anticipating its course was too far south (the ship reached its farthest north at about 85° north latitude)—he put the ship in the hands of his second in command, and on March 14, 1895, set out across the ice with a team of men and dogs. They carried with them two kayaks, necessary if they were to recross open water to landfall on their return journey. The rough pack ice hindered their progress forcing them to turn back just beyond 86° north latitude, some 230 miles from the Pole. Still, Nansen had traveled farther north than anyone before him. Remarkably, he and his team made it back to civilization, via sledge and kayak, and their historic adventure was first told in the pages of the NATIONAL GEOGRAPHIC magazine.

Ten years would pass before Robert Peary would write, in 1909, these memorable (and long-debated) words in his journal: "The pole at last!!! The prize of three centuries... I cannot bring myself to realize it." Peary's reaching of the North Pole—or at least its near vicinity—was the culmination of a 4,500-mile trek that began in New York aboard his ship, the *Roosevelt*. That his rival, Frederick A. Cook, made a similar claim almost simultaneously, set the stage for nearly a century of debate over exactly who arrived where first. In laying my own plans for an unsupported dogsled expedition to the North Pole, I studied everything I could about the Peary-Cook controversy. With the Society's help, I finally launched my expedition on the northern coast of Ellesmere Island on March 8, 1986. We left with 8 people and 5 sleds pulled by 49 dogs. Like Peary we would navigate solely by sextant. We had some advantages, though: The route was known, our wooden sleds were laminated and stronger than those of years ago, and our clothing was the best modern technology could invent. Peary reached the pole on April 6, 1909, but it wasn't until early September that he was able to send word of his success: "Stars and Stripes nailed to Pole" was his simple message. By contrast, when we arrived at the North Pole on May 3, 1986, a small Twin Otter from the National Geographic Society—carrying editor Bill Graves and assistant director of photography Kent Kobersteen— was there to greet us.

The magazine was keen to publish accounts of the race for the South Pole as well. At the turn of the century, the British launched a bold series of expeditions in Antarctica that culminated in the race for the Pole between Norwegian Roald Amundsen and Briton Robert Scott, a race won by Amundsen on December 14, 1911. When Scott and his four companions perished on their desperate haul back from the Pole in March 1912, the tragedy overshadowed the enormous amount of research and exploration the British had accomplished. Scott's *Discovery* expedition of 1901-1904 had been the first major assault. He set up winter quarters on Ross Island within sight of today's American station at McMurdo Sound. Over a two-year period, extensive scientific study was conducted by Scott's team, which included Ernest Shackleton, who would have his own harrowing adventure several years later. On his return to England, Shackleton organized his own expeditions; the first, in 1908-1909, would come within 112 miles of the Pole before the team turned back in exhaustion.

Perhaps the most overlooked Antarctic explorer was the Australian Douglas Mawson. In 1912, even as Amundsen was returning from successfully reaching the South Pole and Scott and his men were pinned down and near death, an expedition led by Mawson made landfall on the western shores of Antarctica. In October 1912 the 18-man expedition split into 3 parties and set out soon after to explore the coastline and the immediate interior. Mawson, with Belgrave Ninnis, Xavier Mertz, and nearly 20 Greenland huskies, set out to find the south magnetic pole. Tragedy struck some 300 miles into the interior when Ninnis and the sled containing the tent, spare clothing, and most of the food disappeared into a hidden crevasse. With no food cached for their return journey, Mawson and Mertz survived mostly on dog meat, which soon ran out as they struggled, tentless, to make it back to camp. Mertz, unknowingly poisoned by eating the livers of the dogs, had to be pulled by Mawson on his sled and eventually died. Mawson continued alone with very little food. He made it back to the coast, only to discover his ship, the *Aurora*, sailing away over the horizon. But several men had been left behind to continue the search for him. When he walked back into the camp in early February 1913, he was so thin his own men did not recognize him.

Douglas Mawson's harrowing ordeal taught later polar explorers an invaluable lesson— namely, not to keep all our eggs in one basket. Nearly 80 years later, my own team traveled with three sleds, each of them self-sufficient.

March 3, 1990 – Day 220
Today we traveled the final 16 miles under perfect, clear skies and temperatures hovering just below zero. Sunlight danced and glared off the icebergs dotting the Indian Ocean, and we crested the hill overlooking the Soviet base just before seven o'clock. As we headed down one last icy slope—men shouting encouragement to their dogs, the dogs howling out of pleasure at the scene spread before them—an aura of peace swept over me as the responsibilities of the past three years and these last 3,741 miles lifted from my shoulders.

The Soviets had marked our entryway with red flags and made a "finish" line. A gathering of one hundred, speaking a dozen different languages, swarmed around us as we came down the flag-bedecked chute. As I called my dogs to a stop one last time and stepped out of my skis I could think only one thing: We had made it!

1920-

1929

Jacques leclerc

The Masses and Tribalism

1920-1929

by Matthew Jacobson
ASSOCIATE PROFESSOR OF AMERICAN STUDIES AND HISTORY, YALE UNIVERSITY

AMONG THE MOST IMPORTANT ACTS OF CONGRESS in the 1920s was the National Origins Act of 1924. With passage of this legislation, the United States turned away from its long tradition of accepting the "huddled masses" fleeing persecution or poverty abroad, establishing instead a system of quotas that would choke the stream of immigrants to a trickle. The immigration quotas reflected presumptions regarding the racial qualities necessary for the making of good Americans. All but the superior, "Nordic" type from northern and western Europe should be turned away because, as Vice President Calvin Coolidge put it in 1921, "Biological laws tell us that certain divergent people will not mix or blend." Especially questionable were newcomers representing what were deemed the "inferior races" of Asia and eastern and southern Europe.

Misgivings about the impact of immigrants on the nation's culture and civilization had been mounting for some time. In the 1870s, for example, San Franciscans periodically rioted against the Chinese—thousands of whom had been arriving since the heady days of the Gold Rush, more of whom were brought in during the 1860s and 1870s to work on building the railroads. By the 1890s race had become the dominant thread in the weave of a growing American nativism. As immigration of Greeks, Italians, and Jews from eastern and southern

Opposite: Uninhibited "flappers," as they were called, signaled the entrance of women into public life.
Preceding pages: Americans' mistrust of foreigners spurred efforts to curb immigration in the 1920s.

Europe reached unprecedented proportions, the Immigration Restriction League, formed in 1894, fretted over the biological outlook for the country in the face of this onslaught of "inferior stock." The newcomers represented "races most alien to the American people," wrote Senator Henry Cabot Lodge of Massachusetts, who believed the immigrants "do not promise well for the [country's] standard of civilization."

Prohibition gave rise to a whole new culture that revolved around speakeasies and bootleg whiskey.

RACE PER SE WAS NOT ALWAYS the ostensible issue. The alleged sedition of German, Irish, and other foreign nationals during World War I, for instance, raised doubts about the loyalty of a polyglot population hailing from nearly every nation on Earth, and the Russian Revolution in 1917 made anyone who espoused "imported" political philosophies, such as socialism and anarchism, especially suspect. Indeed, many saw Warren G. Harding's landslide victory in the election of 1920 as a resounding repudiation of both Woodrow Wilson's internationalism and the various reforms instituted by Progressivism.

However, "eugenics," a pseudoscientific blueprint for the biological engineering of society, became increasingly influential in both official and popular discussions of immigration. Indeed, eugenics supplied the logic for the National Origins Act itself, whose quotas were specifically designed to discriminate against "inferior races." As one eugenics enthusiast put it, after 1924 the nation would evaluate every immigrant's suitability "as a parent of future-born American citizens." To that end, he wrote, "the hereditary stuff out of which future immigrants were made would have to be compatible racially with American ideals. . . ." According to one congressional estimate, the National Origins Act would achieve this goal by reducing the number of incoming Greeks, for example, to next to nothing, from 3,000 persons per year to a mere 100. Italian immigration would plummet more than 90 percent, from 42,000 to just under 4,000 a year. And newcomers from Poland would drop 70 percent, from more than 30,000 to just under 9,000. After the bill had become law, the commissioner of immigration remarked with satisfaction that the immigrants now disembarking at Ellis Island "looked exactly like Americans."

The National Origins Act represented a fundamental paradox in the temper of the decade, and one that would characterize the rest of the century. The Act's underlying supposition of "Nordic" supremacy and its aim of producing a standard American citizen mirrored a certain tension in the country between narrow tribalism and a simultaneous shift toward universal conformity. Even as the 1920s saw a rise in parochialism, intolerance, and race-based politics, they were also years of a maturing consumer capitalism that exposed most Americans to the same set of standardized images and goods, producing a new mass culture for a new mass citizenry.

Increasingly, this citizenry was urban. The census of 1920 marked the first time in American history that more people lived in cities than in the countryside or small towns. And although not all Americans enjoyed the legendary prosperity of the 1920s, American economic life was transformed, as were many of the details of day-to-day living. The nation's manufacturing output rose by more than 60 percent during this period, creating a new landscape of cars and roads and houses, a novel wilderness of electric lights. By decade's end, two out of three American homes were electrified, as compared with fewer than one in ten at the turn of the century. Convenient, labor-saving devices such as refrigerators and washing machines altered the daily rhythms of life. Mass-produced foods such as Rice Krispies, Lender's Bagels, and Mounds Bars influenced the public's tastes even as the titillating pages of such pulp magazines as *Modern Romance* challenged its moral codes. With the proliferation of movie palaces, chain stores, and radio advertising, Bostonians and Angelenos alike heard the jingles and saw the faces of newly familiar advertising icons such as Betty Crocker and Peter Pan, the peanut butter mascot.

THE LANDSCAPE OF THE NATION was not the only thing transformed as traditional values of thrift and austerity gave way before a new consumerism. Americans were buying on credit at an unprecedented rate, casting aside fears of indebtedness and older virtues of forbearance. As one building and loan officer remarked in 1925, "People don't think anything nowadays of borrowing sums they'd never have thought of borrowing in the old days." Spending on recreation tripled during the decade, with most of these dollars going toward mass entertainments such as movies, amusement parks, and professional sports. Indeed, by the end of the decade movie attendance outstripped church attendance, with nearly 100 million people visiting theaters each week.

These changes were not greeted warmly in all quarters. Many critics charged that America's dazzling surfaces masked an inner emptiness, that the burgeoning consumer kingdom was driving Americans into a soulless existence of materialism and conformity. "I'm so beautiful," cried a woman in a short story by F. Scott Fitzgerald. "Why can't I be happy?" The realities of the assembly line and the over-efficient factory system came in for their share of criticism, as did the demise of the individual and the lamentable uniformity created by the hollow triumph of mass-produced gadgetry and merchandising.

In *Babbitt* (1922) Sinclair Lewis decried mass production and consumption for having created a bloodless, loveless, standardized world. The Babbitts' bedroom, Lewis wrote, was "a masterpiece among bedrooms, right out of Cheerful Modern Houses for Medium Incomes," with a color scheme "after one of the best standard designs" and a bedside table that held "a standard electric bedside lamp" and "a standard bedside book." The only thing wrong with the Babbitt house—and the modern American house it parodied—was that, as Lewis declared, "it was not a home."

Materialism and conformity were the watchwords in politics as well. "The business of government is business," Calvin Coolidge announced without irony as he ascended to the Presidency upon Harding's unexpected death in the summer of 1923. Some viewed the decade's three presidents, Harding, Coolidge, and Herbert Hoover, as the perfect figureheads for an uninspired age. Each promoted a powerful government-business partnership as a centerpiece of his administration, putting material prosperity and unhindered corporate power in the forefront of the nation's political life, much as they were in its social and cultural life.

Yet beneath the gleaming surfaces of the consumer culture, all was far from tranquil. The veneer of uniformity and standardization barely concealed a new American tribalism whose animosity took many forms, erupting over what constituted proper Americanism, social custom, morality, and the very future of the country. The decade opened with unprecedented "red raids" in which ten thousand alien radicals (not all of whom were either aliens or radicals) were rounded up in the zealous "dragnet inquiry" instigated by J. Edgar Hoover, then head of the Justice Department's Alien Radical Division. Throughout the decade "wets" battled "drys" over Prohibition, as gangsters and feds shot it out in the streets over the flow of illegal liquor. On the heels of 26 race riots across the nation in 1919 came a powerful resurgence of the Ku Klux Klan, whose politics of hatred this time around targeted not only African Americans in the rural South, but also blacks, immigrants, Catholics, and Jews in the urban North. A Klan march on Washington in 1925 drew 40,000 hooded members. The arrest, trial, and execution of Italian radicals Nicola Sacco and Bartolomeo Vanzetti on charges of murder became occasion for a seven-year-long national orgy of antiradical and anti-immigrant demonstration.

Another form of the tribalism of the twenties was what a later generation would describe as "culture wars"—battles over the school curriculum, over obscenity and censorship, and over depictions of race and sexuality in the theater and in literature. The clash of creationism and modern science was played out in the trial of John T. Scopes, a biology teacher in Dayton, Tennessee, who was tried for teaching the theory of evolution.

ONE OF THE MOST STRIKING ELEMENTS in the nation's tribal mosaic was the flowering of African-American culture in the urban North. During the 1910s, as some half-million black migrants had made their way north to staff the wartime industries, the black populations of many northern cities increased by two, three, and even six times (as in Detroit). The migration continued after the war, and in cities like New York the black population doubled yet again. African Americans—once the only slaves in a free republic, then the most rural group in an industrializing republic—now strode toward the mainstream of an urban industrial nation.

The war itself lent new force to the ideal of making good on the nation's democratic promise. When President Wilson had called upon Americans to help "make the world safe for democracy," blacks had stepped forward and sacrificed mightily for the nation. Surely, then, it was time for America itself to live up to its ideals. The postwar period saw a new stridence in

African-American political life—the emergence of a "New Negro," as the phenomenon was known on both sides of the color line. As W. E. B. Du Bois declared at war's end, "We return. We return from fighting. We return fighting. Make way for Democracy!" Black pride and defiance informed a range of cultural and political forms, from the flamboyant rallies of the black nationalist Garvey movement, to the lyrical writings of Langston Hughes, Nella Larson, and Claude McKay, to the blossoming of jazz, infused with the breath of southern black musical traditions and a spirit of improvisation. In this aspect, the tribal impulse could thus be democratic, as the Harlem Renaissance showed. "I, too, sing America," wrote Langston Hughes. "I, too, am America."

By 1927, when Henry and Edsel Ford sold their 15-millionth car, the automotive industry was beginning to reshape American society.

PERHAPS NOTHING WAS A MORE emphatic signal of the advent of the "modern," however, than the emergence of the "New Woman." Like the phrase the "New Negro," the "New Woman" was easy shorthand for an entire constellation of social changes, including changing occupational patterns, a new female penchant for athletics, enhanced political participation, and the repudiation of physically inhibiting Victorian fashions.

Woman suffrage, the crowning achievement of years of struggle, was won in 1920, but women's public presence became more pronounced still as the decade unfolded. Older notions of "women's place" gave way before the rush of urban life and a flurry of reform activity. The Cable Act granted women equal citizenship rights with men, and the Sheppard-Towner Maternity Act provided public monies for the care of dependent mothers and infants.

Even more striking than direct political gains were changes in the weave of economic and social life. Women were spending less time in the home than ever before. By 1930 fully a quarter of American women over 16 were employed outside the home and five times as many women had attended college as in 1900. The civic realm ceased to be an exclusively male preserve, as ever more women left the parlor to take up activities in the public domain. The city became, as the reform movement put it, "a parlor writ large." And women were frequenting arenas of consumption, too, such as movie theaters, public eateries, and jazz clubs, marking the loosening grip of Victorian moral codes and the strictures on proper femininity.

With the Great War, Americans pulled back emotionally in a state of relative isolationism. Although the United States did intervene in Honduras several times in the 1920s and occupied Nicaragua throughout the decade, the Senate defeated the bill to join the League of Nations. Congress instituted a dramatic scaling back of the U.S. Army and Navy, and a succession of

Presidents refused to recognize the Soviet Union. A trade policy marked by the return of high tariffs further attested to Americans' yearning for national self-sufficiency and aloofness from international affairs.

One symptom of the changing mood in the United States was a reinvigorated national debate over the proper disposition of the Philippine Islands, which had been ceded to the U.S. by Spain as a result of the Spanish-American War in 1898. The U.S. had fought a protracted guerrilla war to put down a popular movement for Philippine independence before finally assuming political control early in the century. Now, in the 1920s, many arguments were advanced for granting Philippine independence. Some strategists worried that the islands represented a military Achilles' heel in Asia. Agricultural interests resented the competition of such Philippine imports as sugar, vegetable oils, and tobacco, and organized labor resented the competition of Philippine workers in agriculture and fisheries. More generally, many worried at the implications for the workings of American democracy if the country held onto the trappings of empire.

At the same time, much of the discussion reflected the period's broader tribalism, with some wondering whether the Filipinos were racially "fit for self-government." Meanwhile, the independence movement escalated in the archipelago itself, and even so venerable an opinion maker as the *New York Times* in 1929 counted the Philippine cause among the major problems in world affairs yet to be handled. However, the issue would not be resolved until 1934, when the Tydings-McDuffie bill finally provided for a ten-year transition to independence.

ELSEWHERE ON THE INTERNATIONAL SCENE, the 1920s saw the ascendance of regimes and figures who would dominate world politics for years to come: the Irish Republican Army in Southern Ireland, the Soviet Union and Stalinism, Adolf Hitler and his Nazi Party in Germany. On the other side of the world, Chiang Kai-shek emerged as the leader of China's Kuomintang Army in 1925, and Hirohito ascended to the Japanese throne in 1926. The decade also witnessed the emergence of newly independent regimes in Egypt, Jordan, Turkey, Albania, and a unified Yugoslavia.

As the world's political landscape was undergoing huge changes, the era of the Roaring Twenties ended on October 29, 1929, when the stock market crash wiped out some 30 billion dollars in U.S. capital and plunged the country into the Great Depression. Within a year much of the wider world was engulfed in the Depression as well. Yet despite the economic hardships that followed, the paradox that had become so clear in 1920s America—the fabrication of a mass culture even as society fragmented into tribes—continued unabated. Indeed, that tension characterizes the nation's social and cultural life today, reflecting the prescience of observers who at the time designated the 1920s the threshold of the "modern" world. ■

Jazz musicians such as "Duke" Ellington turned the world on to the cool sounds of a uniquely American musical style.

Perhaps no other decade in history saw swifter or more far-reaching changes in transportation. The Air Age and the Automobile Age were both in their infancy when the 1920s began. By the end of the decade, life without cars was already unimaginable for most Americans, and aviation was just about to make the leap from an adventure to a commercial transportation system. The NATIONAL GEOGRAPHIC enthusiastically chronicled the transportation revolution. Numerous articles reported on the advancing adventure of automobile travel, while the magazine took an almost proprietary satisfaction in the progress of aviation. "Since Langley pioneered thirty-one years ago; since Alexander Graham Bell flew his man-lifting kite; since the Wright Brothers boldly rode the skies in the first crude, careening biplane," the GEOGRAPHIC proclaimed in 1927, "the growth and progress of air travel have been steadfastly aided and encouraged by the National Geographic Society. In its Magazine there has been told in word and picture, year by year, the graphic, cumulative story of the Conquest of the Air."

Nonstop Across the U.S.

Throughout the decade, the GEOGRAPHIC kept its readers abreast of aviation advances, often in the words of the aviators themselves. Typical was the account in the July 1924 issue by Lt. John A. Macready of the U.S. Army Air Service, who with Lt. Oakley G. Kelly made the first nonstop flight across the United States in May 1923.

Macready and Kelly had tried unsuccessfully twice in 1922 to fly from California to the East Coast. Prevailing winds favored the west-to-east route, but that advantage was offset by the fact that it required the plane to climb over the mountains through dense fog while still laden with a full

THE T-2 ON ITS TRANSCONTINENTAL FLIGHT

load of fuel. After their second failure ("I could easily have crawled under a snake's belly with a high silk hat on, I felt so low," Macready wrote about that disappointment) they decided to try the westbound route, taking off from Long Island, New York, at 12:36 p.m. on May 2, 1923. Their single-engine T-2 transport carried 10,850 pounds at takeoff; at just 150 more pounds, by Macready's calculation, the plane's "absolute ceiling…was the ground."

At daybreak of their second day aloft, they were over New Mexico, where Macready's "strongest impression…was the immensity of the lonely, isolated territory which passed beneath us." At 11:26 a.m. they landed at Rockwell Field in San Diego, to an enthusiastic welcome from spectators crowded on rooftops.

Macready's account appeared with a portfolio of more than 70 aerial photos taken by Macready and Lt. A. W. Stevens in an eight-week series of flights covering 10,000 miles. "No Such Series of Airplane Views Has Ever Before Been Printed," the magazine informed its readers.

Coming of the Automobile Age

"Thirteen million motor cars!" William Joseph Showalter marveled in the October 1923 NATIONAL GOEGRAPHIC.

Like the country, the magazine looked around and saw that the automobile was transforming American life with dizzying speed. Like the country, it found the change a cause for pride and celebration. Showalter listed the benefits: "The broadening experience that travel brings; the development of judgment and decision that automobile driving requires; the spread of mechanical knowledge that car maintenance entails; the demand for initiative and enterprise in those who would own and operate an automobile, are giving to the American people a training the value of which cannot be estimated in dollars and cents."

Cars would mean better education for farm children, for example, since rural students could now travel longer distances to bigger, centralized schools. "What stories the rusty little cars parked around the rural high school could tell of boys and girls who will finish their secondary education, when their parents never got beyond the sixth grade!" Showalter rhapsodized. He was equally enthusiastic about the assembly line that had revolutionized factory work: "Among the marvels of this mechanical age," he wrote, is making automobile workers productive enough to command wages no manual laborer had ever dreamed of.

In this new America being created almost before people could absorb what was happening, commerce was moving goods more quickly and easily than ever before; farmers could save on labor costs while plowing more land more deeply and raising better crops; cities were spreading out and millions of Americans were moving to comfortable green suburbs while remaining within reach of their jobs—all thanks to the automobile engineer; "one of the foremost contributors to human welfare," Showalter concluded, "in all the history of mankind."

MOTOR TRAFFIC, NEW YORK CITY'S FIFTH AVENUE

• Flying Over the Pole

Comparing his pioneering polar flights to the arduous overland journeys of earlier Arctic explorers, Lt. Cmdr. Richard E. Byrd was modest. Robert E. Peary had been out of touch with civilization for 400 days in his effort to reach the North Pole, Byrd wrote, while he and his copilot Floyd Bennett completed their journey in less than 24 hours: "Bennett and I left civilization early one morning, visited the northern apex of the earth, and returned on the afternoon of the same day." Nonetheless, Byrd felt his achievement "added a short paragraph to the story of man's conquest of the globe on which we live." In addition, he pointed out,

BYRD AND HIS TEAM PREPARE FOR THEIR FLIGHT TO THE POLE

the flight demonstrated "the feasibility of using airplanes in any part of the globe."

In a three-engine Fokker with a 63-foot-3-inch wingspan, Byrd and Bennett took off from Spitsbergen just past midnight on the morning of May 9, 1926—a night takeoff because the packed snow was harder in the colder temperatures and thus provided a firmer runway. Magnetic compasses were useless around the Pole, so Byrd used a special sun compass invented by Alfred H. Bumstead, the National Geographic Society's chief cartographer. Besides the two pilots, the plane carried a short-wave radio and a rubber boat, a sledge and a ten-week supply of food, in case they were forced down on the ice.

Flying 2,000 feet over the ice, Byrd and Bennett crossed over the Pole at 9:02 a.m., Greenwich time. "As we flew there," he wrote, "we saluted the gallant, indomitable spirit of Peary." Thirteen minutes later they swerved around and set their course for the return flight over the empty, frozen landscape to Spitsbergen, feeling, Byrd recalled, "no larger than a pinpoint and as lonely as a tomb; as remote and detached as a star."

• Victory Over Disease

"Three announcements of almost unprecedented import to mankind are expected to be made at no distant date," William Joseph Showalter predicted in the September 1922 NATIONAL GEOGRAPHIC.

First would be the news that yellow fever had been eradicated. Next would be the announcement that hookworm, " 'a handmaiden of poverty, an associate of crime and degeneracy, a destroyer of energy and vitality,' " could be eliminated "from any community which has the will to get rid of it." The same would be true of the third scourge on his list, malaria.

Public health had made major advances during World War I, when scientists in the United States and Europe had redoubled efforts to make sure epidemics did not undermine the war effort. Techniques developed during the war were applied in a postwar international preventive campaign against hookworm. Though rife in poor regions, including the southern United States, hookworm was actually quite easy to cure: All it took was a campaign to educate people about the proper medication.

Meanwhile, Showalter explained, mosquito eradication experiments in the American South, in Ecuador, and in other widely scattered sites had shown that relatively simple measures could significantly reduce malaria and yellow fever rates. Improving drains, filling in hollows that collected water, clearing obstructions in streams, and introducing a certain type of minnow had all proved remarkably effective in cutting down the mosquito population and lowering the incidence of disease.

To Showalter, the impending public health successes indicated the start of a better age. "Gradually all the microscopic monsters that have challenged man's dominion on earth are being circumvented," he declared, adding that the combination of preventive medicine and application of the then fashionable theory of selective breeding, or eugenics, "would result in the development and maintenance of a better race, inspired by nobler ideals and moving on to a richer destiny."

• Underground Fantasies

According to local lore, New Mexico's Carlsbad Cavern was discovered at the end of the 19th century by a cowboy who thought he saw smoke rising out of the ground, rode closer, and discovered that what he'd seen was actually a cloud of bats flying up from their underground chamber. After the turn of

STALACTITES AT CARLSBAD CAVERN

95

the century, parts of the cave were used for some years as a commercial guano mine, and then, in October 1923, still mostly unexplored, it was designated a national monument by President Calvin Coolidge.

Soon afterward, in the January 1924 issue, the NATIONAL GEOGRAPHIC published striking photographs of the fantastic world under the New Mexico desert, with its vaulted chambers, curtainlike stalactite formations, and hollowed-out basins left by extinct springs, dotted with onyx formations resembling toadstools or lily pads.

Massive pillars rose as high as 50 feet from bases of dark, smooth stone on the cave floor, writer Willis T. Lee reported, after making the jolting two-hour drive over rutted roads from Carlsbad, 30 miles to the northwest. Lee described some stalagmites as forming slender spires, like totem poles, while others, rounded at the tops, "resemble bareheaded men in ragged clothing."

Geography of the Heart

If the stock in trade of the GEOGRAPHIC's photography was to show its readers distant places, the editors understood that the camera could also explore "the geography of the human heart."

A portfolio of photographs in the October 1920 issue captured a mix of emotions in scenes quite different from the magazine's usual fare.

ANXIOUS MOTHERS OUTSIDE NEW YORK HOSPITAL DURING POLIO EPIDEMIC

Hope mixed with uncertainty shone in the face of an immigrant mother at Ellis Island with her two young children, waiting for admission to her new country. Grief and pride mixed in the expressions of women in black mourning veils at a military funeral for men killed in World War I, while another photo harking back to the war conveyed comradeship in the faces of grinning American soldiers on the back of a truck.

In one of the most striking images (above), smiles masked the dread of women waving to their stricken children from outside the windows of a New York hospital during a polio epidemic. The last photo in the group brought the reader back to the GEOGRAPHIC's more customary themes. It showed three school-age children in the sunroom of their home, intently examining a huge globe and, presumably, fixing in their minds a picture of the larger world outside their windows.

A HOPI INDIAN POTTERY MAKER HAS INHERITED THE SKILL OF ANCIENT PUEBLO DWELLERS.

Home of a Vanished Tribe

Four stories high and with 800 dwelling units, New Mexico's Pueblo Bonito had stood empty in Chaco Canyon for about a thousand years when a National Geographic Society archaeological team led by Neil M. Judd began exploring it in the early 1920s. The site was so remote and the desert landscape so empty that Judd's team had to drive seven hours each way for groceries and traveled 20 miles to get firewood, Judd recalled in the September 1925 magazine.

Many of the pueblo's mysteries remained unsolved, he acknowledged: "One is forced repeatedly to call upon the imagination" to picture its culture and daily life. From beadwork and pottery fragments, he imagined the pueblo's women "sitting in the soft light of their earth-floored dwellings, grinding and kneading and rolling" while also teaching pottery and other crafts to very small children, judging from the tiny fingerprints Judd and his team found on miniature ladles, pitchers, and toy bowls.

One mystery was why the pueblo was abandoned. Attacks by other tribes may have been one reason, Judd speculated, or possibly drought dried out the land and shriveled the corn, beans, and squash that were the pueblo's staple foods.

Honoring Past Explorers

When the GEOGRAPHIC paused in its celebration of contemporary exploration to pay tribute to explorers of the past, it turned to the Polish-born novelist Joseph Conrad, who roamed the world as a seaman for nearly 20 years before turning to literature. Writing in the March 1924 issue, Conrad identified geography's appeal in terms that could apply to the magazine itself: "Of all the sciences," he wrote, "geography finds its origin in action, and, what is more, in adventurous action, of the kind that appeals to sedentary people, who like to dream of arduous adventure..."

Like other sciences, Conrad went on, geography "fought its

way to truth through a long series of errors." Columbus, "the greatest of them all…was at one time loaded with chains and thrown into prison." Balboa, discoverer of the Pacific Ocean, "could not possibly know that this great moment of his life had added suddenly thousands of miles to the circumference of the globe, had opened an immense theater for the human drama of adventure and exploration…"

Conrad's highest praise went to James Cook. Earlier explorers' voyages, he pointed out, "were prompted by an acquisitive spirit, the idea of lucre in some form, the desire of trade or the desire of loot, disguised in more or less fine words. But Cook's three voyages are free from any taint of that sort. His aims needed no disguise. They were scientific"—putting Cook, he went on, in the tradition not of his own century but of the next, with its "single-minded explorers…whose only object was the search for truth."

● Devastation on the Mississippi

In the spring of 1927, the Mississippi River spilled over its banks in the worst flood of its recorded history up to that time. Above New Orleans, demolition teams—under pressure from powerful citizens in the Crescent City—blew up levees. This unnecessarily destroyed the surrounding parishes but prevented New Orleans itself from being pounded by floodwaters that might have hit the city like a high-powered fire hose.

Writer Frederick Simpich, whose September 1927 article was illustrated with photos by Society staff photographer Clifton Adams, traveled the area by boat through "a foul and swirling sea, bearing on its yellow tide the offal, animals, trees, and trash, the fences, bridges, houses, barns, and chicken coops scoured down by 54 flooded tributaries." Bodies of hundreds of dead cows, mules, hogs, and horses littered the water, floating among scenes of utter devastation: "Fallen steel bridges, box

THOUSANDS OF PEOPLE FLED TO LEVEES IN GREENVILLE, MISSISSIPPI.

cars floating. Abandoned railroads. Ruined sawmills and sugar refineries. White-pillared plantation houses in water to their upper verandas."

A bright spot in the tragedy was that new technology—radio, scout planes, motorboats—made it possible to warn "towns, cities, and even whole counties of impending peril…. But for these warnings, made possible by modern invention," Simpich wrote, "more lives must have been lost in this flood than America gave to the battlefields of Europe."

His conclusion echoed the pro-technology, pro-growth spirit of the time. Some thought the area should never have been diked or used for settlement, he wrote, and maybe they were right, but "there is no turning back…. Perhaps perfect defense can never be, for levees are against Nature. But man persists, like the ant whose hill is plowed. He pays for thwarting Nature's laws when he feels the prize is worth the price."

● Report From a Far Place

Of all the adventurers who wrote for NATIONAL GEOGRAPHIC from the world's distant corners, none reached more exotic destinations or spent more time there than Joseph F. Rock. Born

in Austria, Rock was a linguist and botanist who spent nearly three decades, starting in 1920, roaming the backlands of far western China and Tibet. Typical of Rock's articles for the magazine was his November 1928 report from a Tibetan lamasery in Choni, where he lived from 1925 to 1927.

In photos and vivid descriptive prose, Rock wrote about the daily sounds of "deep bass voices of several hundred chanting lamas

PERFORMER IN THE BLACK HAT DANCE AT THE TIBETAN MONASTERY OF CHONI

and an occasional ringing of bells and blowing of trumpets." He spoke about special events such as the dance on the sixth day of the sixth moon, when monks wearing ornately embroidered vestments and papier-mâché masks weighing up to 10 pounds chanted to the accompaniment of drums and 15-foot-long bronze trumpets, while other dancers costumed as living skeletons represented the spirits of the departed.

97

1920 RED SCARE

World War I nourished militant patriotism, distrust of foreigners, and fear of enemy agents behind every lamppost. After the war, the same attitudes fed fantasies that America was endangered by Bolshevism. Strikes and the discovery of a mail-bomb plot heightened the hysteria.

In early January 1920 Attorney General A. Mitchell Palmer ordered a roundup of suspected radicals in cities across the country. Palmer's agents carried out searches, seized evidence without warrants, and held thousands of suspects for days and weeks without charge.

Destined to be the most celebrated targets of the Red Scare were two Italian immigrants, both members of an anarchist group. Nicola Sacco and Bartolomeo Vanzetti were arrested three weeks after payroll robbers killed two men at a Massachusetts shoe factory. The evidence linking them to the crime was questionable, but they were charged, tried (before a judge who all but ordered the jury to convict), found guilty, and sentenced to death. The conduct of the trial left an impression that their real crime was their anarchism. The case became a cause célèbre for anarchists, radicals, and liberals. The two men were executed on August 23, 1927.

▶ LEAGUE OF NATIONS CONVENES

Opening the first session of the League of Nations in Geneva, the British statesman Sir Arthur Balfour noted with regret that the U.S. was still not represented. In Washington a last effort was under way to win Senate ratification of the Treaty of Versailles and the League, but the dispute between President Wilson and his chief adversary, Senator Henry Cabot Lodge, had become so bitter and personal that compromise proved impossible. An overwhelming majority of senators were prepared to vote "aye" when the treaty came back to the Senate floor on March 15, with a substantially modified version of Lodge's accompanying reservations. But Wilson again refused to accept any reservations at all, the same all-or-nothing strategy that had doomed ratification in a first vote the previous November. Once again, the White House called on Democrats to oppose the treaty as long as any reservations were attached. This time a sizable number of Democrats ignored Wilson's demand and supported the treaty, but not enough to reach the two-thirds majority required for ratification.

▶ MARCUS GARVEY

His name was almost forgotten by the time of the great civil rights struggles of the 1950s and '60s, but Marcus Garvey created the first true mass movement among African Americans. The Jamaican-born Garvey preached racial pride, self-help, and separation from whites, who Garvey felt would never give a truly equal chance to blacks.

Garvey's Universal Negro Improvement Association (UNIA), founded in 1914, reached its peak in the early 1920s. Tens of thousands turned out for mass meetings and parades. Seeking to establish a self-sufficient black economic infrastructure, the UNIA organized a chain of retail cooperatives, a publishing house, and other businesses. Best known was the Black Star shipping line, which Garvey hoped would strengthen links between American blacks and Africa. It led instead to his downfall when it failed, due to lack of capital, poor management, and possible corruption. Garvey was convicted of mail fraud in connection with the sale of stock in one of his businesses. He was eventually deported and died in London, poor and almost forgotten, in 1940.

▶ "BLACK" SOX SCANDAL

Maybe a small boy really did cry out "Say it ain't so, Joe!" as Shoeless Joe Jackson left a Chicago courtroom, or maybe a newspaperman made it up. Either way, it summed up the national reaction when, in the last days of the 1920 season, news broke that a grand jury

CHICAGO WHITE (BLACK) SOX

was questioning eight members of the Chicago White Sox, including Jackson and other stars, who were suspected of throwing the 1919 World Series in return for payoffs from gamblers.

Insiders weren't entirely surprised. Many ballplayers, bookies, and sportswriters knew that professional gamblers had put down suspiciously big bets on the underdog Cincinnati Reds. Rumors of a fix had swirled almost from the day of the Reds' unexpected victory. But to the public at large, the news was a shock.

- **JANUARY 5**
Boston Red Sox sell Babe Ruth to New York Yankees for $125,000.

- **MARCH 10**
British Parliament passes the Home Rule bill dividing Ireland into two parts.

- **MAY 21**
President Carranza of Mexico is assassinated.

- **JUNE 4**
Army Reorganization Act calls for American peacetime army of 300,000.

- **AUGUST**
Charles Ponzi's pyramid scheme in which early investors are paid off by later ones, collapses.

- **AUGUST**
Indian independence leader Mohandas K. Gandhi calls for "non-cooperation" with British rule. Strikes and widespread civil disobedience follow.

- **AUGUST 17**
Cleveland Indians' shortstop Ray Chapman dies when hit in the head by New York Yankee pitcher Carl Mays.

- **AUGUST 24**
Olympic Games, the first since 1912, open at Antwerp, Belgium.

The ballplayers were acquitted of criminal conspiracy after a trial that often seemed more intent on covering up baseball's seamy side than on deciding the defendants' guilt or innocence. Despite the acquittals, baseball's new commissioner, Judge Kenesaw Mountain Landis, banned all eight from professional baseball for life.

The "Black" Sox scandal, surfacing just as Prohibition began turning millions of Americans into lawbreakers, deepened the sense of lost illusions and growing cynicism that would mark America's experience in the twenties.

▶ MAIN STREET

If many Americans in the wake of World War I welcomed a "return to normalcy," as President Harding's campaign slogan put it, others found American normalcy small-minded, complacent, and suffocatingly provincial.

Sherwood Anderson's *Winesburg, Ohio,* published in 1919, sketched small-town life in dark colors, but it was Sinclair Lewis's 1920 best-seller *Main Street* that truly ushered in an era of literary assaults on the values, culture, and sentimental myths of the American heartland. Lewis's fictional Gopher Prairie, shown to his readers through the eyes of the town doctor's dissatisfied wife, is architecturally ugly and culturally dead. Its inhabitants are friendly enough to their own kind of people but ignorantly intolerant of anyone "different," and utterly uninterested in ideas or the larger experience of their time. Lewis's literary assault on middle American culture continued with *Babbitt,* whose title character's name passed into the language as the generic word for a certain type of invincibly conventional small-town businessman.

The message of Lewis's fiction was strengthened by his skills as an observer. His portraits of small-town life were "merciless

RADIO DAYS

Radio had been used at sea and for military communications, and civilian engineers and amateurs had experimented with broadcasts of music and news. But the age of commercial broadcasting truly began on the evening of November 4, 1920, when station KDKA, transmitting from the roof of the Westinghouse factory in Pittsburgh, Pennsylvania, reported the returns of that day's Presidential election.

The station, which held the first government-issued broadcast license, stayed on the air until after midnight, announcing returns as they came in by phone. When the broadcast ended, listeners (many of them Westinghouse employees who had been given radio sets for the occasion) knew that Republican Warren G. Harding had carried 37 states with 404 electoral votes—details no one else would know until the morning papers were delivered. Westinghouse's theory was simple. To create demand for radios, broadcast things people want to hear. The plan worked—with amazing speed. Americans spent one million dollars for radios in 1920. Just five years later, the figure was 400 million, and radio's transformation of American culture was well under way.

literary photography," one contemporary said, drawn with great accuracy and a perfect ear for American speech. Lewis attributed his success to "the gift of writing books which so acutely annoyed American smugness that some thousands of my fellow-citizens felt they must read these scandalous documents, whether they liked them or not."

■ TRENDS & TRIVIA

Hercule Poirot debuts in Agatha Christie's *The Mysterious Affair at Styles.*

League of Women Voters, successor to the National American Woman's Suffrage Association, is founded in Chicago.

Waterskiing is pioneered at Lake Annecy, Haute Savoie, France.

The National Negro Baseball League is established by Andrew "Rube" Foster, manager of Chicago's American Giants.

In the first blues recording, Mamie Smith sings "Crazy Blues" for Okeh Records.

F. Scott Fitzgerald's first novel, *This Side of Paradise,* is published.

William Tilden is the first American to win a tennis championship at Wimbledon.

The Baseball Hall of Fame is established in Cooperstown, New York.

Martha Graham makes her professional debut as a lead dancer in the modern ballet *Xochitl.*

A new census report shows the urban population exceeds the rural in the U.S.

The International Dada Fair is held in Germany. Dada artists use shock tactics to rebel against convention. ▶

New York becomes the world's theatrical center, in part because of the influx of theatrical greats to the U.S. after World War I.

Edith Wharton's *The Age of Innocence* is published.

• **AUGUST 26**
Woman suffrage amendment takes effect.

▶ **SEPTEMBER 7-11**
First transcontinental airmail flight.

• **SEPTEMBER 16**
Bomb explosion on New York's Wall Street kills 35.

• **OCTOBER 16**
One million coal miners strike in Britain.

• **NOVEMBER 20**
First municipal airport in the U.S. inaugurated in Tucson, Arizona.

• **DECEMBER 10**
Woodrow Wilson is awarded the Nobel Peace Prize for his work in founding the League of Nations and seeking a fair peace agreement.

By 1921 Russia's civil war had effectively ended. The Bolsheviks were the victors, but the land they ruled was in ruins. Up to two million people had died, many in mass executions carried out with the utmost barbarism by both sides. The economy was devastated.

At the 10th Communist Party Congress in March 1921, Lenin acknowledged that the Bolsheviks' extreme wartime policies had been wrong. Forced confiscation of peasants' crops and the attempted abolition of all private business brought economic disasters that were, Lenin said, more damaging than any battlefield defeats. In a "strategic retreat" from Marxist dogma, Lenin declared a New Economic Policy (NEP), leaving transportation, banks, and basic industries under state control, but ending forced requisitions of food and allowing small private factories and businesses to operate.

The NEP had a dramatic effect during the few years it was in force. Industry and farm production climbed back almost to pre-World War I levels. The NEP era also brought relaxed censorship and a degree of freedom in art, drama, and literature.

▶ DISARMAMENT CONFERENCE

Having rebuffed the League of Nations, American leaders felt the United States needed to make some gesture in support of collective action to secure peace. When Great Britain proposed a conference on limiting naval construction, the new Harding Administration seized the opportunity to host the meeting. Secretary of State Charles Evans Hughes opened the Washington arms conference on November 12, 1921.

The Americans' chief concern was a potential naval arms race with Japan. In return for U.S. pledges not to expand its military facilities in the Pacific, Japan agreed to restrict its warship construction to three-fifths of the U.S. and British tonnages. Companion agreements provided for withdrawal of Japanese troops from Siberia and a reduction of its military presence in China, as well as a mutual commitment by the great powers to respect each others' Pacific island possessions.

Unlike many other post-World War I diplomatic efforts, the Washington agreements made a real, if temporary, contribution to peace. U.S.-Japanese tensions eased significantly (though ill feeling reappeared when racially inspired U.S. laws banned Japanese immigration) and all parties avoided a ruinously expensive buildup of naval power.

▶ THE GREAT LOVER

Men mostly didn't get it. But women across America swooned at the histrionic passion of a young Italian actor named Rodolpho Alfonzo Raffaeli Pierre Filibert di Valentina d'Antonguolla—Rudolph Valentino (above, right), for short.

The great screen lover of the silent-movie era had his first leading role in the 1921 film *The Four Horsemen of the Apocalypse*. Another film later that year

established him as Hollywood's all-star heartthrob. In *The Sheik*, Valentino appeared as the adopted son of an Arab chieftain who wins the heart of a traveling Englishwoman (since he was adopted, Valentino could play the part of an exotic Arab but be racially European, thus observing the taboo against mixed-race romance).

Valentino's acting technique was mainly a matter of smoldering looks, popping eyes, bared teeth, and flaring nostrils. The effect was a bit like an overexcited racehorse, but it sent millions of women out of movie theaters with fluttering hearts. Even while many men found Valentino's pomaded looks and melodramatic lovemaking laughable, his dandified clothes, sideburns, and slicked-back hair set the style for would-be Don Juans—who, particularly if successful, were known in the slang of the time as "sheiks."

▶ IRELAND PARTITIONED

After 400 years of English rule, Ireland won self-government in 1921. Six predominantly Protestant counties in the north, however, refused to join the new Irish Free State and remained part of Great Britain.

The Free State's creation followed several years of violence. Trying to suppress the Irish freedom movement, the British backed up regular military units with a special police force known as the Black and Tans, mostly made up of ex-soldiers. Their brutality toward suspected republicans and their sympathizers embittered most of the Irish public.

- **FEBRUARY 24**
Herbert Hoover becomes U.S.Secretary of commerce.

- **MARCH 4**
Warren G. Harding is first President-elect to ride to his inauguration in an automobile.

- **MAY 31**
More than 85 die in race riot in Tulsa, Oklahoma.

- **JUNE 10**
U.S. Bureau of the Budget is established.

- **JUNE 20**
Alice Robertson of Oklahoma becomes the first woman to preside over the House of Representatives. She holds the gavel for 30 minutes.

- **JUNE**
Chinese Communist Party holds first congress in Shanghai.

- **JULY 1**
Heavyweight championship fight in Jersey City, New Jersey, between Dempsey and Carpentier is first boxing match with million-dollar gate.

More than 1,300 people were killed before British and Irish negotiators signed a treaty on December 6, 1921, giving the Free State dominion status, similar to Canada's at the time, with self-rule under the British throne. Militant republicans opposed the pact, and another year of fighting followed between the Irish Republican Army and the new Free State government.

In Northern Ireland, the seeds of future sectarian conflict were sown by religious discrimination against the Catholic minority, seen by many Protestants as potential traitors to the British crown.

▶ THE COTTON CLUB

The all-black musical revue *Shuffle Along* hit Broadway in 1921 and quickly sparked a craze for African-American music. White New Yorkers flocked uptown to Harlem nightspots, and white bootleggers just as quickly staked out their claims in the new entertainment center. Among them was the Hell's Kitchen gangster Owney Madden, who bought former boxing champ Jack Johnson's Club Deluxe at 142nd Street and Lennox Avenue.

Retaining Johnson as a figurehead manager, Madden reopened it as the Cotton Club. With its lavish shows, a decor of artificial palm trees, and illegal booze at stiff prices, the club became one of Harlem's most popular spots for white audiences.

SANGER

When Margaret Sanger (below) founded the American Birth Control League in 1921, distributing or even teaching about contraception was still strictly prohibited by federal law and by state laws nearly everywhere. But if puritan values still prevailed in American law, they were weakening in the rest of American society.

Although the League was a challenge to still-powerful legal and cultural taboos, it brought Sanger's crusade from the fringes to the American mainstream. Instead of the socialists and rebellious feminists who had been her associates in earlier struggles, the League enlisted respectable, middle-class women, and even more respectable male physicians in the birth-control cause.

Access to legal, safe birth control, Sanger felt, offered more power and new opportunities to women than either economic reforms or woman's suffrage. She was still far from fully respected, in any case. When Boston authorities banned her from speaking there, Sanger appeared anyway, standing on the stage with a band of tape over her mouth.

The performers and service staff were all African American, but with only occasional exceptions, blacks were not admitted as customers. The discriminatory policy angered many blacks, but the segregated entertainment world of the time gave black performers little choice. Among those who inaugurated great careers at the Cotton Club were Duke Ellington, Cab Calloway, Ethel Waters, and Lena Horne.

■ TRENDS & TRIVIA

Census Bureau reports 51 percent of Americans live in towns greater than 2,500.

Federal Highway Act provides federal funds to subsidize seven percent of state road mileage.

Swiss scientist Hermann Rorschach introduces "inkblot" psychological test.

Franklin D. Roosevelt is stricken with polio.

Lie detector is invented by John Agustus Larson and Leonarde Keeler.

Sports hits the airwaves. Radio listeners hear Jack Dempsey and Georges Carpentier battle for the world heavyweight boxing championship. Dempsey wins in the fourth round.

Shuffle Along, an all-black revue by Eubie Blake and Noble Sissle, opens on Broadway and becomes an enormous hit.

First White Castle hamburger stand opens in Wichita, Kansas.

Tomb of the Unknown Soldier is established at Arlington National Cemetery.

Knee-length skirts for women become the standard fashion.

Popular songs are "Blue Moon" and "Look for the Silver Lining."

Armistice Day, November 11, is declared a national holiday.

Rin Tin Tin debuts in Hollywood.

Organ music replaces orchestras in Broadway film theaters.

Eskimo Pie ice cream bars are new.

Coco Chanel introduces the enduring perfume Chanel No. 5.

101

• JULY 14
Sacco and Vanzetti are convicted of murder.

• JULY 21
In a test designed to demonstrate the military potential of air-power, six U.S. planes sink a captured German battleship in the Atlantic.

• AUGUST 2
Great tenor Enrico Caruso dies.

• SEPTEMBER
Labor violence erupts in West Virginia coalfields.

• SEPTEMBER 7-8
First Miss America pageant held in Atlantic City, New Jersey. Margaret Gorman of Washington, D.C. is crowned.

• SEPTEMBER 7
Scandal rocks Hollywood when starlet dies after wild party. Actor Fatty Arbuckle is charged with manslaughter but is eventually acquitted.

• DECEMBER 23
U.S. Socialist leader Eugene Debs is released from prison.

The disillusion and disorder that overtook much of Europe after World War I were particularly intense in Italy. Inflation, unemployment, and strikes roiled the economy. Law and order collapsed. Government was corrupt and inept. With many Italians losing faith in old institutions, new movements arose, among them Benito Mussolini's (below) Fascist Party, which he founded with a few hundred followers in 1919. Mussolini's ideas, which he preached through rabble-rousing editorials in his newspaper, *Il Popolo d'Italia*, were a somewhat incoherent mix of revolutionary reforms, extreme nationalism, and a glorification of order and discipline as the way to recover Italy's lost greatness.

In 1922 gangs of armed Fascist supporters known as Blackshirts took over Milan and several other cities. A weak national government did not react, and Mussolini called on his forces to march into Rome. When King Vittorio Emanuele III refused to declare martial law, the ruling politicians' will to resist dissolved. Summoned by the king, the 39-year-old Mussolini came to Rome on October 30 to form a government, opening the Fascist era.

▶ CAMPAIGN AGAINST LYNCHING

Throughout the 1920s and 1930s, a main goal of the National Association for the Advancement of Colored People (NAACP) and other civil rights organizations was to make lynching a federal crime, since lynch murders were seldom prosecuted and almost never punished in southern courts. In January 1922 the crusade won a symbolic success when antilynching legislation passed the House by a 231-119 vote. As expected, however, the bill died in the Senate, where filibuster rules gave segregationist southern Democrats a stranglehold over any civil rights legislation.

Even though the bill failed, it called national attention to the issue, leading many law-abiding Southerners to recoil from the barbarism of lynch law even while they remained firm believers in segregation. Lynchings, which had taken 3,000 lives from 1890 to 1920, continued to occur, but much less frequently. The antilynching crusade also helped raise the profile of the NAACP, drawing new members and strengthening the organization, financially and morally, for the great civil rights struggles to come in the 1950s and 1960s.

▶ FOUNDING OF MODERN TURKEY

Having joined the losing side in World War I, Turkey faced dismemberment following the Allied victory. French and Italian forces occupied Istanbul, and Greece, Turkey's traditional enemy, seized Smyrna (now Izmir).

Sultan Mehmed VI, the last of the Ottoman rulers who still nominally reigned in Istanbul, might have let the partition become permanent, but Mustafa Kemal (above, right), the hero of Turkey's victory over the British at Gallipoli, began

recruiting a new nationalist army to fight against both foreign forces and the decaying remnants of Ottoman rule. Kemal was willing to relinquish the Ottoman Empire's Arab lands, but insisted that Turkish-speaking regions remain intact.

In September 1922 Kemal recaptured Smyrna from the Greeks. In November his Grand National Assembly declared the end of Ottoman rule. The following year, in the Treaty of Lausanne, the Western powers recognized Turkey within its present borders. Kemal, given the name Kemal Atatürk (Father of the Turks) by the new national parliament, proclaimed a republic and embarked on sweeping reforms aimed at creating a modern, secular Turkish state.

▶ EMILY POST'S ETIQUETTE GUIDE

In an era that seemed mainly interested in breaking taboos, a surprisingly large number of Americans apparently still wanted instruction in the old rules—or so one could conclude from the success of *Emily Post's Etiquette in Society, in Business, in Politics, and at Home.* Using illustrative anecdotes involving upper-crust characters with names like Mrs. Wellborn, Reverend Eminent, and Mrs. Oldname, Post offered her readers guidance on the proper conduct for just about any conceivable activity or situation.

Mrs. Oldname, for example, was the model for how to walk correctly: "Her body is perfectly balanced, she holds herself straight, and yet in nothing suggests a ramrod. She takes steps of medium

- **FEBRUARY 5**
First issue of *Reader's Digest* promises "Thirty-One Articles Each Month from Leading Magazines."

- **FEBRUARY 18**
International Court of Justice established at The Hague, Netherlands.

- **FEBRUARY 25**
Henri Desire Landru, the "modern Bluebeard," is guillotined in Versailles for the murder of ten women and a young boy.

- **FEBRUARY 28**
Egypt gets token independence, though British keep influence.

- **MARCH 18**
British judge sentences Mohandas K. Gandhi to six years in prison.

- **APRIL 16**
Germany and Russia resume relations under Treaty of Rapallo.

- **MAY 12**
Twenty-ton meteor falls near Blackstone, Virginia, leaving a 500-square-foot crater.

INSULIN

length.... On no account does she swing her arms, nor does she rest a hand on her hip!"

Post, a former Baltimore debutante, was already a successful writer of novels, short stories, and magazine articles when she wrote her etiquette guide. Published in 1922, it led the nonfiction best-seller list the following year and has remained popular, in successive, updated editions, ever since.

▶ TUTANKHAMUN'S TOMB

Among ancient Egyptian rulers, Tutankhamun was hardly a major figure. He ascended the throne as a boy and died in his teens, having reigned for only about nine years. Yet it was Tutankhamun—more precisely, his face as carved on the golden death mask entombed with him—that gave the modern world its image of the Pharaohs.

The mask and a breathtaking array of other treasures were unearthed by archaeologist Howard Carter, who discovered Tutankhamun's tomb in the Valley of the Kings in November 1922. Behind an inner door at the end of a rubble-choked, nearly 30-foot-long passage, Carter and his English sponsor, Lord Carnarvon, found a gilded throne and two sentinel statues. The statues were "gold-kilted, gold-sandalled, armed with mace and staff, the protective sacred cobra upon their foreheads," guarding another sealed doorway to the burial shrine where Tutankhamun's coffin had lain for more than 3,200 years.

CARTER OPENS THE ENTRANCE TO THE FOURTH CHAMBER OF TUTANKHAMUN'S TOMB.

Before 1922 a diagnosis of juvenile diabetes was a death sentence. Those who developed the disease lost weight and energy, eventually sank into a coma, and died.

Scientists suspected that the blood sugar buildup in diabetes was caused by the lack of insulin, a hormone from a certain region of the pancreas. But no one found a way to isolate insulin until Frederick Banting of Canada's University of Toronto noticed in a surgeon's report that the insulin-producing "islets" in the pancreas remained intact even after the rest of the organ shriveled.

Banting and his assistant, Charles H. Best, tied off dogs' pancreatic ducts for seven weeks, then successfully extracted insulin from the islets. After biochemist James B. Collip devised a way to purify insulin for injection into humans, Banting and Best injected themselves to make sure it wasn't harmful, and then, in January 1922, administered it to a 14-year-old diabetic who appeared to be nearing his final coma. The boy's condition improved, the first time in history that juvenile diabetes was successfully controlled.

The dramatic circumstances and the richness of the find made the discovery an immediate media event. Keeping the story going for years was the tale of the "Pharaoh's curse," which supposedly doomed those involved in opening the tomb. Starting with Lord Carnarvon, there was a series of mysterious deaths: his halfbrother and Carter's former secretary among them. Carter, however, who should have suffered the worst fate, escaped Tutankhamun's revenge and lived a normal lifespan, dying in 1939 at the age of 66.

■ TRENDS & TRIVIA

Vitamin D is discovered by Elmer McCollum of the Johns Hopkins School of Hygiene and Public Health.

A sociological survey reports just 116 of 1,000 women consider themselves "happy" in marriage.

Mah-jongg becomes a national craze in the U.S.

Fawcett Publications introduces *True Confessions.*

Abie's Irish Rose opens on Broadway in the first of 2,327 performances.

Sinclair Lewis publishes *Babbitt.*

James Joyce's *Ulysses* is published; 500 copies are burned on arrival in the U.S.

Louis Armstrong joins Joe "King" Oliver's Creole Jazz Band in Chicago.

Exuberant young women who bind their breasts, bob their hair, and rebel against convention are known as flappers.

Nanook of the North is a landmark documentary film.

T. S. Eliot's poem *The Waste Land* is published.

New York's postmaster general orders all homes to get mailboxes or relinquish mail delivery.

Douglas Fairbanks, Sr., stars in *Robin Hood.*

Wise potato chips first appear on the market.

King George V opens new concrete tennis stadium at Wimbledon.

The first play-by-play coverage of the World Series is carried by station WJZ in Newark, New Jersey.

103

• **MAY 30**
Lincoln Memorial is dedicated.

• **JULY 24**
League of Nations gives Britain mandate to rule Palestine.

• **AUGUST**
First radio commercial is broadcast by WEAF in New York.

• **AUGUST 2**
Alexander Graham Bell, inventor of the telephone, dies.

• **SEPTEMBER 12**
Bishops of Protestant Episcopal Church vote 36-27 to delete "obey" from marriage vows.

• **OCTOBER 18**
British Broadcasting Company founded. (renamed British Broadcasting Corporation in 1927).

• **NOVEMBER**
White blood corpuscles are discovered by Dr. Alexis Carrel of the Rockefeller Institute.

THE HARDING SCANDALS

Warren G. Harding was a likable president, if hardly a paragon of intellect or energy. "A benign blank," the caustic H. L. Mencken wrote about him. When Harding died on his way back from a vacation in Alaska, public sorrow was manifestly genuine. But sympathy crumbled, with Harding's reputation, as investigators kept finding evidence of bribery and fraud by his drinking and poker-playing companions during his two years and five months as President. Harding knew before he died that trouble was brewing. Two administration officials committed suicide as investigators began to pursue reported abuses. Following Harding's death, Charles R. Forbes, head of the Veterans Bureau, was convicted on corruption charges. The biggest scandal was the Teapot Dome affair (featured on magazine cover, above), in which Secretary of the Interior Albert Fall went to prison for taking bribes in return for oil leases.

No proof emerged that Harding was personally corrupt. "I can take care of my enemies all right," Harding lamented. "But my damn friends...they're the ones that keep me walking the floor nights."

▶ EARTHQUAKE IN TOKYO

The first shock struck just before noon, September 1, 1923. During the next 72 hours, more than 1,700 additional tremors jolted the city of Tokyo. By the end of the second day, nearly the entire eastern region of the Japanese capital had been consumed in fires that roared like great blazing whirlwinds through the wooden houses. Some were started by charcoal or gas stoves that were lit to prepare the midday meal, but many buildings were set afire by chemical or electric causes.

Three-quarters of Tokyo's buildings were destroyed or seriously damaged. Only 1 of 15 wards escaped severe fire damage. Approximately 143,000 people were crushed, drowned, or burned to death. The devastated areas were rebuilt, only to face destruction again more than two decades later in the U.S. firebomb raids of World War II.

▶ THE BEER HALL PUTSCH

Germany was in chaos in 1923. Amid a ruined economy and anger at the punitive Treaty of Versailles, millions turned against the constitutional government. In Munich, a young agitator named Adolf Hitler conceived a plan to force Bavaria's State Commissioner, Gustav von Kahr, to join him in declaring a new government that would then march on Berlin to overthrow the Republic.

Hitler's chance came on November 8, when Kahr and his army and police commanders were attending a mass meeting at a Munich beer hall. As Nazi storm troopers surrounded the hall, Hitler forced Kahr at gunpoint to offer his support. But the moment they escaped, Kahr and his colleagues repudiated the agreement. The next morning, Hitler and the war hero Gen. Erich Ludendorff, whom he had enlisted as a figurehead, led several thousand storm troopers to the war ministry building, ringed by Bavarian police.

.ADOLF HITLER RECEIVES VISITORS IN LANDSBERG JAIL

Someone—on which side, no one ever knew—opened fire. When the shooting ended, 16 Nazis and 3 policemen were dead. Hitler, according to witnesses, fled the scene, leaving his comrades under fire.

Arrested, tried, and convicted of treason, Hitler declared that "the eternal court of history" would acquit him. Given a five-year sentence, he was freed less than nine months later.

▶ THE SAGE OF BALTIMORE

No commentator on America in the twenties spoke with a more distinctive and entertaining voice than H. L. Mencken. In the Baltimore *Evening Sun* and other publications, Mencken punctured puritanism, hypocrisy, and self-satisfaction. "I am not a constructive critic," he once admitted, with considerable understatement.

Mencken waged rhetorical combat with relish and had a gift for colorful invective, as when he wrote about President Harding's speeches: "...He writes the worst English that I have ever encountered. It reminds me of a string of wet sponges; it reminds me of tattered washing on the line; it reminds me of stale bean-soup, of college yells, of dogs barking idiotically through endless nights. It is so bad that a sort of grandeur creeps into it."

Having reached a national audience as coeditor of the literary magazine *Smart Set*, Mencken and his partner George Jean Nathan left the magazine in 1923 to launch a new magazine, the *American*

- **JANUARY**
Army Air Corps orders air crews to wear parachutes at all times during flight.

- **JANUARY 8**
The National Woman's Party launches a national campaign for an equal rights amendment to the federal constitution.

- **MARCH**
First shopping center opens in Kansas City. Country Club Plaza covers 40 acres,with 150 stores, 5,500 parking spaces.

- **MARCH 26**
Legendary actress Sarah Bernhardt dies.

- **APRIL 18**
Yankee Stadium opens in New York.

- **MAY 2-3**
First nonstop transcontinental flight is made, from Long Island, New York, to San Diego, California.

- **JULY 5**
First neon sign installed on marquee of New York's Cosmopolitan Theatre advertises Marion Davies in *Little Old New York*.

Mercury, which became one of the leading intellectual journals of the era.

▶ THE KU KLUX KLAN

American life changed rapidly in the 1920s and, as always, change exhilarated some, threatened others. For many, change wore a foreign face, or a black one. A wave of immigration between 1890 and World War I had filled cities with Catholics and Jews. Wartime mobility scattered immigrants and their children across the country, and drew southern blacks into northern states where few blacks had lived before.

Resentment among old-stock Protestants fueled the reappearance of a Reconstruction-era white supremacy group, the Ku Klux Klan. Greed helped, too. Founded in Georgia in 1915, the reborn Klan had only a few thousand members when, five years later, a pair of operators named Edgar Clarke and Elizabeth Tyler turned bigotry into a business. They sent out salesmen, called Kleagles, to sign up members for a $10 initiation fee, of which the salesman kept a $4 commission. By 1923 the Klan had some four million members and was politically

KLANSMEN MARCH IN A PARADE.

formidable in a number of states, notably overwhelmingly white Indiana, Colorado, and Oregon. The Klan's messages of hate, aimed at blacks, Catholics, Jews, and foreigners, were delivered by cross burnings, night riders, threats, beatings, and murder. Reflecting its roots in rural Protestant culture, the Klan also targeted bootleggers, gamblers, philanderers, and other offenders against its ideas of morality. After peaking in 1924, the movement declined sharply, partly because of scandals in the leadership, partly because the public turned against its outrages—but partly, too, because new immigration restrictions established a piece of the Klan's agenda as national policy.

THE CHARLESTON

Like the raccoon coat, hip flasks, and flapper dresses, the dance that would forever symbolize the Roaring Twenties is invariably associated with college life and the overwhelmingly white, middle-class image of the era's youth culture. In fact, like so much else in American popular music, the Charleston (right) was African American born.

The song that gave the dance its name was written by stride-piano legend James P. Johnson for *Runnin' Wild,* an all-black revue which opened in New York in 1923 as the first-act finale to a sequel to *Shuffle Along (*the first big all-black Broadway hit*)*. "Charleston," with its catchy music and exuberant dance steps, almost instantly sparked a nationwide craze. The 1924 version of George White's *Scandals* featured a Charleston number with no fewer than 60 dancers, while songwriters churned out new songs such as "I'm Going to Charleston, Back to Charleston" and, summing up a widely held opinion, "Charleston Is the Best Dance After All."

Vladimir Ilich Lenin, the steel-willed, ruthless leader of the Russian Revolution and founder of the Soviet state, died at his villa outside Moscow on the evening of January 21, 1924. His country was beginning to recover from years of appalling violence, but Lenin's death left his associates locked in a vicious struggle for power. The principal rivals were Leon Trotsky, commissar of the Red Army, and Joseph Stalin, the Communist Party's general secretary. Disabled by a series of strokes

STALIN (LEFT) AND LENIN

during the last 20 months of his life, Lenin had become concerned at the developing succession struggle. In a "political testament" dictated just over a year before his death (but not published in the Soviet Union until many years later) he criticized both possible successors. Trotsky was capable but too autocratic, Lenin felt; Stalin was "rude" and had accumulated "inordinate power." Lenin intended to remove Stalin as head of the party bureaucracy, but before the next party congress convened, another serious stroke left Lenin unable to speak. Instead of being demoted, Stalin was reconfirmed as general secretary.

▶ LEOPOLD-LOEB CASE

It was meant to be the perfect crime. Eighteen-year-old Richard Loeb, called Dickie, and 19-year-old Nathan Leopold, called Babe, lured their 14-year-old victim into a rented car, murdered him with

CLARENCE DARROW WITH NATHAN LEOPOLD AND RICHARD LOEB

a chisel, and stuffed his body into a culvert. They sent a ransom note, but their motive wasn't money. Loeb and Leopold were both brilliant, both twisted, both the sons of millionaires. Nourishing fantasies of themselves as superior beings above ordinary morality and the law, they killed Bobby Franks to prove it.

As criminals, though, they were hardly geniuses. They hid the body so carelessly it was found almost as soon as the ransom note was delivered, and Leopold dropped an easily traceable pair of glasses near the body. The boys were arrested and they quickly confessed.

The grotesque crime inflamed public opinion. Amid angry outcries for the death penalty, defense lawyer Clarence Darrow tried to save his clients' lives by pleading them guilty and persuading Judge John R. Caverly to accept mental illness as a mitigating factor in sentencing.

It was a novel argument, since at the time defendants were either found sane or acquitted as insane, with no middle ground. But Darrow succeeded. His summation, which took 12 hours spread over 3 days, was one of the most eloquent statements ever delivered against the

death penalty. The world must learn, he declared, "that all life is worth saving, and that mercy is the highest attribute of man." Judge Caverly sentenced both to life imprisonment—though he cited their age, rather than illness, as the reason for sparing their lives.

▶ IMMIGRATION CURTAILED

After significantly tightening immigration laws in 1921, Congress adopted even more drastic restrictions in 1924, reflecting a wide consensus that the United States should not resume accepting nearly a million immigrants a year, as had been the case before World War I.

The 1924 law also explicitly tipped the scales in favor of Anglo-Saxons and against immigrants with Mediterranean, Slavic, Jewish, or Asian origins. Extending a quota system first introduced in the 1921 law, the National Origins Act permitted immigration from different national groups in proportion to their share of the existing American population. Initial quotas were to be based on the 1890 census, excluding the Greeks,

IMMIGRANTS AT ELLIS ISLAND

• **JANUARY 22**
Labour Party wins its first election in Great Britain. Ramsay MacDonald becomes prime minister.

• **JANUARY 25-FEBRUARY 4**
First Winter Olympics held in Chamonix, France.

• **JANUARY 30**
Charles R. Forbes, former director of the U.S. Veterans Bureau, is convicted of conspiracy to defraud the government.

• **FEBRUARY 3**
Former President Woodrow Wilson dies.

• **APRIL 16**
Metro Pictures, Goldwyn Pictures, and Louis B. Mayer Company merge to form MGM.

• **JUNE 15**
Ford announces it has built its ten-millionth car. The first million took seven years; the tenth only 132 working days.

• **SEPTEMBER 28**
U.S. Army aviators complete first round-the-world flight, covering 26,103 miles in 351 hours and 11 minutes flying time over 175 days.

Italians, Slavs, and Jews, who accounted for the majority of immigrants in the two decades before World War I.

▶ RHAPSODY IN BLUE

Bandleader Paul Whiteman had recorded some of George Gershwin's popular songs and had occasionally mentioned that he would like Gershwin (below) to compose something more significant for him. But Gershwin's first inkling that Whiteman had definite plans came when a New York newspaper reported in January 1924 that a Gershwin composition would be featured in the Whiteman orchestra's upcoming

concert of American music at Carnegie Hall—less than six weeks away.

Gershwin sat down at the piano in his family's apartment at 501 West 110th Street, started writing, and somehow managed to finish "Rhapsody in Blue" in time for the concert. It was exactly what Whiteman wanted his program to demonstrate: "serious" music with an American accent.

On the afternoon of February 12, 1924, the jazzy "Rhapsody," with Gershwin at the piano, was the talk of the concert. "Fresh and new and full of promise," the *New York Times* reviewer called Gershwin, and another critic speculated that he had shown the path to the "development of American modern music into a high art form."

▶ FBI ESTABLISHED

The legacy of the Harding Administration scandals made housecleaning at the Justice Department a high priority for Harding's successor, Calvin Coolidge, and the new Attorney General, Harlan Fiske Stone. To repair the tainted image of the department's Bureau of Investigation, Stone turned to

HARLEM RENAISSANCE

As a growing tide of African Americans flowed from the rural South into northern cities, a new black culture began to take shape in the 1920s—most vibrantly in New York. Harlem became a magnet for black writers, artists, and musicians who were consciously engaged, as one historian noted, in "a new awakening of African American culture and creativity."

Major writers of the Harlem Renaissance included James Weldon Johnson, Countee Cullen, Claude McKay, Langston Hughes, Jessie Fauset, and Zora Neale Hurston. Much of their work appeared in *Crisis,* the NAACP's magazine, and *Opportunity*, published by the National Urban League, which sought to give a voice to those "who through poem or story or play or musical composition are passionately striving to bring to the surface...something of the pathos and romance and unflagging spirit" of black Americans. The Harlem writers began to reach white readers as well, with a literature that explicitly protested racial injustice and asserted, in the words of a Langston Hughes poem, "I, too, am America."

29-year-old J. Edgar Hoover, a key aide to former Attorney General A. Mitchell Palmer during the 1919-1920 Red-scare raids.

Hoover would head the bureau, later renamed the Federal Bureau of Investigation, for 48 years. His legacy was mixed. Hoover professionalized the bureau but also compiled a long record of using it against anyone whose political views he didn't like, while keeping secret files on powerful politicians to promote his policies and safeguard his position.

■ TRENDS & TRIVIA

Red Grange, the "Galloping Ghost" of the University of Illinois, and the famed "Four Horsemen of Notre Dame" make college football a big-time, big-money sport.

Publication of *The Crossword Puzzle Book* touches off a national craze.

First modern style open-end mutual fund is founded by Massachusetts Investers Trust.

E. M. Forster's *A Passage to India* is published.

Douglas Fairbanks, Sr., stars in *The Thief of Baghdad.*

The spiral-bound notebook is introduced.

American Heart Association is established.

AT&T and Western Electric jointly create Bell Telephone Laboratories.

Herman Melville's *Billy Budd,* completed just before the writer's death in 1891, is published.

There are 2.5 million radios in the U.S., up from 5,000 in 1920.

First disposable handkerchiefs, later named Kleenex, are sold.

A basic Model T Ford sells for $290.

Surrealism is the dominant art movement. ("Le Domaine" by René Magritte.)▶

Wheaties breakfast cereal is new.

Self-winding wristwatch becomes available.

• OCTOBER 4-10
Washington Senators win only World Series of their history.

• OCTOBER 5
"Little Orphan Annie" appears in *New York Daily News.*

• NOVEMBER 4
Nellie Taylor Ross is elected governor of Wyoming to fill unexpired term of her husband, William Bradford Ross.

• NOVEMBER 4
Calvin Coolidge is elected President with 15.7 million votes to 8.4 million for Democrat James Cox.

• NOVEMBER 27
First Macy's Thanksgiving Day parade is held in New York City.

• NOVEMBER 30
RCA demonstrates wireless transmission of photographs from London to New York.

• DECEMBER 13
American Federation of Labor president Samuel Gompers dies.

THE SCOPES TRIAL

108

When William Jennings Bryan and Clarence Darrow faced each other on a blazing July afternoon on the lawn of a Tennessee country courthouse, it was like no other moment in American legal history, before or since.

Darrow was defending John Scopes, a biology teacher accused of breaking a state law that banned teaching evolution. Bryan was assisting the prosecution. The trial's climax came when Darrow called Bryan as a witness and grilled him on his belief that every word in the Bible was literally true. A flustered Bryan protested: "The only purpose Mr. Darrow has is to slur at the Bible." Darrow replied that he was only examining "your fool ideas that no intelligent Christian on Earth believes." Scopes was convicted, but Tennessee's Supreme Court threw out the verdict on a technicality. The law remained in force, but Bryan's humiliation weakened the antievolution forces—and widened the gap between the two Americas, one rural and fundamentalist, the other modern and skeptical, that were the real antagonists on that sweltering courthouse lawn.

JOHN SCOPES (SEATED, RIGHT) IN CONFERENCE AT THE DEFENSE TABLE

▶ PROPHET OF AIRPOWER

Gen. Billy Mitchell was not a diplomat, to put it mildly. A pioneering Army Air Service pilot in World War I, Mitchell concluded that airpower would be a decisive weapon in future warfare. Ignoring channels and customary protocol, he used newspapers and his friends in Congress to promote development of better aircraft and a separate airpower branch of the armed services. His ideas and his methods antagonized officers who clung to more traditional doctrines. In 1921 Mitchell outraged Navy leaders by arranging a successful test in which bombers sank a captured German battleship, proving, he said, that battleships were obsolete.

His unpopularity with his superiors eventually got him transferred to a do-nothing assignment in Texas, but Mitchell wouldn't be silenced. Following several military aircraft accidents, he blasted the Navy and War Departments for "incompetency, criminal negligence, and almost treasonable administration of the national defense.…"

Court-martialed in 1925 for "conduct prejudicial to good order and military discipline," Mitchell was given a five-year suspension from active duty but resigned his commission instead. He died in 1936.

▶ HITLER'S WARNING

Whatever else can be said against Adolf Hitler, no one could complain that he failed to give the world fair warning of his plans. Eight years before he came to power, his book *Mein Kampf* (*My Struggle*) set out "exactly the kind of Germany he intended to make…," wrote historian William L. Shirer, "and the kind of world he meant to create by armed German conquest." Dictated in the comfortable cell where Hitler served nine months

of a five-year prison sentence for the unsuccessful Munich uprising, the first volume of *Mein Kampf* was published in the fall of 1925. Four hundred pages long and priced at a relatively expensive 12 marks (about $3), it sold exactly 9,473 copies that year, 6,913 in 1926, 5,607 in 1927. *Mein Kampf* was frank about Hitler's thirst for conquest ("soil exists for the people which possesses the force to take it") and about his master race theories ("the stronger must dominate and not blend with the weaker, thus sacrificing his own greatness").

Most chilling of all, perhaps, was his fixation on violence, which he saw as creating its own justification. The strongest and most aggressive, he declared, deserve victory: "Those who want to live, let them fight, and those who do not want to fight, in this world of eternal struggle, do not deserve to live."

▶ THE *NEW YORKER*

Six months after its first issue appeared, the *New Yorker*'s circulation was a meager 2,700 copies. The magazine's chief invester decided in August 1925 to close it down but changed his mind a few hours later. The reprieve gave Harold Ross, the magazine's eccentric, irascible founding editor, time to make the *New Yorker* a showcase for civilized humor by employ-

---

- **JANUARY 20**
Miriam "Ma" Ferguson takes the oath of office as governor of Texas. She campaigned on the slogan "Me for Ma."

- **JANUARY**
President Coolidge declares that "the business of America is business."

- **JANUARY 24**
Total solar eclipse, the first in 300 years, is visible in New York.

- **MARCH 12**
China's President Sun Yat-sen dies.

- **APRIL 15**
American painter John Singer Sargent, known for his elegant portraits, dies of a stroke at 69.

- **MAY**
A. Philip Randolph founds Brotherhood of Sleeping Car Porters.

- **JUNE 6**
Walter P. Chrysler founds his automobile company.

- **JULY 26**
Lawyer William Jennings Bryan dies five days after end of Scopes trial.

ing such writers as Dorothy Parker, John O'Hara, James Thurber, and the incomparable essayist E. B. White, as well as a long line of brilliant cartoonists beginning with Helen Hokinson and Peter Arno.

Even in ads seeking subscribers, the magazine set a relatively high standard of wit. "The most essential feature of a magazine is paper," one ad began, and one particularly useful variety "has been found to be an oblong sheet of green paper issued by the United States Government, and bearing the words: 'Five Dollars.' From this single scrap, enough paper can be procured to print 52 copies [of the magazine]; and to any reader who will submit such a bill to the *New Yorker*, the editors will mail a year's subscription free."

▶ ART DECO

The technology and industrial development of the early 20th century changed not only how people lived and worked but also what people saw and touched. New products and new materials meant new shapes, textures, colors. Not surprisingly, artists and designers responded to the new visual environment by experimenting with new styles. One of the most influential was Art Deco, which took its name from the Exposition Internationale des Arts Décoratifs et Industriels Modernes, held in Paris in 1925.

The Art Deco movement altered the entire visual landscape. It changed the look of lamps, furniture, textiles, pots and pans, and book covers; it also changed the look of ocean liners, office buildings, and factories. In place of the flowery patterns and gingerbread embellishments of the Victorian era,

HAND-PAINTED GLASS BOWL

FITZGERALD

F. Scott Fitzgerald may not have been the greatest writer of his time, but he was its most perfect reflection. He and the twenties were like two facing mirrors, infinitely recreating each other's image until one could not be sure if Fitzgerald invented the Jazz Age, or if it invented him.

His first novel, *This Side of Paradise*, chronicled the experience of a new generation "grown up to find all Gods dead, all wars fought, all faiths in man shaken...." He and his wife Zelda

(above) lived like characters from his fiction: glittery, extravagant, chasing after shallow pleasures, perhaps to escape the emptiness inside. His best portrait of the era was *The Great Gatsby*, whose title character, a bootlegger, tries vainly to use his illegal wealth to win back an old love from her rich but cloddish husband.

Also published in 1925 was Theodore Dreiser's *An American Tragedy,* which probed the power of wealth in America and the corrosive consequences for those who don't have it but crave it.

Art Deco used geometric shapes, industrial materials, and solid bright colors. Its decorative images came from industry, too: cogwheels, construction rigs, machine parts.

American architects were heavily influenced by the movement, especially in New York. The Chrysler Building with its 150-foot stainless steel spire, completed in 1930, still stands at 405 Lexington Avenue as Art Deco's most memorable monument.

■ TRENDS & TRIVIA

Advertising man Bruce Barton's controversial best-seller *The Man Nobody Knows* declares Jesus was the embodiment of "principles of modern salesmanship...."

P. G. Wodehouse's novel *Carry On Jeeves,* featuring the resourceful valet Jeeves and his amiable but dim-witted master Bertie Wooster, lampoons the British class system.

Contract bridge is invented.

Drano is introduced.

207 Americans have incomes of 1 million dollars or more; 7 have incomes above 5 million.

Louis Armstrong makes his first record with his Hot Five band.

Musical comedy *No, No, Nanette* opens on Broadway.

A&W Root Beer becomes the first fast-food franchise.

Josephine Baker's *Negro Review* takes Paris by storm. ▶

The first volume of Ezra Pound's *Cantos* is published.

U.S. national spelling bees begin.

The first air-conditioned theaters open, in New York City.

The U.S. State Department recognizes the right of women to keep their birth names.

The Fayetteville, North Carolina, daily paper stops covering crime, until a survey shows its readers want crime news restored.

The American Medical Association endorses birth control.

- **AUGUST 8**
40,000 Ku Klux Klan members stage march in Washington, D.C.

- **SEPTEMBER 3**
Navy dirigible *Shenandoah* is destroyed in storm near Cadwell, Ohio.

- **NOVEMBER**
Surrealist art show in Paris exhibits works by Ernst, Man Ray, Miró, Picasso.

- **NOVEMBER 21**
David C. Stephenson, Grand Dragon of the Indiana Ku Klux Klan, is convicted of second-degree murder.

- **NOVEMBER 28**
Grand Ole Opry begins Saturday night *Barn Dance* broadcasts over WSM in Nashville, Tennessee.

- **DECEMBER**
Reza Khan becomes Shah of Persia, founding Pahlevi Dynasty.

- **DECEMBER 12**
Milestone Motel, the nation's first motel, opens in Monterey, California.

110

British labor unions tested their strength in the spring of 1926—and found they were not strong enough.

Like many major labor disputes in Britain's history, the 1926 general strike originated in the coal mines. Government subsidies were scheduled to expire, and mine owners planned to cut wages by 13 percent and lengthen shifts by an hour. The miners' union responded with the slogan: "Not a minute on the day, not a penny off the pay." When the owners put the wage cut in effect, about a million miners refused to work. Some two million other British workers went out in sympathy, (right). Public opinion was sharply divided, reflecting in part the class-consciousness still prominent in British culture. Volunteers, including many students from upper-crust Oxford and Cambridge, turned out as strikebreakers to keep essential services going.

Nine days after the sympathy strike began, the Trades Union Council called it off. The miners held out for seven more months but then capitulated, reluctantly swallowing not only the wage cuts but large layoffs as well.

▶ BOOK-OF-THE-MONTH CLUB LAUNCHED
"Entrepreneurs of the word," a Book-of-the-Month Club official once called 1920s publishers such as DeWitt and Lila Wallace, creators of *Reader's Digest*, and Henry Luce, founder of *Time*.

Book-of-the-Month's inventor, Harry Scherman, joined the list when he launched the club in 1926. It was aimed at "the thoughtful people," as Scherman often described his readers—numerous enough, he was convinced, to make a mass audience. The club's first selection, chosen, as was true until 1994, by a panel of well-known literary experts, was *Lolly Willowes*, by an unknown British novelist named Sylvia Townsend Warner. It was sent out in April 1926 to 4,750 members. In the decades to come, the Book-of-the-Month Club introduced American readers to a host of important writers, including Ernest Hemingway, Richard Wright, and George Orwell.

Another was Margaret Mitchell, whom none of the judges had ever heard of before picking her 1936 novel *Gone With the Wind*. (Notified of its selection, an overwhelmed Mitchell wrote back to Scherman: "It was too much to be borne and I went to bed and was ill, with an ice pack and large quantities of aspirin.")

By the time of its 25th anniversary, the club had sent out 100 million books—90 percent of which would never have reached their readers, Scherman believed, if not for the club's creation.

▶ EDERLE SETS CHANNEL RECORD
No woman had ever swum across the 35-mile-wide English Channel. But Gertrude Ederle (above, right), a star Olympic swimmer, was sure she could do it, even

FRIENDS WISH BON VOYAGE TO SWIMMER GERTRUDE EDERLE

though her first attempt, in 1925, had failed. The 19-year-old New Yorker stepped confidently into the choppy surf at Cape Gris-Nez, France, on the morning of August 6, 1926, to begin her second try. Fourteen hours and 31 minutes later, Ederle waded onto the beach at Kingsdown, England. Not only had she become the first woman to swim the channel, she had also beaten the fastest time of any man by nearly two hours. "She stands today as Champion Extraordinary of her sex," declared the magazine *Literary Digest*, adding extravagantly, "Homer would have hymned her victory had it occurred in the days of early Greece, and she would have become a heroine of myth and drama."

▶ FLORIDA LAND BUBBLE BURSTS
"Sit and watch at twilight the fronds of the graceful palm, latticed against the fading gold of the sun-kissed sky," a lyrical Florida banker exhorted property buyers at the height of the dizzying real estate boom that changed the map of the state. Coral Gables, Hollywood, Miami Beach, and dozens of other communities appeared, almost overnight, out of the mangrove swamps. As land values shot up, speculators flooded the state, hoping to buy lots in the next popular resort and resell at huge profits. Many buyers put down deposits for binders on lots they had

---

- **JANUARY 3**
Greek Premier Pangalos declares himself dictator; opposition leaders are exiled.

- **MARCH 16**
Robert H. Goddard flies first liquid fuel rocket in Auburn, Massachusetts.

- **APRIL 11**
American horticulturist Luther Burbank dies. He developed more and better varieties of cultivated plants.

- **MAY 20**
President Coolidge signs Civilian Aviation Act, establishing Bureau of Air Commerce with responsibility for licensing aircraft and pilots.

- **JUNE 14**
Mary Cassat, the only American artist given the privilege of exhibiting with the European Impressionists, dies at 81.

- **JULY 2**
Army Air Corps is established.

- **AUGUST 23**
Screen lover Rudolph Valentino dies in New York; tens of thousands of hysterical mourners throng his funeral.

seen only as outlines on a blueprint, intending to sell the binders before the first payment was due.

Ballyhoo soared with the price of land. The mayors of Miami, Miami Beach, Hialeah, and Coral Gables proclaimed each of their cities as "the most Richly Blessed Community of the most Bountifully Endowed State of the most Highly Enterprising People of the Universe." But the bubble burst as quickly as it had inflated. Defaults by buyers holding unsold binders mounted. Then nature took a hand. On September 18, 1926, a devastating hurricane hit the Gold Coast, flattening thousands of shoddily built houses. About 400 people died, and so did what was left of the land boom, leaving unfinished developments to be overgrown by grass and palmetto.

▶ RELIGION AS SHOW BUSINESS

For faith healer Aimee Semple McPherson, religion was show business, and vice versa. In her 5,000-seat Angelus Temple in Los Angeles, topped by a huge illuminated cross that could be seen for miles, McPherson made the gospels into Hollywood production numbers, complete with sound effects of wind, thunder, and lightning. In one of her extravaganzas, Satan floated in a hot-air balloon through an artillery barrage fired by Christians from the stage.

McPherson's flock consisted almost entirely of recent migrants from the Midwest who had brought their fundamentalist religion with them on their journey west. One of the first successful radio preachers, McPherson reached hundreds of thousands more listeners through her own radio station, KFSG.

On May 18, 1926, McPherson vanished from a Los Angeles beach. She reappeared 32 days later in Mexico, with a melodramatic tale of having been abducted. Evidence quickly accumulated that the kidnapping story was a hoax, and that McPherson had actually spent the time in a beach cottage

with her married lover and radio engineer, Kenneth Ormiston. Those disclosures dimmed McPherson's star but did not extinguish it; through various romantic and financial misadventures, she remained an evangelist until her death in 1944.

WINNIE-THE-POOH

"What about a story?" said Christopher Robin.

"*What* about a story?" I said.

"Could you very sweetly tell Winnie-the-Pooh one?"

"I suppose I could," I said. "What sort of stories does he like?"

"About himself. Because he's *that* sort of bear."

"Oh, I see."

"So could you very sweetly?"

"I'll try," I said.

Thus did A. A. Milne introduce the first of his whimsical tales with characters based on his young son Christopher's toy animals. Possibly no other author ever wrote so artfully while appearing so artless. Milne created personalities so real that they lived in his readers' memories like real childhood friends: The ever-flustered Piglet, gloomy Eeyore, pretentious Owl, and Winnie-the-Pooh himself, the amiable bear of little brain, in perpetual search of "a little something" sweet to eat.

Winnie-the-Pooh won children's and parents' hearts from the day it appeared in October 1926. Nearly three-quarters of a century later, its appeal remains undiminished.

CHRISTOPHER ROBIN AND HIS DAD, A. A. MILNE

■ TRENDS & TRIVIA

Ernest Hemingway's novel *The Sun Also Rises* chronicles the Lost Generation.

R. H. Tawney's *Religion and the Rise of Capitalism* is published.

First records are cut by Duke Ellington and Jelly Roll Morton.

Permanent wave is invented by Antonio Buzzacchino.

The End of Laissez Faire, by John Maynard Keynes, is published.

Basketball performers, the Harlem Globetrotters, are organized by Abe Saperstein.

Paul de Kruif writes *The Microbe Hunters.*

The 1926 Revenue Act gives corporate and income tax cuts.

Norwegian inventor Eric Rotheim devises aerosol spray.

A popular tune is "I Found a Million-Dollar Baby in a Five and Ten Cent Store."

Langston Hughes publishes his famous poem *Weary Blues.*

Miniature golf is a new craze.

Sinclair Lewis declines a Pulitzer Prize for his novel *Arrowsmith*, declaring that prizes tend to make writers "safe, polite, obedient, and sterile."

Paris's Pasteur Institute announces discovery of an antitetanus serum.

Mae West stars in the scandalous comedy *Sex.* New York police shut down the show on morals charges after 375 performances. ▶

111

• OCTOBER 20
Eugene V. Debs, five-time Socialist Party Presidential candidate, dies.

• OCTOBER 31
Magician and escape artist Harry Houdini dies.

• NOVEMBER 1
Joseph Goebbels is appointed head of the Berlin Nazi Party.

• NOVEMBER 15
National Broadcasting Company begins network broadcasting with four-hour special.

• DECEMBER 5
Impressionist painter Claude Monet dies.

• DECEMBER 14
Writer Agatha Christie, missing for four days, is found alive and well after suffering from amnesia.

• DECEMBER 25
25-year-old Crown Prince Hirohito succeeds to Japanese throne on death of his father, Emperor Yoshihito.

On the morning of May 20, 1927, a slim, shy, 25-year-old airmail pilot named Charles A. Lindbergh (below) took off from New York's Roosevelt Field alone in a single-engine plane named the *Spirit of St. Louis.* Thirty-three hours and 29 minutes later, after circling over the Eiffel Tower in the heart of Paris, Lindbergh landed at Le Bourget aerodrome, where a crowd estimated at 100,000 poured out to give him a delirious welcome.

Lindbergh's 3,610-mile flight was an impressive feat of skill and endurance. But that alone did not explain the tidal wave of adulation that made Lindbergh perhaps the most idolized celebrity in American history.

Lindbergh was made a hero for what he was, as well as what he did. Wholesome, hard-working, self-effacing, he embodied old-fashioned virtues that American society in the disillusioned twenties seemed to have lost. He "seemed to have nothing to do with his generation," F. Scott Fitzgerald observed, and for precisely that reason, his flight gave Americans, at least temporarily, a renewed faith in their own ideals.

▶ CHIANG SPLITS WITH COMMUNISTS

It was a partnership that both sides later preferred to forget, but China's Nationalists and Communists began their revolution as allies against the local warlords who controlled most of northern China in the mid-1920s. Under the command of a slim, unsmiling general named Chiang Kai-shek, Nationalist and Communist troops joined in the northern expedition, which set out from the southern city of Canton (now Guangzhou) to bring China under a single government and end years of chaos.

In March 1927, as Chiang's forces neared Shanghai, China's largest city and its financial and industrial capital, Communist-led workers seized control of the city, then welcomed the Kuomintang (Nationalist Party) soldiers. But Chiang, who had links with the business establishment and also with the bosses of Shanghai's criminal underworld, turned on his Communist allies within hours. The Communist militias were disarmed; thousands of party workers were imprisoned; hundreds were shot. Those Communist leaders who escaped arrest slipped out of the city to begin rebuilding their movement, while Chiang established his new national government at Nanjing.

▶ FIRST TV BROADCAST

On April 17, 1927, history appeared on a small screen in the New York headquarters of the American Telephone & Telegraph Company (AT&T). For the occasion, history wore the squarish face of Herbert Hoover, Secretary of Commerce, who was speaking into a camera in his Washington office. "We have long been familiar with the electrical transmission of sound," Hoover told AT&T president Walter Gifford and others gathered around the receiver in New York. "Today we have, in a sense, the transmission of sight, for the first time in the world's history."

The device that transmitted Hoover's image, called Radio Vision by its creator, Charles Francis Jenkins, was one of several designed by inventors working independently of each other. The actual ancestor of modern television was a different system, based on inventions patented in 1923 and 1924 by the Russian-born Vladimir Zworykin, who subsequently became chief of electronic research for RCA.

It's unlikely that Hoover and those watching that first broadcast had any inkling of the profound impact television would have. One participant was thinking about the future, though—Hoover's wife, Lou, who asked Gifford from her husband's office, "What will you invent next? I hope you won't invent anything that reads our thoughts!"

▶ THE IRON LUNG

New hope for patients with polio and other paralyzing illnesses dawned with the invention of the iron lung (below) in 1927. Developed by Philip Drinker and Louis Shaw of the Harvard School of Public Health, the device didn't cure illness, but kept paralyzed patients breathing so they could remain alive and undergo treatment.

The lung was a metal cylinder, large enough so that a patient's whole body could be slid into it. At the neck was a rubber collar, sealing off the chamber inside. An attached pump alternately

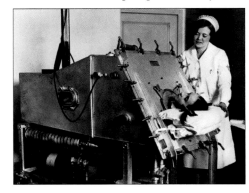

- **JANUARY 5**
Massachusetts becomes first state to require automobile owners to carry liability insurance.

- **JANUARY 7**
Commercial telephone service is inaugurated between London and New York.

- **FEBRUARY 23**
Federal Radio Commission is established.

- **APRIL**
Floods devastate lower Mississippi River Basin.

- **JUNE**
In *The President's Daughter*, Nan Britton describes an affair with the late President Harding and claims he fathered her child.

- **JUNE 2**
Lizzie Borden dies. She was acquitted of murdering her father and stepmother in a sensational trial in 1892.

- **AUGUST 23**
Nicola Sacco and Bartolomeo Vanzetti are executed.

sucked air out and forced it back into the chamber. As air was drawn in and out, the changing pressure expanded and compressed the patient's chest.

▶ THE BAMBINO

It was an age of sports idols. Football in the twenties had Red Grange. Boxing had Jack Dempsey and Gene Tunney, tennis had Bill Tilden. But the star of first magnitude was Babe Ruth. As a crowd-pleaser, no other athlete even came close.

At the start of the decade, Ruth's 54 home runs in 1920, almost double the previous record, electrified fans and helped big-league baseball rub away the tarnish of the "Black Sox" scandal. The next year

BABE RUTH TAKES A SWIPE AT AN ENORMOUS BALL

Ruth hit 59 homers, with a .378 average. An astonishing 60 percent of his 204 hits were for extra bases. Ruth became a national institution. Year after year, he filled American League parks and then played for hundreds of thousands more fans during off-season barnstorming tours.

The Babe was no Greek god, physically or otherwise. Pug-faced, potbellied and spindly-legged, he was also the bad boy who never grew up. He drank and chased women almost as gluttonously as he ate. He was foul-mouthed, crude, and undisciplined, but also open-hearted and so artlessly exuberant in his delight in his skills that no one could help rejoicing with him.

FIRST TALKIE

There was, as it happens, no jazz in *The Jazz Singer.* Nor, notwithstanding that it has gone down in history as the first "talkie," was there much talk. Best known are the few seconds it took for Al Jolson to adlib his trademark phrase, "You ain't heard nothin' yet!" The plot, as virtually all critics agreed then and later, was sentimental slush. But audiences could hear Jolson sing, and that was enough to draw huge crowds from the moment the movie premiered in New York on October 6, 1927.

Movie makers had been experimenting with recorded sound techniques for years. But major studios in the 1920s were hesitant to develop sound systems, among other reasons because sound would end the careers of a number of established stars who had squeaky voices or heavy accents.

Nonetheless, after trying out its new Vitaphone sound system in a couple of experimental short films, Warner Brothers released *The Jazz Singer.* Meanwhile, the Fox theater chain developed a system called Movietone, which soon became the standard process and sealed the doom of the silent era.

In 1927 the Bambino led the Yankees in the greatest season in baseball history. While the team won 110 games, lost 44, and finished 19-and-a-half games ahead of the second-place Philadelphia Athletics, Ruth batted .356 and hit 60 homers, a record that stood for the next 34 years.

■ TRENDS & TRIVIA

Werner Heisenberg formulates the "uncertainty principle," holding that velocity or position of a subatomic particle can be measured, but not both.

Stan Laurel and Oliver Hardy team up in *Putting Pants on Philip,* first of the pair's more than a hundred comedy shorts and feature films.

Sinclair Lewis's *Elmer Gantry* is published.

Bennett Cerf and Donald Klopfer start Random House.

Young women in Chicago and Philadelphia start "slow clubs" where kissing, booze, and jazz are banned.

Georges Lemaitre incorporates the latest discoveries in physics and astronomy into his "Big Bang" theory of an expanding universe.

Herman Joseph Muller discovers that x-rays and ultraviolet light can cause genetic mutations.

Jerome Kern and Oscar Hammerstein's landmark musical *Showboat* opens on Broadway. Paul Robeson's rendition of "Old Man River" is its most unforgettable moment.

Actress Clara Bow, the "It" girl, embodies the flapper ideal.

Gerber baby foods are new.

A Peruvian pilot discovers the ancient and mysterious Nazca lines while flying over Peru's highland desert.

Jazz musician Duke Ellington begins a three-year run at Harlem's Cotton Club.

Wonder Bread and homogenized milk are new conveniences.

Steppenwolfe by Hermann Hesse is published.

◀ **AUGUST**
Work begins on the sculptured faces of four Presidents at Mount Rushmore in South Dakota.

• **SEPTEMBER 14**
Dance star Isadora Duncan dies in freak accident when her scarf snags in turning wheel of car.

• **SEPTEMBER 22**
Heavyweight boxer Gene Tunney defeats Jack Dempsey in the "battle of the long count."

• **NOVEMBER 12**
Holland Tunnel opens, linking New York and New Jersey.

• **DECEMBER 2**
Ford's new Model A is shown to the public. It replaces the Model T or "Tin Lizzie."

• **DECEMBER 17**
U.S. Navy submarine S-4 sinks in collision off Cape Cod; all 40 crewmembers are lost.

Anthropological fieldwork rarely makes for best-sellers, but when 27-year-old Margaret Mead (below) published *Coming of Age in Samoa*, the book was a sensation. Mead's account of adolescent girls in a sexually free culture evoked familiar fantasies about sensuous South Sea islands. But it also struck a chord in America's culture wars. At a time when old taboos were under attack, Mead seemed to put science on the side of sexual rebellion and against moralistic traditions. A quote on the book jacket from a prominent biologist asked "if we shall ever be as sensible about sex as the Samoans are."

Mead's point was that girls in Samoa were taught to approach sex without embarrassment, as a natural part of life rather than something forbidden or sinful. A Samoan girl did not develop guilt or conflicted feelings or face tension with her parents.

By telling Americans that their culture wasn't universal and their values not absolute, Mead raised a central issue in the struggle between tradition and modernism at the heart of American experience in the '20s.

▶ HOOVER VS. SMITH

When Governor Alfred E. Smith of New York won the 1928 Democratic Presidential nomination, it turned the election into a clash of cultures as well as parties and policies. Smith, the first Roman Catholic ever to become a major-party national candidate, embodied the new urban Americans, still close to their immigrant roots, and religiously and ethnically diverse. Herbert Hoover, nominated as the Republican candidate after serving as Secretary of Commerce (but never in any elected national office), typified the native-stock, small-town Protestant majority that still thought of itself as the "real" Americans. Smith's New York accent and an unmistakably urban style of speech and humor emphasized the cultural differences between the two candidates.

In the campaign, Hoover studiously avoided the religious issue. But ugly anti-Catholic prejudice, sometimes open, sometimes whispered, was a constant shadow over Smith's candidacy. "If you vote for Al Smith, you're voting against Christ," an Oklahoma City Baptist minister admonished his congregation. For more than 30 years, until John F. Kennedy's election in 1960, political folklore declared that Smith's defeat proved no Catholic could win the Presidency. But with the country prospering in 1928 and generally satisfied with the policies of the past two Republican administrations, Smith would almost certainly have lost even if religion had not been an issue.

▶ AMOS 'N' ANDY

Blackface comedy, a tradition in American entertainment since the 19th century, hit the airwaves in March 1928 when WMAQ in Chicago broadcast the first 15-minute segment of a new radio serial, *Amos 'n' Andy*.

Invented, written, and performed by two white actors, Charles J. Correll and Freeman F. Gosden (right), the show chronicled the ups and downs of its title characters and their Fresh Air Taxicab Company, so named because its only taxi was a broken-down jalopy without a top. For the next 15 years Amos and Andy were on the air 5 nights a week, with an ever growing cast of supporting characters including the Kingfish, Needle Nose Fletcher, Brother Crawford, and scores of others. Gosden and Correll played every male part, and wrote all the scripts to boot.

So popular was the show that telephone calls dropped off noticeably while it was on the air. Restaurants and department stores set up radios to broadcast it, lest their customers stay home.

Many of the show's characters were sympathetic and its humor was, by the standards of the time, not malicious. Still, *Amos 'n' Andy* reflected crude racial stereotypes, and although it had black listeners, many African Americans found it offensive. Complaints from civil rights organizations mounted in the slowly changing racial climate after World War II, but the show survived on radio until 1958 and on television until 1965.

▶ LADY CHATTERLEY

The British writer D. H. Lawrence, after years of moving restlessly from one country to another, finished his last novel in a

---

• JANUARY 1
Milam Building in San Antonio, Texas, first air-conditioned office building in the U.S., opens.

• JANUARY 11
British novelist Thomas Hardy dies at 87.

• FEBRUARY
The first truly general election is held in Japan. Previous elections were limited to the wealthy and aristocrats.

• MARCH 13
450 are killed when dam bursts north of Los Angeles.

• MAY 7
Britain lowers women's voting age from 30 to 21, the same age as for men.

• JUNE 8
Chiang Kai-shek's Nationalist forces capture Beijing.

• JUNE 18
Amelia Earhart, as passenger, becomes first woman to fly the Atlantic.

115

villa near Florence, Italy. *Lady Chatterley's Lover*, the story of a passionate love affair between an aristocrat's wife and her game-keeper, became possibly the most contro-versial novel ever written in English at that time. Privately published in Florence by an Italian friend of the author's in 1928—less than two years before Lawrence's death—*Lady Chatterley* remained unpublishable in England and the United States for more than 30 years because of its language and graphic lovemaking scenes.

During that time, the novel became a symbol of the conflict between conven-tional taboos and the freedom of artists to explore erotic subjects. In England, it became the centerpiece of a celebrated trial when Penguin Books brought out an unexpurgated version in 1960 and was promptly prose-cuted under the Obscene Publi-cations Act. After prominent authors testified for the defense, the court ruled in Penguin's favor. At almost the same time, American courts overturned an order by Postmaster Arthur Summerfield that had banned the book from the U.S. mails on grounds of obscenity.

▶ KELLOGG-BRIAND PACT

In retrospect it looks like the emptiest international agreement in diplomatic his-tory. In ceremonies in Paris on August 27, 1928, 15 nations, led by the United States, France, England, Germany, Japan, and Italy, signed a treaty solemnly promising never to wage war except in self-defense and to settle all disputes peacefully.

In subsequent years all but a handful of the world's nations accepted the treaty, named the Kellogg-Briand Pact after its originators, U.S. Secretary of State Frank Kellogg and French Foreign Minister Aris-tide Briand. The Nobel committee chose Kellogg to receive the Peace Prize. (Briand

MICKEY MOUSE

"Steamboat Willie" is in the history books for two reasons: It was the first cartoon with synchronized sound, and it also introduced Holly-wood's most enduring cartoon char-acter. Actually, animation pioneer Walt Disney and his associate Ub Iwerks had already used Mickey Mouse in two silent cartoons, but neither had been released when "Willie" showed that drawing and sound could be successfully com-bined. Disney held back the two ear-lier films until sound could be added.

Though Mickey was clearly a mouse, his direct ancestor was a rab-bit named Oswald, a character Dis-ney had originated and used in silent cartoons. After losing the rights to Oswald in a dispute with his partners, Disney gave Mickey many of the rabbit's characteris-tics. Wiry and frenetic in his early films, Mickey became plumper and calmer, even a bit wist-ful, as his cartoon career progressed.

In the ten years after his creation, a new Mickey Mouse cartoon was released at the rate of almost one a month, while an expanding cast of supporting characters entered America's popular culture. Until 1947 Mickey's voice was supplied by Disney himself.

had won the the honor two years previously for negotiating a no-war pact between France and Germany.) Despite its lofty promises, the Kellogg-Briand treaty, lacking any definition of self-defense and with no mechanism to enforce its provisions, proved utterly ineffec-tual in preventing armed conflict.

■ TRENDS & TRIVIA

Vitamin C is isolated by Hungarian biochemist Albert Szent Györgyi.

General Electric begins three days a week of experimental TV pro-grams in Schenectady, New York; the first film drama is shot with three stationary cameras.

Steven Vincent Binet's *John Brown's Body*, an account of the Civil War in verse, is published.

Arturo Toscanini is named con-ductor of the New York Philhar-monic Orchestra.

Lawrence Welk starts his orches-tra and broadcasts from a Yank-ton, South Dakota, radio station.

A. Philip Randolph's Brotherhood of Sleeping Car Porters becomes the first black union chartered by American Federation of Labor.

Pap smear test for cancer is developed by Dr. George Papanicolaou.

Joseph Maurice Ravel's immensely popular composition *Bolero* premiers in Paris.

Playwright Bertolt Brecht and composer Kurt Weill collaborate on *The Threepenny Opera*.

Evelyn Waugh's black comic first novel, *Decline and Fall*, is published.

Luis Buñuel makes his directorial debut with the surrealist movie *An Andalusian Dog.*

The Front Page, Ben Hecht's and Charles MacArthur's classic com-edy about hard-boiled newspa-permen, opens in New York.

Oxford English Dictionary is published.

"You're the Cream in My Coffee" and "Button Up Your Overcoat" are popular songs.

• JUNE 20
Roald Amundsen dies in attempt to rescue Italian Arctic explorer Umberto Nobile, whose air-ship crashed.

• JULY 17
President Alvaro Obregon is assassi-nated in Mexico.

• JULY 30
First color motion picture is demon-strated by George Eastman at Rochester, New York.

• SEPTEMBER
Bacteriologist Alexander Fleming discovers penicillin.

• SEPTEMBER
Haile Selassie stages a coup in Ethiopia and starts a program to modern-ize the country.

• NOVEMBER 6
"The Zipper," the *New York Times'* moving electric sign, begins displaying news bulletins atop the *Times* building.

• NOVEMBER 6
Herbert Hoover uses film and radio in his campaign. He is reelected President, carrying 40 of 48 states.

Up, up, up. Twenty percent in 1927, nearly 50 percent in 1928. As stock prices zoomed higher, investors went into a buying frenzy. Many used borrowed money with shares as collateral. By September 1929 banks and corporations had 8.5 billion dollars paid out in such "margin loans."

Danger signs were ignored: a construction slump, falling car sales, layoffs in auto plants. The market peaked in early September, and the bubble burst on Thursday, October 24. After that day's big sell-off, prices steadied briefly, but went into free fall on Monday, the 28th. The following day, Black Tuesday, 16.4 million shares were sold, five times a normal day's trading. In just five days, stocks had lost one-fourth of their value. Falling share prices wiped out many margin buyers, who could not repay their loans because their stocks were now worth far less than what they had borrowed.

Though it directly affected only the approximately three million Americans who owned stock, the crash reverberated throughout the economy. Within months America was well into the worst depression in its history.

▶ THE LITERATURE OF DISILLUSION

The bloodbath of World War I shattered many of the sentimental myths of war. Most who fought found nothing glorious or romantic in their experience. Poems, novels, plays, and memoirs by former soldiers on both sides often expressed profound disillusion and bitterness at the waste of lives.

Three of the most influential of these works were published in 1929. Erich Maria Remarque, wounded by shrapnel while serving in the German Army, captured the war's horror and hopelessness in *All Quiet on the Western Front*, which was made into a successful film. Ernest Hemingway's *A Farewell to Arms* depicted defeat and chaos on the Italian front, and poet Robert Graves, a badly wounded British veteran, wrote about the British Army's ordeal in the trenches in his savage memoir, *Goodbye to All That.*

All carried the same message: The war was not a heroic sacrifice but a useless slaughter, caused by callous, stupid leaders for unworthy reasons, and nothing on Earth could justify its repetition. That view, widely shared by intellectuals, fed an isolationist mood that would remain powerful in the democracies even as new threats to peace arose with the rise of Japanese and German militarism in the 1930s.

▶ A ROOM OF ONE'S OWN

Imagine that William Shakespeare had a sister who was also a talented poet, and imagine the pain and frustration she would have faced in a literary world shaped and dominated by men.

Using Shakespeare's imaginary sister as her metaphor, novelist Virginia Woolf

(right) explored issues of gender and literature in *A Room of One's Own*. Based on two lectures Woolf had delivered at Cambridge University, the essay appeared in book form in 1929 and became a feminist classic. Many considered it a companion piece to her 1928 novel *Orlando*, whose chief character, a brilliant poet, is born a man in Elizabethan England and eventually ends up as a 20th-century woman.

Reflecting the gender-switching in *Orlando*, Woolf observed in *A Room of One's Own* that a writer seeking to embrace all of human experience needs to be "androgynous," overcoming gender by harmonizing male and female qualities.

▶ MUSEUM OF MODERN ART

For four weeks in November and December 1929, lines formed every day outside the Heckscher Building at 5th Avenue and 57th Street in New York. The attraction was the inaugural exhibition of the Museum of Modern Art. For its first exhibit the museum chose to display works by Cézanne, Gauguin, Seurat, and Van Gogh, in recognition, said museum founder Abby Aldrich Rockefeller, that "the modern movement was started by these men."

The museum's official charter declared its purposes as "establishing and maintaining in the City of New York a museum of modern art" and "encouraging and developing the study of modern arts." Barely three months after the charter application was filed, the first exhibition opened on November 8, in rented space on the Heckscher Building's 12th floor.

• **JANUARY 1-7**
U.S. Army plane remains aloft 150 hours, refueling in the air.

• **JANUARY**
The kingdom of Serbs, Croats, and Slovenes becomes Yugoslavia under King Alexander I.

• **JANUARY 12**
Eight-mile-long Cascade Tunnel, longest railroad tunnel in North America, is finished in Washington State.

• **FEBRUARY 17**
First inflight movie shown on flight from Minneapolis to Chicago.

• **APRIL 16**
American Engineering Council announces plans for uniform traffic signals across the country.

• **MAY**
Artist Georgia O'Keefe moves from New York to Santa Fe.

• **JUNE 27**
Color television is demonstrated for the first time at Bell Laboratories in New York.

The timing could have been better from a financial point of view: The Wall Street crash had happened just ten days earlier. But in terms of public interest, the moment was right. By the time it closed on December 7, the show had drawn more than 47,000 visitors.

As some critics recognized, a museum for new art had to be a new kind of museum. "Stocking masterpieces, we take it, is not the main idea," commented the New York *World*. "The object, apparently, is to acquaint Americans with what is going on."

▶ STALIN DRIVES OUT TROTSKY
Next to Lenin himself, Leon Trotsky (below) was the best known among the architects of the Russian Revolution. As chief commissar of the Red Army during the civil war, Trotsky shuttled from one battlefront to another in a special armored train, rallying the Bolshevik troops with a combination of fiery speeches and ruthless discipline.

Many of his colleagues distrusted Trotsky's ambition, however. After Lenin's death most of them sided with Trotsky's bitter rival, Joseph Stalin. Some, worried about Stalin's growing power, switched back to Trotsky's camp. But Stalin outmaneuvered his opponents. In 1927 Trotsky

was formally expelled from the Communist Party and banished to Soviet Central Asia; in 1929 he was expelled from the Soviet Union altogether. Stalin excised Trotsky from history, too. Textbooks were rewritten with no mention of Trotsky's role in the

revolution; he was airbrushed out of photos so thoroughly that later generations had no idea what he looked like. Even with absolute power in his hands, Stalin did not feel completely safe while Trotsky survived. Soviet agents pursued and finally assassinated Trotsky in Mexico, 11 years after he went into exile.

MOB CRIME

Prohibition made mob crime a big business in American cities. The enduring archetype was the chubby-faced crime boss of Chicago, Al Capone (below), who controlled an illegal liquor trade estimated to bring in 60 million dollars a year. Capone became a celebrity. In frequent interviews, he sounded like an orthodox, pro-business Coolidge Republican. Selling beer would be foolish if people didn't want it, he once said, and as for gambling houses, "I never saw anyone point a gun at a man and make him go in."

Among Capone's many wars with rival mobs, the longest was with an Irish gang led by Dion O'Banion. O'Banion was gunned down outside his flower shop in 1924. Two years later, eight carloads of his cronies sprayed machine-gun fire at Capone's headquarters. Then, on Valentine's Day 1929, Capone's men, dressed in police uniforms, burst into a Chicago garage and executed seven O'Banion gangsters who were waiting there for a liquor shipment.

The St. Valentine's Day Massacre effectively ended the liquor wars, but Capone's time was almost up. In 1931 he was convicted of tax evasion and sent to prison.

■ TRENDS & TRIVIA

Robert S. and Helen Lynd publish their classic study *Middletown*, based on Muncie, Indiana.

First Academy Award ceremony is held in Hollywood. *Wings* wins best picture; Emil Jannings and Janet Gaynor are the winning actor and actress.

Albert Einstein presents his unified field theory.

The "Buck Rogers" comic strip is introduced.

FM broadcasting is successfully tested.

Consumer debt grows as Americans buy furniture and appliances on credit.

Edwin Hubble publishes his theory that the universe is expanding.

The Lateran Pacts make Catholicism the official religion of Italy and the Vatican City an independent country.

Thomas Wolfe's autobiographical novel *Look Homeward, Angel* is published.

Joseph Stalin implements his Five-Year Plan to increase Soviet industrial productivity.

The Sound and the Fury, by William Faulkner, is published.

The Marx Brothers' first movie, *Cocoanuts*, is based on their 1925 Broadway show of the same name.

Babe Ruth hits his 500th major league home run.

The U.S. has 27 million registered cars. ▶

ARTIST'S VIEW OF TRAFFIC JAM

• **AUGUST**
A dispute over the Wailing Wall prompts a Palestinian uprising in Jerusalem.

• **AUGUST**
Graf Zeppelin flies around the world, covering 19,500 miles in 21 days, 7 hours, 26 minutes.

• **SEPTEMBER 24**
Lt. James Doolittle flies a plane on instruments alone.

• **OCTOBER 3**
Amid a wave of riots in American prisons, seven guards and five convicts are killed in an uprising at Colorado State penitentiary.

• **OCTOBER 23**
First transcontinental air service from New York to Los Angeles takes 36 hours with an overnight stop.

• **NOVEMBER 24**
France's Georges Clemenceau, known as the "Father of Victory," dies at 88.

• **NOVEMBER 29**
Richard Byrd flies over the South Pole.

ANIMAL STUDIES

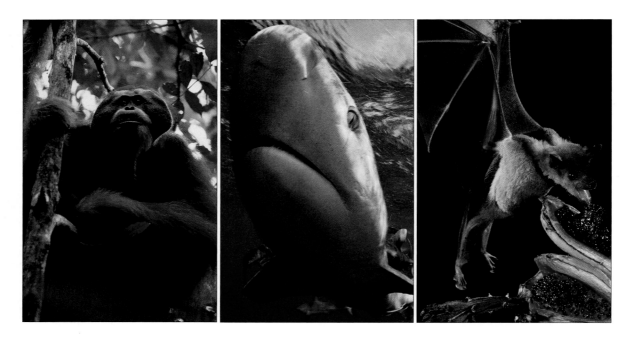

by *Mary G. Smith*

FORMER NATIONAL GEOGRAPHIC SENIOR ASSISTANT EDITOR,
RESEARCH GRANT PROJECTS

"When I was a kid," said Mark Moffett, "I read everything I could find about bugs and other critters. I loved the stories and pictures in NATIONAL GEOGRAPHIC. Some of my favorites were by Paul Zahl." Zahl, who died in 1985, was for many years the National Geographic Society's staff biologist, producing more than 50 illustrated features on subjects ranging from bioluminescent bacteria to gorillas. He was a masterful popularizer of difficult, often obscure animal subjects, and nothing pleased him more than to learn that a child somewhere had been lured into animal research because of his articles.

It's been 15 years since the day I talked with Moffett in my office at NATIONAL GEOGRAPHIC. I was his editor, and we were just getting to know each other. Now a well-known biologist,

Left: Male orangutan, Sumatra   Middle: Gray reef shark, Bikini Atoll   Right: Lesser long-nosed bat, Mexico

Moffett was then a tall, redheaded, and disarmingly young Ph.D. candidate at Harvard. He'd been carrying out ant research in Asia with a small grant from the National Geographic Society's Committee for Research and Exploration, and as he gathered new information about ants, he also did something else that had never before been accomplished: He took fascinating, first-of-their-kind photographs of the behavior of these tiny, very active creatures. Following ants with coverages of spiders, bees, and bugs so strange they almost defy description, Mark has contributed many natural history articles to NATIONAL GEOGRAPHIC. Paul Zahl would be delighted: His torch has been passed into gifted hands.

For a century plus a decade, the National Geographic Society has provided us a strong, captivating link between humans and animals. For every man or woman working with the Society to study and record in words and pictures the world's nonhuman creatures, millions more at home are enthralled by their results in Society books, on television programs, and in old and new copies of the GEOGRAPHIC.

In 1902 Alexander Graham Bell, then President of the fledgling National Geographic Society, told Gilbert Hovey Grosvenor, the young Managing Editor of the Society's monthly magazine, to go to the Caribbean to cover the cataclysmic eruption of Martinique's Mount Pelée. Bell's instructions ended with " . . . give us details of living interest beautifully illustrated by photographs." Grosvenor, following up what turned out to be a prescient description of future NATIONAL GEOGRAPHICS, published in 1906 an entire issue of animal photographs taken by former U.S. Congressman George Shiras III. Shooting in the wild in Canada and the northern United States and using a primitive flash system, Shiras made action pictures, many at night, of lynx, deer, elk, moose, and all kinds of birds. His work set the standard for realistic animal photography. No longer were creatures pictured looking as though they'd just stepped from a taxidermist shop's window. From then on wildlife photographers have labored to show animals behaving normally in their natural habitats.

Of all the subjects covered over the past century by NATIONAL GEOGRAPHIC contributors, perhaps none has drawn more reaction and comment from our readers than the description of how animals live and die. Occasionally such great sympathy has been provoked by stories and television programs on species teetering on the brink of extinction—pandas, mountain lions, Siberian tigers, gorillas, whales, grizzly bears, dozens of others—that many have been given a new lease on life. By the same token, every time a "red in tooth and claw" article appears, a few readers can be counted on to ask—with complete sincerity—why the photographer didn't drop his or her camera to chase away, or even shoot, the lions or bears or African wild dogs that were about to make a meal of some soft-eyed, furry creature.

Since its beginning, the Society's Committee for Research and Exploration has granted millions of dollars in research funds to allow qualified scientists to carry out projects ranging from a study to determine the amount of humidity in camels' breath to the mapping of Mount Everest. But many of the Society's proudest associations have been with animal researchers whose names and faces are familiar to the whole world: Jane Goodall and chimpanzees in Tanzania; Dian Fossey, murdered in 1985 in Rwanda like so many of the mountain gorillas she fought to save; twin scientists John and Frank Craighead, Jr., and their pioneering satellite studies of grizzly bears; Biruté Galdikas, studying orangutans in Indonesia's jungles for more than 20 years. And in 1978 Koko, the "sign language" gorilla took her own photograph in a mirror to give the magazine one of its most memorable covers.

Merlin D. Tuttle's effort to study and publicize the finer qualities of the world's nearly 1,000 species of bats has been aided by Society research grants. His organization, Bat Conservation International, flourishes in Austin, Texas, with a large and enthusiastic membership dedicated to saving bats from their completely undeserved unsavory reputation.

George B. Schaller of the Wildlife Conservation Society, a world-class scientist and dedicated conservationist, has worked for years in some of the most remote places on earth. Readers of NATIONAL GEOGRAPHIC will remember Schaller's remarkable studies of lions and pandas in the wild and his first-time-ever photographs of snow leopards in Nepal. Eugenie Clark, the amazing "shark lady" who swims with underwater creatures that flap, glide, and gnash their frequently terrifying teeth, has written a dozen fascinating reports for NATIONAL GEOGRAPHIC. Most of these stores have been illustrated by David Doubilet, in my experience the world's finest underwater photographer.

Much as I've been impressed for decades by the high-profile projects and articles that appear in NATIONAL GEOGRAPHIC and on television, a corner of my heart is reserved for the ones that occupy a lower rung on the publicity ladder. There was, for instance, a study that looked into the sexual behavior of guppies; and another that featured naked mole rats, creatures that look remarkably like overdone baked potatoes and live in termitelike communities.

Recently NATIONAL GEOGRAPHIC has featured gorillas, tigers, wolves, and many other elusive, reclusive, and dangerous animals in articles illustrated by the world's current crop of leading natural history photographers, including Michael "Nick" Nichols, Frans Lanting, Jim Brandenburg, and Art Wolfe. Despite the danger, the occasional tragedies and mishaps over the years have rarely involved the animals under study. In 1993, for instance, Dieter Plage, a highly regarded photographer and cameraman on assignment in Indonesia with Mary, his wife and professional partner, fell from a towering jungle tree while rigging his camera equipment. He lived only a few hours. A couple of years later, Plage's close friend and colleague, the legendary Australian cameraman Des Bartlett, crashed in an ultralight aircraft in Namibia and escaped death by a heartbeat. Crippling injuries and many surgeries have slowed him down but haven't kept him from returning to work in southern Africa.

As frequently as the GEOGRAPHIC has featured our various mammal kin, the natural history subject it has returned to again and again has been: birds! Hundreds of bird articles, books, and television shows have appeared over the years, many featuring little-known species almost impossible to find in the wild, let alone photograph. In 1951 the Society published

Stalking Birds with Color Camera, a wonderfully illustrated book by Cornell University's Arthur A. Allen. A copy given to me by my father when I was in high school was one of my inspirations to work for NATIONAL GEOGRAPHIC someday. A few years after I was hired, I worked with Allen on the last of his 18 GEOGRAPHIC articles. We became great friends, and that final story about Cornell's Sapsucker Woods bird sanctuary has always been one of my favorites.

Birds have sometimes put GEOGRAPHIC contributors into confrontations with United States customs officials. Marvin Cecil, funded to study the torrent duck, a bright-feathered denizen of swift-running Andean streams, had government permission to bring back a dozen torrent duck eggs from South America for the New York Zoological Society. Cradled in a box on his lap during the flight home, the eggs began to hatch en route. A few hours later a Miami customs officer studied Cecil's papers, then eyed the 12 quacking balls of fluff. "Mister, you can't bring those birds into the country. Your papers say eggs. Them's ducks." After a couple of frantic telephone calls, the ducklings were allowed to proceed. Des Bartlett had a similar encounter years before his near-fatal plane crash in Namibia. In this instance, Des and his wife Jen tried to enter the U.S. from Canada with a trailer load of snow geese, a bird that naturally migrates between the two countries. Stars of an in-progress article and film for NATIONAL GEOGRAPHIC, the birds had been raised from eggs by the Bartletts and were more accustomed to humans than to their own species. After a lively discussion with officials about paying duty on the birds, Des simply released them to fly across the border on their own, demonstrating that they wouldn't need to pay. The birds returned, and the Bartletts continued their journey.

In 1994 I retired from the Society after 37 years on the magazine staff. I had worked primarily with the Society's research grant scientists, encouraging and cajoling them to produce illustrated articles about their Society-supported projects. Although my husband and I now live on a tiny island in the Caribbean, I'll always be wed to science and scientists, and have continued to serve on the boards of several nonprofit organizations, many of them concerned with the great apes. One, the Bonobo Protection Fund in Atlanta, was founded by Sue Savage-Rumbaugh, a scientist who's worked for years with these pygmy chimpanzees, teaching them to communicate with humans. One morning, upon checking my e-mail messages, I found a concerned memo from Savage-Rumbaugh about a Web site on the Internet that touts an association between bonobos and humans that is not only unscientific and untrue but also exploitive and distinctly distasteful. Mulling over the bonobo problem, the years spiraled backward, and I was once again at the National Geographic Society. In 1956, the year I was hired, great ape field research was just a gleam in science's eye, and long-distance human communication then was done by letter, telephone, and telegraph. Now, at the end of this millennium, we find ourselves dealing with bonobos and humans in cyberspace.

What's going to happen to the natural sciences during the next thousand years? Will there be any animals left to study in the year 3000? Will there be anybody left to study them? No one knows, of course. But if humans and animals are here and a National Geographic Society of the future exists, you can bet it will be producing fascinating illustrated reports about the nonhuman occupants of what I fervently hope will be our still lovely planet.

1930-

-1939

The Great Depression

by James Gregory
ASSOCIATE PROFESSOR OF HISTORY, UNIVERSITY OF WASHINGTON

IT SOARS UPWARD WITH A GRACE that defies its size and strength: more than three million cubic yards of concrete, sculpted into a deeply concave curtain, 700 feet tall, holding back one of the continent's mightiest rivers. Hoover Dam on the Colorado River stands today as a marvel of engineering and a worthy monument to America's 1930s. Built between 1931 and 1935 at a cost of 48.9 million dollars, employing upward of 5,000 men and women during much of that time, the dam was part of America's answer to the Great Depression, one of thousands of public works projects that transformed the face of the nation. Dams and bridges, highways and tunnels, water and electrical systems, parks and hiking trails, libraries, schools, courthouses—the legacy of the 1930s stands all around us, an irreplaceable civil infrastructure.

The Great Depression of the 1930s usually evokes images of collapse. The critic Edmund Wilson used the metaphor "American Earthquake" to suggest the era's seismic shifts in values and institutions. It was indeed a great trial, one of the rare periods in American history when the stability and future of the nation seemed in doubt. But it was also a decade of building. Americans built new systems of government and new institutions of public life. Some tried to design new cultural and political values, preaching modernism in the arts, collectivism

Opposite: Interminably long lines of hungry, unemployed men were all too commonplace in the 1930s.
Preceding pages: Families in the American Midwest and around the globe suffered during the Great Depression.

as a social goal. But most of all, Americans built a new physical infrastructure. The 1930s—an era of vibrant ideas and ideologies—was no age of consensus. Indeed, Americans pulled apart more than together. But the works of construction went on, regardless, and were often the glue that kept the society intact.

No nation was prepared for the collapse of investment and consumption following the crash of the U.S. stock market on Black Tuesday, October 29, 1929. But apart from Germany, still suffering from World War I and its aftermath, the United States was probably the least equipped of the industrial powers to meet the emergency. Unlike most of Europe, the U.S. had no social safety net— no unemployment insurance, no old age pensions, no bank insurance to protect the investment funds the economy would need to recover. Moreover, it was blessed—or, in this instance, cursed—with the world's most complicated system of government, in which most responsibilities for economic affairs were reserved to states and local governments.

The Spanish Civil War, which pitted fascism against communism, symbolized the ideological conflicts wreaking havoc in Europe.

In retrospect, what limited powers the federal government did have were often misused in the first years of the Depression. The Federal Reserve Board tightened credit when it should have loosened. Congress passed the Smoot-Hawley tariff, imposing stiffer taxes on imports when it is now clear that freer trade would have helped. President Herbert Hoover used all of the traditional tools of his office trying to engineer a recovery, but moral suasion and an unprecedented grant of loans under the Reconstruction Finance Corporation were not enough to stop the hemorrhaging of investment capital and consumer spending that drove the economy down, down, down in the first three years of the new decade.

BY THE TIME HOOVER LEFT OFFICE in early 1933, 10,000 banks and many more businesses had failed. The gross national product had shrunk by a third and misery was everywhere. More than 12 million people were out of work, about one-quarter of the labor force. Hunger and homelessness followed, especially in the cities where huge squatter camps, dubbed "Hoovervilles," signaled the desperation of many.

Americans had coped with depressions before by relying on local resources. And once again, private charities joined local and state authorities in trying to meet this emergency. Some of these efforts were impressive, but by mid-1932, when the election season opened, it was clear that these measures were not enough. Franklin D. Roosevelt's sweeping victory over Hoover, along with the Democratic Party's new congressional majority, made it clear that most Americans wanted much more from the federal government.

Roosevelt's answer was the New Deal, an incoherent collection of spending programs and reform measures that spilled out of Congress in two surges: first in the hundred days following Roosevelt's March 1933 inauguration, then in a longer session after a new Congress was sworn in in 1935. While only modestly effective as a Depression recovery program, the New Deal proved to be brilliant politically. Although upward of 8 million people (14 percent of the workforce) were still unemployed at the end of 1939, Roosevelt had by then rebuilt the nation's political and governmental systems.

What the New Deal did best was build things. One federal agency, the Works Progress Administration (WPA), constructed or improved 650,000 miles of roads and highways and worked on 125,000 buildings and other public projects, including 2,500 new hospitals, 5,900 schools, 840 airports, 8,000 parks, and nearly 13,000 playgrounds. In the process, the WPA supplied jobs to 8.5 million Americans. Another 2 million people, mostly young men, went to work for the Civilian Conservation Corps (CCC) building roads and trails through the national forests. Other projects were handled by the Public Works Authority (PWA), which contracted with private companies to build New York's Triborough Bridge and Lincoln Tunnel, the causeway to Key West, and port facilities in Brownsville, Texas, among others. The most monumental artifacts of this public works bonanza were the dams, hundreds of them, including the multiple dam systems on the Columbia and Colorado Rivers, in the Central Valley of California, and in the Tennessee River Valley.

HISTORIANS DISAGREE WHETHER THERE SHOULD HAVE BEEN more public works and greater deficit spending, as the economic theorist John Maynard Keynes advocated, or less, on the theory that public projects may have helped dampen private investment and construction. What is clear is that all of this new public infrastructure was an enormous gift to the future. It set up the productivity, prosperity, and new educational and social capacities for the generation to come.

It is ironic that Herbert Hoover was not the one who presided over this great building era. Hoover had trained as an engineer and kept that persona in his political life. By contrast, the man who replaced him in no way suggested the technical skills of the builder. Scion of the nation's most famous political family, he was quite literally a politician by birth. The much younger cousin of Theodore Roosevelt, Franklin had modeled his every move beginning at age 18 after the man he called "Uncle Ted." His attributes turned on personality, not expertise. He managed the Presidency haphazardly, but with common sense and brilliant political skills. Like his cousin and a very few other Presidents, he was able to project a powerful and attractive personality that won the confidence of the great majority of his fellow citizens.

His other great gift was his ability to mediate conflicts and locate compromise, albeit sometimes at the expense of principle. Advisor Raymond Moley once presented FDR with two sharply contrasting policy statements on tariff issues, expecting the President to choose one. Roosevelt instead ordered Moley to "weave the two together." And he wove his way through tougher issues than the tariff. When many thought the banking crisis called for European style nationalization of the financial system, Roosevelt opted for regulation instead. When the Social Security Act to provide unemployment and old age insurance moved through Congress, Roosevelt insisted on formulas that denied eligibility to some of the nation's neediest and that funded the programs out of workers' and employers' contributions instead of general tax revenues. No wonder there was disagreement about where he was headed. While some considered him the enemy of American capitalism, others said he was its savior. He waffled, too, on civil rights. Convinced that he needed the votes of segregationist southern congressmen, he sacrificed nearly everything that had to do with the rights of African Americans, including a federal law against lynching.

MEANWHILE, ALTHOUGH IT BEGAN IN THE UNITED STATES, the Depression quickly became a worldwide crisis. The effects varied widely. Most well-established democracies held up to the challenges of the decade, some doing better than the United States when it came to solving economic problems. Socialist-led democracies in Sweden and the other Scandinavian countries, for example, conquered unemployment with stronger versions of the public works, social welfare reforms, and deficit spending formulas that Roosevelt used inconsistently. Conservative governments in Great Britain and Canada managed to reduce unemployment gradually without either large-scale spending or massive social reforms. France, always the most turbulent of Europe's democracies, had a tougher time contending with the polarizing effects of Depression era politics, lurching from government to government amid much talk of civil war.

The Depression had different trajectories and consequences in colonial Asia and Africa and in semicolonial Latin America. The collapse of agricultural prices and trade in the early 1930s had a devastating initial effect but was often followed by beneficial changes. Argentina, Brazil, Chile, and Mexico adopted strategies of economic nationalism that both relieved distress and paved the way for economic growth. India also began to build industrial capacity.

Nationalist and anticolonial efforts also moved ahead. In India, Mohandas K. Gandhi's All-Indian Congress Party pressed the cause of independence, mounting civil disobedience campaigns and winning some concessions. Nationalists were active as well in Southeast Asia and in the Middle East, where Arab nation-building aspirations had been suppressed by British and French forces. Independence movements would not be successful until after World War II, but in many parts of the world where European empires held sway, the 1930s were a time of opportunity, a time for putting together the political forces that would later bring freedom.

Freedom was very much in jeopardy in Europe's newer democracies, those established after World War I. In Germany, Austria, Spain, and some of the new republics of Eastern Europe, the Depression had catastrophic political consequences, unleashing the forces of authoritarianism and militarism that set up the confrontations of World War II.

German democracy was only ten years old when the Depression struck. No nation suffered more. By the end of 1932, Germany reported 43 percent unemployment and industrial production had been cut in half. Unlike the United States, where economic misery resulted in fairly modest political dislocations, Germany's political situation swirled out of control as parties on both extremes capitalized on the crisis. The ultimate beneficiary was Adolf Hitler's National Socialist Party. Small and ineffective in the 1920s, the Nazis built a huge following in the early 1930s on a program of race hatred, ultranationalism, and most of all anticommunism. On November 6, 1932, just two days before Americans elected Franklin Roosevelt as President, Germans chose their new Reichstag (parliament). Although Socialists and Communists together outnumbered them, the Nazis emerged as the largest single political party and on that basis Hitler negotiated his own appointment as German chancellor.

Hitler's victory and subsequent transformation of Germany into a militarized totalitarian state confirmed what until then had been a singular experiment with fascism in Benito Mussolini's Italy. Absent the Depression, fascism might have remained a minor footnote to world history. But after 1933 it became a force destined to reshape the globe. Even before Germany began conquering its neighbors, fascist movements were destabilizing much of Central and Eastern Europe. In 1935 Mussolini sent troops into Ethiopia, the only independent nation on the continent of Africa. A proud kingdom that had defeated an Italian invasion in 1896, Ethiopia this time stood no chance against tanks and planes.

Spain was the next fascist proving ground. A Popular Front government of Republicans, Socialists, and Communists had won election early in 1936, but a few months later, right-wing generals under the command of Francisco Franco led an army uprising. The government armed its supporters and fought back. Both sides then looked abroad for aid. Germany sent units of its air force to aid Franco; Italy, both air and ground forces. The Soviet Union responded to Republic appeals, supplying airplanes, weapons, and advisors. In addition more than 40,000 volunteers, mostly communists and socialists, from a dozen different countries joined the Republic's International Brigades. Spain by then had become a symbol of the violent ideological conflict that underlay much of European politics in the 1930s. In Spain, left and right,

German youths were especially susceptible to Adolf Hitler's Nazi philosophy of German racial superiority.

communist and fascist, met in a bloody civil war that lasted nearly three years and consumed at least half a million lives. When Madrid finally fell to Franco's forces in March 1939, World War II was less than six months away.

FOR MOST AMERICANS THESE EVENTS WERE SHADOWS ON A WALL, ominous patterns that were sensed but not closely observed. For America the meanings of the 1930s were to be found in the struggles to rebuild at home. And that rebuilding went way beyond jobs and income. No less than Europe with its fiery ideological clashes, the United States was in the midst of a great political change—but one that would invigorate, not destroy, democracy.

We must remember America's "forgotten man," Franklin Roosevelt had told enthusiastic crowds in 1932, pledging then to help the unemployed, the underpaid, the powerless and unrepresented. He kept much of that promise. But the greater significance of the 1930s was that this was the decade when many of those forgotten Americans found ways to represent themselves and in doing so changed how politics and government worked for all Americans.

They did it largely through labor unions. Of all the great building projects of the 1930s, union building was the one with the greatest political consequences for the nation. In a surge of organization that began in 1933 and accelerated after 1935, millions of working people joined unions, seeking not only economic benefits but also a way to be heard. Eight million were members by 1939, on their way to becoming 14 million five years later, when a third of working Americans belonged to unions. Organized labor now became a critical part of the Roosevelt Administration and of the Democratic Party.

The explosive growth of unions was made possible by a three-way synergy between restless rank-and-file workers, ambitious labor leaders, and the Roosevelt Administration, which knew it owed its political future to voters of modest means. In 1935 the Democratic Congress repaid its debt to unions and working-class supporters by passing the National Labor Relations Act, which for the first time guaranteed the right to join unions. In 1936 the brand new Committee for Industrial Organization (CIO), which had separated from the American Federation of Labor (AFL) when the AFL refused to permit industrial style unions, led a new sequence of campaigns. Capped in the winter of 1936-37 by the sensational sit-down strike in General Motors' Flint Michigan assembly plants, the CIO drive achieved major breakthroughs in the hitherto immune automobile, steel, electrical, and rubber industries. Meanwhile the call to "join a union" echoed through the nation's working class neighborhoods, animated by the growing belief that representation in the workplace was as much a part of democracy as representation in Congress.

The emergence of organized labor meant changes that reached far beyond the workplace. In the 1930s and in the decades to come, labor would push to extend the social safety nets that had begun to be strung with the Social Security Act. Never as powerful as organized business interests, the advent of labor nevertheless marked a key shift toward the pluralization of American politics. The United States would not be the same kind of "corporate commonwealth" that it had been before the Depression. No longer would business, social, and educational elites be the only voices heard in the halls of power.

Although the effect was far from revolutionary, a different America was moving into the next decade, more democratic than the one that began the 1930s. Some of America's "forgotten men" had been remembered and could now participate more fully in shaping the nation's future. Other forgotten men of color and many forgotten women would have to wait for their day, but at least now the way forward had been clearly marked. The great surge of political pluralism of the 1930s was setting up the next stage of American democratization. ■

Under the auspices of Franklin D. Roosevelt's New Deal, millions found work building dams like Fort Peck in Montana.

Higher. Deeper. Farther. NATIONAL GEOGRAPHIC in the 1930s took its readers to the frontiers of land, sea, and sky, all dramatically pushed back during the decade. The Society sponsored record-setting deep-sea dives and high-altitude balloon flights, and its representative went along on the most ambitious land-vehicle expedition to date, the 315-day, 7,370-mile French overland crossing from Beirut to Beijing. Meanwhile, the invention of Kodachrome film revolutionized color photography. For the first time, color photos could be enlarged without graininess, and Kodachrome was fast enough to capture action shots that previously could only have been shot in black-and-white.

Penetrating the Ocean's Black Depths

Nearly three-fifths of a mile below the surface of the Atlantic Ocean, the undersea scene looked black beyond the human eye's experience. "It seemed to show as blacker than black," wrote oceanographer William Beebe. "It seemed as if all future nights in the upper world must be considered only relative degrees of twilight."

On August 15, 1934, southeast of Bermuda, Beebe and his partner Otis Barton descended to 3,028 feet, a depth record that would stand for 15 years. Their dive vehicle, called a bathysphere, was no place for claustrophobics. A spherical steel chamber shaped like a large mooring buoy, it measured only four feet nine inches in diameter. With two men cramped inside, it held enough oxygen for eight hours. First used in 1930, when Beebe took it down to 1,426 feet, the two-ton sphere was winched down on steel cables from a barge.

Writing about the record dive in the December 1934 issue, Beebe recalled that the floor felt like a cake of ice and his fingers had grown numb from clutching the steel window frame. Forms of sea life no one had ever seen before swam past the window in the blacker-than-black water.

BEEBE (RIGHT) AND BARTON AFTER THEIR RECORD DIVE

One that utterly mystified Beebe was a deep-sea shrimp that appeared to explode with a bright flash of light (scientists subsequently discovered that the apparent explosion was a sudden burst of luminous fluid that the shrimp released to blind any predators). But Beebe and his companion were also aware that they had seen only an infinitesimal fragment of a mysterious, hidden world. He still felt, as Beebe wrote, "that my ignorance of the world of life beneath our feet was almost complete."

Earhart Honored

On June 21, 1932, the Society presented its Special Gold Medal (below) to aviator Amelia Earhart for her solo transatlantic flight the previous month. Earhart was the eighth person and first woman to receive the medal, first given to Arctic explorer Robert E. Peary in 1906. Following the tradition set when Theodore Roosevelt presented Peary's medal, President Herbert Hoover made the presentation to Earhart, declaring that her achievements "place her in spirit with

RESIDENTS OF LONDONDERRY CHEER EARHART AS SHE LANDS AFTER HER LONG AND DANGEROUS SOLO FLIGHT.

the great pioneering women to whom every generation of Americans has looked up, with admiration for their firmness of will, their strength of character, and their cheerful spirit of comradeship in the work of the world."

Accepting the honor, Earhart recalled that her first Atlantic crossing as a passenger in 1928 had made her a celebrity but had also gotten her compared to a "sack of potatoes" since she had done no flying herself. "That all-too-appropriate appellation, probably as much as any other single factor, inspired me to try going alone," Earhart acknowledged.

"Here Are Numbers!"

"Chief! Here are numbers!" Matthew W. Stirling was surprised that the Mexican workman recognized the row of bars and dots as numerals, but the man was right.

On that morning of January 16, 1939, Stirling and his crew were in the Mexican state of Vera Cruz near the village of Tres Zapotes, where a gigantic carved stone head lay partly buried in the jungle floor. The head had been found more than 80 years before, but not excavated until Stirling's arrival. "Despite its great size," Stirling wrote in the August 1939 GEOGRAPHIC, "the workmanship is delicate and sure, the proportions perfect."

GIANT OLMEC HEAD DISCOVERED BY MATTHEW W. STIRLING

Stirling discovered remnants of a large city dating back to the Olmec civilization, which lasted for about a thousand years until the first century B.C. Hoping to learn more about the Olmecs' civilization and history, Stirling kept an eye out for altar slabs and fallen pillars that might have inscriptions. On that January day the crew found a stone under three feet of dirt, which had protected its inscription.

Stirling compared the carving to known Maya dates and determined that it corresponded to November 4, 291 B.C. A different method put it at 31 B.C., the date favored by most subsequent researchers. Even the later date was still, as Stirling observed, the earliest ever found on any man-made object in the Western Hemisphere.

Vanishing Cultures

The GEOGRAPHIC's coverage of "primitive" peoples in the 1920s and 1930s was relatively enlightened, for its time. The magazine's writers and editors were usually sympathetic, even sentimental, about non-Western peoples whose economy, culture, way of life, and even physical survival were endangered by the spread of modern industrial civilization. Yet the underlying assumption in their reporting was that the weakening or disappearance of traditional cultures was an unavoidable byproduct of "progress"—defined, implicitly or explicitly, as the advance of Western civilization and its technology and social systems.

The long essay about Indians in the Americas that led the November 1937 issue was a case in point. Author Matthew W. Stirling, head of the Smithsonian Institution's Bureau of American Ethnology, ranged over Indian agriculture, religion, rituals, statecraft, and social structures, paying tribute to Indian achievements: "From the fur-clad Eskimo of the frozen Arctic coast, living in his ingenious snow house, to the naked savage of the steaming tropical jungles of the Amazon Basin, with his equally suitable palm-thatched home, the descendants of these first American immigrants demonstrated their adaptability in

countless ways." On the loss of Indian land to white settlers, Stirling sympathetically quoted a member of the Nez Perce tribe: "The earth is our mother, and her body should not be disturbed by the hoe or the plow. Men should subsist by the spontaneous productions of Nature. The sovereignty of the earth cannot be sold or given away."

For all his sympathy, though, Stirling saw displacement of the Indian as sad but inevitable. "His contributions to civilization and toward the betterment of mankind are encountered on every hand," Stirling concluded, "but his story as a separate people now is a subject of history and a record of the past."

Fossil Finds

Between 1922 and 1930, Roy Chapman Andrews led five expeditions to Mongolia—the oldest continuously dry region on the globe, as he noted in his June 1933 article "Explorations in the Gobi Desert," and thus potentially a rich store of information on how plant and animal life evolved on earth. But because of Mongolia's isolation and lack of development, almost no scientific research had been carried out there.

Andrews's goals were sweeping: "To discover the geologic history of Central Asia; to find whether or not it had been the nursery of many of the dominant groups of animals, including the human race; and to reconstruct its past climate, vegetation, and general physical conditions, particularly in relation to the evolution of man."

ANDREWS MAPS THE BADLANDS OF THE GOBI DESERT.

His most publicized find was 18 dinosaur eggs imbedded in a block of sandstone, estimated to be 95 million years old. Andrews and his team also found the skull of a gigantic prehistoric rhinoceros they called *Baluchitherium* (later renamed *Indricotherium*), a huge meat-eating animal resembling a giant hyena, and a mastodon with a jaw like a coal scoop.

Though spectacular, those were not the most important discoveries, in Andrews's view. That distinction belonged to seven tiny skulls from rat-sized animals, which he determined to be the oldest mammal fossils yet discovered.

Teddy Bear Threatened

In a message from Down Under, the NATIONAL GEOGRAPHIC warned its readers that the koala bear, "living prototype of the jolly toy bear that helps make Christmas morning merry in many an American nursery," was in need of protection.

F. Lewis, chief fisheries and game inspector in Victoria, Australia, wrote affectionately about the furry, two-foot-tall marsupials most often found in eucalyptus trees, sometimes clinging like a flagpole sitter to the very top branch. The koala was once one of the most common animals in the Australian bush, Lewis wrote, but they were now under threat from epidemics and hunters who prized their fur.

Trying to explain their appeal, Lewis noted that "in some of their habits they closely resemble human beings. I have seen a mother bear cuff her little one, probably for some transgression of bush law, until it cried as if broken-hearted."

Mapping the Yukon

It seems surprising that as late as 1935, any place in North America would still be unknown enough for explorers to find a previously undiscovered 40-mile-long glacier and two 12,000-foot peaks. But the Society's 1935 expedition to Canada's Yukon Territories found these and other unmapped geographic features in a 5,000-square-mile region lying in Yukon's southwestern corner.

Flying into the area to begin setting up, expedition leader Bradford Washburn recalled in his June 1936 account in the magazine, that the ski-equipped plane passed over "a breath-taking, unforgettable sea of savage snow-clad peaks, which slowly melted from ivory through fiery red and into fearsome darkness as we finally glided down Lake Bennett to a perfect landing just at dusk."

From their base camp, Washburn and his colleagues were to cross the Saint Elias range, photographing and mapping the area as they went, then head for the settlement of Yakutat on the Alaska coast. The expedition was lashed by snowstorms for much of April and well into May, when one blizzard buried all but the top 18 inches of their 8-foot-high tent. To complete the expedition, Washburn paddled an 8-foot rubber boat 55 miles from the head of Nunatak Fiord to Yakutat, sleeping beneath the upturned boat because his tent had burned.

BRADFORD WASHBURN BETWEEN FLIGHTS INTO THE YUKON

Above the Atmosphere

"My impression of the stratosphere was that of being in a profound calm," wrote Capt. Albert W. Stevens after setting a new altitude record of 72,395 feet in the balloon *Explorer II*.

Calm was hardly the word for Stevens's previous ascension

in *Explorer I*, which ripped at nearly 60,000 feet, dropped rapidly to below 3,000 feet, and then exploded, forcing Stevens and his crewmates, Capt. Orville A. Anderson and Maj. William E. Kepner, to parachute out of the plummeting gondola. Fifteen and a half months after that disaster, on the morning of November 11, 1935, Stevens and Anderson took off again from a launch site near Rapid City, South Dakota.

Briefly, it appeared the new flight was headed for trouble, too. Soon after takeoff, the balloon began leaking and sank back toward the ground. The crew dumped ballast and at 50 feet *Explorer II* stopped falling, hovered, then began to ascend

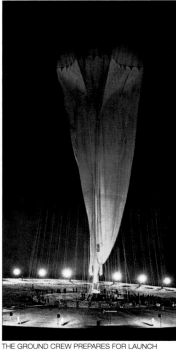

THE GROUND CREW PREPARES FOR LAUNCH

again. At 11:40 a.m. it reached its record altitude, nearly 13 and three-quarters miles. Experiments included measuring cosmic rays, collecting air samples, and photographing the distant horizon, which from that altitude clearly showed the curvature of the earth. The flight carried fungus spores aloft to see if they would still germinate normally back on earth (five of the seven species did so) and dropped collecting tubes to capture spores floating in the atmosphere.

After the flight, sponsored by the National Geographic Society and the Army Air Corps, Stevens and Anderson were given the Society's Hubbard Medal and Gold oak leaf clusters for their Distinguished Service Crosses. After Stevens's account of the flight appeared in the magazine's January 1936 issue, a report on the scientific results followed in May, along with a notice that Society members could write in and receive, at no charge, bookmarks made of cloth from *Explorer II*.

Photographing an Eclipse

Conditions for the National Geographic Society-U.S. Navy team observing the solar eclipse of June 8, 1937, were "practically ideal," the team's scientific leader, S. A. Mitchell, reported in the September issue. In fact, about the only thing lacking was an island midway along the eclipse's path, where totality lasted seven minutes four seconds—the longest since A.D. 699. But only the empty Pacific lay under that point, and no ship would be stable enough or located precisely enough for the measurements scientists hoped to make. So the expedition headed for the closest speck of land, 1,200 miles from the midpoint: a remote atoll named Canton Island, 1,850 miles southwest of Hawaii.

The observers had a variety of goals. One was to determine, through spectrographic analysis, the composition and behavior of the flaming gases above the sun's surface. Another was to check official time signals by recording precisely when the edges of sun and moon first seemed to meet, when the sun disappeared and began to reappear from the moon's shadow, and when it had emerged completely.

When the eclipse began, the sky was clear and free of haze. Capt. J. F. Hellweg, superintendent of the Naval Observatory in Washington, D.C., described it vividly: "...an infinitely small notch appeared on the edge of the sun high up on the right side.... Slowly, steadily, the black shadow descended across the face of the sun.... It did not look like the growing darkness of approaching night, partly because the shadows did not grow longer as they do with the setting sun. A hush spread over the whole place, no birds were in the air where, a short time before, there had been hundreds. All sound seemed to fade out."

● Spain at War

The civil war in Spain was perhaps the most ideologically passionate of the 20th century's major wars, but the GEOGRAPHIC's coverage reflected almost none of that fervor.

The October 1936 issue carried an article entitled "Turbulent Spain," which was essentially a travelogue with only passing references to the fighting, as if the conflict were some other kind of natural feature or cultural attraction. The war's existence, though not its causes or issues, was more prominent in a February 1937 article describing the first months of fighting as seen by an young American in Republican-controlled Madrid.

Gretchen Schwinn (below), a 19-year-old Californian who came to Spain accompanied by her mother to study dance, wrote with a sharp eye for the details of daily life in the besieged Spanish capital. But if Schwinn had any interest in the politics of the war or the ideas over which it was being fought, no inkling of it appeared in her article. She and her mother learned, she wrote, never to wear hats outside because, as she reported with no further elaboration, "only aristocrats wore hats. We had seen a woman stoned by girls because of her hat."

● Across Asia

"The first overland exploration from the Mediterranean to the Yellow Sea since the days of Marco Polo," wrote Maynard Owen Williams about the 1931-32 Citroën-Haardt Trans-Asiatic Expedition, which Williams accompanied as "special staff representative" of the National Geographic Society.

Setting off April 4, 1931, in Beirut, the expedition ended at the French Legation in Beijing ten months and eight days later. The expedition's French organizers, Georges-Marie Haardt and automobile designer Andre Citroën, initially planned a one-way trip from Beirut in a convoy of half-tracked vehicles Citroën had designed especially for the rugged terrain. But even those vehicles couldn't cross the massive barrier of the Karakoram Range at the western end of the Himalaya. So while one group of cars set out from Beirut, another was shipped to the Chinese port of Tientsin and driven across China to wait for the Beirut party, which would complete the mountain crossing on camel and horseback. The two groups successfully made their rendezvous in western Xinjiang, on the ancient Silk Road trade route.

ONLY A FEW LOOSE STONES BETWEEN LIFE AND DESTRUCTION

The Chinese part of the journey presented man-made as well as natural hazards. Local warlords exacted bribes for safe passage, and on one occasion, Williams reported with surprising casualness in his November 1932 account that the convoy came under fire (a "slight misunderstanding," the local authorities explained).

That article, the last of four Williams wrote about the journey, records his interview with a Mongol princess who told him plaintively, "Perhaps your way of life is right for you, but it threatens ours. You are in a hurry, and hence barbaric," the princess told Williams. "You are entranced by mechanical toys, which you haven't mastered.... You are men of auto, railway, radio. You find this a backward land, without roads, speed, a free press, a balanced budget, sanitation, or familiar forms of justice...

"We Mongols," she concluded, "are emancipated. 'A good horse and a wide plain under God's heaven,' that's our desire. And we realize it."

135

136

European rule in southern Asia seemed solidly entrenched. But ideas of independence simmered. In British-ruled India, independence leader Mohandas K. Gandhi (below) led a 200-mile march to the sea to protest the widely hated salt tax. At the coast, Gandhi scooped up a handful of sea salt, violating the official monopoly. He and other Indian National Congress leaders were jailed, but protests continued all across India. More than 60,000 arrests failed to stem the campaign.

Gandhi instructed his followers to remain nonviolent. "Not one of the marchers even raised an arm to fend off the blows," marveled an eyewitness after watching police viciously club down unarmed demonstrators.

Few yet grasped the power of Gandhi's tactics, but less than a year later, he was freed from prison to negotiate with the British viceroy, Lord Irwin. Years of struggle and imprisonment still lay ahead, but Gandhi, with no weapons and no power beyond moral conviction, had established himself as a force the Empire could not suppress or ignore.

COFFEE OR TEA

Shortly after Boeing Transport and National Air Transport merged to form United Airlines, the new company created a new profession for a new industry. Ellen Church, a registered nurse and student pilot, became United's first airline stewardess.

In turn, Church was asked to recruit 7 more nurses meeting these requirements: single, "pleasant personalities," 25 years old, no taller than 5 feet 4 inches, and weighing 115 pounds or less. Besides serving cold meals and beverages, the stewardesses were expected to soothe passengers' anxieties about flying.

WORLD CUP INAUGURATED

Professional soccer had been around for decades, but international competition took its present form when, in 1930, Jules Rimet, the French president of FIFA, the international soccer federation, presented a cup for the world championship.

The first World Cup tournament was played that year in Montevideo, Uruguay; the Uruguayans won by beating Argentina, four goals to two. Italy won the next two championships in 1934 and 1938; the competition was suspended during World War II and not revived until 1950.

PROTECTIONISM BACKFIRES

The start of a new decade found the world sinking deeper into economic disaster. By the end of 1930, nearly five million Americans were unemployed, with thousands more losing their jobs every week. More than 26,000 businesses went broke and closed during the year. Two and a half million were out of work in England, five million in Germany.

The last thing the world needed, most economists thought, was a tighter chokehold on international trade, which was already declining sharply. But American manufacturers, panicked by the shrinking markets for their products, demanded higher tariffs on imported goods.

Congress obliged. The vehicle was a tariff bill sponsored by Representative Willis Hawley of Oregon and Senator Reed Smoot of Utah (below). Originally drawn to support agricultural prices, the bill was amended to raise import duties on a huge number of farm and manufactured goods to the highest levels in American history. A thousand members of the American Economics Association urged a veto, but President Hoover signed it into law on June 17, 1930.

The loss of the U.S. market devastated many European producers, while other countries retaliated against the Smoot-Hawley Act by raising their own tariffs. The value of international trade fell sharply, quickening the downward spiral into worldwide Depression.

A HOME FOR THINKERS

It was to have no students. No classes. No laboratories. The only product of the Institute for Advanced Study was to be ideas—great big ideas about the fundamental nature of the universe.

The institute's founders were Louis Bamberger and his sister, Caroline Bamberger Fuld, who had recently sold their family's department store, the fourth largest retail store in the country. At the urging of educator and educational critic Abraham Flexner, the Bambergers contributed funds for a center located in Princeton, New Jersey, and devoted to pure theory—an "intellectual hotel," longtime director J. Robert Oppenheimer called it, where eminent thinkers could reflect on the most basic questions of science.

Incorporated on May 20, 1930, the

- **FEBRUARY 18**
Astronomer Clyde Tombaugh of Lowell Observatory discovers most distant planet, Pluto.

- **MARCH 7**
Large-scale protest demonstrations by unemployed take place in New York and other cities.

- **MARCH 28**
Turkish nationalists change the Greek name of Constantinople to Istanbul.

- **APRIL 21**
355 prisoners die in a fire in the badly overcrowded Ohio State Penitentiary.

- **MAY 26**
Legislation is signed creating the U.S. National Institutes of Health.

- **JUNE 14**
U.S. Federal Bureau of Narcotics is established.

- **JUNE 30**
France withdraws its last troops from Germany's Rhineland, five years earlier than the date set by the Treaty of Versailles.

institute opened its doors three years later. Its first resident scholar was the best known scientist of the day whose name had already become a synonym for genius: the German-born physicist Albert Einstein.

Einstein, the first of 14 Nobel Prize winners who would eventually come to the institute, was also among the first of many renowned scientists to find refuge in the United States as the Nazi shadow began to darken Europe—a group that contributed decisively to Allied scientific superiority in World War II.

▶ AMERICAN GOTHIC

It would become probably the most recognizable and certainly the most satirized artwork ever painted by an American.

Grant Wood's sister, Nan, and his dentist, B. H. McKeeby, holding a pitchfork, posed for the artist as a dour Iowa farm father and daughter standing in front of a farmhouse. Wood's painting, "American

Gothic" (left), represented the movement that became known as regionalism—emphasizing images, often highly idealized, of rural or small-town American life.

Regionalism was populist art, defying modernism and big-city trendiness and celebrating down-to-earth, unsophisticated, grassroots culture. A left-wing counterpart was the social realism school, favored in the 1930s by artists with socialist leanings, which also rejected abstraction and modernism in favor of heroic workers and farmhands battling oppression in the form of evil, cigar-puffing bosses.

SAM SPADE

Sam Spade didn't just solve the crime. He changed mystery fiction forever. Earlier detectives, à la Sherlock Holmes or Hercule Poirot, solved contrived puzzles in upper-crust drawing rooms where neither the dead nor the living ever seemed to have any real blood. Spade, the cynical private eye in Dashiell Hammett's 1930 novel *The Maltese Falcon*, took crime fiction from the country estate into the gritty urban underworld, where cops and crooks seemed equally lawless, and converted its aristocratic accents into the tough, sardonic, hard-edged speech of big-city streets.

Hammett had spent eight years as a detective for the Pinkerton Agency before becoming a writer and drew on those experiences when he began turning out crime fiction in the '20s. But it was *The Maltese Falcon* and Spade that created the prototype of the hard-boiled detective—following his own rules and seeing the world without illusion, a hero who has no sentiment "and survives," one critic noted, "because he has none."

■ TRENDS & TRIVIA

East Texas oil field, the largest producer in U.S. history, is discovered.

William Faulkner's novel, *As I Lay Dying,* is published.

Sigmund Freud's *Civilization and Its Discontents* is published.

Two alluring European actresses fascinate U.S. audiences: Marlene Dietrich in *The Blue Angel,* and Greta Garbo in *Anna Christie.*

British engineer Frank Whittle patents the jet engine.

Youth Hostels Association is founded in Britain.

More than half of all high-school-age Americans are receiving secondary education, twice the percentage of a decade earlier.

Song "Georgia On My Mind" is popular.

Sinclair Lewis is the first American awarded a Nobel Prize for literature.

"Blondie" comic strip makes its first appearance.

Noel Coward's play *Private Lives* is staged in London.

The Lone Ranger debuts on WXYZ radio in Detroit, Michigan.

First regularly scheduled educational broadcast is made over CBS's *American School of the Air.*

King Kullen Market, the first true supermarket, opens in Jamaica, Long Island, New York.

Flashbulb is introduced.

Minnesota Mining and Manufacturing Company (3M) introduces a soon-to-be indispensable convenience—a transparent cellulose tape called Scotch tape.

• JULY
Surveys begin on route for Pan American Highway through Central America, connecting North and South America.

• JULY 3
U.S. Veterans Administration is established.

• JULY 4
George Washington, the first of four monumental presidential sculptures at Mount Rushmore, South Dakota, is dedicated.

• JULY 7
Sir Arthur Conan Doyle, creator of Sherlock Holmes, dies.

• OCTOBER 26
Getulio Vargas becomes president of Brazil after previous government is overthrown.

• NOVEMBER 2
Haile Selassie is crowned emperor of Ethiopia.

• DECEMBER 11
Bank of the United States fails, erasing the savings of 400,000 depositors. It is one of 1,300 bank failures in 1930.

138

The First Amendment, with its guarantee of a free press, had been in the U.S. Constitution for 140 years. But not until June 1, 1931, did the American press win definitive protection against censorship. That day, in a 5-to-4 ruling, the U.S. Supreme Court threw out a Minnesota law permitting a newspaper to be banned as a public nuisance if a judge found it "obscene, lewd and lascivious" or "malicious, scandalous and defamatory." Minnesota lawyers defended the law as a means of "purifying the press," but Chief Justice Charles Evans Hughes, in the majority opinion, called it "the essence of censorship."

The unlikely First Amendment champion in the case was Jay M. Near, an anti-Semite, scandalmonger, and suspected blackmailer whose newspaper, the *Saturday Press,* had been shut down under the Minnesota law in 1927.

Col. Robert R. McCormick, publisher of the *Chicago Tribune*, financed Near's appeal and later had a passage from the Court's ruling engraved in the lobby of the *Tribune* building, including these words: "The fact that the liberty of the press may be abused by miscreant purveyors of scandal does not make any the less necessary the immunity of the press from previous restraint...."

▶ THE SCOTTSBORO TRIALS

The rape trials of nine black youths in the northeastern Alabama town of Scottsboro turned a harsh national spotlight on Jim Crow justice in the South. Hastily, and on outrageously suspect evidence, an Alabama jury sentenced eight of them to death (the jurors deadlocked on executing the ninth defendant, who was only 13, and a mistrial was declared).

MARCHERS DEMAND FREEDOM FOR SCOTTSBORO BOYS.

The convictions were a textbook example of the Deep South racial codes of the time, under which a black man accused of rape was automatically considered guilty and a white woman accusing a black man was never to be doubted, however unconvincing her testimony might be and without regard to other evidence.

Lawyers affiliated with the Communist Party stepped in to appeal the convictions, while Communist and other groups organized nationwide protests. After years of appeals, reversals, and retrials, charges against four defendants were dropped. The other five were given prison terms. Four were later pardoned; one escaped and was never caught.

▶ THE STORY OF BABAR

To keep her small children amused, Cécile de Brunhoff made up stories about a young elephant in Africa. Her husband, Jean, an author and illustrator, turned those tales into one of the most distinctive and beloved children's books of all time, *The Story of Babar.* Six more Babar books followed.

De Brunhoff, who would die from tuberculosis at only 37, wrote sympathetically but unblinkingly about dying: Babar's mother is killed by hunters; the old King of the Elephants dies from eating a bad mushroom.

His straightforward approach was a message to his young readers, and perhaps also to his own children, that sorrow hurts but can be survived. De Brunhoff's son, Laurent, continued the series after his father's death.

▶ SCRAPING THE SKY

American engineering was still transforming the landscape, even as Depression shadows darkened. In New York City, the Empire State Building (right), then the tallest skyscraper in the world at 1,245 feet above street level, opened May 1, 1931, with President Hoover and former New York Governor Al Smith attending the ceremony.

Five months later, an army of workmen completed building the 8-lane, 4,800-foot-long George Washington Bridge, spanning the Hudson River between New Jersey and upper Manhattan.

▶ JAPAN CONQUERS MANCHURIA

Go back through history to find the very first step on the road to World War II, and you come to the Japanese seizure of Manchuria in 1931.

The conquest was not instigated by the Japanese government, but by ultra-nationalist Imperial Army officers acting on their own. The plotters sent their own troops to dynamite a section of the Japanese-controlled South Manchurian Railway

---

near Mukden (now Shenyang). Then, blaming the explosion on the Chinese, Japanese forces quickly captured the entire region even while the authorities in Tokyo vainly ordered them to halt.

JAPANESE TROOPS MARCH INTO MANCHURIA

Renamed Manchukuo and declared an independent state, Manchuria was in reality a colony of the Japanese army. As a figurehead ruler, the Japanese installed the pliant Puyi, the "last emperor" of China who had been deposed, while still a child, in the overthrow of the Qing (Manchu) Dynasty in 1911.

The easy Japanese success in Manchuria undermined civilian authority and emboldened the militarists, nourishing the dreams of conquest that ultimately led to Pearl Harbor and the Pacific war.

▶ THE GULAG TAKES SHAPE

The dark underside of Stalin's Five Year Plan was a vast, brutal system of slave labor. Mass arrests and deportations were not just a means of political repression; they supplied essential manpower for Stalin's ambitious effort to build up Soviet industry and infrastructure.

Though labor camps existed in the 1920s, the true horrors of the Gulag took shape at the start of the 1930s when Stalin ordered the *kulaks*—rich or slightly well-off peasants—destroyed "as a class." Millions were deported to labor camps in desolate regions of the far north, Siberia, and the Soviet far east.

By 1931 the camp population was more than two million. The Baltic-White Sea Canal, begun that same year, employed 250,000 slave laborers who dug the 168-mile waterway in two years with hand shovels, hauling out stones and frozen dirt in buckets. Doing brutally hard work in a region as far north as Greenland, the workers were fed starvation rations. Sixty thousand died of cold, hunger, exhaustion, or by execution for attempting to escape.

The same murderous conditions prevailed throughout the camps, which were run by the GPU, an earlier incarnation of the KGB. Ostensibly a security force, the GPU was in fact a "vast industrial organization," responsible for a major share of all Soviet manufacturing and public works.

JOY OF COOKING

Irma Rombauer and her daughter Marion were amateurs with "no known qualifications for publishing a cookbook," observed their biographer Anne Mendelson. But that didn't stop the 54-year-old St. Louis widow from paying $3,000 to a local printer to publish the first 3,000 copies of a recipe book she and Marion had put together.

Amateurs they may have been, but circumstances made their tone and timing perfect. Millions of middle-class women who had employed cooks before the Depression were now cooking for themselves. And perhaps because she wasn't a professional, Rombauer's recipes reflected the way people cook in real life, with shortcuts and wild inconsistencies in ingredients and technique.

The Joy of Cooking appeared just in time for Thanksgiving 1931, and immediately proved popular. "Every day has brought ten to twenty orders," Rombauer excitedly wrote to a relative, "and I hope that will keep up for a while." It did. Successive editions sold more than 14 million copies worldwide during the next 65 years.

■ TRENDS & TRIVIA

James Cagney in *The Public Enemy* and Edward G. Robinson in *Little Caesar* establish the gangster movie genre.

Bell Laboratories develops a stereophonic sound system.

Mountaineers Franz and Toni Schmid become the first Alpine climbers to scale the north face of the Matterhorn.

Albert Schweitzer writes *My Life and Thoughts.*

Pearl Buck's epic novel about China, *The Good Earth,* is published.

2,294 banks fail in the United States.

Heavy water is discovered.

Salvador Dali paints "The Persistence of Memory," one of the best known Surrealist paintings.

A 125-foot-tall statue of Christ is dedicated atop Corcovado (Hunchback) Mountain in Rio de Janeiro, Brazil.

Vitamin A is isolated by Swiss chemist Paul Karrer.

Paul Muni's film *I am a Fugitive from a Chain Gang* sparks a movement to reform prison conditions.

The radio program *Fibber McGee and Molly* goes on the air.

American chemist Wallace Hume Carothers finds a polymeric fiber that, when stretched, is stronger than silk. It is eventually called nylon.

"Dick Tracy" comic strip debuts.

Boris Karloff plays the monster in the film *Frankenstein,* and Bela Lugosi appears in *Dracula.*

Bisquick is introduced by General Mills.

139

- **MARCH 31**
Famed football coach Knute Rockne dies in air crash.

- **APRIL 14**
Spain's King Alfonso XIII goes into exile; Spanish republic proclaimed.

- **MAY 11**
Austria's largest bank, Credit Anstalt, fails, causing a financial panic in Austria and Germany.

- **MAY 31**
Pope Pius XI denounces fascism in Italy.

- **SEPTEMBER 21**
Britain suspends gold standard; pound drops sharply.

- **OCTOBER 18**
Inventor Thomas Alva Edison dies at 84 in New Jersey.

- **OCTOBER 24**
Famed mobster Al Capone is jailed for income tax evasion.

- **DECEMBER 7**
Unemployed march in protest in Washington.

1932 THE BONUS ARMY

As the Depression deepened, a 1932 hit song, "Brother, Can You Spare a Dime," echoed the misery of millions of unemployed. That spring, thousands of World War I veterans descended on Washington, seeking cash bonuses for their wartime service. Arriving in freight trains or dilapidated cars or on foot, the men camped at various sites around the capital city.

Thousands of veterans remained after the government ordered the camps cleared. When they resisted police with bricks and stones, President Hoover called in the Army. He ordered restraint, but Gen. Douglas MacArthur ignored the orders. Swinging sabers and hurling tear gas, mounted troops burned the shacks and tents the vets had put up (above). To many, the smoke rising over Washington symbolized the cloud of dread that loomed over the nation. Movie audiences hissed when newsreels showed the Army's assault. Hoover's popularity, already low, sagged even lower. In November, he lost the election to Franklin D. Roosevelt by a resounding seven million votes.

▶ MASSACRES IN EL SALVADOR

"Thirty or forty families own nearly everything...." an American army officer wrote about El Salvador in the early 1930s. "They live in almost regal style. The rest of the population has practically nothing."

As the worldwide Depression and collapsing commodity prices devastated Central American economies, wealthy Salvadoran landowners took more and more land to grow coffee for export, instead of food. Misery in the countryside turned to desperation. A small communist movement called on impoverished peasants to rebel, then tried at the last minute to call off the insurrection, but many *campesinos* never got the word. With few arms except clubs and machetes, the rebels were quickly crushed.

Brutal reprisals followed. In a slaughter that became known as La Matanza—the Killing—as many as 30,000 Salvadorans were executed after the failed uprising. Among them was the Communist leader, Augustín Farabundo Martí, whose name would be adopted 50 years later by rebels in the far longer and bloodier civil war that racked El Salvador in the 1980s.

▶ STARVATION IN RUSSIA

Even the great writer Boris Pasternak could not find words for the famine that ravaged the Soviet Union—especially southern Russia and Ukraine—in 1932-33. "There was such inhuman, unimaginable misery," Pasternak recalled, "such a terrible disaster, that it began to seem almost abstract, it would not fit within the bounds of consciousness."

The famine was man-made, not natural: the result of Joseph Stalin's drive to collectivize Soviet farming. State authorities ruthlessly confiscated hoarded grain, leaving whole villages to starve. Up to 14 million men, women, and children died, but their fate was kept secret: Any mention of the famine could mean death or years in a labor camp, and little information reached the outside world.

▶ *BRAVE NEW WORLD*

In the year 632 A.F. (After Ford) humans are gestated in bottles, pegged into a scientific caste system, and conditioned to perfect, unquestioning conformity. That's the chilling future as imagined in *Brave New World.*

Aldous Huxley's ironic title (taken from Shakespeare's *The Tempest*) passed into the language, and his novel, published in 1932, became one of the most influential books of the era. It explores a dilemma at the heart of 20th-century life: that the technology that solves so many human problems is, at the same time, profoundly dehumanizing.

▶ ELECTIONS IN GERMANY

When German voters went to the polls to elect a new parliament on July 31, nearly 14 million of them—37 percent—voted for the Nazi Party.

Both major parties on the left, the Communists and Social Democrats, had much to fear from a Nazi victory, but failed to unite against their common danger. The Communists, instead, declared the Social Democrats their main enemy, on the dubious logic that moderate socialism would prolong capitalism's final crisis and delay the triumph of the working class.

Hopelessly splintered, the new Reichstag was dissolved almost immediately, and another election set for November. The Nazis lost votes, but they still held more seats than any other party.

• JANUARY 12
Hattie Caraway of Arkansas is first woman elected to U.S. Senate.

• JANUARY 28
The U.S.'s first unemployment insurance law is enacted in Wisconsin.

• JANUARY 28
Japanese heavily bomb Shanghai, China's largest city, killing or wounding thousands of civilians.

• MARCH 7
Four die in violent clashes between unemployed demonstrators and company police at Ford plant in Dearborn, Michigan.

• APRIL 17
Emperor Hailie Selassie abolishes slavery in Ethiopia.

• MAY 7
French President Paul Doumer is felled by a Russian assassin.

• JUNE 22
Reconstruction Finance Corporation is established to help finance industry and agriculture in the U.S.

▶ EARHART FLIES THE ATLANTIC

Shortly after 7 p.m. on the fifth anniversary of Charles A. Lindbergh's flight to Paris, Amelia Earhart took off from Harbour Grace, Newfoundland, in an attempt to become the first woman to pilot a plane across the Atlantic. After crossing as a passenger four years before, Earhart had become a national celebrity; now she hoped to earn fame more legitimately by flying herself.

For much of the 14-hour, 54-minute flight, Earhart battled electrical storms and severe icing. Her fuel gauge stopped functioning, and exhaust flames shot out through a crack in the engine manifold. The next morning, after flying 2,026 miles, she landed her single-engine Lockheed Vega in a meadow near Londonderry, Northern Ireland.

Congratulations poured in, among them a message from President Hoover telling Earhart she had demonstrated "the capacity of women to match the skill of men in carrying through the most difficult feats of high adventure."

▶ "ME TARZAN, YOU JANE"

Invented by novelist Edgar Rice Burroughs, Tarzan, the foundling child of English aristocrats brought up by apes in the African jungle, once again came to the screen in the 1932 movie *Tarzan, the Ape Man* (below).

To play the improbable hero, the moviemakers recruited Olympic swimmer

Johnny Weissmuller. The love interest was actress Maureen O'Sullivan as Jane Parker, an ivory hunter's daughter. Their falling-in-love scene produced the deathless line: "Me Tarzan, you Jane."

Weissmuller "swung, swam, and grunted his way," as one writer put it, through 11 more Tarzan movies in the next 15 years— among them, *Tarzan and His Mate, Tarzan Finds a Son, Tarzan's New York Adventure,* and *Tarzan and the Amazons.*

KIDNAPPED!

When Charles Lindbergh's 20-month-old son (below) was kidnapped from his parents' New Jersey estate on the evening of March 1, 1932, the tragedy befalling a national hero transfixed America.

Letters poured in to Lindbergh and his wife, Anne Morrow Lindbergh, at the rate of a thousand a day, with suggestions and expressions of sympathy. From his jail cell, mobster Al Capone offered to help out if he were released on bail while appealing his conviction for tax evasion. In churches and even at sports events, people paused to pray for the "Little Eagle," as one journalist called the child.

The Lindberghs paid a $50,000 ransom, but some nine weeks after the kidnapping, a truck driver found the baby's body in the woods several miles from the Lindberghs' home, where it had evidently lain since the night of the kidnapping.

Nearly three years later, after a trial based entirely on circumstantial evidence, a German-born carpenter named Bruno Hauptmann was convicted of the murder. The strongest evidence was the recovery of some of the ransom money from Hauptmann's garage. He was electrocuted on April 3, 1936, though doubts about his guilt have lingered ever since.

■ TRENDS & TRIVIA

Plastic is synthesized at Imperial Chemical Industries in Britain.

Laura Ingalls Wilder's *Little House in the Big Woods* is published.

U.S. Route 66 opens from Chicago to Los Angeles.

London Philharmonic Orchestra is founded by Sir Thomas Beecham.

James Chadwick discovers the neutron.

There are 13.7 million unemployed people in the U.S.

Construction of San Francisco's Golden Gate Bridge begins.

Vitamin D is discovered.

Mutiny on the Bounty, by Charles Nordhoff and James Norman Hall, is published.

President Hoover's name becomes synonymous with economic distress, as in "Hooverville" (shacks housing the homeless and unemployed); "Hoover wagon" (vehicle pulled by horses or mules); "Hoover blankets" (newspapers covering people sleeping in parks or doorways).

Zippo lighter is introduced.

Fritos corn chips, Skippy peanut butter, and Three Musketeers candy bars go on the market.

Glacier International Peace Park is established in Montana.

First exposure meter for cameras goes on the market.

The Jack Benny Show debuts on NBC radio.

One Man's Family debuts on radio.

Skater Sonja Henie thrills spectators at the Olympics held in Lake Placid, New York.

• JULY 5
Antonio de Oliveira Salazar becomes dictator of Portugal; will rule until 1968.

• JULY 7
Dow Jones Average hits bottom: 41.22, a 90 percent loss of value from the 381.17 peak in September 1929.

• JULY 31
Bolivia and Paraguay go to war in dispute over the Chaco region.

• SEPTEMBER 20
Mohandas K.Gandhi begins a "fast unto death" to protest India's caste system and discrimination against "untouchables."

• OCTOBER 16
Albert Einstein places the age of the Earth at ten billion years.

• NOVEMBER 8
Franklin D. Roosevelt sweeps the presidential election.

• DECEMBER 27
Radio City Music Hall opens in New York's Rockefeller Center.

142

I f Franklin D. Roosevelt's Presidency were to be remembered in a single phrase, it would be the words from his first inaugural speech March 4, 1933: "The only thing we have to fear is fear itself."

Roosevelt (below, with running mate John Garner) knew that what Americans needed, more than any particular law or policy, was a sense of energy and action. Five days after his inauguration, FDR called Congress into session; its first bill, an emergency banking reform law, was passed the same day.

That was only the start of the whirlwind that became known as the "Hundred Days." In quick succession, Congress created the Civilian Conservation Corps and passed the Federal Emergency Relief Act, the National Industrial Recovery Act, and dozens of other laws. Meanwhile Roosevelt broadcast his first "fireside chat," reassuring the country that change was underway. The New Deal was a revolution. But shaped by Roosevelt's instinct for practical solutions, it was a pragmatic revolution that preserved America's constitutional system and institutions.

MIGRANT AGRICULTURAL WORKER'S FAMILY IN CALIFORNIA

▶ DUST BOWL

After getting caught in a South Dakota dust storm, Eleanor Roosevelt's friend Lorena Hickok described it this way: "It was as though we were picked up in a vast, impenetrable black cloud which was hurling us right off the earth."

Through the mid-1930s, drought dried out the Midwest topsoil and the wind blew it away. Millions of acres of farmland were ruined, and with them, the farmers who lived there. Sharecroppers were put off the land by owners when they couldn't pay their rent, owners by banks when they couldn't pay their mortgages.

Their crops and lives destroyed, families across the Great Plains left their farms in broken-down jalopies and took to the roads, desperately seeking work. Many headed west to California, where the Okies, as they were most often called, traveled from one desolate migrant camp to another, struggling to survive by picking fruit and vegetables for starvation wages.

▶ TAMMANY FALLS

Tammany Hall, the quintessential political machine, had been a power in New York City for nearly a hundred years. But Tammany was discredited when the high-living Mayor James J. Walker (known as "the late Mayor Walker" because he rarely appeared at work before noon) resigned while under investiga-

tion for various forms of official misconduct.

In 1933 the city elected an anti-Tammany candidate, Fiorello LaGuardia, who became one of the most colorful, effective, and popular mayors in New York's history. Tammany managed to survive during LaGuardia's 12 years in City Hall, but it would never regain its former powerful role.

▶ SCREAMS AND SLAPSTICK

Hollywood did its best to take people's minds off Depression woes. Memorable movie moments in 1933 included Fay Wray's scene with a gigantic gorilla in *King Kong* (Miss Wray, one commentator noted, "proved that she could outscream anyone"), and the Marx Brothers' inspired antics in *Duck Soup*.

Variety observed about the new Marx brothers film: "Practically everybody wants a good laugh right now, and this should make practically everybody laugh."

▶ SOVIET TIES RESUMED

For 16 years the United States withheld diplomatic recognition from the Soviet Union, chiefly on political grounds. President Roosevelt, with his customary pragmatism, saw advantages in reversing that policy. The U.S.S.R. was a market for U.S. exports and a potential ally against Japan, then seen as America's most likely enemy.

Negotiating personally with Soviet Foreign Minister Maxim Litvinov, FDR explained that Soviet religious policy was a problem. "In America nobody can understand this idea that people shouldn't have access to religion—any kind they want," the President told Litvinov. Moscow promised that American citizens in

---

- **JANUARY 17**
Over President Hoover's veto, Congress votes to give independence to the Philippines.

- **FEBRUARY 6**
20th Amendment is ratified, changing date of presidential inaugurations.

- **FEBRUARY 15**
Assassination attempt on President-elect Roosevelt fails, but Chicago's Mayor Cermak is fatally wounded.

- **FEBRUARY 25**
USS *Ranger*, first ship designed as an aircraft carrier, is launched.

- **FEBRUARY**
Frances Perkins is named Secretary of Labor, becoming the first woman cabinet member in the U.S.

- **MARCH 6-9**
Banks are closed on FDR's orders.

- **APRIL 3**
British aviators are first to fly over Mount Everest.

the Soviet Union could practice their religion freely (but not Soviet citizens, whose churches throughout Russia were being burned or desecrated). On November 17, Washington and Moscow resumed relations.

► CATHOLIC WORKER MOVEMENT
A new kind of radical movement began on May Day 1933, when a 35-year-old Catholic convert named Dorothy Day appeared in New York's Union Square selling a new newspaper, the *Catholic Worker.* Day believed in socialist ideas rooted in Christian gospel, rather than Marx. Soon she began offering meals and shelter to destitute men and women in her neighborhood—the first "hospitality house."

► HITLER TAKES POWER
His Nazi Party had never won a majority of German votes or seats in Germany's Reichstag. But its opponents were too divided, shortsighted, and morally decrepit to keep Adolf Hitler from power. After weeks of haggling with a motley assortment of right-wing politicians, Hitler was driven to the office of the doddering Paul von Hindenburg, Germany's President, and sworn in as Chancellor on January 30, 1933, in Berlin.

That night, Nazi storm troopers marched in celebration. Flames from their torches lit up the night, foreshadowing the quick

HITLER AND STORM TROOPERS

REPEAL

"It seemed almost a geologic epoch while it was going on," grumped H. L. Mencken, but in fact, Prohibition lasted 12 years, 10 months, and 19 days, during which crime, corruption, and cynicism led a large majority of Americans to conclude that the "noble experiment" had been a disastrous mistake.

MERRYMAKERS CELEBRATE REPEAL OF PROHIBITION.

A repeal amendment, adopted by Congress on February 20, 1933, was easily ratified by the states, where referendum voters backed the amendment by nearly three to one.

Some celebrations were quieter than expected, in part because legal liquor was still in short supply. That gave bootleggers a bit more time to do business. "Liquor has been sold illegally for 13 years," New Jersey's Governor Harry Moore said wryly, "and it will not hurt if this is done a few days more."

destruction of German democracy under Hitler's rule. Less than four months later, pro-Nazi students lit a bonfire near Berlin University and threw into the blaze some 20,000 books written by Jews, or espousing ideas opposed by Germany's new rulers. Among them were works by Freud, Einstein, Thomas Mann, and Erich Maria Remarque.

Meanwhile, under an act grandiloquently titled "Law for Removing the Distress of People and Reich," a cowed Reichstag gave Hitler the authority to legislate by decree. By summer, opposition parties and independent trade unions were banned, and Nazi power was supreme.

■ TRENDS & TRIVIA

First practical contact lens is developed by German ophthalmologist Josef Dallos.

Gertrude Stein's book, *The Autobiography of Alice B. Toklas,* is published.

World's Fair "The Century of Progress Exposition" opens in Chicago; fan-dancer Sally Rand becomes a national celebrity.

Modern Man in Search of a Soul by Swiss psychiatrist Carl G. Jung is published.

Popular songs include "Easter Parade," "Smoke Gets In Your Eyes," and "It's Only a Paper Moon."

Ritz crackers are introduced.

Esquire magazine begins publication.

American League wins major league baseball's first All-Star game, 4-2.

First drive-in movie theater opens in Camden, New Jersey.

Man's Fate, Andre Malraux's novel about the human condition, is published.

Erle Stanley Gardner's first two books featuring lawyer/detective Perry Mason are published.

French visionary Bernadette of Lourdes is canonized.

U.S. journalist, politician, and playwright Claire Booth Luce becomes managing editor of *Vanity Fair* and writes her first novel, *Stuffed Shirts.*

U.S. blues singer Billie Holliday makes her first recording, with Benny Goodman.

The soft drink 7-Up comes on the market.

• APRIL 4
U.S. Navy dirigible *Akron* crashes in a storm off the New Jersey coast with 77 crewmen aboard.

• APRIL 19
U.S. goes off the gold standard.

• MAY 18
Congress approves law creating the Tennessee Valley Authority.

• JULY 22
Aviator Wiley Post sets round-the-world record of 7 days, 18 hours, 49½ minutes.

• OCTOBER
Farmers strike in Midwest against falling farm prices.

• NOVEMBER 30
Eleanor Roosevelt opens White House conference on women's problems.

• DECEMBER
American Newspaper Guild, union for reporters, editors and clerical employees, is founded by columnist Heywood Broun.

144

The century's two most powerful and murderous Communist leaders—one already a world figure, the other still a hunted revolutionary—strengthened their power in 1934.

Joseph Stalin, after vanquishing his main rival Leon Trotsky, ruled the Soviet Communist Party and state. But Stalin would not feel secure until he had destroyed the rest of his possible rivals. His pretext came when a gunman assassinated the Leningrad Communist Party chief, Sergei Kirov. Thousands were accused in the Kirov "plot" and executed—the first big wave of the terror that gripped Stalin's Soviet Union for the rest of the decade.

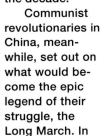

Communist revolutionaries in China, meanwhile, set out on what would become the epic legend of their struggle, the Long March. In October about 80,000 Communists slipped through blockading Nationalist troops and began the trek north that would end a year later. Among the marchers was a 40-year-old visionary named Mao Zedong (above), who became the movement's supreme leader during the trek—a role he never relinquished.

▶ HAITI OCCUPATION ENDS

When U.S. Marines left Haiti in 1934, it ended an era of U.S. interventions, some of them long-lasting, in Central America and the Caribbean. U.S. troops stayed 19 years in Haiti, 21 years in Nicaragua, and 8 years in the Dominican Republic.

The legacy of those interventions was sadly inconsistent with American ideals. Military men Anastasio Somoza in Nicaragua and Rafael Trujillo in the Dominican Republic assumed power after American forces left; both established long, bloody dictatorships.

U.S. occupation brought no lasting benefits to Haiti, either. The hemisphere's poorest nation remained impoverished under a succession of oppressive rulers before a still worse dictator, the sinister "Papa Doc" Duvalier, came to power in the 1950s.

▶ SEC ESTABLISHED

Reflecting the New Deal principle that some regulation of free enterprise is needed to protect the public, Congress established tighter rules for the stock market.

The Securities Exchange Act of 1934 required brokers to register with a new Securities and Exchange Commission (SEC) and banned many deceptive or manipulative sales practices. Stock exchanges, under SEC supervision, were made responsible for enforcing standards and investigating abuses.

▶ THE DIONNE QUINTUPLETS

Less than 48 hours after 5 identical girls were born on a backwoods Ontario farm on the morning of May 28, 1934, setting off an international media frenzy, a representative of the Chicago World's Fair offered Elzire and Oliva Dionne a share of the receipts if they put the quintuplets on exhibit at the fair. The impoverished Dionnes, who had six other children, agreed, but the quints' physician, Allan Dafoe, objected. In the ensuing furor, the girls were made wards of the Canadian government, ostensibly to protect them from being exploited. But Dafoe and government officials proceeded to make them a tourist goldmine.

Three million tourists came to gawk through one-way windows at the quints' nursery, built with government funds. Souvenir shops sprouted along nearby

DR. DAFOE WITH THE QUINTS ON THEIR FIRST BIRTHDAY

roads, and Dafoe grew rich on product endorsements and book royalties. Seven years later, Elzire and Oliva regained custody, but the Dionnes' family life remained deeply troubled. The quints would later describe their childhood as "painfully unhappy."

▶ PURIFYING THE MOVIES

Bent on making the movies wholesome, Hollywood appointed a Production Code administrator to enforce moral purity on film. That meant no more racy dialogue à la Mae West ("Goodness, what beautiful diamonds!" "Goodness has nothing to do with it, dearie"). From 1934 on, the code decreed, "the sanctity of the institution of marriage and the home shall be upheld."

- **JANUARY 7**
The U.S.S.R.'s first ambassador to the U.S. arrives in New York.

- **FEBRUARY 21**
Nicaraguan revolutionary Augusto Cesar Sandino offers to negotiate but is seized by National Guard troops and executed.

- **JUNE 15**
FDR signs a treaty annulling the Platt Amendment of 1903, thus assuring Cuba of independence.

- **JUNE 15**
The National Guard Act makes the National Guard a part of the U.S. Army in time of war or national emergency.

- **JUNE 19**
The U.S. Indian Reorganization Act seeks to return lands to tribal ownership.

- **JUNE 30**
On the "Night of the Long Knives," Adolf Hitler brutally turns on some of his Nazi colleagues, executing hundreds.

- **JULY 4**
French scientist Marie Curie, winner of two Nobel Prizes, dies.

To be given the Production Code seal, a movie had to avoid anything suggestive, or that might undermine conventional morality. Double beds were out. So were "excessive and lustful kissing," profanity, and any portrayal of a clergyman as comic or villainous.

Over the years, only a handful of producers were willing to take the risk of releasing a movie without the seal. The office maintained its puritanical grip for more than three decades, until it was swept away in the cultural and moral upheaval of the 1960s.

▶ PROTEST MOVEMENTS

Though President Roosevelt and the New Deal were widely popular, the discontents of the Depression bred new political movements in the tradition of American populism, with its mix of radical ideas, demagoguery, and, often, appeals to prejudice.

One protest movement was launched by a California physician, Francis E. Townsend, who called for a $200-a-month pension for every American over 60—an utterly implausible amount in 1934—on condition that the pensioner spend all the money the same month, thus generating economic activity that would quickly end the Depression. Within months, Townsend Clubs across the country claimed two million members.

A figure with an uglier edge was the National Union for Social Justice's Father Charles Coughlin. The Detroit radio priest reached an estimated ten million listeners with his anti-Roosevelt broadcasts before turning stridently anti-Semitic by decade's end.

Potentially the most formidable movement was Huey Long's Share Our Wealth program, which promised a guaranteed income high enough to give every family "a home, an automobile, a radio, and the ordinary conveniences." Known as the Kingfish, Long had been virtual dictator of Louisiana, first as governor and then as U.S. senator, and gave every sign that he planned to run against Roosevelt for the

PUBLIC ENEMY

"John Dillinger, ace bad man of the world, got his last night—two slugs through his heart and one through his head."

In the hard-boiled style of 1930s crime reporting, that's how the International News Service led its scoop on the death of the first criminal to be tagged Public Enemy No. 1. Tipped off by a mysterious "woman in red," FBI agents waited for the 31-year-old bank robber and escaped prisoner outside the Biograph movie theater in Chicago, and shot him dead when Dillinger went for a pistol in his pants pocket.

Shootouts between lawmen and outlaws made headlines regularly during 1934 and 1935. In only eight months, G-men or police gunned down a Who's Who of criminals. Beside Dillinger, Bonnie Parker and Clyde Barrow (above) died in a hail of police bullets on a dirt road in Louisiana after a crime spree that included 12 murders. Baby Face Nelson, who succeeded Dillinger as Public Enemy No. 1, was fatally wounded in a gun battle in Illinois. Pretty Boy Floyd was killed in Ohio, and Ma Barker and her son Fred were shot down in Florida.

Presidency—plans cut short when he was assassinated in 1935.

The unlikely trinity of Long, Townsend, and Coughlin was a political threat to Roosevelt but also a help, because their popularity increased pressure for reforms while their programs made FDR's appear moderate and sensible.

■ TRENDS & TRIVIA

Soviet government declares "Socialist realism" the proper form of art.

Henry Miller's *Tropic of Cancer* is published.

Roger Tory Peterson's *A Field Guide to the Birds* is published.

James Hilton writes *Good Bye, Mr. Chips*.

Youth hostel movement is introduced in the United States by Isobel and Maurice Smith in Northfield, Massachusetts.

MUZAK service is launched.

Harlem's Apollo Theater opens.

Laurens Hammond makes the first pipeless organ.

Comic strips "Flash Gordon" and "L'il Abner" debut.

Children's favorite *Mary Poppins*, by P. L. Travers, is published.

George Balanchine establishes the School of American Ballet.

Dell Publishing Co. introduces the modern comic book with the sale of "Famous Funnies." It sells for ten cents and is an immediate hit.

Dancers Fred Astaire and Ginger Rogers star in *The Gay Divorcee*.

Shirley Temple is a new child star. ▶

First laundromat, the Washeteria, with four washing machines, is opened in Fort Worth, Texas.

Ella Fitzgerald, age 16, is a hit on Amateur Night at the Harlem Opera House.

Cole Porter's musical *Anything Goes* comes to Broadway.

145

• JULY 13
SS Chief Heinrich Himmler takes control of Germany's concentration camps.

• JULY 16
General strike in San Francisco is led by International Longshoremen's Association.

• JULY 25
Revolution breaks out in Austria. Chancellor Engelbert Dollfuss is assassinated by Nazis and succeeded by Kurt Schuschnigg.

• AUGUST 19
Following the death of Germany's President Hindenburg, a plebiscite gives Adolf Hitler the presidency.

• SEPTEMBER 8
Passenger ship *Morro Castle* burns and sinks off Asbury Park, New Jersey; 130 die.

• SEPTEMBER 20
Bruno Hauptmann is arrested for kidnapping the Lindberghs' baby; some of ransom money is found in his garage.

• SEPTEMBER 26
Ocean liner *Queen Mary* is launched in Clydesbank, Scotland.

146

If any single program became the lasting emblem of Franklin Roosevelt's New Deal, it was Social Security.

"We can never insure 100 percent of the population against 100 percent of the hazards and vicissitudes of life," FDR declared when he signed the Social Security Act on August 14, 1935. "But we have tried to frame a law which will give some measure of protection to the average citizen and to his family against the loss of a job and against poverty-ridden old age."

The core of the law was the payroll-tax-financed pension system that exists today. In addition, the act provided modest payments (up to $30 a month) for retired workers who were already past 65 when the law took effect. The act also established an unemployment insurance system and aid for needy mothers with children.

Six weeks earlier, Roosevelt had signed another milestone law: the National Labor Relations Act, which for the first time guaranteed workers' rights to join a union and bargain collectively with employers.

Known as the Wagner Act for its sponsor, Senator Robert Wagner of New York, the new law opened the way for unions to organize millions of workers in the steel, automobile, and other basic industries.

ETHIOPIAN TROOPS SWEAR ALLEGIANCE TO THE EMPEROR.

▶ ITALY INVADES ETHIOPIA

Ambitious for imperial conquests, Benito Mussolini for years cast a covetous eye on Ethiopia. On October 3, 1935, striking from Italian Somaliland and Eritrea, Mussolini's forces invaded the kingdom. The seven-month Italian campaign, marked by use of poison gas and devastating air raids on defenseless villages, overcame a brave but hopeless Ethiopian resistance. It also exposed the toothlessness of the League of Nations, which approved sanctions against Italy but failed to enforce them. Ethiopia's Emperor Haile Selassie left the country on May 2, 1936—just days later Italy annexed Ethiopia. From exile, Selassie warned the League that it "would be committing suicide" if it acquiesced in unprovoked aggression against a member country; in retrospect, his anguished words appeared prophetic.

▶ CIO FOUNDED

For 50 years American trade unionism was embodied by the American Federation of Labor (AFL), an organization of craft unions representing elite, skilled workers. With few exceptions, the AFL's barons, men like federation president William F. Green and carpenters' union chief Big Bill Hutcheson, had no interest in the mass of unskilled factory hands working in oppressive and unsafe conditions and for miserable wages in industrial plants.

At the AFL's 1935 convention in Atlantic City, New Jersey, John L. Lewis, the combative head of the United Mine Workers, argued for establishing unions that would represent all the workers in an industry. After a debate enlivened when Hutcheson called Lewis a bastard and Lewis slugged the burly carpenters' leader in the face, the AFL rejected Lewis's plan, fearing industrial unions would undermine the traditional craft organizations.

Lewis and his supporters walked out and established a new group, the Committee for Industrial Organization (later changed to the Congress of Industrial Organizations). With workers' rights to union representation now protected by the new Wagner Act, the CIO sent organizers out to steel, auto, rubber, and other plants across the country, beginning the drive that in just a few years would revolutionize American labor-management relations.

▶ THE POPULAR FRONT

Overnight, Franklin D. Roosevelt was no longer a "social fascist" (the communist label for liberal reformers) but a benevolent ally against real fascism. Elsewhere, Communist parties abruptly stopped preaching revolution in democratic countries and called instead for "popular fronts" with liberal leaders. The change, decreed at the Communist International's 1935 World Congress, mirrored Stalin's concern about the growing threat of Germany. Party members obediently parroted the new line.

In a time when even Harvard's business school dean felt that "capitalism is on trial," the new, less belligerent Communist movement won support from many artists and intellectuals. Eventually, most grew disillusioned with a doctrine that taught, as one repentant fellow-traveler put it, "the most dangerous and ultimately disastrous idea that can lodge within the human mind, namely, that the end justifies the means."

- **JANUARY 29**
Senate refuses to approve U.S. membership in the World Court.

◀ **FEBRUARY 13**
Bruno Hauptmann is found guilty in the Lindbergh baby kidnapping case.

- **MARCH**
Defying restrictions imposed by the Treaty of Versailles, Hitler decrees universal military service in Germany.

- **MAY 11**
Roosevelt issues executive order creating Rural Electrification Administration.

- **MAY 22**
New York State authorities use blood tests as evidence in court.

- **JUNE 10**
Alcoholics Anonymous is founded, in New York City.

▶ THE FEDERAL ARTS PROJECT

"Hell, they've got to eat just like other people," said Harry Hopkins, head of the Works Progress Administration, about the thousands of artists, photographers, writers, dramatists, and musicians employed by the federal government to help them survive in the depths of the Depression.

Some in the federal arts programs were hired to document the era such as Dorothea Lange and other photographers who cap-

WPA WORKERS WIDEN A STREET

tured on film the desperation of unemployed men in breadlines, ruined Dust Bowl landscapes, and gaunt-faced families in migrant labor camps. Other artists were employed painting murals or sculpting friezes in government buildings. Still others were simply paid to practice their art. The government even ran a theater—the Federal Theater Project, which became controversial because of the left-wing slant of some of its productions and was eventually abolished after a congressional investigation.

▶ THE DC-3 REVOLUTIONIZES AIR TRAVEL
On December 17, 1935, the Douglas Aircraft Company tested a new, all-metal, twin-engine passenger airplane—and ushered in a new era of air travel. With 21 seats, the DC-3 was "the first airplane in the world that could make money just by hauling passen-

B MOVIES

When movie theaters began offering double features to bolster sagging attendance, Hollywood studios began churning out low-budget films, many of them Westerns, to fill the second-feature spot. The B movies used assembly-line scripts, unknown or has-been actors, and the cheapest possible locations and production techniques.

Not surprisingly, most were utterly forgettable. The Bs did, however, produce the quintessential American movie hero. John Wayne appeared in nearly two dozen B Westerns for the Monogram and Republic studios in the mid-1930s (for a while, new Wayne films came out nearly once a month)—or perhaps it would be more accurate to say he appeared in the same Western two dozen times, since plots, sets, and scripts hardly changed from one film to the next.

In place of the implausibly wholesome cowboy stars of an earlier era, the Duke created a new archetype. "I was trying to play a man who gets dirty," he recalled, "who sweats sometimes, who enjoys kissing a gal he likes, who gets angry, who fights clean whenever possible but will fight dirty if he has to."

gers," said C. R. Smith, president of American Airlines, which put the new airliner into service in the summer of 1936.

The DC-3 would become the most popular and durable transport plane ever built, so well designed and easy to fly that its basic specifications never changed in the ten years it was in production. In all, more than 10,000 were manufactured for military and commercial use. Thousands flew for 50 years or more; at least 1,000 were thought to be still flying in the early 1990s.

■ TRENDS & TRIVIA

Twenty-two million motor vehicles are registered in the United States; even at the depths of the Depression, one of every two families owns a car, though many are old and dilapidated.

Auto manufacturers display 200 models at New York's annual automobile show.

Radar warning system is devised.

Biochemist Wendell Meredith Stanley isolates and crystallizes a virus for the first time.

Allis-Chalmers develops the first one-man self-propelled combine harvester.

First Howard Johnson's opens in Boston.

Bingo becomes popular.

Alfred Hitchcock's *The 39 Steps* is released.

Beer in cans, packed by Krueger Brewing Co., of Newark, New Jersey, goes on sale for the first time in Richmond, Virginia.

"Passing beam" is devised for automobile headlights.

Board game Monopoly goes on sale.

Jeanette MacDonald and Nelson Eddy team up in *Naughty Marietta,* the first of their eight films together.

First night baseball game is played; Phillies beat Cincinnati Reds, 2-1.

Hit Parade debuts on radio.

Chain letter craze sweeps the country. Postal inspectors declare the scheme illegal.

George Gershwin's folk opera *Porgy and Bess* opens.

147

• JULY
Parking meter invented by Carl C. Magee, first installed in Oklahoma City, Oklahoma.

• JULY 5
U.S. National Labor Relations Act is signed.

• AUGUST 8
Ernie Pyle, later famous for his reporting on World War II, becomes a roving columnist for the Scripps-Howard news service.

• AUGUST 16
Popular humorist Will Rogers dies in Alaska plane crash, with pilot Wiley Post.

• SEPTEMBER 8
Huey Long is assassinated by Dr. Carl Weiss in Louisiana State Capitol.

• SEPTEMBER 15
Anti-Semitic Nuremberg laws are imposed in Germany.

• SEPTEMBER 25
Protestant churches in Nazi Germany are placed under state control.

148

Nowhere in the United States did the New Deal have a more dramatic impact than in the Tennessee River Basin, an isolated region that was home to two million people. Creation of the Tennessee Valley Authority (TVA) brought a multipronged effort to transform the area. Dams were built for flood control and power generation. Building them provided employment in the job-starved hills. TVA also carried out reforestation programs and even constructed regional libraries and operated bookmobiles.

Over the ferocious opposition of private power companies, TVA sold electricity through municipal utilities or rural electricity cooperatives. TVA's experience provided the model for a nationwide program carried out by the Rural Electrification Agency (REA). Established on a temporary basis by executive order, the REA was made permanent by Congress in 1936, the same year TVA's first big dam, the Norris Dam (above) on the Clinch River in southeast Tennessee, was completed.

Fewer than 10 percent of American farms had electricity when REA was created. Fifteen years later, 90 percent of farms had power.

▶ CIVIL WAR IN SPAIN

In 1936, five years after abolishing the monarchy and founding the Spanish Republic, Spain was deeply polarized. A left-wing coalition called the Popular

MILITIA MEMBERS ON A HOMEMADE TANK IN BARCELONA

Front controlled the government but faced bitter opposition from rightists, monarchists, and a conservative Roman Catholic hierarchy. In July a military rebellion broke out. Gen. Francisco Franco assumed command of the uprising.

In the three-year civil war that followed, mass executions of prisoners and other atrocities were common on both sides. Nazi Germany and Fascist Italy openly backed Franco. Using Spain as a training ground for the new tactics and technology of war in the air, German and Italian planes supported Franco's troops with hundreds of bombing missions. (In one raid, bombers destroyed the town of Guernica, a name engraved on the world's memory by Pablo Picasso in one of his and the century's most famous paintings.) The Soviet Union supported the republic and thousands of volunteers from around the world, most, but not all, communists, flocked to Spain to fight alongside the Loyalist forces.

▶ JAPAN'S MILITARY TAKES OVER

In the black predawn of February 26, 1936, a group of extremist Japanese Army officers seized government buildings in Tokyo, assassinated several top officials, and narrowly missed killing Prime Minister Keisuke Okada.

The uprising quickly collapsed, but shaken civilian ministers soon yielded effective power to the country's military leaders—less fanatical than the rebels, but still committed to a massive buildup of the country's armed strength and to expanding Japan's sphere of influence over much of continental East and Southeast Asia and the western Pacific.

Those goals were formally adopted by the cabinet as national policy in August. On November 25 Japan announced the signing of an "Anti-Comintern Pact" with Nazi Germany, linking Japanese ambitions in Asia with Adolf Hitler's in Europe.

▶ HITLER'S OLYMPICS

For Adolf Hitler, the 1936 Olympic Games in Berlin were a chance to dazzle the world with the achievements of the Nazi regime. The government spent far more lavishly than any previous Olympic host on facilities and entertainment for foreign visitors. But the elaborate preparations could not prevent an African-American athlete from becoming the hero of the games, a direct and unanswerable challenge to Nazi racial ideology. Jesse Owens (right) won gold medals in the 100-meter and 200-meter dashes, running broad jump,

- **JANUARY 18**
Writer Rudyard Kipling dies in London at 70.

- **FEBRUARY 26**
The Volkswagen or "people's car" makes its debut in Germany.

- **MARCH**
Devastating floods hit Johnstown, Pennsylvania.

- **MARCH 1**
Boulder Dam, completed on the Colorado River, creates Lake Mead, the largest reservoir in the world.

- **MARCH 7**
German troops reoccupy Rhineland; Britain and France protest but do not act.

- **APRIL 3**
Bruno Hauptmann is executed for kidnapping and murder of Lindbergh baby.

- **APRIL**
Sixteen-year-old Prince Farouk becomes king of Egypt upon the death of his father, King Fuad.

and the 400-meter relay. His black team-mates won eight other golds.

An enduring myth was that Hitler refused to shake Owens's hand. In fact, it was high-jumper Cornelius Johnson who was snubbed. The Olympic Committee asked Hitler to congratulate all athletes or none. Rather than risk a handshake with members of an inferior race, Hitler chose to wait until the games were over, then held a celebration for German winners.

▶ POLLING COMES OF AGE
Besides returning President Roosevelt for a second term, the 1936 presidential election put scientific public opinion polling on America's political map.

The best known polls at the time were those conducted by the magazine *Literary Digest*. In 1936 the *Digest* sent out ten million survey ballots to addresses drawn from lists of telephone subscribers and automobile owners, asking Americans how they would vote. Two million ballots were returned, and after they were tabulated, the magazine announced the result: Republican Alf Landon would be elected; President Roosevelt would get only slightly more than 40 percent of the votes. When the actual ballots were counted, the result was exactly the reverse. Voters had reelected Roosevelt by the biggest landslide in U.S. history. Landon carried just two states, Maine and Vermont.

While *Literary Digest* was wiping the egg from its face, several other pollsters were shown to have called the election correctly on the basis of interviews with much smaller numbers of voters. Demonstrating that it wasn't a sample's size that made it reliable, but its composition, George Gallup's new American Institute of Public Opinion, a *Fortune* survey, and the Crossley Poll had chosen their respondents to make up a statistical cross-section of the whole

ABDICATION

"You must believe me when I tell you that I have found it impossible to carry the heavy burden of responsibility and to discharge my duties as King as I would wish to do without the help and support of the woman I love."

With those words, King Edward VIII (below) told the British public and the world that he was giving up the throne to marry Wallis Warfield Simpson, a twice-divorced American.

Simpson's second divorce was not yet final when Edward succeeded to the throne following the death of his father, George V, on January 20, 1936. But when the decree was issued, the new King informed Prime Minister Stanley Baldwin that he planned to marry her. The cabinet refused to approve, on the ground that remarriage after divorce was prohibited by the Church of England and therefore Edward's marriage to Simpson could not be reconciled with his role as head of the church.

Rather than cause a constitutional crisis, Edward signed the act of abdication and renounced the throne.

voting population—many of whom, in the depths of the Depression, did not have telephones or cars.

Scientific sampling, which had been developed over the previous decade or so by advertisers and market researchers, quickly became a major factor in American political life, not just for candidates assessing their election chances but for Presidents and other officials who wanted to gauge support (or the lack of it) for their policy choices.

■ TRENDS & TRIVIA

Margaret Mitchell's *Gone With the Wind* is published. It will become an all-time best-seller.

Betty Crocker becomes advertising symbol for General Foods products.

Waring blender is invented.

Tampax is introduced.

Consumer Reports magazine debuts.

Poll shows that two-thirds of Americans favor birth control.

Humphrey Bogart has his first major screen role in *The Petrified Forest*.

Oil is discovered in Saudi Arabia.

Oakland Bay Bridge is completed.

Ford Foundation is established.

Life magazine begins publication.

Fluorescent lighting is introduced.

Dale Carnegie's book *How to Win Friends and Influence People* gives tips for success.

Carl Sandburg's epic poem *The People* is published.

Charlie Chaplin plays the Little Tramp for the last time in his film *Modern Times.* The last great silent film, it satirized the Machine Age. ▶

A sit-down strike at General Motors forces recognition of workers' right to organize.

Eleanor Roosevelt begins writing her newspaper column, "My Day."

149

- **MAY 1**
FBI chief J. Edgar Hoover personally arrests Alvin Karpis, suspect in kidnapping and murder cases.

- **JUNE 2**
Anastasio Somoza, commander of Nicaragua's National Guard, takes power and begins 42-year family dynasty.

- **JUNE**
Popular Front government takes power in France; Socialist Leon Blum is premier.

- **JUNE 20**
U.S. Congress passes Merchant Marine Act, subsidizing U.S. merchant fleet.

- **AUGUST 31**
Liner *Queen Mary* arrives in New York after crossing the Atlantic in 3 days, 23 hours, and 57 minutes.

- **OCTOBER 30**
Three-month nationwide dock strike begins in United States.

- **DECEMBER 12**
President Chiang Kai-shek is captured by Communists, but released after promising to cooperate against Japanese aggression.

1937

JAPAN INVADES CHINA

On the night of July 7, 1937, in an area often used for training by foreign troops based in China under agreements dating back to the Boxer Rebellion, a Japanese Army battalion discovered one soldier was missing. When the Japanese demanded to search the nearby town of Wanping, the Chinese refused.

The Japanese made the ensuing skirmish the pretext for extending their presence in the entire area. On July 11 they demanded that the Chinese Army withdraw from all strategic positions in northern China. President Chiang Kai-shek, who had vacillated in previous confrontations, now stood firm. In response, the Japanese launched full-scale war.

JAPANESE BOMB CHINESE CITY.

After capturing Beijing and Shanghai, Japanese troops occupied the capital, Nanjing, on December 13 and went on a brutal rampage that became known as the Rape of Nanjing. Chiang's army, and millions of ordinary Chinese plodded westward in one of history's epic retreats, the beginning of an eight-year ordeal that would test even China's legendary stoicism.

▶ NAZIS TARGET GERMAN CHURCHES
The world remembers Hitler's Germany for its oppression of Jews, but the Nazis also clamped rigid restrictions on Christian churches. Nazi doctrines and institutions were to be supreme in the new Germany, not traditional Christianity or its churches. The Gestapo jailed thousands of Catholic and Protestant clergy and lay leaders, extinguishing any religious authority that might remain independent of Nazi control.

A bizarre concoction of Nazi racial theories, pagan Germanic myths, and adulation of the Führer became Germany's true faith. "National Socialism is the doing of God's will," Hitler's Minister for Church Affairs, lawyer Hans Kerrl, declared in 1937. "Christianity is not dependent upon the Apostle's Creed," Kerrl went on, adding that "true Christianity" was represented by the party and by the Führer, whom Kerrl called "the herald of a new revelation."

Pastor Martin Niemoller, the most prominent Protestant churchman to resist Nazi pressure, was arrested in July and sent to a concentration camp. A year later, Protestant clergymen were ordered to swear a personal oath of loyalty to Hitler. Nearly all complied.

▶ STALIN'S TERROR DEEPENS
In the Soviet Union, Joseph Stalin's reign of terror tightened its deadly grip. Arrests and executions engulfed virtually the entire senior leadership of the Communist Party. Civil war hero Mikhail Tukhachevsky and six other Red Army generals were executed after a secret trial in June; during the next year and a half, almost the whole Central Committee membership and most regional and provincial party officials were shot or disappeared into the labor camps of the Gulag. Millions of lower-ranking party members and ordinary citizens shared the same fate.

The purges swallowed up virtually all those who had created the Communist state. Taking their place were leaders who were products of Stalin's era—the same people, observed historian Martin Malia, "who, after their Leader departed this world, would manage the system until it crumbled in the late 1980s."

▶ TRAGEDIES IN THE SKY
The young aviation industry suffered two tragedies in 1937. On May 6 the 812-foot-long German dirigible *Hindenburg* (below) caught fire and exploded as it approached a mooring tower in Lakehurst, New Jersey, after a 60-hour flight across the Atlantic. Thirty-six people died. The disaster ended regular passenger service by lighter-than-air airships.

On July 2, 39-year-old pilot Amelia Earhart, attempting an around-the-world flight, took off with her navigator Fred Noonan (opposite, left, with Earhart) from Lae, New Guinea, heading for Howland Island, a remote speck in the Pacific Ocean nearly 2,000 miles southwest of Hawaii. Nineteen hours and 12 minutes later, U.S. Navy ships near Howland heard Earhart's broadcast that her fuel was running low.

• **MARCH 15**
Nation's first blood bank is established at Cook County Hospital in Chicago.

• **MARCH 18**
Worst school fire in U.S. history kills about 500 in New London, Texas.

• **APRIL 26**
German bombers supporting General Franco's forces in Spain destroy the town of Guernica.

• **MAY 12**
Britain's George VI crowned, ceremony is broadcast worldwide.

• **MAY 23**
John D. Rockefeller dies at 98.

• **MAY 24**
U.S. Supreme Court upholds Social Security Act.

• **MAY 27**
Golden Gate Bridge opens in San Francisco.

• **JUNE**
American Medical Association approves birth control.

A last faint radio transmission was picked up an hour later. Then they vanished. No trace of Earhart, Noonan, or her twin-engine Lockheed Electra was ever found.

▶ "COURT-PACKING" PLAN FAILS

Frustrated by Supreme Court rulings that threw out major New Deal laws, President Roosevelt on February 5, 1937, asked Congress for a new law that would let the President appoint an additional federal judge for every judge over the age of 70 who had not retired. The bill would have immediately let FDR name six new justices to the Supreme Court. But the plan turned into one of the worst defeats of Roosevelt's Presidency.

"Don't let that wild man in the White House do this dreadful thing," a North Carolina constituent wrote to his senator; columnist Walter Lippmann declared Roosevelt "drunk with power." On July 22, by a resounding 70-20 vote, the Senate sent the "court-packing" bill back to committee, effectively burying it for good.

▶ LABOR STRIFE

Organized labor secured a solid toehold in America's basic industries in 1937, but not without bloodshed. After weeks of sit-down strikes at General Motors plants, GM agreed to negotiate a contract with the United Auto Workers, while U.S. Steel settled with the CIO steelworkers union.

Other employers tried to fight the unions. The bloodiest incident came on Memorial Day at Republic Steel's plant in South Chicago. At a rally of strikers and their families, a clash between steelworkers and police at the plant gate erupted into deadly attacks with clubs, tear gas, and gunfire. Police fired into the unarmed crowd, killing 10 and wounding 90. Though police claimed to have fired in self-defense,

JOE LOUIS

On June 22, 1937, a soft-spoken young boxer named Joe Louis knocked out James J. Braddock to become heavyweight champion of the world. With African Americans still excluded from most professional sports in a rigidly segregated country, Louis became the first black superstar, and an idolized, larger-than-life folk hero to blacks.

Whenever he fought, black neighborhoods across the country fell quiet as people stayed glued to their radios, then erupted in joy when he won. Author Richard Wright recalled the shouts of celebration: "Good God Almighty! Didn't Joe do it?"

Louis would remain champion for a decade. One of his most notable victories was his 1938 two-minute, nine-second knockout of Germany's Max Schmeling, a symbol of Nazi "master race" beliefs.

Writer Russell Baker remembered how blacks poured out of their homes that night and quietly but exultantly marched down West Lombard Street in Baltimore: "It was the first civil rights demonstration I ever saw," Baker wrote later, "and it was completely spontaneous, ignited by the finality with which Joe Louis had destroyed the theory of white superiority."

film taken by a Paramount newsreel cameraman showed victims shot in the back by police officers who were clearly not in danger. Paramount kept the film out of movie theaters for several months, fearing that showing it might cause disorders. The Republic Steel strikers were unsuccessful, but labor made big gains elsewhere; by year's end, nearly eight million American workers were carrying union cards.

■ TRENDS & TRIVIA

Dr. Seuss's first children's book, *And to Think That I Saw It on Mulberry Street* is published after 27 rejections by publishers. Seuss's books would go on to sell more than 200 million copies.

Ballerina Margot Fonteyn makes her debut in *Giselle* at age 18.

Cape Hatteras, North Carolina, is designated the nation's first national seashore.

Radar system developed by the U.S. Army Signal Corps is demonstrated to the War Department.

First jet engines are built and tested on the ground.

Look magazine debuts.

American astronomer Grote Reber builds the first radio telescope.

Spam is introduced.

The Charlie McCarthy Show debuts on CBS.

First issue of *Woman's Day* appears.

Disney releases *Snow White and the Seven Dwarfs*. ▶

First supermarket cart is introduced at Standard Food Store in Oklahoma City.

Insulin is used to control diabetes.

Pablo Picasso paints his famous work "Guernica" inspired by the Spanish Civil War.

The Rodgers and Hart musical *Babes in Arms* introduces classic songs including "My Funny Valentine," "The Lady Is a Tramp," and "Where or When."

Andrew W. Mellon gives his art collection to the United States.

151

• **JUNE 3**
Duke of Windsor and Wallis Simpson marry.

• **JULY 11**
George Gershwin dies.

• **JULY 16**
Germany establishes concentration camp at Buchenwald.

• **AUGUST 2**
Marijuana is outlawed in U.S.

• **SEPTEMBER 26**
Blues singer Bessie Smith dies after a car accident when a segregated hospital refuses to treat her.

• **OCTOBER 5**
FDR calls for "quarantine" against aggressor nations, but isolationism still dominates American attitudes.

• **DECEMBER 11**
Italy quits the League of Nations.

• **DECEMBER 12**
Japanese bombers sink U.S. vessel *Panay* in China, killing two crewmen.

1938

152

German troops seized Austria on March 12, 1938, on the pretext of protecting pro-German Austrians (below) from violent persecution. Britain and France did not lift a finger. Next on the Führer's list was Czechoslovakia.

Knowing that Germany was too weak to fight if Hitler's bluff was called, German military leaders discussed resigning as a group. The chief of the army's general staff resigned but his colleagues lost their nerve. So, however, did the British and French. When Hitler demanded the surrender of Sudetenland, Prime Minister Neville Chamberlain and French Premier Edouard Daladier pressured the Czechs to yield.

At Munich, with no Czech representatives present, Chamberlain and Daladier on September 30 accepted all Hitler's demands. German troops marched into Sudetenland the next day. Chamberlain declared he had secured "peace for our time," but Hitler's promise of no further aggression barely lasted the year. On March 15, 1939, the Nazis seized the rest of Czechoslovakia. The word "Munich" would become a synonym for one of the most disastrous mistakes in history.

THE 40-HOUR WEEK

"The last piece of legislation that could truly be described as a New Deal reform measure," one historian wrote about the Fair Labor Standards Act of 1938.

The measure outlawed child labor in interstate commerce and provided a 25-cent-an-hour minimum wage and a 44-hour work week—changing to 40 cents an hour and 40 hours a week over the next two years. The law contained many exceptions (one congressman sardonically offered an amendment requiring the Secretary of Labor to report to Congress "whether anyone is subject to this bill") but did immediately bring pay raises for some 750,000 workers.

FIBERGLASS INDUSTRY FOUNDED

One of the world's most versatile, useful, and ubiquitous industrial materials is also one of the least visible. Hardly anyone sees fiberglass; they see boats, automobile bodies, insulators, airplane parts, curtains, and thousands of other products.

Craftsmen had long known that glass can be spun into a long, thin, flexible fiber with remarkable strength and other marvelous properties: It will not burn, stretch, or rot. In 1938, however, scientists at two glass manufacturing firms, the Owens-Illinois Glass Company and the Corning Glass Works, developed the first practical process for producing fiberglass commercially. The two companies joined forces as the Owens-Corning Fiberglass Corporation to put the new product into use.

NAZI PERSECUTION OF JEWS WORSENS

For Jews in Germany, the years of Nazi rule were a steady descent into persecution and fear. Within months after Hitler took power, Jews were banned from the civil service, teaching, journalism, theater, and films. In 1935 the infamous

Nuremberg Laws deprived Jews of German citizenship and declared them "subjects," forbidden—among other restrictions—to marry or have sexual relations with Aryans. With official encouragement, signs went up at private businesses everywhere in Germany declaring "Juden unerwuenscht" (Jews Not Welcome).

WORKER CLEANS UP AFTER KRISTALLNACHT.

Buying anything, even food and medicine, became immensely difficult.

Life for Germany's Jews suddenly turned even more terrifying on *Kristallnacht*, or the Night of Broken Glass. Encouraged by Joseph Goebbels, head of Nazi propaganda, storm troopers attacked Jewish homes, synagogues, and businesses on the night of November 9, 1938. Ninety-one Jews were murdered. The outbreak was followed by wholesale confiscation of Jewish enterprises and property—including artworks and jewelry—and by other draconian new measures, such as the expulsion of Jewish children from German schools.

NUCLEAR FISSION DISCOVERED

In the last days of 1938, scientists in Europe and the United States began putting together the pieces of a fateful scientific puzzle.

German chemists Otto Hahn and Fritz Strassmann learned that uranium nuclei could be split by bombarding uranium with neutrons. Lise Meitner, an Austrian scientist working in Sweden with her nephew, physicist Otto Frisch, discovered that when a nucleus split, a small amount of mass was converted into a prodigious

---

- **FEBRUARY 4**
British engineer John L. Baird demonstrates color television in London.

- **MARCH 14**
Hitler returns to his native Austria to announce the "Anschluss," or union with Germany.

- **APRIL 12**
New York passes the country's first law to require medical tests for marriage licenses.

- **APRIL 12**
U.S. students declare a nationwide strike against war and vow not to participate in any future armed conflict.

- **MAY 17**
U.S. Naval Expansion Act is passed by Congress.

- **MAY 26**
House Un-American Activities Committee is established; first chair is Representative Martin Dies of Texas.

- **JUNE 12**
Yellow River dikes burst in China. Catastrophic floods kill 150,000 people.

amount of energy (confirming Einstein's famous $E=mc^2$ formula—energy equals mass times the speed of light squared). French scientists, meanwhile, deduced that a self-sustaining "chain reaction" could be created by fissioning the uranium isotope U-235.

When the new discoveries were demonstrated at a Washington conference early in the new year, scientists quickly grasped the implications. Within days, physicist J. Robert Oppenheimer made a crude sketch of a bomb. And a Columbia University colleague found the great Enrico Fermi one day standing at a window overlooking New York City. "A little bomb like that," Fermi said, cupping his hands in the shape of a ball and looking out over the busy streets, "and it would all disappear."

▶ JAZZ GOES UPTOWN

"You must be out of your mind!" Benny Goodman (below) told the publicist who first suggested a swing concert in Carnegie Hall. But when Goodman led his musicians onstage on January 16, 1938, every seat was sold, plus 100 overflow seats. Prices ranged from 85 cents for the upper balcony to $2.75 for boxes, a slight discount from prices charged for Philharmonic concerts.

Goodman, the first well-known band-leader in America to use black and white musicians together, brought an integrated group to the Carnegie performance, including such stars as trumpeter Harry James, pianist Teddy Wilson, drummer Gene Krupa, and vibra-phonist Lionel Hampton. Goodman opened with "Don't Be That Way" and went on through a program that included a memorable jam with Count Basie and Lester Young, among

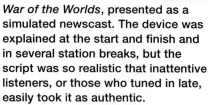

WAR OF WORLDS

"Incredible as it may seem, both the observations of science and the evidence of our eyes lead to the inescapable conclusion that those strange beings who landed in the Jersey farmlands tonight are the vanguard of an invading army from the planet Mars." The voice was authoritative, and nearly two million radio listeners believed they were hearing a real news announcement. Hundreds of thousands fled their homes. Terror-stricken people in cars and on foot brought New York City's Riverside Drive to a standstill.

There was no invasion. For Halloween night on CBS's *Mercury Theater*, actor Orson Welles (right) and his writers had chosen to dramatize H. G. Wells's *War of the Worlds*, presented as a simulated newscast. The device was explained at the start and finish and in several station breaks, but the script was so realistic that inattentive listeners, or those who tuned in late, easily took it as authentic.

The panic was testimony to radio's influence and authority in American life. Not only the uneducated were fooled; research found that nearly a third of college graduates in the audience thought they were hearing actual news.

others—but the number no one would ever forget was the ender, "Sing Sing Sing," with breathtaking solos by pianist Jess Stacy.

The concert opened Carnegie to other jazz musicians: In short order, Ethel Waters, Louis Armstrong, and blues singer Big Bill Broonzy appeared there.

■ TRENDS & TRIVIA

Bugs Bunny makes his screen debut.

Hungarian brothers Ladislaw and Georg Biro invent the ballpoint pen.

Nylon is patented; the next year the toothbrush is the first commercial product to use nylon.

Famed jockey Eddie Arcaro wins his first Kentucky Derby on Lawrin.

The Cloisters, part of New York's Metropolitan Museum of Art, is built to house medieval art.

Jefferson-head nickel is introduced.

Nestle comes out with instant coffee.

Thornton Wilder's play *Our Town* opens.

Johnny Vander Meer of the Cincinnati Reds becomes the only pitcher in history to pitch two successive no-hit games.

Popular songs are "You Must Have Been a Beautiful Baby" and "Jeepers Creepers."

Cabins are pressurized in passenger airlines.

Action Comics introduces Superman, the first in a long line of comic book superheroes, such as Wonder Woman and Batman. ▶

The Adventures of Robin Hood, starring Errol Flynn, is released by Warner Brothers.

Vitamins E and B are identified.

● JUNE 23
Civilian air transportation comes under federal control with establishment of the U.S. Civil Aeronautics Authority.

● JULY 3
FDR dedicates Gettysburg National Monument on 75th anniversary of the battle.

● JULY 13-15
Howard Hughes circles the planet in record time of 3 days, 19 hours, 14 minutes in his twin-engine Lockheed.

● JULY 18
"Wrong Way" Corrigan, forbidden to make a solo transatlantic flight, takes off from New York for California but flies to Ireland instead.

● SEPTEMBER 15
American novelist Thomas Wolfe dies.

● NOVEMBER 7
Jewish refugee from Nazi Germany assassinates German diplomat Ernst von Rath in Paris.

● NOVEMBER 14-18
The CIO is now called the Congress of Industrial Organizations. John L. Lewis is unanimously elected president.

154

Just past 11 p.m. on the night of August 21, 1939, the music coming over radios in Nazi Germany suddenly stopped. A stunning announcement followed: "The Reich government and the Soviet government have agreed to conclude a pact of nonaggression with each other. The Reich Minister for Foreign Affairs will arrive in Moscow on Wednesday, August 23, for the conclusion of the negotiations."

The pact promised peace between two dictators who had been the bitterest of enemies. With it, peace in Europe was doomed. Nine days later, at dawn on September 1, Hitler's army—now assured it would not have to fight a major enemy in the east—stormed into Poland while German bombers aimed toward Polish cities. Britain and France, having repeatedly backed down from Nazi aggressions in the past, honored their commitment to Poland. On September 3, both declared war on Germany. By then, Nazi forces were already deep inside Poland. Their swift advance added a new phrase to the world's vocabulary: Blitzkrieg or "lightning war."

► A-BOMB PROGRAM CONCEIVED

Six weeks after war broke out in Europe, a former Roosevelt adviser named Alexander Sachs came to the White House with a letter for FDR explaining the recent discoveries about atomic fission and the possible development of "extremely powerful bombs of a new type." It carried Albert Einstein's signature, though most of it was actually written by the Hungarian-born scientist Leo Szilard.

After a somewhat roundabout preliminary conversation, Sachs read aloud the opening paragraph and the last, which hinted that Nazi Germany might try to build atomic weapons. That, and the prestige of Einstein's name, got the message through. Handing the letter to his aide, Brig. Gen. Edwin ("Pa") Watson, Roosevelt said: "This requires action." America's atomic bomb project was, if not born, at least conceived.

► ROMANCE AND FANTASY

Harsh memories of the Depression lay just behind, and clouds of war lay ahead. But Hollywood marked the year with one of its greatest romantic epics and one of its greatest fantasies.

Gone With the Wind premiered in Atlanta, with the theater decorated as a plantation house and ushers and ticket-takers in antebellum costumes. The film contributed one of the most famous lines

CLARK GABLE AND VIVIEN LEIGH IN *GONE WITH THE WIND*

of dialogue in movie history. When Scarlett O'Hara asks, "If you go, where shall I go, what shall I do?" Clark Gable, in the role of Rhett Butler, responds: "Frankly, my dear, I don't give a damn."

In *The Wizard of Oz*, 16-year-old Judy Garland (right), as Dorothy, led the Cowardly Lion, the Scarecrow, the Tin Woodsman, and enchanted audiences down the yellow brick road to the Emerald City. After the first previews, the producers had considered cutting one of Dorothy's

songs to shorten the movie—but came to their senses in time. The song was titled "Over the Rainbow."

► THE PAPERBACK REVOLUTION

The rather scholarly looking kangaroo was named Gertrude. She wore spectacles and was reading a book, with another sticking out of her pouch. (The glasses later disappeared, lest anyone get the idea that books caused eyestrain.) Gertrude was the trademark for a new line of 25-cent paperbacks called Pocket Books, launched by publisher Robert de Graff.

Paperbacks were not a new idea. Dime novels in soft covers had flourished for a time, but died out when copyright laws began to be more strictly enforced. But it was de Graff, promising "genuinely good and enduring books at irresistibly low prices, with almost universal distribution," who made paperbacks a permanent part of the American publishing industry.

Pocket Books changed Americans' book-buying habits almost immediately. A cigar stand near de Graff's office sold 110 books in a day and a half after the first titles were released. The list began

---

- **JANUARY**
Italy annexes Albania.

- **JANUARY 26**
Gen. Franco's troops capture Barcelona.

- **JANUARY 28**
Irish poet W. B. Yeats dies.

- **MARCH 2**
Cardinal Eugenio Pacelli is elected Pope Pius XII. He succeeds Pius XI.

- **MAY 16**
Food Stamp plan to dispose of agricultural surpluses is inaugurated in Rochester, New York, for recipients of relief.

- **MAY**
A ship carrying 937 Jewish refugees is denied entry by Cuba and the U.S. Returned to Europe, most of the refugees die in the Holocaust.

- **MAY 17**
British government imposes limits on Jewish immigration to Palestine.

with James Hilton's best-seller *Lost Horizon* and included, among others, *Bambi*, *Wuthering Heights*, Agatha Christie's *The Murder of Roger Ackroyd*, and a collection of five Shakespeare tragedies.

Sales quickly soared into the millions, especially when World War II put vast numbers of Americans on the move and fueled demand for cheap, easy-to-carry reading matter.

▶ MARIAN ANDERSON AT LINCOLN MEMORIAL
The invitation was from Howard University. But Howard clearly could not accommodate the expected Easter Sunday audience for the celebrated contralto Marian Anderson. The university approached the Daughters of the American Revolution, owners of Constitution Hall, but the DAR would not permit a black artist to perform there.

A storm of criticism followed; among those protesting was Eleanor Roosevelt, who announced in her newspaper column

that she was giving up her DAR membership. With President Roosevelt's approval, federal authorities offered the Lincoln Memorial as an alternative. Before a mesmerized crowd of 75,000 blacks and whites, Anderson sang for 20 minutes from the steps below Abraham Lincoln's statue (above). "My heart beat like mad," she recalled, "…loud and strong and as if it wanted to say something."

After the concert, the NAACP's Walter White noticed a young black woman in the crowd with tears streaming down her face. White recalled: "If Marian Anderson could do it, the girl's eyes seemed to say, then I can, too."

BASEBALL

Lou Gehrig (below), after ending his streak of 2,130 consecutive games, told fans at Yankee Stadium that despite being diagnosed with an incurable disease, "I consider myself the luckiest man on the face of the earth." The first baseball game was broadcast on a new gadget called television. And a lumberyard clerk in Williamsport, Pennsylvania, started the Little League.

All these events occurred in 1939, which had been successfully promoted as the 100th anniversary of baseball's invention by the Civil War hero Abner Doubleday. No actual evidence connects Doubleday with baseball (the game is nowhere mentioned in the 41 volumes of his diary) but, in a triumph of promotional myth-making over historical fact, a years-long campaign by civic boosters in Cooperstown, New York, won organized baseball's support for declaring the centennial and establishing the National Baseball Hall of Fame on the site of Doubleday's supposed creation.

▶ CIVIL WAR ENDS IN SPAIN
The Spanish loyalists had held out against Gen. Francisco Franco for nearly three years, but time—and Soviet support—ran out for the republic in 1939. Madrid fell in March; the last remnants of the Republican Army surrendered April 1. With the end of the fighting, Franco established a dictatorship that would last until his death in 1975. Bitter memories, too, would last for many years. Much of the country had been devastated, and hundreds of thousands had died, not just in battle but in mass executions carried out by both sides.

■ TRENDS & TRIVIA

John Steinbeck's *The Grapes of Wrath* is published.

Glenn Miller and his band have a big hit with "In the Mood."

Conscription begins in Britain.

First reflector radio telescope is built in Wheaton, Illinois.

C. S. Forester's *Captain Horatio Hornblower* is published.

After six years of the New Deal, ten million Americans are still unemployed.

Senate committee issues a report on widespread intimidation and illegal antiunion activities by U.S. employers.

United Jewish Appeal is founded.

Batman makes his first comic book appearance.

New York World's Fair opens. The "World of Tomorrow" theme features new technology and an upbeat vision of the future.

Ted Williams plays his first game for the Boston Red Sox.

Radio soap operas such as *Search for Tomorrow* and *Our Gal Sunday* captivate millions, especially housewives.

Jimmy Stewart stars in *Mr. Smith Goes to Washington*.

Director John Ford's Western *Stagecoach* opens.

Recent invention of nylon brings affordable nylon stockings to women.

Ernest O. Lawrence wins the Nobel Prize for physics for inventing and developing the atom smasher (cyclotron).

Rockefeller Center opens in New York City.

• MAY 22
Nazi Germany and Fascist Italy conclude military alliance, known as "Pact of Steel."

• AUGUST 2
Hatch Act becomes law, barring U.S. government employees from political activity.

• AUGUST 24
Germans test a jet airplane.

• SEPTEMBER 23
Sigmund Freud, the father of psychoanalysis, dies at 83.

• SEPTEMBER 27
Warsaw falls to German invaders.

• OCTOBER 11
NAACP Legal Defense and Education Fund is established to pursue legal battle against racial segregation.

• NOVEMBER 30
Soviet Union invades Finland.

PHOTOGRAPHY

by Sam Abell
NATIONAL GEOGRAPHIC STAFF PHOTOGRAPHER

In 1961, when I was 16, my father took me across Ohio to attend an illustrated lecture by Albert Moldvay, a NATIONAL GEOGRAPHIC staff photographer. I was impressed—not only by the quality of his work but also by the way he answered photographers who questioned the 'relevance' of the GEOGRAPHIC's photography. "Who cares about rain forests?" was one typical question. "Rain forests matter," Moldvay replied. "So do deserts and oceans and the Arctic—if they don't matter, what does?" His answer, like his photographs, was ahead of its time.

I thought of GEOGRAPHIC photography next in 1963. I was a senior in high school and another Ohioan was in the news. GEOGRAPHIC staff man Barry Bishop, of Cincinnati, was one of the first Americans to climb Mount Everest. He had miraculously survived for a night near the summit in an

Left: Testing a Speed Graphic, Nova Scotia   Middle: Covering monsoons, Nepal   Right: Studying monk seals, Hawaii

open bivouac—no tent, sleeping bag, or oxygen—managing to return minus only his toes, which were lost to frostbite. When I saw Bishop's riveting photographs in the GEOGRAPHIC, I redoubled my dedication to photography. Four years later, in 1967, I won a summer internship and set foot in the Society's photography division for the first time. My first assignment was to photograph an archaeological dig in Arizona. Digs are very safe assignments for interns—nothing moves. But I worked hard to bring that dig alive photographically. At the end of each week I sent off film shipments and anxiously awaited word from headquarters on my progress. I worked hard because I felt I was part of something larger than myself, part of one of the most innovative, imaginative, and accomplished group of photographers in the world. I wanted my work to live up to their standards.

It was a lot to ask. The NATIONAL GEOGRAPHIC's photographic history—an almost unbroken monthly record, stretching back to 1895—includes some of the most remarkable photographs ever made. It also claims some of the most enterprising, inventive, artistic, and self-sacrificing photographers in the world. As Gil Grosvenor, Chairman of the Board of the National Geographic Society, and himself a photographer for the magazine, wrote in 1994: "By staying in the forefront of new technology in photography and printing, the GEOGRAPHIC has maintained both continuity and change during an amazing century—the world's longest time exposure."

That "long time exposure" was begun by Gil's grandfather, Gilbert Hovey Grosvenor, the first full-time editor of the NATIONAL GEOGRAPHIC and one of photography's genuine pioneers and most ardent advocates. For the first ten years of the magazine's existence, however, it published few photographs. The GEOGRAPHIC resembled a text-heavy scholarly journal. Then came changes in printing and in the emerging enterprise of photography, and after the turn of the century photographs began to dominate the pages of the magazine, gradually edging out halftone reproductions of gravure prints and paintings. The turning point came in July 1906 when the GEOGRAPHIC published a set of 74 remarkable photographs of wildlife by George Shiras III. Using magnesium-powder flash to illuminate his subjects and stealthy approach by flat-bottom boat in darkness, Shiras made original images of wild animals that are still worthy today. Shiras's work established the expectation, among editors and readers alike, that GEOGRAPHIC photographers would bring back pictures never seen before.

Still, there were no full-time staff photographers until the 1920s. Until then GEOGRAPHIC editors searched the world for photographs, amassing in the process a deep archive of images from the start of the century. The first "assigned" photographers were explorers, scientists, and writers who took cameras along, or who sought out local photographers in remote locations and bought their work.

I often think of those pioneering photographers—Joseph F. Rock in the mountains of China and Herbert G. Ponting with Robert Falcon Scott in Antarctica—and of the ordeals they endured. Their equipment was bulky and awkward: cameras and tripods; fragile glass plates; perishable chemicals for developing pictures in improvised darkrooms. In 1911 Ponting had to carry all that on a crossing to Antarctica in seas so violent that tethered horses were swept overboard. Then came two winters of pitch-dark and bitter cold. Through it all he photographed, developed film, and produced portraits that are, to me, unrivaled in their artistry and humanity. But his photographs are also documentary, the only photographic record we have of Scott's ill-fated expedition. In this mastery of the art of realism, Ponting, like Shiras before him, set the standard for generations of GEOGRAPHIC photographers to come.

That next generation constituted the first "staff" photographers—men who regularly went out on assignment around the world for the Society. Their assembly in Washington coincided with the creation of American publishing's first color photography laboratory in 1920. The lab was dedicated to producing autochromes—delicate glass plates that held an equally delicate pastel image. Autochromes were the first successful commercial method of making color photographs, but they were expensive and finicky, requiring a very long exposure even in direct sunlight. Nonetheless, the GEOGRAPHIC published more than 1,500 autochromes between 1921 and 1930, more than any other publication.

One of the pioneers of color photography was the young Edwin (Bud) Wisherd. In 1923, on his first assignment, he rode a horse and led a mule loaded down with more than 50 pounds of equipment through the American Southwest, becoming the first GEOGRAPHIC photographer to expose natural color plates in the field. Some four decades later, as manager of the photography lab, Wisherd checked cameras out to me for my first assignment—also to the American Southwest.

Such career longevity is not exceptional at the National Geographic Society. Wisherd was part of a pioneering generation of prolific photographers that includes Charles Martin, Maynard Owen Williams, Clifton Adams, W. Robert Moore, Luis Marden, B. Anthony Stewart, and Volkmar (Kurt) Wentzel, all of whose work illustrated the pages of the GEOGRAPHIC for decades. Marden, still active today as a writer, was instrumental in moving GEOGRAPHIC photography into the modern era of small, light cameras that allowed more informal and intimate photography. In 1934, as a 21-year-old, he had written *Color Photography With the Miniature Camera*. Based on the book, GEOGRAPHIC hired him, but at first would not publish pictures taken with his 35-mm Leica because the quality wasn't there. Then Kodak improved the character of Kodachrome film. "It was changeover time," Kurt Wentzel recalls. "The generation change, from large-format to 35 mm, came with Luis Marden's vision."

Marden's other lasting contribution to the history of GEOGRAPHIC photography was his pioneering work in taking pictures underwater—a chapter of photographic history almost entirely written by GEOGRAPHIC photographers. Marden didn't make the first color photograph underwater; Charles Martin accomplished that once-impossible feat in 1926. Rather, Marden's accomplishment was to collaborate with Jacques-Yves Cousteau, the pioneering underwater explorer. Together they refined the revolutionary Aqua-Lung—in effect, the underwater equivalent of the 35-mm camera. With it divers (and photographers) could more easily maneuver, and work longer, underwater.

The connection between Martin, Marden, and Cousteau, is an example of the linkage between generations of photographers at the GEOGRAPHIC. Building on Marden's accomplishment in the 1950s, an enterprising, and influential photographer, Bates Littlehales, established that accurate, artistic photographs could be taken at ever greater depths. His work paved the way for the current generation of underwater photographers including David Doubilet, Bill Curtsinger, Flip Nicklin, and Emory Kristof. Taken together, their work constitutes a stand-alone chapter of exceptional exploration, enterprise, and accomplishment. Perhaps more than any contemporary photographer, Kristof represents the classic GEOGRAPHIC connection between inventiveness, exploration, and high achievement in image making. Because of his interest in very deep ocean exploration, NATIONAL GEOGRAPHIC readers have seen the first photographs of the submerged *Titanic* (and numerous other sunken ships), as well as the first photographs of newly discovered life forms existing on the edge of deep-ocean volcanic vents.

Kristof's career is an example of the accomplishments possible for a photographer who specializes. Unlike Doubilet, Curtsinger, and Nicklin, most photographers don't begin that way. The generation of photographers hired by the legendary Bob Gilka in the '60s, '70s, and early '80s were almost all generalists, able to handle any photographic assignment anywhere on Earth. People such as Win Parks, Tom Abercrombie, Jim Stanfield, Dean Conger, Bruce Dale, Joe Scherschel, George Mobley, Robert Madden, Gordon Gahan, Jodi Cobb, David Alan Harvey, William Allard, Jonathan Blair, Robert Sisson, Sisse Brimberg, Jim Amos, and James P. Blair did whatever was asked of them. In the process, they set a standard for accomplishment in editorial photography that would be hard, ever, to match.

Some of them did develop photographic specialties, however. Conger's work in the U.S.S.R., for instance, constitutes an unmatched record of life in that vast, closed country. Others who devoted themselves to one subject were Robert Sisson, insect and animal life; William Allard, the American West and cowboy culture; David Harvey, the Hispanic culture; and Jodi Cobb, the life of the Geisha. The opportunity to delve, sometimes for decades, into a single subject is the priceless and distinctive gift the National Geographic Society has made to photographers—and to photography.

The men and women who have taken advantage of this opportunity have repaid the GEOGRAPHIC and its readers by their extraordinary work. But uncommon devotion to photography comes at a price. Ten years after he climbed Mount Everest, Barry Bishop spoke of his thoughts the night he spent exposed near the summit. "Well," he said, "We knew it was unsurvivable—that this was the end. But we'd been to the summit and I still had my camera with me. The film was in it. They'd find that." Bishop survived, and his effort and accomplishment remain in my mind a model for what GEOGRAPHIC photography stands for, as one generation teaches and inspires the next. Chris Johns and Michael "Nick" Nichols photograph wildlife today in the spirit of Shiras. Maria Stenzel, in the shadow of Ponting, photographs in Antarctica. Sisse Brimberg and Karen Kasmauski photograph with the conviction of Jim Blair and Dean Conger. Sarah Leen and Joanna Pinneo photograph with the determination of George Mobley, and Robert Caputo has distinguished himself as the heir to Kurt Wentzel in Africa.

I have my own connection. Sitting alone with my doubts in Arizona on that first assignment in 1967 there was a knock on my door. It was Western Union with a telegram from the Society. It read: "Good sharpshooting on shipments one and two. A tip of the hat." It was signed: "Moldvay"—the same photographer I'd once seen from a distance in Ohio. My feelings then were true: I was part of something much, much larger than myself.

1940-

1949

Birth of the Atomic Age

■ **1940-1949** ■

by Paul Boyer

DIRECTOR, INSTITUTE FOR RESEARCH IN THE HUMANITIES
UNIVERSITY OF WISCONSIN–MADISON

THE 1940S, A DECADE OF TOTAL WAR, saw the emergence of a new weapon of mass destruction—the atomic bomb—that would profoundly shape the future. Amid all the complex crosscurrents of the 1940s, and its moments of high achievement and human promise, the central theme of the decade must, sadly, be war and the sweeping social, political, and technological changes that follow in its wake. Although World War II ended in 1945, having killed some 17 million soldiers and even more civilians, the peace that followed was uneasy at best, for the world now faced the war's grim aftermath. Not only was the planet now threatened by nuclear weapons but also the Western democracies now faced a new global struggle against a new foe: the Cold War confrontation with the Soviet Union.

The seeds of World War II had been sown in the punitive peace that followed World War I, when victorious England and France imposed harsh terms on the vanquished Germans. In the ensuing economic and social chaos, dictatorial regimes arose. In Italy, Benito Mussolini gained power in 1922. In Germany, Adolf Hitler's nationalistic and rabidly anti-Semitic National Socialist (Nazi) Party assumed control in 1933. Rebuilding the German *Wehrmacht*, or war machine, Hitler solidified his dictatorship, expanding into surrounding regions, and persecuting Jews and dissidents at home. Meanwhile, in Japan, a military

Opposite: Bombing by both sides in World War II laid waste such European landmarks as England's Coventry Cathedral.
Preceding pages: Adolf Hitler's overweening political ambitions plunged the world into a war that killed millions.

regime intent on gaining access to raw materials and markets grew increasingly warlike, invading Manchuria in 1931 and China in 1937. Germany, Italy, and Japan formed a military axis, and in 1939 Hitler invaded Poland. World War II had begun.

Initially, isolationist sentiment prevailed in the United States. Convinced that bankers and industrialists had inveigled America into World War I, many Americans had sworn "never again." But with Japan's surprise attack on the U.S. base at Pearl Harbor in Hawaii on December 7, 1941, killing 2,400 U.S. servicemen, isolationist sentiment evaporated. America was at war, and the nation rallied around President Franklin D. Roosevelt.

President Franklin D. Roosevelt guided the U.S. first through the Depression and then through a world war.

Total war meant civilian mobilization as well as military. On the American home front, Depression-era unemployment was soon a thing of the past as war plants operated around the clock. The media and the government built support for the war effort. Norman Rockwell produced a memorable series of paintings illustrating the "Four Freedoms" that President Roosevelt and British Prime Minister Winston Churchill had proclaimed as the Allies' war aims. The redoubtable singer Kate Smith and other entertainers raised millions in war-bond drives. Bing Crosby's 1942 hit song "White Christmas" expressed a nation's longing for peace.

Some war propaganda had an ugly tinge. Racist cartoons portrayed the Japanese as vermin or subhuman brutes. On the West Coast, authorities rounded up 110,000 Japanese-Americans and imprisoned them in remote internment camps. Meanwhile, African-American servicemen and industrial workers endured racial prejudice in many forms. In 1941, facing a protest march on Washington, President Roosevelt issued an executive order barring racial discrimination in war plants; enforcement proved lax, however. Amid heightened racial tensions, conflict erupted in Detroit and other cities. A 1943 Los Angeles riot targeted young Hispanic men. *An American Dilemma*, a 1944 study of U.S. race relations by Swedish economist Gunnar Myrdal, noted the irony of America's fighting racism abroad while tolerating it at home.

As Japan swiftly occupied much of Southeast Asia, the Philippines, and Pacific island groups, Allied war planners initially focused on Europe. The German Army in North Africa surrendered in May 1943, and in July, Allied forces landed in Sicily. Italy surrendered in October, but German troops in Italy fought on. On June 6, 1944, D day, a vast Allied armada under U.S. Gen. Dwight D. Eisenhower swarmed across the English Channel at Normandy. While Allied troops, including Gen. George S. Patton's Third Army, drove across France, Allied bombers battered Berlin, Hamburg, Dresden, and other German cities. Meanwhile, Russia's army, having repelled Hitler's invasion at horrific cost, including a five-month Nazi siege of Stalingrad, pushed across Eastern

Europe, driving toward Germany. On April 30, 1945, as the Russians closed in, Hitler committed suicide in his underground bunker in Berlin. A week later, on May 7, Germany surrendered. In the U.S., celebrations of V-E (Victory in Europe) Day were muted, however. President Roosevelt had died on April 12 of a cerebral hemorrhage, and a grieving nation watched uneasily as Vice President Harry S. Truman moved into the White House.

Full attention now turned to the Pacific war, an arena of naval battles and island-hopping campaigns. Three years earlier, in May 1942, the Battle of Coral Sea had checked Japan's move toward Australia, and the Battle of Midway the following month had produced a morale-boosting U.S. victory. In October 1944 the Battle of Leyte Gulf set the stage for the recapture of the Philippines. Slowly G.I.s leapfrogged from one island chain to another—the Solomons, the Marshalls, the Marianas—fighting battles that would resonate in the annals of U.S. military history: Guadalcanal, Tarawa, Iwo Jima, Okinawa. A photograph of GIs raising the flag at Iwo Jima produced one of the war's most memorable images.

By early summer 1945, as U.S. B-29s regularly bombed Japanese cities, unleashing firestorms that killed many thousands, Japan was on its knees. Although some Japanese military leaders insisted on carrying on, Emperor Hirohito made clear that the war must end. Peace feelers went out from Tokyo by way of Moscow. Then on August 6, 1945, a U.S. warplane, the *Enola Gay*, dropped a new weapon, the atomic bomb, on Hiroshima. The city was pulverized. Scores of thousands of men, women, and children perished instantaneously. Thousands more died later of radiation poisoning. On August 9 a second atomic bomb was dropped on Nagasaki, and five days later, on August 14, Japan surrendered. The atomic bomb had forestalled a U.S. invasion of Japan, President Truman claimed, and amply repaid Japan for Pearl Harbor and for wartime atrocities.

WILD CELEBRATIONS MARKED JAPAN'S SURRENDER, but the euphoria faded as Americans learned more about the atomic bomb and its potential. First proposed to FDR in 1939 by Albert Einstein and other physicists, the bomb had been built by a secret wartime undertaking, the Manhattan Project, operating at several locations, including Los Alamos, New Mexico. When President Truman, in Germany for a conference with America's wartime allies, learned of a successful atomic-bomb test in New Mexico in July 1945, he toughened his bargaining with Soviet leader Joseph Stalin. Although some Manhattan Project scientists urged an initial demonstration shot, Truman authorized the bomb's immediate military use. Historians, and the American people, would long debate whether the President's sole objective in bombing Japan was to force that country's surrender, or whether he also intended to intimidate Russia.

The early postwar era brought a wave of fear over the atomic future. Radio commentator H. V. Kaltenborn called the bomb a "Frankenstein monster." *Life* magazine published "The Thirty-Six Hour War," a scenario of atomic conflict illustrated with drawings of New York City in ruin. Religious writers linked the bomb to the fiery destruction of Earth foretold in the Bible. As the bomb gripped the popular imagination, bartenders mixed "atomic" cocktails, and General Mills offered kids an "Atomic Bomb" ring for 50 cents and a Kix cereal boxtop. A 1946 U.S. atomic test at Bikini Atoll in the Pacific inspired the skimpy swimsuit called a bikini.

To allay atomic fears, Washington proposed civil-defense plans and promoted atomic energy as a source of limitless power as well as of medical wonders and futuristic atomic cars, ships, and airplanes. David E. Lilienthal, head of the Atomic Energy Commission, tirelessly portrayed the bright Utopia that lay ahead as scientists harnessed the power of the atom.

The atomic bomb was not the war's only technological legacy. Jet engines, a wartime invention, would soon transform civilian air travel. Mainframe computers, whose development was spurred by wartime antiaircraft and ballistics research, became commercially available to governments and big corporations in the late 1940s. The V-1 and V-2 rockets, developed by Nazi scientists to carry bombs to England, laid the groundwork for both nuclear missiles and for space exploration. On the other hand, the war slowed the growth of television, which had actually made its public debut at the 1939 New York World's Fair. But with the 1946 advent of popular variety shows such as Ed Sullivan's *Toast of the Town* and Arthur Godfrey's *Talent Scouts*, and of the first TV soap opera, *Faraway Hills*, the television era began.

MANY LOOKED TO THE UNITED NATIONS, launched at a 1945 conference in San Francisco, to control atomic energy and assure world peace, but that hope faded as the United States and the Soviet Union, once wartime allies, became bitter adversaries divided by their ideology, their economic and political systems, and their global aspirations. In February 1946 Stalin, announcing a rearmament plan, predicted a mortal struggle with the capitalist bloc, led by the United States. A month later, speaking in Missouri, Winston Churchill foresaw a grim conflict pitting the Christian West against atheistic communism, centered in Moscow. From the Baltic to the Adriatic, declared Churchill, an Iron Curtain now divided Europe. In March 1947 President Truman, raising the specter of global communist domination, persuaded Congress to vote millions in economic aid to help Greece and Turkey resist Soviet-backed communist insurgencies. In June of that year, as Moscow's grip on Eastern Europe tightened and as western European Communist Parties gained strength, the United States announced a program of economic aid, the Marshall Plan, to promote European recovery and check communism's advances.

The divided city of Berlin, deep in the Soviet occupation zone, became the focus of conflict in June 1948 when the Soviets, seeking to prevent the emergence of a separate West German government, blockaded land access to the city. For nearly a year, until the Soviets lifted the blockade in May 1949, U.S. and British airplanes supplied all of West Berlin's needs. That same year, the United States and its European allies created a military alliance, the North Atlantic Treaty Organization (NATO); the Russians responded with the Warsaw Pact.

Cold War alarms reverberated at home. In the late 1940s, the House Un-American Activities Committee investigated atomic scientists, civil-rights activists, and Hollywood writers in a quest for Communists. In 1947, responding to growing pressure, the Truman administration launched a loyalty program to ferret out subversives in government. The climate of paranoia increased in 1948 when ex-Communist Whittaker Chambers accused Alger Hiss, a State Department diplomat in the 1930s, of having been a Soviet spy. These developments helped spawn the Red Scare that swept the nation in the early 1950s, whipped up by Senator Joseph R. McCarthy.

With the Cold War, too, came a deadly nuclear arms race. When the Soviets tested their first atomic bomb in 1949, President Truman responded with a program to develop the far more powerful hydrogen bomb, and the nuclear arms race was under way. In the 1951 film "The Day the Earth Stood Still," extraterrestrial visitors warn Earthlings to abandon their insane course, but it would take more than a Hollywood movie to halt the nuclear competition.

From the ruins of war came a new global economic and social order. U.S. occupation forces in Japan imposed a new democratic political system. U.S. aid to its former enemies Japan and Germany helped both to become economic powerhouses and formidable trading rivals of the United States. The postwar political map changed radically as well. The Jewish state of Israel, reinforced by refugees from Nazism, arose in 1948, planting the seeds of conflict with displaced Palestinians and Israel's Arab neighbors. The war weakened Europe's colonial grip in Africa and Asia. With the defeat of the occupying Japanese, independence movements arose in French Indochina, including Vietnam, laying the groundwork for a future war. India gained independence from a war-weakened Great Britain in 1947, and as conflict erupted between Hindus and Muslims, a separate Muslim state, Pakistan, emerged as well.

With Japan's defeat, a long civil war resumed in China. In 1949 Chinese Communists under Mao Zedong came to power in Beijing. Mao's foe Chiang Kai-shek fled to the island of Taiwan, where, with U.S. backing, he proclaimed the Republic of China as the nation's legitimate government. In Korea, a Japanese colony from 1910 to 1945, the United States and the Soviets established separate spheres of influence, divided at the 38th parallel. The Cold War turned hot in June 1950, as Soviet-armed North Korean troops stormed across the 38th parallel and the Korean War began.

The horrors of Germany's racist policies came to light as the Allies liberated millions from concentration camps.

In the United States, World War II spurred sweeping social changes. The educational benefits provided to veterans by the 1944 Servicemen's Readjustment Act (the GI Bill) contributed to a postwar surge in college enrollments. Encouraged by the government, millions of women had joined the military (in noncombat roles) or worked in war plants, and they were not all willing to relinquish this newfound independence. Wartime prosperity and pent-up consumer demand also contributed directly to a postwar economic boom. By 1950 U.S. factories were producing six million refrigerators and automobiles annually. Nearly five million new houses were built in 1945-1950, inaugurating the postwar explosion in suburban housing. A surging birthrate produced the celebrated "baby boom" generation that would spur spending on diapers, toys, and new schools in the 1950s; flood college campuses in the 1960s; and stir worries about Social

Security and Medicare in the 1990s as the Baby Boomers contemplated retirement.

The war and its aftermath also profoundly affected American race relations. While white families moved to the suburbs, blacks and other minorities remained behind in the inner cities, often without jobs or decent housing. But African Americans who had helped win the war as soldiers or factory workers were unwilling to accept a return to segregation and second-class citizenship. Further, as the United States sought the support of darker-skinned peoples in the Cold War struggle, racism at home proved an increasing embarrassment. The full horror of Hitler's anti-Semitic program, which murdered as many as six million Jews and other minorities, and which became fully known only after the war, provided a shocking revelation of where racism had ultimately led. Responding to these developments, President Truman in 1946 set up a Committee on Civil Rights, which published its report, *To Secure These Rights*, in 1947. The following year (an election year, by no coincidence), Truman submitted a major civil-rights program to Congress. When Congress stalled, the President in July 1948 issued an executive order forbidding racial segregation in the military. Thus, while the full-scale civil-rights movement lay ahead, its beginnings date to the 1940s, as one aftereffect of the war.

As the 1948 election loomed, a Republican presidential victory seemed likely. Republican hopes increased when southern white delegates at the Democratic nominating convention, protesting Truman's civil-rights program, withdrew and formed the States Rights party (nicknamed the Dixiecrats), nominating Governor J. Strom Thurmond of South Carolina for President. Another splinter party, the Progressives, headed by former Vice President Henry Wallace, opposed the administration's Cold War policies. With the opposition thus divided, the Republican candidate, New York governor Thomas E. Dewey, seemed certain to win. But Truman undertook a national campaign tour, diverting voter discontent from himself to the "do nothing" Republican Congress. Truman's civil-rights program drew black voters, and his opposition to the antilabor Taft-Hartley Act of 1947 appealed to union members. His role as a Cold War leader helped as well. On election day, Truman eked out a narrow victory—one of the great upsets in U.S. electoral history. The next year the President proposed a far-reaching program of domestic reform. Known as the Fair Deal, it got nowhere at the time, but it did foreshadow the Great Society programs of President Lyndon B. Johnson 20 years later.

With the end of the decade, the world faced grave uncertainties as two nuclear superpowers maneuvered for supremacy. The U.S. economy was booming, but anticommunist alarms poisoned the political climate, and profound changes were afoot that would soon transform America. Few decades in American history witnessed such violence and conflict or brought such portentous changes as the 1940s. The era that spawned a technology of horrifying destructive power reminds us how deeply war and conflict are embedded in the human condition, how unexpected the consequences of war can be—and how difficult is the struggle to achieve a world of peace. ■

One of the century's greatest leaders, British Prime Minister Winston Churchill flashes V for victory.

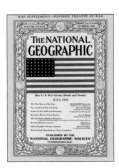

Until July 1942 the cover of National Geographic magazine, known for the quality of the photographs in its pages, simply listed the issue's contents. The cover was rimmed with oak leaves encompassed in a bright yellow border. In this issue the magazine added an illustration of the American flag, reflecting the patriotism of the war years. This was the first step toward individualizing each cover.

Lascaux Cave Prehistoric Art

In the hills of Dordogne, France, caverns riddle the soft rock like holes in Swiss cheese. Beside the River Vézère is the Lascaux Cave. On its walls, almost as fresh as the day they were created, is cave art at least 20,000 years old. Discovered by four boys in 1940, Lascaux revealed the most extraordinary array of prehistoric paintings and drawings that anyone had yet seen. In the December 1948 issue of the Geographic, Norbert Casteret, a noted cave explorer, wrote, "The grotto of Lascaux—by far the finest and best-preserved gallery of prehistoric art—was introduced to me, a veteran of more than a thousand underground galleries and abysses, by a reporter for the National Geographic magazine. After more than 30 years of globe-trotting for National Geographic magazine to scenes of geographic, historic, and artistic interest the world over, my old friend, Maynard Owen Williams, invaded my chosen field and hustled me off to the choicest prehistoric prize of all."

Casteret described the scenes in this ancient art gallery, but the photographs by Williams let readers see for themselves. Casteret re-created the picture of Williams taking photographs underground. "It took two hours of breathing and polishing to warm the lenses enough so that they would not mist over completely. Now standing on tiptoe and leaning back at a crazy angle, now kneeling and curled up in tight corners, our photographer went through bending and stretching exercises.... Mountain photography is a job for trained athletes, but underground toil is aggravated by the fact that one aims in the dark, focuses in the dark, and has to banish this darkness with the exactly measured light of flashlights. Williams has faced Mother Earth without losing his smile."

EXPLORER NORBERT CASTERET ENTERS CAVE.

The Curlew's Secret

The opening sentence in this December 1948 article announced the discovery: "Up to June 12, 1948, one bird—and only one—of all the 815 species of North American birds had successfully hidden the secret of its meeting place and summer home from the eyes of man."

The mysterious bird was the bristle-thighed curlew, a member of the sandpiper family. It was first observed and collected on Tahiti in 1769 by the naturalist Joseph Banks. For one hundred years after its discovery, naturalists thought it must nest on some island other than whichever one they were studying at the time. Then, in 1869, a bristle-thighed curlew was collected at Kenai, Alaska, across the Kenai Peninsula from Seward. Further sightings occurred through the years, but the curlew continued to keep its nesting site a secret.

In the summer of 1947 Warren M. Petersen, an Alaska Native Service schoolteacher, and Henry Kyllingstad, also a teacher, wrote Arthur A. Allen, professor of ornithology at Cornell University, telling of their efforts to solve the mystery.

The Society's committee on research had listed Alaska as an objective for bird study. "I immediately wrote Dr. Gilbert Grosvenor, president of the National Geographic Society, suggesting a cooperative expedition with Petersen, Kyllingstad, and the Arctic Institute of North America to find the bristle-thighed curlew's nest. By return mail this proposal received Dr. Grosvenor's cordial approval."

On June 12, 1948, north of Mountain Village, Alaska, the last of all North American birds to give up the secret of its nesting place revealed its summer home in the tundra moss.

Farewell to Bikini

"About the middle of February 1946, modern civilization suddenly overtook the natives of Bikini Atoll in the Ralik Chain of the Marshall Islands." The author of the July 1946 article, Carl Markwith, on leave from the National Geographic Society, was a photographer's mate, 3rd class, U.S.N.R., when he went to Bikini as a member of a Navy photographic team to film the last days of the people on their island. When the U.S. Navy decided that Bikini was the place to test the atom bomb, the native people suddenly found themselves in the atomic age.

They were to be moved to the island of Rongerik, about 125 miles to the east. "Bikini, as I first saw it from the air," the author wrote, "was something to remember. I'd been seeing South Sea islands as they looked after both we and the Japs had had our innings—hot, dirty heaps of coral overrun with military installations, roaring with gasoline engines, reeking of Diesel oil, and almost completely treeless. Bikini Island was a long, narrow crescent of gleaming sand, well grown with palms and other vegetation and framing one side of a lagoon of

BIKINI ISLAND WOMEN CARRY POSSESSIONS TO A SHIP THAT WILL TAKE THEM TO THEIR NEW HOME.

incredibly blue and green water."

Markwith spent the next few days recording everyday life, as the islanders prepared to move and planned ceremonies to say goodbye to the only home most of them had ever known. Acting as the film crew's interpreter was James Milne, a native of Tarawa in the Gilbert Islands.

"While helping to pick up mike cable after the [farewell church service], I noticed one of the younger men in an earnest conversation with Jimmy, which, from their gestures, seemed to involve me," wrote Markwith. "Investigation disclosed that Laiboei [a local man] wished Jimmy to ask me if I had enough film to spare for a shot of himself and family at the grave of his sister. We all moved down the shore to the grave where they grouped around the headstone and I made my shots....the expressions on the faces of that family were so sincere that I suddenly found there was an unusual amount of dust in the air."

• King Solomon's Mines

The Holy Land and the Holy Book are closely intertwined, and archaeologists have frequently followed clues in the Bible to locate long-lost cities. As author Nelson Glueck put it in the February 1944 issue, "The spade is sometimes mightier than the pen in throwing light on facts long buried under the debris of centuries." Archaeological finds continue to substantiate the details and general background of biblical accounts.

In a series of expeditions from 1936 to 1943, Glueck found the ruins of Ezion-geber on the Gulf of Aqaba. The Bible says that Ezion-geber, King Solomon's seaport, was situated "on the shore of the Red Sea, in the land of Edom" (I Kings 9:26). Digging at an ancient mound called Tell el-Kheleifeh, Glueck's expedition quickly found pottery fragments from the tenth to fifth centuries B.C., the age of David and Solomon; of Elijah,

Isaiah, and Jeremiah; of the House of David from its founding until its two Great Exiles and the return of the Jews to Jerusalem. A full-page map accompanying the article gave biblical place names, with modern equivalents in parentheses.

King Solomon's copper mines were a grail to researchers. It had been thought that there was no copper or iron in greater Palestine. Discoveries in Wadi Araba proved the passage describing the Promised Land, "And you shall inherit a land whose stones are iron, and out of whose hills you can dig copper" (Deuteronomy 8:9). It is now clear that along the entire length of Wadi Araba there are deposits of copper and iron that were worked extensively during the time of King Solomon.

Ezion-geber was not only a port and naval base guarding the crossroads to Arabia and Egypt but also an industrial center. Capturing the scope of trade and the sophistication of ancient civilization, the author wrote, "Solomon traded copper and iron to Arabia in return for...spices, incense, and other precious objects.... It is probable that the Queen of Sheba came to Jerusalem not merely to bask in the brilliance of Solomon, but also to arrange trade treaties with him and to delimit spheres of interest."

The article ended prophetically. "Oil is already being pro-

ARABS TRAVEL ON THEIR "SHIPS OF THE DESERT."

duced in tremendous quantities along both sides of the Persian Gulf and in Arabia. The islands of Bahrein, off the northeast end of the Persian Gulf, are little more than plugged faucets which need only to be opened to spout, and the great desert of Arabia is thought to be a sandy surface over a sea of oil."

• Across Tibet from India to China

Traveling through valleys more than two miles high, the author, Lt. Col. Ilia Tolstoy, and his companion, Capt. Brooke Dolan, traversed Tibet from India to China. They made the 1,500-mile journey in 1942, following the loss to the Japanese of the Burma Road. They were seeking new routes to transport supplies to China. Roads were few, bridges were precarious, and bandits were rumored. Their yaks, carrying gear, negotiated snow-clogged passes by relay plunges. Sent by the Office of Strategic Services (OSS), the men were admonished by Director William "Wild Bill" Donovan to "keep in touch if you can."

In an August 1946 article, Col. Tolstoy described their first glimpse of Tibet from Natu La, first pass over the Himalaya at 13,500 feet, "For a while we were in the clouds and could see neither behind nor ahead of us. Then the mists parted for a moment, allowing us to take our last look back at India and our first ahead into the thick, evergreen forests below us and the sea of ranges in the distance. We were looking down into mysterious Tibet."

En route they met with many officials, observing the finely nuanced etiquette of greeting and gift giving. One merchant asked them when the United States would again buy Tibetan wool. Before the war Tibetan wool had been sold in great quantities to the U.S. for the manufacture of auto rugs, but the war had cut off the export. As Tolstoy reported, "We soon realized that Tibetans who knew of the United States were interested in the outcome of the war and had a sympathetic feeling toward us. They had, however, great doubt as to our ability to defeat Japan, since at the time Japan was almost at their border."

They also met the Minister of Finance in Lhasa, the only Tibetan member of the National Geographic Society, whose reception room was lined with the Society's maps of the world.

The high point of their reconnaissance was the public meeting and private audience with His Holiness the Dalai Lama, then an 11-year-old boy, at his palace in Lhasa. In a carefully choreographed ceremony, the two American explorers presented the Dalai Lama with gifts and a letter from President Roosevelt.

ROOSEVELT'S PHOTO TRAVELED RUGGED TERRAIN TO ARRIVE AS A GIFT FOR THE DALAI LAMA.

Map of Germany and Its Approaches

The magazine enclosed a ten-color supplement map in its July 1944 issue that showed Hitler's so-called "Fortress Europe," comprising the Reich homeland and "the fringe of conquered and enslaved peoples around pre-war Germany." The supplement was the latest in a series of maps tracing the changing face of Europe from the time of the peace conferences of 1919-1920 to the Allied invasion of 1944. "Members who have retained their ten general maps of Europe, from that of August 1914, and now receive this revealing chart of July 1944, have a complete running account of the surging politics and racial rivalry from the beginning of World War I to the big drive of World War II."

A feature of special interest on this supplement was the mapping of the network of military highways Hitler had built since coming to power. "…These remarkable roads," said the Society, "resemble the Pennsylvania Turnpike between Pittsburgh and Harrisburg." They are described thus: "These double-lane speedways, marked by double red lines, by-pass cities and towns. No grade crossings slow up traffic. There are hundreds of overpasses and underpasses. No traffic lights cut down speed. Streams of trucks move swiftly over the entire system."

The map also shows railroads and canals. "Thus the map enables the 1,250,000 members of the National Geographic Society to follow all transportation systems—highway, canal, and rail—which feed supplies to the Nazi armies. Nearly every place on all three systems is a potential bombing target."

Women at Work

A week before Pearl Harbor women made up a fraction of one percent of the total labor force. Two years later 475,000 women constituted nearly 35 percent of industry.

La Verne Bradley, author of "Women at Work" in the August 1944 issue, wrote, "The balance of power rests in women's hands. Literally. Behind the whine of sawmills and roar of blast furnaces, the hammer of arsenals and thunder of machine shops—in shipyards, factories, foundries, slaughter-houses, and laboratories—women are manipulating the machinery of war."

In aircraft production, for example, women made up more than 45 percent of the workforce at Douglas Aircraft. Women had trained for months for one of the most crucial jobs in the business: the final ground testing and adjusting of every functioning part of a patrol bomber. "Engine, instruments, controls—theirs is the final check before men take it aloft." The author noticed one "small taffy blonde, wearing a blue hair ribbon" reading on her lunch hour *Pneudraulic Power Machine and Riveters*. "She suddenly figured a couple of years ago that maybe the talents of her toolmaker father might be developed in her. They were."

The author mentions Anne Hollman, who is "46 and helps make one of the hottest fighter planes in the Army. She is the only woman flash welder in the East. And she is an Amazon. In the last war she was a machine operator in a knitting mill; then she did housework for 20 years. Now she is back, master of a difficult trade and proud of her skill.…"

Women worked in shipyards. They welded and riveted and handled the big cranes. Women physicists and engineers in the Acoustics and Special Problems Division of the Naval Ordnance Laboratory at the Washington Navy Yard came as close as women got to going to sea. They worked on ships tied at docks; they went on field assignments with officers and men to Key West, New London, and Miami.

USING A WHEEL STICK, WOMEN ROLL A BROKEN BOXCAR TRUCK IN CHICAGO.

Women worked for the Army. When this article appeared, some 29 percent of the 84,000 civilians supporting the Army engineers were women. They measured the depth of the Columbia River; operated radios to Mississippi River boats; and computed soil erosion, levee seepage, and silting. They charted evaporation rates and wave action on breakwaters. They went almost everywhere the engineers went, except overseas.

Women worked in all manner of civilian jobs: flagpole painters, cabbies, bus drivers, trolley motormen, and messengers. They were also milkmen, postmen, firemen, street cleaners, and traffic cops. Women trained as meteorologists, geologists, engineers, physicians—all found work.

The author observed, "At war's end, the country will emerge with a vast pool of skilled, semiskilled, and professional women." She concluded, "It's a man's and woman's world."

● The British Way

After the war, and at the time when money began flowing to Europe under the Marshall Plan, the NATIONAL GEOGRAPHIC devoted the entire April 1949 issue to an overview of the history, science, and culture of America's wartime ally, Great Britain. "The British Way"—with some 20 illustrations and 50 paintings—sought to tell the story of Great Britain's contributions to Western civilization. "I write…," said author Sir Evelyn Wrench, founder of the English-Speaking Union, "with the hope that the readers of the NATIONAL GEOGRAPHIC magazine…may derive inspiration from this review of some of the events which have helped fashion our joint civilization."

The bulk of the issue is composed of two-page spreads—artwork on one page and a story on the facing page—that review significant events and people in British history, from the building of the Roman Wall (A.D. 121-211) to Winston Churchill

(1874-1965). There is Alfred the Great (849-899). "To him is due the conception that England is an island realm and must be defended at sea and not on land. He regarded the North Sea and the English Channel as the national frontiers."

There is William Shakespeare (1564-1616). "Thomas Carlyle declared that the British would rather lose India than the writings of Shakespeare. Recently, India gained control of its own destiny, but what Carlyle esteemed the greater treasure still belongs to England."

There is Isaac Newton (1642-1727). "He made known to a world which still believed in witchcraft the laws of gravitation," and "by means of a prism bought at a fair…discovered secrets of light."

There is James Watt (1736-1819), who grew up in the fishing town of Greenock, Scotland, and gave the world the modern steam engine, which powered the Industrial Revolution.

There is William Blackstone (1723-1780), who codified English law and whose four-volume *Commentaries*, "undoubtedly one of the most influential books in the English language," says the author, was read in 1835 by Abraham Lincoln. Lincoln said, "I read until I devoured them."

There is Joseph Lister (1827-1912), the founder of antiseptic surgery, who ranks with Edward Jenner (1749-1823), who conquered smallpox, among the greatest benefactors of humanity.

There is Florence Nightingale (1820-1910), "the Lady of the Lamp," whose compassion and powers of organization relieved the suffering of soldiers on the battlefield in the Crimean War in the 1850s.

Finally, there is Winston Churchill. "No one who was in London," writes the author, "during the spring and summer of 1940 will ever forget those months.… Surely no other leader in history has ever more successfully instilled into his hearers his own supreme confidence." His words of truth and determination rallied a nation—"I have nothing to offer but blood, toil, tears, and sweat."

173

THE BRITISH OPEN THE LEGAL YEAR IN THE TRADITIONAL MANNER.

174

In the spring of 1940 Germany continued its blitzkreig, or lightning war, against stunned targeted nations. German panzer divisions—tanks, mechanized infantry, and motorized artillery—supported by coordinated air strikes from the Luftwaffe's dreaded screeching "Stukas," penetrated slower-moving armies. Nazi forces rolled into Denmark and Norway, then turned to the Netherlands, Belgium, and Luxembourg. The panzers overran northern France, and resistance in the Alps and at the Maginot Line could not withstand the thrust into the heartland. Paris capitulated—a prize that the Germans had failed to grasp in the First World War. One victory eluded Hitler: The British Army had been successfully evacuated from Dunkirk, and Britain stood alone in defiance, holding out for the day, as Churchill said to Parliament, when "the New World, with all its power and might, steps forth to the rescue and liberation of the old."

Yet for the American people in 1940 the overriding concern was whether they should become embroiled in a European conflict. The danger was that if they did not involve themselves, Americans might find their democratic form of government alone in a hostile fascist and totalitarian world.

▶ MIRACLE AT DUNKIRK

Hitler issued a "stop order" that halted all panzer divisions for two days in May, a time that in retrospect was strategically critical for the outcome of the war. In those two days, May 24 through May 26, the British Expeditionary Force, along with remnants of the French First Army, were evacuated from the coast around Dunkirk by the "Skylark Navy"—little ships from ports along eastern England that heeded the call for all hands and crossed the Channel on a life-or-death mission. The impromptu navy managed to take 338,226 officers and men, 139,097 of them French, off the beach and convey them to Britain. Exultation at the return of the men was such that Churchill had to warn in Parliament that "wars are not won by evacuations."

▶ THE SWASTIKA FLIES OVER PARIS

With the German panzer divisions advancing, the French government abandoned Paris without a fight, and on June 14, the German Army entered the undefended capital. Henri Philippe Pétain, a World War I hero, petitioned for peace—at humiliating cost. When emissaries sent by Pétain met their counterparts near Tours on June 20, they were transported eastward. They alighted from their train to find themselves outside the railway coach in which German delegates had signed the armistice of November 1918. Entering the coach, the French were faced with the Nazi leadership: Hitler, Ribbentrop, Hess, Göring, Keitel, and Raeder. The Germans left no room for negotiation, demanding signatures or the panzers would roll again. Ashen-faced, the chief French delegate, Gen. Charles Huntziger, obliged.

France was now three-quarters occupied by the Germans. The swastika flew from the Eiffel Tower. Pétain's government moved to the spa town of Vichy.

HITLER AND GENERALS PARADE IN FRONT OF THE EIFFEL TOWER.

As Churchill's representative to France flew out, he took with him Gen. Charles de Gaulle, almost the only member of the French government determined to carry on resistance.

▶ BATTLE OF BRITAIN

The Battle of Britain was a revolutionary confrontation in that it was to have been won by air superiority alone. On July 16 Hitler issued his Führer Directive (No. 16), demanding more, it developed, of the Luftwaffe than the air arm could deliver.

It was not for want of trying. The Battle of London—the war in the air over the city from the 7th to 30th of September, the climactic phase of the Battle of Britain—saw dense formations of Heinkel, Dornier, and Junkers bombers, escorted by Messerschmitt 109s and 110s, run a gantlet of barrage balloons, antiaircraft guns, and the opposing force of "The Few," the pilots and crew of the RAF's Spitfires and Hurricanes.

Victory was close. The use of radar, invented in the 1930s by Robert Watson-Watt, conferred an important advantage on the hard-pressed RAF. The victory, however narrow, handed Germany its first defeat and would bear fruit in time with the downfall of Hitler's regime.

▶ A WINTER WAR IN FINLAND

In October 1940 the Soviet Union demanded naval base rights and land cessation from the Finnish government. The Finns stonewalled and in November the Soviets invaded. Eventually, the Soviet Union was to commit a million men to the effort. The Finns fought back effectively, although their total strength never exceeded 175,000. Before their population was simply overpowered, the stalwart Finns became a source of inspiration to enemies of the Axis powers, with whom the Soviets were associated after the Molotov-Ribbentrop Pact. Fortunately for the future of Western-Soviet relations, the Finns petitioned for peace before Britain and France sent ground troops to help.

▶ NATIVE SON

Richard Wright, an American novelist born in 1908 near Natchez, Mississippi, published his novel *Native Son* in the spring of 1940. He began reading widely at the age of 15, when he handed a forged note to a librarian at the whites-only public library that read, "Dear Madam: Will you please let this nigger boy have some books by H. L. Menken?" Wright's novel became an instant best-seller, was a Book-of-the-Month-Club selection, and was adapted for the stage by Orson Welles and for film by Wright himself. Wright said he wanted to write a book "so hard and deep that they would have to face it without the consolation of tears." It is the story of Bigger Thomas, a young black man in Chicago who articulates his rage at the racism that marks his life through acts of violence. Challenging the conscience of a

THE DRAFT

With war breaking out in Europe, U.S. leaders saw the need for a buildup of the armed forces. This implied a draft. Conscription was not only unpopular but also unprecedented in American history while the country was at peace. Nevertheless, early in 1940, Senator Edward R. Burke (Democrat, Nebraska) and Representative James W. Wadsworth (Republican, New York) presented a bill to Congress. Bipartisan support was underscored by the endorsement of Republican presidential candidate Wendell Willkie. The Selective Training and Service Act, approved September 16, required that all males between the ages of 21 and 35 register. Those drafted—or selected—would serve for one year only and only in the Western Hemisphere. Tin Pan Alley—a source of popular songs—came out with "Don't Worry, Dear, I'll Be Back in a Year." But as the year wore on, many realized that their stint in the service was just beginning.

nation, *Native Son* was a breakthrough for writers of African-American descent. Wright won the prestigious Spingarn Medal from the National Association for the Advancement of Colored People in recognition of his achievement. Five years later, Wright published his own story, *Black Boy*, now considered an American classic.

■ TRENDS & TRIVIA

For Whom the Bell Tolls by Ernest Hemingway and *Of Mice and Men* by John Steinbeck are published.

"You Are My Sunshine" and "When You Wish Upon a Star" become favorite songs.

Composers Stravinsky and Schönberg flee from Europe to the U.S. to escape persecution.

Jazz pianist and composer Duke Ellington wows U.S. audiences.

Children enjoy the first tactile book, *Pat the Bunny,* by Dorothy Kunhardt.

Old-age pensions are granted to women age 60 and over in Britain.

The Wurlitzer plays any selected song for a coin.

Cartoon characters Tom and Jerry come to life under Joe Barbera and William Hanna.

Walt Disney releases *Pinnochio* and *Fantasia.*

The *BBC Radio Newsreel* begins broadcasts.

Winston Churchill is caricatured as a toy bulldog wearing a steel helmet with "Hitler terror" stamped on it.

Barn fans come into use for drying crops.

Power brakes are available for trucks.

The *New York Times* begins running a box on the front page called "The International Situation."

The Rh factor in blood is discovered by Karl Landsteiner of New York's Rockefeller Institute.

175

• JUNE 28
Alien Registration Act goes into effect requiring registration and fingerprinting of aliens in the U.S.

◄ SEPTEMBER
The Lascaux Cave is discovered by four boys in southwestern France.

• OCTOBER
Princess Elizabeth makes her first radio broadcast to child evacuees.

▶ NOVEMBER 5
FDR's reelection campaign is successful.

176

Throughout 1941 the Kriegs-marine under Adm. Karl Dönitz ordered its U-boats to use wolfpack tactics against Allied shipping in the central and western Atlantic, beyond the scope of British air cover. The extended U-boat warfare in the Atlantic proved success-ful for the German Navy, sink-ing 1.5 million tons of Allied shipping at a time when Britain was launching less than 1 mil-lion tons of new ships annually.

Mussolini's vision of an Italian empire in Africa floun-dered as Britain claimed its first complete success of the war—the liberation of Ethiopia from Axis occupation and the restoration of Emperor Haile Selassie to his throne.

Hitler came to Mussolini's aid in Greece and within three weeks the swastika was waving over the Acropolis. Hitler's Balkan campaign carved up Yugoslavia in less than a month. The Führer's attention turned furi-ously on Russia, where he had long desired *Lebensraum*, living space, for the German people.

Before the year was out, Japan attacked the United States at Pearl Harbor. The fol-lowing day the United States declared war on Japan, and Germany and Italy, in keeping with the terms of the Tripartite Pact they had signed with Japan, declared war on the United States.

▶ FOUR FREEDOMS

In his State of the Union address on Janu-ary 6, President Franklin D. Roosevelt defined democratic principles that became the ideological cornerstone of the war's aim. "In the future days, which we seek to make secure, we look forward to a world founded on four essential free-doms.... The first is freedom of speech and expression—everywhere in the world. The second is freedom of every person to worship God in his own way—everywhere in the world. The third is freedom from want...everywhere in the world. The fourth is freedom from fear...anywhere in the world." These vague, but popular free-doms charged the wartime purpose.

▶ LEND-LEASE

"Give us the tools, and we'll finish the job," said Winston Churchill in an effort to secure war supplies from the United States for his war-ravaged country. President Roosevelt heard the plea and attempted to rally the American people; but for Americans, the war was still far away. To buy time, Roosevelt skirted public resistance and the Neutrality Act of 1935 by trading 50 old destroyers for 99-year leases on naval and air bases in places such as Newfoundland and Trinidad. Then he campaigned for a pro-gram that would allow the U.S. to lend war supplies to countries fighting the Nazis.

Congress debated for two months before passing Lend-Lease on March 11, 1941. Three hours after signing the bill, Roosevelt released 28 PT boats and PT submarine chasers to Churchill. By the end of the war some 40 countries received aid, mostly in the form of munitions, aircraft, and ships, totaling more than 50 billion dollars.

▶ OPERATION BARBAROSSA

In a stunning move that would prove to be a turning point in the war, Germany invaded Russia on June 22, 1941. It was the largest attack in history. Three million German troops advanced along a 1,250-mile-long front that stretched from the Baltic to the Black Sea. In an address to his generals on March 30, Hitler had stressed that the war against Russia "will have to be conducted with unprecedented, unmerciful, and unrelenting harshness." Operation Barbarossa brought German panzer divisions to within 220 miles of Moscow in six weeks, when Hitler, inter-fering with his generals over the conduct of the operation, ordered his tanks southward to destroy the Soviet Fifth Army. The blunder fatally wounded the Führer's ambition.

RUSSIAN REFUGEES HEAD EAST AFTER GERMAN INVASION.

▶ THE SEARCH FOR ROSEBUD

Orson Welles, the enfant terrible of Amer-ican radio, burst upon Hollywood with his directorial debut, *Citizen Kane*. Starring in his own production, the 25-year-old Welles created what is still considered one of the century's path-breaking movies, and perhaps its greatest.

William Randolph Hearst, the arche-type of the American mogul on whose oversize life the movie is based, took offense and ordered a boycott of its cover-age by his newspaper empire. The boycott failed dismally as huge crowds turned out to see the film. In the story of a reporter's attempts to track down the meaning of the

- **JANUARY 20**
FDR is inaugurated for unprecedented third term as Presi-dent of the U.S.

- **FEBRUARY 19**
Work begins on a third of six sets of locks at the Panama Canal.

- **FEBRUARY 26**
A strike called at Bethlehem Steel plants starts in motion the CIO's greatest victory to date.

- **MARCH 17**
The National Gallery of Art opens in Washington, D.C.

- **MARCH 28**
Author Virginia Woolf drowns herself rather than face another nervous breakdown.

- **APRIL 28**
U.S. Supreme Court rules blacks are entitled to all first class services on railroad trains.

- **APRIL 30**
FDR buys the first savings bonds for the defense fund.

ORSON WELLES DAZZLES MOVIEGOERS WITH *CITIZEN KANE.*

last word, "Rosebud," spoken by the man-who-had-it-all, Welles vindicated his reputation as a genius.

▶ DAY OF INFAMY

Sunday, December 7, dawned bright and peaceful, like any other morning at Pearl Harbor, the major U.S. naval base in Hawaii. In peacetime the Pacific Fleet observed Sunday as a holiday, and the officers and men expected a relaxed beginning to the day.

For the attack on Pearl Harbor (below), Japan committed its entire first-line strength of six carriers with more than 460 aircraft to a two-strike plan. Nineteen U.S. ships, including six battleships, were sunk or disabled; some 2,400 soldiers, sailors, and civilians were killed. Japan thought it was delivering a blow that would demoralize and divide the American people. From the moment most Americans learned of

the attack over the radio, however, they united behind the President who declared December 7 a date that would live in infamy.

FAIR EMPLOYMENT

At the urging of Eleanor Roosevelt and to head off a march on Washington planned by A. Philip Randolph, president of the Brotherhood of Sleeping Car Porters, President Roosevelt signed Executive Order 8802 on June 25. The mandate called on employers and unions "to provide for the full and equitable participation of all workers in defense industries, without discrimination because of race, creed, color, or national origin." The Fair Employment Practices Commission was empowered to investigate grievances and publicize findings. The President acted to counter widespread discrimination by defense contractors and in government employment.

When the President signed the executive order, the Chicago *Defender* wrote, "Faith in a democracy which Negroes had begun to feel had strayed from its course was renewed throughout the nation."

▶ BIRTH OF COMMERCIAL TV

In the 1920s astronomical costs, tiny screens, and fuzzy pictures made TV broadcasting cumbersome. In 1939 NBC broadcast President Roosevelt's opening address at the World's Fair. In 1941 NBC and CBS were both granted commercial licenses to broadcast from their New York stations.

By the fall of 1947, there were only 60,000 television sets in U.S. households. Fears that the new medium would disrupt domestic life ran strong. A *New York Times* TV critic wrote "the wife scarcely knows where the kitchen is, let alone her place in it…. The reason is television." Many bars and store windows attracted customers with their new sets. By the 1950s, the sale of television sets exploded around the world.

■ TRENDS & TRIVIA

Mickey Mouse gas masks are issued to British children. Two million children are sent to the countryside for their safety.

Road to Zanzibar opens, starring Bing Crosby, Bob Hope, and Dorothy Lamour.

Hans Haas pioneers underwater photography.

U.S. government freezes Japanese assets in the United States.

The United Service Organizations (USO) is formed to entertain troops around the world. Performers are stars such as Bob Hope, Fred Astaire, and Marlene Dietrich.

U.S. Air Raid Volunteers wear armbands and white helmets and enforce blackout rules, including dimming Broadway's lights.

The jeep, developed a year earlier, makes its combat debut.

The world's first aerosol can is patented. It contains bug spray.

The BBC launches Britain's "V for Victory" campaign.

Americans wear red, white, and blue pins lacquered with "Remember Pearl Harbor."

Elementary schools teach U.S. children to spot enemy planes.

Labor leaders swear off strikes during the war years in order to keep industry strong.

Parade magazine begins publication.

Glen Miller and his orchestra are featured in the movie *Sun Valley Serenade.* ▶

Teenagers popularize slumber parties.

● **MAY 24**
The *Bismarck* sinks the *Hood*, pride of the Royal Navy. On May 27 the British sink the *Bismarck*, pride of the German Navy.

● **JULY 2**
New York Yankee Joe DiMaggio sets record, hitting safely in 56 straight games.

● **AUGUST 5**
An earthquake measuring 6.8 on Richter scale strikes Pelileo, Chile, killing more than 6,000.

● **AUGUST 14**
The Atlantic Charter is adopted by Churchill and Roosevelt.

● **SEPTEMBER 6**
All Germany's Jews over the age of six must wear the Star of David in public.

● **SEPTEMBER 20**
FDR signs largest tax bill to date, increasing U.S. coffers by 35 billion dollars.

● **OCTOBER 16**
40,000 perish in Bengal, India, after hurricane hits.

In the Pacific the first six months of the war saw Japan embark on a wild run that gained it supremacy over 20 million square miles of Asia and the Pacific, a realm five times as great as Germany's at its height of conquest. This quick success was in keeping with the words of Adm. Isoroku Yamamoto, commander in chief of the Combined Fleet, who said, "If I am told to fight regardless of the consequences, I shall run wild for the first six months...." But he also warned, "I have utterly no confidence for the second or third year."

Six months later the tide began to turn at the Battle of Midway, when Adm. Chester W. Nimitz's Pacific Fleet challenged Admiral Yamamoto's fleet, inflicting a matériel loss from which Japan would not recover and altering the course of war in the Pacific.

For Nazi hopes, the high mark was also reached in 1942. German troops occupied 14 European sovereign states: France, Belgium, Holland, Luxembourg, Denmark, Norway, Austria, Czechoslovakia, Poland, Greece, Yugoslavia, and the Baltic states of Estonia, Latvia, and Lithuania. But as the German military arm reached into Russia, Nazi generals began to realize that their reach exceeded their grasp.

▶ SHOOTOUT AT MIDWAY

Listening posts throughout the Pacific picked up a lengthy radio signal in code on May 20, from Admiral Yamamoto to his fleet. U.S. intelligence deciphered the message, and U.S. and Japanese ships began to converge on a tiny speck in the immense Pacific called Midway Island. It was shaping up to be a engagement of aircraft carriers. In a fortuitous climax to the Battle of Midway, which raged from June 3 to 6, American dive bombers spotted four Japanese carriers with planes refueling and rearming. In just five minutes, from 10:25 to 10:30 a.m., on June 4, the air crews crippled three of the four carriers and, with them, the dreams of Japan's New Order in Asia.

▶ BATTLE TO THE DEATH AT STALINGRAD

From August 19, 1942, to February 2, 1943, the Battle of Stalingrad raged. More than a million people died in a struggle marked by close-combat ferocity. The entire city was laid waste. The German Sixth Army, under Gen. Friedrich von Paulus, surrendered. Of the 108,000 men taken prisoner, only 5,000 ever saw Germany again. On the news of Paulus's capitulation, bells rang in the Kremlin, celebrating the first undeniable Russian victory in the war, which, though horrendous, gave hope to the Allies that Germany would be defeated.

▶ TORCH IN NORTH AFRICA

The Battle of El Alamein in Egypt, directed by Lt. Gen. Bernard Montgomery, pushed the Germans, under Field Marshall Erwin Rommel, into retreat on November 4. Four days after the British victory, the Allies launched the largest amphibious invasion the world had yet known. More than 500 ships carried more than 100,000 troops and thousands of tons of supplies to the beaches of Morocco and Algeria. Code-named "Torch," the operation was led

BRITISH TROOPS CAPTURE GERMAN TANK AND SOLDIER.

by U.S. Lt. Gen. Dwight D. Eisenhower. The aim was to squeeze Axis forces out of North Africa and force a change of allegiance from France's Vichy government.

Although the Vichy Deputy Prime Minister Pierre Laval changed sides on November 10, he was disowned by Vichy Prime Minister Pétain, who was still subject to the German occupation of France. But the balance of military power in North Africa ultimately shifted to the Allies.

▶ THE MANHATTAN PROJECT

On a visit to FDR's home in Hyde Park, New York, in 1942, Winston Churchill brought up the subject of "tube alloys," the British code name for atomic weapon research, to Roosevelt. The President agreed to undertake the research in the United States and to fund the program, which became known as the Manhattan Project. Brig. Gen. Leslie R. Groves was put in command, and physicist J. Robert Oppenheimer became scientific director. Scientists gathered secretly at Los Alamos, New Mexico, and the race was on to beat the Germans in finding a way to split the atom and release a destructive force hitherto unknown to humans.

▶ *ENDLÖSUNG*

In January a secret meeting was held at the headquarters of Interpol, of which Heinrich Himmler was president, in the suburbs of Berlin. Deputy Chief of the

---

- **JANUARY 1**
U.S. Office of Production Management bans sale of new cars in the U.S.

- **JANUARY 29**
The U.S. office of Civil Defense is established.

- **JANUARY 30**
Emergency Price Control Act takes effect, giving the Price Administration the power to place ceilings on rents and prices in the U.S.

- **FEBRUARY 9**
War time goes into effect, moving U.S. clocks an hour ahead.

- **FEBRUARY 15**
Singapore surrenders to the Japanese—more than 130,000 British troops are captured.

- **MARCH**
The BBC begins broadcast of a daily Morse code news bulletin to the French Resistance.

- **APRIL 10**
Bataan Death March begins. Japanese force American and Philippine prisoners to march northward under horrific conditions; 10,000 will die.

SS Reinhard Heydrich proposed and received authority to institutionalize the massacre of the Jews, a program to be named *Endlösung* (the Final Solution). Until then most Jews had been killed by mass shootings, which Himmler condemned as inefficient. Now work camps became extermination camps, such as Treblinka and Sobibor, where Jews were gassed on arrival. Auschwitz, in southern Poland, served both the purposes of working people to death and gassing them. The machinery of the Final Solution and Nazi domination were profoundly connected, enabling the Nazis to rule by terror and sadistic brutality.

▶ WOMEN PITCH IN

The Women's Army Auxiliary Corps was created in May, giving women the opportunity to serve with the Army as clerks, telephone operators, cooks, airplane spotters, telegraphers, secretaries, and drivers. The response was astounding. On the first day of registration, more than 13,000 applied—

an "infinite variety," *Life* noted, "college girls and career women, shop girls and stenographers, housewives and widows." In time, 350,000 women would serve in the Women's Army Corps and the Women Accepted for Voluntary Emergency Service in the Navy (WAVES). On a visit to Fort Des Moines the following year, Eleanor Roosevelt admired the adventurous spirit of the "army behind the fighting forces."

▶ JAPANESE INTERNMENT

War hysteria swept the United States after the Japanese attack on Pearl Harbor. Panic and rumors particularly infected the West Coast

RATIONING

In a fireside chat, President Roosevelt explained the need for comprehensive rationing, designed to ensure, as he said, "an equality of sacrifice." Also, to combat inflation, prices were fixed at the highest price charged for the item in March 1942. Rationing of gasoline, rubber, sugar, meat, and other items frustrated shoppers and changed ways of life. Yet the rationing cards reminded every citizen of the reason for sacrifice—the redirection of the economy toward the production of airplanes, tanks, and other equipment necessary to support the war effort. To cope with the restrictions of rationing, families began growing Victory Gardens, and the Sunday drive became a memory of prewar days.

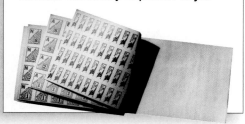

where fears of a Japanese attack on coastal communities led to roundups of immigrant Japanese and their American-born children. The pressure led President Roosevelt, on February 19, 1942, to issue Executive Order 9066, permitting areas "from which any or all persons may be excluded."

Families hastily packed personal belongings and sold their possessions at rock bottom prices to scavengers. They left their fields unharvested, closed their shops, and said goodbye to friends before reporting to the War Relocation Authority, which took them to camps where a 20 by 25-foot room was allotted per household. The order was rescinded in 1944, and the last of the camps closed in March 1946.

■ TRENDS & TRIVIA

Bing Crosby's recording of Irving Berlin's "White Christmas" is a huge hit.

James Cagney stars in *Yankee Doodle Dandy*.

Jacqueline Cochran founds the Women's Air Force Service Pilots (WASPs).

Stars and Stripes, the daily paper for U.S. GIs in Europe, is published in Britain.

Magnetic recording tape is developed.

Bell Aircraft tests first jet plane.

Albert Camus writes *The Stranger*.

Dannon Yogurt and Raisin Bran hit the grocery store shelves.

Soldiers can expect Spam, powdered eggs, and baked beans on the mess-hall menu.

A "Dear John" letter comes to mean a letter of rejection from a former sweetheart.

Pleasure driving screams to a halt due to gas rationing. A, B, and C windshield stickers determine amount of gasoline allotted.

Women simulate hosiery by painting their legs with makeup and drawing black "seams" on their calves.

Polyester clothing is introduced.

Selman Waksman discovers Streptomycin, an antibiotic effective against tuberculosis.

Humphrey Bogart and Ingrid Bergman star in the classic World War II film *Casablanca*. ▶

Irving Berlin's musical, *This Is the Army* premiers at New York City's Broadway Theater.

• MAY 29
Legendary actor John Barrymore known as "The Great Profile" dies at 60.

• JUNE 22
First V-Mail, letters transferred to microfilm, are sent from New York to London.

• JUNE 21
A Japanese submarine shells the Oregon coast.

• AUGUST 7
U.S. Marines land on Guadacanal, beginning the first major U.S. amphibious operation in the Pacific.

• NOVEMBER 18
Vichy France cuts off diplomatic relations with the United States.

• NOVEMBER 29
Cocoanut Grove fire, the worst in modern times in the U.S., kills 487 at a Boston nightclub.

• DECEMBER 2
American physicist Enrico Fermi achieves the first sustained nuclear chain reaction.

• DECEMBER 21
U.S. Supreme Court rules that Nevada divorces are valid in all states.

During 1943 the balance of power began to shift in favor of the Allies. In the ongoing Battle of the Atlantic, March was a decisive month, as German U-boat strength reached a peak, but better convoy methods resulted in safer crossings. Air coverage improved, and June was the quietest month since the battle in the gray North Atlantic began. While U-boats did not give up the fight, it became clear that the Allies could limit losses, better detect U-boats, and produce more tonnage than they lost.

British Gen. Bernard Montgomery and American Gen. Dwight D. Eisenhower finally pushed German Field Marshall Erwin Rommel—the Desert Fox—out of North Africa. The Allies swept on to Sicily, then to the Italian mainland.

Agonizing struggles took place in the Pacific as the Allies began island-hopping toward Japan.

In Japan-occupied China, European colonialism came conspicuously and symbolically to an end as the foreign community was rounded up and marched away to prison camps. Such scenes were now familiar throughout Japan's new Pacific empire as the British and Dutch colonial authorities faced public humiliation before their former subjects.

▶ ALLIES INVADE AXIS HOME FRONT

Following a planned deception involving a corpse bearing false papers that convinced Hitler that an enemy invasion fleet would be heading for Greece, Corsica, or Sardinia, the Allies landed in Sicily—the first Allied troops to set foot on Axis home ground. The British and Americans had disagreed about the invasion of Italy, in the "soft underbelly," as Churchill phrased it. The U.S. agreed to the plan only if it did not distract from eventual landings in northern France. While the invasion of Sicily led to the downfall of Mussolini, and a change of allegiance of the Italian government, the Allies' slog up the backbone of Italy would be bloody.

AMERICAN TROOPS ENTER PALERMO, SICILY.

▶ GREATEST TANK BATTLE IN HISTORY

Considered by many to be the turning point of the war in Europe, the Battle of Kursk marked the first time that a defending force checked a German blitzkrieg. More than 6,000 tanks clashed in the muddied fields around the Russian city of Kursk, where defenders had dug a staggering 3,750 miles of antitank trenches. In the end, Marshal Georgi Konstantiovich Zhukov withstood the German onslaught by using battle techniques from earlier wars—trench labyrinths and massed artillery—coupled with minefields. After Kursk, Germany's blitzkrieg would never again win a major offensive on the Eastern Front.

WOMEN AND CHILDREN OF WARSAW, POLAND, UNDER NAZI CAPTORS

▶ WARSAW GHETTO UPRISING

The Warsaw Ghetto had been walled in by the Germans in 1940. The Jewish inhabitants were permitted little food or contact with the outside world. In July 1942 deportations of Jews began, at the rate of more than 6,000 a day. A young prisoner named Abraham Krzepicki escaped from the death camp of Treblinka and warned the people. The Jews took up what arms they could and fought heroically street by street against the overwhelming force of German bombs, shells, and fire under SS Gen. Jürgen Stroop. From April 19 to May 16, the struggle continued. About 70 fighters escaped through the sewers; some 7,000 died among the ruins; and more than 56,000 were transported to Treblinka or work camps. Yet their heroic resistance won a moral victory.

▶ RACE RIOTS BREAK OUT

As Americans went on the move, migrating from rural areas to cities to work in war plants, racial tensions escalated over competition for housing, transportation, and recreation. Race riots occurred in Mobile, New York City, and Los Angeles. One of the worst erupted in Detroit on June 20, where 300,000 whites and blacks had recently moved to work in factories. The governor of Michigan did not ask for federal troops until almost a day into the rioting. Finally, some 3,800 federal troops arrived, impos-

---

• **FEBRUARY 7**
Shoe rationing is set at three pairs per year in the U.S.

• **FEBRUARY 9**
FDR orders a minimum 48-hour workweek in war plants.

• **FEBRUARY 13**
U.S. Marine Corps adds a women's unit.

• **APRIL 8**
Missionary Mary Reed, who worked with lepers in India for almost 50 years, dies.

• **APRIL 17**
Essential U.S. workers are prohibited by War Manpower Commission from leaving their jobs.

• **MAY 27**
Striking Akron, Ohio, rubber workers are ordered back to work by FDR.

• **JUNE 14**
The U.S. Supreme Court rules that children need not salute the flag in schools.

ing order but not before 25 blacks and 9 whites had been killed, nearly a thousand injured, and hundreds arrested.

▶ MASSACRE IN THE FOREST

In the spring of 1943, a horrible discovery was unearthed in the Katyn Forest near the Russian city of Smolensk. Peasants reported that in the early months of 1940 they had seen men being dragged out of railway cars and taken into the forest. Germans, who held the territory, investigated and discovered the graves (right) of Polish officers, hands bound, all shot in the back of the head. An international team of scientists concluded that the victims had been killed in 1940 when the Russians held sway in the area. The dead— about 4,500—had

probably refused Communist indoctrination. The fate of another 11,000 who disappeared remains unknown.

▶ PENICILLIN IS MASS PRODUCED

A researcher working in a government laboratory in Peoria, Illinois, noticed that mold on a cantaloupe at a local market grew rapidly. His observation led to new deep-fermentation techniques that yielded ten times as much penicillin as the original mold obtained by Sir Alexander Fleming in England in 1928. The new ability to produce mass amounts of penicillin meant that every wounded soldier and every civilian needing treatment against infection could now receive it.

▶ THE GI IN THE POPULAR IMAGINATION

Since 1941, readers back home had been following the movements, experiences, and

AUTOMATIC TAXES

"A revolution in American public finance," wrote journalist David Brinkley, about a change in the method of collecting taxes signed into law in 1943. Before the war, individuals paid their taxes in quarterly installments on the income they had earned the previous year. That system had worked well enough when relatively few people paid relatively little in taxes. But now, with millions of people being taxed to support the war effort, a change was needed. In the new "Pay As You Go" system, workers had their taxes withheld from their paychecks as they earned the money. Since everyone began the year free from tax debt, and because people were now paying their taxes with money they never actually held, there was less opposition to increasing taxes.

emotions of the troops away at war through newspaper columns. War correspondent Ernie Pyle became an American folk hero as he chronicled the lives of the servicemen overseas, giving their families at home a sense of what their boys were going through. Cartoonists Bill Mauldin (below) and George Baker created their own popular characters for the armed forces newspapers. In "Up Front with Mauldin," two dog-tired, war-weary GIs named Willie and Joe gave face to

the men fighting in Europe. Their humor carried a bitter edge. "Just gimme th' aspirin. I already got a Purple Heart." Baker drew "The Sad Sack," a messy but well-intentioned GI always in trouble.

■ TRENDS & TRIVIA

The first telephone answering machines take calls in Switzerland.

The slang word, "snafu," slips into daily language. It means "situation normal, all fouled up."

The first kidney machine is developed.

Betty Smith writes *A Tree Grows in Brooklyn*.

Nobel Prize is awarded for the discovery of Vitamin K .

Hepcats and other music fanatics, look hip in zoot suits with pleats.

The Allied slogan "Use it up, wear it out, make it do, or do without" echoes throughout the home front.

The All American Girls' Baseball League is founded. It will eventually attract one million spectators.

Shivering transatlantic flying-boat passengers drink an Irish chef's new beverage—Irish coffee.

Classes at Harvard go coed.

Oscar Hammerstein and Richard Rodgers collaborate for the first time, on *Oklahoma!*

Jacques Yves Cousteau and Émile Gagnan successfully test their underwater device, the Aqua-Lung.

The American Broadcasting Company (ABC) is created.

The Pentagon is completed at a cost of 83 million dollars. It is the world's largest office building.

As vegetables become scarce, communal plots known as Victory Gardens become popular on the home front.

Judy Johnson becomes the first female jockey to win a professional race, in Maryland.

- **JULY 19**
The Big Inch, the world's longest oil pipeline to date, extending from Texas to Pennsylvania, is dedicated.

- **OCTOBER 5-11**
The World Series celebrates its 40th birthday; the New York Yankees defeat St. Louis Cardinals four games to one.

- **OCTOBER 17**
Chicago subway formally opens.

- **NOVEMBER**
Leonard Bernstein makes his debut conducting the New York Philharmonic Orchestra.

- **NOVEMBER**
American troops take Tarawa Island, an atoll in the Gilbert Islands, from the Japanese.

- **DECEMBER 22**
British children's writer Beatrix Potter, creator of *Peter Rabbit*, dies.

- **DECEMBER 24**
American Gen. Dwight D. Eisenhower is named Supreme Commander of Allied forces for invasion of Europe.

ALLIES PRESS THE ADVANTAGE

On the Eastern Front, Russia made relentless but costly advances against the Germans. Bitter fighting in Italy raged for months, one of the most hard-fought clashes taking place at the mountain stronghold of Monte Cassino and the medieval Benedictine abbey above the town. But on June 4, Rome was liberated.

On June 6 (D day), Operation Overlord landed 155,000 Allied troops on the northern coast of France. The Allies pushed on, aiming to free Paris. By year's end, Americans stood within reach of Germany's borders.

Japan, faced with an enervating war in China and a perilous hold on its island possessions, saw its defensive perimeter begin to shrink. The Axis war-making capabilities, nevertheless, were still formidable. The Germans launched their "secret weapon," V-1 pilotless bombs, against London, while the Japanese, fighting suicidally almost to the last man, inflicted horrendous casualties on U.S. forces.

AMERICANS DEBARK ON D DAY.

WAR ABOVE BERLIN

The Royal Air Force's Bomber Command, in night raids on cities, and the U.S. Eighth Air Force, in daytime attacks on industrial targets, strangled German war production, especially its oil supply, and established mastery in the air. With the deployment of the P-51B Mustang, a long-range fighter equipped with a Rolls-Royce engine, the Allies now had fighter coverage with the endurance to reach Berlin. Some one million of Berlin's four-and-a-half million inhabitants fled; those remaining endured the most sustained attack from the air of any population in World War II. By April 1944, some 1.5 million Berliners were homeless, and 2,000 city acres had been leveled.

GREATEST AMPHIBIOUS ASSAULT

Under Gen. Dwight D. Eisenhower, Supreme Allied Commander, Operation Overlord, history's most complex amphibious invasion, placed 155,000 U.S., British, Canadian, and French troops on the beaches of Normandy on June 6.

In bad weather the seaborne assault forces, transported and supported by some 5,000 ships covered by more than 3,000 planes, went ashore at points between Cherbourg and Le Havre at beaches codenamed Sword, Juno, Gold, Utah, and Omaha. It was on Omaha that two U.S. divisions faced the fiercest opposition from an unanticipated crack anti-invasion force, but by nightfall, at the cost of 3,000 casualties, the Americans had established a two-mile-deep beachhead.

In the coming months the Allies would have to punch through the hedgerows of Normandy, earthen banks dating from the Middle Ages that surrounded every field. Despite the advantage of almost impregnable defensive lines every few hundred yards, the Germans would succumb to an Allied breakthrough at the town of St. Lô.

ANNE FRANK

"In spite of everything, I still believe that people are really good at heart," wrote a 14-year-old Jewish girl named Anne Frank (above) in her diary, a record of the more than two years she and her family and four other people spent hiding from the Nazis in the backrooms of an Amsterdam warehouse. Friends brought them food, but someone betrayed them, and the Gestapo broke down the door. Anne died of typhus at Belsen camp in March 1945. Of the family, only the father survived the war. Anne's diary is vivid and haunting. First published in Dutch in 1947, in English in 1952, and ultimately in more than 30 languages, *The Diary of Anne Frank* has kept her memory—and the memory of the individual horrors of the Holocaust—alive.

BATTLE OF THE BULGE

In the winter of 1944, Hitler launched his last offensive on the Western Front in what became known as the Battle of the Bulge—named for the deformation in Allied lines caused by the German advance. On the morning of December 16, the Fifth and Sixth panzer divisions fell like a thunderstorm on the unsuspecting American defenders in the Ardennes. Eisenhower suspected a major offensive was in the making and ordered two armored divisions to the area. The capture of the town of Bastogne was key to German success, and

---

• **JUNE 4**
Allied troops enter Rome. Since it is a holy day, they wait until the following day to occupy the city.

• **JUNE**
Napalm is used for the first time in warfare by the UK.

• **JUNE 22**
Serviceman's Readjustment Act (GI Bill) is signed, granting returned servicemen broad benefits.

• **JULY 22**
Nazis reveal plot of army officers to overthrow Hitler's regime.

◄ **AUGUST 25**
Paris is liberated by allied troops. Grateful French bestow kisses on U.S. soldiers.

on Christmas Day Bastogne was surrounded by German troops. But progress against the defiant and reinforced Allies proved elusive, and by January 16 the Allied front was restored.

▶ LIBERATION OF PARIS

After four years of German occupation, Parisians sensed that liberation was at hand. As resistance in the streets mounted against the Germans, Allied leaders felt obliged to come to the aid of the insurgents. The French 2nd Armoured Division, which owed allegiance to Gen. Charles de Gaulle and was under the command of Gen. Philippe Leclerc, received orders from Eisenhower to advance to the city. Hitler

GEN. DE GAULLE LEADS A PARADE CELEBRATING LIBERATION.

had ordered the German commander, Gen. Dietrich von Choltitz, to leave the city "a field of ruins," but he agreed to a cease-fire instead. On August 25 Allied troops swept into Paris on "a physical wave of human emotion," wrote American Maj. Frank Burk, riding through "fifteen solid miles of cheering, deliriously happy people...."

▶ POSTWAR PLANNING

With a vision of Allied victory clearly in sight, the world's non-Axis nations met at a resort called Bretton Woods in New Hampshire from July 1 to 22, to ensure an open postwar economy through the creation of new global economic institutions. The

ROSIE'S RIVETS

Few characters of World War II folklore enjoyed more immediate recognition than Rosie the Riveter. Fictional Rosie was honored in the words of a popular song, "It's the girl that makes the thing that holds the oil that oils the ring, that works the thingamabob that's going to win the war." Norman Rockwell painted her portrait for the May 29, 1943, cover of the *Saturday Evening Post*, her right foot making a stool out of *Mein Kampf*, a riveter slung across her lap like a machine gun.

Her real-life counterparts numbered in the millions. By 1944, 35 percent of American women were counted in the workforce. Women were laid off or fired as the war wound down, expected by society at large to return to the home. But a profound change had been wrought. Women remembered and valued the independence, the pay, and the respect they had earned in the workplace.

framework for the International Monetary Fund was established to help stabilize currencies. The International Bank for Reconstruction and Development (now known as the World Bank) was intended to lend money to member nations for long-term capital improvements.

From August 21 to October 7, the United States, Great Britain, China, and the Soviet Union met at a Washington, D.C., estate called Dumbarton Oaks to frame the structure of a postwar security organization. In time, that vision became the United Nations.

■ TRENDS & TRIVIA

Quinine is used to ward off malaria.

The Maquis, French underground resistance fighters, number 35,000.

Pilots can direct guns, rockets, bombs, and torpedoes automatically with the new Pilot's Universal Sighting System.

First eye bank opens for business.

First high-fidelity recordings are released.

Tennessee Williams's *The Glass Menagerie* is published.

The cost of living climbs almost 30 percent in the U.S.

Massachusetts lifts its ban on the novel about interracial love, *Strange Fruit,* by Lillian Smith.

National Velvet stars 11-year-old Elizabeth Taylor.

The U.S. Army Air Corps takes the first night reconnaissance photos.

Ballet *Appalachian Spring*, with music by Aaron Copland and choreography by Martha Graham, premieres.

30,000 fans gather to hear Frank Sinatra sing at New York's Paramount Theatre, where he makes young girls swoon.

World's first underwater oil pipeline is laid beneath the English Channel.

The International Red Cross is awarded Nobel Peace Prize.

Going My Way wins Academy Award for best picture.

Joe Nuxhall, 15-year-old Cincinnati Reds pitcher, is the youngest-ever major league baseball player.

I Remember Mama opens at the Music Box in New York City.

183

• AUGUST
Britain passes an education act that provides all British children with free education.

• OCTOBER 20
General MacArthur lands on Leyte, fulfilling his promise, "I shall return."

• NOVEMBER 1
Quadruplets are delivered by cesarean section for the first time.

• NOVEMBER
U.S. surgeon performs first successful heart operation on a newborn infant.

• NOVEMBER 7
FDR wins a fourth term as President.

• DECEMBER
Civil war breaks out in Greece.

• DECEMBER 16
Glenn Miller's plane, en route from Paris to London, is reported missing.

"Fighting all over the globe reaches a climax of fury," said President Roosevelt in his January 1945 budget address to Congress. A monumental year, 1945 saw the end of the war in Europe and Asia and the beginnings of the atomic and electronic age. In Berlin, fighting was street to street, house to house, but on

May 2, Germany surrendered to Soviet Marshal Zhukov. On May 8 Prime Minister Winston Churchill and the new American President, Harry S. Truman, declared V-E (Victory-in-Europe) Day (above).

Japan fought on. Kamikaze (divine wind) suicide bombers reinforced American dread about the cost in lives involved in invading the home islands. In the spring and summer, U.S. B-29 Superfortresses fire-bombed Japan's wood-built and crowded cities. On August 6 the U.S. dropped an atomic bomb on the city of Hiroshima. A second bomb three days later scorched Nagasaki. Japan surrendered on August 14.

▶ FIREBOMBING DRESDEN AND TOKYO

On February 13-15, 1945, RAF and USAF bombers created a firestorm that reduced Dresden, the last undevastated city of the Reich, to rubble and consumed perhaps 60,000 civilian lives. The inscription on a mass grave in Dresden asks, "Who knows the number?"

On March 9-10, Bomber Command attacked Tokyo with 325 aircraft, armed with highly inflammable jellified gasoline, flying at low altitude under cover of darkness. The sun rose on a city engulfed in flames, some 16 square miles, with more than 80,000 dead. The temperature was so hot in the heart of the firestorm that the water in the city's canals boiled.

▶ THE BIG THREE AT YALTA

In February 1945, Churchill, Roosevelt, and Stalin (below) met at Yalta in the Crimea to determine the shape of postwar East and Central Europe. Each leader had his own priorities. Roosevelt wanted an accord on the new international security organization and Russia's agreement to declare war on Japan. Churchill wanted to maintain the British Empire and keep a

balance of power in Europe. Stalin particularly wanted to control the borders of Poland, make Germany bear costly reparations, and grab land in the Far East. In the end, Roosevelt gave way over the matter of Poland's borders. In time, the Yalta

Conference came to be criticized as a failure in foreign policy—perhaps due in part to Roosevelt's clearly failing health.

▶ AMPHIBIOUS BATTLE IN THE PACIFIC

With the retaking of the Philippines in October 1944, and the capture of the Marianas in November 1944, the war in the Pacific entered its final climactic phase. Now, operations would combine the amphibious skills of sailors, soldiers, and airmen. On February 19, the 3rd, 4th, and 5th Marine Divisions assaulted Iwo Jima in what would become the Marines' worst landing experience of the Pacific war. War correspondent Robert Sherrod said that men died "with the greatest possible violence." The enemy, heavily gunned and well garrisoned, had dug into the basaltic bedrock and had honey-combed the island with tunnels. Before the island was secured, on March 16, 6,800 Americans had been killed and 20,000 wounded. The 21,000 Japanese defenders died almost to a man.

Iwo Jima gave Americans a foretaste of what would happen when U.S. Marines invaded Okinawa, a large island on the approaches to Japan's heartland. On April 1, an armada of 1,300 ships, including 18 battleships, 40 carriers, and 200 destroyers, supported the 1st and 6th Marines and 7th and 96th Divisions in their race to the shore. The Japanese had fortressed themselves in the hills of the 80-mile-long island, and on April 6, kamikazis attacked the support ships in dense waves. Not until late June was Okinawa declared taken. The American forces had lost 12,500 and the Japanese 110,000, with 7,400 refusing to surrender.

▶ HOLOCAUST HORROR EMERGES

Early in 1945, even Heinrich Himmler, chief of the Gestapo and Minister of the Interior responsible for the death camps,

184

• JANUARY 27
Auschwitz concentration camp, in Poland, is liberated.

• MARCH 9
Les Enfant du Paradis premieres in France.

• APRIL 18
Beloved war correspondent Ernie Pyle is killed by machine gun fire in the Pacific.

• APRIL 18
Dachau concentration camp, in Germany, is liberated.

• MAY 1
Nazi propaganda mastermind Joseph Goebbels commits suicide.

• MAY 8
V-E Day for victory in Europe.

• JUNE 26
The United Nations Charter is signed in San Francisco.

recognized that Germany would not win the war. But he was determined that Jews and slave laborers should not fall into Allied hands to tell their tale, and he ordered all prisoners to be herded west ahead of the Soviet advance. Of the 10,000 from camps around Danzig, only a dozen survived the forced march. Thousands died of starvation and disease in the older concentration camps inside Germany such as Belsen and Dachau. One Dachau prisoner recalled how he felt when the tanks rolled in, "We were free! We broke into weeping, kissed the tank. A Negro soldier gave us a tin of meat, bread, and chocolate. We sat down on the ground and ate up all the food together. The Negro watched us, tears in his eyes."

▶ SIEGE OF BERLIN

Eisenhower ordered his troops to stop at the Elbe and Mülde Rivers on April 25 as Soviet forces encircled Berlin and fought to the steps of the Reich Chancellery and the Reichstag. On April 30, as heavy Russian shells demolished the Chancellery, Hitler, 55 feet underground in a bunker, took poison and shot himself with a service revolver. On April 26 Mussolini had been caught trying to flee. On the 28th he was shot by partisans and, with his mistress, hung upside down in a city square in Milan. The Red Army lost more than 300,000 men in the Battle of Berlin. About 125,000 Berliners died during the siege.

▶ WAR ENDS IN ASIA

On the morning of August 6, the B-29 *Enola Gay* (right) dropped an atomic bomb on Hiroshima and in a matter of minutes 78,000 people lay dead or dying in the ruins. More would die later of radiation sickness. The White House called on the Japanese to surrender or "they may expect a rain of ruin from the air." No word was received, and on August 9, another B-29 delivered an atomic blast on the city of Nagasaki, killing 25,000. Six days later, Emperor

Hirohito broadcast to his people the news that Japan had surrendered the day before. On September 2, aboard the battleship *Missouri* in Tokyo Bay, Gen. Douglas Mac-Arthur accepted the papers of surrender. The war was over.

FDR IS DEAD

Winston Churchill once said that to encounter Franklin Roosevelt with his buoyant sparkle, his iridescent personality, and his inner élan, was like opening your first bottle of champagne. "He was one of the few statesmen in the twentieth century, or any century," the British philosopher Isaiah Berlin wrote, "who seemed to have no fear of the future." Yet having occupied the Presidency into an unprecedented fourth term, from the Depression through the darkest day of the Second World War to the Yalta Conference and plans for a postwar world, Roosevelt had begun to show the toll.

At the "Little White House" in Warm Springs, Georgia, where he had gone to rest, the President suffered a cerebral hemorrhage and died at 3:35 p.m. on April 12.

At 5:30 Vice President Harry Truman was summoned to the White House. Eleanor Roosevelt stepped forth to greet him, saying gently, "Harry, the President is dead." When Truman asked if there was anything he could do for her, she is reputed to have replied, "Is there anything we can do for you? For you are the one in trouble now."

■ TRENDS & TRIVIA

The world's first water supply with fluoride is available in Michigan.

Dr. Claus Maertens invents Doc Marten shoes after suffering a ski injury.

First microwave oven is patented in the U.S.

U.S. farm prices reach their highest levels since 1920.

Tupperware is developed.

Bumper stickers are new, manufactured in Kansas.

Hairstyles such as the Tony Curtis, the Boston Box, and the flattop are flaunted by teenage boys.

After the war, black markets that trade food, clothing, and cigarettes develop in Europe.

America laughs at "Who's on First" routine by Abbott and Costello. ▶

Frozen orange juice and frozen dinners are offered in the U.S.

Warner Brothers popularizes Sylvester the Cat.

Fluorescent lighting is first used, in Europe.

Benadryl is developed to treat colds and allergies.

World Bank becomes an agency of the UN to promote loans for needy countries.

The first post-war Volkswagen Beetles come on the market.

Joan Crawford stars in *Mildred Pierce.*

Silly Putty is accidentally discovered.

▶ **JULY 8**
DDT is sprayed on Jones Beach, New York, in the first public test of the Todd Insecticidal Fog Applicator.

● **JULY 16**
First atomic bomb is tested in Los Alamos desert.

● **JULY 28**
B-25 bomber crashes into Empire State Building, killing 14.

● **AUGUST 18**
Truman orders restoration of civilian economy, including free market.

● **SEPTEMBER 2**
Ho Chi Minh declares Vietnam a republic.

In an "election speech" on February 9, Stalin made clear that the Soviet Union would turn to itself to rebuild its war-devastated economy in a series of Five-year plans that would require sacrifice on the part of the people. Consumer goods must "wait on rearmament." Stalin, thus, rejected the international economic arrangements set forth at Bretton Woods. A war between capitalism and communism, he said, was inevitable. U.S. Supreme Court Justice William O. Douglas characterized Stalin's speech as "the declaration of World War III." On March 5, former British Prime Minister Winston Churchill (above left, with Truman), in a speech given in Fulton, Missouri, declared that "an iron curtain has descended across the Continent." Churchill called for the United States to stand with the British Commonwealth in opposing the spread of Soviet influence. U.S. policymakers were hesitant about accepting the reality of Churchill's image, but before the year was out, American attitudes toward the Soviet Union, its wartime ally, began to change.

▶ INDEPENDENCE OF THE PHILIPPINES

On the morning of July 4, 1946, a flag nobly ascended into the morning sky proclaiming the independence of the Republic of the Philippines. Church bells rang across the war-ravaged islands. Japan's five years of occupation during World War II had been difficult. Manila, the capital and soul of the country, lay close to ruins. Cholera raged unchecked, and economic disparity further tested the new independent nation whose struggle for autonomy had lasted 425 years. In 1521 Spain had claimed the islands and had remained in control for 333 years. Despite resistance to foreign rule, it wasn't until the Spanish-American War of 1898, when the underground resistance joined forces with the United States, that plans for Spain's fall seemed imminent. Yet, four hours after U.S. troops rushed into Manila, they raised the United States flag—instead of the Philippine flag. It took until March 1934 to agree on a ten-year transition period to independence. Three years before promised autonomy, Japan attacked the Philippines. During the occupation, 10,000 men perished in death marches to prison camps and more than a million died by the end of World War II. With peace established, the Philippines finally became an independent nation.

▶ THE KEYNESIAN REVOLUTION

John Maynard Keynes was a British economist who achieved prominence with the publication in 1919 of *The Economic Consequences of the Peace*, which criticized, correctly as it turned out, the reparations imposed on Germany. Keynes advanced the innovative idea that national governments had financial responsibilities beyond balancing budgets and had a role to play in influencing market forces. In an economic depression, he argued, governments should increase their public spending, even incurring deficit spending if necessary. Keynes's 1936 book, *The General Theory of Employment, Interest, and Money*, influenced postwar government policies. Keynes played an important part in the Bretton Woods Conference of 1944, and his economic theories held sway in the policies and thinking of Western governments into the 1980s. He died April 21, 1946, at age 63.

▶ TRUMAN'S EMPLOYMENT ACT

A landmark piece of legislation from the Truman Administration, the Employment Act of 1946, incorporated Keynesian ideas of the role of governments in the employment levels of their people and gave hope of jobs to the millions of returning GIs. Though failing to call for full employment, as Truman had wished, the bill nevertheless gave the federal government the power to "use all practical means" to foster "maximum employment." The bill also set up a President's Economic Council, the first of its kind, to assess the economic outlook, analyze the effects of government programs and policies, and provide an annual economic report.

▶ JUDGMENT AT NUREMBERG

Held in the city where only a dozen years earlier Hitler's speeches had whipped crowds into a frenzy, the Nuremberg trials brought 21 defendants—from the German general staff, government, and Nazi Party—to answer charges of war crimes, crimes against peace, and crimes against humanity. The trials continued, with brief recesses, from November 1945 to August 1946. The evidence brought to the world's conscience the unspeakable atrocities at

---

- **JANUARY 1**
Japan's Emperor Hirohito declares his divinity is a myth.

- **FEBRUARY 12**
U.S. report finds Nazis have been given refuge in Argentina.

- **MARCH 22**
First U.S.-built rocket leaves Earth's atmosphere, reaching a 50-mile height.

- **APRIL 1**
Tsunami kills 179 people in Hawaii and wraps railroad tracks around trees.

- **MAY 1**
U.S. and Britain draw up plan to divide Palestine into separate Jewish and Arab states.

- **JUNE 3**
Supreme Court in *Morgan* v. *Commonwealth* rules that buses must allow seating without regard to race in interstate commerce.

- **JUNE 25**
Ho Chi Minh travels to France to discuss Vietnamese independence.

camps such as Dachau, Buchenwald, and Belsen. The defense was usually, "I was only following orders." The judgments acquitted two, sentenced eight to prison terms, and condemned eleven to death. Among the last was Hermann Göring, commander of the Luftwaffe, who poisoned himself on the eve of execution.

In Tokyo the Allies tried 25 of Japan's leaders for general war crimes, and 7 were sentenced to death, including Gen. Hideki Tojo, Japan's Minister of War.

▶ ENIAC GOES INTO ACTION

Weighing in at 30 tons, a new computer called ENIAC (below), for Electronic Numerical Integrator and Calculator, was built by J. P. Eckert and J. W. Mauchly at the University of Pennsylvania. ENIAC had 18,000 vacuum tubes and could accomplish 5,000 steps a second, adding, multiplying, dividing, and calculating square roots. The

War Department planned on using ENIAC for, among other things, artillery calculations, while International Business Machines (IBM) aimed to design a less powerful calculator for commercial use.

▶ THE GI BILL

In 1946 returning veterans found that the "GI Bill of Rights," signed into law by President Roosevelt in June 1944, not only helped them ease back into civilian life but

DR. SPOCK

"The cry of the baby was heard across the land," wrote historian Landon Jones of the baby boom that followed World War II. By year's end, 3.4 million babies were in their bassinets. Just in time to help their parents, in 1946 a new book appeared on the scene—*The Common Sense Book of Baby and Child Care*, by Benjamin Spock, M.D. (right). "Trust yourself. You know more than you think you do," his book began. His advice to "be natural and play with your baby" was a departure from prevailing rigid childrearing practices.

The book was one of the publishing world's all-time success stories. It sold millions throughout the second half of the century, spawned countless similar books, and guided generations of Americans and others with its flexible, practical advice.

also expanded their educational horizons and gave untold millions a secure grasp on middle-class life. The GI Bill, designed to provide the returning veteran with access to education, training, and status he could not otherwise have experienced, provided numerous special benefits. It helped buy houses and secure loans, gave those who could not find a job $20 a week for 52 weeks, and financed construction of additional hospitals. The veterans made the most of this extraordinary empowering legislation in the years following the war.

■ TRENDS & TRIVIA

The first car with electric windows impresses consumers.

China leads the world's population with 455 million people.

The pilot ejector seat is tested.

The first bikini debuts in Paris.

Estimates put lives lost in the war at 35 million, plus 10 million more deaths in Nazi concentration camps.

Radios play the tunes "Zip-a-dee-doo-dah" and "Shoo-fly Pie and Apple Pan Dowdy."

At a medical symposium at the University of Buffalo, it is suggested that smoking and lung cancer may be linked.

The longest on-screen kiss wins Cary Grant and Ingrid Bergman notoriety.

Adm. Richard E. Byrd explores and maps the Antarctic. He discovers nine mountain ranges.

The U.S. Central Intelligence Agency (CIA) is established.

It's a Wonderful Life, starring Donna Reed and James Stewart, appears in theaters.

Annie Get Your Gun, starring Ethel Merman, opens on Broadway.

Eastman Kodak introduces Ektachrome color film.

The "Eisenhower jacket" becomes fashionable. Women wear it as a blouse.

French singer Edith Piaf becomes an international star with her recording of "La Vie en Rose." ▶

Tide laundry soap is introduced by Proctor & Gamble.

● **JULY 7**
Mother Cabrini, founder of the Missionary Sisters of the Sacred Heart of Jesus, is canonized by Pope Pius XII.

● **JULY 30**
U.S. joins UNESCO (United Nations Educational, Scientific, and Cultural Organization).

● **AUGUST 1**
The U.S. Atomic Energy Commission is created.

● **SEPTEMBER 7**
U.S. announces it will build an atomic submarine.

● **OCTOBER 30**
Shoe rationing ends in U.S.

● **NOVEMBER 25**
Oregon's Indians are granted land payment rights.

● **DECEMBER 7**
A fire kills 127 and injures nearly 100 at the Winecoff Hotel in Georgia.

President Harry S. Truman delivered the speech that set forth what came to be called the Truman Doctrine in the House chamber before a joint session of Congress on March 12. Asking Congress for 400 million dollars to support the governments of Greece and Turkey, which were losing British financial support and were vulnerable to subversion by the Communists, Truman went even further: "At the present moment in world history nearly every nation must choose between alternative ways of life," he declared. Never mentioning the Soviet Union by name, he said that "one way of life is based upon the will of the majority.... The second way of life is based upon the will of a minority forcibly imposed upon the majority.... I believe that it must be the policy of the United States to support free peoples who are resisting attempted subjugation by armed minorities or by outside pressures."

A straightforward address lasting only 18 minutes, the speech laid the basis on which America would resist the spread of communism over the coming decades. The policy of containment that Truman articulated provided the rationale for the Cold War in Europe and throughout the world for five decades, until the dissolution in the 1990s of the Soviet Union.

▶ LEVITTOWN, U.S.A.

Responding to an insatiable demand for housing after the war, William Levitt, an enterprising salesman, and his brother Alfred, an architect, applied assembly-line techniques to house building. Lumber for Levitt houses came from Levitt-owned forests. Levitt workers were organized into teams, each with specific tasks. They could erect a house, using preassembled materials, in 16 minutes.

The first "Levittown" sprang up in a field on Long Island, 30 miles from New York City—then, and even now, the largest single housing development put up at one time by an American builder. It had 17,000 Cape Cod-style houses, 7 village greens and shopping centers, 14 playgrounds, 9 swimming pools, 2 bowling alleys, and a town hall. When a Levitt house came up for sale, buyers would line up overnight. The bylaws of the community, however, stipulated that those buyers had to be white.

▶ THE NEW LOOK

When Christian Dior showed off his first Paris collection in 1947, his "New Look" (below) took the fashion world by storm. Gone was the wartime austerity. Here was a new silhouette that involved softly rounded bodices, tight waists, and very full skirts. It was a striking change, right down to the high-heeled shoes worn with the outfits. With rationing still in place in many parts of Europe, the yards of material required to make the full skirt were not readily available. Nevertheless, many women approximated the look, luxuriating in the new feeling of extravagance. Acceptance was not universal, as some criticized the New Look as indulgent and picketed the House of Dior. In Texas, resistance found a leader in Mrs. Bobbie Woodward, who formed the Little Below the Knee Club, a group whose cry of protest was, "The Alamo fell, but our hemlines will not."

▶ THE TAFT-HARTLEY ACT

Led in the Senate by Robert Taft of Ohio and in the House by Fred Hartley from New Jersey, Republican majorities in Congress, supported by conservative Democrats, overrode a presidential veto and a barrage of invective from organized labor to pass the Taft-Hartley Act on June 23. The legislation weakened the pro-labor gains of the 1935 Wagner Act and the New Deal. The act, proposed in response to postwar labor strikes and unrest, allowed the President to call for an 80-day "cooling off" period before strikes that might affect national interest. It also banned the closed shop and gave management greater power in opposing organizing drives. Labor leaders condemned the act as "fascistic" and as a "slave labor act," but in time labor learned to live within its bounds.

▶ WESTWARD IN THE KON-TIKI

To prove a theory that South American Indians reached South Pacific islands such as Tahiti, anthropologist Thor Heyerdahl set to sea on April 21 from Callao, Peru, with five fellow Norwegians and a Swede in a craft modeled after the rafts of the ancient Peruvians. Named the Kon-Tiki after a Peruvian god, she was 45 feet long and built of buoyant balsa wood from the rain forest of Ecuador. All parts were lashed together by rope, as the early people would have done it.

The cultures of South America and Polynesia have similarities: Both regions

• **JANUARY 25**
U.S. gangster Al Capone dies of apoplexy.

• **MARCH 25**
John D. Rockefeller, Jr., donates 8.5 million dollars to purchase a site for the United Nations in New York City.

• **APRIL 7**
Henry Ford, builder of the automobile dynasty, dies at 83.

• **APRIL**
Fighting erupts between Hindus and Muslims in India.

• **APRIL**
French put down a native revolt in Madagascar.

• **APRIL 7**
Writer Willa Cather dies at 73.

• **APRIL 16-18**
Ship explosion kills some 500 people, injures 2,000, and nearly annihilates Texas City, Texas.

have stepped pyramids, megalithic structures, feathered dress, and related words. Prevailing winds and ocean currents, both moving east to west, would have helped ancient voyagers from Peru reach the South Seas. On August 11, some three months and 4,000 miles later, the *Kon-Tiki* sighted land—the island of Puka Puka, easternmost of the Tuamotu archipelago. Tahiti was dead ahead. The *Kon-Tiki* sailed on, but its journey ended a week later when the vessel ran aground on a reef. It was later towed to Tahiti.

▶ THE CARBON 14 CLOCK
Radiocarbon dating, developed by Willard F. Libby, provided the first real way of measuring the age of prehistoric artifacts. Libby's method, for which he won the Nobel Prize for chemistry in 1960, uses carbon 14, a radioactive form of carbon, as a yardstick. All living things take in traces of carbon 14 during their lifetimes. At death, the unstable carbon 14 atoms, like all radioactive materials, begin to decay at a predictable rate. By measuring the amount of carbon 14 remaining, Libby was able to show the age of bones, seeds, ashes, or anything once living. Since 1947 ancient objects have routinely undergone carbon 14 testing, often dramatically changing or confirming ideas about early human life and evolution.

▶ BLOODY BIRTH OF INDIA AND PAKISTAN
August 15 should have been a day of celebration on the Indian subcontinent, as at midnight India had gained its independence from Great Britain after 75 years of struggle. In the capital city of New Delhi, India's first Prime Minister, Jawaharlal Nehru, rode through cheering crowds with Britain's last Viceroy, Lord Louis Mountbatten. But in Calcutta, Mohandas K. Gandhi, the 77-year-old "father of the country," was desperately trying to keep Hindus and Muslims from massacring each other. A united India had been his dream, and that vision was

BROKEN BARRIER

Jackie Robinson (below), son of a Georgia sharecropper and grandson of a slave, broke the barriers of racial discrimination that had held in major league baseball for 60 years when he played for the Brooklyn Dodgers in the 1947 season.

Robinson served in the war as an Army lieutenant in the 27th Cavalry and was a football star at the University of California-Los Angeles. He played baseball for Montreal, leading the International League in hitting and runs scored. Dodgers general manager Branch Rickey signed Robinson in 1945 to a contract with a Dodger farm club as pressure grew to open up sports regardless of color.

Robinson took the field in April 1947. He was greeted with threats and jibes, but he silenced the bigots by his self-contained bearing and by batting .297. He was named Rookie of the Year.

disintegrating as the country split into a Muslim Pakistan and a Hindu India.

There were two Muslim regions, one in the northwest, the other in the northeast corners of India. Partition, insisted upon by Muslim leader Mohammed Ali Jinnah, compelled some 14 million people to uproot themselves and flee for their lives and their futures. Hindus and Sikhs hiked southward, Muslims headed north, and along the way at least 600,000 died, preyed upon by marauding bands of fanatics. Within a few months the two nations, India and Pakistan, were at war, quarreling over the Muslim state of Kashmir in the first of several armed confrontations.

■ TRENDS & TRIVIA

Communist "witch-hunt" begins in Hollywood. Many actors' careers never recover.

Miracle on 34th Street puts Santa Claus on trial.

The last trolley cars in New York City are replaced by buses.

Aluminum foil and food processors are introduced and will revolutionize kitchen work.

A Streetcar Named Desire by Tennessee Williams opens on Broadway.

More than a million U.S. veterans enroll in college under the "GI Bill of Rights."

Racing car driver John Cobb sets world ground speed record at 394.196 mph.

The polaroid camera develops its first snapshot.

Hewlett-Packard Company incorporates in California.

Epoxy glue is developed.

The tubeless tire is introduced by Goodyear.

All the King's Men by Robert Penn Warren is awarded the Pulitzer Prize for fiction.

The polio virus is isolated.

Bubblegum-blowing contests are popular.

U.S. Air Force is established as a separate branch from the Army.

Princess Elizabeth, heir to the British throne, marries Philip Mountbatten, in London.

Peter Paul introduces Almond Joy candy bars.

Congress establishes Everglades National Park in Florida.

• JULY
Remains of dinosaurs that lived 200 million years ago are uncovered.

• JULY 26
U.S. National Securities Act is signed, uniting all branches of the armed services under the Department of Defense.

▶ OCTOBER 14
Pilot Chuck Yeager breaks the sound barrier in a Bell X-1 rocket plane.

• NOVEMBER 9
Wage and price controls are lifted except for rent and sugar.

• DECEMBER 23
Truman grants pardons to 1,523 who evaded the WW II draft.

• DECEMBER 27
Record-breaking storm in the eastern U.S. brings New York State 25.8 inches of snow.

On April 3 President Truman signed the Marshall Plan, which allocated billions to rebuild war-ravaged Europe, a keystone in the global strategy to limit the expansion of communism. The plan had been urged by Secretary of State George Marshall, who had seen that Europe's slow recovery from the war left it, as Winston Churchill described, "a rubble heap, a charnel house, a breeding ground of pestilence and hate."

With the Marshall Plan, the United States took upon its shoulders the leadership of the world. Prewar feelings of isolationism, of not becoming embroiled in European affairs, which had been characteristic of an American outlook since the nation's founding, were finally laid to rest. The American leadership and people realized that unless the United States acted, Western democracy would collapse. "We grabbed the lifeline with both hands," said British Foreign Minister Ernest Bevin. The plan averted starvation on a massive scale, precluded an economic depression, and set Western Europe on its feet again.

▶ APARTHEID IN SOUTH AFRICA

The Afrikaners, the Dutch-descendant population of South Africa, swept into power in parliament in 1948, formally ushering in the policy of apartheid, or apartness, between blacks and whites. Apartheid became the way of life in South Africa, with strict racial segregation in land ownership, residence, marriage, work, education, religion, sport, and public places. After 1948 apartheid was expressed in law, jobs, and political representation. The policy applied not only to whites and blacks but also to people of mixed ancestry and those from other ethnic groups. "Homelands" were set up and blacks were forcibly moved to them or to separate townships on the edges of cities. As world opinion mounted against the policy, South Africa withdrew from the British Commonwealth, and sanctions were voted against the country in the United Nations. Internal opposition was fierce, and the government brutally tried to still it. As a ruling policy governing all aspects of life, apartheid lasted 42 years, until the early 1990s when it was abolished. Nelson Mandela, imprisoned for more than 27 years for opposing apartheid, was elected president in 1994.

▶ STATE OF ISRAEL PROCLAIMED

At precisely 4:00 p.m. local time on May 14, the voice of longtime leader David Ben Gurion came over the radio to read, "...By virtue of the national and historic right of the Jewish people and the resolution of the United Nations: [We] hereby proclaim the establishment of the Jewish State in Palestine—to be called Israel." Outraged at having a non-Arab nation set up in their midst, the nearby Arab states attacked the next day. Israel defeated them and increased its land by one-quarter. More than 600,000 Palestinian Arabs fled to refugee camps in Lebanon, Jordan, Gaza, and Syria. Some formed the Palestine Liberation Organization (PLO), dedicated to achieving a homeland, by violence if necessary. Conflict between the Arabs and Israelis has marked the second half of the century, and even at the close of the century, peace is elusive.

▶ ASSASSINATION OF GANDHI

The man who had practiced nonviolence while leading India to independence was assassinated on January 30 by a fanatical Hindu who resented Mohandas K. Gandhi's attempts to bring peace between Hindus and Muslims. Known as Mahatma (Sanskrit for "Great Soul") Gandhi, India's national and spiritual leader was born into a family of Hindu Bania (merchant) caste in Porbandar, was educated in India and Britain, and qualified as a barrister in London. Returning to India in 1915, he led the country's quest for independence, and was frequently arrested by the British. One of his most dramatic actions was a 200-mile march to the sea with hundreds of followers in 1930 where they extracted salt from seawater in protest of the British Salt Act which required people to buy salt from the government. He adopted a way of life and used symbols that appealed to ordinary Hindus, such as the loincloth and the spinning wheel. He championed the rights of the poor, and before and after his death was revered as the father of his country.

A QUIET MOMENT BEFORE THE FUNERAL PROCESSION FOR MAHATMA GANDHI

- **JANUARY 4**
  After 62 years of British rule, Burma gains independence.

- **JANUARY 23**
  Czech Communists take control of Slovakia.

- **MARCH 8**
  U.S. Supreme Court rules that religious instruction in public schools is not constitutional.

- **MARCH 15**
  In the U.S. more than 200,000 soft-coal miners strike for a more liberal old-age pension plan.

- **APRIL 24**
  The Berlin Airlift begins.

- **MAY 25**
  General Motors and the United Auto Workers sign the first sliding-scale contract, which ties wage increases to the cost of living.

- **JUNE 18**
  Currency reform replaces the Reichs-mark, prompting Russians to suspend trade between the two German sectors.

KINSEY REPORT

Alfred Kinsey (below), an zoologist at Indiana University, published his first report on American sexuality in 1948, *Sexual Behavior in the Human Male*. It relied on thousands of interviews he had conducted beginning in 1938, and its 804 pages were filled with charts, graphs, and jargon. Nevertheless, it quickly soared to the top of the best-seller lists. Kinsey's report, for the first time, offered insights and statistics about Americans' sexuality.

Many critics disputed the figures. The Indiana Roman Catholic Archdiocese said the report helped "pave the way for people to believe in communism." One minister said that Kinsey "would lead us, like deranged Nebuchadnezzars of old, out into the fields to mingle with the cattle and become one with the beasts of the jungle." Literary critic Lionel Trilling agreed that straight talk might help dispel old myths but objected to Kinsey's reduction of sex to physical activity, especially his emphasis on orgasm. The Rockefeller Foundation felt the heat and cut off funding. Yet five years later Kinsey produced his second report, *Sexual Behavior in the Human Female*.

▶ INTEGRATION IN THE ARMED FORCES

President Truman issued an executive order on July 30 to end discrimination in the military "as rapidly as possible." He established the President's Committee on Equality of Treatment and Opportunity in the Armed Services to study compliance to the order. Nearly a million blacks had served their country in World War II, and now recognition of equal footing in the services was the law of the land. Truman had also taken another major step for racial equality just a few days earlier, ordering an end to discrimination in federal hiring practices.

▶ POLLOCK'S ABSTRACT EXPRESSIONISM

Born on a ranch near Cody, Wyoming, Jackson Pollock gained prominence with a show that opened January 5 at the Betty Parsons Gallery in New York City. His 17 enormous canvases were unlike anything anybody had ever seen. In the atmosphere of anxiety and alienation that permeated the cultural world following the war, Pollock had focused on the act of painting itself. He spread huge strips of canvas on the floor and attacked them with paint. The result was multilayered swirls with no beginning and no end. His show stirred the art world, and he became the unofficial leader of a group of Abstract Expressionists, so-called because of their emphasis on the actual act of painting rather than on subject matter. Among those he influenced were Mark Rothko, Willem de Kooning, Arshile Gorky, and Robert Motherwell.

▶ HOLLAND'S PYRRHIC VICTORY

The independence movement in the former Dutch colony of Indonesia, launched upon the defeat of Japan, was suppressed by returning Dutch forces. The Dutch retook Indonesia, capturing independence leaders Sukarno and Hatta in December. It proved to be a short-lived victory, however, as the naked attempt to reassert colonial control sparked an international outcry. Under pressure from the United Nations and from aggressive guerrilla attacks, Holland would soon withdraw from the region, leaving Sukarno to lead one of Asia's most populous nations.

■ TRENDS & TRIVIA

First self-service McDonald's opens in California.

England's Cambridge University begins granting full degrees to women.

The long-playing (LP) vinyl record is invented.

The United Nations deems lack of food the number one world problem.

Poet W. H. Auden's *Age of Anxiety* is awarded the Pulitzer Prize.

"All I Want For Christmas Is My Two Front Teeth" and "Buttons and Bows" are favorite songs.

The word game Scrabble is launched in the U.S.

Bell Laboratories announces the invention of the miniature transistor. It will revolutionize electronic equipment by replacing vacuum tubes. ▶

Bernard Baruch coins the term "Cold War."

Norman Mailer's war novel, *The Naked and the Dead*, is published.

A 200-inch reflecting telescope at Mount Palomar is the largest in the world.

Kiss Me Kate opens at New Century Theatre in New York City.

The Voice of America begins radio broadcasts overseas.

Cubist painter Georges Braque wins first prize at the Venice art festival (Braque painting, "Violin and Glass,"). ▶

• JUNE 24
The Selective Service Act is signed, requiring men aged 18-25 to register for military duty.

• JUNE 30
New York City subway fare doubles to ten cents.

• JULY 5
Britain offers free "cradle to grave" health care services.

• NOVEMBER 2
Harry S. Truman wins a full term and surprises many by beating Thomas E. Dewey in the presidential election.

• NOVEMBER 14
Princess Elizabeth gives birth to Prince Charles, heir to the British throne.

• DECEMBER 10
The United Nations adopts its universal declaration of human rights.

• DECEMBER 29
Scientists announce discovery of a drug that prevents the tsetse fly from causing sleeping sickness in cattle.

192

With the end of World War II in August 1945, hostilities resumed between the Nationalists under Chiang Kai-shek and the Communists under Mao Zedong. U.S. attempts to mediate failed, and full-blown civil war erupted in June 1946. At the outset the Nationalists outnumbered the Communists four to one, had superior weapons, and could wield an air force. But corruption and incompetence bedeviled the Nationalists, and defeats and defections mounted.

FRONTIER GUARD

The decisive battle of the civil war began in November 1948 at Hwai-Hai, a key railroad junction in central China. An epic battle, the conflict lasted 65 days, as half a million troops on each side faced off. In the end, the Nationalists were nearly annihilated, and Chiang Kai-shek fled with his surviving supporters to the offshore island of Taiwan, protected by the U.S. Navy.

On October 1, the victorious Mao Zedong, having prevailed against decades of battle and hardship—such as the Long March in 1934-35—declared the establishment of the People's Republic of China. Mao set about revolutionizing China's rural and industrial economies and silencing his opposition.

▶ FAIR DEAL

Harry S. Truman's surprise victory over strongly favored New York governor Thomas E. Dewey was won through the support of blacks, organized labor, and farmers. Truman delivered his State of the Union address on January 5 to the new 81st Congress. He had outlined a program in 1948, but few had paid much attention. Now he had the public's ear, and he coined a new name for his domestic program. The "Fair Deal" was an attempt to extend the social progressivism of Roosevelt's "New Deal." It would repeal the Taft-Hartley law, enact generous farm price supports, expand Social Security, aid local school systems, increase low-rent housing availability, and broaden civil rights. Truman's ideas constituted the blueprint for Democratic Party policies for subsequent administrations.

Two weeks later, on January 20, Truman was sworn in as President in his own right. For the first time, television carried the inauguration as far west as Sedalia, Missouri, connecting 14 cities by coaxial cable and reaching some ten million people—the largest number of people thus far in history to watch a single event.

Truman outlined a four-point program, devoted exclusively to foreign policy. He pledged that the U.S. would continue to support the United Nations; it would join a new "defense arrangement" with the freedom-loving nations of the North Atlantic; it would keep its "full weight" behind the Marshall Plan; and—his final point which caught everyone by surprise—it would advance a "bold new program" to bring scientific and economic progress to "underdeveloped countries." It was the first mention of what became

known as the Point Four Program, and it heralded a new emphasis on promoting the well-being of less developed nations. Democracy, Truman declared, was a "vitalizing force" in the world.

▶ SOVIETS DETONATE ATOM BOMB

On September 23 President Truman announced that the Soviet Union had made and exploded an atomic bomb of its own. The United States' monopoly of the bomb ended, and the arms race would now accelerate. Research went forward in earnest on the hydrogen bomb, a thermonuclear device that would be 500 times more powerful than the atom bomb.

▶ *DEATH OF A SALESMAN*

On February 10 *Death of a Salesman* by 34-year-old Arthur Miller opened at the Morosco Theatre, starring Lee J. Cobb. The drama, which won the Pulitzer Prize and the New York Drama Critics Award,

SCENE FROM *DEATH OF A SALESMAN*

concerned the disillusion of Willy Loman, a 63-year-old salesman whose dream of better times—his American dream—has proved elusive. All Willy has to show for a life "way out there in the blue, riding on a smile and a shoestring," is a long-suffering wife and two sons who have not grown up.

▶ BERLIN AIRLIFT

For 321 days the Berlin Airlift brought food, clothing, fuel, and other necessities to the people of the Allied section of Berlin, whose land routes had been blockaded by the Soviets. "How long do you plan to keep it up?" asked a top U.S.

- **FEBRUARY 19**
First Bollingen Poetry Prize is awarded to Ezra Pound.

- **MARCH 2**
First nonstop flight around-the-world is completed; the plane is refueled in the air.

- **APRIL 20**
Scientists develop a way to produce cortisone commercially.

- **MAY 17**
Britain reasserts Belfast's dependence on the UK, but recognizes Dublin's independence.

- **MAY 31**
Trial of Alger Hiss begins.

- **JUNE 28**
The last U.S. combat troops are called home from Korea, leaving only 500 advisers.

- **AUGUST 3**
U.S. Congress designates June 14 as Flag Day.

ORWELL'S 1984

George Orwell's last novel, *1984,* stunned and frightened the post-war world with its nightmarish depiction of a totalitarian future. Neither the political right nor left could take comfort in Orwell's vision of a world where the concept of the individual was obliterated under the never-blinking eye of Big Brother, a faceless, computerized bureaucracy that hoarded secret information about every man, woman, and child.

Winston Smith, the hero with no especially heroic qualities other than a vague yearning for privacy and love, has a brief, doomed love affair, is arrested by the thought police, tortured, and released. In the end, he acquiesces in his own submission.

The novel showed a world where the past was constantly altered to accord with the present and where language, "Newspeak," was narrowed to channel the range of ideas. Its depiction of a society dominated by slogans—"War Is Peace," "Ignorance Is Strength"—gave readers much to think about as the nations' political structures in the aftermath of war hardened along ideological lines.

CHILDREN CHEER THE AMERICAN PLANE THAT BRINGS THEM FOOD.

official of a Soviet general, who replied, "Until you drop plans for a West German government." If the United States retreated from Berlin, Secretary of State George Marshall warned President Truman, it would mean the "failure of the rest of our European policy." Truman ordered the airlift to feed the 2.5 million West Berliners. In winter weather and despite crashes and huge logistical challenges, Western pilots under Gen. Lucius Clay landed almost minute by minute in the minuscule West Berlin airfields to deliver more than 1.5 million tons of food and supplies to the beleaguered residents. Finally, under a UN-brokered agreement, the Soviet authorities reopened the city on May 12.

▶ NATO ESTABLISHED

By a vote of 82 to 13, the U.S. Senate ratified the North Atlantic Treaty on July 21. The treaty committed the United States to a defense alliance with 11 other countries. This was the first time since 1778 that the United States had entered into a military arrangement in peacetime. The historic move indicated the nation's willingness to assume a leading role in the Cold War. The signatories to the North Atlantic Treaty Organization (NATO) were the U.S., Canada, Great Britain, France, Italy, Denmark, Portugal, Norway, Iceland, Belgium,

the Netherlands, and Luxembourg. They agreed "that an armed attack against one or more of them…shall be considered an attack against them all." The pact was drawn up under Article 51 of the UN Charter, which allowed for countries to make their own regional security plans. The West felt that a strong unified defense would help counter the aggressive policies of the Soviet Union as manifested in the Communist coup in Czechoslovakia, the attempts to subvert Greece and Turkey, and the blockade of Berlin.

■ TRENDS & TRIVIA

RCA introduces the 45 rpm record.

Paddipads, the first disposable diapers, go on sale in Britain.

Northwest is the first U.S. airline to serve alcoholic beverages in flight.

The Samba, a Brazilian dance, is fashionable.

Linus Pauling finds the molecular flaw that causes sickle-cell anemia.

"Bali Ha'i" and "Rudolph the Red Nosed-Reindeer" become hit songs.

The board game Clue debuts.

Prepared cake mixes become an option for bakers.

Ingrid Bergman creates a scandal by leaving her husband for film director Roberto Rossellini.

Supporters of communism risk excommunication from the Catholic Church.

Simone de Beauvoir breaks ground with her book *The Second Sex.*

Holographs (3-D photographs) are new.

Gary Davis begins a campaign to expand limits on conscientious objector status.

Philip Johnson builds his famous glass house. ▼

• **SEPTEMBER 17** In the greatest ship loss since the *Titanic,* the Canadian liner *Noronic* burns, killing 207.

• **OCTOBER 1** Pittsburgh steel strike begins—500,000 quit.

• **OCTOBER 16** Civil war in Greece ends.

• **OCTOBER 26** Truman raises minimum wage from 40 to 75 cents an hour.

• **DECEMBER 10** 50,000 French troops mass at Vietnam's border to prevent Chinese invasion.

• **DECEMBER 26** Albert Einstein presents his generalized theory of gravitation.

• **DECEMBER 28** Dutch grant independence to Indonesia.

UNDERWATER EXPLORATION

by Sylvia A. Earle
OCEANOGRAPHER AND NATIONAL GEOGRAPHIC EXPLORER-IN-RESIDENCE

In the very early years of the century, when my parents were children growing up in southern New Jersey, the ocean was something they only heard about. Mysterious and blue, it lay somewhere over the horizon, beyond easy reach in an era of few roads and no automobiles. By the time I came along, commercial air travel across the country was common and my family made frequent summertime trips to the Jersey shore in a sturdy Ford sedan. Encountering craggy horseshoe crabs, starfish, urchins, jellyfish, clams, eels, and fragrant piles of seaweed hopping with sand fleas, I badgered my mother with questions that seemed to have no answers—until she suggested I look through the family's well-thumbed collection of GEOGRAPHICS. There I discovered Roy Waldo Miner's wondrous articles about marine life, written in the 1930s and illustrated with glorious paintings by Else Bostelmann. For the

Left: Swedish warship, Baltic Sea   Middle: Diving, Pacific Ocean   Right: Larval lobster atop jellyfish, Pacific Ocean

first time, I experienced the thrill shared by millions of people over the past century: Diving into a stack of NATIONAL GEOGRAPHIC magazines is an adventure, a chance to tag along vicariously on expeditions with great explorers—and dream about how to get there yourself.

I learned about the early days of flight, read of expeditions into the deep sea, and admired the first color images of live reef fish in an article by W. H. Longley and NATIONAL GEOGRAPHIC photographer Charles Martin, written in 1927, the same year that Charles Lindbergh made the first solo flight across the Atlantic. Later practitioners of the art of underwater photography can confirm what Martin discovered years ago: To capture fine images underwater is a mix of science and art, of technological wizardry and dogged determination—all filtered through an indefinable twist of mind and blessed with more than a little luck. Pioneering photographers have forged enduring partnerships in the pages of the magazine with a diverse collection of ocean scientists and writers, including poet and naturalist Diane Ackerman, archaeologist George Bass, and several who share an intimate knowledge of whales, including Roger Payne, Jim Darling, Hal Whitehead, and Victor Sheffer. Without a doubt, these explorers have forever transformed the way humankind views the ocean.

Going under the ocean was not easy, but in a 1934 story, zoologist William Beebe explained what made it worthwhile. Beebe went below the surface near Bermuda, crouching with engineer Otis Barton inside the bathysphere, a hollow steel ball lowered on a cable 3,028 feet down—deeper than anyone had been before. Beebe described what he saw—"swivel-toothed dragonfish pursuing luminescent squid . . . silver hatchetfish drifting through the abyssal darkness . . . pygmy round-mouths"—and Else Bostelmann produced vivid paintings to complement his prose.

In the 1940s, as World War II swept the planet, undersea technology advanced quickly with particular emphasis on the strategic advantages of submarines and the acoustic techniques developed over millions of years by marine mammals. Stories began to appear in the NATIONAL GEOGRAPHIC early in the 1950s by a charismatic Frenchman, Capt. Jacques-Yves Cousteau, a man who loved to dive and who coinvented a self-contained underwater breathing apparatus — the Aqua-Lung. As Cousteau put it, "The best way to observe fish is to become a fish." Cousteau and his many collaborators inspired millions not only to look to the sea but also to follow the "oceanauts," onward—and downward.

Meanwhile, an ingenious Swiss engineer, Auguste Piccard, known to readers of the GEOGRAPHIC for his record-breaking ascents in hot-air balloons in the 1930s, applied his knowledge of buoyancy and pressure to develop underwater counterparts. Lt. Comdr. G. S. Houot reported in the GEOGRAPHIC the results of exploration to as much as 7,500 feet down using Piccard's bathyscaphe, and Paul Zahl mesmerized readers with his descriptions of deep-sea life. But the first photographs of the nature of the abyssal realm were made possible by systems developed by the Massachusetts Institute of Technology "wizard," Harold E. Edgerton.

In 1959, polar waters were breached when the U.S. nuclear submarine *Skate* surfaced at the North Pole, 50 years after Comdr. Robert E. Peary laboriously attained that point by dogsled. Twenty years later Gilbert M. Grosvenor, then Editor of the magazine and soon to be President of the Society, dived under the Pole with diving doctor Joseph MacInnis and photographer Al Giddings. On January 23, 1960, U.S. Navy Lt. Don Walsh and Jacques Piccard descended to the deepest crack in the ocean floor—nearly seven miles down in the Mariana Trench near the Philippines. The same year, the U.S.

nuclear sub *Triton* sailed 30,752 miles around the world in 60 days 21 hours—underwater—a year before the first person orbited Earth in space. Tragedy struck in 1963, with the loss of the nuclear sub *Thresher* in 8,490 feet of water 260 miles off the coast of New England. Aviation pioneer Edwin A. Link observed in the GEOGRAPHIC the following year that the *Thresher* disaster "changed the course of our study of the ocean, greatly increased its impetus, and dramatized the need for a new science: oceanology." Link responded to the challenge himself, pioneering techniques for living underwater and developing submersibles that let divers swim from a special chamber directly into the sea.

Since then, stunning new images of the deep-sea floor have come into focus, and maps produced as inserts in the NATIONAL GEOGRAPHIC magazine have set new standards for portraying the Earth. Previously, the sea was typically depicted as featureless blobs of blue; now, its rugged underwater mountain chains, high peaks, broad valleys, and deep canyons have been revealed in splendid detail.

But what is really there? What does it look like along the central rift at the crest of the Mid-Atlantic Ridge, where new ocean floor spews forth? What are the mechanisms underlying plate tectonics, deep-sea volcanoes and other ocean processes? In 1974 three submersibles—*Alvin*, from the Woods Hole Oceanographic Institution (WHOI), and the French subs, *Cyana* and *Archimède*—took dozens of scientists along a 30-mile stretch of ocean floor to find out, helping spark a revolution in earth sciences. Within a decade, the once-scorned theory of continental drift was widely accepted as fundamental, recovery of offshore oil and gas spurred substantial investments in ocean technology, and engineers from many nations considered how to extract minerals from the deep sea.

Geophysicist Robert D. Ballard emerged as a key member of a 1977 expedition sponsored by the National Geographic Society and WHOI to explore a rift area near the Galápagos Islands. He and others who traveled one and a half miles down for a close-up view found more than they ever dreamed of: vents in the seafloor gushing mineral-laden hot water, surrounded by bizarre tube worms, pale crabs, clams, and numerous other creatures. This discovery marked the birth of a new field of biology to study creatures dwelling in the absence of sunlight who derive energy directly from hydrothermal vents. Soon after his return from the Galápagos, Ballard was elated at the discoveries—but keenly aware of how little is really known. "Less than one-tenth of one percent of the deep sea has been explored," he lamented. He favored the development of remotely operated systems that could quickly scope out large areas, then follow up, if necessary, with manned subs.

He soon put his vision to work in a project that many believed to be a foolish, impossible goal: finding the remains of the luxury liner, *Titanic*, sunk deep in the frigid waters of the North Atlantic after a collision with an iceberg in 1912. Encouragement and support came together in a cooperative U.S.-French expedition involving the U.S. Navy; WHOI; the French research organization, IFREMER; and the National Geographic Society. Against great odds, there was success. Soon, everyone could see this most famous of all shipwrecks through extraordinary still, video, even 3-D IMAX images crafted by Emory Kristof, Al Giddings, and others.

Discovery of the *Titanic* was part of yet another revolution—that of recovering human history. Thousands of ships and countless human artifacts, including great treasures, once thought forever lost at sea, have become accessible for the first time. Ballard began to make archaeological expeditions to the Mediterranean Sea and elsewhere with an added bonus: sharing the view with schoolchildren by linking live images from underwater to museums and classrooms worldwide.

I wonder, sometimes, what William Beebe would think of such armchair exploration, or what his reaction would be to a 1998 issue of the NATIONAL GEOGRAPHIC featuring close-up images of Mars and the *Titanic*—in vivid color, and in three dimensions. Or what he would say if he could join crittercam inventor, Greg Marshall, and biologist John Francis to travel vicariously with sperm whales deep in the ocean. Or step aboard a space shuttle and gain a view of Earth that made dramatically visible this planet's uniquely aquatic nature. Beebe's astonishment over the pace and scope of discovery might be matched by just one thing: the swift decline of ocean health. When Thor Heyerdahl first sailed from Peru to Tahiti in 1947 on a raft made of balsa logs, the sea was nearly as pristine as when Christopher Columbus ventured to North America nearly five centuries earlier. Scarcely two decades later, Heyerdahl's report in the NATIONAL GEOGRAPHIC of the 1970 *Ra II* expedition sounded the alarm: debris, tar balls, and other trash littered the Atlantic. Many were skeptical, but soon the evidence was inescapable. Whatever we put into the sea is literally injected into the system that supports us all, the system that governs climate, produces oxygen, and absorbs carbon dioxide—shaping the very chemistry of Earth and making life here possible.

Other damage has been wrought by what we take out of the sea—hundreds of millions of tons of wildlife removed in the past century, yielding what Michael Parfit, in a November 1995 issue of the NATIONAL GEOGRAPHIC, termed "diminishing returns." More than 100 marine species—cod, capelin, haddock, bluefin tuna, and others once thought to be infinitely resilient—are proving vulnerable to new technologies and short-sighted policies. Hope is on the horizon, though, as reported by Douglas H. Chadwick in a 1998 issue of the magazine. Chadwick noted efforts to develop a system of protected areas in U.S. waters comparable to actions early in the century to establish for the land a system of national parks and wilderness areas.

If the greatest threat to the sea is ignorance, the most promising cure is exploration coupled with effective communication. The National Geographic Society now enlists television and radio "expeditions"—live transmissions from polar ice, ocean depths, and shallow reefs—as well as large format films, the Internet, and other modern methods to complement the tried-and-true power of conventional print to inform, inspire, and motivate. Yet, what Roy Waldo Miner wrote in 1935 about one of Earth's largest creatures, the giant squid, is still true as the century closes: "No one knows how large they grow, how long they live, or how deep they dwell." Most of Earth's mountains have not been seen, let alone climbed, though one must descend to their peaks and work downward. Gardiner G. Hubbard's 1888 observation in the first issue of the NATIONAL GEOGRAPHIC remains timely: "When we embark on the great ocean of discovery, the horizon of the unknown advances with us and surrounds us wherever we go. The more we know, the greater we find is our ignorance." The greatest era of exploration of this ocean planet has just begun.

1950-

The Cold War and McCarthyism

1950-1959

David Oshinsky
BOARD OF GOVERNORS PROFESSOR OF HISTORY, RUTGERS UNIVERSITY

ON FEBRUARY 9, 1950, AN OBSCURE REPUBLICAN SENATOR from Wisconsin delivered a speech about "Communists in government" to a women's club in Wheeling, West Virginia. Waving a piece of paper in the air, he uttered the words that would make him both an instant celebrity and the symbol for an age. "I have here in my hand," Senator Joseph R. McCarthy told his audience, "a list of 205 Communists that were made known to the Secretary of State and who nevertheless are still working and shaping the policy of the State Department."

McCarthy had no list. He knew nothing about "Reds" in the federal government—or anywhere else. An erratic freshman senator, facing a tough reelection fight in 1952, McCarthy needed a sensational issue to revive his faltering career. Sensing the potential of "Communist subversion," he slapped together the Wheeling speech from a variety of questionable sources, adding embellishments of his own. In the following days, McCarthy changed his "205 Communists" into "207 bad risks," followed by "57 card-carrying Communists," and then "81 loyalty risks." It didn't seem to matter. The newspapers gave him front-page headlines and the public was aroused. To millions of Americans, McCarthy provided a logical explanation for their country's growing troubles in the world. The Communists were gaining ground, he charged, because traitors

Opposite: School children duck and cover in a bomb drill, a new activity for a world where atomic attacks were possible.
Preceding pages: Fueled by widely available cars and housing, Americans created a new suburban culture in the 1950s.

in the U.S. government were aiding their cause. The real enemy was not in Moscow, but rather in Washington, D.C.

McCarthy soon became the Cold War's dominant politician. His genius lay in his ability to simplify complex world events, to manipulate the media, and to boldly provide names, documents, and statistics—in short, the appearance of diligent research. Though the nation's fear of communism neither began with McCarthy nor ended with his political collapse, the senator exploited this fear in ways that dramatically altered the American landscape of the 1950s, and beyond.

Republican Senator Joseph R. McCarthy vowed to sweep all Communists out of Washington.

The roots of "McCarthyism"—a word coined by the cartoonist Herblock to describe the senator's baseless charges—can be traced to the widening rift between the United States and the Soviet Union following World War II. To American eyes, the defeat of Nazi Germany and Japan had not made the world a safer place. Soviet aggression in Europe had robbed them of the fruits of victory, and one form of totalitarianism had been replaced by another. Growing fear of Stalin's Russia and erosion of public tolerance for left-wing activity in the U.S. was spurred on by public officials who claimed that Communists were infiltrating labor unions, universities, the motion picture industry, and the government itself. "They are everywhere," warned Attorney General Tom C. Clark. "In factories, offices, butcher shops, on street corners, in private businesses—and each carries with him the germ of death for society."

In fact, the American Communist Party was far weaker in 1947 than it had been in 1937, and its numbers were dwindling daily. However, the public's sense of vulnerability was heightened by the fall of Eastern Europe to Stalin's army, coupled with a series of staggering surprises at home. In 1948 one of America's leading public servants, Alger Hiss, was accused of spying for the Russians. The next year China fell to Communist rule, and a few months later, the Soviet Union tested an atomic bomb, ending America's nuclear monopoly.

The news quickly got worse. On January 21, 1950, Hiss was convicted of perjury and sent to federal prison. In February British authorities arrested Klaus Fuchs, a physicist who had worked on the Manhattan Project, for passing atomic secrets to the Russians. On June 25 Communist North Korea crossed the 38th parallel to invade anti-Communist South Korea. A week later, without consulting Congress, President Harry S. Truman dispatched American ground troops to halt the North Korean advance. That same summer FBI agents arrested Julius and Ethel Rosenberg on charges of conspiracy to commit atomic espionage. In November Communist China entered the Korean War, routing American troops at the Yalu River.

The Hiss Case, the fall of China, the Russian A-bomb, the Rosenberg arrests, the Korean War—all sent shock waves through the nation. Some Americans feared an all-out Soviet assault;

others suspected destruction from within. An extreme display of mass anxiety occurred in Mosinee, Wisconsin, on May Day 1950, when American Legionnaires disguised as Russian soldiers staged a mock takeover of the town. The mayor, the ministers, and the "capitalist merchants" were all herded into a makeshift stockade on Main Street, renamed "Red Square." The local newspaper printed Communist propaganda, the library banned objectionable books, and local restaurants served potato soup, black bread, and dark coffee. After being "liberated" that evening by "freedom fighters," the townspeople held a large rally amid the burning of Communist literature and the singing of patriotic songs.

State and local governments were also on guard. Indiana forced professional wrestlers to sign a loyalty oath; Ohio declared Communists ineligible for unemployment benefits. Tennessee imposed the death penalty for conspirators seeking to overthrow the state government, and in New Rochelle, New York, an ordinance to register Communists snared one perplexed resident who came to police headquarters thinking the ordinance applied to commuters.

A SENSE OF DREAD CREPT INTO EVERYDAY LIFE. With U.S. soldiers battling communists in Korea, and Russia armed with the A-bomb, public opinion polls showed a clear majority expecting an atomic showdown in the near future. In New York City, schoolchildren were given metal "dog tags" and taught to dive under their desks in simulated "take cover drills." One youngster explained his tag this way: "If a bomb gets me in the street, people will know what my name is." In Washington, D.C., real estate advertisements read: "Small farm—out beyond the atomic blast." The mayor of Toledo tried to calm anxious residents by joking that he would put up neon signs directing Soviet pilots to Cleveland and Detroit.

Early in 1951 the Rosenbergs were convicted of conspiracy to commit atomic espionage; trial judge Irving R. Kaufman, a master of hyperbole, accused them of "putting" the A-bomb "into the hands of the Russians." In June 1953, following numerous appeals, the Rosenbergs were executed at Sing Sing State Prison, just north of New York City. Evidence released since their deaths—particularly the decrypted Soviet intelligence cables from World War II known as the Venona files—reinforces the conclusion that Julius Rosenberg was guilty as charged, while Ethel Rosenberg knew about her husband's activities but played a lesser role.

That Klaus Fuchs, charged with a similar crime in England, received only a 14-year prison sentence underscores the deep anxiety about communism permeating American society in this era. Not surprisingly, Americans who lived and traveled abroad were amazed and appalled to find how "McCarthyism" was perceived elsewhere. During a junket to Australia, Senator Ralph Flanders found himself deluged with questions about his Wisconsin colleague. "I discovered then for the first time," he recalled, "that there was a strong impression abroad that McCarthy was something like a new Hitler, and that the United States might be following the Nazi path." Both Winthrop Aldrich, the U.S. Ambassador to England, and C. Douglas Dillon, the U.S. Ambassador to France, sent cables home warning of "McCarthyism's" negative impact on American prestige. From Paris, author Rebecca West wrote to a friend, "I have been here a week and a situation that depresses me profoundly is driving me into the Seine with a brick around my neck. You cannot believe the effect of McCarthy on the French populace. They do not see why [we] don't take him by the neck and throw him into the Potomac." To Europeans, McCarthy had become a convenient symbol of their perception of the new America—the free-world colossus, arrogant and inflexible. As one American noted after completing a tour of Austria, Germany, and Switzerland, "I was shaken when I found myself obliged to answer arguments implying that the threat of war was greater from us than from Russia. I soon discovered that this was a widely shared view."

MCCARTHY WAS EASILY REELECTED TO THE SENATE IN 1952. With Republicans now in control of Congress, a mad scramble ensued over the direction and control of the Communist issue. Nearly 200 of the 221 Republican congressmen applied for duty on the House Un-American Activities Committee (HUAC), where Chairman Harold Velde, a zealous ex-FBI agent, promised to hunt down Communists in every walk of life. "They are foreign to our nation and to our God," he thundered. "In the world of humanity, they are aliens."

Meanwhile, Senate Republican leaders, fearing McCarthy's well-earned reputation for mayhem, offered him the chairmanship of a minor committee called Government Operations. McCarthy accepted, knowing that it had a Permanent Subcommittee on Investigations with the stated though little used authority to scrutinize "federal activities at all levels." He filled his staff with former prosecutors, FBI agents, and professional Red-hunters. For chief counsel, the key position, he chose Roy M. Cohn, a shrewd, abrasive young attorney from New York who had aided the Rosenberg prosecution. With a large budget and the power to hold hearings, call witnesses, and issue subpoenas, McCarthy and Cohn began their investigations of "Communist influence" in government. Their early targets included the Foreign Service, the State Department's overseas libraries, and the Voice of America. At the same time, other congressional bodies such as the HUAC and the Senate Internal Security Subcommittee searched for Communists in America's schools, churches, and labor unions.

McCarthy got much of his information from the FBI, which secretly opened its files to his investigators. Other material came from "patriotic" or disgruntled federal workers, who kept the senator well stocked with rumor and classified documents. McCarthy's hearings did not uncover any Communists, but they did ruin a number of careers and undermine the morale of countless government workers. The worst damage was done to the U.S. Army. In the fall of 1953 McCarthy and Cohn literally paralyzed the Army Signal Corps at Fort Monmouth, New Jersey, by charging that a spy ring was in operation there.

Panicked by the publicity, the Army immediately suspended 42 scientists, engineers, and technicians who worked at the fort. Not one of them, it turned out, was guilty of espionage, subversion, or anything resembling disloyal behavior. Indeed, their FBI files—obtained years later through the Freedom of Information Act—demonstrated not only the wild exaggerations employed by Senator McCarthy, but also the level of snooping and harassment carried out by government investigators in the name of national security. A typical dossier read:

"You favored the leftist policies of columnist Max Lerner, who was affiliated with a number of organizations cited . . . as Communist fronts.

You listed as a reference_____, who reportedly was a member of the Young Communist League.

Your brother_____, with whom you have been in close and continuing association, attended a rally at Yankee Stadium in 1948 at which Paul Robeson spoke."

McCarthy's attacks on the Army escalated in 1954. In public hearings, he berated several officers for their alleged failures to halt Communist penetration of the military, telling one decorated war hero that he was "not fit to wear the uniform" of his country. President Dwight D. Eisenhower was furious. Vowing to avoid a direct confrontation—"I will not get into the gutter with that guy," he told his aides—the President insisted that Republican leaders televise the Senate's pending investigation of the Army-McCarthy feud.

It proved to be a wise strategy. For 36 days the senator entered America's living room as a belligerent guest. The cumulative impression of his performance—his windy speeches, frightening outbursts, endless interruptions, and crude personal attacks—was simply devastating.

Vice President Richard Nixon argued for capitalism during the "kitchen debate" with Soviet Premier Nikita Khrushchev.

The climax came on June 9, 1954, when McCarthy challenged the patriotism of a young attorney who worked in the law firm of Army Counsel Joseph Welch. As McCarthy paused, Welch said to him: "Let us not assassinate this lad further, Senator. You have done enough. Have you no sense of decency, sir? At long last, have you left no sense of decency?" There was a second or two of silence, then a thunderous burst of applause. McCarthy sensed he had come off poorly, though he didn't seem to understand why. "What did I do?" he kept asking the people around him. "What did I do?" A few months later, the Senate censured McCarthy for conduct "contrary to Senatorial traditions." The vote was 67-22, with only Republican conservatives opposed.

Many linked this condemnation to the easing of Cold War tensions at home. The Korean War had ended in 1953, Stalin was dead, and the radical right was temporarily in shambles. For McCarthy, life went downhill with blinding speed. The press now ignored him and his influence disappeared. When he rose to speak in the Senate, his colleagues drifted away. Shunned and humiliated, he spent his final days drinking in private, railing bitterly against those who had deserted his cause. McCarthy died of acute alcoholism in 1957, virtually alone, at the age of 48.

The death of McCarthy symbolized a shift in Cold War thinking. Old anxieties about Soviet espionage and aggression were replaced by new concerns about Russian progress in science, technology, and military affairs. On October 4, 1957, when the Soviets launched *Sputnik*

(Traveling Companion), the first artificial satellite, weighing less than 200 pounds, American reaction was volcanic. A month later, the Soviets stepped up the pressure by orbiting *Sputnik 2*, an 1,100-pound capsule carrying a small dog. Americans had always taken their technical superiority for granted. Even the Soviet atomic bomb was seen as an aberration, built from stolen U.S. blueprints. But *Sputnik* shook America's confidence and wounded its pride. "The time has clearly come," said one alarmed senator, "to be less concerned with the depth of pile of the new broadloom or the height of the tail fin of the new car and to be more prepared to shed blood, sweat, and tears."

IN THE MCCARTHY YEARS, AMERICA'S SCHOOLS had been portrayed as a hotbed of left-wing radicalism. Now they were lambasted as a bastion of mediocrity. In a series of issues devoted to this "crisis" in American education, *Life* magazine followed a 16-year-old Russian student and his American counterpart through a typical high school day. Alexi studied math and science, spoke fluent English, played chess and the piano, exercised vigorously, and studied four hours after class. Stephen, meanwhile, spent his day lounging through basic geometry and learning how to type. The students around him read magazines such as *Modern Romance* in English class. No one bothered to study. The end result, warned *Life*'s editors, was a generation of young Americans ill-equipped "to cope with the technicalities of the Space Age."

The embarrassments continued. In December 1957 millions watched on television as the U.S. Navy's much-publicized Vanguard rocket caught fire on takeoff and crashed to the ground. A month later, the Army used its new Jupiter rocket to launch a satellite named *Explorer 1*, which weighed all of 10 pounds. President Eisenhower insisted, correctly, that the United States was ahead of the Soviet Union in nuclear research and delivery systems. But Americans were skeptical, especially after the Russians orbited a third satellite weighing almost 3,000 pounds. For the first time, Eisenhower saw his public approval rating fall below 50 percent.

Intense competition—from Berlin to Cuba, athletics to chess, the arms race to the space race—would drive Soviet-American relations for decades to come. It was fitting, perhaps, that the 1950s ended with Soviet Premier Nikita Khrushchev heatedly debating Vice President Richard Nixon, one of McCarthy's former allies, about the consumer gap in their respective societies. Standing nose-to-nose in a "model" American kitchen, they argued the merits of their respective nation's electrical appliances. Looking grumpily at a self-loading dishwasher, Khrushchev asked: "Don't you have a machine that puts food in your mouth and pushes it down?" When he bragged that Russia would soon "come alongside America, salute her, and move on ahead," Nixon merely responded that it was "better to compete in the relative merits of washing machines than in the strength of rockets." The Cold War would continue for years, but the battlefield was now a far different place. ■

Mushroom-shaped clouds, like this one over Bikini Atoll, symbolized humankind's potential to destroy itself.

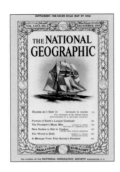

By the mid-1950s, a few of NATIONAL GEOGRAPHIC's original staffers were still in control of the magazine. As a result, the publication had changed little since it first appeared in 1888. A makeover was long overdue.

That finally came in 1957, when Melville Bell Grosvenor became Editor. He allowed designers to use more white space in layouts. He put color pictures on the cover permanently. And he looked to the heavens above and watery depths below for exciting new stories. Many on the GEOGRAPHIC staff referred to his ten-year reign as "the golden years."

Saving the Majestic Whooping Crane

Birds garnered 36 articles in the 1950s—more than in any other decade in the Society's history. The reason was simple; they were Gilbert H. Grosvenor's favorite subjects. They also illustrated beautifully the GEOGRAPHIC's dedication to educating its readers about the importance of conservation.

The plight of the majestic whooping crane was a wonderful example of the magazine's concern. In "Whooping Cranes Fight for Survival," Robert Porter Allen, research director of the

YOUNG WHOOPING CRANE STRETCHES ITS WINGS.

National Audubon Society, and Frederick Kent Truslow, a veteran bird photographer, profiled these birds on the brink of extinction for the November 1959 issue. The two men crouched in Texas marshes for weeks to observe the only 33 such cranes then known to exist in the wild. Allen spent almost a month in a remote corner of Canada's Northwest Territories looking for the birds' breeding grounds.

"I look back on these hard-working days with the whooping cranes...as among the most rewarding of my life," he wrote. "Few birds, and for that matter few animals of any kind, can match their nobility and natural dignity. Everything we learn about them adds to our respect and admiration."

Exploring Watery Realms

Exploration was the major focus for the magazine, especially when it allowed readers the vicarious thrill of swimming through ancient shipwrecks in the filmy blue deep or meeting magnificent tropical fish face-to-face. Underwater adventure

BOUNTY'S ANCHOR FLUKE PROTRUDES FROM SAND LIKE A BROAD ARROW.

produced some famous moments in the 1950s. Many readers met French aquatic explorer Jacques-Yves Cousteau for the first time in the pages of NATIONAL GEOGRAPHIC. "The best way to observe fish is to become a fish," he wrote in the October 1952 article "Fish Men Explore a New World Undersea." "And the best way to become a fish...is to don an underwater breathing device called the Aqua-Lung," which he co-invented.

Magazine writer-photographer Luis Marden was less concerned with self-promotion. He had discovered the remains of the legendary H.M.S. *Bounty* in January 1957 off Pitcairn Island in the South Pacific. This was a historic find, the answer to a riddle that had confounded scholars for two centuries.

The magazine knew it would be a newsbreaking event. So until the piece was thoroughly researched for publication in the December 1957 issue, Marden could not discuss his discovery. "The gestation of one of our stories is even longer than a man's," he told *Newsweek* after the article appeared.

Once the story ran, the ship's ruins made international headlines—167 years after the mutineers burned it to avoid capture. Marden and Melville Grosvenor appeared on television to talk about the *Bounty*. This gave Grosvenor the impetus to explore another exciting realm—a National Geographic television division.

Color on the Cover

Color pictures could fill the GEOGRAPHIC's pages and ads, but it was not standard policy to put color on the magazine's cover. When asked why, a staff member deferred to a higher authority; "If the Lord had meant the GEOGRAPHIC to have a picture on the cover, He would have put one there in the first place."

Melville Bell Grosvenor disagreed. Not long after he succeeded his father as Editor in 1957, he asked several staff members to pick out the most recent issue from a pile of magazines tossed on the floor of his office. When nobody could do so, he pointed out that the covers were virtually indistinguishable.

No more, he insisted. Emblazoned in full color across the July 1959 cover was Old Glory, with a star for the new 49th state of Alaska. August's cover reverted to black and white, but color appeared again in September and has never left. From then on, the magazine that had benefited so much from color photography tipped its hat to the technology right up front.

The Friendly Atom

With characteristic optimism, NATIONAL GEOGRAPHIC decided to look for silver linings in the mushroom clouds caused by atomic energy. "You and the Obedient Atom" (September 1958) and "Man's New Servant, the Friendly Atom" (January 1954) devoted an exhaustive number of pages to explain the nicer side of science's newest, scariest development. Somehow, the atom became more palatable.

"So small are nature's basic building blocks that you could put 36 billion atoms on the head of a pin," Allan C. Fisher, Jr., wrote in the 1958 article. "Yet these unimaginably tiny particles work like genii at man's bidding. Their peaceful energy is gradually shaping our world into a far better place."

This was a very different perspective from other publications that saw atomic energy leading to a nuclear Götterdämmerung. But the GEOGRAPHIC's take was legitimate, the result of two years of reporting and photography. Fisher described the atom's medical applications and ended the 49-page article on a poignant note with a young leukemia patient who hoped that atomic research might cure him.

The GEOGRAPHIC did not ignore atomic energy's negative side. Before Fisher's article, staff writer Samuel W. Matthews covered a nuclear explosion on a Nevada army base.

"The spreading mushroom became bright pink...," he wrote in the July 1953 issue. "Within 24 hours this cloud, carrying its... radioactive particles, was to be tracked across Utah,

URANIUM ATOM'S TIGHTLY CLUSTERED CORE IS THE MAIN SOURCE OF ATOMIC ENERGY.

Colorado, Kansas, Missouri, and into southern Ohio." The structure nearest the explosion was "crumbled into matchwood."

Top of the World

Man first reached the top of Mount Everest in 1953, and the GEOGRAPHIC illustrated the historic ascent of the world's highest mountain the next year in the July issue.

The coverage was extensive: An article by the British expedition's organizer, Sir John Hunt; another by Sir Edmund Hillary, one of the two men who climbed to the top; and a brief piece about President Dwight D. Eisenhower's presentation to the expedition of the Society's highest honor, the Hubbard Medal.

Everest's treacherous peaks had long tempted climbers from outside the Himalaya. Natives believed the mountains were the sacred dwellings of gods, off-limits to mortals. This began to change in the early part of the 20th century, as foreigners were willing to pay natives well to join expeditions.

Hunt's party was the eighth to attempt Everest since 1921 when Tibet first granted access to outsiders. He sent his two strongest climbers, Hillary and Tenzing Norgay, to make the ascent to the top.

"I'm not one of those blokes who says to himself, 'I'll get up, come hell or high water,'" Hillary told the GEOGRAPHIC audience. "Mountains mean a lot to me, but not that much."

TENZING NORGAY STANDS ON TOP OF THE WORLD.

The New Zealand beekeeper's realistic attitude was appealing to the end. "I feel no great elation at first, just relief and a sense of wonder. Then I turn to Tenzing and shake his hand.... He throws his arms around my shoulders, and we thump each other, and there is very little we can say or need to say."

Surviving the Big One

In 1950, 30,000 people lost their lives in a massive earthquake that rocked portions of India, Tibet, and Burma. The GEOGRAPHIC did not rush to cover the disaster; any other publication could tell readers that story. Instead, it waited almost two years, until March 1952, to gain a different perspective on what happened through the firsthand account of a British naturalist.

Dr. F. Kingdon-Ward was collecting botanical specimens in the Luhit Valley of southeastern Tibet on August 15 near the village of Rima. He was sitting outside his tent before going to bed when the quake began.

"It was as though the keystone had fallen out of the universe, and the arch of the sky were collapsing," he wrote. Ward, his wife, two sons, and servants hugged the ground until the first tremors were over. Nobody in the village was killed, but much was damaged.

"Almost every hillside had been torn open," he observed. "Strips of green pasture half a mile long had peeled off, leaving dead-white scars."

Ward and his family struggled for two and a half months to reach the nearest Indian city. His photos of the wrecked landscape were significant because almost none were available from that remote corner of the world. "It was not destruction," he concluded. "It was complete annihilation."

Eye in the Sky

The government's renewed interest in aerospace technology was leading up to something spectacular in the 1950s. The Society

THE MOON, PHOTOGRAPHED BY TELESCOPE

made a major contribution to the field when it completed the first *Sky Atlas* in 1956, a joint venture with the California Institute of Technology. The survey contained 1,758 pictures and mapped more of the universe than had ever been shown before. Astronomers still turn to the atlas as a reliable resource.

The magazine previewed a few of the pictures in the January 1953 issue. The black-and-white photos were taken by what was then the world's largest telescope at the Institute's Palomar Observatory. For many readers, it was the first time they'd ever seen Saturn's rings and Jupiter's giant eye.

"Face to Face with the Moon!" a legend trumpeted over a full-page shot of the lunar landscape pockmarked by craters and high mountains. "The Big Eye Shows Our Satellite as if 200 Miles Away."

The Scrolls' Scribes

The discovery of the Dead Sea Scrolls in 1947 fascinated scholars and laymen alike. For in those fragile pages was an

THE GREAT ISAIAH SCROLL FROM CAVE ONE, BEST PRESERVED OF THE ANCIENT DOCUMENTS

unprecedented glimpse into the early history of Christianity and Judaism from around the time Christ was born.

The GEOGRAPHIC took a close look at the first ten years of scholarship on the scrolls in December 1958. As was their practice, the editors asked an academic to write "The Men Who Hid the Dead Sea Scrolls." A. Douglas Tushingham oversaw art and archaeology for the Royal Ontario Museum. To report the story, he spent weeks with scholars in Khirbat Qumran, a ruin overlooking the Dead Sea. The scholars believed that Qumran was the home of the Essenes, authors of the scrolls.

The Essenes were an ascetic Jewish sect that came to Qumran around 100 B.C. to await the Messiah. They apparently abandoned their monastery more than 150 years later when Roman troops stormed Israel to quash rebellion. Before the Essenes fled, they hid their manuscripts and hymns in nearby caves until the fighting was over, then vanished from history.

"The Essenes, however, are far from forgotten," Tushingham wrote. "The scraps of leather that flow into the Palestine Archaeological Museum are at last restoring them to their rightful place in the chronicles of religious development."

Since the article's publication, some scholars have proposed that a different sect inhabited Qumran. The identity of the scrolls' authors is as intriguing at the century's end as it was in the middle.

Radiocarbon Dating

A new scientific tool, radiocarbon dating, came into use by the 1950s, one very important for an archaeologically oriented magazine like the GEOGRAPHIC.

Two writers described how the tool worked in the August 1958 issue. Scientists had recently used radiocarbon dating to determine the ages of Stonehenge and a Neandertal skeleton unearthed in the mountains of Iraq.

Dr. Willard Libby pioneered radiocarbon dating in 1947 and

won the 1960 Nobel Prize in chemistry for his discovery. His method of estimating an object's age by comparing the radioactivity in its carbon with that of modern carbon was explained through art, anecdotes, and the wisdom of the ancients.

"When man contemplates his own youth and insignificance in the face of such incomprehensible age," the article said, "he can but recall the words of the Psalmist: 'For a thousand years in thy sight are but as yesterday when it is past, and as a watch in the night.'"

211

Covering the Korean War

The GEOGRAPHIC's coverage of the Korean War began before the war itself.

"The arbitrary division into Northern and Southern Zones, which began as a military expedient for disarming of Japanese troops by American and Russian forces, became Korea's real tragedy," writer Enzo de Chetelet said in the June 1950 issue.

He then launched into descriptions of Koreans at work and play more typical of GEOGRAPHIC country stories. Still, the article seemed eerily prescient when the U.S. declared war on North Korea a month later.

Coverage of the war adopted a tone of upbeat boosterism. "Here Come the Marines" (November 1950) showed male and female leathernecks readying for battle. Objectivity went by the wayside in Adm. Arthur Radford's October 1953 article "Our Navy in the Far East." The photo coverage was uplifting; frowns were almost nonexistent throughout the 40-page story.

Frowns were more evident in the photographs accompanying "'Known But to God,'" (November 1958). The article was a tribute to the unknown U.S. soldiers killed in World War II and Korea. Assistant Editor Beverley Bowie's experience as a WW II veteran gave the short piece a personal, moving touch.

"A good place to learn [fear] would have been Taejon... where the bruised and reeling Eighth Army traded space for time," he wrote. He ended the piece in true military funeral style—with "Taps."

LATITUDE 38 STILL DIVIDES KOREA
AFTER THE GI'S ARE GONE.

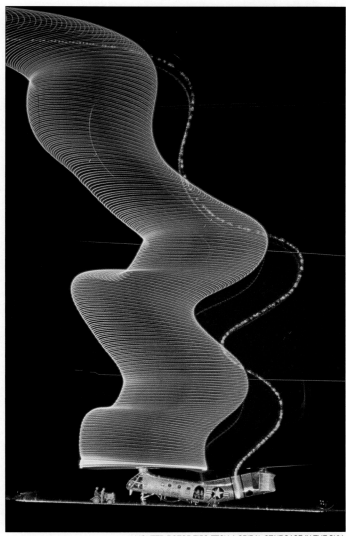

LIGHTED ROTOR TIPS ETCH A SPIRAL STAIRCASE IN THE SKY.

In Praise of the Whirlybird

While the rest of the world praised transatlantic jet passenger service, the GEOGRAPHIC took a new look at the trusty helicopter. Writer Peter T. White flew up and down, side to side, to see how many ways whirlybirds served people.

White's April 1959 article began and ended with Igor Sikorsky, who built one of the first usable helicopters in 1939. The inventor sent White on a cross-country flight aboard a military copter. Garbed in a fireproof flight suit and earplugs, the writer, along with a Marine pilot, took off.

"I wished he'd given me a bucket of cotton to put over my head...everything vibrated, especially my teeth. When I tried to write on a pad, my notes had that vibrant look, too."

White saw choppers do everything from fight fires to herd cattle. Something he and readers took for granted became something much more vital. "No, nothing about helicopters could surprise me anymore," he concluded.

212

Eleven days into President Harry S. Truman's second term, he faced one of the toughest decisions of any President's career—whether the U.S. should develop a weapon that had the power of 500 atomic bombs. He tackled it in a seven-minute meeting.

"Can the Russians do it?" Truman asked his three top advisers on the hydrogen bomb. "Yes," they replied. "We have no choice," the President said. "We'll go ahead."

The pressure on Truman was tremendous. To create the "Super," as the hydrogen bomb was called, was to introduce to the world an implement of war that could explode into a fireball three miles wide. J. Robert Oppenheimer, who helped build the atomic bomb, was one of many respected scientists who

ATOM BOMB TEST IN NEVADA

argued against the Super as immoral and impractical. Most of Truman's cabinet and a few other scientists countered that disaster would strike if the Russians made the bomb first.

On January 31 the President gave the go-ahead. The nuclear arms race was on.

▶ ALONE IN THE CROWD

The Lonely Crowd took a hard look at the American middle class and found it more alienated and artificial than ever. It was a society that valued conformity more than individuality. And that shocking revelation made the book a hot topic.

Sociologist David Riesman, along with Nathan Glazer, and Reuel Denney, wrote that many Americans had become "other-directed" people living by the community's standards rather than their own. In the past, Americans had been "inner-directed," motivated by their own beliefs.

This change in "social character" happened for many reasons. Families were smaller by 1950, so peer groups played a larger role in personal development. People also had more money and more leisure time to spend absorbing what they were seeing and hearing in an expanding number of media outlets. And they took cues from this new "family" of peers.

"Men are created different," the book warned. "They lose their social freedom and their individual autonomy in seeking to become like each other."

▶ FAULKNER'S CONCERN

William Faulkner's acceptance speech for the Nobel Prize for literature still resonates as one of the award's finest. The man best known for his writing about endurance and the triumph of the human spirit decided to address another emo-

tional subject— nuclear holocaust.

"Our tragedy today is a general and universal fear.... There are no longer problems of the spirit," he said. "There is only one question: When will I be blown up?"

WILLIAM FAULKNER

Few attending the banquet on December 10 could understand the speech. Faulkner stood far from the microphone and spoke too fast because he didn't want to be there at all. He was a farmer, he told reporters, and he could not leave the farm. Finally, his wife had persuaded him to go to Stockholm. So the author of such works as *Light in August* and *The Sound and the Fury* reluctantly accepted the accolade most writers dream of—in a rented tuxedo.

▶ CHINA INVADES TIBET

Tibet's brief period of independence ended on October 7 when her old enemy China attacked Tibet's eastern frontier.

More than a week slipped by before news of the fighting reached Tibet's capital, Lhasa. By then, Chinese troops were far into the country, and Tibetan soldiers were surrendering, unable to match the invaders' might.

TIBET'S YOUNG DALAI LAMA

The Chinese Quin (Manchu) Dynasty ruled Tibet from the late 18th century until 1911 when Tibet proclaimed its independence. Mao wanted to "liberate" or recapture the mountainous country along the Indian border for security and material reasons, and for historical considerations as well. The Chinese insisted that Tibet had always been theirs.

Tibetan leaders unsuccessfully pleaded their case to the UN, which was already having difficulty fighting the Chinese in North Korea. Tibet became part of China in 1951 and remains so today.

- **JANUARY**
India becomes the world's largest democratic republic.

- **FEBRUARY 9**
U.S. Senator Joseph R. McCarthy claims to have a list of 205 communists working for the State Department.

- **FEBRUARY 15**
The Soviet Union and China formally become allies through signing the Sino-Soviet pact.

- **MARCH 1**
Klaus Fuchs is sentenced to 14 years in prison in England for passing atomic bomb secrets to the Soviets.

- **APRIL 8**
Russian choreographer and ballet dancer Vaslav Nijinsky dies in London at 60.

▶ **MAY 11**
President Harry S. Truman dedicates Grand Coulee Dam in Washington State.

NSC-68

The defense business got a huge boost from the National Security Council's paper entitled "NSC-68," a document that essentially formed the underpinning of the Cold War. The council was created in the late 1940s to "create a unified military establishment" and hit its stride in the next decade.

Written in 1950, primarily by State Department officials detailed to the council, NSC-68 found that the U.S. could and should increase defense spending to keep the Soviet Union from gaining the upper hand. Not to do so "would result in a serious decline in the strength of the free world." NSC-68 did not explain how the military should build up or the costs necessary. Truman asked to have those questions answered in three subsequent papers.

When NSC-68 was presented in April, the council was only three years old. But its importance as an advising and policy-making entity was already apparent. The papers it had produced through 1950 set the course of American diplomacy for years to come.

BEGINNING OF THE KOREAN WAR

The Korean War began June 25 when North Korean soldiers in Soviet tanks burst across the 38th parallel, the line that separated the communist north from the noncommunist south. Days later, under a UN mandate to protect South Korea, President Truman sent in troops commanded by

U.S. MARINES BOARD A TRANSPORT BOUND FOR KOREA.

Gen. Douglas MacArthur. Through brilliant strategy, the general pushed the enemy back behind the parallel. But that was not enough for MacArthur; he wanted to free all Korea of communist forces. He assured Truman that he could do so without alarming North Korea's neighbor and ally, China.

But MacArthur grossly underestimated China's concern. In November the Chinese attacked, killing thousands of U.S. troops and forcing survivors to retreat south of the 38th parallel. It was one of the worst reversals in American military history.

"PEANUTS"

Charles Schulz (below) learned cartooning through a correspondence course. After several years of fine-tuning his skills, he introduced Charlie Brown, Lucy, Snoopy, and the rest of the "Peanuts" gang in seven newspapers on October 2.

His cartoons were uncluttered. His characters were children who behaved like children, not like the stereotyped cartoon characters of the period. Schulz's brainchildren flew kites, played ball, and, more often than not, lost the game. "Most of us are acquainted with losing," Schulz later told a reporter. "Very few of us ever win."

That vulnerability, combined with a razor-sharp wit, made "Peanuts" a hit. Shultz eventually put the Peanuts gang on lunch boxes and sweatshirts and in television specials and full-length movies. Almost five decades later, 2,600 papers in 75 countries carry Schulz's cartoons, which he continues to draw himself.

■ TRENDS & TRIVIA

"Frosty the Snowman" becomes a popular song.

Billy Wilder directs *Sunset Boulevard.*

L. Ron Hubbard's *Dianetics* is published.

Associated Press reporters name the racehorse Man O'War "horse of the first half of the century."

Diners' Club introduces the first credit card.

Oxford University professor C. S. Lewis introduces the enchanted land of Narnia in *The Lion, the Witch, and the Wardrobe.*

England observes the centennial of the bowler hat.

The George Burns and Gracie Allen Show debuts on television.

What's My Line goes on the air.

Nat King Cole's "Mona Lisa" sells more than three million records.

New York City opens the Port Authority Bus Terminal.

Minute Rice is introduced.

Delta bluesman Muddy Waters releases "Rollin' Stone"—from which the singing group and magazine take their names.

Rev. Billy Graham airs his weekly radio show, *The Hour of Decision.* ▼

213

- **JUNE 11**
French artist Henri Matisse wins grand prize at Venice Biennale. He is 81.

- **JUNE 17**
American surgeon R. H. Lawler performs first human kidney transplant.

- **AUGUST 8**
U.S. swimmer Florence Chadwick breaks the women's record, swimming the English Channel in 13 hours, 23 minutes.

- **OCTOBER 6**
World's longest oil pipeline is completed, between the Persian Gulf and the Mediterranean Sea.

- **OCTOBER 23**
Al Jolson, American film star and singer, dies at 67.

- **NOVEMBER 4**
The UN rescinds its 1946 resolution to bar Spain from all UN activities.

- **DECEMBER 25**
Scottish nationalists steal the sacred coronation Stone of Scone from Westminster Abbey. It is later recovered.

214

President Harry S. Truman had only one regret after he fired Gen. Douglas MacArthur (below)—that he had not done it sooner. "We might have got out of Korea six months earlier and not been…on the brink of a third world war," he told a biographer.

One of the last straws was MacArthur's announcement that he was ready to meet the Chinese and North Koreans to discuss ending the war. If they refused the meeting, MacArthur said his forces would attack China. "There is no substitute for victory," he wrote a Republican congressman.

His problem wasn't China, however; it was Truman, whom he never consulted on the issue. MacArthur's expansionist stand ran counter to what the President and the UN wanted—a settlement in Korea. Truman relieved MacArthur of his command on April 11.

Many Americans felt the President had fired a national hero. Years later, Truman said he knew he'd made the right decision: "Somebody has to be in charge who has been freely and legally chosen…by a majority of the people."

▶ PRESIDENTIAL TERM LIMITS

Passed by a Republican Congress in reaction to Democratic President Franklin Roosevelt's four terms in office, the 22nd Amendment to the U.S. Constitution limited a President's tenure to two terms. It was ratified February 26, four years after it surfaced as a bill on Capitol Hill.

The amendment set restrictions on the Vice President also. If he inherited a term less than two years long, he could be re-elected twice. If the term was longer, however, only once.

The controversial amendment was seen by some as harmful to a second-term President because it curtailed his effectiveness. Those in favor of curbing presidential power cited a tradition established by George Washington. The first president did not seek a third term because he did not think one person should hold such a powerful office for so long. That tradition was unbroken until FDR's second reelection in 1940.

▶ POWER OF TELEVISION

Television's power as a kingmaker and opinion-shaper became evident during Senator Estes Kefauver's investigation of organized crime. The lanky congressman from Tennessee went from obscurity to fame largely because of a lack of daytime programming.

Organized crime had become too big to combat on the local level, several mayors told Kefauver. "The Mob" had to be fought nationally, and Kefauver saw this fight as his ticket to the Vice Presidency. New York was one of the 14 cities where he planned to hold investigations. It was also the only city in the world where more people owned television sets than not. The networks wanted to give those owners, and others elsewhere, something to watch in the daytime.

Kefauver's hearings in March more than filled the bill. They were mesmerizing. "There in eerie half-light, looking at millions of small frosty screens, people sat as if charmed," *Life* magazine wrote. "For days on end and into the nights they watched with complete absorption…the broadcast from which all future uses of television in public affairs must date."

Kefauver never became Vice President. But he did win an Emmy.

▶ DAWN OF THE COMPUTER AGE

The world's first electronic digital computer designed for commercial use debuted June 14 in Philadelphia. The Universal Automatic Computer (UNIVAC) was designed by two engineers, John Mauchly and John Presper Eckert. Five years before, they had built ENIAC, one of the earliest large-scale electronic computers, at the University of Pennsylvania.

UNIVAC (below) was smaller, slower, and used less power than ENIAC. The new machine weighed 8 tons, performed about 2,000 calculations per second, and consumed about 100 kilowats of power. Its predecessor weighed 30 tons, accomplished 5,000 calculations per second, and used

• **JANUARY 10**
Nobel and Pulitzer-Prize winner Sinclair Lewis dies at 65 in Rome. He wrote *Babbitt* and *Main Street*.

• **JANUARY 18**
German automobile engineer Ferdinand Porsche dies at 75 in Stuttgart.

• **FEBRUARY 12**
The Shah of Iran, Reza Pahlevi, marries 19-year-old Soraya Esfandiari, daughter of a rebel chieftain.

• **FEBRUARY 14**
Sugar Ray Robinson defeats Jake "Raging Bull" LaMotta for the world middleweight boxing championship.

• **APRIL 26**
President Truman's daughter, Margaret, makes her radio debut in the NBC comedy *Jackpot*.

• **MAY**
South Africa removes all blacks from the electoral rolls so they cannot vote.

• **MAY 29**
American comedienne Fanny Brice dies at 59.

almost twice as much power as UNIVAC.

Mauchly and Eckert started to build the computers on their own, but ran into financial difficulties. In 1950 Remington Rand Co. bought their business and kept the engineers on board to oversee the UNIVAC project. Rand's first customer for UNIVAC was the U.S. Census Bureau. The computer helped analyze the 1950 census results.

▶ A KINDER, GENTLER ATOM
Scientists put atomic power to a peaceful use in December when a nuclear reactor generated electricity for the first time.

At a power plant built in Idaho under the auspices of the federal Atomic Energy Commission, the reactor used nuclear fission to run the plant's lights. It was successful because it made more plutonium, a highly fissionable element, from less uranium, an element of limited quantity.

Atomic energy was the hope of the future, an abundant source of economical power that lessened America's need for oil. But as time went on, these plants turned out to be more expensive to build and maintain than expected. The question of waste storage and disposal became increasingly problematic and the possibility of long-lasting, horrific effects from accidents at nuclear power plants made them unpopular. Even in peaceful applications, the power of the atom fell short of expectations.

▶ CATCHER IN THE RYE
J. D. Salinger's *The Catcher in the Rye* pulled no punches in explaining the teenage experience. The language was authentic, the situations real and often rough. These elements made it different from other books about teen angst. *Catcher*'s readers rarely came away ambivalent. Many schools made it required reading, while others banned the book from their shelves.

The protagonist, Holden Caulfield, became an icon for teens who identified

WE LOVED LUCY

When Lucille Ball suggested that her husband, Desi Arnaz, play her husband on the television show she was pitching to CBS, executives there said no. Nobody would believe that a woman from upstate New York would marry a Cuban bandleader. Besides, one consultant pointed out, nobody could understand him.

But Lucy *had* married a Cuban bandleader, one whose accent turned out to be one of the show's signature comedic devices. Shortly after *I Love Lucy* debuted on October 15, people tuned in to watch the zany redhead "splain" her antics to her husband. Desi turned out to be the perfect foil for Lucy.

I Love Lucy was one of the first television shows filmed in Hollywood instead of New York City. It helped launch another standard—reruns. The use of high-quality film ensured that viewers could love Lucy long after the show's demise in 1957.

with his disgust for "phonies" and the realization that growing up involved becoming one. "I'm always saying 'Glad to've met you' to somebody I'm not at *all* glad I met," Holden said. "If you want to stay alive, you have to say that stuff, though."

Salinger first published stories in the *New Yorker* in the '40s, but his work was largely unnoticed until 1951. The acclaim was overwhelming; he moved to New Hampshire where he lives reclusively, refusing all requests for interviews.

■ TRENDS & TRIVIA

The first section of the New Jersey Turnpike is opened to trafffic.

The United Nations complex in New York City is completed.

Richard Rodgers and Oscar Hammerstein's *The King and I* is a Broadway hit.

An Wang founds Wang Laboratories in Boston, Mass.

Cleveland disc jockey Alan Freed coins the term "rock 'n' roll."

Herman Wouk's *The Caine Mutiny* is published.

Chrysler Corporation introduces power steering.

Comic strip kid "Dennis the Menace" begins to irritate Mr. Wilson.

Jet magazine debuts.

The Roy Rogers Show airs.

Pete Seeger releases "On Top of Old Smokey."

Irving Gordon's song "Unforgettable" is popular.

Citation becomes the first racehorse to win a million dollars.

Television's first coaxial cable stretches across the country.

James Jones's *From Here to Eternity* is published.

Super Glue is introduced.

Bobby Thomson's three-run homer—the "shot heard 'round the world"—clinches the pennant for the New York Giants.

WCBS-TV in New York broadcasts the first baseball game in color.

AT&T becomes the first company with over a million stockholders.

215

● MAY
Guy Burgess and Donald MacLean, two high-ranking British diplomats, escape before they're arrested as Soviet spies.

● JUNE 13
Eamon de Valera, an American-born Irish nationalist, is re-elected Ireland's premier after three years out of office.

● JULY 20
Jordan's King Abdullah is assassinated as he enters a mosque in Jerusalem.

● DECEMBER 6
Harold Ross, editor and founder of the *New Yorker*, dies at 59.

▶ DECEMBER 11
Joe DiMaggio retires from baseball.

● DECEMBER 24
Libya gains its independence from Italy.

216

Gen. Dwight D. Eisenhower was elected President by people in need of a hero. The nation that had survived the Depression and two World Wars now worried that another war had the potential to end in atomic annihilation. Who better to get America through this menacing time than the soldier who'd rescued Europe from Hitler?

"Ike" told Republican and Democratic suitors that he wasn't interested in the Presidency. He was content as NATO's commander, a job more suited to his extensive military experience.

The Republicans managed to woo the conservative general to their ticket after rumors surfaced that Gen. Douglas MacArthur, a man Eisenhower vehemently disliked, was a potential candidate.

His opponent, eloquent and patrician Illinois Governor Adlai Stevenson II, was a favorite with the press and intellectuals.

Ike's appeal was broader. He came across as a friendly, small-town guy, a man who could cradle the war-weary nation like a father.

Eisenhower defeated Stevenson in a landslide. In doing so, he won more votes than any previous candidate.

▶ INVISIBLE MAN

Critics lauded Ralph Ellison's *Invisible Man* as the perfect Cold War novel, the story of an individual's struggles to realize himself fully as an American.

Ellison's unnamed hero faced his biggest challenge from a group called the Brotherhood, an underground organization most critics equated with the Communist Party.

What made Ellison's only published novel so compelling was his perspective. It emphasized the richness of black culture, even in an alienating, stifling urban setting. "It is drenched in Negro life, talk, music," gushed the *Nation*'s book review in May. "What white man could ever have written it? It tells us how distant even the best of whites are from the black men that pass them on the streets...."

Invisible Man won the 1953 National Book Award. A decade later, scholars voted it the most important book in 20 years.

▶ ELIZABETH II ASCENDS THE THRONE

When Elizabeth II inherited the British throne after her father died suddenly on February 6, she was prepared. The 25-year-old princess had been training for the job

GUARDSMEN PALLBEARERS CARRY THE COFFIN OF KING GEORGE VI.

for 15 years, ever since her father, George VI, took the throne upon the abdication of his brother, Edward VIII, in 1936.

"She loves her duty and means to be a queen," said Parliament member and future Prime Minister Harold Macmillan, "and not a puppet." Winston Churchill, then the prime minister, was more poetic; "A fair and youthful figure, princess, wife, and mother, is heir to all our traditions and glories."

During the war, Elizabeth had been an auto mechanic in the British Army. Her conscientious demeanor and her marriage to Philip Mountbatten, an able man who assisted her in official duties, endeared her to her subjects.

▶ HYDROGEN BOMB TEST

The first casualty of thermonuclear testing was Elugelab, a small atoll in the Marshall Islands of the South Pacific. There, on November 1, the U.S. government detonated a 65-ton thermonuclear device nicknamed Mike. The explosion blew the island off the face of the earth, leaving behind a crater that was two miles wide and half a mile deep.

The Soviet Union tested a thermonuclear device a year later, just as Edmund Teller, the determined scientist in charge of the American effort, had feared. Both countries tested more advanced H-bombs next, the U.S. in 1954 and Russia in 1955.

▶ MAU MAU REBELLION

The Mau Mau rebellion pushed open the doors for Kenya's independence. The Kenyan peoples, like others all over Africa, resented European rule and cried out for self-government.

Kenya as a country did not exist until the 20th century. Many different tribes, each with its own government, culture, and territories, lived in East Africa. Great Britain took over much of the region, and

The button reads: **LET'S BACK IKE**

• **FEBRUARY 17**
Dorothy Maynor becomes first black to sing at DAR's Constitution Hall in Washington, D.C.

• **FEBRUARY 29**
New York City installs its first four "Don't Walk" signs in Times Square; eight out of ten pedestrians obey them.

• **MARCH 7**
U.S. signs military aid pact with Cuba.

• **MARCH 7**
Fulgencio Batista takes control of Cuba for a second—and last—time.

• **APRIL 8**
President Truman orders the government to take over the nation's steel mills.

• **APRIL 15**
President Truman signs a treaty with Japan, granting Japan full sovereignty.

• **JULY 26**
Eva Perón, wife of Argentina's President Juan Perón, dies of cancer at 33.

A NIGHT RAID SEARCHES FOR MEMBERS OF THE MAU MAU.

renamed it Kenya in 1920. To lure colonists to the new nation, the colonial government set aside half of the best farmland for whites.

The tribes were outraged. The expropriation threatened their culture as much as it did their economic livelihood. Thousands of members of the large Kikuyu tribe formed a secret society called the Mau Mau to overthrow the English.

By October 1952 the Mau Mau had killed 43 people and hundreds of cattle, and set the countryside ablaze. Great Britain dispatched troops to Kenya to enforce martial law. Four years of fighting ensued, and some 13,000 people died. The Mau Mau was defeated, but its struggle was instrumental in Britain's decision to grant independence to Kenya in 1963.

▶ THE CHECKERS SPEECH
Richard M. Nixon opened his financial records and his heart to about 58 million Americans on national television September 23. Defending his handling of campaign contributions on TV was an extreme measure. But the Republican vice presidential candidate's future on Gen. Dwight D. Eisenhower's ticket depended on his ability to convince voters of his trustworthiness. Going on the air after *The Milton Berle Show* seemed the best way to reach the most people.

For 30 minutes, Nixon pulled out all the political stops—his war record, his family's slim finances, and how the enemies he made while fighting to save his country from communism wanted to ruin him two months before the election. No donor received special favors, he insisted, nor

A NEW WESTERN

High Noon was not a typical Western. It was shot in black and white, had no orchestral fanfares, and most of the action was psychological. And the hero cried.

To those who picketed theaters showing the film, this was downright un-American. Yet peeling away the Western facade revealed something very American—a look at how people behaved during the McCarthy years.

Gary Cooper won his second Oscar for his portrayal of Will Kane (below), a marshall left by his friends to face four outlaws alone. Their excuses were plausible—fear of retaliation or loss of income. This mirrored the situation on Capitol Hill, where many members of the Hollywood community were called to testify before the House Un-American Activities Committee. Few were willing to put aside the threat of personal ruin to stand up to the committee. Several of those who did were blacklisted.

had he spent campaign funds on his family. In fact, the only campaign contribution he kept was a black-and-white puppy that his daughter Tricia named Checkers.

"The kids love the dog," he said, as his wife, Pat, stood at his side. "Regardless of what they say about it, we're going to keep it."

Many viewers found Nixon's speech moving, and others were appalled that he would use his family to gain sympathy. Eisenhower called his running mate "a courageous and honest man" and kept him on the ticket.

217

• **AUGUST**
Crown Prince Hussein of Jordan, 16, succeeds his father, King Talial, who is declared mentally unfit to rule.

• **SEPTEMBER 26**
George Santayana, writer and philosopher, dies at 88 in an Italian convent.

• **NOVEMBER**
Archaeologists in Cyprus discover a 2,000-year-old mosaic depicting Homer's *Iliad*.

• **DECEMBER 10**
Dr. Albert Schweitzer wins the Nobel Peace Prize for his work in Africa.

◀ **DECEMBER**
London's killer fog is blamed for 12,000 deaths.

• **DECEMBER**
President-elect Eisenhower makes a three-day visit to U.S. troops in Korea.

SOVIET LEADER STALIN DIES

People greeted news of the death of Soviet despot Joseph Stalin (below) with tears or cheers. The former seminarian who killed millions of people and reshaped the face of Eurasia died of a brain hemorrhage in early March.

His death had the potential to cause chaos throughout the Soviet Union. When the Kremlin released the story the morning after he died, the country's new leaders reasserted their unity and readiness to prevent any possible coups or rebellions. Party Secretary Georgi Malenkov replaced Stalin, and another powerful party member, Nikita Khrushchev, replaced Malenkov.

Stalin's mummified body was displayed next to Lenin's until 1961 when de-Stalinization was in full swing. An old party member said that the ghost of Lenin himself was ashamed of Stalin's evil legacy. "I do not like being next to Stalin, who inflicted so much harm on the party," the spectral leader had supposedly told the man.

Lenin may have gotten his wish; Stalin's remains were placed in the wall surrounding the Kremlin along with others who had been instrumental to the Soviet cause.

▶ **KOREAN ARMISTICE**

The Korean War ended July 27 without obvious winners. The losers were more obvious—more than three million casualties during the three-year period.

Negotiators from the UN, China, and North and South Korea had been trying to end the war since 1951. At issue was the exchange of prisoners; the communists disagreed with the UN's policy that no POW should be forced to return to his army.

Just as an armistice was on the horizon, South Korea's President Syngman Rhee threw a wrench into the works by secretly arranging the mass "escape" of 25,000 North Korean POWs. His purpose was to torpedo the peace talks and thus prevent the permanent division of Korea.

Despite Rhee's actions, the armistice was signed. Politically and physically, little had changed on the Korean Peninsula. The boundary was roughly the same. Rhee controlled the south and Kim Il Sung ruled the communist north.

▶ **CIA HELPS OUST IRANIAN LEADER**

Prior to World War II, Great Britain exerted considerable influence in Iranian affairs. After the war, however, Britain's diminished power as a world leader emboldened Iran to seek more control over its destiny.

Britain acquired a controlling share of Iran's oil supply early in the century. The Iranians received a small share of the profits but could not even be certain of their portion because the books were closed to them. Fed up with the inequity, the Iranian government nationalized the oil business in 1951. The new premier, Muhammad Mossadegh, ordered all

British oil workers out of the country, and his troops took over the main refinery.

U.S. intelligence experts worried that in the ensuing chaos Iran's Communist Party would dethrone the Shah, its young, pro-Western ruler, and gain control of the country. In the summer of 1953, President Eisenhower gave the Central Intelligence Agency the go-ahead to orchestrate Mossadegh's ouster. It was one of the agency's first covert operations. Code-named "Ajax," the coup was an inexpensive success. Mobs supportive of the Shah overthrew Mossadegh August 19.

American oil companies gained about 40 percent of Iran's oil. In return for several million dollars in U.S. military and economic aid, the Shah allowed the U.S. to establish surveillance stations along Iran's border with the Soviet Union.

▶ **ROSENBERGS EXECUTED**

Convicted spies Julius and Ethel Rosenberg (opposite, top) gave the Soviet Union more than military secrets. They gave their lives, and became martyrs to a world sickened by McCarthyism.

A U.S. court handed the Rosenbergs the death penalty in 1951 after they were convicted on charges of passing important information about nuclear weapons to the Soviet Union. On June 19, 1953, they were electrocuted. In New York, where the couple had lived with their two young boys, thousands of people protested. The French government condemned the act as "barbarism." U.S. Supreme Court Justice William O. Douglas, who had granted the couple a stay of execution, faced charges of official misconduct.

The Rosenberg case continued to be controversial. As the Cold War thawed, the U.S. and the Soviet Union began to release information about the extent of damage the Rosenbergs had done to American security.

- **JANUARY**
The Yugoslav Parliament appoints Marshal Tito (Josip Broz) president.

- **FEBRUARY**
Dikes in Holland burst, killing 1,000 people. Another 300 die in related flooding on England's east coast.

- **MARCH 5**
Sergei Prokofiev, composer of *Peter and the Wolf*, dies at 61 near Moscow.

- **MARCH 31**
Swedish official Dag Hammarskjold becomes UN secretary general.

- **APRIL 15**
Film star Charlie Chaplin gives up his U.S. re-entry permit rather than face accusations of being a communist.

- **APRIL 15**
Pope Pius XII approves psychoanalysis for Catholics.

- **MAY 18**
American aviator Jacqueline Cochran becomes the first woman to fly faster than the speed of sound.

DNA DISCOVERY

A group of scientists centered around a brilliant British physicist named Francis Crick made the most important biological discovery of the 20th century: the physical structure of the genetic code.

Crick and James Watson, an American biochemist, hypothesized about the structure of the molecule deoxyribonucleic acid (DNA), then compared their theory with x-ray diffraction photos of DNA taken by two British biophysicists. It looked like a match. Crick and Watson then built a three-dimensional model that resembled a twisted spiral staircase.

Prior to this discovery, scientists knew that each cell of an organism carried genes, hypothetical structures that explained how traits were passed down from generation to generation. But nobody knew how those structures were designed. Crick and Watson used beads, wire, and cardboard to set up a double helix. It incorporated two identical strands of DNA. When a cell reproduced, the strands unraveled and became independent blueprints for two new cells.

"…They played a very minor role," said a retired Soviet spy. "…More important than their spying activities was that the Rosenbergs served as a symbol in support of communism and the Soviet Union."

Most scholars concluded that Julius, but not Ethel, was guilty of some degree of espionage.

▶ EAST GERMAN UPRISING
What began as a strike by thousands of East German workers against high production quotas accelerated into a pro-democracy riot June 16. The Soviet-run government retaliated by sending in tanks and troops the next day. The message was crystal-clear; behind the Iron Curtain was an iron fist ready to smash any uprisings instantly.

The high quotas were soon rolled back. The next year, the Soviet Union gave East Germany full sovereignty and no longer required it to pay stiff war reparations.

▶ GLORIFICATION OF BACHELORHOOD
Playboy was not merely a girlie magazine. It was a guide to a sophisticated lifestyle. In its pages, men learned how to re-create themselves as suave bachelors who knew what wine to order, car to drive, and cuff links to wear. The articles were enlivened by color photographs of stunning, often naked, women.

The magazine's creator, Hugh Hefner,

saw that America was ready for something like *Playboy*. He consumed Alfred Kinsey's recent reports that detailed what was going on in bedrooms across the country. He interpreted their findings as a sign that sexuality was about to become something to enjoy instead of hide.

Women were central to *Playboy*'s success. Hefner's first centerfold was Marilyn Monroe, who had posed for the picture when she was an unknown extra in 1949. By the time he bought the rights to the photo in 1953, she was a star. Her career survived the centerfold; Hefner's was made.

■ TRENDS & TRIVIA

TV Guide begins publication.

Hollywood spreads out onto wide-screened movies.

White Rose Redi-Tea is the first instant ice tea mix.

Mary Norton's classic children's book, *The Borrowers*, is published.

Spike heels (aka "stilettos") are popular.

Swanson serves up the first TV dinner.

Arthur Miller's *The Crucible* is staged.

"The Doggie in the Window" is a hit song.

Larry Rivers paints "Washington Crossing the Delaware."

Chevrolet introduces the sexy Corvette.

New York Curb Exchange becomes American Stock Exchange.

Maureen "Little Mo" Connolly becomes the first woman to win tennis's Grand Slam.

First kidney transplant is performed.

Radial tires are new.

Samuel Beckett's *Waiting for Godot* debuts in Paris.

Marlon Brando stars in *The Wild One*. ▶

James Baldwin's *Go Tell It on the Mountain* is published.

Jane Russell and Marilyn Monroe star in *Gentlemen Prefer Blondes*.

▶ JUNE I
Edmund Hillary and Tenzing Norgay are the first to reach the top of Mount Everest.

▶ JULY
U.S. golfer Ben Hogan wins his third major pro golf tournament in one year.

• AUGUST
Earthquakes and tidal waves kill a thousand in the Greek Ionian islands.

• NOVEMBER 9
Welsh poet Dylan Thomas dies in New York at 39.

• NOVEMBER 27
Playwright Eugene O'Neill dies at 65.

• DECEMBER
An English expedition leaves to search for Nepal's legendary Yeti, or abominable snowman.

220

"We conclude that in the field of public opinion, the doctrine of separate but equal has no place. Separated educational facilities are inherently unequal."

With those words, U.S. Supreme Court Chief Justice Earl Warren outlawed racial segregation in public schools. The practice had been challenged for more than a hundred years in the courts. But it finally died after the nation's highest court reviewed cases from South Carolina, Virginia, Kansas, Delaware, and the District of Columbia. The decision was known as *Brown* v. *Board of Education* after the Kansas suit.

The separate-but-equal policy came from an 1896 high court decision that ruled blacks were entitled to ride in a railroad car similar to one used by whites, but separate.

Separate became very unequal. Some states spent far less money on black facilities than white ones. To end this long-tolerated practice, Warren knew that his court had to present a unanimous front to impress upon the nation how badly the change was needed. The other eight justices concurred.

The ruling "deprived segregationist practices of their moral legitimacy...," wrote historian David Halberstam. "It instantaneously broadened the concept of freedom...."

▶ MCCARTHY'S DOWNFALL

U.S. Senator Joseph R. McCarthy's tirades were becoming tiresome by the summer of 1954. His relentless charges against alleged communists frequently turned out to be untrue. The Wisconsin Republican was even going after members of his own party.

An Army lawyer finally called him on the carpet before millions of television viewers on June 9. "Have you no sense of decency, sir?" Joseph Welch asked McCarthy after he'd attacked one of Welch's employees. "At long last, have you left no sense of decency?"

JOSEPH R. MCCARTHY WITH HIS ASSISTANT ROY COHN

The room erupted with applause. The ripple effects of Welch's rebuttal were widespread and sustained. FBI Director J. Edgar Hoover withdrew his support for McCarthy's probe. Eventually, reporters stopped taking his calls. Then the embarrassed U.S. Senate censured him. The man who had wrecked thousands of lives and convinced millions more that communism led to Armageddon was finished.

▶ THE "RESCUE" OF GUATEMALA

In June the CIA carried out its second successful coup d'etat. The Guatemalan effort had the two-pronged effect of fighting communism and protecting the interests of an American company closely tied to members of President Eisenhower's cabinet.

Two years earlier, Guatemalan President Jacobo Arbenz Guzman launched agricultural reforms designed to give farmland to impoverished peasants. The nationalized land program confiscated more than 400,000 acres from United Fruit Company, the American company that virtually controlled Guatemala.

The fruit conglomerate retaliated by pressuring the U.S. not to sell arms to Guatemala. Threatened by his country's hostile neighbors, Arbenz turned to arms dealers in communist Czechoslovakia. At last, Eisenhower had a reason to intervene; a nation in America's backyard was doing business with the communists.

The CIA coup used about 400 well-paid Guatemalan nationalists, a few planes, and a radio announcer who made a few troops sound like thousands. As the "rebel army" prepared to "rescue" Guatemala City, Arbenz angrily resigned.

U.S. Secretary of State John Foster Dulles called the coup "a new and glorious chapter for all the people of the Americas." Latin Americans saw it as another example of unwanted U.S. intervention.

▶ BREAKING BARRIERS

Roger Bannister did what nobody thought a human could do; he ran a mile in less than four minutes. After his feat (below), others broke the barrier, causing people to reevaluate the human body's limitations.

The British medical student won his first race when he was 13 years old. He participated in the 1952 Olympics, then took a year off from competition. Bannister soon convinced himself that he could break the previous record of running a mile in less than four minutes. His positive attitude was crucial because his studies gave him little time for training. Coaches told him that breaking the record could kill him. "I was prepared to die," Bannister said later.

The day his team was scheduled to race against the British Amateur Athletic Association was windy enough to cause

◀ **JANUARY 21**
The U.S. launches the *Nautilus,* the world's first atomic submarine.

• **JANUARY**
President Eisenhower proposes lowering the voting age in the U.S. to 18.

• **MARCH 1**
Four Puerto Rican nationalists open fire in the U.S. Capitol and wound five Congressmen after the island votes against independence.

• **APRIL**
Col. Gamal Abdal Nasser becomes Egypt's premier.

• **APRIL 4**
Famed conductor Arturo Toscanini retires at 87, ending a 68-year career.

• **APRIL**
Juan Péron is reelected president of Argentina.

Bannister to consider withdrawing. But he stayed in and ran the mile in 3 minutes, 59.4 seconds. Once across the finish line, he fainted.

▶ DIEN BIEN PHU

By 1954 France had begun to give up on Vietnam. Its struggle to hold that portion of its colonial empire had become *la guerre sale,* the dirty war.

Begun in 1947, it had gone on too long, killed too many people, and cost too much money. France wanted out. French commanders planned to show a spectacular display of military muscle to scare the Viet Minh, as the Vietnamese communists were called, into a settlement. The showdown

FRENCH PRISONERS CAPTURED AT DIEN BIEN PHU

would take place in a little valley near the Laotian border called Dien Bien Phu.

The location was, in the words of a skeptical French general, "a battalion meat grinder." The French had consistently underestimated the Viet Minh's size, capability, and determination. Led by Gen. Vo Nguyen Giap, the Vietnamese surrounded the French by taking the highlands around Dien Bien Phu. After a two-month siege,

ELVIS IS KING

Elvis Aaron Presley was a shy 19-year-old in 1954 when he cut his first record, "I'm All Right, Mama," in Memphis. He played the guitar, was a tolerable mimic, and he loved the beat of black music.

Black artists had begun to "cross over" to white stations, pulled along by teenagers. Elvis's first producer, Sam Phillips, said Elvis was exactly what black music needed to go mainstream—a white man who could sing like a black man.

Within two years, Elvis clinched his arrival on *The Ed Sullivan Show.* His timing was impeccable. Teens could afford the cheaper new transistor radios and portable record players, and more families owned cars with radios. Fans screamed for Elvis's pouty good looks. Known as "the Pelvis," he could whip his audience into a frenzy with a thrust of his hips.

the French surrendered May 7.

Both countries came to the negotiating table in Geneva in July. With British and Soviet approval, France and the Viet Minh signed a treaty that divided the country into two zones; the one north of the 17th parallel would be occupied by the communists and the south, by the French. The two would reunite to elect a leader in 1956.

France promptly gave control of the south to anti-communist Vietnamese forces who then formed the Republic of Vietnam. America's support of the new nation's refusal to acknowledge the Geneva treaty led to the Vietnam War.

■ TRENDS & TRIVIA

Time Inc. publishes *Sports Illustrated,* a weekly devoted to sports.

Marilyn Monroe marries baseball legend Joe DiMaggio.

The U.S. Air Force Academy is established.

First Newport Jazz Festival is held.

"Papa Loves Mambo" makes it easy to cha-cha.

William Golding's *Lord of the Flies* is published.

RCA begins selling color TV sets for $1,000 each.

Alfred Hitchcock directs *Rear Window.*

Robert Young stars in TV's *Father Knows Best.*

Ludwig Mies van der Rohe and Philip Johnson collaborate on the Seagrams Building in Manhattan.

Sun Myung Moon founds his Unification Church in South Korea.

Mercedes Benz introduces fuel-injected engines.

J. R. R. Tolkien's *The Fellowship of the Ring,* the first of the much-loved *Lord of the Rings* trilogy, is published.

NBC's *The Tonight Show* debuts on television.

Folkway Records releases a four-record set of the songs of the legendary Huddie Ledbetter, aka Leadbelly.

American singer Frank Sinatra wins an Oscar as Best Supporting Actor in *From Here to Eternity.* ▶

• APRIL 7
President Eisenhower announces his "domino theory;" if one Asian country falls to communism, the rest are sure to follow.

• MAY
Photojournalist Robert Capa dies after stepping on a land mine in Vietnam.

• JUNE 27
The Soviet Union opens the world's first atomic power station with enough power to supply a town of 5,000.

• JULY 11
Gen. Alfredo Stroessner, an anti-communist dictator, takes control of Paraguay. He will rule for the next 35 years.

• OCTOBER
Comic book publishers form the Comics Code Authority to regulate violence in response to claims that violent comics harm children.

• OCTOBER
Hurricane Hazel, worst to hit North America in recorded history, whips the U.S and Canada.

• NOVEMBER 3
Henri Matisse dies at 84.

T he civil rights movement made further inroads against racial segregation in December when a black seamstress, worn out from a long day's work, refused to relinquish her seat on a Montgomery, Alabama, bus to a white man. Her courageous action was upheld by the U.S. Supreme Court a year later.

Rosa Parks (below) had waited for an uncrowded bus because she wanted to sit on her ride home. When one finally came along, she sat in the back, the only section where

blacks were allowed. Soon, all seats were taken in both black and white sections. When a white man boarded, the driver ordered the first row of blacks to give up their seats. Parks was the only passenger who refused and for this, she was arrested.

The arrest led to a black boycott of Montgomery's buses. A young minister named Martin Luther King, Jr., organized carpools to keep the boycott alive until the Supreme Court rendered its decision during the following year.

AFL-CIO MERGE

The nation's two largest labor organizations joined forces in December to present a united front to a conservative President and an unsympathetic Congress.

The American Federation of Labor merged with the more left-wing Congress of Industrial Organizations and the AFL's tough, cigar-smoking George Meany became the new organization's first president. The AFL-CIO represented 16 million workers, or 30 percent of employed Americans. Its primary task was to champion labor's cause with politicians. It also provided a number of other services to its members, such as educational and economic research information. The individual unions continued to create their own guidelines. But they had to keep their practices and books clean, or risk expulsion from the organization.

Membership did not fluctuate much until about 1970 when it began to drop. Deindustrialization meant fewer union jobs, so more people pursued white collar or service industry jobs. By the century's end, the AFL-CIO represented about 16 percent of the nation's employment rolls. The organization created by the trend toward conservatism was powerless in halting it.

ROCK 'N' ROLL HITS THE BIG TIME

Rock 'n' roll exploded like a firecracker in July when "Rock Around the Clock" hit the top of *Billboard* magazine's chart. The tune stayed there for eight weeks, a major accomplishment for the new musical form.

"We were lucky," singer Bill Haley told a reporter. "We [with his band the Comets] came along at a time in which nothing new was happening in the music field. The big band era had faded. We had an open market. It was easy to hit a home run."

Haley's song mixed country-western bop with rhythm and blues. The energetic

BILL HALEY REHEARSES WITH HIS COMETS.

tune got even more exposure when it was featured in the soundtrack for *Blackboard Jungle*, a movie about teenagers. Haley, a balding, family man, found himself an unlikely symbol for the film's fans. He made the most of the song's popularity and made his own movie in 1955 entitled, of course, *Rock Around the Clock*.

THE BEAT GENERATION

"You don't have to be right," poet Allen Ginsberg said. "All you have to do is be candid."

His candor made him the poet laureate of the Beats, a group of young writers disgusted with American society in the 1950s. The core members—Ginsberg, Jack Kerouac, William S. Burroughs, and John Clellon Holmes—met in New York City where all but Burroughs attended Columbia University. In their quest to escape what they thought was a culture of irresponsible materialism, they turned to sex, drugs, jazz, and writing. The word "beat," meaning physically or emotionally exhausted in their parlance, summed up their sentiments perfectly.

Ginsberg, who was openly gay when few people were, followed fellow Beat, Neal Cassady, to San Francisco. There, in 1955, he wrote "Howl," the poem that made Ginsberg a hero for future generations. Critics praised the work, but the San Francisco Police Department condemned it as obscene. Ginsberg went to

► **JANUARY 7**
Contralto Marian Anderson is the first black to sing at the Metropolitan Opera House in New York City.

• **JANUARY**
RCA demonstrates a music synthesizer in New York City.

• **JANUARY 14**
Hubert C. Booth, inventor of the first vacuum cleaner, dies at 83 in England.

• **MARCH 12**
Jazz musician Charlie "Bird" Parker dies at 34.

• **APRIL 18**
Albert Einstein dies at 76 in Princeton, New Jersey.

• **MAY**
The Allies admit West Germany into NATO.

court to defend his freedom of expression two years later.

The strength of lines like "I saw the best minds of my generation/destroyed by madness" was not wasted on Judge W. J. Clayton Horn. Dismissing the charges, he noted "Howl" was "a plea for holy living."

▶ THE WARSAW PACT

The Warsaw Pact was the communist response to the North Atlantic Treaty Organization. Signed on May 14, the agreement bound the Soviet Union and its eastern European satellites (except Yugoslavia) together in a military alliance against their Western enemies.

The pact was triggered in part by NATO's admission of West Germany, which the Soviets saw as an armed threat on the fringes of the Iron Curtain. Wary of any Western influences trickling across the borders, the Soviets wanted to reassert their authority over their satellites by stationing troops throughout Eastern Europe. The pact enabled them to do this in the name of mutual defense.

▶ FEEDING THE MASSES IN MINUTES

Ray Kroc was a fastidious visionary. As he waited in line at the McDonald brothers' sparkling-clean hamburger restaurant in San Bernadino, California, he saw lots of people placing lots of orders with tidy attendants an hour before lunchtime. This mob was no fluke, the brothers assured him. It would stay crowded until the doors closed that night.

Kroc decided it was time to stop selling milkshake makers and start selling restaurants. He became the McDonalds' franchising manager in 1954, then opened his own franchise a year later in Des Plaines, Illinois, near his home in Chicago.

The McDonalds had devised a successful formula that Kroc knew not to tinker with. Experience taught the brothers to

POLIO CRIPPLED

Dr. Jonas K. Salk's development of the first effective polio vaccine helped bring the crippling disease to its knees in 1955.

Poliomyelitis struck thousands, particularly children, causing paralysis and death. Its most famous victim was President Franklin D. Roosevelt, who contracted the disease as an adult and was left partially paralyzed.

Salk made a vaccine with "killed" or inactivated strains of the three viruses known to cause polio. Other researchers believed only live viruses triggered the body to make the necessary immunities. This meant exposure to the virus; several who tried it died. Using an inactive virus reduced that possibility. Salk inoculated himself first, then conducted massive field trials in 1953 and 1954. The government approved his vaccine in April 1955.

limit the menu; this cut down on prep time and supplies. Everything was done in an assembly line with each person performing a specific job. Customers could be served in minutes, which allowed high turnover. By the time the McDonalds met Kroc, they'd opened nine franchises in 15 years and wanted to open just a few more.

Kroc was more ambitious. He bought out his employers in 1961 and continued to spread the gospel of the fast-food hamburger throughout the world. "It requires a certain kind of mind to see the beauty in a hamburger bun," he said later. Today, there are more than 21,000 McDonald's in more than 106 countries.

■ TRENDS & TRIVIA

Christian Dior introduces A-line skirts in his spring collection.

Disneyland opens in Anaheim, California.

The U.S. Air Force announces that there is no evidence of flying saucers or other unidentified flying objects (UFOs).

University of Maryland freshman Jim Henson introduces his Muppets on a local show.

Captain Kangaroo and *The Lawrence Welk Show* debut.

Kentucky Fried Chicken is introduced.

Kenner Toys sells Play-Doh.

The Ladies Professional Golf Association (LPGA) holds its first tournament.

Johnny Cash releases "Folsom Prison Blues."

Sloan Wilson's *The Man in the Gray Flannel Suit* is published.

Tennessee Williams's play *Cat on a Hot Tin Roof* is staged.

The game show *The $64,000 Question* goes on TV.

Vladimir Nabokov's *Lolita* is published.

A presidential press conference is televised for the first time.

Coonskin caps are the rage. ▶

223

• **MAY 16**
U.S. signs a treaty giving Cambodia military aid.

• **JUNE 13**
Pressure from the League of Decency forces theaters to remove posters of Marilyn Monroe holding down her dress in *The Seven-Year Itch.*

• **JULY**
Frenchman Louison Bobet wins the Tour de France for the third time.

• **JULY**
Jazz trumpeter Miles Davis gains stardom after appearing at the Newport Jazz Festival.

• **SEPTEMBER 19**
Argentine leader Juan Perón is overthrown and replaced by Gen. Eduardo Lonardi.

• **SEPTEMBER 30**
Actor James Dean dies in a car crash at age 24 in California.

• **OCTOBER 26**
Ngo Dinh Diem announces that he is president of the newly formed Republic of South Vietnam.

Soviet leader Nikita Khrushchev's blistering condemnation of his predecessor, Joseph Stalin, in a closed-door speech to Communist Party members, was interpreted by some of Russia's satellites to mean that the days of short-leashed governance were over. Perhaps, they hoped, the new regime would be more tolerant of nationalism.

This interpretation of Krushchev's de-Stalinization program proved to be fatal for many Hungarians. On November 1, Hungarian Prime Minister Imre Nagy withdrew his country from the Warsaw Pact and announced Hungary's neutrality. Three days later, 2,500 Soviet tanks rolled into Budapest to quash the rebellion; 207,000 people were killed, and another 150,000 fled the country. Nagy was captured and later executed.

The Hungarian rebellion of 1956 "showed that the Soviet Union would use force to keep its new empire intact," a *New York Times* editorial said. "It also made clear, for the first time, that the West would not send military aid even to a broadly supported, armed anti-Communist uprising."

▶ CINEMATIC ROYALTY BECOMES REAL

It was a storybook event hailed as the wedding of the century. Real royalty married cinematic royalty on April 19 when Prince Rainier III of Monaco took actress Grace Kelly of Philadelphia to be his wife (right). More than 1,200 guests attended, while another 30 million watched on television as the elegant, taffeta-clad American became a princess.

Kelly was the daughter of a wealthy businessman who'd begun his career as a bricklayer, a good example of the American dream come true. She starred in a number of films in the early '50s, such as *High Noon*, *Rear Window*, and *The Country Girl*, for which she won the Academy Award for Best Actress. While filming *To Catch a Thief* on the French Riviera in 1955, Kelly met Rainier, who ruled a tiny principality known for its glamorous casinos. The two were engaged by the year's end.

After the lavish wedding, Princess Grace left show business. She devoted herself to her three children and charitable works. In 1982 she was killed when she lost control of her car on a mountain road in Monaco.

▶ SINKING OF THE ANDREA DORIA

The *Andrea Doria* was supposed to be unsinkable. The Italian ocean liner had state-of-the-art equipment and a hull divided into watertight compartments. Despite these modern trappings, the ship sank less than 12 hours after it was broadsided by another ship. Fifty-two people died.

The disaster was one of the costliest and most controversial in maritime history. The New York-bound *Andrea Doria* was carrying 1,134 passengers from Genoa. As it rounded Nantucket July 25 and headed southwest, the Swedish liner *Stockholm* approached from the opposite direction. With a mighty prow designed to break icebergs, the *Stockholm* rammed into the Italian ship's hold. Several passengers were crushed in their berths.

After admiralty courts could not decide which ship was at fault, the ships' owners established a fund to settle 40 million dollars worth of claims.

▶ THE SUEZ CRISIS

Egypt's nationalization of the Suez Canal in July pitted the U.S. against Great Britain, France, and Israel.

Egypt, under the leadership of President Gamal Abdel Nasser, had become the center of Arab nationalism, a key component of which was opposition to Western colonialism. This made it difficult for Nasser to get funding for a new dam at Aswan. When the U.S., suspicious that neutrality was as evil as communism, withdrew its offer to help fund the dam, Nasser looked to the Suez Canal as a revenue source. The crucial link between the Mediterranean and the Indian Ocean was a cash cow. He informed stockholders in the Suez Canal Co. that they would be compensated for their investment based on values set by the Cairo stock market.

This infuriated Britain and France, two of the largest stockholders. In October France and Israel devised a plan to seize the canal and invited the British to take part. The plan called for Israel to invade Egypt's Sinai Peninsula, which would prompt Egypt to respond with force. France and Great Britain would then demand that Israel and Egypt pull back from the canal zone, knowing full well that Egypt would refuse. The Europeans would have a pretext to intervene and take back the canal; Israel would gain new territory.

The U.S. was appalled, mostly because its two allies had undertaken the operation behind its back. The government pressured Israel, France, and Great Britain to back off,

SUNKEN SHIPS BLOCK THE ENTRANCE TO THE SUEZ CANAL.

which they did. By the next spring, Israel had left the Sinai, Britain and France's influence in the Middle East was destroyed, and Egypt remained in charge of the canal.

▶ PEYTON PLACE

Grace Metalious had a feminist vision before the term came into widespread use. The heroines of her best-selling novel *Peyton Place* were independent women who wanted control over their lives and desires.

"They wanted more than to simply find the right man....," historian Kenneth Davis said of the book. "For perhaps the first time in popular fiction a writer was saying that women wanted sex and enjoyed it but they wanted it on their terms."

Metalious was a housewife in New Hampshire with little to lend to a writer's vocation except great self-discipline and a keen sense of the superficiality of small-town life. "It's like turning a rock over with

ROAD NETWORK

The largest public works project in U.S., the Highway Act, emphasized how important the automobile had become to American society. The multibillion-dollar, 41,000-mile network of roads would link all cities with more than 50,000 residents. Theoretically, one could drive across the continent without stopping.

"More than any single action by the government since the end of the war, this one would change the face of America," President Eisenhower wrote.

The improved highways meant greater mobility for the military in emergencies—a logical reason why the project began when a former general lived in the White House. The federal government was responsible for 90 percent of building costs; the states would assume the remaining 10 percent.

The law was a huge boon for the trucking industry, which took over more than a quarter of the country's shipping business during the next four decades. Passenger trains were the losers. The number of passengers dropped precipitously while the number of automobile registrations soared.

your foot," she said. "All kinds of strange things crawl out."

It was the "strange things" about *Peyton Place* that made it a euphemism for respectable-looking towns haunted by scandalous secrets. Rape, incest, adultery—these were things upstanding citizens did not discuss, let alone commit. But 60,000 of them bought the book within ten days of publication to read about those who did. *Peyton Place* became a popular book, movie, and television show.

■ TRENDS & TRIVIA

James Baldwin's *Giovanni's Room* is published.

Pampers disposable diapers are introduced.

Comet, the powdery blue-green cleanser, goes to work.

Proctor & Gamble introduces Crest, the first fluoride toothpaste.

Brigitte Bardot electrifies moviegoers with her sensuality in husband Roger Vadim's *And God Created Woman.*

First transatlantic telephone cable system goes into operation.

My Fair Lady, a musical rendition of playwright George Bernard Shaw's *Pygmalion,* is staged.

Harry Belafonte's "Calypso" turns the U.S. on to Caribbean rhythm.

W. H. Whyte's *The Organization Man* is published.

Two soap operas debut, *The Edge of Night* and *As the World Turns.*

Charleton Heston and Yul Brynner star in *The Ten Commandments.*

John F. Kennedy's *Profiles in Courage* is published.

New York Yankee Don Larsen pitches the first and only perfect World Series game in history.

The Teflon Company introduces the first nonstick cookware.

David Brinkley and Chet Huntley anchor NBC's *Huntley-Brinkley Report.* ▶

First transcontinental helicopter flight is made.

Little Richard releases "Tutti Fruitti."

• MARCH
France grants independence to Morocco and Tunisia.

• MARCH 17
Radio comedian Fred Allen dies at 61.

• AUGUST 14
German playwright Bertolt Brecht dies in Berlin at 58.

• AUGUST 17
Democratic presidential candidate Adlai Stevenson II names Senator Estes Kefauver as his running mate.

• NOVEMBER 6
Dwight D. Eisenhower is reelected President of the U.S.

• NOVEMBER 9
French writer Jean-Paul Sartre breaks with the Communist Party.

• NOVEMBER 26
Jazz musician Tommy Dorsey dies in Greenwich, Connecticut.

1957

SOVIETS LAUNCH SPUTNIK

When the Soviet Union sent the world's first satellite into space on October 4, the U.S. watched with shock and apprehension. *Sputnik* (Russian for "traveling companion") gave space exploration the jet-propelled boost necessary to start the race to the next frontier, and the Soviets were in the lead.

Each branch of the military wanted to be the one chosen to develop a satellite. The Army's group was headed by rocket scientist Werner von Braun, who was instrumental in developing Germany's missile program during World War II. Although his group's satellite was almost ready, the Defense Department gave the job to the Navy. When that satellite, later nicknamed "Kaputnik," exploded on the launch pad, the Army's team got the nod to finish its project.

Explorer I went into orbit January 31, 1958, two months after the Soviets launched *Sputnik II*.

The U.S. was determined not to lag behind in science and technology again. In order to better train future scientists, the government entered the college loan business, offering grants and loans to students and schools under the auspices of the National Defense Education Act.

PAPA DOC TAKES OVER HAITI

Haiti's new president looked good on paper. François Duvalier directed his country's efforts to eradicate malaria and yaws, a disfiguring disease that afflicted many Haitians.

"Papa Doc," turned out to be one of the most oppressive dictators in the Western Hemisphere. Surrounded by murderous thugs called *tontons macoutes* (Creole for "bogeymen"), Duvalier killed 2,000 people and sent many more into exile. He proclaimed himself president for life in 1964.

The U.S. cut diplomatic ties with Haiti. Tourism all but disappeared. The isolated country was under a voodoo curse, kept spellbound by the bloodthirsty tontons.

Duvalier died in 1971 and was succeeded by his inept son, Jean-Claude, or "Baby Doc." By 1986 enough Haitian exiles had spread the word about the Duvaliers' miserable tyranny to make it an international issue. When Baby Doc was overthrown in February, he fled to France.

BASEBALL MOVES WEST

The year ushered in a new era for one of the most fundamental pieces of American pie—baseball. The New York Giants and the Brooklyn Dodgers traded their historic identities for California, becoming the first major-league baseball teams headquartered west of the Rocky Mountains.

Dodgers owner Walter O'Malley and Giants owner Horace Stoneham together decided to follow current migration patterns to California. The Dodgers moved to Los Angeles; the Giants chose San Francisco. New Yorkers were outraged, particularly because O'Malley was making a good profit in New York.

"It had always been recognized that baseball was a business," veteran

SAN FRANCISCO GIANT WILLIE MAYS CATCHES A FLY BALL.

sportswriter Red Smith wrote. "O'Malley was the first to say out loud that it was all business—a business that he owned and could operate as he chose."

INDEPENDENCE FOR GHANA

Ghana became sub-Saharan Africa's first country to achieve independence on March 6, as representatives of more than 50 countries participated in the celebration. The former British colony's declaration galvanized other African colonies to seek their freedom. By the next decade, the continent's political face was dramatically different.

Ghana's road to independence was not smooth. Riots and strikes had erupted in the small country on the Atlantic coast in 1948. To end the troubles, Britain gave its colony a greater role in self-governing. The gradual transition to freedom that followed was less volatile.

The newest U.N. member seemed to

- **JANUARY 14**
Actor Humphrey Bogart dies at 57.

- **MARCH 29**
Teamsters Union Vice President Jimmy Hoffa is indicted for bribery and other charges.

- **APRIL 9**
Italian auto manufacturer Fiat decides to enter the U.S. market.

- **AUGUST**
Malaya becomes independent after 170 years of British rule.

- **AUGUST 7**
Oliver Hardy, the stout half of Laurel and Hardy, dies at 65.

- **AUGUST 29**
South Carolina Senator Strom Thurmond filibusters for 24 hours to prevent the Civil Rights Act from passing. He is unsuccessful.

have a bright future. There were some industries, such as mining, and a healthy cacao crop. Prime Minister Kwame Nkrumah, an avowed Christian, was educated in the U.S. and England. But to the dismay of Western leaders, he gradually turned to China for political inspiration. He was a despot until overthrown by the military in 1965.

▶ EUROPEAN ECONOMIC COMMUNITY

Six European nations (France, West Germany, Luxembourg, Italy, Holland, and Belgium) came together in March to promote economic integration. The European Economic Community hoped that by doing so, it could avoid any more world wars and global depressions.

The EEC worked to eliminate trade barriers within the countries' borders and establish a tariff for goods imported from outside the bloc; within ten years members were trading four times as much as before.

In 1967 the EEC merged with other groups to form the European Community. Three decades later, the now 15-member organization had renamed itself the European Union and was a strong economic competitor to the U.S. and Asia.

▶ THE CAT IN THE HAT

A mischievous cat in a tall striped hat started a crusade in 1957. This crafty animal (and its creator, writer Theodor Geisel—aka Dr. Seuss) showed that learning to read could be fun. To do that, Seuss strung together about 220 words, accompanied by fantastic, cheery art. The results delivered what columnist Ellen Goodman called "a karate chop on the weary little world of Dick, Jane, and Spot." Geisel's book about a cat, two children, and a self-righteous fish left alone on a rainy day differed from his other works

because he wanted children to be able to read it by themselves. He used rhymes they could easily sound out such as, "Look at me now! It is fun to have fun, but you have to know how." His hair-raising plot kept kids on the edges of their seats wondering if the cat's mess could be cleaned up before the children's mother returned.

Along with Dr. Seuss's other 1957 book, *How the Grinch Stole Christmas*, *The Cat in the Hat* became a staple in first-grade classrooms and in American households—with or without children.

BOOMERS!

The number of new Americans born in 1957 reached 4.3 million, the most in almost 30 years. A baby was born every seven seconds, increasing the demand for housing, schools, and diapers.

Veterans had returned from the war eager to start more peaceful lives with wives and children. The economy was strong, and new housing developments mushroomed to accommodate the new families. School construction was a high priority as the number of elementary and middle school students jumped.

The swell in population reverberated for years. The 29 million Americans born in the 1950s, dubbed the "baby boomers," would attend college in greater numbers than any previous generation. Many became the student activists of the '60s who fought for radical changes in the American way of life.

• **SEPTEMBER 4**
The Arkansas National Guard is called out to prevent nine blacks from enrolling in Little Rock's all-white Central High School.

• **SEPTEMBER 20**
Finnish composer Jean Sibelius dies at 91.

• **OCTOBER 24**
French designer Christian Dior dies at 52.

• **OCTOBER 24**
The AFL-CIO suspends the Teamsters on the grounds of corruption.

• **OCTOBER 29**
Movie magnate Louis B. Mayer dies at 72.

• **NOVEMBER 5**
The British government allows women to sit in the House of Lords.

• **DECEMBER 10**
French writer Albert Camus wins the Nobel Prize for literature.

China's Great Leap Forward turned out to be the exact opposite. Mao Zedong's scheme to industrialize the country killed 20 million people.

Mao (below with Zhou Enlai) wanted his leap to accomplish many things, not the least of which was to supplant Soviet communism with his own philosophy. To modernize, Mao called on China's one great resource—its people.

Peasants were put to work around the clock to create a better infrastructure. They built furnaces in their yards to make steel. Their farms became parts of bigger communes. "The achievements of a single night surpass those of several millennia," crowed Chinese propagandists. Output increased, but the West did not consider Chinese figures reliable.

This new push was a death knell for agriculture. The diversion of farm labor left the country under a famine. By 1962 millions had starved to death, many of them children.

Mao refused to apologize for the Great Leap, but he temporarily lost stature and authority within the Chinese leadership as a result.

He remained in the background until the Cultural Revolution in 1966.

▶ NASA TAKES OVER U.S. SPACE PROGRAM
Four decades before *Sputnik* dashed America's hopes of launching the first satellite into space, Smithsonian Secretary Charles D. Walcott saw the need for a federal agency to kick-start an aeronautics industry. His vision became the National Aeronautics and Space Administration (NASA), which was established in October.

NASA gathered the research done by various branches of the military together under one roof. Congress intended that the agency explore nonmilitary aeronautical and space uses; the director would be a civilian. Its first project was to investigate the planet and its atmosphere with the *Explorer* satellites, which also debuted in 1958. Information from these satellites led to the discovery of the Van Allen belts, rings of electrically charged particles surrounding earth.

NASA made some great advances and suffered some equally great tragedies in space exploration. The U.S. soon zoomed to the field's forefront as it developed an industry that employed thousands and earned billions.

▶ PASTERNAK FORCED TO REFUSE PRIZE
Boris Pasternak, the first Soviet writer to win the Nobel Prize for literature, became the first writer in history not to accept it. "I must reject this undeserved prize...," he wrote the Swedish organization in October. "Please do not receive my voluntary rejection with displeasure."

Few believed it was voluntary. The *New Yorker* magazine had called his prizewinning novel, *Dr. Zhivago*, "one of the great events in man's literary and moral history." Pasternak himself knew it was a masterpiece: "I completed my chief and most important work, the only one I am not ashamed of," he wrote.

The Soviet government felt otherwise and pressured Pasternak to turn down the Nobel. The book's hero was a doctor disillusioned with Soviet ideology who sought fulfillment in Christianity. For a Soviet citizen to accept an award for such a story was to admit flaws in the system. The 68-year-old writer was a traitorous "pig" in the eyes of the party. He lost his membership in the Union of Translators, which threatened his livelihood as one of the country's foremost literary translators.

Despite the campaign against Pasternak, crowds of people attended his funeral in 1960. It took the Soviets another 18 years to accept *Dr. Zhivago*. But even then, the party was cautious; the novel appeared as installments in a literary magazine.

▶ JET SET
The world became much smaller on October 4 as British Overseas Airways Corp. (BOAC) launched the first transatlantic passenger jet service from New York to London. The trip took a little more than six hours, about two-thirds as long as the same trip via prop plane.

The U.S. was not far behind. Pan American World Airways sent a Boeing 707 to Paris on October 26. Mass air-transit had a speedy, smooth, and remarkably quiet start. Once passengers realized that going to Europe or North America did not entail a wearisome nine-hour flight, they were more inclined to go.

Aircraft manufacturers rose to the occasion. Soon the skies were streaked with white plumes of jet exhaust, which caused another form of air pollution. More people flying farther than ever before also led to a new proliferation in airborne diseases, some scientists theorized. Many of these flu strains seemed to originate in the Far East.

• JANUARY
Linus Pauling presents a petition signed by 9,000 scientists asking the UN to halt all nuclear testing.

◀ MARCH
Nikita Khrushchev becomes Soviet premier.

• MARCH 24
Elvis Presley is drafted into the U.S. Army.

• APRIL 18
Poet Ezra Pound pleads insanity to treason charges in the U.S.

• APRIL
American pianist Van Cliburn, 23, wins the International Tchaikovsky Piano Competition in Moscow.

• MAY 14
Vice President Richard Nixon cuts short his Latin American tour after demonstrators in Peru and Venezuela protest his visit.

Speedy jet travel made quick trips abroad feasible—for those who could afford it. The new form of travel brought forth a new class of people: the "jet set."

▶ FRANCE'S COLONIAL STRUGGLES
Algeria's struggle for independence brought France to the brink of civil war in 1958 and toppled the Fourth Republic.

Holding on to the North African colony had become an economic strain for France, and many people were reluctant to pay for a war that benefited a small number of French colonists in Algeria. However, the *colons*, as the colonists were called, were equally reluctant to relinquish control of the land they had ruled since the early 19th century to Algerian Muslims. The French military supported the colons and was eager to keep Algeria an integral part of France.

To rescue France from bloodshed, President René Coty turned to well-loved war hero Charles de Gaulle. The former general agreed to assume control as premier on the condition that he be allowed to present a new constitution. De Gaulle and other like-minded French nationalists wanted to do away with the corrupt and inefficient Fourth Republic, and resolving the Algerian rebellion gave them that opportunity. De Gaulle's constitution, which was approved in September, transferred decisive power from parliament to the executive branch. Two months later he became president of the new Fifth Republic.

De Gaulle began taking steps to allow Algeria to leave the French fold, despite the opposition of rogue French military officers. In 1962 Algeria became independent.

REBELS IN THE DESERT

THALIDOMIDE

The thalidomide scare that began in the late 1950s led to vast improvements in the way drugs are tested in the U.S. The potent drug caused 10,000 babies to be born with deformed or missing limbs (below).

The drug, first produced by a German pharmaceutical company in 1953, soothed nausea in the early stages of pregnancy and induced sleep.

In 1958 it was available over the counter in many European countries and Canada.

Rules governing pharmaceutical testing were almost nonexistent in 1958. In the U.S., the onus of proving a drug's safety fell to the government instead of the manufacturer. If the Food and Drug Administration did not report any deficiencies within 60 days, the drug went on the market.

Thalidomide was the first drug Dr. Frances Kelsey, a new FDA employee, reviewed in 1960. Sensing the drug was problematic, she and her colleagues questioned the manufacturers. Her determination to get answers delayed the process for months—long enough to establish a solid link between thalidomide and an epidemic of deformed babies in countries where it was sold. The manufacturers withdrew their application.

■ TRENDS & TRIVIA

Pelé, a 17-year-old Brazilian soccer star, dazzles the world with his ability to score goals.

French designer Yves Saint-Laurent impresses fashion writers with his first line.

Artist Jasper Johns introduces his form of Abstract Expressionism in New York.

BankAmericard and American Express issue credit cards.

Sweet 'N' Low sweetener debuts.

The Grammys—the Oscars of the recording industry—are given for the first time.

Eugene Burdick and William J. Lederer's *The Ugly American* is published.

Truman Capote's *Breakfast At Tiffany's* is published.

American Bobby Fischer becomes the world's youngest chess grand master at 15.

Maurice Chevalier sings "Thank Heaven For Little Girls" in the film *Gigi*.

The conservative John Birch Society is established.

Eddie Fisher leaves Debbie Reynolds for Elizabeth Taylor.

Leon Uris's *Exodus* is published.

"The Purple People Eater" and "Catch a Falling Star" are popular songs.

Ten-year-old Mimi Jordan is national Hula Hoop champion. ▶

229

• JUNE 28
The world's longest suspension bridge opens in Michigan. The Mackinac Bridge measures 8,614 feet long.

• JULY
King Faisal II, Iraq's crown prince and prime minister, is assassinated in a coup by the army, which establishes a republic.

• SEPTEMBER 12
An engineer at Texas Instruments invents the computer microchip.

• SEPTEMBER 22
Sherman Adams, a top Eisenhower adviser, resigns in the wake of charges that he accepted numerous gifts.

• NOVEMBER 8
Jeweler Harry Winston donates the 44.5-carat Hope Diamond to the Smithsonian Institution in Washington, D.C.

• NOVEMBER 15
Actor Tyrone Power dies at 44.

Cuban revolutionary Fidel Castro (below) was a charismatic leader worth befriending, Vice President Richard M. Nixon concluded after meeting him. "Because he has the power to lead, we have no choice but at least to try to orient him in the right direction," Nixon told President Eisenhower.

But Eisenhower suspected that Castro was a red in olive clothing and wanted little to do with him.

Castro's predecessor, Fulgencio Batista, was good to American businesses like United Fruit, which dominated the island's sugarcane industry. Castro, an ardent nationalist, threatened those relationships. After forcing Batista to resign in January, he launched agrarian nationalization that expropriated almost 1.7 million acres from American firms.

Many Cubans were delighted with this and by their bearded leader who earned the support of the downtrodden masses.

Castro soon hitched Cuba's wagon to the Soviet star, establishing a communist beachhead a mere 90 miles from the U.S.

▶ ST. LAWRENCE SEAWAY OPENS

In a good expression of Canadian-American cooperation, the St. Lawrence Seaway opened June 26, permitting ships on the Atlantic Ocean to sail to the continental heartland near the Great Lakes. Regional harbors such as Cleveland and Toronto became international ports.

Twenty-two thousand people spent four years building the 2,300-mile-long waterway. But the idea behind making the St. Lawrence more navigable had been around since French explorers first reached its mouth in 1534. Canada and the U.S. agreed to build the waterway in 1932. But when the agreement went to Congress for ratification 12 years later, the railroad and seaport lobbies, afraid of losing business, blocked its passage.

After the war, new obsessions with national defense made the waterway more attractive. Canada covered 71 percent of the costs in return for the same percentage of toll revenue. The St. Lawrence Seaway continues to be one of the continent's most important shipping routes.

▶ THAT MOTOWN SOUND

Motown was the first black-owned company to capitalize on black music. Ex-boxer Berry Gordy, Jr., turned a frame house in a nondescript part of Detroit into a talent factory the likes of which remained unparalleled in modern music.

Diana Ross, Marvin Gaye, the Temptations, and Stevie Wonder were just a few of the stars who cut their teeth at Motown. Detroit's booming auto industry had lured many blacks to the city; Gordy himself worked on Ford's assembly line. The large black population gave rise to a lively music scene deeply rooted in gospel and the blues.

Gordy decided that writing and recording music was a more exciting future than building cars. His first hit was "Lonely Teardrops," recorded by Jackie Wilson in 1959. The experience taught Gordy that the way to make money in the industry was to have total control. He made sure that Motown owned the rights to its songs and extended his control over the singers by managing them personally. Because many were poor, unsophisticated kids, he started a charm school to help them acquire grace and polish.

Motown's music was infectious. It was hard not to tap toes or snap fingers to Marvin Gaye's "Hitchhike" or Smokey Robinson's "Shop Around." By 1966, 75 percent of Motown's releases had crossed over onto traditionally white pop charts.

Gordy was a millionaire many times over when he sold Motown to MCA in 1988. Hailed as an entrepreneur and condemned as a thief by some former employees, he let his music speak for him. In a rare public statement written in 1990, Gordy passed along his mother's advice: "Keep developing people and getting hit records...you'll be fine."

▶ THE KITCHEN DEBATE

To a presidential hopeful like Richard Nixon, the chance to stand up to the Soviet premier was too good to miss. He could impress voters as a tough communist-buster once again.

Unfortunately, Khrushchev proved to be a indefatigable sparring partner who was just as hell-bent on preserving communism as Nixon was on vanquishing it. The two leaders battled it out verbally in front of television cameras in what went down in history as the "kitchen debate."

Khrushchev was testy when Nixon arrived in Russia July 23. The U.S. was in the midst of Captive Nations Week, during which Eisenhower asked Americans to pray for "captive" peoples forced to live under communist oppression. Nixon's arrival to host Moscow's first U.S. Exhibition—an extravaganza designed to whet Soviet appetites for all the things capitalism could buy—had plucked Khrushchev's last nerve.

As the two men surveyed a model American kitchen, Nixon lauded the gadgets. "Anything that makes women work less is good," he said. "We don't think of women in terms of capitalism," retorted Khrushchev. "We think better of them."

The leaders soon began jabbing each other in the chest. The argumentative Khrushchev came away smiling; to him, the routine debate wasn't worth a mention in his memoirs.

But not Nixon. He understood how pointless it was to argue the merits of communism versus capitalism because, in leaders such as Khrushchev, communist supremacy was a fact of life.

▶ PRESERVING ANTARCTICA

Twelve nations joined hands to preserve the pristine vastness of Antarctica as the decade came to a close. Signed on December 1, the Antarctic Treaty recognized that "it is in the interest of all mankind that Antarctica shall continue for ever to be used exclusively for peaceful purposes and shall not become the scene or object of international discord."

The original signers were Argentina, Australia, Belgium, Chile, France, Japan, New Zealand, Norway, South Africa, the Soviet Union, the U.S., and the United Kingdom. They operated more than 50 research stations on the southernmost continent. In this snowy wilderness, these countries and the 30 more who later signed the treaty could put their political

NEW WAVE CINEMA

Identifying a movie with its director instead of the genre or star was a direct result of French new wave cinema, or *la nouvelle vague*.

A group of young French movie critics working for the magazine *Les Cahiers du Cinema* started the movement. To them, movies had become old-fashioned. Filmmaking had missed the wave of modernism that was breathing new life into other art forms. The industry was too hierarchical; few people got the chance to direct until they were in their 50s. The founders of nouvelle vague did not want to wait that long. They began making  their own low-budget films, picking up the best techniques of past and present masters such as Orson Welles and Alfred Hitchcock. The filmmaker himself became the celebrity or *auteur* (author).

Nouvelle vague came to international attention in 1959 when critics at the Cannes Film Festival lauded Alain Resnais's *Hiroshima, Mon Amour* (above) and François Truffaut's *The 400 Blows.* The critics-turned-directors created a refreshing, individualistic style for the future.

differences aside in the name of scientific research.

It was in Antarctica that scientists first discovered a gaping hole in the ozone layer of the atmosphere. Toward the century's end, treaty signers grappled with yet another threat to the continent—tourism.

■ TRENDS & TRIVIA

Rodgers and Hammerstein hit another home run with *The Sound of Music.*

James Michener's *Hawaii* is published.

In *Ben-Hur,* Charlton Heston portrays a gladiator-turned-Christian.

The Solomon R. Guggenheim Museum, designed by Frank Lloyd Wright, opens in New York.

Phone booth packing craze hits the U.S. from South Africa.

Beat writer William S. Burroughs's *Naked Lunch* is published.

A Raisin in the Sun is the first Broadway play by a black writer to win the New York Drama Critics' Circle Award.

Rod Sterling hosts *The Twilight Zone.*

Japanese Crown Prince Akihito marries a commoner, Shōda Michiko—the first time any crown prince of Japan has done so in 1,500 years.

William Strunk, Jr., and E. B. White's *The Elements of Style,* a bible for writers, is published.

Electrocardiograph and internal pacemaker are developed.

Soviet spacecraft *Lunik II* sends back the first photos of the moon's dark side.

Mattel Inc. introduces Barbie. ▼

• JUNE 18
Ethel Barrymore, grand dame of the theater, dies at 79.

◀ JULY 17
Blues singer Billie Holliday dies at 44, weeks after being arrested for narcotics possession.

• AUGUST 21
Hawaii becomes the 50th state.

• SEPTEMBER
During his U.S. visit, Soviet Premier Khrushchev is told he cannot visit Disneyland for "security reasons."

• NOVEMBER 2
Television quiz show *Twenty-One* is investigated by the federal government after a contestant, Charles Van Doren, admits cheating.

• NOVEMBER
Hutu tribes overthrow the ruling Tutsi minority in the UN mandate of Rwanda.

MAPPING OUR WORLD

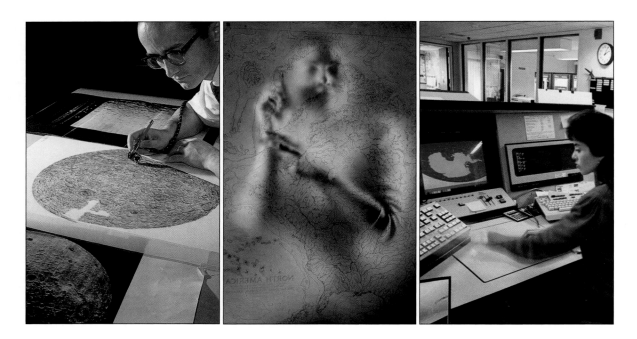

by Allen Carroll
MANAGING DIRECTOR, NATIONAL GEOGRAPHIC MAPS

Eleven years before the dawn of the 20th century, an obscure geography professor at the University of Vienna named Albrecht Penck stood before an international conference to put forward what was regarded as a revolutionary notion. Penck proposed that a multinational effort be launched to compile a comprehensive map of the world at a scale of 1:1,000,000. At that scale, an inch on paper is equal to about 16 miles on the ground, and a globe would be about 42 feet in diameter. Penck's idea, which came to be called the International Millionth Map, was envisioned more precisely as a series of sheets, each covering a small patch of the globe, all compiled to the same map projection and representing the Earth's features in a consistent style.

This seemingly innocuous proposal was, in an important sense, a bellwether for the century to

Left: Revealing the moon's relief   Middle: Inking rivers and shorelines   Right: National Geographic map-drafting database

come. For hundreds of years before Penck's time, maps had served the practical purposes of navigation and orientation on land and sea. But maps of the world had also served other powerful mandates. The earliest world maps were more often than not a means of expression of religion, myth, and worldview—peopled with dragons and half-human monsters, ruled by mythical kings—as much an exercise of imagination as of measurement. Maps were also powerful expressions of political hegemony. They were often carefully guarded repositories of state secrets—knowledge of the world that could be used for military and economic gain. In the 19th century, however, a new phenomenon arose: the explorer as naturalist and scientist, bent on mapping the unknown corners of the world not for political and military conquest and plunder but as a scientific and intellectual quest. Penck's vision carried that impulse to a new level. The world, though not completely explored, was now a knowable entity. Continuing improvements in surveying instruments and techniques made scientists capable of mapping it in its entirety with an accuracy and detail never before imagined.

Meanwhile, the blank spaces on the map had shrunk to a few of its remotest corners—the Arctic north, the dusty interior of Australia, the icy barrens of Antarctica. The beginning decades of the 20th century would see a mad scramble to conquer these inaccessible remnants. Well into the 1930s, Rear Adm. Richard E. Byrd was mapping for the first time thousands of square miles of Antarctica and remote reaches of the South Pacific under the auspices of the National Geographic Society.

The depths of the oceans were almost completely uncharted through mid-century, and remain today the most extensive terra incognita—no small statement, given that the oceans cover seven-tenths of the Earth. Humans have reached only tiny corners of the ocean floor. Yet technology has opened remote views of the abyssal depths to us. Sonar returns echoes of plains and mountains, and satellites can read the gravitational echoes of submarine features by measuring subtle variations in the height of surface waters. Thus are revealed some of the Earth's most dramatic features—its deepest canyon in the Mariana Trench at 35,827 feet below sea level, and its longest mountain range by far, the Mid-Ocean Ridge, running from the North Atlantic around Africa's southern horn into the Indian Ocean.

Even as the blank spaces receded, the tumult of the 20th century further delayed the fulfillment of Penck's vision. Armed conflict interrupted peacetime mapping projects, but it also spurred technological advances, bringing powerful new tools to the making of maps.

The most important of these was aerial photography. The advent of the airplane carried the camera skyward, first as a curiosity, then as a vital reconnaissance tool during World War I. Aerial photography was slow to become a standard tool of cartographers, however. Photographs invariably distort: Lenses tilt; images warp toward edges of frames; airplanes bounce around in air turbulence; and mountain peaks, because they are closer to the camera, appear larger than valleys. Photogrammetry, the exacting science of correcting these distortions, developed rapidly between the World Wars, and eventually gained acceptance among mapmakers as its efficiencies became apparent.

Meanwhile, the National Geographic Society was establishing itself as a leader in bringing maps to a public eager to chart the new century's rapid political changes. The Society's Cartographic Division, established in 1915, listed among its early titles a May 1918 map of the "Western Theater of War" on which many Americans followed the agonizing progress of U.S doughboys in the trenches. The Society's political map of the world—far and away the most popular and familiar of the

Cartographic Division's titles—was first published in 1922 and has become a visual icon of the 20th century. In an effort to represent the round Earth on a flat printed sheet with a minimum of distortion, the Society's cartographers abandoned the traditional Mercator projection, which enormously enlarges polar areas. Their quest for the ideal map projection continued as recently as 1998, when the National Geographic Society adopted the Winkel Tripel projection for its world maps. This projection's overall shape conforms well to the proportions of a poster-size sheet, and its landform outlines are not stretched into grotesque shapes and sizes.

On the eve of World War II, much of the world remained poorly mapped. Unfamiliar to most people, for example, were the remote Pacific islands that were to become household names during the Allies' bloody island-hopping campaign against the Japanese. The Society's published maps, intended for reference use by the general public, sometimes found service in more urgent circumstances. Adm. Chester Nimitz, commander of the U.S. naval forces in the Pacific, became lost when a storm struck during an airplane flight over the Solomon Islands. Luckily a Marine on board was carrying the Geographic's map of the Pacific Ocean. The pilot managed to fly beneath the clouds and, using the map, to identify the islands below and navigate to a military airfield. Indeed, the armed services relied heavily on the Society's vast collection of maps during the Second World War. They were posted at German intersections to aid Patton's troops, and were on the conference table as Franklin D. Roosevelt and Winston Churchill met to plot strategy in 1944.

The division of Europe by the victorious Allies, followed later by the global decline of colonialism, brought dramatic changes to world maps. The postwar era also brought a dramatic expansion in the uses of maps and the tools for making them. A burgeoning global economy fueled mapping efforts to aid in the exploitation of natural resources. Oil exploration ranged from desert sands to Arctic tundra. Large corporations plotted global strategies, and laid continent- and ocean-spanning communication lines. The superpowers used maps to trace the cat-and-mouse games of submarines beneath Arctic ice and to plot nuclear missile trajectories over the North Pole. As the superpowers looked upward into space, the bird's-eye capabilities of aerial photography were eclipsed by satellite imagery.

Did these rapid developments mean the fulfillment of Albrecht Penck's vision? Well…yes and no. A computerized version of Penck's Millionth Map, called the Digital Chart of the World (DCW), is available on four CD-ROMs to anyone with a few hundred dollars. Its one-to-a-million-scale maps are the fruits of the Department of Defense's Cold War mapping efforts. Yet the 2,094 "tiles" that make up the DCW are something of a mess. Much of the information is old—up to 35 years old in some cases. Preparation of the National Geographic Society's new digital map database, for instance, which now uses the DCW as a primary source, required the DCW to be considerably updated, corrected, and technically modified.

As we near the new millennium, the big blank spaces on the map of the world have long been filled in. But the map of the world is by no means complete. Less than 10 percent of the Earth has been mapped at the detailed scale of 1:50,000. And maps that purport to be accurate don't agree with one another. Jack Estes, a professor of geography at the University of California at Santa Barbara, refers to the current state of affairs as "the myth of the map." Indeed, the widely held belief that the world is fully known and completely mapped is grossly incorrect. It's safe to say that Penck would be shocked to discover how sophisticated our mapping tools have become. But he'd be even more shocked to realize that, more than a century after he articulated his vision, his map is at best imperfect, at worst far from complete.

And yet, the tools are there. In fact, the new tools of cartography are so potent that maps in the 21st century will have a visibility, utility, and mutability that was inconceivable a century ago, and is even now difficult to imagine. Mapmakers are putting together several late 20th-century inventions to create a second fin de siècle revolution in mapping.

THE TOOLS:

1. Computers. Mapmakers used to draw with ink on paper or scratch lines into chemically treated film. Now maps are created on computers, making them malleable and mobile. Computers can also turn the map's traditional flat plane into three-dimensional landscapes.

2. Geographic Information Systems. The specialized computer software known as GIS combines mapping and manipulation of information. With GIS, a point, line, or area on a map takes on numerical value that makes it subject to statistical and scientific analysis. Maps thus become a powerful aid to planning and problem solving, for purposes ranging from crime prevention to agriculture, from mineral exploration to disease control.

3. Satellite imagery. Satellites view our changing planet with unblinking eyes, transmitting reams of data that can be interpreted by mapmakers in countless ways. For the public, maps that were once abstractions take on the vivid detail of photography. For specialists, the satellites' electronic eyes make measurements in many colors and with ever greater detail.

4. Navigation technology. A network of Global Positioning System (GPS) satellites enables individuals with inexpensive, handheld devices to locate themselves nearly instantly on the Earth's surface. Combined with accurate maps, GPS can help manage fleets of commercial trucks, keep airplanes safely separated, and guide families to weekend destinations.

5. The Internet. By linking thousands of computers around the globe, the Internet allows map information to move from place to place, and to be combined with other maps. Maps that used to lie dormant on library shelves now race to and fro across the globe.

These exciting innovations raise possibilities that even the experts are only beginning to understand. In the future, a global "hypermap" may exist as a kind of vast, multilayered sphere in cyberspace. This virtual globe—linking students, families, professionals, and institutions with one another and with spatial information at rates of thousands of times a second—could bring new forms of knowledge and understanding to many millions of people. It's a breathtaking vision, one that Albrecht Penck would applaud, and one that the staff members of the National Geographic Society's Cartographic Division welcome, in our continuing quest to provide the public with the most accurate, legible, and informative maps available.

1960-

1969

Challenging the Establishment

1960-1969

by *Clayborne Carson*
PROFESSOR OF HISTORY, DIRECTOR MARTIN LUTHER KING, JR., PAPERS PROJECT
STANFORD UNIVERSITY

MORE FILLED WITH SOCIAL TUMULT than any other decade of the 20th century, the sixties began with a period of calm before a storm of mass protest and rebellion that swept through many parts of the world. In the early years of the decade in the United States, social and economic trends with long-term implications appeared to be forging a more homogeneous nation, one in which regional, ethnic, religious, and racial differences would blur. The Supreme Court's unanimous 1954 decision in *Brown* v. *the Board of Education of Topeka, Kansas,* ruled that all school segregation was unconstitutional, prompting scholar and activist W. E. B. Du Bois to write, "I have seen the Impossible happen. It did happen on May 17, 1954." For many Americans, the Jim Crow system of segregation seemed a regional anachronism that was vulnerable to external economic and political forces. Martin Luther King, Jr.'s historic address at the 1963 March on Washington for Jobs and Freedom symbolized a convergence of African-American aspirations and the egalitarian ideals that most white Americans shared.

The convergence was illusory. The United States were never truly united, but during the 1960s American society fractured in ways it never had before— not only along the color line but also along lines that were scarcely visible at

Opposite: John Kennedy, Jr.'s poignant farewell to his father in 1963 crystallized the tragic loss of a young President. Preceding pages: America's involvement in the Vietnam War sparked a wave of demonstrations on college campuses.

the start of the decade. Social divisions stood out in stark relief as a host of rapid social and political challenges tested the viability of nearly every institution. The African-American struggle for equal treatment stimulated a series of other struggles to reshape the identity of Americans, both collectively and as members of distinctive groups. In the course of those multiple efforts, the conviction of some people that "We Shall Overcome" was overwhelmed by a wave of unresolvable arguments over who, exactly, "we" were.

Dr. Martin Luther King, Jr.'s nonviolent efforts to gain black equality, such as the 1963 March on Washington, made him an international hero.

The apparent placidity of American society at the start of the 1960s obscured hints of the changes that were in store. When the southern black college students who initiated the lunch counter sit-in movement in February 1960 politely asked for racial integration and citizenship rights, they sparked a mass movement that in time became increasingly militant and developed its own set of values. By the time of the March on Washington, student activists affiliated with the Student Nonviolent Coordinating Committee (SNCC) and the Congress of Racial Equality (CORE) had grown impatient with the snail-like pace of racial reform. They criticized President John F. Kennedy for not acting forcefully against southern segregationists.

The President who had backed the unsuccessful Bay of Pigs invasion of Cuba and who had mobilized the nation to win the "space race" against the Soviet Union was reluctant to take a stand against southern segregation for fear of alienating southern white Democrats. But when African Americans asserting their rights were confronted by intransigent southern officials willing to use force to deny those rights, Kennedy was finally prodded to act. In the fall of 1962, when Governor Ross Barnett resisted the admission of Air Force veteran James Meredith as the only black student at the University of Mississippi, Kennedy sent in federal marshalls. The following spring he confronted an even stronger challenge in Alabama when Birmingham officials used water hoses and police dogs to suppress youthful black protesters and Governor George Wallace personally stepped in to prevent two black students from registering at the University of Alabama.

Soon after forcing Wallace to back down, Kennedy belatedly identified his Presidency with the civil rights cause when he announced support for the legislation that would become the Civil Rights Act of 1964. In his televised address to the nation on June 11, 1963, Kennedy noted that the black struggle had unleashed expectations that could not be readily restrained or reversed: "If an American, because his skin is dark, cannot eat lunch in a restaurant open to the public, if he cannot send his children to the best public school available, if he cannot vote for the public officials who represent him, if, in short, he cannot enjoy the full and free life which all of us want, then who among us would be content to have the color of his skin changed and stand in his place? Who among us would then be content with the counsels of patience and delay?"

John Kennedy's belated support of civil rights did not stop protests involving African Americans and other groups from escalating as the decade unfolded. Festering resentments broke through the placid surface of American life. The social unrest and conflict of this period, both in the United States and in many other countries, were the result of the breakdown of traditional beliefs and social patterns arising from extensive migration, rapid technological change, and the influence of an increasingly pervasive, worldwide mass culture.

In the United States, the beat poets of the 1950s had revealed early signs of disaffection with mainstream mass culture. In the sixties this alienation was expressed in such books as Paul Goodman's *Growing Up Absurd* (1960), which found American society wanting because of its failure to offer meaningful work for young people. Similarly, Betty Friedan's *The Feminine Mystique* (1963) expressed the discontent of middle-class, college-educated women whose lives were not fulfilled by their assigned roles as housewives. Goodman, Friedan, and other writers of the time gave voice to a variety of social inequities and the dissatisfactions experienced by many individuals. Outside the civil rights struggle, however, such discontents remained isolated and submerged during the early 1960s rather than mobilized in mass movements.

THE POLITICAL CONFORMITY IMPOSED BY COLD WAR challenges from abroad significantly dampened dissent at home—until a series of major unexpected events revealed the fragility of the country's institutions. Kennedy's assassination in November 1963 shocked the nation, and the lingering questions about the tragedy fostered increasing distrust and uncertainty. If such a thing could happen here, was the United States as exceptional as Americans had believed? Black nationalist Malcolm X gained notoriety when he compared the Kennedy assassination to those that the United States had encouraged elsewhere, such as the assassination of Patrice Lumumba in the Congo or the coup against Ngo Dinh Diem and Ngo Dinh Nhu in South Vietnam. "Chickens coming home to roost never did make me sad; they've always made me glad," Malcolm declared in what was a preview of the embittered rhetoric of the late 1960s.

Although Lyndon B. Johnson, upon stepping into the Presidency, succeeded in enacting the pending civil rights legislation, he would preside over the disintegration of the liberal coalition that made possible not only racial reform but also his own Great Society programs. Delegates to the Democratic Party's convention in August 1964 were prepared to back the President's bid to retain his office, but a chasm that would last beyond the decade opened between Kennedy-Johnson liberals and civil rights activists. The break occurred when Johnson's supporters refused to advocate the seating of Mississippi Freedom Democratic Party (MFDP) delegates in place of the "regular," all-white Mississippi delegation. MFDP backers such as Fannie Lou Hamer, Bob Moses, and Stokely Carmichael subsequently repudiated the conventional liberalism of Johnson, Hubert H. Humphrey, and Walter F. Mondale.

Johnson's landslide win over Barry M. Goldwater in the 1964 election marked the last major victory for the national liberal coalition. It would be the last presidential election of the century in which most white Americans voted for the candidate favored by the majority of black Americans. After the spring 1965 Selma-to-Montgomery voting rights march, Johnson proclaimed "We Shall Overcome" in mobilizing support for new voting rights legislation. But the Voting Rights Act of 1965 and the Economic Opportunity Act of 1964 were not enough to ameliorate the festering racial grievances that would explode in the Watts neighborhood of Los Angeles during August 1965 and in many other cities afterward.

IN ADDITION TO THE RACIAL DIVISIONS of the mid-1960s, a number of other conflicts served to fracture American society. Women who supported the African-American struggle against racial discrimination discovered in the process their own long-buried resentment of gender-based restrictions on opportunity, a resentment they would begin to express with increasing frequency and vigor. While Friedan and other reformers established the National Organization for Women (NOW) to spearhead the struggle for women's rights, two white veterans of the civil rights movement, Casey Hayden and Mary King, initiated discussions and debates that culminated in the emergence of a grassroots women's liberation movement.

And just as the women's movement adopted tactics from the African-American civil rights movement, so too did the youth rebellion of the 1960s. During the fall 1964 Free Speech Movement at the University of California–Berkeley, students demonstrated against a host of in loco parentis campus restrictions through sit-ins and mass rallies. Soon college students elsewhere began to use direct action tactics to express opposition to the military draft and the war in Vietnam. To some extent, the antiwar protests of young people became aspects of generalized rebellion against the "Establishment."

The spread of militant activism to predominately white universities was only one facet of a broader upsurge of rebelliousness among young people around the world. The new youth counterculture that arose in the mid-1960s was an amalgam of political protest and cultural rebellion. The jeans worn by civil rights organizers in the South became the new style of dress that would increasingly distinguish young people from their elders. The birth of rock-and-roll during the 1950s had prepared the way for new styles of popular music that reflected and encouraged the social and political changes of the 1960s. Widespread use of psychotropic drugs—especially marijuana and LSD—was both a response to and a product of social and cultural experimentation, especially among young people.

In various ways, the leading popular artists of the 1960s reflected these attitudes of political dissent and cultural rebellion. Bob Dylan pioneered in creating a form of protest music that built on the social criticism of earlier folk singers and on the infectious energy of rock-and-roll. British groups such as the Beatles and the Rolling Stones continued the transformation of what had been known as "race music" into music that crossed racial lines and developed a huge international following. At the same time, Jimi Hendrix, Nina Simone,

CAPTAIN COUSTEAU POPS OUT OF THE DIVING SAUCER DS-2 AFTER A DESCENT TO 1,000 FEET.

• Living Beneath the Breakers

Jacques-Yves Cousteau (above) was a successful diver and inventor when he first appeared in NATIONAL GEOGRAPHIC's pages in 1952. Ten years before, he and an engineer named Émile Gagnan had invented the Aqua-Lung, a lightweight, self-contained underwater breathing device. Aqua-Lungs were well-known, but Cousteau was not.

By the end of the 1960s, however, his name began to exceed his device in fame. Anybody who watched television could identify his lilting French accent and the images of his watery domain. Blessed with a wiry frame and aquiline Gallic features, Cousteau was the quintessential merman, more at home in the sea than not. Recognizing this, the GEOGRAPHIC came out with an article and television documentary in April 1966. Under Cousteau's supervision, six sea-floor technicians spent almost one month 328 feet beneath the azure surface of the Mediterranean Sea installing an oil well head.

Photographed by Cousteau's son, Philippe, the divers persevered in their underwater colony. They inhaled a special brew called "heliox," ate bland frozen dinners, and collapsed at the day's end five at a time in bunks, leaving one to stand watch. It was an exhausting but successful venture.

The adventure also spun off a popular television documentary. "The World of Jacques-Yves Cousteau" concluded the Society's first foray into television production in 1965 and 1966. CBS carried the four documentaries, which were co-sponsored by *Encyclopaedia Britannica* and the Aetna Insurance Company. Melville Grosvenor now had another medium through which he could spread the Society's mission.

• Jane Goodall's World

Jane Goodall became one of the magazine's most enigmatic subjects—a willowy blonde who left the civilized world of England to live in the wilds of Africa to study chimpanzees. Her observations and concern for her subjects charmed readers.

"I cannot remember a time when I did not want to go to Africa to study animals," she said in her first article, published in August 1963. "Therefore, after leaving school, I saved up the fare and went to Nairobi, Kenya."

Dr. Louis Leakey asked her if she would consider doing a field study of chimpanzees. She leaped at the challenge and spent the next 19 months hunting down grants. When the Kenyan authorities expressed reservations about sending a single white woman into the bush alone, Goodall's mother joined her. The women set off for Lake Tanganyika in pursuit of their furry subjects. They found many. Goodall spent hours sitting quietly, trying to gain the animals' trust.

"To be accepted...by a group of wild chimpanzees is the result of months of patience...," she wrote. "At last I sat among them, enjoying a degree of acceptance that I had hardly dreamed possible.... Most astonishing of all, I saw chimpanzees fashion and use crude implements—the beginnings of tool use. This discovery could prove helpful to those studying man's rise to dominance over other primates."

CHIMPANZEE DAVID GREYBEARD GETS A HANDOUT OF BANANAS FROM JANE GOODALL.

1960

PRINCE CHARMING

John Fitzgerald Kennedy's charm and family money helped him win the presidential election.

He was the picture of confidence and health when he debated his Republican opponent, Vice President Richard M. Nixon, on television. The Vice President, who was generally the healthier of the two, looked worn-out and uncomfortable.

The four debates were not the only reasons Kennedy won the election. He was an inspiring speaker who promised to shake the country out of its lethargy and meet the New Frontier of "uncharted areas of science and space, unsolved problems of peace and war, unconquered pockets of ignorance and prejudice, unanswered questions of poverty and surplus."

Kennedy focused on key voting groups. His running mate, Texas Senator Lyndon B. Johnson, wooed southern voters. Kennedy's brother and campaign manager, Robert F. Kennedy, went after the black vote by helping free Dr. Martin Luther King, Jr., from a Georgia jail where he had been sent on charges of driving with an invalid license.

Kennedy won by a mere 118,574 votes, becoming the nation's first Catholic and second-youngest President.

▶ SIT-INS FOR EQUALITY

Like most college students, the college freshmen seated at the counter of Woolworth's in Greensboro, North Carolina, on February 1, wanted a cheap meal. But these students wanted something more—the right to be served in any section of any restaurant regardless of their skin color. Instead, they were ignored.

The next day, 25 other students joined the sit-in. Within days, blacks throughout North Carolina went to lunch counters in their towns and demanded the same. One black college grad in Charlotte spoke for many: "All I want is to come in and place my order and be served and leave a tip if I feel like it."

The sit-ins swept the South. In most places, they were passive, with blacks sitting on one side waiting for recognition and whites on the other ignoring them. But in Chattanooga, Tennessee, the management of one restaurant pelted the demonstrators with plates and flowerpots. Firefighters in Marshall, Texas, turned their hoses on protesters.

Back in North Carolina, the Student Nonviolent Coordinating Committee was established in Raleigh to keep the protest's momentum alive. The group's main adviser, Ella Baker, believed blacks had a better chance to gain civil rights by changing the laws of individual communities. This differed from the national approach favored by her former employer, Dr. Martin Luther King, Jr.'s Southern

Christian Leadership Conference. Although occasionally at odds on how to get there, both groups helped to blaze the trail toward black equality.

▶ LIGHT USED RIGHT

American physicist Theodore Maiman (below) generated the world's first operational laser pulse in May, ushering in one of the most important technological advances of the era. Using a tightly focused beam of light, lasers have lent themselves to medical, musical, and electronic applications.

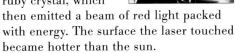

Maiman passed a bright light through a ruby crystal, which then emitted a beam of red light packed with energy. The surface the laser touched became hotter than the sun.

Although he made the first usable laser, Maiman could not take credit for inventing it. Two other scientists battled over that claim for years. Charles Townes, who had discovered the maser or "microwave amplification by stimulated emission of radiation" in 1953, said the laser was a similar concept except it used light instead of microwaves. Physicist Gordon Gould said he had developed a similar concept. But Townes reached the patent office first. By the time the case was settled, laser was a household word.

▶ TWISTIN' THE NIGHT AWAY

Dancing solo went mainstream in 1960. No partners needed for the Twist—just a supple pelvis to corkscrew one's body in time with the beat.

Rhythm-and-blues musician Hank Ballard made the Twist the rage for hip young blacks in 1959. Chubby Checker, a former chicken plucker from South Carolina,

SIT-IN AT A LUNCH COUNTER IN GREENSBORO, NORTH CAROLINA

• JANUARY
Alvin Ray "Pete" Rozelle becomes commissioner of the National Football League.

• JANUARY 4
Nobel Prize-winning writer Albert Camus dies at 46 in a car accident southwest of Paris.

• JANUARY 7
Abdel Nasser lays the cornerstone for the Aswan High Dam in Egypt.

• FEBRUARY 13
France tests its first atomic device in the Algerian portion of the Sahara.

• MARCH 1
Morocco is hit by an earthquake, tidal wave, and fires that kill more than 12,000 near the resort of Agadir.

• MARCH 30
South Africa declares a state of emergency after police kill 62 people during anti-apartheid protests.

• APRIL 2
NASA launches the first weather satellite.

turned on the rest of the world. He took "The Twist" to the top of *Billboard*'s charts in 1960. A year later he twisted away on *The Ed Sullivan Show*, and the song soared to the top of the charts again. Twisting (above) was easy—no lessons, and no touching. It became the rage in discotheques and school gymnasiums everywhere.

▶ THE FRANCIS GARY POWERS CRISIS
The Soviet Union's capture of U.S. pilot Francis Gary Powers was a diplomatic disaster for almost everyone involved. The international incident made President Dwight D. Eisenhower look like a liar and Soviet leader Nikita Khrushchev like a fool for trusting him.

Powers, the CIA pilot who flew the first U-2 jet in 1956, was shot down on April 30 during a covert mission to observe a Soviet missile installation. Such missions had been going on for several years, to the Soviets' great frustration. But they had no proof.

Eisenhower wanted the missions stopped. He was about to attend a crucial summit with the Soviets and with France and Great Britain. He hoped to negotiate for more peaceful relations between the superpowers, thus ending his Presidency on a triumphant note. "If one of these aircraft were lost when we were engaged in apparently sincere deliberations, it could...ruin my effectiveness," he told an aide.

His subordinates convinced him to permit one more flight. This time, a Soviet missile detected the plane and brought it down. Powers survived but was captured.

Khrushchev was furious. The incident proved to his detractors that Eisenhower, whom Khrushchev insisted was trustworthy, was not. He publicized the incident, but not the fact that Powers had survived.

THE PILL IS BORN

The sexual revolution gained millions of new soldiers in 1960 when birth control pills went on the market, putting women in control of their reproductive systems.

Two women helped make the pill reality. Margaret Sanger, the founder of Planned Parenthood, located the scientists who created it. And her friend, heiress Katherine McCormick, paid for their work.

Endocrinologist Gregory Godwin Pincus came to Sanger's attention in 1950. He was working on an oral contraceptive with tepid support from his main sponsor, Searle Pharmaceutical Corp. Sanger introduced him to McCormick, and the three agreed to join forces. "You have the power to change the world by doing this," Sanger told Pincus.

In 1960, he did. His pill, known as Envoid, combined a synthetic version of the hormone progesterone with a similar substance called mestranol to block conception. Within three years, 2.3 million women were on it.

The U.S. fell into the trap; the plane, Eisenhower's men insisted, was monitoring the weather. Khrushchev then trotted out his trump card—Powers.

Once the truth was out, the summit turned into a nightmare and so did Powers's life. After two years on a Soviet prison farm, he returned home to find that he'd been labeled a traitor by many for not killing himself to avoid capture. He was vindicated in 1987 when the government awarded him the Air Force's Distinguished Flying Cross. It was a little late; Powers had died ten years earlier in a helicopter crash.

■ TRENDS & TRIVIA

Lerner and Loewe's musical *Camelot* brings King Arthur's court to Broadway.

Joy Adamson's *Born Free* immortalizes Elsa the lioness.

Brasília, Brazil's modern capital, opens. Cookie-cutter apartment buildings take away all class distinctions with their uniformity.

Alfred Hitchcock's thriller *Psycho* keeps people out of showers.

The Fantasticks opens on Broadway and enjoys that fabled street's longest run for 37 years.

Felt-tipped pens are marketed for the first time.

The Dave Brubeck Quartet releases "Time Out," jazz for the masses.

Drinks are first packaged in aluminum cans.

Ethiopian Abebe Bikila becomes first African to win an Olympic gold medal in track and field.

John Knowles's *A Separate Peace* is published.

The Andy Griffith Show and *The Flintstones* air on TV.

Lucy and Desi Arnaz file for divorce.

England's Princess Margaret Rose marries Anthony Armstrong Jones at Westminster Abbey.

"Itsy Bitsy Teenie Weenie Yellow Polka Dot Bikini" is a hit song.

Former polio victim Wilma Rudolph wins three Olympic gold medals in track and field for the U.S.

A British jury rules that *Lady Chatterley's Lover* is not obscene.

251

• **APRIL 27**
A congressional committee starts looking into whether record companies pay disc jockeys to play their records.

• **MAY 11**
John D. Rockefeller, Jr., the Standard Oil magnate, dies at 86 in Tucson, Arizona.

• **MAY**
Israeli Nazi hunters capture Adolf Eichmann, a mastermind of the Jewish Holocaust, in Argentina.

• **JUNE 30**
Belgium gives the Congo its independence.

• **AUGUST 16**
The island nation of Cyprus becomes an independent republic.

• **OCTOBER 12**
At the U.N. General Assembly, Soviet Premier Nikita Khrushchev angrily bangs his shoe on his desk over an anti-Soviet speech.

• **NOVEMBER 16**
Movie star Clark Gable dies at 59 of chronic heart problems, leaving behind his fifth wife, pregnant with his only child.

1961

In 1961 the Soviet Union and the U.S. sent men into space for the first time.

On April 12 the Soviets got there first when 27-year-old Yuri Gagarin (below) orbited Earth in 89 minutes. After landing safely, he emerged from the experience a hero and cheerfully boyish example of Soviet aeronautic superiority.

President John F. Kennedy was less enchanted. The Soviets had sent the first animal into space several years before, and now they again had beaten the U.S. in the race for manned spaceflight. No more, he declared to Congress. America would land on  the moon first. The costs, he estimated, could run as high as nine billion dollars. But that, he insisted, was a small price for "the key to our future on earth."

Shortly before Kennedy's announcement, Alan B. Shepard, Jr., became the first American in space on May 5. The naval commander did not orbit Earth, nor was he aloft for as long as Gagarin.

The Soviets continued to lead the way to the next frontier. In August Gherman Titov spent a day in space. Four years later fellow astronaut Aleksei Leonov became the first man to walk in space.

252

▶ LET US BEGIN ANEW

John F. Kennedy's inaugural speech was an invigorating cry for action. "Ask not what your country can do for you," the handsome new President said. "Ask what you can do for your country.

"So let us begin anew…," he stated. "Let us never negotiate out of fear, but let us never fear to negotiate…. Let both sides seek to invoke the wonders of science instead of its terrors. Together let us explore the stars, conquer the deserts, eradicate disease, tap the ocean depths, and encourage the arts and commerce…. Let both sides join in creating…a new world of law."

KENNEDY AND EISENHOWER

Within six weeks, Kennedy established the Peace Corps, an organization that dispatched volunteers to underdeveloped countries to teach residents to become self-sufficient.

The Peace Corps was also a helpful political device for spreading the American message to countries that seemed vulnerable to communism. By the century's end, thousands of Peace Corps volunteers of all ages and backgrounds were working in more than 90 nations.

▶ THE BAY OF PIGS FIASCO

The Kennedy Administration suffered a major setback in April when a CIA-sponsored invasion of Cuba at the Bay of Pigs went down in flames.

Like his predecessor, Dwight D. Eisenhower, President Kennedy underestimated Cuban leader Fidel Castro. The cigar-smoking radical was popular with the masses whose lives had improved under his reforms.

The CIA had been plotting the invasion since the Eisenhower Administration with Cuban exiles in the U.S. who insisted that an invasion would trigger anti-Castro uprisings across the island.

A handful of Kennedy advisers were wary of the plan. Kennedy, however, believed what the CIA was telling him and was anxious to flex his new muscles on the international stage. So he authorized the invasion. Within 72 hours, Cuban forces had killed 400 invaders and held the rest captive. The U.S. admitted defeat. Castro, in return, formally allied Cuba with the Soviet Union.

▶ THE ALLIANCE FOR PROGRESS

The Alliance for Progress was President Kennedy's attempt to keep democracy alive in Latin America. He envisioned the alliance as a way to improve education, health care, and economic opportunities and perhaps to prevent another Cuban revolution from taking place in the Western Hemisphere.

Unfortunately, most of the money earmarked for these goals wound up augmenting a military build-up throughout the region, which then experienced a record number of coups between 1961 and 1967. Big businesses on both sides of the Equator and corrupt local officials managed to get a chunk of the 100 billion dollars. While some hospitals and schools were built during the alliance's 13 years, its emphasis shifted to subsidizing crowd-control gear and military training. Tired of facing criticism for what the alliance had become, the U.S. stopped all funding in 1974.

▶ THE FREEDOM RIDERS

The freedom riders brought the civil rights movement to the attention of millions of Americans. The group of black and white antisegregationists rode into bus stations throughout the South to prove that federal

- **JANUARY 31**
  The U.S. sends Ham, a chimpanzee, into space. He survives and is rewarded with an apple.

- **FEBRUARY 24**
  In Africa, Louis and Mary Leakey find the oldest known human bones—more than 600,000 years old.

- **FEBRUARY 26**
  King Mohammed V of Morocco dies after surgery and is succeeded by his son Hassan.

- **MARCH 21**
  The U.S. announces it will give the Laotian government aid to fight communists.

- **APRIL 7**
  The UN unanimously votes to censure South Africa for apartheid, 83-0.

- **MAY 30**
  Army officers assassinate Gen. Rafael Trujillo, dictator of the Dominican Republic.

- **JUNE 16**
  Russian ballet dancer Rudolf Nureyev defects in Paris.

integration laws had failed. They were brutally beaten by angry racists.

In 1960 the U.S. Supreme Court outlawed segregation in interstate bus terminals. But without enforcement, bus stations in the South continued to have whites-only facilities. The civil rights group called the Congress of Racial Equality (CORE) wanted to prove that segregation still flourished. "Our intention was to provoke the Southern authorities into arresting us and thereby prod the Justice Department into enforcing the law of the land," said James Farmer, the group's national director.

Thirteen CORE volunteers—seven black and six white—first rode out in June. After reports about the initial carnage were publicized, the number of riders swelled to 300. President Kennedy ordered a host of federal marshals to escort the demonstrators. He then ordered his brother, Attorney General Robert F. Kennedy, to work out a deal with civil rights leaders that would end

PROTESTERS IN MISSISSIPPI INSPIRED BY THE FREEDOM RIDERS

the embarrassment. The final agreement established a tax-exempt voter education program to enroll blacks.

▶ POP POET

Bob Dylan intellectualized popular music. With him, lyrics became literary compositions set to music. Critics first noticed Dylan in Greenwich Village coffeehouses in 1961.

A HOUSE DIVIDED

The Berlin Wall was a Cold War symbol, a stark reminder of how far one side would go to prevent the other from gaining the upper hand.

Communist soldiers began building the 30-mile barrier on August 13, using concrete blocks and barbed wire to separate East from West Berlin. Like Germany, the capital had been carved in two after World War II. The Soviets controlled East Germany, the Allies oversaw West Germany, and Berlin, which was in the middle of the new Soviet satellite, was uncomfortably split between the two spheres of influence.

The differences between the Soviets and the West were nowhere more apparent than in Berlin. The western city was vibrant and colorful; its eastern neighbor was drab and depressing.

By 1961 East Berlin was losing about 2,000 residents a day. The government hoped the wall would halt the westward flow. For the next 28 years, the wall remained a grim boundary between two worlds.

They called him a folksinger—the first of many labels that stuck and later wore off.

"I played all the folk songs with a rock-and-roll attitude," he said. "That's what made me different. It allowed me to cut through all the mess and be heard."

He wrote about love, but also about hatred and war. Songs such as "Like a Rolling Stone" presaged the decade of protest. Dylan, said poet Allen Ginsberg, proved that great art could come from the jukebox.

■ TRENDS & TRIVIA

Audrey Hepburn stars in *Breakfast at Tiffany's.*

IBM introduces the Selectric typewriter.

Racing-car driver A. J. Foyt revs his engine to a record of 139.13 mph in the Indianapolis 500.

Patsy Cline releases "I Fall to Pieces."

Joseph Heller's *Catch-22* is published.

N.Y. Yankees Roger Maris hits 61 home runs, breaking the record Babe Ruth set in 1927.

The 23rd Amendment gives the District of Columbia representation but no vote in Congress.

Walt Disney produces *101 Dalmatians.*

Stand-up comic Lenny Bruce is arrested for the first of many times on obscenity charges.

Tennessee Williams's *Night of the Iguana* is staged.

Eugene Ionesco's *Rhinoceros* debuts.

Muriel Spark's *The Prime of Miss Jean Brodie* is published.

First electric toothbrush becomes available.

Certificates of deposit are introduced.

South African Gary Player becomes the first foreign golfer to win the Masters.

Norton Juster's *The Phantom Tollbooth* is published.

Studies of the seafloor support continental drift theory almost 60 years after Alfred Wegener proposed it.

• JULY 2
Ernest Hemingway commits suicide in Ketchum, Idaho, at 61.

• AUGUST 26
Burma becomes world's first Buddhist republic.

• SEPTEMBER 11
The World Wildlife Fund is established in Switzerland.

• OCTOBER 17
Albania is banished from the Soviet bloc of nations for adhering to Maoism.

• NOVEMBER 2
Cartoonist James Thurber dies at 66 in New York.

• NOVEMBER 16
Former Speaker of the House Sam Rayburn dies of cancer at 79. His 17-year speakership was the longest in U.S. history.

• DECEMBER 13
Artist Grandma Moses dies at 101 in Hoosick Falls, N.Y.

254

The Cold War got hot during the Cuban missile crisis. For 14 days in October, John Kennedy and Nikita Khrushchev figuratively stared at each other over sleek Soviet missiles—aimed at the U.S.

Khrushchev quietly installed the missiles to protect the Soviet's new ally from the U.S. and in response to American missile sites in Turkey. A U-2 first photographed the Cuban installations on October 14, and Kennedy was stunned. He swiftly assembled a group of advisers. To keep the potential disaster under wraps, the group shuttled in and out of the White House through secret tunnels and spoke over secure telephone lines.

Almost a week later Kennedy announced the crisis everyone feared—an atomic face-off. "I have directed the armed forces to prepare for any eventuality," he said.

The news caused panic. People jammed supermarkets to stockpile their bomb shelters and school children practiced diving under their desks.

Then, as Secretary of State Dean Rusk later said with relief, "the other fellow just blinked." On October 28 Khrushchev backed down. He started to ship missiles back to the Soviet Union, and the U.S. later began removing its missiles from Turkey.

▶ THE ELEVATION OF EVERYDAY OBJECTS
The banal became inspirational for a group of English and American artists who were tired of Abstract Expressionism's anguish and hidden meanings. For the practitioners of Pop art, subject matter was on the surface of anything from comic strips to Coke bottles.

Artist Andy Warhol created art with Coca-Cola by filling a canvas with rows of the same bottle. He then did the same for a can of Campbell's soup and Marilyn Monroe's face (below) in 1962.

Warhol's approach was novel, but not new. He and other Pop artists like Claes Oldenburg and Roy Lichtenstein drew upon the traditions of the Ashcan school of art, an American style of the early 1900s, which focused on the everyday aspects of life. By the late 1950s, everyday life was inundated by commercial culture, and the Pop artists chose to capitalize on it rather than condemn it.

▶ STRIKING DOWN PRAYER IN SCHOOL
The U.S. Supreme Court once again reaffirmed the separation between church and state in a landmark decision that rendered prayer in public schools illegal.

The court's decision in *Engel* v. *Vitale* rocked the nation when it came down in June. "School Prayer Unconstitutional" screamed the six-column headline of the New York *Herald Tribune*.

The case began in 1958 after the Herricks, New York, school board adopted

a short, noncompulsory prayer. Lawrence Roth, a nonpracticing Jew and father of two boys, viewed this as a dangerous crack in the wall between church and state. He and several other parents enlisted the American Civil Liberties Union to remove the prayer.

The New York courts upheld the school board, however, because the prayer was not compulsory. When the Supreme Court agreed to hear the case in April 1962, ACLU lawyer William Butler centered much of his argument on showing that noncompulsory prayers were not realistic for an age group that valued conformity above all else.

"Little children want to be with other little children," he argued. "It can be sustained that, in effect, the children are coerced into saying this prayer because of these reasons."

A majority of the justices ruled that school prayer indeed violated the First Amendment. That important amendment, wrote Justice Hugo Black, "was written to quiet well-justified fears...arising out of an awareness that governments of the past had shackled men's tongues to make them speak only the religious thoughts that the government wanted them to speak...." Writing prayers, he added, was something that people, not the government, should do themselves.

▶ THE PEOPLE'S POPE
The genial son of Italian peasants ushered the Roman Catholic Church into the 20th century. Pope John XXIII brought together 2,540 Catholics and Protestants in October to find a way to make the church part of the modern world. Three years later, it was well on its way with some major reforms on the books.

The Second Vatican Council was the Church's first assembly of its leaders in more than 90 years. The Pope asked those

invited to suggest topics for discussion, and they ranged from contraception to improving Christian-Jewish relations. He solicited topics from Protestant and Orthodox priests who were also asked to attend.

Pope John's wish to inject some modernity into Catholicism came true. Mass no longer had to be said in Latin, which made it more accessible. Anti-Semitism and nuclear weapons were condemned. In order to become a bigger part of the global community, the Roman Catholic church had to share the "grief and anguish of contemporary humanity...."

The Church did not reverse its anti-contraception policy, nor did it end clerical celibacy, as some had hoped. And both of these issues caused more Catholics to leave the fold as time passed. Still, Pope John's attempt to step forward was recognized. When he died in 1963, he was one of the most beloved popes in modern history.

▶ THE PERFECT COLD WAR HERO
He was suave. He was cool. He killed his enemies without wrinkling his impeccably tailored dinner jackets. He was Bond, James Bond, Agent 007, the Cold War's

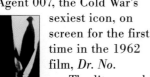

sexiest icon, on screen for the first time in the 1962 film, *Dr. No.*

The literary child of Ian Fleming, Bond did not fall far from the tree. The handsome English writer had been attracting women like flies to honey since his teens. Fleming learned the art of espionage while serving as a naval intelligence officer during World War II. He tried journalism afterward, but was annoyed when the facts ruined a good story. So he invented a spy. Fleming's first Bond novel,

Casino Royale, was published in 1953. Here was a hero for a new era with wacky weapons that would have been far-fetched in the pre-nuclear age. Bond was made for the movies, and a Scottish coffin polisher named Sean Connery (left) was made for James Bond. The producers of *Dr. No* were wowed by his ironic, sexy presence.

Fleming was less impressed by Connery and urged the producers to use David Niven or Noel Coward instead. But he changed his mind after seeing Connery in *Dr. No* and *From Russia With Love* (1963).

Fleming died in 1964, but Bond kept going, portrayed by 6 actors in 20 films.

SILENT SPRING

The modern environmental movement began in 1962 with Rachel Carson's meticulously researched book, *Silent Spring.* Her prosaic treatise on DDT and other pesticides galvanized millions to take up the cause against chemical destruction. So strong was the public's reaction to the book that numerous countries, including the U.S., eventually banned DDT.

"Chemicals are the sinister and little recognized partners of radiation in changing the very nature of the world," the marine biologist (right) wrote. "Non-selective chemicals that have the power to kill every insect, the good and the bad, to still the song of birds and the leaping of fish in the streams—to coat the leaves with a deadly film and to linger on in soil.... Can anyone believe it is possible to lay down such a barrage of poison on the surface of the earth without making it unfit for all life?"

■ TRENDS & TRIVIA

Madeline L'Engle's *A Wrinkle in Time* is science fiction for children.

Ingri and Edgar Parin d'Aulaire write and illustrate their magnificent *Book of Greek Myths* for children.

Helen Gurley Brown's *Sex and the Single Girl* is published.

David Lean directs *Lawrence of Arabia.*

Michael Harrington's *The Other America* reveals that 25 percent of Americans live in poverty.

Amnesty International is founded.

AT&T launches Telstar I, the first communications satellite. ▶

The film *West Side Story* wins ten Oscars.

"Love Me Do" introduces the Beatles in England.

Johnny Carson becomes host of *The Tonight Show.*

Edward Albee's *Who's Afraid of Virginia Woolf?* opens in New York City.

The Beach Boys record "Surfin' Safari," the sun-and-surf set's anthem.

K Mart and Wal-Mart open.

Wilt "the Stilt" Chamberlain scores 100 points in one game for the Philadelphia Warriors—an unbroken pro basketball record.

U.S. bans discrimination in housing.

Dulles Airport opens in Centreville, Virginia, the first civilian airport designed for jets.

255

● APRIL 26
Seven major steel mills in the U.S. cancel a price hike under presidential orders.

● AUGUST 14
Tunnel linking France and Italy under Mont Blanc is completed.

● AUGUST 5
Marilyn Monroe commits suicide at 36.

● SEPTEMBER 12
Richard M. Nixon begins his run for governor of California.

● SEPTEMBER 30
The University of Mississippi admits its first black student, James Meredith.

● OCTOBER 10
Mariner 2 reveals the presence of solar wind. Two months later, it sends back close-up photos of Venus.

● NOVEMBER 7
Eleanor Roosevelt dies.

● NOVEMBER 7
Ethiopian Emperor Haile Selassie absorbs the formerly autonomous region of Eritrea into his country.

1963

ONE MAN'S DREAM

The civil rights movement reached a sublime peak on August 28 when more than 200,000 people (below) assembled in Washington, D.C., heard the speech of a lifetime delivered by one of the country's greatest orators, the Rev. Dr. Martin Luther King, Jr. His electrifying words highlighted a day of demonstration for blacks and whites who sought racial equality.

King looked out over the sea of faces in the summer heat. Realizing that the end of the speech he'd written wasn't good enough, he ditched it and went into preaching mode.

"I still have a dream," he said slowly. "It is a dream deeply rooted in the American dream. I have a dream that one day this nation will rise up and live out the true meaning of its creed: 'We hold these truths to be self-evident, that all men are created equal.' When we let freedom ring...we will be able to speed up that day when all of God's children, black men and white men, Jews and Gentiles, Protestants and Catholics, will be able to join hands and sing in the words of the old Negro spiritual, 'Free at last! Free at last! Thank God Almighty, we are free at last!' "

▶ I AM A BERLINER

President John F. Kennedy's memorable speech in Berlin on June 26 played well. Some 150,000 Germans cheered as the uncrowned king of the free world denounced the Soviet Union.

Kennedy essentially drew a line in the sand, pledging that the U.S. would do whatever was necessary to preserve West Germany and Berlin from communism.

"There are many people in the world who really don't understand, or say they don't, what is the great issue between the free world and the communist world," he said from a podium festooned with the American flag in front of the city's town hall. "Let them come to Berlin!... There are even a few who say that it's true that communism is an evil system, but it permits us to make economic progress. Let them come to Berlin!"

The crowd roared with approval—and a few chuckles. Kennedy's translator was unaware of the fact that Berliner was also a colloquialism for a certain type of dessert. So when the president announced proudly, "Ich bin ein Berliner!" he was also saying, "I am a puff pastry!"

▶ SOUTH VIETNAM'S LEADER IS MURDERED

The assassination of South Vietnamese Premier Ngo Dinh Diem in November deepened America's involvement in Indochina. The chaos that followed the murder only increased South Vietnam's dependency on U.S. aid. As Kennedy had forewarned, the country had become "our offspring."

Diem, an autocratic anticommunist,

had become a liability for the Kennedy Administration. He was a dictator whose main advisor was his ruthless brother Nhu. The two presided over a corrupt and often oppressive government. A Buddhist monk performed self-immolation to protest Diem's policies, and that horrific image, displayed in publications immediately afterward, showed many Americans how miserable the regime their country supported really was.

Kennedy and his father, Joseph, had supported Diem; they had befriended him several years before when he lived in a monastery in New York. But for a President about to begin his reelection campaign, the alliance became politically unwise, especially after reports began circulating that Diem was interested in a settlement with the North Vietnamese government.

Kennedy's advisers discreetly told members of Diem's military that the U.S. would not oppose a coup nor would it withdraw its support in the fight against the communist north. So on November 2, the generals killed Diem and Nhu. Three weeks later, Kennedy was killed. Two months after that, Diem's murderers were overthrown.

▶ KENNEDY IS ASSASSINATED

John F. Kennedy's assassination was a devastating tragedy that replayed itself over and over again in the American psyche. The President was shot twice as he rode through Dallas on November 22 in a convertible with his wife.

"I guess that we thought that we had a little more time," said Daniel P. Moynihan, a cabinet member and later a U.S. senator. "[Columnist] Mary McGrory said to me that we'll never laugh again. And I said, 'Heavens, Mary. We'll laugh again. It's just that we'll never be young again.' "

Youth had indeed come to the White House with Kennedy, the youngest man

---

- **FEBRUARY 8**
Iraq's premier, Abdul Kassim, is ousted in a military coup.

- **FEBRUARY 19**
Seeking autonomy, Kurds begin peace talks with Iraq.

- **FEBRUARY 22**
Earthquakes hit Libya, killing 300 and leaving 12,000 homeless.

- **MAY 1**
Sir Winston Churchill announces that he will not run again for Parliament, ending a 61-year career.

◀ **MAY 6**
Police in Birmingham, Alabama, arrest 1,000 civil rights protesters.

- **JUNE 5**
British Secretary of War John Profumo resigns as a result of an affair with a prostitute who was also involved with a Soviet naval officer.

- **JUNE 12**
A sniper kills civil rights leader Medgar W. Evers in Jackson, Mississippi. Hundreds of blacks riot throughout the South.

ever elected President and the second youngest to take office. The handsome man, along with his glamorous wife, Jacqueline, and two young children, made many Americans proud. Jackie herself later compared her husband's brief term with Camelot, the legendary court of Britain's heroic King Arthur and his beautiful queen, Guinevere.

Figuring out who really killed the 35th President became an obsession for some and an industry for others. Most evidence pointed to one man, Lee Harvey Oswald. He got a job in the Texas Schoolbook Depository, a building that overlooked the route, and studied the planned motorcade route days before. On the morning of Kennedy's visit, Oswald climbed to the building's sixth floor and positioned himself near a window. Shortly before 12:30 p.m., he brought the President's head into view with a telescopic site mounted on a high-powered rifle, then fired.

Within the hour, Oswald was arrested, and Vice President Lyndon B. Johnson was soon after sworn in as President (below). Oswald's connections with the Communist Party and with supporters of Fidel Castro gave the assassination the appearance of a grand conspiracy, especially since Kennedy himself was linked with plans to assassinate the Cuban leader. But before police could obtain much information from Oswald, a nightclub owner named Jack Ruby shot him to death.

Ruby's underworld connections made some believe the Mafia paid Oswald to kill

Kennedy in return for some past slight. For all of his charm, Kennedy had made a number of enemies through questionable business deals, indiscreet liaisons with women, and his family's consuming quest for power.

In 1964 the government-appointed Warren Commission announced that Oswald alone killed Kennedy. Despite the commission's report, numerous unbelievers continued to crank out articles, books, and movies, outlining conspiracy theories galore. Some conspiracy theorists believe the Soviet KGB masterminded the assassination in retaliation for the Cuban missile crisis. Other theorists implicate the CIA, Castro, segregationists, or Cuban exiles.

FEMALE RIGHTS

Betty Friedan's *The Feminine Mystique* was a breath of fresh air. She articulated what millions of women were feeling—that there had to be more to life than raising children and running a household.

"I and every other woman I knew had been living a lie," Friedan (below) wrote in her controversial feminist manifesto. "If women really were *people*...then all the things that kept them from being full people in our society would have to be changed."

Friedan hit a nerve with women, many of whom identified with the civil rights movement because they too felt

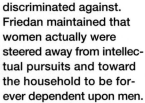

discriminated against. Friedan maintained that women actually were steered away from intellectual pursuits and toward the household to be forever dependent upon men.

"The feminine mystique," she wrote, "...kept us passive and apart, and kept us from seeing our real problems and possibilities." In 1966 Friedan co-founded the National Organization for Women (NOW). Her pioneering efforts inspired countless women.

■ TRENDS & TRIVIA

Maurice Sendak's *Where the Wild Things Are* is published.

Tab cola is introduced.

Touch-Tone telephones and cassette tape recorders debut.

Elizabeth Taylor and Richard Burton fall in love while filming *Cleopatra*.

Peter, Paul, and Mary's song "Puff the Magic Dragon" is condemned by some who incorrectly insist it is about drugs.

Weight Watchers International is incorporated.

Alfred Hitchcock directs *The Birds*.

The Spy Who Came in From the Cold, John Le Carré's first spy novel, is published.

Motown releases *Little Stevie Wonder, the 12-Year-Old Genius*, his first album.

Soviet astronaut Valentina Tereshkova is the first woman in space.

Scientists put the finishing touches on the measles vaccine.

Roald Dahl's *Charlie and the Chocolate Factory* is published.

The Beatles release their first album, *Please Please Me*.

General Hospital and *Let's Make a Deal* air on American television.

First metal tennis racket is patented in U.S. by René Lacoste.

Pope Paul VI sets precedent by inviting five women to attend Vatican II as delegates.

Sylvia Plath's *The Bell Jar* is published.

257

• **JUNE 3**
Pope John XXIII dies after a lengthy battle with cancer.

• **JULY 26**
Earthquake in Yugoslavia kills more than 1,000 people near the city of Skopje.

• **AUGUST 25**
South Vietnamese police arrest 1,000 students protesting against the government.

• **SEPTEMBER 15**
Four black girls die after a bomb explodes during Sunday School at a church in Birmingham, Alabama.

• **OCTOBER**
British Prime Minister Harold Macmillan resigns, another casualty of the Profumo scandal.

• **NOVEMBER 22**
British author C. S. Lewis dies at 64.

• **DECEMBER 10**
Zanzibar regains its independence from Britain after 73 years.

258

President Lyndon B. Johnson's promise of a "Great Society" became the most ambitious collection of social changes since the New Deal.

"The Great Society rests on abundance and liberty for all," he said. "It demands an end to poverty and racial injustice. But that is just the beginning."

Johnson (below, left, with Vice President Hubert H. Humphrey, Jr.) outlined his vision in 1964. The Economic Opportunity Act was one of the first measures enacted. The bill created a Job Corps for school dropouts and VISTA (Volunteers in Service to America), a domestic version of the Peace Corps. Other innovations included Medicare, Medicaid, food stamps, and the federal Department of Housing and Urban Development.

Between 1959 and 1969, the number of Americans living below the poverty line dropped by almost half.

"The brilliant court and flashing pennons of Camelot are not his," acknowledged a historian. "Rather...the small farmer's son become president has plotted out in his Great Society the contours and tracelines of the next major social development in America."

▶ LBJ'S POWER GRAB

The Gulf of Tonkin Resolution gave President Johnson broad powers to wage an undeclared war in Vietnam without the normal congressional checks and balances. His use of that power triggered a rash of antiwar demonstrations and loss of congressional allies. It eventually led to his departure from the White House.

The justifications for the resolution were shaky. American ships had been patrolling the Gulf of Tonkin for the South Vietnamese during the summer of 1964 to monitor the North Vietnamese. On August 2 U.S. officials reported that the North Vietnamese had attacked the U.S.S. *Maddox* without provocation. Two days later, the *Maddox* and the U.S.S. *Turner Joy* reported more unprovoked fire.

Johnson immediately asked Congress for the authority to "take all necessary measures including the use of armed forces to prevent further aggression" by the Viet Cong. Congress overwhelmingly granted his request; only two members voted against the resolution.

But Congress—and the American public—became unhappy with the Gulf of Tonkin Resolution after the news leaked out that the first attack by the North Vietnamese was not unprovoked and the second probably never happened. Prominent Johnson supporters felt duped; they had given him almost unlimited power to conduct a distant war for reasons that he could only poorly articulate. Four years later, Johnson, angered and hurt by bipartisan criticisms of his Vietnam policies, announced that he would not seek a second term or continue to bomb North Vietnam.

▶ AT LAST, CIVIL RIGHTS ACT PASSES

The Civil Rights Act of 1964 was an idea whose time was long overdue. When President Johnson signed the bill into law that July, he exhorted the public to "close the springs of racial poison" and erase "the last vestiges of injustice in America."

The Civil Rights Act struck down discrimination based on race, creed, national origin, or sex. Sex was added during House debates as a poison pill to kill the bill by a segregationist who tried to disguise it as a "chivalrous action." His plan backfired, though, when five female representatives rallied around the bill and refused to accept anything less than victory. "We were entitled to this little crumb of equality," said one.

Johnson was happy to take credit for the act, although a limited version had been in the pipeline since the Kennedy Administration. Momentum picked up after Kennedy's assassination because many saw the bill's passage as a fitting tribute to the late President. That, and some last-minute lobbying by an impressive group of religious leaders helped Johnson push the bill through the Senate.

▶ I'M THE GREATEST

Nobody could believe it. The rhymin', jivin' Cassius Marcellus Clay had knocked out world heavyweight champ Sonny

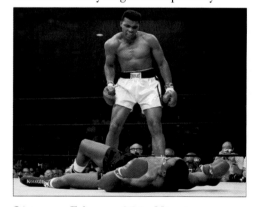

Liston on February 25 in Miami.

"Eat your words!" the new champ yelled to the 46 reporters outside the ring, 43 of whom predicted he would lose. "I'm the greatest! I'm gonna upset the world!"

Nicknamed the "Louisville Lip," Clay

was a colorful character whose speech was an unbelievable stream of hype. "Float like a butterfly, sting like a bee, his hands can't hit what his eyes can't see!" His physical presence mimicked his chatter. He danced around his opponents' blows, then peppered them with punches.

Clay, an Olympic gold medalist, had only fought 19 professional boxing matches before he challenged Liston. A year later, in a rematch that many said was staged, Clay beat Liston again, this time with the so-called "invisible punch" in the first round in a fight held in Lewiston, Maine (opposite, right).

The young champ converted to Islam and changed his name to Muhammad Ali in 1967, the same year he refused to enter the Vietnam War—for religious reasons. "I ain't got nothing against no Viet Cong," he said. The boxing commission rewarded his religious fervor by taking away his title. But to millions of young blacks and conscientious objectors, Ali remained the Champ.

▶ SMOKING GUN

The verdict on cigarettes finally came down in 1964 when the U.S. Surgeon General found them guilty. "Many kinds of damage to body functions, and to organs, cells, and tissues occur more frequently and severely in smokers," Dr. Luther Terry's report said.

The number of smokers had been growing since the turn of the century. During World War I, tobacco companies made the patriotic gesture of giving free smokes to soldiers. A cigarette was the perfect way to calm the nerves, and it looked glamorous to boot. By 1963, 70 million Americans smoked—39 percent of the population. Tobacco was the nation's fifth-largest cash crop.

But sentiment and money could not erase the fact that lung cancer fatalities had increased almost proportionally to the number of smokers. While the disease killed only 2 percent of the population, it was the most prevalent form of cancer.

The tobacco industry refuted the report and worked hard to soften the language of a warning label that the government required be placed on every pack of cigarettes. But the report's damage still managed to do a slow burn on the industry. The number of smokers in the U.S. has dropped to about 25 percent near the century's end.

THE FAB FOUR

The Beatles (below) transformed pop music. The spokesmen of the peace-and-love generation pushed their creative limits with every new album, infusing each experiment with their beautiful harmonies and witty, beguiling lyrics.

"Rock," wrote the renowned critic Greil Marcus, "became, in the shape of the Beatles, a way of life."

John Lennon, Paul McCartney, George Harrison, and Ringo Starr had been drawing crowds in England since 1961. But it was their American tour in February 1964 that made them superstars. Police in New York had to hold back a swarm of hysterical teens at the airport when the Beatles landed. It was utter pandemonium—the British invasion.

"The chemistry was there," McCartney told interviewer David Frost 27 years after the group disbanded in 1970. "It was four...personalities. It wasn't just John; it wasn't just me...without the Beatles, it would have been a very different world."

■ TRENDS & TRIVIA

America's first disco opens on Los Angeles's Sunset Strip, called "Whiskey-a-Go-Go."

Geraldine Mock of West Germany becomes the first woman to fly around the world solo.

Sidney Poitier becomes the first black to win the Oscar for best actor for his role in *Lilies of the Field.*

Ford Motor Company introduces the Mustang.

Motown's Supremes are hot.

Race riots start in New York and New Jersey.

Marc Chagall paints the ceiling of the Paris Opera House for free.

Op art is hip.

A Hard Day's Night is the first Beatles film.

Julie Andrews stars in *Mary Poppins.*

Peter Sellers stars in *The Pink Panther.*

CBS airs *The Munsters* and *Gilligan's Island.*

Carol Channing stars in *Hello Dolly!* on Broadway.

Jazz musician John Coltrane releases *A Love Supreme.*

Topless bikini or "monokini" hits the beach.

GI Joe is a doll for boys.

Barbra Streisand immortalizes Fanny Brice in the play *Funny Girl.*

A Fistful of Dollars is the first spaghetti Western (a Western filmed in Italy or Spain by an Italian director).

259

MISSING CALL FBI

◀ **JUNE**
The FBI distributes thousands of flyers throughout the South in the search for three missing civil rights workers.

● **JUNE 14**
Black lawyer Nelson Mandela begins a life sentence for plotting to overthrow South Africa's government.

● **AUGUST 12**
Ian Fleming dies of a heart attack at 56, the same day his son celebrates his 12th birthday.

● **AUGUST 17**
Teamsters leader Jimmy Hoffa gets a five-year jail term and $10,000 fine for defrauding the union.

● **OCTOBER 15**
Soviet leader Nikita Khrushchev resigns under pressure. Leonid Brezhnev becomes First Secretary.

● **DECEMBER 10**
Martin Luther King, Jr., receives the Nobel Peace Prize.

VIETNAM WAR ESCALATES

America's involvement in Vietnam deepened in 1965 when President Johnson dispatched two Marine battalions to protect an air base in Da Nang. These were combat soldiers, unlike the 23,500 troops already there who were designated "advisers."

American fighter pilots dropped more bombs on North

Vietnam (above) that year alone than the previous generation had dumped on Japan in World War II. In the south, U.S. and South Vietnamese pilots unleashed 1,000 tons of explosives on an alleged Viet Cong outpost near the Cambodian border. Thousands of civilians died, and many more were wounded.

Americans began dying too—1,130 in 1965. At the end of July, there were 125,000 GIs in Vietnam, up from 75,000. The draft doubled also, calling for 35,000 more soldiers per month. Many draftees were poor; higher-income young men were often able to avoid combat duty through deferments.

▶ DEATH OF MALCOLM X

Malcolm X's speech to the crowd packed in a Harlem ballroom on February 21 was disrupted by a yell. A man close to the podium claimed that another was trying to pick his pocket. "Hold it!" the black leader said. "Don't get excited. Let's cool it, brothers!"

Three men immediately leaped onto the stage and shot Malcolm. He was assassinated at the age of 39, just as his more peaceful counterpart, Martin Luther King, Jr., would be three years later.

Malcolm's exhortations for peace were the precise reason for his death. Only months before the assembly in Harlem, the Muslim revolutionary had returned from a *hajj*, or pilgrimage, to Mecca and advocated "an honest black-white brotherhood." This outraged his former colleagues in the Nation of Islam.

Malcolm Little had joined the group in 1952 and changed his surname to X. He soon became the group's star orator. Some thought he threatened the authority of the Nation's leader, Elijah Muhammad, who suspended Malcolm in 1963 for making inappropriate comments about President Kennedy's assassination.

Malcolm traveled to the Middle East, where he embraced the basic Islamic tenet that all men are brothers. Upon returning to America, he established the Organization of Afro-American Unity. "There can be no black-white unity until there is first some black unity," he once said. "We cannot think of being acceptable to others until we have first proven acceptable to ourselves." His assassination, however, showed that black unity was still elusive.

▶ RACE RIOTS RAVAGE LOS ANGELES

To many blacks, Dr. Martin Luther King, Jr.'s policy of nonviolence was not working fast enough. Racism was slow to die, and violent action looked like the best way to accelerate the process.

The Watts riot that occurred in August was a fiery example of this new tack and a harbinger of summers to come. The disturbance began on August 11 when a Los Angeles police officer argued with the mother of a man arrested for drunken driving in the predominantly black neighborhood of Watts. The argument attracted onlookers, who began jeering at the officer. Relations between the police and Watts residents were abysmal; white patrolmen assigned to the beat called their nightsticks "nigger knockers."

The arrest escalated into a full-blown riot that raged for five days. King came to survey the scene and asked a looter what he thought he'd achieved. The young man responded, "We made the whole world pay attention to us."

Whites certainly paid attention to the televised rampage. White terrorist groups were formed, urban police departments added riot-control gear to their arsenals, and California voters, disgusted by the riot, traded their liberal governor, Pat Brown, for conservative Ronald Reagan in hopes of regaining law and order.

As a race riot, Watts was not new. But those of the past typically were instigated by whites who perceived blacks or other minorities as threats to neighborhoods and jobs. The Watts riot and others that followed in the mid-1960s were different. Blacks now were retaliating in an expression of hopeless rage.

• **JANUARY 30**
Sir Winston Churchill dies of a stroke at 90 in London.

• **FEBRUARY 15**
Silky-voiced singer Nat King Cole dies at 45 of lung cancer.

• **FEBRUARY 23**
Stan Laurel, the slim half of Laurel and Hardy, dies at 74 in Santa Monica, California.

• **MARCH 18**
Soviet astronaut Aleksei Leonov becomes first man to walk in space.

• **APRIL 6**
NASA launches *Early Bird*, the world's first commercial satellite.

• **APRIL 23**
Edward R. Murrow dies at 56 of lung cancer.

• **MAY 11**
Cyclone in Pakistan kills 5,000 people and leaves 5 million more homeless.

POLICE CHECK SUSPECTED LOOTERS IN WATTS.

"I regret it, yes," said a black college student who had rioted in Watts. "But deep down inside I know I was feeling some joy while it was going on, simply because I am a Negro."

▶ DOMINICAN DEBACLE

Any gains the Alliance for Progress had made for the U.S. in Central America were lost during a springtime coup in the Dominican Republic. Fearing that the island nation would become another communist stronghold, President Johnson dispatched 22,000 soldiers to prevent a liberal reformer from regaining office. This overreaction cost Johnson credibility at home and abroad.

The Dominican Republic's troubles had begun in the 1930s when Gen. Rafael Trujillo began his dictatorial reign. He was assassinated in 1961 and eventually the people elected Juan Bosch, a poet and social reformer, as president. He was deposed in 1963 by a military junta, which held office for only two years before restive young officers staged a countercoup in 1965 and sought to reinstate Bosch.

The overthrown junta turned to the U.S. for intervention. Reacting to exaggerated reports from the American ambassador, Johnson responded with force. From his Puerto Rican exile, Bosch called the invasion a ridiculous example "of a

NEW VOTERS

The Voting Rights Act transformed American politics and the lives of black Americans. By guaranteeing blacks the right to vote, the law forced politicians to consider and include a growing constituency.

Literacy tests and poll taxes effectively shut blacks out of the voting process in several states. In the South, where half of the nation's 19 million blacks lived, the overwhelming majority could not elect their representatives.

Civil rights leaders demanded an end to the gross inequity in 1965. President Johnson, an ardent anti-segregationist, supported them. But it would take violent action to prod other politicians to act. That happened in March during a peaceful protest in Selma, Alabama. Police there clubbed and teargassed a group led by Martin Luther King, Jr.

Johnson pressed his congressional cronies to pass a voting rights bill that he signed on August 6. Within ten years, the number of black voters in the South had soared by more than 50 percent, and 3,500 blacks had been elected to public offices.

great big elephant afraid of a mouse."

By June the Dominicans—with U.S. assistance—were preparing themselves for an election that would be held the following year. But they, and others throughout Latin America, resented the intrusion on their sovereignty as another example of American imperialism. Adlai Stevenson II, a respected statesman, spoke for many Americans when he said, "When I consider what the administration did in the Dominican Republic, I begin to wonder if we know what we're doing in Vietnam."

■ TRENDS & TRIVIA

Miniskirts and the Mod look come into fashion.

The Who releases "My Generation."

Skateboarding becomes popular.

Britain bans cigarette advertising on television.

Houston Astrodome opens as the world's largest air-conditioned arena.

Britain adopts the metric system.

The Beatles release "Yesterday."

The Rolling Stones monster hit "[I Can't Get No] Satisfaction" brings fame and a bad-boy image to the group.

Movie theaters are alive with *The Sound of Music.*

The Byrds trade folk for psychedelia in "Eight Miles High."

Sonny and Cher release "I Got You Babe."

Ralph Nader's *Unsafe at Any Speed* is published. ▶

Neil Simon's *The Odd Couple* debuts on Broadway.

NADER PROMOTES HIS BOOK.

Nutra-Sweet is introduced.

Eero Saarinen's Gateway Arch in St. Louis is completed.

The Warlocks form a folk rock group that is later renamed the Grateful Dead.

Drug guru Timothy Leary preaches "Drop out, turn on, tune in."

Poet Allen Ginsberg organizes first "Be-In" in San Francisco.

• JULY 14
U.S. Ambassador to the U.N. Adlai Stevenson II has a heart attack on a London street and dies at 65.

• JULY 25
Crowds boo Bob Dylan off the stage at the Newport Jazz Festival for using electric instruments.

• AUGUST 9
Singapore splits from Malaysia to become independent.

• AUGUST 20
Thousands riot in Greece as new government takes over.

• NOVEMBER 12
Ferdinand Marcos wins presidential election in the Philippines.

• DECEMBER 10
UNICEF wins Nobel Peace Prize.

• DECEMBER 31
Central African Republic President David Dacko is ousted by his cousin Jean Bedel Bocassa.

1966 MAO'S LAST REVOLUTION

In an effort to control the huge country he had profoundly changed and to dislodge his enemies, the aging Chairman Mao Zedong (below) launched China's "great proletariat cultural revolution" in the spring of 1966.

Over the next three years 400,000 would perish as the Cultural Revolution, under the command of Mao's ruthless wife Jiang Qing and a group of radical reformers later called "the Gang of Four," assaulted anything that smacked of capitalism. Millions of students called Red Guards marched in the streets, proudly hoisting Mao's picture. Anyone opposing them faced public humiliation or death.

What was good for Mao was not good for his country. Agricultural and factory production dropped. Secondary and higher education almost came to a halt. The revolution caused havoc in the lives of intellectuals, Buddhist monks, and young people who didn't join the Red Guards.

In three years the zealous guards irreparably damaged thousands of years of history by destroying monasteries, manuscripts, and priceless works of art. Mao's revolution was a cultural disaster.

▶ PANTHER POWER

Huey Newton did not mince words in articulating what black Americans wanted. "We want power…full employment… land, bread, housing, education, clothing, justice."

Newton was the self-proclaimed minister of defense of the Black Panthers, an organization founded in Oakland, California, in the fall of 1966. Newton and Panther Chairman Bobby Seale urged blacks to arm themselves in the war against racism and capitalism. Political power, they stressed, "comes through the barrel of a gun."

Panther ideology was a fusion of socialism, Marxism, and black nationalism. "Black Power" had become the catchphrase of the day, often accompanied by an arm raised in a clenched-fist salute.

The Panthers offered power. Recruits, usually from the ghetto, were issued guns, black uniforms, and a beat. They patrolled the ghettos to protect residents and to monitor police activities. The group also opened schools and medical clinics, organized free breakfasts for children, and worked with the homeless.

These peaceful activities were overshadowed by the prevailing image of armed Panthers, inscrutable behind their dark sunglasses. Most whites were terrified of the group. When Newton's replacement, Eldridge Cleaver, called for a free, communist Vietnam and advocated a wholesale overthrow of the U.S. government, the FBI responded with a covert, illegal crusade against the Panthers. Police in several cities used massive force to kill Panther leaders and squelch the movement on a local level.

By the mid-1970s, the Panthers suffered from internal struggles and legal problems. The group gradually dropped into oblivion.

▶ OPENING THE BEDROOM DOOR

Sex was again in the public eye in 1966 when William Masters and Virginia Johnson introduced *Human Sexual Response*.

The two researchers spent 11 years listening to the sighs and moans of 694 men and women. They reported their findings in straightforward language, often going into clinical detail, about how patients responded to sexual stimulation. Packed with solid scientific data, the study gave doctors and therapists something concrete to work with as they helped patients grapple with "the widespread problem of sexual inadequacy."

▶ MOTHER INDIA

On January 19 Indira Gandhi became prime minister of India, the country her father had helped create 21 years before.

She proved to be a tough leader who tried to keep Asia's great experiment with democracy on course. But the country she inherited was poor and vastly overpopulated by peoples of different ethnicities and religions. Her heavy-handed methods of maintaining control led to her assassination 18 years later. "My father was a saint," she once said. "I am not."

Gandhi was Jawaharlal Nehru's only child and closest confidante. *Bharat Mata* (Mother India) attached no special importance to the fact that she was a woman because Indian women were often active in politics. More than 50 served as members of parliament. Others held responsible government jobs; Gandhi herself had served as the minister of information and broadcasting

- **JANUARY 8**
American forces launch biggest attack to date against Viet Cong northwest of Saigon without consulting South Vietnamese allies.

- **FEBRUARY 3**
The Soviet Union's Luna 9 makes the first non-crash landing on the moon.

- **FEBRUARY 27**
Peggy Fleming wins her first of three consecutive world championships in figure skating.

- **MARCH**
French President Charles de Gaulle pulls France out of NATO.

- **MARCH 12**
With the support of the U.S. government, Indonesian President Suharto overthrows President Sukarno.

- **APRIL 17**
LSD guru and former Harvard professor Timothy Leary is arrested in New York City for possession of marijuana.

- **MAY 11**
Joseph Hirshhorn gives his 35-million-dollar modern art collection to the U.S.

under her father's successor. "I am just an Indian citizen and the first servant of my country," she shrugged to a reporter after her election.

▶ THE RENAISSANCE UNDER SEIGE
Necessity truly became the mother of invention for art preservationists in November when the Arno River flooded Florence, Italy. In a rare example of global cooperation, scholars, students, and art lovers from around the world raced against time to figure out how to save some of the most important works of the Italian Renaissance.

FLOODWATER LEAVES ITS MARK.

Swollen by unusually heavy rains that deluged northern Italy, the Arno River reached record heights as it spilled into the city. High-speed winds whipped the waves into watery fists that forced open the Baptistery's huge bronze doors, carved in the 15th century by Lorenzo Ghiberti. Priceless frescoes by masters like Cimabue appeared to be soaked beyond salvation. Thousands of ancient books were buried in mud. The Uffizi Gallery's staff had managed to hustle its masterpieces to the top floors. But much of the city's artistic heritage had been stored at or below street level.

Swarms of people who descended on the city to rescue the art rolled up their sleeves and put on waders. In one library, volunteers spent days inserting blotting paper between the pages of sopping books.

MIRANDA RIGHTS

Ernesto Miranda gave his name to one of the Supreme Court's most controversial decisions. *Miranda v. Arizona* protected persons accused of a crime from self-incrimination and guaranteed their right to a court-appointed attorney if they could not afford to hire their own. The Court was divided over the decision, and so was the country. It underscored an important right, but at the same time was seen as a protective device for those who potentially were the least deserving—accused criminals.

Miranda's confession to kidnapping and raping a teenager, obtained after a two-hour interrogation, became the most incriminating evidence against him in the subsequent trial. The lawyer later assigned to Miranda argued that the police had obtained the confession illegally since they had never informed him of his constitutional right to silence or to have an attorney present.

Chief Justice Earl Warren agreed. "…The right to have counsel present at the interrogation is indispensable to the protection of the Fifth Amendment privilege…," he wrote. "Our aim is to assure that the individual's right to choose between silence and speech remains unfettered throughout the interrogation process."

Art historians and preservationists brainstormed together. Frescoes were peeled off walls so the mold growing behind could be destroyed. To prevent mold from spreading in old books, conservationists placed them in airtight boxes with mold-killing chemicals. These innovations became standard preservationists' tools for years to come.

263

■ TRENDS & TRIVIA

Roman Catholics in the U.S. are allowed to eat meat on Fridays, except during Lent.

Chemical structure of DNA is discovered.

Paul Scofield stars in *A Man for All Seasons.*

Frank Sinatra, 50, marries Mia Farrow, 21, in Las Vegas.

Simon and Garfunkel release "The 59th Street Bridge Song [Feelin' Groovy]."

Italian film star Sophia Loren and director Carlo Ponti hold a second wedding ceremony to assure their union's legal status.

Bill Russell becomes the highest paid and first black coach in pro sports. The Boston Celtics pay him $125,000.

Robert Indiana unveils his "Love" sculpture.

Star Trek, Family Affair, and *Hollywood Squares* debut on American TV.

Beatles release "Eleanor Rigby."

Truman Capote's *In Cold Blood* is published.

MasterCharge debuts.

Cabaret opens on Broadway.

New York City's historic Pennsylvania Station is torn down.

Frank Zappa releases *Freak-Out!* rock's first double album.

Massachusetts elects Edward Brooke, the first black senator since Reconstruction.

Congress passes "truth in packaging" law, requiring manufacturers to list a product's ingredients on the package.

• MAY 11
U.S troops shell Cambodia for the first time during the Vietnam War.

• MAY 26
British Guiana becomes independent nation of Guyana.

• JUNE 15
Three days of anti-establishment rioting end in Amsterdam.

• JULY 19
Richard Speck is charged with killing eight nurses in Chicago. He is later convicted.

• AUGUST 1
From a 27-story tower on the University of Texas campus in Austin, Eagle Scout Charles Whitman kills 12 and wounds 33 others.

◄ NOVEMBER
Students burn their draft cards to protest Vietnam War conscription.

264

Israel quadrupled its size after crushing a multinational Arabic army over the course of six days in June.

The Six-Day War started with squabbles along Israel's border with Lebanon, Syria, and Jordan. Guerrillas and soldiers from all sides had been sniping at each other since the mid-1950s. Many fighters were Palestinians who resented the creation of Israel in 1948.

Israel sent soldiers to the northern borders to protect Jewish settlers. Egyptian President Gamal Abdel Nasser, sensing a chance to broaden his appeal in the Arab world, dispatched his troops to Israel's southern border on the Sinai Peninsula. He then applied pressure from the east by blockading the Strait of Tiran, Israel's sole entrance to the Red Sea.

Israel responded with a show of strength, pushing across the Sinai to Egypt. In Jordan, the historic cities of Bethlehem, Jericho, and all of Jerusalem fell into Israeli hands. To the north, they captured Syria's Golan Heights.

The stunning victory left Israelis more confident, but it intensified international disagreements over the balance of power in the Middle East. Israeli settlers poured into the captured land, laying the groundwork for future strife.

▶ STARVATION IN BIAFRA

Starvation in Africa became an all-too-common image in 1967 as photos of emaciated children poured out of the breakaway nation of Biafra. They were the most recent victims of the tribal warfare that had plagued the continent before and after the demise of colonialism.

Biafra was carved out of the former British colony of Nigeria, which was the home of the Igbo people. Before Nigerian independence in 1960, the Igbo had assimilated easily into colonial society. Other tribes resented the Igbo's importance, particularly the Hausa people who traditionally dominated the north.

The situation finally boiled over in 1966, when soldiers, the majority of whom were Igbo, overthrew the Nigerian government and installed military rule. The Hausa responded to the coup by killing 30,000 Igbo in the north and forcing a million to flee to their traditional homeland in the south. They renamed the region Biafra and declared independence in 1967.

Great Britain and the Soviet Union, afraid that Biafra's action might start a rash of successions all over the volatile continent, supported Nigeria. France, Portugal, and South Africa weakly supported Biafra. Nigerian bombs ruined Biafra's food supply, while Nigerian blockades prevented any relief shipments. One million Igbo died—mostly starved children—before Biafra surrendered in 1970.

▶ HERE'S TO YOU, MRS. ROBINSON

Women moved into the driver's seat in *The Graduate* when a middle-aged housewife seduced a younger man. The role reversal was a daring move for American filmmaker Mike Nichols.

The film broke ground musically as well. Nichols asked the pop singer-songwriter duo of Paul Simon and Art Garfunkel if he could use their music—the first use ever of pop music in a major motion picture. One of the songs, "Mrs. Robinson," became a huge hit.

The male lead was an unremarkable-looking actor named Dustin Hoffman. His everyday appearance and the fact that he was not a big star made him all the more plausible as Benjamin Braddock, a

WEDDING SCENE FROM *THE GRADUATE*

confused college grad trying to make sense out of what society expected from him. Again, Nichols had defied convention with great results. His movie was poignant and funny, and would be immensely appealing to several generations of young audiences who identified with Braddock.

▶ FIRST BLACK ON THE BENCH

Grandson of a slave, Thurgood Marshall became one of the Supreme Court's most liberal judges. Appointed in 1967, the first black on the bench brought a crucial perspective to the challenges posed by the civil rights movement.

"The position of the Negro today in America is the tragic but inevitable consequence of centuries of unequal treatment," he wrote in a 1978 opinion. "Measured by any benchmark of conduct or achievement, meaningful equality remains a distant dream for the Negro."

Marshall's struggles to make the dream a reality began in college, when he

---

● **FEBRUARY 5**
Gen. Anastasio Somoza Debayle is elected president of Nicaragua.

◀ **MARCH 9**
Svetlana Alliluyeva, daughter of Joseph Stalin, defects to the U.S.

● **MARCH 13**
Former Vice President Richard Nixon authorizes his presidential campaign committee.

● **APRIL 19**
West Germany's first chancellor, Konrad Adenauer, dies at 91.

● **APRIL**
Military junta takes over Greece and establishes Western Europe's first post-war dictatorship under George Papadopoulos.

● **MAY 1**
Elvis Presley marries longtime girlfriend Priscilla Beaulieu.

successfully organized a protest against a segregated movie theater. During his 22-year career as a lawyer with the NAACP, Marshall gained national attention as he took 32 cases to the Supreme Court, including the one that overturned school segregation, *Brown* v. *Board of Education*.

"He was a very courageous figure," a NAACP colleague said. "He would travel to the courthouses of the South, and folks would come from miles...to see the nigger lawyer who stood up in white men's courtrooms."

Marshall served as a federal appellate judge and U.S. Solicitor General before President Johnson appointed him to the nation's highest court. The nomination passed overwhelmingly in the Senate, 69 to 11. Marshall's concern for the rights of minorities and poor people meshed well with Chief Justice Earl Warren. But as the social pendulum swung toward conservatism, he was often a lone dissenter. His opinions, some of the most readable in the court's history, are moving examples of American liberalism at its most expansive.

▶ THE SUMMER OF LOVE
The much-anticipated "Summer of Love" turned out to be a major downer for the counterculture. The extended "be-in" attracted some "uncool" types—disturbed youths and dope dealers who injected a heavy dose of violence into what was supposed to be a series of peaceful events.

It had auspicious beginnings. In April the largest public demonstration in American history took place when 300,000 people marched for peace.

On the West Coast, "hippies" piled into their Volkswagen buses and drove to the Haight-Asbury section of San Francisco where several peace rallies were scheduled.

Not everyone enjoyed peaceful drug trips, nor did everyone know when to stop. Drug addiction and crime soared in the hippie enclaves, and, because many of the

NEW HEART

The first successful human heart transplant took place on December 3 in Cape Town, South Africa. Christiaan Barnard and his team performed the groundbreaking surgery on Louis Washkansky, a 55-year-old grocer. The heart was obtained from a young woman who had been mortally wounded in a car accident.

Barnard was hailed as a "miracle worker" by some while others condemned him as too eager to play God. Physicians argued that the end of life could no longer be said to occur when the heart ceased to beat. Death was now best defined as the moment when all electrical activity in the brain ended.

Washkansky died from lung problems 18 days after the surgery. But Barnard and other surgeons continued to perform heart transplants.

HEART TRANSPLANT PIONEERS CHRISTIAAN BARNARD, MICHAEL DE BAKEY, AND ADRIAN KANTROWITZ

victims were runaways, the crimes went unreported. The neighborhood turned into a dangerous slum until a new generation swept in 20 years later. Proof that the summer of love backfired was never more evident than in 1998 when Haight residents rejected the installation of a huge peace sign as too likely to attract "youths searching for a lost era."

■ TRENDS & TRIVIA

Rolling Stone magazine begins publication.

Corporation for Public Broadcasting is established.

Amana markets the first compact microwave oven.

Quartz watches are new.

English model Twiggy inaugurates the emaciated look for women. ▶

Britain introduces the breathalyzer test for drunken drivers.

Aretha Franklin releases "Respect" and is named top female vocalist of the year by *Billboard* magazine.

The Doors release "Light My Fire."

Luis Buñuel directs *Belle du Jour*.

Tom Stoppard's play *Rosencrantz and Guildenstern Are Dead* debuts.

Aleksander Solzhenitsyn's *Cancer Ward* is published.

Gabriel Garcia Marquez's *One Hundred Years of Solitude* is published.

The Carol Burnett Show and *The Flying Nun* air on American TV.

Walt Disney Studios produces *Doctor Dolittle.*

Day-Glo paint colors debut.

U.S. Supreme Court upholds legality of interracial marriages.

William Styron's *The Confessions of Nat Turner* is published.

The hundred millionth telephone is installed in the U.S.

• JUNE
American radio and television stations that carry cigarette ads must also include information about related health risks.

• JUNE 18
50,000 people attend Monterey International Pop Festival in California, largest rock concert to date.

• JULY 8
British actress Vivien Leigh dies of tuberculosis at 53.

• JULY 31
French President Charles de Gaulle infuriates Canadian government by endorsing Quebec separatists' calls for secession.

• OCTOBER 3
Folk singer Woody Guthrie dies at 55 after a 13-year struggle with Huntington's chorea.

◀ OCTOBER 8
Bolivian soldiers ambush and kill Latin American revolutionary Che Guevara.

266

North Vietnam may have lost the battle in the Tet Offensive, but it helped them win the war. The Viet Cong's massive strike against the south showed they were not close to defeat, as Americans had been led to believe.

Both sides had declared a truce in late January to observe Tet, Vietnam's traditional New Year's celebration. North Vietnamese guerrillas broke the truce on January 31, when they attacked several sites in the south. Although their attempts to capture the U.S. embassy in Saigon failed, the fact that they had entered the embassy grounds was a shocking development.

The offensive cost the Viet Cong 40,000 lives. Although the Americans lost far fewer, January's casualty figures were the highest ever in one month, fueling the growing antiwar fires at home. People of all ages and backgrounds took part in demonstrations.

The Tet Offensive prompted some of President Johnson's advisers to push for de-escalation, and he acquiesced. He refused Gen. William Westmoreland's request for an additional 206,000 troops and ordered an end to all bombing above the 20th parallel. By October both sides began to discuss terms for peace, but the war would drag on for years.

▶ PRAGUE'S BRIEF SPRING

The Czechs made a brave attempt to achieve "socialism with a human face" in 1968, only to be squelched by their omnipresent political overlord, the Soviet Union. "Prague Spring" threatened Soviet Communist hegemony in Eastern Europe,

CZECH STUDENTS DISTRIBUTE UNDERGROUND LITERATURE.

and Soviet leaders could not tolerate a rip in the Iron Curtain.

The challenge began in January when Alexander Dubcek replaced Antonín Novotný, an ardent Stalinist, as first secretary of Czechoslovakia's Communist Party. Dubcek then began liberalizing the country with reforms aimed at renewing personal freedom. He relaxed government controls over the press and other industries. He withdrew from the Warsaw Pact. There was even talk of tolerating other political parties.

Soviet Party Chairman Leonid Brezhnev summoned Dubcek to warn him to end his flirtation with democracy. Dubcek declined. Brezhnev then enlisted the support of other satellite leaders against him. Still Dubcek refused to change, widely supported by his people.

Brezhnev was fed up. On August 20 he sent some 500,000 Soviet troops to yank Czechoslovakia back into the fold. Students in Prague tried to fight, but their rocks and bottles were no match for the mighty tanks. Thirty died and another 300 were wounded before Dubcek surrendered. Brezhnev then issued a doctrine that gave

the Soviets the right to intervene in any socialist country they deemed was in trouble.

▶ MY LAI'S UGLY SECRET

The My Lai massacre was a horrific example of wartime atrocities at their worst.

My Lai, a village near the South Vietnamese coast, was thought to be home to Viet Cong sympathizers. On March 16 a platoon of American infantrymen stormed in to rid the village and surrounding hamlets of the enemy. All they found were women, children, and old men—unarmed.

"We were mad and had been told that the enemy was there," one soldier recalled. "We were going in there to give them a fight for what they had done to our dead buddies."

The soldiers made no effort to distinguish friend from foe; women often fought with the Viet Cong, and their children, the soldiers had been told, laid land mines.

An officer, Lt. William Calley, Jr., ordered the men to round up villagers. "We made them squat down," Priv. Paul Meadlo described later on national television. "The mothers was hugging their children...we kept right on firing. They was waving their arms and begging...." More than 300 people were killed.

The massacre remained hushed up until the next year when a soldier threatened to go public with what he knew. The Army court-martialed Calley in hopes of settling the breach of conduct internally. But the story was out, and soon *Life* magazine published grizzly pictures of the bodies piled in pits after the slaughter.

Many Americans were reluctant to hold Calley responsible. He was a soldier following orders, they argued, a scapegoat. Not long after President Nixon asked to review Calley's life sentence, the Army commuted it to ten years. Within six months, he was free on parole.

• JANUARY 30
North Korea seizes U.S.S. *Pueblo*, which the Korean government says is doing surveillance in international waters.

• FEBRUARY
The Kerner Commission's report warns that the U.S. has split into two "separate and unequal" nations.

• APRIL 20
Pierre Trudeau is sworn in as Canada's prime minister.

• APRIL 22-23
Students for a Democratic Society take over Columbia University buildings to protest against war and racism.

• MAY
Students seeking to overthrow France's "capitalist government" and striking laborers bring the country to a halt.

• JUNE 1
Helen Keller, 87, dies in her sleep at her home in Connecticut.

• JUNE 5
Jordanian Sirhan Sirhan assassinates presidential candidate Senator Robert F. Kennedy in Los Angeles.

▶ VICTORY FOR NIXON

Richard M. Nixon achieved his life's goal when Americans, fed up with war and its destructive impact on the home front, elected him President in 1968.

With an adroit campaign team and sizable war chest in place, the former Vice President went after the middle class, his "forgotten Americans." They were tired of Vietnam, but uncomfortable with defeat. They saw the "Great Society" as an intrusive waste unappreciated by those it was supposed to aid. To them, Nixon's pledge of "peace with honor" sounded like a winner.

Middle-class voters were not the only ones turned off by Johnson. Eugene J. McCarthy, a Democratic senator from Minnesota opposed to the war, tossed his hat in the presidential race and almost beat Johnson in the pivotal New Hampshire primary. Such a successful challenge from a relative unknown in a hawkish state showed the President his vulnerability. In March he announced he would not seek re-election.

Former Attorney General Robert F. Kennedy and then Vice President Hubert H. Humphrey entered the fray; Kennedy appeared to be the early front-runner, but his assassination in June left the field in disarray once again.

The Democrats' last hope collapsed at their August convention in Chicago. Americans watched in horror as television

PRESIDENT-ELECT NIXON WITH HIS FAMILY

KING IS DEAD

Martin Luther King, Jr., the American apostle of Gandhian civil disobedience, was a victim of the violence he fought so valiantly to end. Escaped convict James Earl Ray shot King on April 4 in Memphis, Tennessee, where the civil rights leader had gone to lend his support to striking garbage collectors. The act triggered yet more violence as riots erupted in several cities where blacks rose up in retaliation for the loss of their leader. King had made many enemies while crusading for equality for blacks. Segregationists hated his desire for integration. J. Edgar Hoover, the FBI's omnipotent

KING'S COMPANIONS INDICATE SOURCE OF THE SHOTS THAT FELLED HIM.

director, thought King was a communist revolutionary and launched a campaign to destroy him. When King condemned the Vietnam War, the military community turned against him.

"I'd like to live a long life," King told followers the night before he died. "Longevity has its place, but I'm not concerned about that now. I just want to do God's will...and I've seen the Promised Land. So I'm happy tonight.... I'm not fearing any man."

cameras recorded police beating antiwar protesters outside, while inside, the party reaffirmed Johnson's pro-war policy and nominated Humphrey.

Humphrey rebounded in September when he announced that he would withdraw troops from Vietnam. But his pledge was too late. Nixon gained the White House by a very narrow margin.

■ TRENDS & TRIVIA

Black militant leader Eldridge Cleaver's *Soul on Ice* is published.

Arthur Ashe is first black to win major tennis title in the U.S. Open.

Spanish tenor Placido Domingo debuts at the Metropolitan Opera House in New York.

New York elects Shirley Chisholm America's first black congresswoman.

Kurt Vonnegut's *Welcome to the Monkey House* is published.

Marvin Gaye releases "I Heard It Through the Grapevine."

Stanley Kubrick directs *2001: A Space Odyssey*.

Diahann Carroll is first black actress to get her own TV sitcom, *Julia*.

60 Minutes and *The Dick Cavett Show* debut.

Waterbeds are introduced.

Hair! is Broadway's first rock hit.

Pulsars are discovered.

Laugh-In socks it to America.

U.S. begins rating movies.

Jacuzzis debut.

Cunard introduces its newest star, the *Queen Elizabeth II*.

Arthur Miller's play *The Price* is staged.

Nehru jackets are the rage.

Tom Wolfe's *Electric Kool-Aid Acid Test* is published.

Katharine Hepburn and Peter O'Toole star in *The Lion in Winter*.

The Beatles release "Hey Jude."

267

- **AUGUST** Week-long flood in India kills 1,000.
- **SEPTEMBER 29** Military junta in Greece strips the parliament of almost all its power.
- **OCTOBER 12** Bloodless coup ousts Panamanian President Arnulfo Arias and replaces him with Lt. Col. Omar Torrijos.
- **OCTOBER** Jacqueline Kennedy marries Greek shipping magnate Aristotle Onassis.
- **NOVEMBER 20** Leaders of non-communist European countries meet to solve currency crisis.
- **DECEMBER** North Koreans release *Pueblo* crew after its commander admits to spying.
- **DECEMBER 27** U.S. astronauts on Apollo 8 complete man's first orbit of the moon.

268

Neil Armstrong carefully stepped off the ladder's last rung and onto the moon. "That's one small step for man, one giant leap for mankind," he told the 600 million people who were listening to him some 250,000 miles away.

Armstrong's step on July 20 was a huge victory for American technology. It was also a well-timed psychological boost. The Vietnam War and the protests against it, racism and the urban riots it ignited, and the loss of three leaders to assassins—all of these gave the American psyche every reason for despair.

The road to victory had been bumpy. Some two years before Apollo 11, tragedy struck NASA when three astronauts burned to death in their capsule. There were many detractors, too, who argued that money spent exploring space was better used addressing problems below the stratosphere. But to most of the millions enchanted by

the moonwalk by Buzz Aldrin (left) and Armstrong, it was a stupendous achievement for all humanity. As one London clerk said, it was "absolutely bloody marvelous."

▶ CHAPPAQUIDDICK

The Kennedy clan's last hope of regaining the White House in the 20th century died in July with a young woman named Mary Jo Kopechne. She was trapped in a car driven by Edward M. Kennedy, the family's only surviving son.

The circumstances surrounding the accident on Chappaquiddick Island continued to dog him. Although Massachusetts voters sent him back to the Senate repeatedly, many Americans had difficulty believing that he could save himself but not Kopechne.

The senator and Kopechne were invited—separately—to attend a small party on July 18 off Martha's Vineyard. Kopechne had worked for Kennedy's late brother Robert. Before midnight, she left with Kennedy. While crossing a narrow bridge that spanned a small pond, his car ran off the road and overturned in about ten feet of water.

The story then became as murky as the dark water. Kennedy reported the accident ten hours later. He told police his efforts to save his passenger were in vain. He did not go to a nearby house for help because he said he was in shock at the time.

Kopechne's body was recovered, embalmed, and whisked away to her family in Pennsylvania before the district attorney could request an autopsy. Kennedy later was allowed to plead guilty to leaving the scene of an accident.

"By acting the way he did during and after the Chappaquiddick affair," wrote John Davis, a cousin of Jacqueline Kennedy Onassis, "Teddy destroyed an image that the Kennedys had paid a vast fortune and spent many years to create...."

▶ MANSON'S "FAMILY"

Cults took on a monstrous new face in 1969 as Charles Manson's wild visage was emblazoned across newspapers and television screens.

The longhaired ex-con with a hypnotic stare convinced his devoted followers to kill seven people in Beverly Hills. Most of the 14 members remained true to their leader, even after they were sentenced to spend much of their lives in jail because of him.

Manson (below) held special terror for parents, who already distrusted longhaired hippies. Nine of his disciples were young girls. He seduced them with drugs and promises of familial love that so many adolescents thought they lacked. After he'd conquered their bodies, Manson moved into their heads. "I am just a mirror," he said. "Anything you see in me is you."

Manson's "family" lived in the desert near Los Angeles where they armed themselves for a race war their leader saw as imminent. On August 9 Manson sent them to the home of movie director Roman Polanski. (He claimed to have been slighted by a previous tenant.) There, they slaughtered Polanski's pregnant wife, actress Sharon Tate, and four

other people. The next night, the cult killed Leno and Rosemary LaBianca, who lived near Polanski.

Police caught up with the family in December. Manson, who represented himself in trial, was convicted even though he had not participated in the murders, and was given the death penalty. That eventually turned into a life sentence after California abolished capital punishment. Manson has been up for parole a few times but has been turned down each time.

• **FEBRUARY 3**
Yassir Arafat takes over the Palestine Liberation Organization.

• **MARCH 17**
Golda Meir is sworn in as prime minister of Israel.

• **MAY**
Student activists seize college campuses across U.S. to protest the Vietnam War.

• **JUNE 20**
Georges Pompidou succeeds Charles de Gaulle as French president.

• **JUNE**
Danish parliament votes to legalize pornography.

• **JUNE 22**
American singer-actress Judy Garland is found dead at 47 in London.

• **JULY**
Honduras and El Salvador wage an undeclared, four-day war over a soccer match dispute.

• **AUGUST 2**
In a visit to Romania, Richard Nixon becomes the first U.S. President to visit a communist country in 25 years.

▶ TROUBLES FLARE IN NORTHERN IRELAND

Age-old hatreds boiled to the surface in Northern Ireland as Catholics and Protestants violently fought for what each thought should be theirs in the British province.

Irish Catholics comprised about a third of the country's population, yet their rate of unemployment was three times higher than that of their Protestant neighbors. This kept Catholics too poor to buy property, which kept them out of the political system; only property owners in Northern Ireland could vote. Protestants feared that if more Catholics could vote, their next move would be to reunite with the very Catholic Republic of Ireland. Northern Ireland's Protestants had made their corner of the island home for three centuries and were reluctant to relinquish control.

In 1969 Catholics from Londonderry to Belfast took their demands to the streets. When police brutally squelched the protesters, they fought back. In Belfast, 7 were killed and 400 wounded while buildings burned to the ground.

Realizing that local police were contributing to the riots instead of stopping them, the British government dispatched troops to Northern Ireland in August. Still the rioting continued. By the middle of 1970, political extremists from both sides had joined in, hoping to overthrow the government.

▶ PUTTING THE SUPER IN THE SUPERBOWL

When Joe Namath announced that his team would win football's world championship in 1969, nobody believed him. The New York Jets were part of the American Football League, the upstart whose teams were considered to be poor matches for those in the established National Football League. Namath's bold assertion prompted some football fans to turn on their televisions on January 12 to see if the handsome quarterback could deliver.

He did. The Jets vanquished the NFL's formidable Baltimore Colts 16-7. The historic upset prompted the leagues to rename football's last game of the season the Superbowl.

"There was $15,000 a player at stake, and there was this beautiful ring," Jets coach Weeb Ewbank later said. "But there were also the instincts of football in motion. And human nature—beat the man across from you. Especially if you keep getting told how much better he is than you."

WOODSTOCK

Thousands of fans flocked to rock extravaganzas held in New York and California in 1969. They didn't care if the toilets overflowed or rain soaked them to the skin. All that mattered was drugs, love, and rock 'n' roll.

Woodstock was as successful as Altamont was disastrous. The New York event spawned a popular movie and album, which more than covered any losses the August concert cost its promoters.

The Rolling Stones wanted a piece of this action and held a free concert in December at the Altamont Speedway southeast of San Francisco. Instead of paying security guards, they let a motorcycle gang, the Hell's Angels, do the job in exchange for beer.

The bikers relished the task. They stabbed one fan to death and beat others. The show was a sad look at what the counterculture had become.

■ TRENDS & TRIVIA

Julie Nixon marries David Eisenhower, grandson of her father's former boss, President Dwight D. Eisenhower.

Mario Puzo's *The Godfather* is published.

Oh! Calcutta debuts on Broadway.

Yale University admits female undergraduates.

Monty Python's Flying Circus debuts on British television.

Saturday Evening Post ceases publication after 148 years.

Long-running television shows *The Brady Bunch* and *Hee Haw* debut.

Butch Cassidy and the Sundance Kid is a screen hit.

Penthouse magazine begins publication.

New York's Chemical Bank experiments with first automatic teller machine.

Thor Heyerdahl sets off to circumnavigate the world in a papyrus-reed ship.

Claes Oldenburg sculpts the monumental "Lipstick."

B. J. Thomas releases "Raindrops Keep Fallin' On My Head."

Sly and the Family Stone release "Everyday People."

Rubella vaccine is introduced.

Sesame Street debuts. ▶

Boeing comes out with the 747 jumbo jet.

Star Trek goes off the air.

ORIGINAL CAST OF *SESAME STREET*

269

• **SEPTEMBER 1**
Col. Muammar Qaddafi, 29, overthrows King Idris I of Libya.

• **SEPTEMBER 4**
Viet Cong leader Ho Chi Minh dies at 79 of a heart attack.

• **OCTOBER**
Beatles fans panic over rumors that Paul McCartney is dead until he reassures them that is not the case.

• **OCTOBER 16**
The New York Mets, one of the biggest losers in baseball, wins the World Series by beating the Baltimore Orioles 5-3.

• **NOVEMBER 18**
Joseph P. Kennedy, head of Kennedy dynasty, dies at 81 of heart problems.

• **NOVEMBER 24**
Apollo 12 makes America's second moon landing.

• **DECEMBER 18**
British Parliament abolishes capital punishment.

SPACE AND FLIGHT

270

by Michael Collins
APOLLO 11 ASTRONAUT AND MEMBER, NATIONAL GEOGRAPHIC BOARD OF TRUSTEES

At the turn of the century, aerial locomotion, as it was called, was making the exciting and dangerous transition from conjecture and experimentation to practical flight. Balloons had been flying since the 18th century, kites longer than that, and gliders were moderately successful in this country and abroad. But powered flying machines were stymied by overweight, underpowered engines, inefficient construction materials and techniques and—perhaps worse—a skimpy knowledge of how to guide a craft subject to the upsetting motions of yaw, pitch, and roll. "Stability and control," in the lexicon of the modern test pilot, was an unknown art.

The first major aeronautical figure in the United States, Professor Samuel Pierpont Langley, was doing his best to overcome these problems. As early as 1896 he had successfully flown an

Left: Antique biplanes, Iowa   Middle: Air-safety test flight, California   Right: Space walk in Earth orbit

"aerodrome," an unmanned tandem-wing machine powered by a one horsepower steam engine. Langley was Secretary of the Smithsonian Institution and conducted many of his experiments nearby, from a barge in the Anacostia River. When he enlarged his aerodrome and added a pilot, it twice flopped ignominiously into the water. No one was hurt, but the machine and his dream of flight were destroyed. Then, on December 17, 1903, a bicycle shop owner from Dayton, Ohio, made the world's first manned, powered flight. While his brother Wilbur watched, Orville Wright took off in the *Flyer* and skimmed the sands of Kill Devil Hills, North Carolina, for all of 12 seconds. Later that day the machine was wrecked, but, as Orville wrote later, ". . .the age of the flying machine had come at last."

No mention of the Wrights' achievement appeared in the GEOGRAPHIC for several years, perhaps because of the Wright brothers' penchant for secrecy before their first patent was granted. In January 1907, the Society's former President, Alexander Graham Bell (himself an ardent aerial experimenter, primarily with kites) tipped his hat to the Wrights, the first mention of them in the magazine ("the first practical flying-machine. . ."). But it is clear that Bell remained a kite proponent, pointing out that "men have launched themselves into the air on wings, and most have met with disaster to life or limb," and "there is always an element of instability in a horizontal aeroplane."

By 1911 the Society had seen the light: The theme of its annual banquet was "In Honor of the Army and Aviation." Speaking that evening, Wilbur Wright noted of aviation that "the leading nations of earth are taking up the subject, our own nation being the first of all to begin it. But unfortunately there seems to be some hesitation at present." The hesitation probably referred to the U.S. Army, which had been slow to acquire the Wrights' radical new invention as a weapon. Eventually, Orville convinced the Army of aviation's utility by a series of flights from Fort Myer, Virginia. Unfortunately on one of these a passenger was killed—the first fatality in powered aviation.

On the eve of World War I, the scope of aviation expanded dramatically in the United States. One of the best known new names was that of Glenn Curtiss. In 1916 several Curtiss designed biplanes participated in the Mexican Punitive Expedition against Pancho Villa. In the region's high mountains and hot deserts, the underpowered airplanes were nearly useless in reconnaissance roles. Lt. James L. Collins, my father, who took part in the expedition as aide-de-camp to Gen. John J. ("Black Jack") Pershing, used to snort with derision at this combat debut of the "flyboys" whose flimsy gadgets couldn't even make it over Mexico's mountain passes.

During World War I, the Society followed aviation's development closely, devoting more than a hundred pages in the January 1918 magazine to the air war in Europe. An accompanying photograph shows Maj. William A. Bishop, Britain's premier air ace, on the steps of the Society's headquarters in Washington, D.C. For the next 80 years the Society assisted the fledgling aviation industry by publishing popular accounts of flying: higher, faster, farther—even into space.

In the aftermath of the war, surplus airplanes were put to a variety of uses. The U.S. Air Mail Service was inaugurated in 1918, with generally sorry results, but by 1921 a letter could be flown from San Francisco to New York in 33 hours. At the same time, airplanes became a main attraction at county fairs, where a dollar or so bought a few terrifying moments aloft with a daredevil pilot.

Then there were the great air races. Jimmy Doolittle won the 1925 Schneider Trophy with a speed of 232.5 miles an hour. Six years later it took 340 miles an hour to win the Schneider, the victor a

British Supermarine, the progenitor of the World War II Spitfire. The GEOGRAPHIC persuaded many of the participants to write about their exploits. The July 1924 issue featured "The Non-stop Flight Across America," by Army Lt. John A. Macready, who shared piloting duties with Lt. Oakley G. Kelly on the flight from Long Island to San Diego in nearly 23 sleepless hours. The same issue showed the "highest altitude photograph ever made," taken by Macready 32,220 feet over Dayton, Ohio.

The Society celebrated the first flight to the North Pole not only with an article by Lt. Comdr. Richard E. Byrd but also by awarding him its most prestigious honor, the Hubbard medal. Commander Byrd, a member of the Society, thanked Society President Gilbert Hovey Grosvenor for his support and gift of two sun-compasses: "...without these compasses it would have been impossible for us to have steered a straight course to the pole." A Hubbard medal went to Charles A. Lindbergh for his 1927 solo crossing of the Atlantic. Lindbergh was honored by a reception to which the Society could admit only 6,000 members despite a throng of 30,000 outside. The first two women to receive Society medals were Amelia Earhart in 1932 for the first solo Atlantic crossing by a woman, and Anne Morrow Lindbergh for her aerial survey flights in 1931 and 1933, during which she was her husband's copilot and radio operator.

The Society's avid interest in flying can be measured by the 30 articles in the magazine during the decade of the twenties and by its sponsorship of some record attempts, such as that of the stratospheric balloon *Explorer II*. On Armistice Day, November 11, 1935, this pressurized metal ball carried two men to an altitude of more than 13 miles, a record that stood for many years. Valuable cosmic ray and ozone measurements were made in the thin, frigid (-80°F) air.

When *Explorer II* set its record, Adolf Hitler had been in power two years. As war in Europe loomed, the United States again found itself with woefully small military forces, but aeronautical research in this country was strong. Thanks in part to competitions such as air races, the period between the World Wars had produced a solid technology base. In the Second World War, a German report on our North American P-51 admitted that "the Mustang is far superior aerodynamically to all other airplanes." Production was our problem, but American entrepreneurs were ready. Names such as Boeing, Lockheed, Douglas, Vought, Grumman, Martin knew how to compete and produce. When President Franklin D. Roosevelt ordered a production of 50,000 aircraft, America truly did become the Arsenal of Democracy. By the end of the war, despite a German lead in the new field of jet propulsion, American airpower was dominant, both in Europe and the Pacific.

The postwar Society embraced the supersonic age with a barrage of enthusiastic articles: "New Frontier in the Sky," "Our Air Age Speeds Ahead," "Flying in the Blowtorch Era." Chuck Yeager broke Mach 1, the sound barrier, in 1947, and his X-1 rocket plane started a series that led to the X-15, whose pilot, Joe Walker, wrote an article for the magazine. By the end of the '50s, more Americans crossed the country by plane than by train, and more flew the Atlantic than took ships.

The pace of aeronautics was dizzying enough, but above the Earth's atmosphere the rocket motor opened up a whole new domain. In October 1957 the grapefruit-size *Sputnik* rocketed into orbit, causing near pandemonium below: How had the U.S. fallen behind the Soviets? We did not catch up quickly. In 1961 Yuri Gagarin made a 90-minute circle of the earth, while Alan Shepard was tuning up for a mere suborbital lob. Finally John Glenn's Mercury capsule did produce three orbits and one Hubbard medal. The race for the moon was on. The magazine followed closely as the Mercury developed into the two-seated Gemini and the three-man moon craft. On Christmas Eve 1968, the crew of Apollo 8 (Frank Borman, Jim Lovell, Bill Anders), the first humans to break the bond of Earth's gravity, circled the moon and took turns reading the first ten verses of Genesis, concluding their broadcast with a Merry Christmas to "all of you on the good Earth." To me, listening in Mission Control, it was powerful stuff. I had been assigned to the crew of Apollo 8, but back surgery caused me to be switched to Apollo 11, the first landing flight.

My flight to the moon with Neil Armstrong and Buzz Aldrin began on a scorching Florida morning, July 16, 1969. We blasted into Earth orbit, made a brief equipment check, then accelerated to escape velocity, 25,000 miles per hour, and aimed for the point in the sky where the moon would be three days later. As we arrived, the moon was transformed: no more a pale yellow disk but a bulging, ominous sphere, with light cascading around its rim and with us in the shadows, in an eerie bluish glow. Neil and Buzz descended to the lunar surface in their fragile lander, *Eagle*, while I remained in *Columbia*, our base camp. My worst fear was that something would go wrong with our rendezvous, and that I would have to leave them stranded and come home by myself. But the rendezvous went precisely as written in the procedures checklist I wore around my neck, and after blasting out of lunar orbit we coasted on home. Five lunar landings followed ours, and some surplus Apollo parts were used to build our country's first space station, *Skylab*.

The press usually called our Mercury, Gemini, and Apollo craft "capsules," a term that annoyed many of us astronauts. Capsules were swallowed; we flew spacecraft. Finally, in 1981, we got a craft that no one could call a capsule—a machine with wings and wheels, the space shuttle. Part aircraft, part spacecraft, no part capsule, this versatile machine has flown nearly a hundred times. Although in most respects highly successful, in 1986 the shuttle *Challenger* exploded in flight, killing its crew of seven. The history of air and space is pockmarked with tragedy, and I'm sure always will be.

To reach beyond the moon, NASA explores with telescope and unmanned probes. The resulting images have enriched the pages of the magazine and will, I think, become even more important as the geography of the Earth, above and below the waterline, becomes increasingly familiar. NASA's instruments such as the Hubble Space Telescope have become more powerful, and unmanned spacecraft will return detailed profiles of planets and moons that heretofore have been not much more than blurry blobs. Mars is of special interest to me, as I wrote in the November 1988 issue. It is the closest to a sister planet that we Earthlings have, and I'm hoping for an expedition and an eventual colony there. If that happens, I'm sure the Society's flag will make the trip, given the Society's dedication to "the increase and diffusion of geographic knowledge"—even if the geography is extraterrestial. I know that when the Apollo 11 crew received the Hubbard in 1969, I felt doubly honored, first because of the august company I was joining, but also because the award came from a unique institution that has so enthusiastically chronicled the exploration of air and space.

1970-

1979

Watching the World on TV

1970-1979

by Susan J. Douglas

PROFESSOR OF COMMUNICATION STUDIES, UNIVERSITY OF MICHIGAN—ANN ARBOR

THE SEVENTIES. JUST MENTION THE DECADE, and the memory is flooded with kitschy images of platform shoes, the Fonz, pet rocks, disco, the Village People, shag haircuts, people on CBs yelling "breaker-breaker," and body-convulsing therapy fads from primal scream to est. During this decade, one President resigned from office, another handed out "WIN" buttons to combat inflation, and yet another had a brother hawking his own beer on national television. Do we really want to remember this particular ten-year period?

What makes the 1970s so fascinating, and so painful, to review is that it was a crucial transition decade for America. In these years, the country moved from an era of optimism, characterized by a faith in progress and idealistic crusades for reform at home and world betterment abroad, to an era of pessimism, marked by a collapse of trust in national institutions, a new isolationism epitomized by the "Vietnam Syndrome," and narcissistic quests for self-actualization and personal advancement. As idealism was replaced by disillusionment, many people in the United States in the 1970s stopped looking outward to society and the world, and turned their gazes inward.

When people think back to the 1970s, flickering images on television illustrate their mental time lines. And it was definitely not all kitsch. From the

Opposite: Photographs like this one taken during a bombing raid in 1972 dramatized the plight of Vietnamese civilians.
Preceding pages: Richard M. Nixon left the White House in 1974, his troubled Presidency brought to an early demise.

shocking sight of our own National Guardsmen shooting students at Kent State University in the spring of 1970, to the relentlessly dispiriting newscast tapes of Americans held hostage in Iran at the decade's end, television gave national and international events a sense of immediacy and urgency. The increasing globalization of TV in the 1970s, especially of the news, indelibly shaped most people's perceptions and memories of the period.

Thanks to video technology, satellite transmission, and "live" reporting, the 1970s saw the merger of instantaneous news with an almost total saturation of television ownership: In the United States and much of Western Europe and Japan, few households were without at least one TV set. The 1970s were the first decade in which people around the world were simultaneous witnesses to the same events. These changes in TV technology compelled American viewers to focus on international affairs despite the widespread desire in the post-Vietnam era to retreat into isolationism.

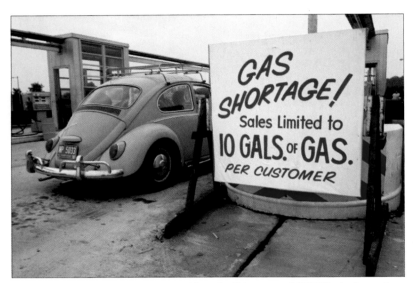

In retaliation for U.S. support of Israel, all but one of OPEC's Arab members imposed an oil embargo in 1973 that triggered gas shortages around the world.

The ability to tape and transmit news instantly from the scene, instead of having to go back to the studio to process film, meant that more news stories, from more locations, could be broadcast more quickly and more cheaply than before. When coupled with mobile ground stations, usually installed in vans, and the ability to transmit TV images via satellite halfway across the globe, the new video technology meant that people could watch international events as they happened, often over live feeds. The explosion in national and international news showed us environmental disasters and activism around the world; brought the Middle East to the center of international diplomacy; and made hijackings and other forms of international terrorism a worldwide concern. Television news took us to China with Nixon, to the frantic collapse of Saigon, to the Soviet Union's own "Vietnam" in Afghanistan; to IRA bombings in London; to the seizure of the U.S. Embassy in Iran.

Television was also the medium—again, thanks to satellite transmission—through which the rest of the world experienced what came to be called American "cultural imperialism": the massive export of American films and TV shows to other countries. Not everyone abroad was thrilled to have *Kojak* or *Three's Company* beamed into their homes, however. For the United States, on the other hand, the 1970s was a decade in which huge national audiences could regularly share common experiences, whether they were watching the massacre of Israeli athletes at the 1972 Munich Olympics, or *Roots*, or *Dallas*.

Perhaps no event more dramatically illustrated the triumph of television in America than when *Life*, a magazine with one of the largest circulations in the country for more than 30 years, ceased publication in 1972. TV had stolen its market. Now the nation's most popular magazine, with a circulation of 20 million, was *TV Guide*.

Despite the turning of the calendar to 1970, what we think of as the activist sixties weren't over. A number of major social movements persisted or got their start in the early 1970s, their growth fanned by TV. The antiwar movement, for example, was widely covered on television in early May 1970, as a hundred student strikes around the country protested the Nixon Administration's invasion of Cambodia. On May 4 the sickening images of National Guardsmen shooting 13 students at Kent State, killing 4, sparked student strikes or demonstrations at more than 1,200 college campuses.

In the midst of this, a new social movement—this one for women's liberation—also began to make the nightly news, culminating in the national Women's Strike For Equality on August 26, 1970. New words and concepts—such as "equal pay for equal work," "sexism," "male chauvinist pig," and "Ms."—became part of the American lexicon. So did the concept of "coed toilets," the bugaboo raised by Phyllis Schlafly, a conservative antifeminist activist who led the backlash against feminism and the fight to defeat passage of the Equal Rights Amendment. New television shows, from *Maude* and *The Mary Tyler Moore Show* to *Charlie's Angels* and *Wonder Woman*, sought to address women's new aspirations by intermixing images of new roles—and power—with wet T-shirts and string bikinis.

IN FEBRUARY 1974 THE KIDNAPPING OF PATTY HEARST turned into a four-month-long television news drama as the quiet, apolitical heiress metamorphosed into the beret-clad "Tania," latest recruit into the Symbionese Liberation Army (SLA). In April, with a gun-toting Tania at their side, the SLA robbed a bank, a robbery captured by video surveillance cameras and repeatedly rebroadcast, often in slow motion, on TV. In May Americans witnessed the shoot-out, when police stormed the SLA's house and killed five members of the group, a grisly event that was also conveniently captured by and replayed on the nightly news. The whole bizarre episode was emblematic of TV journalism's new addiction to sensationalism.

In 1973 and 1974 many Americans were already glued to their sets consuming another unprecedented drama: the Senate hearings investigating the Watergate scandal. In June 1972 five men hired by President Nixon's reelection committee were caught breaking into the Democratic National Committee headquarters in an effort to install listening devices. Bob Woodward and Carl Bernstein, investigating the story for the *Washington Post*, uncovered evidence that pointed to "dirty tricks," "hush money," and a cover-up involving those at the highest levels of the administration. The American public stayed tuned as the House Judiciary Committee, on July 30, 1974, recommended that Richard Nixon be impeached. The hearings turned politicians Sam Ervin, Howard Baker, Barbara Jordan, and Peter Rodino into TV stars and household names. And the revelations about the White House's contempt for the law and its elaborate cover-up instilled in the public a deep cynicism about the government which, at century's end, has hardly abated. In addition to the episode's sweeping historic implications, its other legacy was to attach the suffix "gate" to the name of every political scandal.

Not only did television allow viewers in all parts of the country to follow events in the nation's capital, it also brought international crises into the living room. Viewers grew accustomed to having close-up shots of remote conflicts and disasters flashed in front of their faces at dinnertime. In April 1975 images of Americans being airlifted out of Saigon, as South Vietnamese desperate to escape dangled from the helicopters' skids came to symbolize the American defeat. Combined with the memory of the 58,000 American lives lost in the war, such images contributed heavily to the Vietnam Syndrome—the profound and lasting reluctance to become militarily involved in the internal disputes of other countries.

Still, the nation could hardly revert to isolationism. Television's nightly dose of news from around the world had the effect of making events in distant lands seem increasingly bound up with American interests, an effect that was not lost on terrorists. Suddenly governments were faced with diplomatic problems far outside the standard framework of the Cold War, confounded by combatants who used terrorist tactics to advance political goals.

A SERIES OF ATTACKS, HIJACKINGS, AND WARS in the Middle East focused the world's attention on the region. After watching on television as armed Arab terrorists, faces covered with ski masks, paced the balcony of the Israeli athletes' quarters in the Olympic Village in Munich and learning of the bloody outcome of the hostage-taking, many everyday Americans with little knowledge of the issues developed strong anti-Arab sentiments. Animosity toward the Arab world in much of America and Europe was only reinforced by a spate of airplane hijackings, many by Palestinian guerrillas. In September 1970, for example, members of the Popular Front for the Liberation of Palestine held more than 50 airline passengers hostage in the Jordanian desert; they blew up three planes while demanding the release of hundreds of prisoners from jails in Israel, Great Britain, and Germany. In the wake of the hijacking, airports around the world instituted security devices, and ever since, travelers have had to walk through metal detectors and have all their luggage screened before getting on a plane. The most famous hijacking of the decade was one that was foiled. On July 4, 1976, Israeli commandos stormed the airport in Entebbe, Uganda, and shot all of the hijackers, who had demanded the release of 53 Palestinian and pro-Palestinian prisoners. The "Raid at Entebbe" prompted at least one made-for-TV movie and inspired the plots of a host of action movies and thrillers.

Attitudes toward the Arab countries were hardly enhanced by the Arab Oil Embargo of 1973, imposed on the United States and its allies by the Organization of Petroleum Exporting Countries (OPEC) to protest American support for Israel during the Yom Kippur War in October 1973. In that conflict, Egypt and Syria staged a surprise attack on the Golan Heights and the east bank during the holiest Jewish holiday of the year, only to be pounded back to the cease-fire lines drawn at the end of the 1967 Six-Day War. Enraged by America's assistance to Israel, the Arab nations insisted they would maintain the embargo until Israel relinquished the land it had captured in 1967.

The embargo did not achieve that goal. But it did cause gas prices in the U.S. to soar from

40 cents to 70 cents a gallon—sometimes even higher—and produced huge lines at gas stations. And with the new global news, people saw how the cut in oil production was felt worldwide. Britain, for example, imposed a three-day workweek to deal with the shortages and high prices. The embargo, which lasted until March 1974, also fanned inflation, which affected everything from the price of sugar and butter to the cost of borrowing money. By 1975 Britain's inflation rate was 25 percent. The economic problems in the U.S. in the 1970s were characterized by the new word "stagflation," in which double-digit inflation rates combined with the highest unemployment rate since the Great Depression. Stagflation bedeviled the economy and the Presidents who tried to alleviate it. As higher prices at the pumps made American drivers more conscious of fuel efficiency, the big American auto companies—which began giving rebates in a desperate effort to compete with high gas mileage Volkswagens and Toyotas— also began redesigning their cars to make them more energy efficient.

President Jimmy Carter's inability to liberate 52 Americans held hostage in Iran for more than a year contributed to his failure to win a second term.

To many environmentalists, the OPEC embargo was just the wakeup call that America needed to learn how to be more energy conscious. It also heightened a growing awareness of the need to preserve and protect the nation's—and the world's—environment and natural resources. That people were becoming increasingly concerned about the environment was evidenced in the first Earth Day on April 22, 1970, when millions of Americans gathered in the nation's capital, on college campuses, and in parks around the country. Environmental activism in Europe and the U.S. remained strong throughout the decade, only reinforced by highly publicized disasters such as the 1978 *Amoco Cadiz* oil spill off the coast of Brittany, France, and the discovery of lethal toxic waste at Love Canal in upstate New York that same year. A near-disaster at Pennsylvania's Three Mile Island nuclear power plant in 1979 helped stop the construction of nuclear power plants in America. Major films like *The China Syndrome* and *Silkwood* spoke to the public's anxiety about environmental contamination.

The optimism of the 1960s civil rights movement gave way to frustration and despair in 1974 and 1975 as Americans watched cities like Boston ripped apart as a result of the forced busing of school children. At the same time, in an event that made television history, 100 million Americans, the largest audience to date, tuned in to watch the miniseries *Roots*, the chronicle of a family's intergenerational history from slavery to freedom.

Roots was the perfect blend of exposé and fairy tale for the 1970s—it drew from the old optimism and faith in the American Dream and from the newly heightened awareness of

America's sins, past and present. The television Nielsen ratings for the decade—a kind of Rorschach test of the national psyche—reveal the contradictory impulses of the period. Americans made hits out of shows that were filled with often biting social commentary such as *All in the Family*, *Sanford and Son*, and *Maude*. At the same time, viewers also flocked to shows that took them back to the allegedly simpler, more hopeful eras depicted in *Happy Days* and *Little House on the Prairie*. The international blockbuster *Dallas*, which combined fantasies of unlimited wealth and power with stories that cast the rich and powerful as just as miserable as everybody else, epitomized how successful the export of American pop culture had become. All over the globe, as the series closed its second season, people wondered "Who shot J.R.?"

In reaction against the liberal activism of the early 1970s, religious evangelicalism swept much of the country; by decade's end 40 percent of Americans claimed they had been "born again." Jerry Falwell, exemplar of that new sort of man of the cloth, the "televangelist," formed the right wing lobbying group Moral Majority, Inc. The extensive grassroots organizing of such groups, coupled with widespread disappointment in President Jimmy Carter's administration, helped pave the way for Ronald Reagan's election in 1980.

WITHOUT DOUBT, BOTH THE MOST HAUNTING and the most humiliating images on TV near decade's end came, once again, from the Middle East. President Carter achieved a foreign policy triumph when he brought Egypt's Anwar Sadat and Israel's Menachem Begin together in September of 1978 and helped them negotiate the Camp David Accords. This historic peace treaty, signed in March 1979, earned both Sadat and Begin the Nobel Peace Prize. Only 8 months later, Iranian fundamentalists captured the U.S. embassy in Tehran and held 52 embassy employees hostage for 444 days. On the nightly news, Americans saw Iranians burning the American flag and waving placards labeling the U.S. "the Great Satan." These images, and the daily nature of the crisis, prompted ABC to launch *Nightline*, whose mission was to grip viewers in a sado-masochistic daily count of how long "America [was] Held Hostage."

In his 1964 bestseller, *Understanding Media*, Marshall McLuhan saw the advent of a "global village"—a world bound together by new communications technologies. This vision was indeed realized in the 1970s, but the village was far from unified. Watching the world on television did as much to provoke suspicion, fear, and animosity—especially between the Western and the Arab worlds—as it did to bring people together through common concerns or through common cultural texts. We saw stories that bred a deep distrust, especially of the federal government. We also witnessed the birth of long-lasting social movements that forever changed the nation's politics and culture. This contradictory mix— of cynicism and a longing for public politics—is a 1970s legacy we have with us still, at the turn of the new millennium. ■

President Carter's Camp David Accords brought Israel and Egypt together in peace for the first time in modern history.

A new Grosvenor became Editor in 1970 and stayed throughout the decade.

Gilbert M. Grosvenor originally wanted to go to medical school. But between his junior and senior years in college, he went to Holland, packing a camera with him. "I guess that's when I was bitten by the bug," he recalled later. He started working for the Society in 1954 and remained, except for two years of military duty, until he retired more than 40 years later.

His first years as Editor were often tumultuous. Grosvenor wanted to reflect the times, while longtime conservative board members clung to the principles of the past. "Basically, some people don't like the way the world is changing, and they want *something* to stay the way it is," Grosvenor once told a writer. "But we can't stand still…. Unless you constantly evolve a publication, you're in trouble."

He began that evolution ever so slowly in the '70s. As many members of the staff quipped, the name of the game at the Society was evolution, not revolution.

● Rescuing the Eagle

Articles on animals always scored high with GEOGRAPHIC readers. Few other mainstream publications devoted the same amount of space to the animal kingdom as the magazine did. It continued to meet that demand, seasoning its fare with the now-fashionable dose of advocacy.

BALD EAGLES OFTEN RETURN TO THE SAME NESTING SITE.

America's national bird was in dire need of advocacy in 1978. Wildlife biologist Thomas C. Dunstan estimated the number of bald eagles in North America had dropped to fewer than 84,000, down from about 250,000 in the previous century.

"More than most creatures, the bald eagle's survival hinges on man, whose reshaping of the landscape and intrusion on wild places put unrelenting pressure on the bird…," he wrote in the February 1978 issue. "The eagle's decline can't be pinned on any single element of environmental degradation: It results from loss of feeding and nesting sites due to human activities, from chemical contamination of food supply, from poaching and accidental shooting, and from electrocution on power lines used as perches."

To see how how another country tackled the problem of animal extinction, author John Putnam went to India.

"The predators have become the hunted…," he wrote in September 1976. "So great has been the slaughter of animals, so entrenched the pattern of destruction of habitat, that many came to believe that India's treasure of wildlife was doomed." Not so, he concluded, as he listed the various measures enacted since the decade began. But the creatures' future there was as insecure as it was in the U.S. The plight of animals continued to be a major source of stories for the magazine throughout the century.

● The Hazards of Taking a Stand

"You cannot run a 'hearts and flowers' story from South Africa when you get daily television news about Soweto…," Gil Grosvenor told a group of Society trustees in 1977. "We felt it was time to publish a 'country story' on South Africa…. We did not go in with the idea of doing a hatchet job…."

But a "hatchet job" was exactly what the South African government felt the June article was. "South Africa's Lonely Ordeal" incurred the wrath of the apartheid government, as well as of some conservative Society members and trustees. The story examined how the apartheid system affected the country's majority—blacks. The photos selected were realistic, which was unflattering to the government.

South Africa struck back with an ad campaign denouncing the GEOGRAPHIC's "maiden attempt to enter the realm of advocacy reporting." Melvin Payne, Chairman of the Society's Board of Trustees, brought one of those ads to a board meeting in June. He and others had strong reservations about Grosvenor's editorial judgment in the story, as well as others about Harlem and Cuba. The board ultimately had the right to fire the Editor regardless of family ties.

The tempest on 17th Street did not go unnoticed in the publishing world. "The dispute goes to the basic question of how boldly the society, with its tradition of Victorian delicacy,

SOUTH AFRICA'S HOMELANDS POLICY RELOCATES TRIBAL MEMBERS TO A NEW TOWN.

284

will pick its way through a global landscape where life's harsher realities, as one staff writer put it, often 'leap right out at you,' " the *Washington Post* reported in July.

Grosvenor managed to quell the dissension with a reaffirmation of the Society's mission. He spelled out his vision in the January 1978 issue, "As journalists committed to objective, impartial reporting of what we can report, we accept the opportunity to reflect our times...," he wrote. "To some people, failure to denounce is the same as silent praise, and objective statement of fact amounts to advocacy—if fact fails to coincide with prejudice.... We will continue to travel the world unencumbered by ideology...."

WESTERN GREBE SWIMS THROUGH AN OIL SLICK.

Environmental Advocate

The environmental movement of the 1970s was tailor-made for NATIONAL GEOGRAPHIC. The magazine had been extolling Mother Nature's virtues since its inception. But tackling pollution broke one of Gilbert H. Grosvenor's cardinal rules—no articles "of a controversial nature." It also posed another thorny issue; some of the industries contributing the most pollution advertised in NATIONAL GEOGRAPHIC.

Despite these obstacles, the magazine published "Our Ecological Crisis," a package of two articles and a map-and-painting supplement in the December 1970 issue. James Blair's photos were grim: an oil-covered bird (above), bare hills ravaged by strip mining, and piles of fish killed by pollutants.

Staff writer Gordon Young's coverage echoed this bleakness. "We have been brought up to equate growth with success," he wrote. "A town should grow, we feel, so each town vies to attract more business and more inhabitants. But many ecologists point out that each resident's share of land and air and water is reduced by growth. At some point, the quality of life declines."

Pushing Canadian Unity

The issue of Quebec separatism was one Gilbert Grosvenor took seriously. He was the sixth generation of a family that had spent much of its leisure time in Canada.

"I have always thought of myself as part Canadian...," he told readers in the April 1977 issue. "Is it possible that our good neighbor to the north will come apart, as the United States once did?... We pray that the day will never come when a Canadian Prime Minister must decide, as Abraham Lincoln had to do, whether to preserve a country by force of arms."

The Editor's plea for Canadian unity introduced an article on Quebec. In any other publication, the story would have been a typical, balanced piece about the province on the verge of secession. But in a magazine known for its avoidance of any controversy, the very existence of such an article was shocking. One reader insisted that the whole Quebec problem was made up.

Grosvenor was buffeted by criticism from within as well as from the outside. "The *Magazine* is not changing," he told his detractors. "The *world* is changing."

Journey Inside the Cell

In its nearly hundred-year history, there wasn't much of the world that NATIONAL GEOGRAPHIC had not explored. The time had come to seek new frontiers, starting with the smallest of living organisms, the cell. This journey was made possible by an explosion of new insights into the life sciences that began in the 1950s. Rapid advancements in technology helped push these discoveries along.

The magazine brought readers up-to-date with a three-part article, "Exploring the New Biology" in September 1976.

"Little more than a generation ago the cell, the living capsule from which all plants and animals are built, was largely uncharted territory," Rick Gore wrote. "Nor was science sure what a gene, the basic unit of heredity, was made of. Today the cell has been mapped, and biologists know that our genes are made up of that marvelous chemical, DNA.... One cell in my toe, say, has all the data in its DNA for making another man physically identical to me."

The GEOGRAPHIC's roll-up-the-sleeves attitude toward explaining science lent itself to good television coverage, too.

MOLECULAR MODEL OF AN ANTIBODY

285

A year before the biology series ran, the Television Division had produced *The Incredible Machine*. The documentary about the human body kicked off the Society's new series with PBS and was a runaway success; it earned the highest ratings of any show in the history of public television and edged out the networks in a few markets.

At Home in Harlem

"To Live in Harlem" was a milestone. Written and photographed by two black freelancers, the February 1977 article was the first GEOGRAPHIC story about black Americans.

"I am in love with Harlem," wrote Frank Hercules. "It is a replica in miniature of the human condition. To live in Harlem is sometimes to hear the siren song of success, often to be denied by heaven and disdained by hell, yet always to hope anew each morning, whatever yesterday's despair."

THE STREET IN HARLEM SERVES AS A SOCIAL CENTER.

Hercules's affinity for his neighborhood made the story. He moved easily among the residents, from preachers to sinners. And LeRoy Woodson, in addition to photographing the abandoned tenements many associated with Harlem, found a side unknown to outsiders. A group gathered for dinner under a cut-glass chandelier. Men played checkers on a sunny street. And children scampered through uncapped fire hydrants to cool off.

Demystified, Harlem became another American town, with its own set of assets and problems. But it was something more—a metaphor for all urban areas. "Harlem is going through far-reaching changes...," an Episcopal minister told Hercules. "What is wrong with Harlem is also wrong with New York City, and wrong with the whole country and, if you like, the world." So, Hercules concluded, "to love the United States....is, for better, for worse, to love Harlem."

Showing Famine's Face

Famines in Africa and Bangladesh alerted millions to the horrible problems of starvation. Photographs of emaciated children filled magazines, television screens, and newspapers.

In July 1975 the GEOGRAPHIC went behind the immediate problem to look at the bigger issue—supplying food for the world's burgeoning population. The subject was not unprecedented for the magazine; the entire January 1916 issue had covered how the world fed itself. Nearly 60 years later, it revisited the subject.

"As many as 1.5 *billion* people may suffer some degree of malnutrition...," Gil Grosvenor wrote in his introduction. "Recent international conferences on both population and food have reminded the world that the people of poorer nations may view with suspicion programs to limit human numbers." That suspicion, combined with religious beliefs and old-age security needs, was a major stumbling block to population control.

To drive his point home, Grosvenor dispatched photographer Steve Raymer to Bangladesh. "The scene is chilling, horrifying," Raymer wrote. "Several thousand starving Bengalis wait patiently, it seems, to die.... A woman clad in rags clutches an infant so thin his ribs look like a birdcage beneath his peeling skin.... This is the face of famine...."

Space Age Fantasy

Like everything else in the U.S. in 1976, the GEOGRAPHIC had a bicentennial moment. With a majestic bald eagle gracing July's cover, the magazine looked at the country's past, present, and future. For the future look, the editors indulged in a little science fiction, written by Isaac Asimov.

Asimov chronicled an imaginary journey to an American space colony in 2026. The story, however fanciful, was rooted in reality. About 30 engineers, social scientists, and physical scientists had outlined the feasibility of space colonies for NASA. Their findings were the grist for Asimov's article.

"As we moved in toward the docking module, L-5 stopped being a torus in space and became a habitat, a world with 10,000 people," he wrote. "...L-5 was a little more than 1.1 miles across."

His observations were often humorous. "Do the women and children stay indoors?" he asked after noticing that most of the

COMPACT AMERICAN COMMUNITY ON SPACE COLONY L-5

pedestrians he saw were men. When his somewhat humorless guide offered to take him on a tour of L-5's waste treatment plant, he replied, "Perhaps not."

Asimov was one of several dignitaries whose words appeared in the bicentennial issue. Engineer Buckminster Fuller, city planner Edmund Bacon, and Richard Babcock, a lawyer who focused on housing law and urban planning, shared their views on where the U.S was headed.

And for the readers who wanted something lighter, the magazine served up its traditional feel-good fare with "Kansas City, Heartland U.S.A."

ROBYN DAVIDSON AND HER COMPANIONS BRAVE THE ELEMENTS IN AUSTRALIA'S OUTBACK.

Crossing the Outback

In the May 1978 issue, readers met Robyn Davidson, a plucky young woman who trekked across some 1,700 miles of Australia's outback on foot and camel.

"Why cross it by camel?" the 28-year-old wrote. "Why not? Australia is a vast country, and most of us who live there see only a small fraction of it.... Beyond the roads, in the area known...as the outback, camels are the perfect form of transport."

In six months Davidson, her four camels, and her dog Diggity walked between Alice Springs and the Indian Ocean—through mountains, desert, and stretches of sandhill country. They befriended an Aborigine named Mr. Eddie, who joined them for three weeks. "He taught me to laugh at my predicaments," Davidson wrote, "and not to be handcuffed by my obsession with time."

But time was passing. On October 20 the caravan reached the ocean. With much reluctance, the camels cautiously followed Davidson into the surf. A week later, friends adopted the camels, and Davidson prepared to fly home. "How do you say farewell to camels that have crossed a desert with you?" she wrote. "I found no right way except to take them for one last swim... For a second I was tempted to saddle the camels and start over. But no. The trip is not meant to be repeated except in my memory—over and over again."

New Life-Forms in Galápagos Rift

New life-forms in the deep were discovered in the 1970s, and NATIONAL GEOGRAPHIC dove into the watery abyss to report on them. Scientists discovered the new creatures in the Galápagos Rift, west of Ecuador. Here, a mile and a half beneath the surface of the Pacific Ocean, hydrothermal vents from the seafloor made the area warmer and more hospitable to life. The magazine covered this new realm twice, once in October 1977 and again in November 1979.

"In the Galápagos Rift—a boundary between separating plates of oceanic crust—lava erupts, cools, and cracks," the first article explained. "Cold seawater penetrates into fractures and, growing hot, drops off some elements while picking up others."

This unusual environment was host to creatures and plants never seen before. The life-forms had formed a food chain based on energy from within the earth, rather than from the sun. The discovery of this process, which the scientists called chemosynthesis, opened up a whole new field of study—life in oceanic rifts.

Discovering Butterflies' Winter Retreat

For years zoologists wondered where the monarch butterfly wintered. The colorful creatures spent the summer in the U.S. and Canada, only to vanish at the onset of cold air.

Canadian zoologist Fred Urquhart had been puzzling over this mystery since 1937. In 1975 a couple in Mexico found millions of monarchs (below) in the evergreens of the Sierra Madre mountains. Urquhart and his wife, Norah, headed south the next year and traveled 10,000 feet up.

In the August 1976 issue, Urquhart described their encounter, "Then we saw them. Masses of butterflies—everywhere! In the quietness of semidormancy, they festooned the tree branches, they enveloped the oyamel trunks, they carpeted the ground in their tremulous legions. Other multitudes...filled the air with their sun-shot wings, shimmering against the blue mountain sky and drifting across our vision in blizzard flakes of orange and black."

SITE CO-DISCOVERER CATHY BRUGGER

Urquhart believed that the monarchs chose the Sierra Madre because the temperatures there hovered around freezing. "Inactivated by the chill, they burn up almost none of the reserve fat they'll need on their northward flight," he wrote. The Urquharts tagged about 10,000 monarchs to test the theory. Months later, two turned up in Texas.

287

288

Six college students who never saw a day of combat duty became casualties of war in May. They were killed during demonstrations against the U.S. invasion of Cambodia.

President Nixon first launched bombing raids over Cambodia in 1969 to stop Viet Cong based on the Vietnam-Cambodia border from attacking South Vietnam. In April 1970 he announced he had sent 32,000 troops into Cambodia to stabilize it and to eradicate enemy camps.

College students exploded with frustration. Some cried for Nixon's impeachment, while others staged massive, often violent demonstrations. At Kent State University in Ohio, National Guardsmen opened fire on a demonstration May 4, killing four people and wounding nine (above). A week later, at a protest at Jackson State University in Mississippi, state patrolmen shot and killed two students and wounded nine.

By now, millions of Americans had joined the antiwar movement. Pressured by angry constituents, Congress terminated the Tonkin Resolution's broad presidential powers. In June, Nixon pulled troops out of Cambodia.

▶ FARM WORKERS UNITE

Grapes were redeemed in 1970 after a five-year boycott. The fruit had been driven into the doghouse by striking farmworkers who sought better wages and working conditions. Millions of Americans championed the cause and refused to buy grapes.

Cesar Chavez brought the plight of migrant farmworkers to national attention in the 1960s. The former field hand knew personally how miserable their conditions were—bad facilities, poor wages, and no job security. To give these disenfranchised workers a voice, in 1962 Chavez organized what would eventually become the United Farm Workers.

The fledgling union's first big attempt to right wrongs began in 1965 with the grape boycott. A year later the group formed an important affiliation with the powerful AFL-CIO. By 1968 the boycott was in the news, and grape growers were retaliating against the strikers, occasionally with violence.

The boycott ended in 1970 when the growers and pickers reached a settlement. For the first time in years, farmworkers had some bargaining leverage.

▶ COLLEGIATE WIT TAKES OFF

Garry Trudeau had entertained readers of the *Yale Daily News* with his satirical strip, "Bull Tales," since 1968. He combined the Yale word for likable goof "doone" with a roommate's name, Pillsbury, to invent "Mike Doonesbury," a character who mixed effortlessly with real campus figures and stereotypes alike. So when Universal Press Syndicate asked him to introduce Mike to real-life national figures, Trudeau agreed to try.

"Doonesbury" was controversial almost from the beginning. Some papers dropped the strip, only to pick it up again when devoted readers protested. Soon, more than 400 papers ran it every day.

No person or ideology was safe from Trudeau's lampoons. President Nixon appeared often, to his dismay. The wry commentary prompted several papers to move "Doonesbury" onto the editorial pages as an important barometer of what concerned—and tickled—young, educated Americans. It became the first comic strip to win a Pulitzer Prize.

▶ GOING GREEN

By 1970 Earth was *the* cause, a link between people who shared little else other than the scary realization of their planet's fragility. Environmental and wilderness groups signed up hundreds of new members. Recycling became hip, and littering a mortal sin.

"The ecology issue has assumed the dimensions of a vast popular fad," wrote economist Robert Heilbroner. Unlike other fads, however, he continued, this one "may indeed constitute the most dangerous and difficult challenge that humanity has ever faced."

On April 22 millions of Americans pledged to take that challenge in parades, marches, and demonstrations held across the country. The first Earth Day was an overwhelming affirmation of a new social revolution, organized by Senator Gaylord

EARTH DAY CELEBRATION IN WASHINGTON, D.C.

- **JANUARY 12**
Biafra surrenders to Nigeria.

- **JANUARY 16**
Col. Muammar Qaddafi becomes premier of Libya.

- **FEBRUARY 25**
Abstract Expressionist artist Mark Rothko commits suicide at 66 in New York.

- **MARCH 28**
New York townhouse used by the radical Weathermen group blows up, killing three.

- **APRIL 10**
Paul McCartney announces that he's leaving the Beatles, thus disbanding history's most successful pop group.

- **MAY 4**
Freelance writer Seymour Hersh wins the Pulitzer Prize for international reporting for breaking the My Lai massacre story.

- **JUNE 28**
Thousands of homosexuals stage an antidiscrimination protest in New York.

Nelson and activist Denis Hayes. The *New Republic* called the event "an awakening to the dangers in a dictatorship of technology."

The government recognized the environmental movement's political clout, as well. Two months after Earth Day, the Environmental Protection Agency opened. Building on the National Environmental Policy Act in the late 1960s, new laws like Superfund and the Endangered Species Act were passed.

A year after Earth Day, 11 other countries had formed environmental regulatory agencies; that number grew almost tenfold by 1980. Despite this increased awareness, the environment continued to take a beating. It would take more than three decades of concern to begin to right the wrongs inflicted for more than a century.

▶ CHILE'S SOCIALIST EXPERIMENT
Chile became the first country in the Western Hemisphere to elect a Marxist president in September. Dr. Salvador Allende Gossens, former minister of health, senator, and three-time presidential candidate, launched aggressive reforms designed to restructure Chile's economy.

Because many landowners exported their produce and because control of the country's most valuable export, copper, was shared with U.S. companies, South America's oldest democracy was forced to rely on imports and foreign capital for survival. Allende forced large landowners to redistribute their holdings among the poor and nationalized all U.S.-owned copper mines without offering compensation.

Improving wages and social services made Allende popular with Chile's poor and working class but not, however, with the wealthy or the U.S government. President Richard Nixon canceled all loans to Chile, and its economy plummeted. The CIA funneled money to Allende's detractors to foment rebellion. And the Chilean middle class—one of Latin America's

ROCK AND DRUGS

Rock 'n' roll's infamous link with drugs took on a deadly pallor in the fall when Jimi Hendrix (bottom) and Janis Joplin (top) died of drug overdoses. Both were 27 years old.

They were two of rock's brightest, most flamboyant stars. Joplin was a hard-living Texan who belted out the blues as nobody believed a white woman or man could. Hendrix coaxed his electric guitar to snarl or croon as though it were alive.

Fans admired their decadence almost as much as their music. Hendrix and Joplin careened along the fast lane that opened up in the late 1960s. They indulged their appetites for sex and drugs with abandon. Their lifestyles exemplified the extreme edge of hippiedom. Those lifestyles were too much for even extraordinary mortals. In September Hendrix choked in his sleep on a lethal cocktail of barbituates and alcohol. Joplin's body was found a month later, her arm punctured by needle marks.

largest—wearied of the inflation and the supply shortages that accompanied their leader's "transition to socialism."

On September 11, 1973, one of Allende's advisors, Gen. Augusto Pinochet, led a junta against him. When Allende's corpse was found later in the palace, Pinochet called it a suicide; Allende's widow called it murder. It was not long before thousands were dead, and the country's formerly democratic tradition collapsed into iron-fisted authoritarianism.

■ TRENDS & TRIVIA

Italy legalizes divorce.

New York City holds its first marathon.

FDA approves lithium as an antidepressant.

Diane Crump is the first female jockey to compete in the Kentucky Derby.

New York City's World Trade Center is completed.

Midi-length coats, dresses, and skirts come into fashion.

Dee Brown's *Bury My Heart at Wounded Knee* is published.

Simon and Garfunkel release "Bridge Over Troubled Water."

The Partridge Family, The Mary Tyler Moore Show, and the daytime soap *All My Children* debut on American television.

Robert Altman directs *M*A*S*H.*

Medicine bottles adopt childproof safety tops.

The New English Bible translates the sacred text into modern language.

Laurence Olivier is the first actor to be named to the peerage.

The voting age drops to 18 in U.S.

Richard Bach's *Jonathan Livingston Seagull* is published.

George C. Scott stars in *Patton.*

U.S. Congress passes the Occupational Safety and Health Act.

Tom Wolfe's *Radical Chic & Mau-mauing the Flak Catchers* is published.

Monday Night Football debuts on ABC.

289

• JULY 21
Egypt's Aswan Dam is completed.

• JULY 27
Portugal's authoritarian premier, Dr. Antonio Salazar, dies of a heart attack at 81 after almost 40 years of rule.

• AUGUST 12
The Soviet Union signs a non-aggression pact with West Germany.

• SEPTEMBER 27
Jordan's King Hussein and Palestine Liberation Organization leader Yassir Arafat agree to stop fighting each other.

• SEPTEMBER 28
Egyptian leader Gamal Abdel Nasser dies at 52 of a heart attack. Vice President Anwar Sadat succeeds him.

• OCTOBER
Radical French-Canadian separatists kidnap two Quebec officials.

• NOVEMBER 9
Charles de Gaulle dies.

PENTAGON PAPERS

The publication of the Pentagon Papers was almost more important than their content. They set in motion a chain of events that ended in President Richard Nixon's resignation.

Classified as "top secret," the exhaustive report spelled out in critical detail how the U.S. conducted policy in Southeast Asia during three administrations.

In June a former Defense Department consultant leaked the study to the *New York Times* and the *Washington Post*. Daniel Ellsberg (left) did so in hopes that the revelation would embarrass the government into retreating from Vietnam.

Nixon sought an injunction against the *Times* to stop it from publishing the full report and was denied. He then asked aides to form a team of "plumbers" to investigate the leak. "If a conspiracy existed, I wanted…to find out," he said later, even if it had to be done "surreptitiously."

Nixon and his advisers used "plumbers" again. In August 1972 police arrested five men as they tried to bug the Democratic National Committee's headquarters in Washington, D.C. Nixon denied direct involvement but was forced to resign in 1974.

▶ MARS—UP CLOSE AND PERSONAL

Another world opened up in December as Mariner 9 began mapping the surface of Mars. The images were tantalizing: cracks that resembled riverbeds, volcanoes—one the size of Arizona—and a canyon ten times the length and four times the depth of the Grand Canyon. Earth's closest planetary neighbor suddenly seemed closer. "Mars may be red, but it certainly isn't dead," mused astronomer Carl Sagan.

Mariner was the ninth in a series of space probes NASA launched to explore the inner solar system beginning in 1962. Powered by four solar panels, the probe used radio transmissions to communicate with scientists on Earth. Earlier probes had revealed a good deal of information about Mars's atmosphere and structure. But until Mariner 9 sent back more than 7,000 pictures, the planet's surface was a mystery.

The Soviet Union's probe made the first successful landing on Mars on December 2 during a turbulent dust storm. Twenty seconds after touching the ground, Mars 3 went dead—and joined Mars 2 as the planet's first bits of man-made debris.

Orbiting Mars from a safe distance, Mariner 9 escaped the dust storms. From there, the probe continued to observe Mars until it lost contact with Earth in 1972.

▶ AMERICA'S FAVORITE FATHEAD

People didn't know what to make of *All in the Family*. In a world of bland, comfortable sitcoms, Archie Bunker's fatheaded bigotry was shocking. His Polish son-in-law, Mike, was "Meathead." His black neighbors were "jungle bunnies." Puerto Ricans were "spics." He hurled these epithets without compunction while his scatterbrained wife, Edith aka "Dingbat," scurried to heed his every whim.

Norman Lear's takeoff on Britain's *Till Death Do Us Part* succeeded in part because it appealed to two very different

audiences—people who relished seeing racism skewered and those who identified with Archie. Within six months, the CBS series was the most-watched show on television and continued to be for the next five years.

The sitcom spawned others. Edith's cousin Maude got her own show in 1972, and the Bunkers' black neighbors moved on up to

CAST OF *ALL IN THE FAMILY*

Manhattan's East Side three years later to star in *The Jeffersons*.

Lear rediscovered established stars like Carroll O'Connor and Jean Stapleton, and created others like Rob Reiner and Sally Struthers. When *All in the Family* went off the air in 1991, O'Connor was the only original cast member remaining. His character by then was an American icon.

▶ BUSING COMBATS SEGREGATION

Riding a bus to school was nothing new in the U.S.; almost 40 percent of the country's children did it. But when the Supreme Court upheld busing as a reasonable way to integrate public schools in 1971, the familiar yellow school buses suddenly became pariahs. Many whites turned to private schools, concerned that their children would not get a good education in previously all-black schools.

The *Swann* v. *Charlotte-Mecklenberg Board of Education* decision took its name from a case in Charlotte, North Carolina, where about 30 percent of the school population was black. Despite a court-ordered desegregation plan, many of those students attended black schools. A federally appointed consultant suggested that busing elementary school students in white schools to black schools, and vice-versa

• JANUARY 10
French fashion designer Gabrielle "Coco" Chanel dies at 86 in Paris.

• JANUARY 14
Jury acquits Hell's Angels member Allen Passaro of killing Altamont concertgoer despite filmed evidence of the event.

• MARCH 24
South Vietnamese forces withdraw from Laos, 44 days after invading.

• APRIL 10-14
In China, Premier Zhou Enlai welcomes American table-tennis team to world championships; press calls it "ping-pong diplomacy."

• APRIL 24
200,000 antiwar protesters, 700 of whom are veterans, demonstrate on Capitol Hill.

• APRIL 25
East Pakistan becomes the independent country of Bangladesh.

• MAY 31
Queen Elizabeth outrages some subjects by asking for an additional 1.14 million dollars on top of her yearly, nontaxable, income.

would solve the problem. The school board challenged this on the grounds that it would be hard on the students.

Warren Burger, whom President Nixon appointed to succeed retired Chief Justice Earl Warren in 1969, wrote the opinion. A conservative Republican, Burger nonetheless disagreed with Nixon's antibusing policies. "School authorities are traditionally charged with broad power to formulate and implement educational policy, and might well conclude that in order to prepare students to live in a pluralistic society each school should have a prescribed ratio of Negro to white students," he wrote. "Desegregation plans cannot be limited to the walk-in school."

▶ HANDHELD REVOLUTION

A tiny bit of silicon called a microprocessor transformed the future in 1971. The revolutionary tool allowed computer designers to wrestle their creations down to a more manageable, affordable size.

Engineers at Intel, a fledgling company in California, invented the first microprocessor. A Japanese firm had hired Intel to make 12 different chips for calculators. Worried that its small staff could not churn out so many chips, Intel engineers instead developed one chip that performed 12 functions. The general-purpose logic chip would be programmed by software, which was cheaper and faster than having to use hardware.

Nine months later, the Intel 4004 was

MICROCHIP

perfected. The integrated circuit was mounted atop a silicon chip that measured 1/8 of an inch wide by 1/6 of an inch long. This complex sandwich was layered with 2,300 transistors interconnected by fine slivers of aluminum; the transistors stored and used data to perform whatever function was needed.

Intel added more transistors to increase capabilities. In 1981 IBM installed Intel's invention as the "brains" for its first personal computers. Within 15 years, billions of microprocessors were whizzing away in computers, automated teller machines, home appliances, streetlights, and almost anything electronic.

CAT SCAN

A British engineer combined the power of computers with conventional x-rays to revolutionize medicine. Godfrey Hounsfield had figured out the theory behind computerized axial tomography (CAT) scanning several years before. Computer technology finally caught up with him in 1971.

Hounsfield attached an x-ray machine to a state-of-the-art computer. The device passed a myriad of x-rays through a patient's brain at different angles; the computer then turned these cross-sectional images into a three-dimensional picture (right). This allowed doctors to pinpoint a tumor without surgery.

Physicist Allen MacLeod Cormack had published his formulas for combining multiple x-ray measurements in 1963 and 1964. Although Hounsfield's theories came to fruition first, Cormack's contributions did not go unnoticed. The two shared a Nobel Prize for medicine in 1979.

■ TRENDS & TRIVIA

Ralph Nader establishes Public Citizen, a lobbying and litigating center for consumers.

The Soviet Union legalizes long hair on men.

Loretta Lynn releases autobiographical song "Coal Miner's Daughter."

Masterpiece Theater debuts on PBS.

Environmental group Greenpeace is founded.

Look magazine folds after 34 years.

U.S. bans cigarette ads from television.

Smilies—the original yellow happy faces—become popular.

Jerzy Kosinski's *Being There* is published.

The film industry opens to blacks with the "blaxploitation" genre exemplified by *Shaft*.

Three Dog Night release "Joy to the World."

Walt Disney World opens in Orlando, Florida.

Gene Hackman stars in *The French Connection*.

Clint Eastwood becomes *Dirty Harry*.

Marvin Gaye's song "What's Going On?" makes social commentary.

Colombo and *The Sonny and Cher Comedy Hour* debut.

John Updike's *Rabbit Redux* is published.

Amtrak begins operations.

291

- **JUNE 28**
Supreme Court decides the government wrongfully drafted Muhammad Ali, the prizefighter and conscientious objector.

- **JULY 6**
Musician Louis Armstrong dies.

- **AUGUST**
To strengthen the dollar and halt inflation, President Nixon announces the U.S. will no longer convert dollars abroad into gold.

- **SEPTEMBER 9-13**
Inmates seize control of New York's Attica State Correctional Facility for four days of rioting and fires; 28 inmates and 9 guards die.

- **OCTOBER 28**
Great Britain joins the European Common Market.

- **NOVEMBER 15**
The People's Republic of China attends its first United Nations meeting as a member.

- **DECEMBER 14**
New York City Police Detective Frank Serpico testifies about corruption before the Knapp Commission.

Richard Nixon summarized his trips to Beijing and Moscow as pivotal steps "toward a more peaceful world."

The President saw a chance to play one communist enemy against the other. To gain leverage with the Soviet Union, he would befriend China. "For the long run, it means pulling China back into the world community," Nixon told an interviewer, "...as a great and progressing nation, not as the epicenter of world revolution."

Nixon visited China in February (below), after months of clandestine planning. The summit went well; acknowledging their differences, he and Chinese leader Mao Zedong pledged to work toward the relaxation of tension in Asia and the world.

Three months later, the Soviets welcomed Nixon to Moscow. There, he and Soviet leader Leonid Brezhnev signed the Strategic Arms Limitations Treaty (SALT I), which limited each superpower's number of nuclear weapons. In addition to the treaty, Brezhnev agreed to use his influence with the North Vietnamese to end the war.

▶ ALIENATION OF UGANDA

The repercussions of colonialism continued to plague Africa long after Europe relinquished control. In Uganda, English overseers had exacerbated tribal rivalries by favoring the Ganda people and by allowing Indians to control most of the East African colony's commerce.

Ten years of independence did not improve the situation. By 1972 the Ugandan Army had forced the Gandan political party into exile and installed a bloodthirsty ex-boxer named Idi Amin as prime minister. In an attempt to bolster the economy, Amin expelled all Asians who were not Ugandan citizens. He then gave their businesses—among the country's most successful—to military cronies. Amin's bigotry was not limited to Asians. He deported all Israelis, thereby severing an alliance he'd once cultivated. He also went after the Lango and Acholi peoples because they had supported his predecessors. Before he was ousted in 1979, Amin had slaughtered some 300,000 Ugandans and alienated his country from the rest of the world.

▶ BLOODY SUNDAY REDUX

The violent suppression of a peaceful protest led to a 15-month suspension of Northern Ireland's House of Parliament.

In Ireland's second "Bloody Sunday," 10,000 unarmed Catholics marched in Londonderry on January 30 to protest Northern Ireland's policy of internment—imprisonment without trial. The Protestant-controlled government adopted the policy in 1971 as a way of keeping hundreds of alleged Irish Republican Army members in jail.

When the protesters approached Londonderry's Bogside neighborhood, soldiers used guns instead of the customary tear gas or water cannons to disperse the crowd. Thirteen protesters died. Tempers flared in both Irelands. A furious crowd

CONFRONTATION BETWEEN PARATROOPERS AND PROTESTERS

torched the British Embassy in Dublin on February 2. A month later, a bomb ripped through a shopping district in Belfast, killing 6 people and wounding 30. Within days, another bomb exploded in Belfast, this time injuring 70 people in a train station.

Britain seized direct control of Northern Ireland on March 24 and suspended the Protestant-controlled parliament. This thrilled many Catholics and outraged Protestants, who saw it as a concession to "terrorist violence."

The following year, a new parliament comprising Catholics and Protestants took over; four years later, they abolished internment.

▶ VIETNAM'S CHRISTMAS BLITZKRIEG

By October 1972 the U.S. had almost freed itself from Vietnam.

The number of American soldiers stationed in South Vietnam had dropped to about 25,000 from 1967's high of 540,000. If the U.S. government recalled those remaining troops, North Vietnam would release its American prisoners. Furthermore, the Viet Cong leaders were ready to negotiate a cease-fire if they could keep the territory they occupied in the south.

South Vietnamese Premier Nguyen Van Thieu balked at this. And Nixon, unwilling to be the President who let that country fall to communists—supported

● **JANUARY 30**
Sheik Mujibur Rahman becomes Prime Minister of Bangladesh after months in jail for his role in independence movement.

● **FEBRUARY 24**
The North Vietnamese government walks out of peace talks in Paris to protest U.S. air raids.

● **MARCH 13**
Writer Clifford Irving admits that he made up an "autobiography" of reclusive millionaire Howard Hughes.

● **APRIL 22**
John Fairfax and Sylvia Cook are the first people known to have rowed across the Pacific Ocean. The 8,000-mile trip took one year.

● **MAY 1**
The *New York Times* wins a Pulitzer Prize for its coverage and publishing of the Pentagon Papers.

● **MAY 2**
J. Edgar Hoover, the first head of the FBI, dies at 77 in Washington, D.C.

● **MAY 28**
Edward, the Duke of Windsor, dies at 77. The former English king abdicated in 1936 to marry Wallis Simpson.

him. He authorized the "Christmas Bombings," a display of explosives designed to scare the North Vietnamese into further concessions. During the 11-day blitz, U.S. fighter planes dropped almost 40,000 tons of bombs on Hanoi and Haiphong, killing 1,600 civilians and 93 American airmen.

Nixon canceled the attacks after the Viet Cong agreed to resume negotiations in January. The ensuing Paris Accords offered essentially the same terms as those outlined in October. Thieu again refused to sign the treaty, but the U.S. pressured him not to oppose it. The accords went into effect January 27, 1973, leaving the fundamental question of who would govern South Vietnam unanswered.

Like the French before them, the U.S. could not secure the country's independence. Nixon's "peace with honor" was merely another way of saying withdrawal without victory.

▶ WOULD-BE ASSASSIN SHOOTS WALLACE According to a passage Arthur Bremer had scribbled in a notebook, happiness was "having George Wallace arrested for a hit-and-run accident."

The itinerant worker shot the Democratic presidential candidate in the chest May 15 during a campaign stop in Laurel, Maryland. The assassination attempt left Wallace paralyzed below the waist and forced him to quit the race.

Before the shooting, Wallace, the vitriolic governor of Alabama, was making strides in his second quest for the White House. His lively condemnations of busing and "pointy-headed intellectuals" appealed to right-wing Democrats and southern Republicans who agreed with his segregationist views. More than half the Democrats voting in the Michigan primary chose Wallace—after Bremer shot him. These weren't all bigots, pollsters discovered. Many were working-class people frustrated by the

OLYMPIC TERROR

The 1972 Summer Olympics in Munich were the most tragic in modern history. Seven Palestinian terrorists stormed a dormitory in the Olympic Village, killing two Israeli coaches and taking nine others hostage. Before the day was over, the hostages, four of their captors, and a German policeman were dead as well. The terrorists (right) belonged to Black September, an arm of the Palestine Liberation Organization. They threatened to kill the hostages unless Israeli Prime Minister Golda Meir released 200 Palestinian prisoners. She refused, and a day of tense negotiations unfolded. As 12,000 policeman and millions of cameras watched, the terrorists turned down one alternative after another.

Toward nightfall, they agreed to fly—with their captives—to Cairo. When the hatch on the helicopter that transported them from the dormitory to the runway opened, German gunmen opened fire. Within minutes, several bullet-riddled bodies sprawled on the tarmac. Three days later Israel raided Palestinian training camps in Syria and Lebanon.

national status quo. They represented another kind of protest movement—and one that commanded a sizable voting bloc.

Wallace ran again in 1976 without success. He then returned to state politics. During his fourth tenure as governor, he shed some of his racist policies and managed to gain a degree of credibility with black voters. He bowed out of the political spotlight altogether in 1987.

TRENDS & TRIVIA

David Halberstam's *The Best and the Brightest* is published.

Don McLean releases the song "American Pie."

Pandas Hsing-Hsing and Ling-Ling are given to the National Zoo as a gift from China.

293

Francis Ford Coppola directs *The Godfather.*

Grease introduces the fifties fad on Broadway.

The Environmental Protection Agency bans the pesticide DDT.

Federal Express is started.

Jogging or warm-up suits become popular.

Home Box Office debuts.

Alex Comfort's *The Joy of Sex* is published.

Ms. magazine debuts.

Oregon passes the U.S.'s first returnable bottle law.

Robert Moog patents the Moog synthesizer.

Life magazine ceases publication.

Soviet gymnast Olga Korbut popularizes her sport.

Pope Paul VI abolishes the tonsure haircut for seminarians—a requirement since 6 A.D.

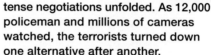

Liza Minelli stars in *Cabaret.*

U.S. swimmer Mark Spitz wins an unprecedented seven gold medals at the Olympics. ◀

• JUNE 17
Five men are arrested and charged with breaking into the Democratic National Committee's headquarters in Washington, D.C.

• JUNE 29
The U.S. Supreme Court rules 5-4 that the death penalty is unconstitutional.

• JULY 31
After admitting to undergoing electric shock therapy, Senator Thomas Eagleton withdraws as Senator George McGovern's running mate.

• SEPTEMBER 3
U.S. chess player Bobby Fischer defeats Soviet Boris Spassky in the world championship in Iceland.

• SEPTEMBER 15
G. Gordon Liddy and E. Howard Hunt are indicted on charges of conspiring to break into Democratic National Headquarters.

• NOVEMBER
President Richard Nixon is reelected after defeating Senator George McGovern, 45.9 million votes to 28.4 million.

• DECEMBER 24
Nicaragua is rocked by a series of earthquakes that leave 10,000 dead.

294

The Arab oil embargo of 1973 transformed a little-known Third World organization into a major world power. Oil was a commodity that could no longer be taken for granted.

With the exception of Iraq, the Arab members of the Organization of Petroleum Exporting Countries (OPEC) imposed the six-month embargo in October in response to U.S. military support for Israel. The embargo suspended all shipments to countries supportive of Israel and its allies. Two months later, OPEC voted to raise the price of oil.

OPEC's actions strained America's relations with Western Europe and Japan. The majority of those countries imported most of their oil supply, whereas only 12 percent of oil consumed in the U.S. came from the Arab world.

Americans still had to endure some austerity measures. President Richard Nixon cut all shipments of home heating oil by 15 percent and urged people to turn down their thermostats. Congress lowered the national speed limit to 55 miles per hour. Drivers queued up to get gas before supplies were exhausted.

The Arab states lifted the embargo in March after the U.S. agreed to seek an accord between Israel and Syria.

▶ WATERGATE MELTDOWN
Millions of Americans watched the Nixon Administration go on a televised trial in the summer of 1973. White House employees squirmed in their seats as a Senate committee grilled them in its quest to discover who had approved breaking into the Democratic National Committee's headquarters in Washington's Watergate office building.

Sam Ervin (above, right), a North Carolina Democrat, chaired the bipartisan committee. Dismissing Nixon's requests not to televise the hearings, Ervin announced his intention to "spare no one, whatever his station in life might be."

Former White House Counsel John Dean III and Former Special Assistant Alexander Butterfield gave some of the most damaging testimony. Dean insisted Nixon himself attempted to cover up the break-in. When Butterfield testified later that the President taped almost all Oval Office conversations, the committee saw a way to prove Dean's allegations. Ervin was not the only one trying to get those tapes. So was Archibald Cox, a patrician legal scholar appointed by the government to investigate whether the President had broken the law. Infuriated by Cox's persistent requests for the tapes, Nixon ordered Attorney General Elliott Richardson to fire him. Richardson and his deputy, William Ruckelshaus, resigned in protest, leaving Solicitor General Robert Bork to do the job. The debacle

became known as the "Saturday Night Massacre."

Nixon could not get rid of District Judge John Sirica, who had presided over the trial of the Watergate burglars. The Republican judge publicly expressed his doubts that the men had acted alone.

Nor could Nixon fire the two Washington Post reporters who uncovered the scandal. Bob Woodward's and Carl Bernstein's remarkable reporting inspired scores of young people to pursue careers in journalism.

▶ RISE AND FALL OF WOUNDED KNEE
The 71-day siege at Wounded Knee, South Dakota, was a telling sign that the era of activism so symbolic of the '60s was on the wane. While many sympathized with the Native Americans, there were no organized marches or major demonstrations to show support for the cause.

On February 27 about 300 members of the American Indian Movement (AIM) seized Wounded Knee, where the U.S. Army massacred some 200 Sioux in 1890. As camera crews descended into the valley, AIM issued its demands to the government: sovereignty over tribal affairs, improved conditions on Indian reservations, and a thorough investigation of some 300 treaties AIM said the government had made with Indians, then broken. If those demands were not met, AIM

OSCAR RUNNING BEAR AT WOUNDED KNEE

• JANUARY 5
Airports in U.S. begin inspecting luggage and travelers in wake of problems with airborne terrorism.

• JANUARY 22
Lyndon B. Johnson dies of a heart attack at 64 in Texas.

• FEBRUARY 14
First American POWs return to U.S. from North Vietnam.

• APRIL 8
Spanish painter Pablo Picasso dies at 92 in France.

• MAY 11
Citing government misconduct, a federal judge acquits Daniel Ellsberg of theft-related charges for releasing the Pentagon Papers.

• JUNE 24
The world's oldest head of state, Irish President Eamon de Valera, retires at 90 after 57 years in that job.

• JULY 10
The Bahamas become independent from Britain.

• AUGUST 4
Astronomers in Houston use radar to pierce through the clouds of Venus for the first time.

would kill its 11 hostages. "We definitely are going to hold [Wounded Knee] until death do us part," one leader threatened.

The Sioux's tribal chairman, Richard Wilson, condemned AIM for interfering in the tribe's affairs. Wilson, AIM retorted, was a corrupt half-breed. This dispute hurt AIM's position; other Indian tribes distanced themselves from the fracas, and so did the rest of the country. Soon, AIM members began evacuating the site. Those who remained surrendered May 8.

▶ HERO IN THREE WHITE SOCKS
One of America's best-loved heroes raced onto the scene in the spring and summer of 1973. A lanky, three-year-old chestnut colt named Secretariat (below) became the first horse in 25 years to win racing's Triple Crown. He won the Belmont Stakes by an unprecedented 31 lengths and his jockey, Ron Turcotte, never once used his crop.

With his three white socks and amiable personality, Secretariat was a winner on and off the track. Young girls and old men sent him fan mail. When his van drove by, people lined the road to glimpse "Big Red."

One of Secretariat's most devoted fans was sportswriter Bill Nack, who covered racing for Long Island *Newsday*, the horse's hometown newspaper.

"The nation was beginning to suffer the effects of Watergate," Nack wrote. "Secretariat represented everything [the Watergate conspirators] did not—honest, generous, simple, and incorruptible."

▶ MAKING OF A DICTATOR
The new Philippine constitution adopted in January legitimized Ferdinand Marcos's

ROE V. WADE

The Supreme Court's divisive decision to impose constitutional protections on abortion went to the heart of an ongoing debate over when life begins (right). In the most basic sense, *Roe* v. *Wade* was about the unwritten but long acknowledged constitutional right to privacy.

Norma McCorvey, a single woman from Texas, became pregnant. Because abortion was illegal in the state, she arranged an adoption. In the process, she met Sarah Weddington, a young attorney eager to challenge Texas's abortion law.

To prevent McCorvey's family from discovering her pregnancy, Weddington listed her as "Jane Roe"—the first name listed in a class action suit against Texas on behalf of any woman seeking an abortion. Gradually, the case wound its way up to the nation's highest court, and, early in 1973, that court legalized abortions for women in the first trimester of pregnancy.

unbridled control of the Pacific archipelago.

Marcos already had served the two terms that the constitution allowed. To extend his reign, he secretly ordered a rash of bombings in 1972, which he then blamed on communists. Under the guise of cracking down on the dangerous insurgents, he declared martial law in September.

After imprisoning most of his detractors to silence any opposition, Marcos clinched his control at the constitutional convention in January. The constitution he proposed sailed through, and Marcos became prime minister with no term limits.

■ TRENDS & TRIVIA

Kurt Vonnegut, Jr.'s *Breakfast of Champions* is published.

Equus shows on Broadway.

Barbra Streisand releases "The Way We Were."

Paul McCartney & Wings release "Band On the Run."

Ingmar Bergman directs *Scenes From a Marriage* with Liv Ullman.

Baseball's American League adopts the designated hitter rule.

Supermarket bar codes debut.

Pink Floyd releases "Dark Side of the Moon," which spends a record 741 weeks on U.S. charts.

Marlon Brando stars in Bernardo Bertolucci's *Last Tango in Paris.*

University of Miami is first to offer athletic scholarships to women.

Chicago's Sears Tower is world's tallest building (1,454 feet).

Daredevil motorcyclist Evel Knievel leaps over 52 wrecked cars in Los Angeles.

Tool unearthed in Yukon indicates that humans have been in the New World since 27,000 B.C.

Marvin Gaye releases "Let's Get It On."

American Psychiatric Association declassifies homosexuality as a mental illness.

Tony Orlando and Dawn release "Tie a Yellow Ribbon Round the Old Oak Tree."

Linda Blair is possessed in *The Exorcist.*

Telly Savalas is a lollipop-licking N.Y. cop on *Kojak.*

- **SEPTEMBER 11**
A coup in Chile ousts President Salvador Allende. He is found dead in the presidential palace.

- **SEPTEMBER 20**
Billie Jean King trounces Bobby Riggs in a "battle of the sexes" tennis match in the Houston Astrodome.

◀ **OCTOBER 10**
Vice President Spiro T. Agnew resigns after pleading no contest to charges of income tax evasion and accepting bribes.

- **NOVEMBER 14**
England's Princess Anne marries Capt. Mark Phillips in London.

- **DECEMBER 1**
David Ben Gurion, Israel's first premier and one of its founders, dies at 87 of a brain hemorrhage in Tel Aviv.

- **DECEMBER 14**
After six months, captors in Italy release J. Paul Getty III when his grandfather, oil millionaire J. Paul Getty, pays about $750,000 in ransom.

NIXON RESIGNS

At 9:01 p.m. on August 8, Richard Nixon (below) became the first President in American history to announce his resignation.

"I have always tried to do what was best for the nation," he said in his televised appearance from the Oval Office. "Because of the Watergate matter, I might not have the support of the Congress that I would consider necessary to make the very difficult decisions and carry out the duties of this office in the way the interests of the nation will require. Therefore, I shall resign the Presidency effective at noon tomorrow."

Nixon's 37th speech from the White House drew a bigger audience than any other political speech; about 150 million people tuned in to watch. That he would leave office was not surprising. The question was how he would go.

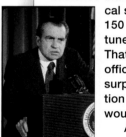

As he boarded a helicopter the next day on his way back to California, Nixon choked back tears. Then, pulling himself together, he turned to the crowd and flashed his trademark "V for Victory" sign. Minutes later, his successor, President Gerald R. Ford, said, "Our long national nightmare is over."

▶ GREEK LEADERSHIP LOSES

Democracy returned to its ancient birthplace in 1974 when Greek civilians overthrew the harsh military dictatorship that had held sway for seven years. The breaking point actually occurred in Cyprus, where the junta proved unable to protect Greek Cypriots from invading Turks.

Greece and Turkey had fought to control the Mediterranean island since it became independent in 1959. Greek Christian Cypriots outnumbered Turkish Muslims four to one, and relations between the two groups were as rocky as the land itself. Yet Greece had the advantage because Cyprus's president, Archbishop Makarios, supported *enosis* (union with Greece). When he abandoned that policy, the Greek junta had him deposed in July 1974.

Threatened by the new regime's blatant support of Greek annexation, Turkey invaded Cyprus on July 20. Within a month, it controlled almost 40 percent of the island and named the territory the Turkish Republic of Northern Cyprus. All attempts to broker a peace agreement failed. At the century's end, the island was still divided.

The Greek junta's inability to win the the war in Cyprus caused the government to collapse. The leaders were forced to resign, and former Prime Minister Constantine Karamanlis returned from exile to restore Greece to democracy.

▶ "SHUTTLE DIPLOMACY"

The U.S. achieved some measure of success in its ongoing search for peace in the Middle East when Secretary of State Henry Kissinger (above, right) brokered a Syrian-Israeli truce in May.

For 32 days Kissinger flew between the two countries, an exhausting process that the press called "shuttle diplomacy." Then, days after he informed

President Richard Nixon that the whole thing was hopeless, everything changed. Israeli Premier Golda Meir and Syrian President Hafez al-Assad signed a disengagement to formalize an end to the Yom Kippur War, in which Syria and Egypt attempted to regain land taken by Israel eight years before. Under the disengagement plan that Kissinger created, Israel relinquished all Syrian territory captured since October 1973, along with Quneitra, the provincial capital of the Golan Heights. UN troops would monitor a buffer zone there.

The timing of Kissinger's diplomatic victory was excellent for Nixon, whose role in the Watergate scandal was becoming more apparent. The Secretary of State now occupied the spotlight, casting the beleaguered administration in a rosy light for the first time in months. He was called a "national asset," a shining example of Nixon's good judgment after so many bad ones.

Kissinger's truce held, despite Israel's annexation of the Golan Heights in 1981.

▶ STRANGE SAGA OF PATTY HEARST

Kidnapped heiress Patricia Hearst refused to leave her captors, trading freedom for felony in a highly publicized case which dominated the news for much of 1974.

The 19-year-old granddaughter of publishing millionaire William Randolph Hearst was abducted from her apartment on February 4 in Berkeley, California. The kidnappers identified themselves as the Symbionese Liberation Army (SLA), a group of about 15 terrorists led by two ex-convicts. As ransom, they demanded that Hearst's father distribute two million

---

- **JANUARY 23**
Experts report an 18.5-minute gap on a taped conversation between Nixon and H. R. Haldeman was not made by accident.

- **FEBRUARY 11**
Communist insurgents in Cambodia kill 139 people and wound 44 more in Phnom Penh.

- **MARCH 20**
News anchor Chet Huntley dies at 62 of cancer in Montana.

- **APRIL 10**
Israeli Premier Golda Meir resigns.

- **MAY 6**
German Chancellor Willy Brandt resigns in wake of a spy scandal.

- **MAY 4**
Duke Ellington dies at 75.

- **MAY 15**
A. H. Robins Co. takes the Dalkon Shield off the market after reports that the contraceptive is dangerous and not successful.

dollars' worth of food to California's poor. After he complied, they asked for more money and refused to release their hostage.

Almost two months later, the kidnapping took a bizarre turn when Hearst announced she had joined her captors' fight for "the freedom of oppressed people" and changed her name to Tania. The pretty art student was then caught on film wielding a gun (below) as the SLA robbed a bank. In another incident, "Tania" opened fire on a storefront to help her shoplifting cohorts escape.

Hearst disappeared in June not long

after five SLA members—one of whom she described as her lover—were killed in a police raid. She was arrested in 1975 and charged with armed robbery. Famed litigator F. Lee Bailey argued that the SLA had brainwashed his client, and therefore, she could not be held responsible for her deeds. The jury disagreed, however, and found her guilty. Less than a year into her prison term, Hearst obtained a presidential pardon and left jail to marry her former bodyguard.

▶ ETHIOPIAN EMPEROR OVERTHROWN
Ethiopian Emperor Haile Selassie's impressive efforts to bring his country into the 20th century were not enough to sustain him.

A military junta deposed the 82-year-old autocrat in September, charging that his corrupt regime had bankrupted the country. After almost six decades of opulent rule, Selassie was taken away in a Volkswagen.

One of the few African nations that

HANK AARON

Hank Aaron was not a social activist or radical. He was a baseball player. But in the course of doing his job in the spring of 1974, he found himself at the center of a maelstrom of racism. He was a black man poised to break a record that a white man had set 39 years before.

Despite death threats and hate mail, the Atlanta Braves outfielder stepped up to bat on April 8, ready to give the hometown crowd something to see. "Hammerin' Hank" whacked the ball and took off for his 715th home run, thereby besting Babe Ruth's record by one. "All I could think about was that I wanted to touch all the bases," Aaron said.

To honor the achievement, officials stopped the game against the L.A. Dodgers for about 15 minutes so Aaron could accept plaques, handshakes, and hugs from well-wishers. Then it was back to business; the Braves beat the Dodgers 7-4. And Aaron went on to score another 40 home runs before retiring in 1976.

was never a European colony, Ethiopia took great strides toward modernity under Selassie. He enacted a constitution, emancipated slaves, and founded an education system. World leaders admired his diplomacy and called upon him to mediate several international disputes.

Still, Ethiopia remained poor, a fact exacerbated by a horrible famine that killed 20,000 in 1973. Fueled by demonstrations and rumor that Selassie's regime kept the famine a secret from the rest of the world, the military turned against him. The new government adopted a course of socialism that gave way to communism before it too was overthrown in 1991.

■ TRENDS & TRIVIA

Fashion model Beverly Johnson becomes first black to appear on the cover of *Vogue*.

The Heimlich Maneuver is introduced.

CBS's "Good Times" introduces the catch phrase "Dy-No-Mite!"

Chicano comic Freddie Prinz stars in NBC's *Chico and the Man*.

Bob Woodward and Carl Bernstein's *All the President's Men* is published just before Nixon resigns.

Martin Scorsese directs *Alice Doesn't Live Here Anymore*.

Streaking becomes a craze.

ABC's *Happy Days* debuts.

Calculators become affordable.

Roman Polanksi directs *Chinatown*.

Harry Chapin releases "Cat's In the Cradle."

Paul Newman stars in *The Towering Inferno*.

Aleksandr Solzhenitsyn's *The Gulag Archipelago* is published.

Stephen King's first novel, *Carrie*, is published.

Laura Ingalls Wilder's children's books become a TV show, *Little House on the Prairie*.

Bob Chandler of Hazlewood, Missouri, builds Bigfoot, the first "monster truck."

Clothing is made of can pop-tops.

James Garner appears in *The Rockford Files*.

Tom Stoppard's *Travesties* debuts on stage.

297

◀ **JUNE 30**
Russian ballet star Mikhail Baryshnikov (left) defects in Toronto.

● **JULY 1**
Argentinian President Juan Perón dies and is succeeded by his wife and vice president, Isabel.

● **JULY 30**
U.S. Supreme Court rules that Nixon must release tapes requested by the special prosecutor investigating Watergate.

● **AUGUST 29**
Moses Malone becomes first high school athlete to bypass college and go straight into pro basketball.

● **SEPTEMBER 16**
President Gerald Ford pardons former President Richard Nixon and grants immunity to Vietnam draft-dodgers.

● **NOVEMBER 12**
UN votes to suspend South Africa for its apartheid policy.

● **DECEMBER 29**
Earthquake in Pakistan kills 4,700 and injures 15,000.

A mid declining U.S. support, South Vietnam's resistance to the North crumbled, bringing an end to the Vietnam War.

The U.S. Army had evacuated the few remaining GIs from the roof of the American embassy in Saigon only a few hours before the city fell to the Viet Cong on April 30. It was renamed Ho Chi Minh City.

The new government formed an alliance with the Soviet Union—a major blow to China, which had hoped to gain a strategic satellite in Southeast Asia. Neighboring Laos followed.

In response, China threw its weight behind a newly triumphant Khmer Rouge government in Cambodia, an ancient enemy of Vietnam. Led by the ruthless and fanatical Pol Pot, the Khmer Rouge began a systematic terror campaign against the Cambodian people that would result in the murder of more than one million.

Refugees from war-torn Indochina soon flooded countries around the world.

SKULLS OF KHMERS AT AN EXTERMINATION CAMP

▶ END OF THE PORTUGUESE EMPIRE

The once-vast Portuguese empire faded out of existence in 1975 after five centuries. Europe's first great colonizer was forced to relinquish its African holdings because they had become too costly to maintain.

Portugal's three African colonies—Mozambique, Angola, and Portuguese Guinea—had sought freedom for more than ten years. By the mid-1960s, Portugal was the only European country that kept its African holdings, partly because it had not played a big role in World War II. However, maintaining a grip on the rebellious colonies was absorbing more than 40 percent of the national budget. When a junta led by seven army captains overthrew the government in April 1974, people celebrated with wine and flowers; most were thrilled to see 40 years of strict authoritarianism end.

The new leaders granted Portuguese Guinea its independence in September. Mozambique became independent in June, and Angola followed in November. But freedom did not come with peace in the latter two countries. Mozambique's white-controlled neighbors attacked it for supporting antiapartheid freedom fighters. In Angola, the communist-backed government continued to fight rebels who were supported by South Africa and occasionally the U.S. It was not until 1997 that all sides were able to forge a coalition government.

▶ JUAN CARLOS BECOMES KING OF SPAIN

Spain's new ruler, King Juan Carlos (above, right), had to play his cards close to the chest. He had been handpicked by Gen. Francisco Franco to carry on the dictator's legacy. But the young Bourbon king was more inclined toward democracy and, to achieve such reforms without antagonizing the military, he had to tread carefully.

When Franco died in November, Spain

was in the midst of a recession. Basque separatists continued to fight for independence, as did groups in Catalonia, the last province to surrender to Franco 40 years before. Workers and students demanded more freedom. And the Catholic Church, a longtime Franco ally, was criticizing the king's policies.

Juan Carlos did not announce his intentions to make Spain a constitutional democracy. Instead, he worked behind the scenes to form new coalitions with political leaders. The king replaced Franco's fascist premier with a man who shared his own views. Within a few years, Spain had a multiparty parliament and was well on its way to political reform.

▶ HELSINKI ACCORDS SIGNED

Détente and human rights prevailed in August when the U.S., Canada, the Soviet Union, and each European country except Albania signed the Helsinki Accords. In addition to recognizing each signer's sovereignty, the 35 nations pledged to guarantee the "freedom of thought, conscience, religion, and belief" of those they governed.

The accords were the culmination of a two-year international forum organized to soothe tensions and improve life within Europe. But the original concept behind the Conference on Security and Cooperation in Europe (CSCE) was less noble; in 1953 Soviet Foreign Minister Vyacheslav Molotov thought such a conference would be a good way to legitimize his country's absorption of Eastern Europe.

- **JANUARY 10**
Ugandan Bernadette Olowo becomes first female ambassador to the Vatican.

- **FEBRUARY 11**
Great Britain's Conservative Party elects its first female leader, Margaret Thatcher.

- **MARCH 25**
King Faisal of Saudi Arabia is assassinated by a nephew in Riyadh.

- **APRIL 5**
Chinese Nationalist President Chiang Kai-shek dies of a heart attack at 87 in Taiwan.

- **MAY 27**
The Bolshoi Ballet makes its first appearance in the U.S. in ten years.

- **JUNE 5**
Egypt reopens the Suez Canal after eight years.

- **JULY 11**
Chinese archaeologists announce the discovery of a 2,000-year-old pottery army in northwestern China.

Critics of the accords argued that it essentially did just that. By pledging to respect all existing European borders, the West acknowledged the Soviet Union's control of the East, and left Germany, as well as Berlin, divided. Furthermore, critics said, the Soviet Union's human rights record was atrocious. It was doubtful that a nonbinding document could effect much change. The Soviets soon ignored the human rights provisions.

But the accords were not in vain. One country's abuses became the concern of many. The U.S. began linking all foreign aid to human rights. The resulting trade sanctions hit abusers where it hurt most.

▶ NEW YORK ON THE ROCKS

The young lawyer looked at his client's cast-encased ankle, then at the photos he'd taken of the foot-deep pothole in New York's First Avenue that caused the break. His client had a clear-cut case against the city for damages resulting from her injury. But New York had no money. If she pursued her case, she would be another creditor in the interminable line flowing out of City Hall.

The nation's financial nerve center was the first city the federal government had to bail out in modern history. Many observers said New York's government was bloated beyond necessity after years of trying to be all things to all people. As taxpayers and businesses began leaving the city, officials made up the difference by borrowing money from private lenders and floating municipal bonds. When the notes and debts came due, the coffers were empty.

President Gerald Ford initially refused to help New York out; "FORD TO CITY: DROP DEAD," screamed the *Daily News* on October 30. However, to avoid the repercussions that a one-billion-dollar default would have on international banking and New York's future, he relented. Two months later, he approved

LIVE FROM NY

Staying home to watch TV on Saturday night was no longer a shameful admission, thanks to *Saturday Night Live*. Within months of the show's October debut, it was far worse to admit missing the zany comedy. Everybody assembled at the watercooler or outside the classroom Monday morning was exchanging lines from the hilarious skits.

The roster of players read like a comedic *Who's Who*: (left to right, below) Laraine Newman, John Belushi, Jane Curtin, Gilda Radner, Garrett Morris, Dan Ackroyd, and Chevy Chase. The characters they created—the Coneheads, the Bees, the Blues Brothers—were just as well loved.

Within three years, *Saturday Night Live* had eclipsed *The Tonight Show* as the most-watched show of late-night television.

almost two billion dollars in loans.

Conservative Republicans turned New York's fiscal woes into one of their favorite battle cries—big government is bad. "Liberalism had become the party of undisciplined government spending on behalf of undisciplined interest groups," wrote journalist E. J. Dionne. "The result was fiscal chaos." This became a standard theme in GOP campaigns for the rest of the century.

■ TRENDS & TRIVIA

Thomas Mann's notebooks are opened at his wish—20 years after his death.

Jack Nicholson and Louise Fletcher star in *One Flew Over the Cuckoo's Nest*.

The Doobie Brothers release "Old Black Water."

Earth, Wind, and Fire release "That's the Way of the World."

Jaws terrifies moviegoers.

Van McCoy's hit single "The Hustle," becomes a dance craze.

Bruce Springsteen and the E Street Band release "Born to Run."

Customized vans are new.

Junko Tabei of Japan is first woman to ascend Mount Everest.

Three American automakers offer rebates to buyers for the first time.

The Wizard of Oz goes soul—in Broadway's musical hit, *The Wiz*.

The cattle industry introduces "Beefalo" (a crossbreed of cattle and bison).

Automakers begin installing catalytic converters.

Lyme disease is first diagnosed in Lyme, Connecticut.

ABC's *Welcome Back, Kotter* and *Barney Miller* debut.

James Clavell's *Shōgun* is published.

E. L. Doctorow's *Ragtime* is published.

A Chorus Line becomes a Broadway hit.

299

◀ JULY
A joint U.S.-U.S.S.R Apollo-Soyuz mission docks in orbit.

● AUGUST 15
Bangladesh's President Sheik Mujibur Rahman is overthrown and killed in a coup led by former ally Khondaker Moshtaque Ahmed.

● OCTOBER 1
Muhammad Ali beats Joe Frazier after 14 rounds in the "Thrilla in Manila."

● NOVEMBER 14
Spain agrees to leave the Spanish Sahara to Morocco.

● NOVEMBER 20
A Senate committee reports for the first time that assassination has been used in foreign policy. The evidence stems from CIA plots to kill two foreign leaders.

300

Electing a small-town peanut farmer President underscored America's disgust with Washington insiders. Many Americans hoped that Jimmy Carter (below) would be the proverbial new broom who would make a clean sweep of the mess made by men who'd spent too much time inside the Washington, D.C. Beltway. Carter was no political neophyte. The former governor of Georgia was a member of the Trilateral Commission, the international consortium assembled by David Rockefeller to ensure global economic stability. Once elected, Carter filled his cabinet with advisers from another influential Rockefeller group, the Council on Foreign Relations.

With his soft drawl and easy grin, Carter was hard not to like. He vowed to replace the "bloated bureaucracy" with an efficient, moral, and comprehensible government.

And he was human. "I've committed adultery in my heart," he confessed in an interview with *Playboy*. "This is something that God recognizes I will do... and God forgives me for it."

Voters forgave him too. He won with 51 percent of the vote.

▶ RAID AT ENTEBBE

Israel struck a major blow against terrorism on July 4. Israeli commandos swarmed into the airport in the Ugandan town of Entebbe where Palestinian terrorists held 105 hostages. The daring raiders killed 7 terrorists and rescued 102 hostages.

The Palestinians had hijacked an Air France jet in Athens en route to Paris on June 27. The plane headed south to Uganda, where Idi Amin's pro-Arab government received them.

In return for the hostages, the hijackers demanded the release of 53 Palestinian and pro-Palestinian prisoners held in Israel and Europe. Despite Amin's public attempts to free the hostages, his involvement was suspicious. Four of the prisoners whose release the terrorists sought were Ugandan.

While the rest of the world believed that Israel was negotiating with the hijackers, three planeloads of Israeli commandos slipped into Entebbe. They set off explosives at one end of the airport to draw attention away from the hostage scene, then went to work. Three hostages were killed, but the rest were whisked to safety.

▶ CHINA'S SECOND REVOLUTION

The death of the Chinese Communist Party's two most prominent leaders, Mao Zedong and Zhou Enlai, triggered a new power struggle among the party's aging elite. Zhou's protégé, Hua Guofeng, who succeeded him in February, gained Zhou's title and also Mao's after the chairman's death in October.

Ostensibly, his titles gave the new chairman-premier more power than his predecessors. For a previously obscure party functionary to control the government, the party, and the military was unprecedented. Over the next two years it would prove unsustainable against mounting competition from the wily Vice Premier Deng Xiaoping whom Hua promoted. But Hua moved successfully to arrest Mao's powerful widow and other key radicals, later known as the Gang of Four, who had instigated the Cultural Revolution (below).

Hua and Deng quietly started to abandon some of Mao's most cherished policies. To boost agricultural output, peasants were allowed to farm their own plots instead of massive collectives. "Dare to be rich" was the new catchphrase, and farmers leaped at the chance. Food production grew by 50 percent between 1978 and 1984. Books and music banned during the Cultural Revolution reappeared. Deng hailed the reforms as China's "second revolution."

YOUNG CHINESE CARRY A PICTURE OF MAO ZEDONG.

▶ ARGENTINA'S "DIRTY WAR"

Thousands of Argentines were killed or placed under arrest during the Latin American nation's "dirty war" in 1976. Up to 20,000 more disappeared.

The internal war started in March when a repressive military junta overthrew President Isabel Perón. The ex-dancer was far less able to lead the country than her late husband, Juan. Terrorist attacks, a 335-percent cost of living increase, and rampant strikes pockmarked her two-year rule.

She managed to abort an air force coup in December, but could not withstand the army. On March 24, Lt. Gen. Jorge Rafael Videla placed Perón under house arrest on corruption charges. He

• JANUARY 12
Dame Agatha Christie dies at 85.

• FEBRUARY 7
U.S. Census shows that Sunbelt cities are the only ones showing any growth since 1970.

• MARCH 14
Egyptian President Anwar Sadat ends friendship pact with Soviets.

• APRIL 5
Billionaire Howard Hughes dies of a stroke at 70 aboard his private plane.

• JUNE 1
Syria invades Lebanon, and Americans leave.

▶ JULY 4
Bicentennial celebrations are held throughout the U.S.

suspended the constitution, dissolved the legislature, and announced that democracy would return only when Argentines had been sufficiently reeducated in "morality, uprightness, and efficiency."

"Reeducation" was another word for eradication. Videla's death squads slaughtered thousands of alleged leftists, whose bodies were never found. Their families mourned the loss of the *desaparecidos,* the disappeared.

► TRAGEDY IN SOWETO

Ten thousand black schoolchildren forced South Africa to relax some of its racist policies in June, something which international sanctions and embargoes had not been able to accomplish for years. The step forward was imprinted in blood, however; 25 children died and another 200 were hurt during the uprising in Soweto.

South Africa's policy of apartheid—Afrikaans for racial separation—segregated almost every aspect of life. Unlike whites, blacks had to pay to send their children to inferior schools where they studied a limited number of subjects. Secondary school classes were taught in English, while primary classes were taught in several regional languages, which intensified tribal rivalries.

In 1975 this changed for the worse. The government decreed that 50 percent of all instruction had to be given in Afrikaans. Few teachers spoke the language, and blacks scorned it as the tongue of their oppressors. The next year, students in Soweto, Johannesburg's black ghetto, staged a peaceful demonstration against the new rule. As they marched to the stadium where the rally would be held, police opened fire under orders to restore peace "at all costs."

Blacks erupted over the harsh measures. A poignant photograph of the blood-spattered body of the first victim, Hector Peterson, was flashed around the world,

QUINLAN CASE

The parents of a 22-year-old comatose patient prevailed over medical technology in 1976. Julia and Joseph Quinlan (below) won the right to take their daughter Karen Ann off a respirator that they believed was hurting her and prolonging her life unnecessarily. The New Jersey Supreme Court decision set the standard for a rash of other "right-to-die" rulings across the U.S.

Karen Ann lapsed into a coma after mixing Valium and gin at a party in 1975. Doctors said the brain damage was irreversible but refused her parents' request that she be removed from life support.

The couple sued. On March 31, 1976, the state's highest court unanimously ruled that a person's right to privacy included the choice to forego life-extending medical treatment.

After she was taken off the respirator, Karen Ann miraculously breathed on her own until succumbing to pneumonia in 1985. By then, several states had redefined death as the cessation of brain activity.

outraging the international community. Businessmen feared the wave of violence would further damage the country's international status and pressured the government to relax some of the apartheid laws. Prime Minister John Vorster abolished the 50-percent rule as well as several restrictions on sports and public amenities.

Although two decades would pass before apartheid itself was abolished, Soweto marked the end of the Afrikaners' attempts to impose cultural dominance.

■ TRENDS & TRIVIA

Sylvester Stallone stars in *Rocky.*

Jessica Lange stars in a remake of *King Kong.*

Leon Uris's *Trinity* is published.

Alex Haley's *Roots* is published.

In Thailand, the earliest example of bronze work is discovered and dated to 3600 B.C.

Rod Stewart releases "Tonight's the Night."

Football star O. J. Simpson runs 273 yards in a game, breaking his own record of 250 yards.

Scientists at MIT make the first synthetic gene.

The Tall Ships sail into New York's harbor to celebrate the U.S. Bicentennial.

Dorothy Hamill's "wedge" and Farrah Fawcett's "wings" become popular hairstyles.

Peter Frampton's "Frampton Comes Alive" is best-selling double live album to date.

Citizens Band (CB) radio craze is launched by C. W. McCall's hit single "Convoy."

ABC hires Barbara Walters as the first female national news anchor.

Females are eligible for Rhodes scholarships.

The Muppet Show and ABC's *Charlie's Angels* are popular TV shows.

Call waiting becomes available.

The VCR debuts. ▼

301

- **JULY 18**
Romanian gymnast Nadia Comaneci, 14, scores the first perfect score of 10 in Olympic gymnastics history.

- **JULY 20**
Viking 1 lands on Mars and transmits photos back to U.S.

- **AUGUST 26**
Death toll from mysterious disease that afflicted an American Legionnaires convention in Philadelphia reaches 28.

- **SEPTEMBER 16**
Episcopal Church approves ordination of women.

- **SEPTEMBER 19**
Sweden's Social Democrats lose control for first time in 44 years.

- **OCTOBER 6**
Military coup takes over control of Thailand.

- **NOVEMBER 16**
The Parti Québécois wins election in Quebec, a major step for the independence movement.

302

The Panama Canal was an engineering marvel. Yet to many Latin Americans, it was U.S. imperialism at its worst. The ten-mile-wide swath that split Panama was U.S. territory, where U.S. citizens had the best jobs and earned the most money. That domination only worsened relations between the region and its powerful neighbor to the north.

President Johnson started discussing a possible transfer of control in 1964. Thirteen years later, another Democrat, Jimmy Carter resumed talks. In the two treaties he signed with Panamanian leader, Omar Torrijos Herrera, Panama would have full control of the canal by 1999; the U.S. retained the right to intervene to protect the zone's neutrality. "Fairness, not force, should lie at the heart of our dealings with the nations of the world," Carter said.

His actions made conservatives apoplectic. "There is *no* Panama Canal," railed the American Conservative Union. "There is an *American* Canal in Panama!"

To blunt criticism, Carter enlisted prominent statesmen such as Henry Kissinger to explain the importance of restoring good relations in Latin America. Slowly, public opinion tilted in the President's favor. Congress ratified the treaties in 1978.

▶ Sadat's Step Toward Peace

Egyptian President Anwar Sadat's step into enemy territory was as much a loss as it was a gain. Arab leaders condemned his November visit to Israel as traitorous, while other leaders in the rest of the world praised his courage. Treason or bravery aside, Sadat (below) took a major step toward normalizing relations between two bitter enemies.

It seemed preposterous that an Arab leader would consent to visit a country whose existence he and his brethren refused to recognize for almost 30 years. Yet Sadat did. His speech to the Israeli Parliament was the most eloquent of olive branches.

"If you want to live with us in this part of the world, in sincerity I tell you that we welcome you among us with all security and safety," he told members of the Knesset. "…We accept to live with you in a lasting and just peace."

There were caveats, the Egyptian president added. Israel had to withdraw from the Arab lands it had taken and recognize Palestinian rights. In a follow-up speech, Israeli Prime Minister Menachem Begin deftly refused his guest's request, stressing that Israel (and the occupied territories) was the manifestation of a sacred promise, the biblical homeland of the Jewish people.

Sadat's pursuit of a separate peace with Israel lost Egypt its position as the center of the Arab world. It later would cost Sadat his life.

▶ Alaska Pipeline Opens

On June 20 crude oil began coursing through the Alaska pipeline from the North Slope oil fields to refineries in

TRANS-ALASKA PIPELINE TERMINAL

Valdez 799 miles away. Oil companies estimated the multimillion-dollar project would be able to supply 1.2 million barrels of oil a day, almost 10 percent of the U.S. daily consumption.

Environmentalists opposed the pipeline, fearful that it would leak and contaminate pristine Arctic wilderness. Many Alaskans, however, supported the project because of the new jobs and money it would bring to the state. Without the pipeline, oil companies argued, the vast oil fields near Prudhoe Bay would be unreachable. Ice covered the bay most of the year, thereby locking ships out.

The 1973 OPEC oil embargo broke the stalemate. The need for oil seemed to outweigh any risks involved. Construction began the next year.

▶ Punk Prodigies

Punk rockers took rock 'n' roll back to its rebellious roots and threw it back out with a loud, raw sound. Clad in torn T-shirts, dog collars, and stuck with safety pins, the wild-looking punkers railed against what rock had become—formulaic, heavy, and far too corporate. All one really needed was a nihilistic attitude and a lot of volume.

In the U.S., New York City was the incubator for innovative punk artists like Patti Smith, Talking Heads, and Televi-

• **JANUARY 17**
The U.S. carries out its first death sentence in ten years when a firing squad in Utah shoots convicted murderer Gary Gilmore.

• **FEBRUARY 25**
Ugandan President Idi Amin detains 240 Americans and accuses U.S. of plotting against him. They are freed four days later unharmed.

• **MARCH 27**
Two 747s collide on the runway at the airport in Tenerife, Canary Islands, killing 574. The accident is the worst in aviation history.

• **APRIL 23**
Ethiopia expels U.S. citizens and diplomats in retaliation for aid restrictions based on human rights violations.

• **MAY 17**
Menachem Begin becomes Israel's prime minister.

• **JUNE 16**
Rocket scientist Werner von Braun dies of cancer at 65 in Alexandria, Virginia.

• **JULY 13-14**
25-hour blackout in New York unleashes crime spree.

sion. Across the Atlantic, in England, the Clash fused their hyper-driven sound with Jamaican reggae.

But the most outrageous were the Sex Pistols, a group assembled by British clothing entrepreneur Malcolm McLaren. "McLaren understood that rock and roll was the most important, perhaps the only, kind of culture the young truly cared about," wrote critic Greil Marcus. "Everything else (fashion, slang, sexual style) flowed from rock and roll."

To front the Pistols, McLaren chose a pimply faced youth whose disdain for personal hygiene begat his stage name, Johnny Rotten. It didn't matter that he couldn't sing because the rest of the band couldn't play. What mattered was their shock value. The Pistols spit on the audience, smashed bottles on critics' heads, and caused mayhem wherever they went. "I don't understand it," Rotten mused to a reporter. "All we're trying to do is destroy everything."

The Pistols destroyed themselves within two years. Punk outlived them only to become one of the things it hated most—a commercially viable form of music.

▶ SON OF SAM

Heat wasn't the only reason women in New York City wore their hair up or short during the summer of 1977. They did it to save their lives.

For more than a year, the city and surrounding suburbs lay in the grip of a maniacal serial killer who called himself "Son of Sam." He killed seven people and wounded nine others. Most of his victims were women with long hair. He hunted his prey at night, usually stalking couples parked in secluded spots. His preferred weapon was a .44-caliber revolver. Beside his choice of gun, the killer left other clues—incoherent, misspelled letters written neatly in black ink.

"I am the 'monster'-'Beelzebub'-the

ROOTS

ABC's gamble on a fictionalized family history called *Roots* became the most-watched television drama in history. Almost half the country was glued to their sets for eight nights in January to watch the saga of an African slave named Kunta Kinte and his descendants.

Independent producer David Wolper bought the rights to film *Roots* from author Alex Haley and convinced ABC that the popular book would make an equally popular miniseries.

Roots outstripped all expectations.

CICELY TYSON AND MAYA ANGELOU IN *ROOTS*

Wolper's production was a graphic tour de force. Critics attacked it as pseudo-history, the "shackles, whips, and lust" view of slavery. But the sheer number of viewers—100 million—said much more. ABC aired the show again in 1978, then spun off *Roots: the Next Generations* the following year. Tracing one's roots became important to many.

chubby behemouth (sic)," he said in a letter addressed to an officer investigating the crimes. "I love to hunt. Prowling the streets looking for fair game… The wemon (sic) of Queens are the prettyist of all… I don't want to kill any more."

The pudgy 24-year-old smiled when police arrested him on August 10 near his apartment in Yonkers. "Well, you've got me," he said. In exchange for his guilty pleas, David Berkowitz was sentenced to spend life in jail.

"I am so glad I've been apprehended," he wrote during a psychiatric evaluation. "I am not well not at all."

■ TRENDS & TRIVIA

Fleetwood Mac releases the album *Rumours*.

J. R. R. Tolkien's *The Silmarillion* is published.

Writing found in Mesopotamia dates back to 10,000 B.C.

Clogs are popular shoes for men and women.

The Rocky Horror Picture Show and *Monty Python and the Holy Grail* become cult classics.

Toni Morrison's *Song of Solomon* is published.

Woody Allen's *Annie Hall* makes menswear popular for women.

Magnetic resonance imaging (MRI) is introduced.

Generic products become a cheaper alternative to brand-name products.

Jimmy Carter is the first U.S. President to walk in his inaugural parade.

The U.S. tests first space shuttle.

Volkswagen announces it will no longer make the Beetle.

Astronomers discover rings around Uranus.

Debby Boone releases "You Light Up My Life."

The Love Boat sets sail on TV.

George Lucas directs *Star Wars*.

CHEWBACCA AND HAN SOLO IN *STAR WARS*

303

● AUGUST 16
Elvis "The King" Presley dies in Memphis, Tennessee, at 42.

● AUGUST 19
Bushy-browed comic Groucho Marx dies at 77.

● SEPTEMBER 21
Director of U.S. Office of Management and Budget Bert Lance resigns because of financial improprieties.

◄ OCTOBER 21
Ali Maow Maalin of Somalia contracts smallpox—believed to be the last naturally occurring case.

● NOVEMBER 28
Rhodesia's Prime Minister Ian Smith says he will give blacks voting rights.

● DECEMBER
Amnesty International wins Nobel Peace Prize.

● DECEMBER 25
Charlie Chaplin dies at 88 in Switzerland.

The Camp David Accords brought Israel and Egypt together in a remarkable example of summit diplomacy.

The two nations had reached an impasse in 1978 because Israel would not relinquish the West Bank and the Gaza Strip and refused to stop building new settlements in those areas. As relations between the two nations worsened, U.S. President Jimmy Carter planned a rescue mission. He invited Israeli Prime Minister Menachem Begin (right) and Egyptian President Anwar Sadat (left) to visit him at Camp David in September.

At first, they met together. But when Carter realized his guests did not get along, he met each one separately. For days, the President and Secretary of State Cyrus Vance scurried between the leaders' cabins to relay demands. Finally, after Carter agreed to help Israel build new airfields in the Negev Desert, Begin relinquished full control of the Sinai. Sadat, in turn, gave Israel access to the Suez Canal, Strait of Tiran, and the Gulf of Aqaba. The leaders pledged to resolve the issue of self-government for Palestinians living in the West Bank and Gaza Strip within five years.

304

▶ POLISH PONTIFF

The Catholic Church elected its first non-Italian pope in four centuries, a charismatic, 58-year-old Pole named Karol Wojtyla (below). The first pontiff from behind the Iron Curtain was a visible threat to the Soviet Union because it proved that despite the most concerted efforts, communism had not dislodged God from people's hearts.

John Paul II, as Wojtyla became, was a conservative theologian uninterested in sweeping reforms. He refused to lift bans on abortion, birth control, or women in the priesthood. Instead, he devoted his considerable energy to reaching out to every corner of the globe. A pontiff for the jet age, John Paul visited more than 150 countries to establish what one biographer called "an omnipresent papacy."

His willingness to travel increased the church's visibility in the Third World, where it had been losing members to Marxist ideology and Protestant missionaries. "Having lived in a country that had to fight for its existence...I have understood exploitation," he told an interviewer. "I put myself immediately on the side of the poor, the disinherited, the oppressed...and the defenseless."

▶ JONESTOWN MASSACRE

The U.S. experienced a religious revival in the 1970s, and a host of charismatic sects cropped up to meet the new need for spirituality. While many were harmless, some were dangerous cults run by unbalanced fanatics who demanded total obedience.

One such leader was Jim Jones, who led the People's Temple in San Francisco. The self-proclaimed reincarnation of Jesus and Lenin led his 900-member flock to a new promised land in South America. There, in the sweltering jungles of Guyana, they built a commune they named Jonestown.

About a year after the 1977 exodus, California Congressman Leo Ryan started getting reports that Jones kept members against their will and forced them to rehearse a mass suicide as a "loyalty test."

Ryan flew to Guyana to investigate, accompanied by a reporter, two photographers, and an observer. When several cult members begged Ryan to help them escape, Jones ordered the deaths of Ryan and his team, then announced that "the time has come to meet in another place." Cult members lined up to drink a lethal cyanide punch, then collapsed in each other's arms. Jones surveyed the carnage he'd caused, then shot himself in the head.

▶ DISCO FEVER

Disco fever, the trend that engulfed a nation, was based on a made-up story written by a writer who let his journalistic ethics slip. Yet even though the names and situations described in Nik Cohn's *New York* magazine cover story were fictitious, the concept behind them was not.

The New York metro area—indeed most of America—was filled with people who toiled away in menial jobs all week to save up for that one Big Night Out at the disco. There, on the multicolored lighted dance floor, in their tight polyester clothing and platform shoes, they let their dancing prowess turn them into momentary kings and queens.

Cohn sensed this, yet was unwilling to spend time reporting the story. He visited

• **JANUARY 4**
Chilean President Augusto Pinochet wins vote of confidence after UN condemns his regime for human rights violations. Elections are suspended until 1986.

• **FEBRUARY 15**
Leon Spinks dethrones Muhammad Ali as the heavyweight champ. Ali wins it back in November.

• **MARCH 19**
Amoco Cadiz runs aground off the coast of France and unleashes the worst oil spill to date–24 million gallons.

▶ **MAY 9**
Italian Prime Minister Aldo Moro's body is found eight weeks after he was kidnapped by Red Brigade terrorists.

• **JUNE 6**
Californians stage a tax revolt by voting in Proposition 13, designed to eliminate 7 billion dollars in property taxes.

• **JUNE 10**
Affirmed wins the Triple Crown, ridden by 18-year-old Steve Cauthen.

a Brooklyn disco twice, then returned in the daylight to get a feel for local culture. The rest was nothing more than hunches and good writing.

New York published Cohn's story in June 1976. One of the many readers was Robert Stigwood, the producer of *Jesus Christ Superstar*. Stigwood was looking for a vehicle for his new client, John Travolta (below), and playing an Italian disco dancer seemed a natural. Cohn's article became *Saturday Night Fever*, the smash-hit movie and soundtrack of 1978.

"Fevermania… was something I'd never bargained for…," he confessed two decades later. "*Fever* had taken on a life of its own…. 'Stayin' Alive' and Travolta's white suit, above all, with the tight vest and billowing flared trousers, and his right hand pointing to the stars…had entered pop mythology, embedding themselves in the collective memory, until they came, for many, to define a whole decade."

▶ REFINING RACIAL DISCRIMINATION
Allan Bakke's fight to get into medical school came to define reverse discrimination. Race could no longer be the decisive factor for school admission, the Supreme Court ruled, although it could play an important role in promoting diversity.

Bakke, a white man in his early 30s, tried twice to get into medical school at the University of California's campus at Davis. After the second rejection, he hired a lawyer. He contended the school's quotas for "disadvantaged students" illegally excluded qualified candidates like himself because of his race. In the wake of the Civil Rights Act, most universities had adopted affirmative action policies to recruit minority candidates with, at times, weaker qualifications than other applicants.

Four years after Bakke filed suit, the Supreme Court handed down its decision. Four justices ruled in favor of Bakke, another four ruled against him, and one, Lewis Powell, seemed to do a bit of both.

"Preferring members of any one group for no reason other than race or ethnic origin is discrimination for its own sake," Powell wrote. "Ethnic diversity is…only one element in a range of factors a university may properly consider in attaining a goal of a heterogeneous student body."

TEST-TUBE BABY

Like most babies, Louise Brown was a miracle to her parents. Healthy and dainty, she looked nothing like a groundbreaking scientific experiment. But she was; Louise was the first human conceived outside the womb.

Her mother, Lesley Brown, was unable to conceive because of defective fallopian tubes. She and her husband, John, turned to gynecologist Patrick Steptoe and his colleague, Robert Edwards, for help. The doctors were well known in England for their pioneering experiments with artificial insemination, a process that involved creating an embryo in a laboratory dish and inserting the fertilized egg into a woman's uterus. To date they'd had no success.

Louise's birth on July 25 was a shocking revelation. "Making reproduction synonymous with manufacturing is an abhorrent picture coming into view," thundered one theologian. The hubbub did not stop scientists from exploring the new field of genetic engineering. In vitro became a safe, if not reliable, alternative.

• JUNE 30
Public opposition forces U.S. government to halt construction of nuclear power plant project in Seabrook, New Hampshire.

• OCTOBER 13
Police in New York charge Sex Pistols' guitarist Sid Vicious with the murder of girlfriend Nancy Spungeon.

• NOVEMBER 8
American painter Norman Rockwell dies at 84 at his home in Stockbridge, Massachusetts.

• NOVEMBER 15
Anthropologist Margaret Mead dies of cancer at 76.

• DECEMBER 8
Former Israeli Prime Minister Golda Meir dies at 80 of viral hepatitis.

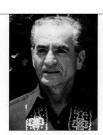

◀ DECEMBER 29
Millions march against the Shah in Iran.

I ran became the world's first Islamic republic in 1979 after a revolution against the Shah. The country's new leader was a 78-year-old cleric, Ayatollah Ruhollah Khomeini.

To Khomeini and his devout Shiite followers (below), the Shah's path of modernization through Westernization went against the tenets of Islam. Exiled in 1964, Khomeini continued to inspire his followers from afar, preaching through recorded messages. Fourteen years later, the revolt he advocated began. A strike by millions of Iranian workers flared into wholesale rebellion. The

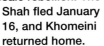

Shah fled January 16, and Khomeini returned home.

When President Carter allowed the Shah to enter the U.S for medical treatment in November, students in Tehran stormed the American embassy and took 66 hostages. They released 13 two weeks later, but refused to free the rest until the U.S. delivered the Shah.

Carter's failure to free the hostages torpedoed his chance for reelection. Hours after his successor, Ronald M. Reagan, took the oath of office, Iran released the 52 hostages. The 444-day crisis was over.

▶ SOVIETS INVADE AFGHANISTAN

The rugged mountainous landscape bore little resemblance to the lush jungles of Southeast Asia. Still the similarity was striking; as a Soviet writer noted (below), the 1979 Soviet invasion of Afghanistan looked like a potential Vietnam.

AFGHANISTAN: SOVIET VIETNAM

TEXT AND PHOTOGRAPHS BY Vladislav Tamarov

Soviet leaders said the Afghan Marxist government sought its assistance in quashing a formidable guerrilla group called the Mujahidin. Though poorly equipped, the rebels controlled almost all of the country's 28 provinces. The threat of losing an important border state to Islamic extremists was too real for the Soviets. After toppling a weak puppet-leader in Kabul, 80,000 Soviet troops dispersed to secure the rest of the country.

The U.S., China, and Pakistan demanded an immediate withdrawal, at which the Soviets thumbed their noses. But the Mujahidin could not be dismissed as easily. For them, the fight was a *jihad*, an Islamic holy war against the infidels. "The Russians can't stay in Afghanistan," said one fighter. "Even the animals hate them."

Through sheer will—and the assistance of Great Britain, China, and the CIA—the Mujahidin defeated their enemy nine years later. Afghanistan wobbled to its feet, then fell again into civil war in the 1990s.

▶ BRITAIN'S IRON LADY

The victory of British Conservatives in the 1979 elections helped usher in an era of economic conservatism. Tory Prime Minister Margaret Thatcher (below) was one of the first in a string of world leaders who took office toward the century's end promising fewer taxes and less government.

The shopkeeper's daughter swept the country with promises to break the labor unions' powerful grip and revitalize the economy. Her Labour predecessors had courted union support to maintain social cohesion. As a result, the rate of productivity was one of the lowest in the industrial world.

The "Iron Lady" warned of tough times ahead, and she was correct. During her first year, England suffered the worst recession in more than 50 years. Unemployment rose at a time when decreased government spending meant fewer social services. Thatcher curtailed wage increases and slashed taxes for higher income groups. Inflation spiked at 22 percent, then declined.

The "Thatcher Revolution" lasted 11 years. As she promised, the unions' power had diminished and so had the welfare

- **JANUARY 25**
Former Vice President Nelson Rockefeller dies at 70 of a heart attack in New York City.

- **JANUARY 31**
The U.S. and China resume diplomatic relations.

- **MARCH 29**
Ugandan rebels seize country and force Idi Amin to flee.

- **APRIL 4**
Pakistan hangs former Prime Minister Ali Bhutto, convicted for attempting to kill a political rival.

- **APRIL 16**
Bill Rodgers sets new record for the Boston Marathon— 2 hours, 9 minutes, and 27 seconds.

- **MAY 25**
American Airlines DC-10 crashes after taking off from Chicago's O'Hare Airport, killing 272.

- **JUNE 10**
Pope John Paul II ends a nine-day visit to his homeland of Poland. His is the first papal visit to a communist country.

state. But those accomplishments came at a cost. Many old coal mines and shipyards closed, and the working-class way of life in some industrial towns never recovered.

▶ A SAINT AMONG US

An angel came to earth in the petite form of Mother Teresa (below). The frail, 69-year-old nun accepted the Nobel Peace Prize as she did everything else—in the name of the poorest of the poor.

The former Agnes Gonxha Bojaxhiu entered a convent when she was a teenager in Albania. She then moved to Calcutta to teach young girls in a convent school. There, in 1946, she received what she described later as her "call within a call" to serve the city's poor. Rome gave her mission its blessing, and she soon opened a hospice and orphanage. In 1950 she established an order, the Missionaries of Charity.

The order's ranks swelled to about 3,000 women who carried out Mother Teresa's mission on five continents in 87 countries. Her devotion to and respect for the world's cast-offs was unfailing. "I have been told I spoil the poor…," she said. "Well, at least one congregation is spoiling the poor, because everyone else is spoiling the rich."

▶ USING GOD FOR GAIN

Televangelists were not new in 1979. Billy Graham had been preaching via radio and TV since 1950; Jerry Falwell's "Old-Time Gospel Hour" debuted six years later. However, televangelists who formed their own

THREE MILE ISLAND

The Three Mile Island debacle in late March incorporated everyone's fears about the "friendly" atom. When one of the valves at a plant near Harrisburg, Pennsylvania, malfunctioned, coolant leaked out of one reactor, leaving its radioactive core partially exposed. If the reactor exploded, it would release radioactive fall-out in the atmosphere. Twelve days later, engineers had fixed the problem.

TEST OF RIVER WATER NEAR THREE MILE ISLAND

The atmosphere was unharmed, but the nuclear industry was damaged almost beyond repair. The Nuclear Regulatory Commission tightened standards for plant design and construction. Costs became so prohibitive that several projects already under way were scuttled. The energy source of the future had become an expensive, unpopular, and unsafe problem.

political action groups were novel, and Falwell was the maverick.

"This country is fed up with radical causes," the Baptist minister said, "fed up with the unisex movement, fed up with the departure from basics, from decency, from the philosophy of the monogamous home."

To rescue America from sinking into a 20th-century Sodom and Gomorrah, Falwell founded the Moral Majority in 1979. His goal was to build a formidable voting bloc of Christian conservatives that pushed for appropriate legislation. "Get them saved, baptized, and registered," he told his staff.

The Moral Majority and other groups like it on the religious right soon exercised enormous power in the Republican Party.

■ TRENDS & TRIVIA

Sony introduces the Walkman.

Trivial Pursuit becomes a popular board game.

The U.S. Treasury issues the Susan B. Anthony dollar coin.

Donna Summer releases "Bad Girls."

Pink Floyd releases "The Wall."

Nadine Gordimer's *Burger's Daughter* is published.

Henry Kissinger's *The White House Years* is published.

Dustin Hoffman and Meryl Streep star in *Kramer vs. Kramer.*

Sigourney Weaver stars in *Alien.*

CBS's *Knots Landing* debuts as a nighttime soap opera.

Larry Bird and Earvin "Magic" Johnson glamorize college basketball in the NCAA championship.

William Styron's *Sophie's Choice* is published.

Treat Williams stars in Milos Forman's film version of *Hair.*

Voyager I sends back first pictures of Jupiter.

Elaine Pagel's *Gnostic Gospels* is published.

Art imitates life too closely in *The China Syndrome.*

Dudley Moore and Bo Derek star in *10.*

Sylvester Stallone directs and stars in *Rocky II.*

Performance art becomes a new art form.

"Palimony" suits are in the news.

307

- JUNE 11
Actor John Wayne dies of cancer at 72.

- JULY 5
Parliament on England's tiny Isle of Man turns 1,000 years old.

- AUGUST 3
U.S. Secretary of Health, Education, and Welfare's Patricia Harris becomes the first black female Cabinet member.

- AUGUST 30
India's last viceroy, Earl Mountbatten, dies when an IRA bomb blows up his fishing boat.

- OCTOBER 29
Police arrest 1,045 "No Nukes" protesters on Wall Street, the 50th anniversary of the 1929 stock market crash.

- NOVEMBER
Former California Governor Ronald Reagan announces he will run for President.

- DECEMBER 27
U.S. government loans the Chrysler Corporation 1.75 billion dollars. The car manufacturer repays the loan in 1984.

ENVIRONMENT

by John G. Mitchell
NATIONAL GEOGRAPHIC SENIOR ASSISTANT EDITOR, ENVIRONMENT

In the May 1901 issue of NATIONAL GEOGRAPHIC, an article on Alaska appeared under the byline of Henry Gannett, the Chief Geographer of the United States Geological Survey. Gannett, whose efforts had helped establish Yellowstone as the world's first national park, had recently cruised the coast of the great northern territory and pronounced it a glorious wonder. But he was troubled, too. Gannett had looked behind the fetching littoral scenery and found that some of Alaska's natural resources were being drastically depleted. "The gathering of furs and skins," he wrote, "has been prosecuted so actively that the fur trade is now of comparatively little consequence." The sea otter had become rare, he warned, and fur seals, reduced to a fraction of their former number. "Even the great brown bear has become scarce and shy," he went on, "and hides in the fastness of the interior."

Left: Redwood National Park, California   Middle: Poison-arrow frogs, Costa Rica Right: Pumping the aquifer, Nebraska

Henry Gannett served as president of the National Geographic Society from 1910 until his death in 1914. If his observations and alarms did not immediately shape the course of resource conservation in this country—protection for marine mammals, for instance, would have to wait until 1972—his concern surely presaged how persistently the Society and its magazine would cover the environment story through the rest of the 20th century.

That story, of course, had opened even before Gannett's Alaskan tour, not in Alaska but in the hills of the Northeast and the wilderness valleys of California, where lumbermen were cutting down some of the nation's last great forests. Gannett himself had warned, in May 1899, that "the clearing away" of the redwood forests of the Pacific Coast might well lead to "the end of the species as a source of lumber." Others at the time feared the loss of forests because they recognized trees as anchors of the soil, purifiers of water, and fonts of refreshment for the human spirit. In reaction to industrial abuses in the woods, thousands of Americans began to protest, swelling the membership rosters of the Sierra Club, the Association for the Protection of the Adirondacks, and sundry other organizations of the conservationist persuasion. And then there was Theodore Roosevelt.

"The preservation of the forests is vital to the welfare of every country," President Roosevelt declared in a 1905 speech reprinted in NATIONAL GEOGRAPHIC. "If we permit the natural resources of this land to be destroyed so that we hand over to our children a heritage diminished in value, we thereby prove our unfitness to stand in the forefront of civilized peoples." TR acted on his convictions. In his 8 years in office (1901-1909), he established some 20 national monuments and parks and the nation's first wildlife refuges, and he added millions of acres to the forest reserves.

But the lumber industry's appetite for big trees still threatened the giant sequoias of California. In 1915 Gilbert H. Grosvenor, then Editor of NATIONAL GEOGRAPHIC, photographed 20 of his colleagues joining hands to encircle the largest of them all, the General Sherman tree, the "king of all treedom," in Sequoia National Park. In an article accompanying that photograph the following year, the GEOGRAPHIC warned that a thousand acres of the best sequoias still remained at risk on private lands. Inviting donations from its members, the Society raised $20,000 to purchase several of the private tracts, and turned them over to the National Park Service.

Throughout the first half of the 20th century, the effort to create new parks and protect old forests dominated much of the nation's conservation agenda. But for many activists, no place was truly wild without wildlife, and that wildlife needed protection no less than trees. In what might seem to modern minds an ironic twist, the earliest leaders of the wildlife conservation movement were hunters, and avid ones at that. George Bird Grinnell, a founder of the big-game trophy-scoring Boone & Crockett Club, had launched the first Audubon Society in 1886, two years before the debut of the National Geographic Society. William T. Hornaday of the New York Zoological Society also cherished the smell of gunpowder and the taste of wild flesh. But in 1907 he posted 12 captive bison to one of Theodore Roosevelt's new refuges in Oklahoma, achieving what no individual or government had ever attempted—the recovery of a creature that, a few years earlier, had been on the brink of extinction.

NATIONAL GEOGRAPHIC's attitude toward wildlife at the turn of the century leaned more toward consumptive use than conservation, as illustrated by the multiple dispatches appearing in the magazine in 1910-11 to celebrate the hunting prowess of our former President, Theodore Roosevelt, on safari in Africa. It wasn't long, however, before the Society's heroes would be stalking animals with cameras rather than rifles, and celebrating efforts to save the tigers of India, the elephants of Africa, the brown bears of North America, and the great whales of the seven seas. As the magazine pursued the global story of wildlife's last hurrahs, the Society began to post its burgeoning book and television divisions afield to cover the story as well. From George Shiras's two-volume 1898 epic, *Hunting Wild Life With Camera and Flashlight*, to photographer Joel Sartore's and writer Douglas Chadwick's *The Company We Keep*, a 1996 opus on the Endangered Species Act, Geographic's Book Division has explored the habits and habitats of creatures great and small in every continent and clime. National Geographic Television first ventured into conservation programming in 1991.

Even before television brought raw nature to the living room, before the phrase "environmental protection" replaced "conservation" in the vernacular of government and the media, a number of events would begin to cause some Americans to wonder if they, too, might soon qualify as an endangered species. Among the warning signs at mid-century was the fact that the ambient air in some cities had become difficult to breathe, and the water in both city and rural communities unfit to drink. Possibly the most ominous event occurred in 1948, in Pennsylvania's coke- and steel-making Monongahela Valley, when a weeklong atmospheric inversion nailed a lid of brown smoke over the little city of Donora. By the time the lid lifted, 20 Donorans were dead.

As the century turned 60 and the United States entered a long decade of doubt and dissent, a new generation of environmentalists came of age to challenge some of the assumptions of the postwar feel-good years. Was the American Dream truly a home in the shade-tree suburbs, or were suburbs merely the prelude to urban sprawl? Why did interstate highways always skewer so many parks—or poor neighborhoods? Why did coal stripminers seem to have a right to decapitate the hilltops and poison the creeks? Did pesticides promise agricultural abundance—or a path to a "silent spring"?

These questions framed some of the major environmental issues of the 1960s, but there were other battles brewing on territory long familiar to readers of NATIONAL GEOGRAPHIC. In Arizona the Sierra Club squared off with the U.S. Bureau of Reclamation, which wanted to turn the Grand Canyon into a reservoir. GEOGRAPHIC had first sung the praises of the canyon in 1893 and would continue to do so in some 20 articles over the next 104 years. Protective of its status as a tax-deductible, nonprofit organization, the magazine did not take sides in this fray; it didn't have to. The Sierra Club won the battle of the Grand Canyon (but lost its own tax-deductible status, plus Glen Canyon upstream, in the process).

In South Florida developers and federal transportation planners proposed to build a huge international jetport athwart one of the crucial headwaters of Everglades National Park. Proponents managed to sneak in a "training" runway before their scheme was spiked, largely because of the efforts of one organization, the National Audubon Society, and one influential Floridian, Nathaniel P. Reed (now a trustee of the National Geographic Society). By then, the ecological values of the Everglades should have been well known to readers of the magazine. Since 1896 Geographic, had taken them there, at least vicariously, more than a dozen times.

In California the last of the redwoods were at risk. After Henry Gannett's cautionary tale in 1899, Geographic writers and photographers had visited the tall trees periodically to acclaim their magnificence and the ongoing effort to save them from destruction. In 1964 Melville Bell Grosvenor and Paul A. Zahl reported that a Society expedition had measured the "Mt. Everest of All Living Things" on a horseshoe bend of Redwood Creek in Humboldt County. The discovery of the world's tallest tree, at 367.8 feet, in no small measure boosted the long campaign to create a Redwood National Park, which was finally established in 1968.

The first Earth Day, April 22, 1970, marked a sea change in the environmental protection movement: It was going professional, staffed with environmental lawyers and eco-technicians chasing down dozens of newfangled issues. But National Geographic managed to keep track of it. A chronological selection of magazine stories over the past quarter century more or less mirrors the march of major environmental events and issues.

December 1970: Geographic devotes 62 pages to "Our Ecological Crisis," a follow-up to Earth Day. The focus is on air and water pollution. April 1979: "The Promise and Peril of Nuclear Energy." Within a few days of that story's publication, a reactor melts down at Pennsylvania's Three Mile Island. February 1980: "The Pesticide Dilemma." By poisoning the pests, asked the Editor, "are we also unwittingly poisoning ourselves?" February 1981: Following a revolution in Iran and waiting lines at the gas pumps, a special issue on "Energy," examining the nation's profligate use of nonrenewable energy resources. November 1981: "Acid Rain." January 1983: "Tropical Rain Forests." March 1985: "Hazardous Wastes. . . Storing Up Trouble." In December 1988, at the end of the Society's centennial year, the magazine asked, "Can man save this fragile Earth?" Geographic editors and contributors filled that month's issue searching for answers, from the rain forests of Brazil to the Arctic slope of Alaska, among whale researchers, nature-conserving businessmen, and human population biologists.

The Society continued to probe the most crucial environmental issues through the final decade of the 20th century. The oil-stained aftermath of Operation Desert Storm. The continuing destruction of wetlands in the U.S. (despite political promises of "no net loss"). The tragic lesson of Chernobyl and the legacy of industrial pollution in Eastern Europe. The imperfect present and perilous future of ocean fisheries, marine sanctuaries, coral reefs, and barrier islands. The unregulated scourge of poison runoff. Another special issue, this one on "The Power, Promise, and Turmoil of North America's Fresh Water." Between 1994 and 1998, moreover, Geographic examined the state of the United States' public lands, revisiting the policies and problems of the national parks, forests, wildlife refuges, and wilderness areas previously treated systematically in the magazine in the 1970s.

Staying up to speed with this much-embattled idea called the environment was not easy. In his introduction to the December 1988 centennial issue, on saving the fragile Earth, Gilbert M. Grosvenor, then President and Chairman of the Society's Board, confessed that he was worried. "I worry," he wrote, "that we did not do enough soon enough to warn our members about what was happening." Therefore, he went on, "The responsibility lies squarely with us. Will future generations praise our foresight or look back in anger and dismay at what we had, and what we lost forever?"

1980-

1989

"All Right We Are Two Nations"

by Michael Kazin
PROFESSOR OF HISTORY, AMERICAN UNIVERSITY

THE LOS ANGELES COLISEUM ON JULY 28, 1984, felt like the center of the world. President Ronald Reagan, former Hollywood actor, opened the Olympic Games on a warm, smogless afternoon to the cheers of 93,000 spectators (each of whom had paid at least 50 dollars per seat) and a television audience of more than a billion. Earlier that day, the President had met with the U.S. team and urged the athletes to "Set your sights high, then go for it. Do it for yourself, for your family, for your country." He didn't need to remind them that 15 communist nations were boycotting the Games in an act of symbolic revenge. Four years earlier, the U.S. and *its* closest allies had snubbed the Olympics in Moscow to protest the Soviet invasion of Afghanistan.

Despite the echoes of the Cold War, or perhaps because of them, the Los Angeles Games were a star-spangled triumph. U.S. athletes won 174 medals, three times more than competitors from any other nation. A horde of unpaid local volunteers ensured that the Games would make a profit, and a security network costing 50 million dollars helped keep them free of trouble. That fall, as Reagan ran for reelection, his campaign aired video clips of Olympic crowds chanting, "U.S.A! U.S.A.!" while yet another young American ran, jumped, swam, or dribbled to victory. The sheen of those glorious summer days helped the ever

Opposite: Ronald Reagan's affability and strong conservatism helped him retain the Presidency for most of the decade.
Preceding pages: Berliners demolish the wall between communism and capitalism in 1989, marking the end of the Cold War.

buoyant incumbent to crush his Democratic rival, Walter F. Mondale, by a margin of 512 electoral votes.

Not all residents of Los Angeles in the mid-1980s were in a mood to wave flags and cheer for the President, however. About a mile from the coliseum, gangs of young blacks and Latinos waged deadly battles to control the booming market for crack cocaine, an inexpensive and frequently lethal drug. Elsewhere in California, the aerospace, computer, and entertainment industries produced decent wages for many and fortunes for a few. But in Los Angeles, unemployment among black youths averaged 45 percent, and a majority of the jobless were high-school dropouts. In the much ballyhooed "information age," a college education was the indispensable ticket to a comfortable future. One day in the mid-1980s, when the port of San Pedro, near Los Angeles, advertised a few entry-level jobs, 50,000 eager young Californians lined up to apply. Meanwhile, in downtown L.A., homeless people proliferated, begging handouts from lawyers and accountants.

Reforms by Premier Mikhail Gorbachev in the 1980s led to the collapse of the Soviet Union in 1991.

DURING THE 1980S SUCH CONTRASTS between anguish and ambition became increasingly commonplace. Though still one society under law, Americans increasingly lived inside subcultures that shared little beyond a common government and, usually, the English language. In the 1920s, the novelist John Dos Passos had written about the United States, "...all right we are two nations."

Sixty years later the divisions still ran along lines of wealth and race, moral values, and political ideology. Ronald Reagan's America was predominately white and overwhelmingly Christian; it was not unified by economic class but by a faith in property rights and military prowess and a deep mistrust of liberals and all their works. The other America was a more fragmented place: Its members clustered around one or more proud, if embattled, identities—gay, lesbian, feminist, African American, environmentalist. They did, however, share a fierce defense of gains made by social movements in the 1960s and 1970s that the Reagan Administration wanted to reverse: federal programs for the poor and racial minorities, opposition to military adventures abroad, and a mass culture that prized self-expression.

In this contest, the President and his supporters usually had the upper hand. Reagan's electoral triumph in 1980 brought to national power a conservative movement that had been growing inside and outside the Republican Party since the 1950s. The American right was an amalgam of the well-heeled and the morally outraged: corporate executives who chafed at strong unions and federal regulators, evangelical Protestants concerned about abortion and sexual permissiveness, tradition-minded intellectuals unhappy with the leftward drift of the academy. Both the National Association of Manufacturers and the Southern Baptist Convention (the largest Protestant body in the nation) lent prestige and resources to the conservative cause. Once dismissed as "extreme," the American right had learned to emphasize mainstream concerns about rising taxes and violent crime. Conservatives had their differences, but these faded before the need to unite against the Soviet Union and its clients around the world.

Reagan was the perfect figure to bridge the gap between the ideology of the right and ordinary voters who cared little for any species of political doctrine. A former Democrat and union president (of the Screen Actors Guild), the President touched cultural chords in many white voters who had soured on liberal Democrats but were uncomfortable with the wealthy image of the traditional right. With a natural, quip-ready style honed during decades of acting and public speaking, Reagan skewered both left-wing dictators abroad and liberal "special interests" at home. But he was also the consummate optimist: unfailingly upbeat about what America had done in the past and, if only government would "get off their backs," the great things its citizens could accomplish in the future. The President's calming wit after being wounded in an assassination attempt just two months after taking office—"please tell me you're all Republicans," he told surgeons—also endeared him to many Americans. Not since John F. Kennedy had the White House been occupied by a man who looked and sounded so good. For Reagan, the image-making was all. In private meetings, relying on notes prepared by aides, he got lost when the discussion went beyond the material on his three- by five-inch cards. Critics scorned his "no-hands" approach to the office. But American conservatism had never had so skillful a spokesman. "He knows so little," marveled one adviser, "and accomplishes so much."

REAGAN'S MAIN DOMESTIC PRIORITY WAS ECONOMIC. Unemployment, poverty, and inflation had all increased during the 1970s, as had the taxes paid by middle-class Americans. Soon after taking office, Reagan proposed a major tax cut and a huge boost in military spending to challenge adversaries abroad. Both measures passed Congress rather easily, despite fears they would hike the budget deficit. But the President and many other conservatives had embraced the "supply-side" theory, developed by economist Arthur Laffer, which predicted that lower overall tax rates, for both individuals and businesses, would spur a surge in growth. The happy consequence, Reagan expected, would be a torrent of actual revenues, enough to pay for both a stronger military and a "safety net" for any Americans who remained poor.

The results were not quite so glorious. The national debt climbed steadily through the decade, quadrupling to 2.7 trillion dollars by the time Reagan left office. And the economy got sicker before recovering. A recession that began in 1981 and ended in 1983 pushed unemployment over 10 percent—the highest level since the Great Depression. The suffering was worst in the industrial Midwest; steel and auto companies, battered by foreign competitors, laid off thousands of workers who had expected their unionized jobs to last until they retired. Reagan's popularity rating dipped as low as 41 percent. By 1984 military contracts and high-technology industries were feeding a boom, particularly in the Sunbelt states where the

Republican Party had its base. But the gap between rich Americans and all others grew wider.

During his years in office, Reagan and his allies in Congress moved aggressively to weaken "special interests" that resisted their agenda. In 1981 he fired and blacklisted 12,000 unionized air-traffic controllers who had walked off their jobs. As federal workers, the controllers had no right to strike, but Reagan's action was meant to deliver a stern message to all of organized labor: The days of government neutrality in industrial relations were over. The President issued a similar challenge to environmental and civil rights groups. He appointed men and women to run the Interior Department and the Environmental Protection Agency who wanted to open public lands to corporate development and were disinclined to spend federal money cleaning up toxic waste dumps. Federal judgeships and key posts in the Justice Department were filled with opponents of affirmative action. As for abortion, a major issue for the Christian right but one that divided the Republican Party, Reagan gave the pro-life cause a handful of supportive speeches but did almost nothing to promote its Human Life Amendment in Congress.

In foreign policy, the administration combined militant rhetoric with actions designed to make any foes of the U.S. perpetually nervous. Since the U.S. defeat in Vietnam, revolutionary forces in the Third World had gained strength, and the bloc of nations dominated by the U.S.S.R. had supplied many of them with arms and counsel. Determined to redress the balance, the administration funneled arms and money to counterrevolutionary guerrillas in Afghanistan and Angola. Militaries in the Central American nations of El Salvador and Guatemala were backed to the hilt as they fought to defeat left-wing rebels sympathetic to Fidel Castro's Cuba. In the fall of 1983, 5,000 U.S. troops invaded the tiny Caribbean island of Grenada to oust a radical regime mired in internal bloodletting. The odds were ridiculously lopsided, but the American victory marked a change from previous U.S. policy: a pro-communist government had been toppled, not merely "contained."

The crusade against the Red menace occasionally boomeranged. The White House appeared callous toward human rights when it refused to pressure the rulers of South Africa—stalwart anticommunists—to abandon their brutal system of apartheid. And the administration defied laws passed by Congress in order to help the Nicaraguan Contras, the guerrilla army it had helped organize to overthrow the Sandinista government. In late 1986 one phase of this secret project, involving a scheme to use money from illicit weapons sales to Iran, blew up into a major scandal that would dog the administration's foreign policy till the end.

Although the President could not take on the Soviet Union militarily without incinerating the planet, he and his policymakers sought to keep the Kremlin off balance. As some Pentagon officials mused about the advantages of waging a "limited nuclear war," new U.S. missiles were deployed in Western Europe, despite the vocal opposition of millions of Europeans. In 1983 Reagan announced a Strategic Defense Initiative, intended to protect the U.S. against nuclear attack with a vast network of small missiles and sensing devices. The very prospect of having to match so costly a program (which the U.S. media quickly dubbed "Star Wars") alarmed Soviet officials, who were struggling to modernize their sclerotic economy. That same year, during an address to evangelical ministers, the President labeled the U.S.S.R. an "evil empire" and suggested its demise was imminent.

Conservatives were thrilled that the U.S. was on the march again. Representatives from the other America vigorously disagreed. Antiwar activists feared the administration was flirting with nuclear war and argued that developing nations like Nicaragua should be free to choose their own allies and shape their own economies. A broad movement persuaded voters in several states to pass resolutions demanding a "nuclear freeze," and many liberal churches vowed to give sanctuary to any serviceman or woman who refused to serve in Central America. College students staged sit-ins demanding that no university funds be invested in companies that did business in South Africa.

The right's attempt to remake domestic politics met with an equally robust response —but an uncoordinated one that did little to alter national policy. Such groups as the Sierra Club and the National Organization for Women boosted their memberships but could not budge Reagan's stand on the environment or stem the growth of the right-to-life movement. Labor unions turned out a quarter of a million "solidarity" demonstrators in Washington, D.C., but seemed helpless to slow the erosion of their membership and political influence. The separatist Nation of Islam, led by Minister Louis Farrakhan, gained new stature among young blacks who had lost confidence in the dream of a color-blind society. Homosexual activists promoted "safe sex" as AIDS struck down thousands. President Reagan devoted no speech to the epidemic until 1987, preferring, in the words of his White House physician, to believe "it was [like] measles and would go away."

In 1989 the Chinese government brutally crushed a student-led demonstration for democratic reform in Beijing's Tiananmen Square.

The conflict between the two Americas was not merely a matter of political choices; clashing cultural tastes also played a part. A key terrain was popular music. Reagan's backers found comfort in spirituals and applauded country music hits like Merle Haggard's "Are the Good Times Really Over for Good?" (sample line: "Stop rollin' downhill like a snowball headed for hell.... Stand up for the flag and let's all ring the liberty bell"). Reagan detractors preferred Bruce Springsteen's bitter songs about plant closings and Vietnam veterans who had "Nowhere to run, got nowhere to go" or raps whose nervous beat and frank talk about drugs and sex evoked the realities of life in black urban neighborhoods.

Reagan's many opponents held fast to their convictions but, except during the recession of the early 1980s, they were never able to counter his appeal to millions of white Americans who trusted him to protect their security and economic interests and to endorse their spiritual beliefs. The President was also fortunate to be in office during a period when free-market ideology was on the rise throughout the developed world. Welfare states in both capitalist and socialist nations were crumbling almost everywhere under the weight of budget deficits and the market discipline imposed by global corporations.

Then, with remarkable speed, the "evil empire" unraveled. In 1985 Mikhail Gorbachev became leader of the Soviet Union and attempted to transform his nation into a more democratic and open society. He encouraged his fellow rulers in Eastern Europe to do the same. But few Communists were motivated to give up their power and privilege. By the end of the decade, their opportunity had passed. Under the pressure of grassroots movements, East Germany dissolved as a separate nation, and anticommunists rapidly, and, for the most part, nonviolently, seized power in Czechoslovakia, Bulgaria, Poland, Hungary, and Romania.

Could the Reagan administration take most of the credit for the demise of European communism? Certainly the President's ardent belief that such a fate was possible emboldened his allies on both sides of the Iron Curtain. "Mr. Gorbachev, tear down this wall," Reagan demanded in 1987 at the barrier separating East and West Berlin. Two years later, with George Bush in the White House, joyful Berliners themselves composed the demolition crew. But the other side, long depicted as implacable, essentially surrendered without a fight. Perhaps the true victor of the Cold War was consumer capitalism. Its promise and products trickled into minds and across heavily fortified borders, rendering absurd the claim that Communist rule provided a better life for ordinary people.

Ronald Reagan did preside over a sea change in American political life. During the 1980s most Americans came to agree with key elements of his conservative ideology: Business is overregulated, welfare programs are a waste of money, affirmative action is unfair to white people, communism is immoral and must be defeated. The huge budget deficit stymied the passage of new social programs. And conservative Republicans became politically competitive in almost every state in the nation—something liberal Democrats had never been able to claim.

Yet Reagan and the movement he led into power failed to address many social ills and exacerbated others. During the tenure of the supreme optimist, the poverty rate for children increased by more than 20 percent, AIDS claimed 55,000 lives, and an eightfold increase in the number of millionaires occurred while real wages remained stagnant. And the cultural gulf between the two Americas was wider than it had been at the beginning of the decade. In the spring of 1992 the black and Mexican-American neighborhoods of Los Angeles erupted in the worst urban riot since the 1960s.

Nevertheless, when Reagan left office at the age of 77 to return to California, he was more popular at the end of his tenure than any President since Franklin D. Roosevelt. That liberal icon was, ironically, also Reagan's first political hero. It had been quite a performance. ■

In Romania, and elsewhere in Eastern Europe, Vladimir Lenin's communism fell out of favor—and so did his memorials.

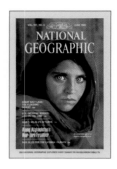

When Gilbert M. Grosvenor became the Society's President in 1980, he turned over the Editor's reins to Wilbur E. Garrett, a man with talent and imagination who had worked for the magazine since 1954. Grosvenor hated to give up "the best job in the world," but he wanted to oversee the organization's expansion into other areas. Garrett believed the GEOGRAPHIC should be as readable as it was beautiful. He opened the door to more provocative topics. A 1986 article on the human immune system angered some readers for its reference to AIDS. A year before, angry creationists canceled memberships over an article about prehistoric man.

Controversies did little to rain on Garrett's parade. In 1984 the GEOGRAPHIC won the magazine world's equivalent of a Pulitzer Prize—the National Magazine Award for General Excellence. It was an important achievement for the Society and for Garrett.

• Space Cowboys

To cover America's first manned spaceflight in six years, the GEOGRAPHIC hired a man already steeped in astronaut lore. Tom Wolfe profiled the country's space cowboys in his classic book, *The Right Stuff*. In the October 1981 issue he put the space shuttle *Columbia* in historic context.

"To me there was a touch of Rip Van Winkle about it all," he wrote. "After $54\frac{1}{2}$ hours in earth orbit an airplane—not a capsule or a command module but an airplane, a ship with wings—descends above the high desert of California.... The ship makes a perfect touchdown and rolls to a stop. At last the commander emerges. He is 50 years old. He has grown old and farsighted waiting for this flight. He had to wear glasses to read the instrument panel."

John Young was 41 when work on *Columbia* began. The 122-foot-long shuttle was designed to take satellites into space, and to carry astronauts to satellites already in orbit to make adjustments. However, the shuttle itself needed some work, and officials postponed its launch several times. Once the glitches had been fixed, *Columbia* was ready for liftoff April 12, 1981. Two days later the

SPACE SHUTTLE *COLUMBIA* LIFTS OFF.

two-man crew became the first American astronauts to return to dry land instead of a splashing down into the ocean. "What a way to come to California!" said copilot Robert Crippen after reaching Edwards Air Force Base. Their mission was a success.

"I hope to have a few more flights on the shuttle myself," Crippen wrote in an article he and Young penned for the October 1981 issue. "You know, right after landing, John said it all: 'We're really not that far, the human race isn't, from going to the stars.'"

• Exploring Oldest Known Shipwreck

Exploring shipwrecks continued to be a staple of the NATIONAL GEOGRAPHIC in the 1980s. The vessels and their cargoes became a tangible link to the misty past that intrigued so many readers.

Marine archaeologist George Bass was perfect for GEOGRAPHIC stories and research grants. The intrepid explorer's numerous dives made great copy and lent themselves to spectacular photography. He chronicled one of his most important expeditions to the world's oldest shipwreck in the December 1987 issue. The 50-foot vessel had sunk more than 3,000 years before off the coast of Turkey and had taken with it a king's ransom of treasures.

"Almost at once the wreck fulfilled our expectations," Bass wrote. "The first dives yielded disk-shaped copper ingots,...a mace head of stone, a Canaanite amphora full of glass beads, and a second amphora filled with orpiment, a yellow sulfide of arsenic once used as pigment.... We later brought up samples of a grayish brittle material that later proved to be 99.5 percent pure tin—the very substance that spurred on the Bronze Age."

During the next several years, Bass's team retrieved from the sunken vessel more priceless objects made in Greece, Nubia, Egypt, and Cyprus. The vessel's international cargo was strong proof of the economic ties that existed between the ancient kingdoms of Africa, Asia, and Europe. It was obvious that she carried important cargo; "This is no tramp steamer we're dealing with," Bass quipped.

The ship's identity and itinerary remained shrouded in mystery. "Even I would never have imagined a site with such an

POTTERY FROM A BRONZE AGE SHIPWRECK

abundance of new information for scholars from so many fields—Egyptologists, geographers, Homeric scholars, students of ancient metallurgy," Bass concluded. "We were salvaging the greatest of all treasures—the treasure of knowledge."

Mount St. Helens Blows Its Top

Rowe Findley decided to take a break from volcano-watching May 18, 1980. The NATIONAL GEOGRAPHIC editor had been observing Mount St. Helens since the end of March on a reliable tip that it would soon erupt. But the huge mountain in Washington's Cascade Range lay dormant, occasionally rumbling and spitting forth some smoke. A little day trip away from the snoozing giant seemed appropriate.

His decision may have saved his life. Mount St. Helens erupted after he left. More than 50 people died in the first volcanic eruption in the contiguous U.S. since 1917.

"Ten megatons of TNT…," Findley wrote in the January 1981 issue. "That 5.0 quake does it. The entire mountainside falls as the gases explode out with a roar heard 200 miles away. The incredible blast rolls north, northwest, and northeast at aircraft speeds. In one continuous thunderous sweep, it sycthes down giants of the forest, clear-cutting 200 square miles in all. Within three miles of the summit, the trees simply vanish—transported through the air for unknown distances."

Findley was one of many journalists and photographers who came to the mountain in hopes of witnessing the event. He was also one of the lucky ones; two photographers he'd befriended

TWO VICTIMS WERE ASPHYXIATED IN THIS TRUCK, TEN MILES FROM THE MOUNTAINTOP.

were killed in the eruption. Freelancer Robert Landsburg managed to shoot four pictures before he was suffocated in hot ash. The magazine printed the photos as a tribute to a man who gave his life to document the world around him.

Getting to Know Gorillas

Dian Fossey's landmark studies of Rwanda's mountain gorillas gained international fame partially because of three articles she wrote for the GEOGRAPHIC. In the last one, published four years before she died in 1985, the American anthropologist acknowledged that her subjects could be violent as well as peaceful.

"The initial concept of gorilla killing gorilla was too horrid for me to accept," she wrote in the April 1981 issue. "Yet I now believe infanticide is the means by which a male instinctively seeks to perpetuate his own lineage by killing another male's progeny in order to breed with the victim's mother."

But the world's largest apes faced a much bigger threat from man than they did from each other. Fossey said poachers were responsible for two-thirds of the dead gorillas she'd found since coming to the Virunga Mountains in 1967. To protect the creatures from extinction, she established a research center in a region where Rwandan laws protected gorillas.

The need for land and meat to feed an overpopulated country

DIAN FOSSEY COAXES TUCK TO TURN AROUND FOR A PHOTO.

whittled away at its reserves. Fossey's ongoing struggles to save her gorillas may have killed her. On December 22, 1985, her lifeless body was found in her cabin. Officials suspected poachers but could never prove their allegations.

Fossey's grasp of her subjects' intellect gave her hope for their survival. "Perhaps we will find—we may hope, at least—that the gorillas' own strategies of group growth and maintenance will circumvent group disintegration caused by man's encroachment," she wrote in 1981. Seven years later, her life and cause were immortalized in the film *Gorillas in the Mist*.

Red-Letter Anniversaries

The GEOGRAPHIC had brought the world to its members' armchairs since the first issue came out. Portfolios of nations or "country stories" as the staff called them were expected features. In the 1980s country stories took over entire issues as the editors fêted France and Australia.

Both countries had some historical link to the U.S. In 1989 France was observing the bicentennial of its revolution, which had been partially inspired by America's break from England. In 1988 Australia commemorated the 200th anniversary of the landing of the first European settlers, 12 years after the U.S.

323

celebrated its bicentennial.

"…No two nations so far apart geographically are so close culturally…," Editor Bill Garrett said in reference to Australia and the U.S. "Both nations were founded by those rejected by Europe or who had rejected Europe."

He approached the undertakings as the massive projects they were. The magazine established an outpost in Sydney and dispatched freelancers to capture the essence of the world Down Under for the February 1988 issue. Several members of the staff also traveled for the plum assignment. "We decided that Australia was a great place to visit—and we *would* like to live there," said Senior Assistant Editor Betsy Moize.

France was covered in a similar fashion. More than a score of photographers and writers fanned out across the Texas-size

"WE'RE FULL OF HOPE AND DEFIANCE," SAYS AUSTRALIAN ACTIVIST PETER GARRETT (CENTER).

country to prepare the July 1989 issue. "Our team found the French less aloof than reputed," reported Senior Assistant Editors Mary Smith and John Putnam. "[They were] upbeat, and keen on getting an American view of their lives and their country."

Almost Busted

Magazine researchers at the GEOGRAPHIC never knew what they'd find in the mound of goods Peter White would give them. The much-loved writer was capable of bringing back anything to support his story, from elephant dung to poppies. He took his reporting seriously and was always on the lookout for tangible proof.

While doing fieldwork for an article on cocaine, White accompanied police officers when they raided a drug den in New York City. He asked the officers if he might keep one of the confiscated crack pipes, and they obliged. He then carefully wrapped the dishwashing liquid bottle and plastic pen casing in his suitcase for the flight back to Washington, D.C.

The outline of the objects in his luggage raised some eyebrows. Airport security officers asked White what he was carrying, and he replied in a matter-of-fact tone, "Those are devices for smoking cocaine."

White managed to return to Washington without a criminal record and with his pipe. His story ran in the January 1989 issue, accompanied by a profile of a drug rehabilitation program for teens. The comprehensive package examined coca, its transformation into a potent drug, and society's struggles with chemical abuse.

"I should have liked to end this article on an optimistic note," White wrote. "But it would not be helpful to pretend that cocaine can be brought under control anytime soon. Alas, it's more persistently entrenched than most of us imagine."

Scratch 'N' Sniff

The sense of smell was as mysterious as any place or thing the magazine could ever cover. And it was perhaps more difficult to convey with words and pictures.

Boyd Gibbons's article in the September 1986 issue covered just about everything a layman needed to know about smell—what caused odors, how they were detected, and how other creatures used their olfactory sense. When readers finished, they had the chance to put their own noses to the test in a smell survey. They were asked to scratch, sniff, and comment on six scents to help scientists learn more about the sense of smell.

"Odors reach into all our emotional life, drawing from the deepest caves in our minds," Gibbons wrote. "Odors suggest, stimulate associations, evoke, frighten, and arouse us, but they seem to lie below conscious thought until someone… parts the curtain…."

To depict what one could only smell required imagination. Photographer Louis Psihoyos found a wine "nose" testing bouquet in a moldy French wine cellar and a cheetah spraying its territory in Africa. But he had to go only as far as Ohio for one of the most sensational photographs ever to appear in the GEOGRAPHIC. There he found Thelma Williams and three other odor judges in clinical white coats gingerly sniffing men's armpits to determine the efficacy of a deodorant. The *New York Daily News* ran the picture on its front page, and the *Washington Post* profiled it in an article headlined "Geographic's Call to Odor."

Seeing the Titanic

At 1:05 a.m. on September 1, 1985, a team of French and American marine geologists stared into a video screen and saw what was left of the R.M.S. *Titanic*. The ship that supposedly God himself could not sink struck an iceberg April 14, 1912, and sank to the bottom of the icy North Atlantic in a matter of hours, taking with her 1,522 lives.

Expeditions to find the *Titanic* since then were fruitless. But people continued to search, some in pursuit of the treasures, others perhaps wanting closure to one of modern history's great tragedies.

TEAM MEMBERS SURVEY VIDEO SCREENS DURING *ARGO*'S SEARCH FOR THE *TITANIC*.

"I have never seen the ship—nor has anyone for 73 years—yet I know nearly every feature of her...," Bob Ballard wrote in the December 1985 issue. "The sea has preserved her well."

For two months, the marine explorer and other members of a Franco-American expedition swept the ocean floor south of Newfoundland with a search vehicle called *Argo*. Loaded with video cameras and a side-scan sonar, the bullet-shaped contraption finally picked up the first glimpse of the *Titanic*—one of its giant boilers—13,000 feet below the surface.

Readers who did not know nautical terminology were at a disadvantage. Terms like capstans and windlass sent many people to their dictionaries. And years of exposure to marine elements had taken a toll on the wreck, making it hard to discern what was being shown in the murky blue images.

In cases like this, the magazine's art department got the chance to demonstrate its immense value. Diagrams and artistic renderings made everything crystal-clear. Pierre Mion's painting of the *Titanic* in her watery grave gave Ballard's December 1986 article tremendous punch. The picture amplified Ballard's observations: "The stark sight of her immense black hull towering above the ocean floor will remain forever ingrained in my memory."

The Issue of Energy

The gas lines of the late 1970s were gone. But the reality that lay behind them remained.

One of Gilbert M. Grosvenor's last decisions as Editor was to publish a special supplement on the energy crisis in February 1981. Throughout the 115-page report, writers and scientists outlined a "state-of-the-union" report on what caused the problem, as well as new technologies and resources that might solve it. To keep the focus on energy, the issue did not run any advertising.

Putting out such a lengthy 13th issue required a lot of extra energy from the staff assigned to it. When the last proofs had been shipped to the printer, the crew donned special T-shirts—"We Survived the Energy Issue."

Giants of the Sea

The plight of the world's whales became an important subject for the GEOGRAPHIC in the '70s and '80s. To help save the giants of the sea, the Society cultivated the talents of several scientists who studied these ocean mammals.

Hal Whitehead is a soft-spoken Canadian who specializes in sperm whales, smaller only than the mammoth blue whales. Whitehead's reverence for his subjects shone through in his first article in the December 1984 issue.

"It is at night that I feel closest to the sperm whales," he wrote. "During this three-hour watch my four fellow crew members aboard the research vessel *Tulip* are asleep, and I am alone with the sounds. Through a sensitive hydrophone suspended beneath *Tulip*, I hear the clicks of a family group of about 15 whales.... To me, these clicks resounding in the depths give a clearer sense of the life of the sperm whale than do the strange, wrinkled bodies we see in daylight on the surface."

For centuries, men hunted down sperm whales for the fine oil encased in their foreheads. Whalers mistook the oil for sperm, which is how the creatures got their name. Biologists speculated that Moby Dick, the ferocious white whale of Herman Melville's imagination, was a sperm whale.

The sperm whales Whitehead studied were anything but ferocious. But they were still under attack from whalers and other people who preferred to study sperm whale carcasses. Whitehead said this was no longer necessary. If one were willing (and financially able) to spend time observing live sperm whales, the rewards would be incalculable.

"Now, whenever I put on the headphones and hear the whales sounding the mysteries of their strange world," he wrote, "I pray that the oceans may never be silent."

THE FLUKES OF A BLUE WHALE APPROACH 20 FEET IN BREADTH.

One of America's most popular Presidents came to power in an election that attracted the smallest voter turnout in modern history.

Slightly more than half of registered voters went to the polls in 1980, and 50.7 percent of them voted for Ronald Reagan (below, with Margaret Thatcher). The former governor of California was a conservative who promised an end to New Deal liberalism, less government, and more opportunities for private enterprise.

"He holds, as a matter of faith, that a dollar spent privately creates more wealth than a dollar spent by Government," a *New York Times* editorial said in 1981.

The new President was the first professional actor in the White House, and the skills he developed on the set lent themselves well to his new position. Reagan came across as an affable uncle, cheerful and quick with one-liners. To his followers, he was the Great Communicator. Others nicknamed him the "Teflon President" because nothing bad seemed to stick to him. Reagan left office with higher approval ratings than when he was elected.

EL SALVADOR'S CIVIL WAR

El Salvador's relentless civil war put President Jimmy Carter's human rights policies to the test in 1980. Toward the end of his term, the contradictions of supporting an oppressive regime were apparent. But, by then, it seemed too late to back out.

In El Salvador, the discrepancies between the very rich and very poor were

ANTIGOVERNMENT GUERRILLAS IN EL SALVADOR

vast. Few peasants owned land, and much of the existing farmland was off-limits, held as pasture or kept fallow by the owners. The succession of military governments that controlled El Salvador treated alleged dissenters with violence, giving the country an abysmal record of human rights violations. One of the most famous examples of this occurred in March, when right-wing terrorists murdered Archbishop Oscar Romero, an outspoken critic of the government, as he performed Mass.

Despite human rights violations, the U.S. had supplied the Central American nation with military and economic aid since the 1960s with a few breaks in between. Carter halted the aid early in 1980, several months after Salvadoran national guardsmen raped and killed three American nuns and a social worker. The victims were accused of collaborating with leftist antigovernment militants.

In 1981 a new U.S. President reversed Carter's decision. Republican Ronald Reagan was more concerned about keeping El Salvador out of the hands of com-

munist rebels than with its human rights abuses. He resumed sending aid that year, and El Salvador's civil war raged until 1991.

IMAGINE THERE'S NO LENNON

John Lennon's murder on December 8 was a low point of the year for his many fans. A deranged fan shot the former Beatle seven times as he and his wife, Yoko Ono, were returning to their Manhattan apartment from a recording session. Within hours a crowd had gathered outside the building to mourn the loss (below).

Rolling Stone called Lennon "the Beatles' most committed rock & roller, their social conscience, and their slyest verbal wit." He and the other members of the Fab Four took the world by storm during the '60s. The group disbanded in 1970 because of artistic differences. Lennon then moved beyond the pop songs of his youth and into advocacy rock with Ono, his second wife.

"All we need is love…," Lennon told a *Rolling Stone* writer three days before he died. "It's damn hard, but I absolutely believe it. We're not the first to say, 'Imagine no countries' or 'Give peace a chance,' but we're carrying that torch…passing it from hand to hand, to each other, to each country, to each generation."

At 2 p.m. eastern standard time December 14, people around the world observed a ten-minute silent vigil. It was a moving demonstration that Lennon himself would have been proud to inspire.

ALL NEWS ALL THE TIME

News junkies got their fix in 1980 when Ted Turner launched the first 24-hour TV news channel on June 1.

CNN, his underdog network, broadcast

- **JANUARY**
Brazilian rancher discovers gold on his property, and the news triggers a huge gold rush into the Amazon.

- **JANUARY 6**
Indira Gandhi regains power in India after being ousted 33 months before.

- **MARCH 10**
Jean Harris, head-mistress of girls' prep school, kills her lover, Dr. Herman Tarnower, creator of the Scarsdale Diet, after he jilts her.

- **APRIL 17**
White-ruled Rhodesia becomes black-ruled Zimbabwe.

- **MAY 4**
Yugoslavian President Josip Tito dies at 87, leaving a dangerous power vacuum in the communist country.

◀ **MAY 18**
Mount St. Helens in Washington erupts, spewing ash 60,000 feet into the air. It was the most violent volcanic eruption in the continental U.S.

ON THE SET OF CNN'S ALL NEWS CHANNEL

a steady stream of news via satellite to the many cable systems cropping up all over the country. CNN's ability to cover breaking news as it unfolded put the Big Three networks constantly behind. And it was able to do so with a fraction of the other networks' budgets.

Turner plowed money from his family's billboard business into an ultrahigh frequency (UHF) television station in Atlanta and used it to transmit programs to cable systems. Cable subscribers now wanted variety in addition to good reception, and cable providers were scrambling to fill the airtime.

WTBS's success taught Turner much about the fledgling cable industry. He tested his all-news format during the 1980 presidential elections and liked the feedback. Ten years later, CNN truly came into its own with its excellent coverage of the Gulf War.

▶ FREEDOM FLOTILLA
The "dramatic exodus" from Cuba that American officials hailed as proof of Fidel Castro's failed revolution was an embarrassment—for the U.S. When the wily leader asked Cuban-Americans to retrieve friends and relatives still on the island, he neglected to mention a crucial catch: the exiles also had to ferry across some extra passengers, a number of whom were mentally ill or ex-cons. What had been billed as a "freedom flotilla" was a handy way for Castro to unload his problems or, as he

SMALLPOX

After it had killed millions of people since the beginning of history, smallpox itself was at death's door in 1980. The World Health Organization pronounced it dead in May.

Smallpox was a contagious virus transmitted usually through liquid discharged from the nose or mouth. Victims developed high fever and muscular pain, followed by skin rash. Many of them died; a few went blind.

By the mid-20th century, between 10 and 15 million people came down with smallpox annually, and more than 2 million of them died.

Determined to eradicate the disease, the World Health Organization launched a global vaccination campaign in 1967.

"The world and all its peoples have won freedom from smallpox...," the organization proclaimed at the 33rd World Health Assembly. "This unprecedented achievement in the history of public health... [demonstrates] how nations working together in a common cause may further human progress."

described the deportees, "scum."

Some 125,000 Cubans crossed the Straits of Florida between April and August. They flocked to Miami, which soon ranked second to Havana as the largest Cuban urban center. The U.S. had welcomed Cubans as refugees from a communist country since 1959. Castro's housecleaning forced the U.S. to reverse its open-arms policy, however. President Jimmy Carter declared the flotilla illegal, and many of the refugees went straight into detention camps. By mid-decade, most had been released, and Congress passed laws to halt immigration.

■ TRENDS & TRIVIA

Rely tampons are linked to toxic shock syndrome.

3M Corp. introduces Post-it Notes.

Rollerblade in-line skates are introduced.

Dallas fans ponder "Who shot J.R.?"

Umberto Eco's medieval whodunit *The Name of the Rose* is published.

David Lynch directs *The Elephant Man.*

Americans wear or display yellow ribbons to commemorate the Iranian hostages.

The Philadelphia Phillies win their first World Series in 98 years.

ABC's hostage-watch program continues as *Nightline.*

Kool & the Gang release "Celebrate!"

French pharmaceutical company invents RU-486, the abortion pill.

Mark Medoff's *Children of a Lesser God* opens in New York.

Preppy clothing is in fashion.

Martin Scorsese directs *Raging Bull.*

The U.S., along with Japan and West Germany, boycotts the Summer Olympics, held in Moscow.

One thousand paintings by Pablo Picasso are shown at the Museum of Modern Art in New York.

George Lucas directs *The Empire Strikes Back.*

The U.S. ice hockey team defeats the Soviet Union team and wins the gold at the Winter Olympics, held at Lake Placid, New York.

327

• JULY 2
The U.S. Supreme Court upholds the right of the press and public to attend criminal trials in *Richmond Newspapers v. Virginia.*

• JULY 17
Military junta, backed by cocaine barons, takes over Bolivia.

• JULY 26
The deposed Shah of Iran dies at 60 of cancer in Egypt.

• AUGUST
Fernando Belaunde Terry is Peru's first freely elected president in 12 years.

• AUGUST 31
Gdansk Accords give Polish workers union and strike rights. They agree not to challenge Communist Party supremacy.

• SEPTEMBER
Iraq invades Iran in a territorial dispute and begins decade-long war between Arabs and Persians.

• SEPTEMBER 11
Military government takes control in Turkey after strikes, terrorism, and rising unemployment beset the country.

• DECEMBER
Milton Obote is reelected president in Uganda, where a constitutional government is restored for the first time in 18 years.

SOLIDARITY IN POLAND

Solidarity, the Polish labor movement that achieved so much in 1980, was in trouble a year later. The Communist government had banned the union, imprisoned its leaders, and reneged on several promises.

The Poles had long-bristled under Soviet domination and refused to forsake Catholicism. The Catholic Church remained influential in Poland, evidenced by the overwhelmingly positive response to the papal visit in 1979. Native son John Paul II was much loved, and his message of "the inalienable rights of man" triggered a new wave of nationalism.

The country's economic situation reached a breaking point in 1980 when food prices went up. Ignoring government sanctions prohibiting strikes, Poles stopped working. They formed Solidarity, and chose an electrician named Lech Walesa (above) as its leader.

He forced the government to recognize the union and won several key concessions. However, in 1981, Solidarity had become increasingly revolutionary, and the government decided to crack down. It placed Poland under martial law and drove Solidarity underground.

▶ MODERN-DAY PLAGUE

A deadly epidemic that entered the lexicon in 1981 threatened to be the 20th century's bubonic plague. Nobody could pinpoint the microbe responsible for AIDS (acquired immunodeficiency syndrome). And nobody could find a cure.

Dr. Peter Piot saw his first AIDS cases in the late 1970s, but the mysterious illness had no name until 1981. During a conference in the U.S., the Belgian physician noticed strong similarities between a disease American doctors observed in gay men and intravenous drug users and an illness he'd seen in patients who traveled from Africa to seek his help. The unidentified virus attacked the body's immune system, thereby leaving the victim vulnerable to disease. An international commission later called the virus HIV (human immunodeficiency virus) and called AIDS the disease it caused.

Because most of the victims in the U.S. were homosexual men, researchers believed HIV and AIDS were somehow linked to their sexual practices. But Piot had seen the symptoms in enough heterosexuals to know this was not so. To prove his point, he took a group of American researchers to Africa where men, women, and children were infected. Nobody was safe.

This revelation tossed ice water on America's sexual revolution. Advertisements urged people to practice "safe sex." The gay community pressed the government and private enterprise to fund AIDS research. Scientists discovered treatments, but no solutions. By the century's end, AIDS or HIV had claimed more than six million victims around the world; four times as many now are infected.

▶ WOMAN ON THE U.S. SUPREME COURT

The women's movement scored a huge victory in September when Sandra Day O'Connor (right, with Chief Justice War-ren Burger) became the first female jurist on the U.S. Supreme Court. Her ability to chart the course of the country's legal decisions made her one of the most influential women in modern American history.

Almost half the women in the country were working outside the home by 1981. Yet few held high-ranking jobs in the political and legal arenas. O'Connor knew this all too well; although she graduated at the top of Stanford University's law school class in 1952, law firms offered her only secretarial jobs. She went to work in the Arizona attorney general's office and rose up in the public sector.

O'Connor was President Ronald Reagan's first Supreme Court appointment. By choosing her, the President could support women's rights and leave his conservative stamp on American society.

Initially, she reflected his views. She dissented in an opinion upholding abortion and expressed skepticism about the legitimacy of racial quotas. But Reagan's conservative appointments soon polarized the bench, and O'Connor was often alone in the center.

▶ A ROYAL WEDDING

The fairy-tale wedding that joined the heir to the English throne and his golden-haired princess in July seemed blessed. The world cheered as the former Diana Spencer appeared with her new husband, Charles, on a balcony overlooking Buckingham Palace's courtyard (opposite, top).

Charles's proposal to his distant cousin ended years of speculation about whom he would marry. The 32-year-old Prince of Wales had been linked to sev-

---

THE PC

Until 1981 computers were usually clunky objects that inhabited sterile-looking labs or classrooms. International Business Machines changed that. The New York-based company introduced the first generation of personal computers (later called PCs) in 1981, a streamlined contraption with 64 kilobytes of memory. The hefty price of $2,665 made it a luxury item. Nevertheless, IBM sold 25,000 that year, and millions more soon after.

The PC utilized Intel's microprocessor and enabled users to run other programs through an operating system designed by Microsoft, a computer company headquartered near Seattle. Because IBM did not retain exclusive rights with the licensees, Intel and Microsoft were free to sell their products to other companies.

The market became flooded with IBM "clones." A decade later, IBM was having financial woes. But the machine it helped develop was flourishing.

TRENDS & TRIVIA

Jane Fonda's workout book debuts.

Pac-Man video game is new.

Walter Cronkite leaves the air as CBS's popular evening anchor.

Mozart comes to Broadway in *Amadeus.*

John Updike's *Rabbit Is Rich* is published.

Harvey Fierstein's play *Torch Song Trilogy* debuts off-off Broadway.

Dynasty and *Hill Street Blues* air on American TV.

To respond to cuts in school lunch budgets,the U.S. Department of Agriculture announces that ketchup is a vegetable.

FDA approves the sweetener aspartame for consumer use.

Kim Carnes releases "Bette Davis Eyes."

Washington Post returns Pulitzer Prize after learning that reporter Janet Cooke fabricated her story about a child heroin addict.

Susan Brown is first female coxswain in Oxford-Cambridge boat race—and steers Oxford to victory.

Steven Spielberg's *Raiders of the Lost Ark* opens in theaters.

France's high-speed train, TGV, capable of 236-mph speeds, makes its maiden run from Lyon.

Warren Beatty directs and stars in *Reds* with Diane Keaton.

Pablo Picasso's "Guernica" returns to Spain under provisions of his will.

Christian Dior opens boutique in Beijing, China.

---

eral women, including Diana's older sister. His decision to marry Diana was well received. The demure 19-year-old woman had a spotless reputation. She came from a fine, old family, and she was head over heels in love with her fiancé.

About 750 million "guests"—some even in formal attire—watched the royal wedding on the telly and gushed over Diana's veil beaded with 10,000 mother-of-pearl sequins and Charles's gold-trimmed military regalia.

Their romance soured several years and two children later. Charles returned to an old flame, and Diana sank into a deep depression. After an acrimonious separation, the couple divorced in 1995.

▶ I Want My MTV

One of the most remarkable things about Music Television—MTV—was that it had not taken hold sooner. The cable channel harnessed two of the most powerful forms of entertainment—music and television—to reach a huge audience made up of teens and 20-somethings. The all-music video channel set trends, made careers, and influenced an entire generation.

The brainchild of former radio executives, MTV played videos made by pop singers 24 hours a day. With the advent of rock 'n' roll, television producers realized the music's tremendous potential to reel in young viewers and brought singers onto

shows like *American Bandstand* and England's *Ready Steady Go!* Bands too busy to appear on the air would send film clips made by the record company. The shows got free programming, and the record companies got free exposure.

MTV's creators knew how much advertisers wanted to reach affluent young people who watched less television and read fewer publications than any other age group. They succeeded in selling the idea to their bosses at Warner Brothers in 1981. On August 1 the new channel took off with the perfect anthem—the Buggles' "Video Killed the Radio Star."

▶ MAY 12
Jailed IRA activist Bobby Sands, 27, dies after 66-day hunger strike to protest treatment by British authorities.

• JUNE 21
Police in Atlanta implicate Wayne Williams in the murders of 28 black children and adults over a two-year period.

• JUNE
Baseball players begin seven-week strike over free-agent dispute.

• AUGUST 6
President Reagan fires 12,000 striking air-traffic controllers.

• OCTOBER 6
Islamic fundamentalists assassinate Egyptian President Anwar Sadat.

• NOVEMBER 29
Screen star Natalie Wood drowns off the California coast.

330

Lebanon was a microcosm of the problems that plagued the Middle East. Christians and Muslims fought against each other, and wave upon wave of Palestinians came to Lebanon, using it as a base from which to fight Israel.

The turmoil reached critical mass in June when Israel invaded Lebanon in hopes of destroying the Palestine Liberation Organization's formidable presence there. Israeli Prime Minister Menachem Begin's initial goal was to secure Israel's border with Lebanon. But he expanded the scope to rid the country of all Palestinians and their sympathizers, as well as reinstate a government friendly toward Israel.

Begin's relentless attacks on Palestinian enclaves incurred the wrath of other world leaders, as well as liberal Israelis. He ignored his critics. But he could not ignore charges that Israeli forces stationed in West Beirut allowed Lebanese Christian extremists to massacre hundreds of Palestinian civilians in September. The Israeli government later determined that Defense Minister Ariel Sharon and other officials bore "indirect responsibility" for the killings. Two years later, Israel withdrew its troops from Lebanon, leaving a small force in the south.

FALKLANDS WAR

Argentina's long-standing dispute with Great Britain about who had sovereignty over the Falkland Islands led to war in the spring. The leaders of both countries expected to win handily, thereby reversing their political declines at home.

The question of who ruled the 200 islands off the east coast of South

BRITISH TROOPS ARRIVE IN THE FALKLAND ISLANDS.

America and their 1,800 inhabitants dated back to 1833 when Great Britain evicted all Argentinean colonists there. Almost 150 years later, Argentinean President Leopoldo Galtieri decided to sound the war cry in hopes of taking the country's mind off its poor economy and oppressive government. His troops invaded the archipelago on April 2; he doubted that Great Britain would fight very hard for a small number of sheep farmers and fishermen so far away.

He underestimated British Prime Minister Margaret Thatcher, however. She dispatched more than a hundred ships to the Falklands. They soon recaptured one of the larger islands, then sank a submarine and warship. Argentineans rallied fervently to the cause, as Galtieri had hoped, and condemned Britain's aggression. Other Latin American countries concurred.

Argentina proved to be no match for England. After losing more than 700 men, Galtieri surrendered June 14. The displays of national pride turned into

outrage, and the president stepped down in disgrace. Within two years, Argentineans elected a civilian government in free elections, ending almost a decade of brutal military rule.

BELL BREAKUP

For years AT&T was another word for the telephone company. The company had virtually controlled the telecommunications industry since the beginning. But in 1982 it lost the monopoly, ending years of legal battles with the U.S. government. The Bell family breakup was one of the most significant antitrust settlements in history.

Allegations of trust violations first surfaced in 1909 when AT&T bought Western Union. Complaints continued to surface, and the government tried to grapple with the giant in several ways, including banning its entry into any unregulated business. Despite this, AT&T remained one of the world's largest and most profitable companies.

In 1974 the Department of Justice asked the courts to dismember the communications company in one of two antitrust suits filed against AT&T. After several years of expensive haggling, both sides reached an agreement. In return for relinquishing control of the 22 regional phone companies, AT&T kept its long distance and manufacturing businesses, as well as Bell Laboratories.

ACID RAIN

Acid rain dropped into the public consciousness in 1982 after Canada blamed massive fish kills on pollution released by American factories. Countries around the world began to attack this dangerous new by-product of industrialization.

The problem manifested itself when hundreds of dead fish surfaced in Ontario lakes. Scientists eventually made the link between the waters' high degree of acidity and pollution originating across the border from the industrial regions of the northeastern U.S. Fossil-fuel burning factories and power plants belched out oxides of sulfur and nitrogen. Once in the air, these gases mixed with moisture, then fell to the ground as acid rain. This toxic brew killed fish and stripped plants and soil of vital nutrients.

Subsequent studies done by the U.S. government proved that American industry was the primary source of the acid rain. In 1989 President George Bush agreed to cut back the noxious emissions by almost 50 percent before the century's end. But many wondered if this was too late.

▶ THE END OF ERA

The Equal Rights Amendment had been dividing those it was designed to help since its conception in 1923. Women were among the most vocal opponents of the proposal, and one in particular helped engineer its demise in 1982.

To Phyllis Schlafly, ERA's promise that "equality of rights under the law shall not be denied or abridged…on account of sex" was a dangerous threat to a woman's role in society. She formed a lobbying group called

PROMINENT FEMINISTS MARCH IN SUPPORT OF THE ERA.

MEMORIAL

Out of America's most hated war came one of its most moving monuments. The Vietnam Veterans Memorial was dedicated Nov. 13 in Washington before 150,000 people.

The black granite tablets were inscribed with the names of almost 60,000 American soldiers killed or missing in the war. Placed between the Lincoln Memorial and the Washington Monument on the Mall, the Vietnam Memorial was designed to be a link between the nation's past and present. The designer, Maya Lin, conceived the idea when she visited the site during a college break in 1980. Her design was chosen out of 1,420 entries in a national competition.

"I had an impulse to cut open the earth…an initial violence that in time would heal," she told NATIONAL GEOGRAPHIC in 1985. "The names would become the memorial. There was no need to embellish."

Stop ERA, which then formed strong ties to conservative organizations.

Schlafly's group faced an uphill battle in the mid-1970s. Congress had approved the ERA almost unanimously in 1972. Within six years, 35 state legislatures had ratified the proposal, three short of the three-quarters majority of 38 required to become the country's 26th Amendment. Bowing to constituent pressure, Congress extended the deadline for ratification another three years.

By 1982 Stop ERA had rallied enough opposition to kill the proposed amendment, and it died May 30. But the idea behind it lived on; 16 state constitutions now guaranteed sexual equality.

■ TRENDS & TRIVIA

Halcion sleeping pills are new.

Steven Spielberg produces *E.T. The Extra-Terrestrial.*

USA Today debuts.

Plastic surgeons begin performing liposuction.

John Naisbett's *Megatrends* is published.

David Letterman moves his talk show to late night.

Cheers debuts on television.

Japanese carmaker Honda begins manufacturing cars in Ohio.

Gender confusion abounds in *Tootsie* and *Victor/Victoria.*

Stevie Wonder and Paul McCartney release "Ebony and Ivory."

Richard Attenborough directs *Gandhi.*

Braniff International Corp. is the first major U.S. airline to file for bankruptcy.

The Go-Go's bring back miniskirts.

Alice Walker's *The Color Purple* is published.

Michael Jackson's "Thriller" establishes the former child singer as a megastar.

Madonna Louise Ciccone aka "Madonna" releases her first single, "Everybody."

Jimmy Connors defeats John McEnroe at Wimbledon in the longest men's singles' final—4 hours and 14 minutes.

Andrew Lloyd Webber's *Cats* makes its New York debut.

• JUNE 12
More than 800,000 march in Manhattan to protest nuclear proliferation.

• JUNE 22
Prince Charles and Princess Diana announce the birth of their first son.

• JULY 16
Rev. Sun Myung Moon performs wedding ceremony for 4,150 followers in Madison Square Garden.

• SEPTEMBER 9
Monaco's Princess Grace dies in a car accident at 52. Her daughter, Stephanie, survives.

• OCTOBER 1
West German conservatives elect Helmut Kohl to be the country's new chancellor.

• NOVEMBER 10
Soviet leader Leonid Brezhnev dies at 75 from heart and lung problems. Yuri Andropov, former head of the KGB, succeeds him.

• DECEMBER 2
Barney Clark, 61, is the first recipient of an artificial heart, in Salt Lake City, Utah. He dies three months later.

332

The assassination of Philippine opposition leader Benigno Aquino triggered a storm of protest against President Ferdinand Marcos that helped end his regime.

Many Filipinos suspected that Marcos's henchmen had arranged to have the former senator killed as he returned to his homeland after three years in exile. A committee assigned to investigate the murder later confirmed those suspicions and charged 26 people, many members of the military, with the crime, including Marcos's confidante Gen. Fabian Ver.

Aquino hoped to rescue his country from despotism. Marcos's longtime opponent spent eight years in prison on trumped-up charges, then three years in the U.S. He knew that returning to the Philippines could be fatal but was willing to take the risk. He was shot within seconds of landing in Manila.

Thousands of Aquino loyalists (left) protested and rallied behind his widow, Corazon. Three years later, she became president after the international community pressured Marcos to leave the country.

"We are finally free," Aquino proclaimed at her inauguration. "A new life starts for our country."

THE U.S. EMBASSY IN BEIRUT AFTER BOMBING

▶ MARINES KILLED IN BEIRUT

"The sending of Marines to Beirut was the source of my greatest regret and my greatest sorrow as President," Ronald Reagan said in his autobiography. He was referring to the 241 men who died when terrorists blew up the Marine headquarters on October 23. Lebanese allies of Iran and perhaps Syria were blamed.

The tragedy changed America's policy toward the Lebanese civil war. The U.S., Britain, France, and Italy sent troops to Lebanon to end the fighting. But their presence had little effect. The fighting continued as Israel, Syria, and Lebanese factions fought for control.

In April 1983 an Iranian-sponsored Islamic group bombed the American Embassy, killing 40 people. Six months later, another Islamic group smashed a truck full of dynamite into the Marine headquarters and leveled the four-story building. Within minutes, the French troops' compound exploded, killing 58 people inside. "I haven't seen carnage like that since Vietnam," said one survivor.

Reagan dispatched 300 more soldiers to Lebanon to maintain what he believed was America's credibility. But political opponents and the unchanging hopelessness of the situation changed his mind. He moved the last remaining troops offshore in February 1984.

The war was over in 1990. During its 15-year course, between 130,000 and 150,000 people died, about as many were wounded, and Lebanon's economy was in ruins.

▶ TAKING THE CUP DOWN UNDER

The longest winning streak in the history of modern sports ended September 26, when *Australia II* became the first non-American yacht to win the America's Cup in 132 years. The folks Down Under whooped with joy as the Australian crew slipped past America's *Liberty* to break the tie and take the coveted trophy.

Owned by businessman Alan Bond, the victorious boat was a point of controversy before the race began. *Australia II*'s revolutionary winged keel increased her agility and speed. Her crew was so confident of the design that they brought aboard a golden spanner to loose the bolts that had bound the silver cup to a table

AUSTRALIANS CELEBRATE THEIR VICTORY.

in the New York Yacht Club since 1870. The club was loath to lose the cup and fought a losing battle to disqualify Bond's yacht.

Australia II was not flawless, but she came through when it mattered—during the tie-breaking seventh heat against Dennis Conner's *Liberty*. What had been America's Cup now was Australia's Cup.

▶ SOVIETS DOWN PASSENGER PLANE

Cold War tensions bristled in September when a Soviet missile brought down a Korean Airlines jet, killing all 269 people on board. President Ronald Reagan called the attack "barbarous," and Congress demanded reparations for the victims' families. One of the 61 Americans aboard the plane was U.S. Representative

---

• FEBRUARY 28
Israeli Defense Minister Ariel Sharon resigns after commission determines he was involved in massacres in two Palestinian refugee camps.

• MARCH 8
In a speech before a group of evangelical Christians, President Reagan denounces Soviet Communism as "the focus of evil in the modern world."

• APRIL 27
Soviet leader Yuri Andropov asks U.S. to join in ban on space weapons.

• MAY 11
The much celebrated 60-volume set of Hitler diaries are proved to be a hoax.

• JUNE
Britain's Conservative Party wins a landslide victory, which guarantees Margaret Thatcher her second term as prime minister.

▶ JUNE 18
Astronaut Sally Ride is the first American woman to travel in space.

Larry McDonald (R-Ga.).

The Soviets pushed the blame back on the U.S. The plane was shot down in a restricted air zone over Sakhalin Island, home of a Soviet military base. Officials said they tried in vain to reach the pilot, then fired at what they believed was a spy plane. The U.S. and Japan often flew covert surveillance missions in the area because of the numerous Soviet military installations around the Sea of Okhotsk. Flight 007, the Soviets concluded, was doing just that.

Investigators believed the key to establishing culpability lay in the plane's flight recorder or "black box," which the Soviets released in 1992. The information gleaned from the recorder was minimal. And the question of what a civilian plane was doing in a restricted air zone remained unanswered.

▶ STAR WARS

Designing a shield that could protect the U.S. against nuclear weapons was one of President Ronald Reagan's fondest dreams. He insisted such a device would eliminate the threat of nuclear devastation.

On March 23 he challenged the scientific community to make his dream a reality and asked the American public to support it.

His Strategic Defense Initiative (SDI)— nicknamed "Star Wars" because of the element of space-age fantasy it possessed— came at a time when the arms race was universally unpopular. The two nations most responsible for it—the U.S. and the U.S.S.R.—disagreed on how to end it. Reagan's intense dislike of communism made him distrust his Soviet counterparts as much as they distrusted him.

Star Wars was the brainchild of politicians, not scientists, a fact Reagan himself

PRESIDENT REAGAN PROMOTES SDI.

readily admitted. The technology necessary was not yet available. It would be expensive. Because there was no way of testing the entire system, it had to work perfectly the first time.

Politically, SDI was fraught with problems. It violated the 1972 U.S.-Soviet ban on antiballistic missile defense systems, exacerbated the already frosty relations between the two countries, and seemed to escalate the arms race it purported to end.

Reagan refused to let go of SDI. Some 30 billion dollars poured into the project before it was canceled in 1993. The collapse of the Soviet Union rendered Star Wars obsolete.

CRACK COCAINE

Crack cocaine blindsided the U.S. in the early 1980s. It was cheap, profitable, and it wrecked lives. The smokable form of cocaine was far more addictive and potent. Dealers discovered they could stretch their dollars by mixing about $1,000 worth of cocaine hydrochloride solution with baking soda over the stove. The two formed a chunk that could be chipped into hundreds of tiny "rocks," which had a street value of a few dollars per rock. Thus the dealer turned his $1,000 investment into about $7,000. And because the rocks were so cheap, anyone could buy them, unlike cocaine.

Crime was one of crack's most constant companions. Drug dealers armed with combat weapons killed each other—and anyone who got in their way. Addicts sold themselves or goods they had stolen to get another hit. At the end of the decade, violent crime was up by 33 percent, and crack addiction showed no signs of slowing down.

333

■ TRENDS & TRIVIA

The compact disc is introduced.

Cabbage Patch dolls are a hot Christmas gift.

The federal government recognizes Martin Luther King, Jr.'s birthday as a holiday.

Apple computers are the first to use a "mouse."

Stanley Karnow's *Vietnam: A History* is published.

Ingmar Bergman directs *Fanny and Alexander.*

The Police release "Every Breath You Take."

Flashdance introduces a cutoff sweatshirt craze.

Last episode of *M*A*S*H* garners 125 million viewers.

National Commission of Excellence in Education releases "A Nation at Risk," a critical look at the country's education system.

Jack Nicholson and Shirley MacLaine star in *Terms of Endearment.*

Chicago motorists are the first to use cellular phones in their vehicles on a regular basis. Phones sell for $3,000 plus $150 in monthly service fees.

Vanessa Williams is the first black Miss America.

First Lady Nancy Reagan unveils the "Just Say No" program to combat drug use.

Michael Jackson releases "Beat It."

Challenger carries the first black astronaut, Lt. Col. Guion Bluford.

National Council of Churches publishes a Bible in which references to God are gender-free.

• JULY
Latin American leaders ask that all foreign countries relinquish bases in their region to end wars there.

• AUGUST
France sends troops into Chad to fight Libya-backed rebels.

• SEPTEMBER 2
Israeli Prime Minister Menachem Begin resigns. He is replaced by Yitzhak Shamir.

• OCTOBER
U.S. invades Grenada to restore island's democratic government and attack Cuban troops.

• OCTOBER
Millions of Europeans demonstrate against nuclear weapons.

• DECEMBER
President Reagan announces the U.S. will withdraw from UNESCO.

• DECEMBER 10
Polish Solidarity leader Lech Walesa wins Nobel Peace Prize.

334

The Democratic Party's nomination of Geraldine Ferraro (below) for Vice President was a watershed for American women. It signaled recognition of the clout they now wielded in the political process.

"She's a woman, she's ethnic, she's Catholic," said an adviser to Walter Mondale, the party's presidential candidate and former Vice President himself under Jimmy Carter. "We have broken the barrier."

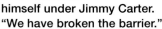

The 48-year-old Democratic Congresswoman from New York was the first woman vice-presidential candidate nominated by a major political party in the U.S. She was a moderate liberal who favored abortion rights, women's equity, and tuition tax credits and opposed mandatory busing.

Perhaps because she was a first, Ferraro was placed under intense scrutiny. Her husband's plea to a misdemeanor charge in connection with the couple's real estate business and her unimpressive performance in a televised debate with Vice President George Bush added more drag to the sagging Mondale campaign. The 1984 election was a Republican landslide.

▶ BHOPAL GAS LEAK KILLS THOUSANDS
The gas leak at a chemical plant in India that killed more than 3,000 people underscored concerns about the chemical industry and the moral responsibilities of international corporations doing business in the Third World.

It occurred the morning of December 3 at Union Carbide's plant in the central Indian city of Bhopal. Water seeped into a 45-ton underground tank of methyl isocyanate, a chemical used to make insecticides. The two combined to form a lethal gas that suffocated hundreds of sleeping residents. Others woke up feeling dizzy, their throats sore from gasping for breath. Animals dropped dead in the streets and in nearby fields from exposure to the air-borne poison.

"This is worse than war," one soldier said as he surveyed the devastation.

Union Carbide critics accused the company of cutting corners abroad to save money at home. But the allegation lost some steam when the federal Environmental Protection Agency announced in January that Union Carbide's West Virginia plant had leaked 28 times since 1980.

After five years of litigation, Union Carbide settled all criminal charges stemming from the incident by paying the Indian government 470 million dollars.

▶ LIVE AID
In December British rockers came together under the name of Band Aid to raise money to help feed millions of Africans who were enduring one of the continent's worst famines in years. A year later, American singers followed suit. The groups cooperated—via satellite—to host

the "Live Aid" concert in July 1985. That 17-hour event and the groups' earlier recordings raised more than 70 million dollars for famine victims.

The great agricultural advances made in the latter half of the century eluded Africa. Civil wars were rampant, hampering farmers and discouraging foreign investment. These problems, combined with overpopulation and a drought, led to the horrific famine of the mid-1980s.

Bob Geldof (above) was appalled by pictures of famine victims he saw on TV. The Boomtown Rats' lead singer gathered about 40 pop stars to record a song, the proceeds from which went to alleviate the famine. "Do They Know It's Christmas?" raised more than ten million dollars.

▶ BODYGUARDS ASSASSINATE GANDHI
Indian Prime Minister Indira Gandhi's handling of religious separatists led to her assassination. She was killed by two of her Sikh bodyguards who sought revenge for the Indian Army's slaughter of hundreds of Sikhs earlier in the year.

Practicing a fusion of Hinduism and Islam, Sikhs were a small but powerful minority in India. Most lived in the northwestern state of Punjab, where Sikh extremists had struggled violently to establish their own country. Identifiable by their turbans, unshaven faces, and common name of Singh (lion), Sikh men were renowned as brave, incorruptible soldiers. With this reputation in mind, Gandhi employed several as bodyguards.

In June Gandhi sent the Indian Army to the Punjab city of Amritsar to quash a rebellion. The mission was called

---

- **JANUARY 13**
McDonald's Ray Kroc dies at 81 in San Diego.

- **FEBRUARY 29**
Canadian Prime Minister Pierre Trudeau announces his resignation after leading the Liberal Party for 15 years.

- **MARCH 25**
Salvadorans vote in first presidential election since 1977.

- **APRIL 1**
Singer-songwriter Marvin Gaye is shot dead by his father in Los Angeles.

- **APRIL 30**
President Reagan signs cultural and scientific agreements with Chinese leaders.

- **MAY 1**
Federal Department of Housing and Urban Development announces that up to 350,000 Americans are homeless.

- **JUNE 30**
American playwright Lillian Hellman dies at 79 on Martha's Vineyard, Massachusetts.

"Operation Bluestar." The Indian Army approached the rebels' stronghold—the sacred Golden Temple—and was surprised to discover they faced a well-prepared group. After three days of hard fighting, hundreds lay dead inside the temple, and the vast majority were Sikhs. The sacrilege outraged the Sikh community. Several of Gandhi's advisers urged her to fire all Sikhs in her household. But she refused. She could not be a secular leader, she argued, if she singled out any one group.

Her attempts to bridge religious tensions were too late, however. Two bodyguards had already joined a small conspiracy formed to avenge Operation Bluestar. Beant Singh and Satwant Singh opened fire on Gandhi as she passed their posts on the way to a television interview October 31. She died instantly.

▶ CONTRA CONTROVERSY

President Ronald Reagan's desire to overthrow Nicaragua's leftist Sandanista government became an obsession. When Congress curtailed U.S. funding of the armed right-wing contra opposition group in 1984, Reagan acquiesced publicly. But privately, he worked to keep the contras going.

The Sandinista government Reagan opposed came to power in 1979 after overthrowing Anastasio Somoza. The Sandinistas promised to replace almost half a century of repression with democracy. The U.S. and other Western nations were pleased with the auspicious beginning and sent financial aid in 1980. But it was not enough to offset Nicaragua's 1.5 billion dollar debt. The new leaders began to shop around for other sources, and negotiated a 100 million dollar trade agreement with the Soviet Union.

This alliance bothered President Reagan. In his first term, he'd begun quietly supporting the contras, whom he called "freedom fighters." The Sandinistas, he

SUBWAY SHOOTING

To many Americans, Bernhard Goetz's shooting of four young men on a New York City subway in December epitomized urban decay and racial tension. Goetz (below) was white and his victims were black.

Goetz contended that he fired his gun in self-defense when the four men attempted to rob him. They denied his story, however, and said his attack was unprovoked. The incident left one of the men permanently paralyzed.

The New York subways had long been perceived as dangerous. Riders kept close tabs on their wallets and avoided the trains at night. To many, Goetz's story was very plausible. For blacks, however, racial tensions were as palpable as the fear of crime. They saw Goetz's vigilantism as another example of white oppression.

After three years in court, Goetz was convicted of criminal weapons possession. He served eight months of a one-year sentence.

said, were exporting Marxism throughout Central America and had to be stopped. In January 1984 a U.S. ship started mining Nicaraguan harbors at his command. This continued until April when the *Wall Street Journal* reported the story.

On Capitol Hill, Democrats and Republicans condemned Reagan's violation of national and international law. Congress outlawed all aid to the contras and passed the Boland II amendment that prohibited any administration agency involved in intelligence activities from "supporting, directly or indirectly, military or paramilitary operations in Nicaragua." Reagan signed it into law October 12.

■ TRENDS & TRIVIA

Stonewashed jeans are popular.

Arnold Schwarzenegger becomes *The Terminator.*

Milan Kundera's *The Unbearable Lightness of Being* is published.

Bruce Springsteen releases "Born in the U.S.A."

Lee Iacocca's autobiography is published.

Don Johnson and Philip Michael Thomas make pastels cool for men in *Miami Vice.*

Bill Cosby stars in *The Cosby Show.*

The horrors of the Khmer Rouge are on-screen in *The Killing Fields.*

Tina Turner makes a comeback sans Ike with "Private Dancer."

Saturday Night Live stars Bill Murray and Eddie Murphy appear in blockbuster movie hits, *Ghostbusters* and *Beverly Hills Cop* respectively.

Frozen tofu "Tofuti" rivals ice cream.

Underwear becomes outerwear, thanks to Madonna.

Tom Clancy's *The Hunt for Red October* is published.

Olympics holds the first marathon for women.

Surgeons transplant baboon's heart into human baby; Baby Fae dies 20 days later.

South African Anglican Bishop Desmond Tutu wins Nobel Peace Prize for his antiapartheid stand.

79 banks fail in the U.S., the largest number since 1938.

PG-13 movie rating is adopted.

335

▶ JULY 28
Gina Hemhill, granddaughter of Jesse Owens, carries the Olympic flame in Los Angeles.

• JULY 21
James Fixx, author of best-selling book on running, dies of a heart attack at 52 while jogging.

• JULY
Soviet Union and other communist countries boycott Summer Olympics in Los Angeles.

• SEPTEMBER 26
Britain agrees to return Hong Kong to China in 1997.

• OCTOBER 17
Congress discloses a CIA manual used in Nicaragua to teach contras how to plan assassinations and manipulate the economy.

• NOVEMBER 1
Rajiv Gandhi succeeds his late mother, Indira, as India's Prime Minister.

In March the Soviet Communist Party anointed a leader who would change the world. Mikhail Gorbachev's sweeping reforms undid many of the controls that kept the Soviet Union together.

Communism was the only way of life Gorbachev (below) had ever known. The lawyer from Stavropol joined the Communist Party in 1952 and moved gradually up through the ranks. He and his wife, Raisa, were charming and adroit, the antithesis of America's perception of Soviets. But beneath his polish was a tough politician. "This man has a nice smile, but he has got iron teeth," one party member said. Gorbachev introduced perestroika (restructure) and glasnost (openness).

The former installed free market reforms, and the latter freed the media from its role as a party house organ. His policies helped fan the flames of nationalism that were rippling across the Soviet Union. In 1989 the Eastern European satellites began pulling out, and other republics followed suit. Gorbachev's ideologies soon destroyed the very thing he was charged with preserving—his country.

▷ HOLE IN THE SKY

Something meteorologists had suspected for several years was confirmed in 1985. British scientists pinpointed a hole in the ozone layer, the portion of the Earth's upper atmosphere that absorbs 99 percent of the sun's ultraviolet rays. If too much ultraviolet radiation reached the planet's surface, it could cause skin cancer and have serious repercussions on food production.

The hole was located 15 miles above Antarctica. The primary culprits in ozone depletion were man-made substances called chlorofluorocarbons (CFCs). They were used as propellants in aerosol sprays, as well as in refrigerators and air conditioners. Some scientists believed CFCs contributed to the "greenhouse effect," in which air pollution was heating up the Earth's temperature.

Two years later, in 1987, 53 nations signed a treaty pledging to reduce the amount of CFCs in the atmosphere. Forty more signed onto the Montreal Protocols in 1989, and in 1990, all signers agreed to eliminate the dangerous chemicals by 2000.

▷ DISASTROUS MOVE

Eleven people were killed and 200 more left homeless after police in Philadelphia bombed the headquarters of a black radical group called MOVE. Critics condemned the city's black mayor, Wilson Goode, for sanctioning the use of excessive force. He responded that the bombing, though tragic, was unavoidable.

MOVE's relations with the city government were tense long before May 15. The self-described black revolutionary group lived a communal existence in West Philadelphia, eschewing all establishment trappings and adopting the surname of Africa. After one bloody shoot-out with police left an officer dead and several

others wounded, nine MOVE members were convicted and imprisoned.

The remaining members' ongoing efforts to free their "brothers and sisters" continued to irritate city officials. In 1985 police tried once again to disband MOVE, who then barricaded themselves and their children inside a row house. After a daylong siege, police bombed the roof. Fires from the explosion rippled across the roofs of neighboring houses. Eleven MOVE members, including a few children, died, and 61 homes burned to the ground (below).

The MOVE incident only temporarily hurt Goode's reputation. He was re-elected to a second term in 1988.

▷ THE RAINBOW WARRIOR INCIDENT

The environmental group Greenpeace often used confrontational methods to create a greener, more peaceful world. Its exploits to save whales and seal pups and to stop nuclear power generated a lot of press and criticism from people who found them too extreme. Some of that skepticism turned into sympathy in July, however, when French intelligence agents caused the death of a Greenpeace photographer.

The group's flagship, *Rainbow Warrior*, had dropped anchor in Auckland, New Zealand, before sailing to French Polynesia to protest France's nuclear

RAINBOW WARRIOR SINKS IN AUCKLAND HARBOR.

weapons testing. A French agent attached two bombs to the 160-foot trawler's hull, then swam away before they went off. Fernando Pereira drowned as the ship sank.

Police later caught the agent and charged him and an accomplice with murder. The French government denied complicity at first. Two months later, faced with overwhelming evidence to the contrary, Prime Minister Laurent Fabius admitted his government's guilt. He dismissed the intelligence chief and accepted the resignation of the minister of defense. New Zealand allowed the agents to plead guilty to manslaughter.

▶ GRAMM-RUDMAN

The Gramm-Rudman-Hollings Act was a well-intentioned attempt to eliminate the federal deficit. Cosponsored by U.S. Senators Phil Gramm (R-Tx.), Warren Rudman (R-N.H.), and Ernest Hollings (D-S.C.), the law mandated a gradual ratcheting down of the deficit through annual budget cuts agreed upon by Congress and the President. If the two parties could not agree, all government programs would be cut by the same percentage automatically.

Support for Gramm-Rudman, as it came to be known, was bipartisan. Legislators had to respond to the public's growing concern about the federal deficit. President Ronald Reagan's call for increased security meant spending more money on defense at a time when his resolve to cut taxes meant

TERRORISM

Terrorism had become an uncomfortable fact of life by 1985. Religious extremists and political groups were inclined to use its destructive ploys, making international travel a risky venture.

In October, members of the Palestine Liberation Front seized the cruise ship *Achille Lauro* after it left Egypt. The incident was a marked departure for Palestinians, whose previous attacks had been directed only at Israeli targets. The ship was Italian, and the casualty was an American, Leon Klinghofer, who was shot, then pushed out of his wheelchair into the sea and drowned.

The hijackers surrendered to Egyptian authorities (below) who, unaware of Klinghofer's murder, agreed to fly them to Tunisia. The U.S. learned of the murder and intercepted the Egyptian plane over Sicily, forcing it to land. The terrorists were arrrested and tried by the Italian courts.

there was less money available. The government borrowed, and by the end of 1985, the deficit had soared to two trillion dollars, almost double the amount in 1981.

Gramm-Rudman's intent was to eliminate the deficit by 1991. But belt-tightening proved as tricky after the law was in place as it was before. Congress could not agree on what programs to cut, Reagan refused to consider raising taxes, and the U.S. Supreme Court ruled that the law's automatic cutting procedures were unconstitutional.

■ TRENDS & TRIVIA

An extra second is added to the calendar year.

Nintendo video games debut.

Anne Tyler's *The Accidental Tourist* is published.

American singers release "We Are the World" as a fundraiser for African famine victims.

The Discovery Channel and the Home Shopping Network debut.

Whitney Houston releases "Saving All My Love For You."

Garrison Keillor's *Lake Woebegone Days* is published.

Aretha Franklin releases "Who's Zoomin' Who?"

Victor Hugo's *Les Miserables* is staged in London.

Boris Becker, 17, is the youngest man to win Wimbledon.

Bret Easton Ellis's *Less Than Zero* is published.

Montgomery Ward discontinues its catalog.

Libby Riddles is the first woman to win the Iditarod.

Larry McMurtry's *Lonesome Dove* is published.

Meryl Streep and Robert Redford star in *Out of Africa*.

Capital Cities Communications buys ABC for 3.5 billion dollars.

John Huston directs *Prizzi's Honor.*

Bea Arthur, Rue McClanahan, and Betty White make aging seem hilarious in *The Golden Girls.*

General Electric buys NBC and RCA for 6.3 billion dollars.

337

• MAY 27
Cyclone in Bangladesh kills 10,000 people.

• AUGUST
South Africa suspends trading on its stock and currency markets in response to protests against the apartheid government.

• SEPTEMBER 1
A French and American research team locates the *Titanic* several miles off the coast of Newfoundland.

• SEPTEMBER
The Plaza Accords among the world's central bankers sharply reduces the value of the U.S. dollar against the Japanese yen.

▶ OCTOBER 2
Film star Rock Hudson dies of AIDS at 59.

• NOVEMBER 14
Volcanic eruption in Colombia kills some 20,000 people.

1986

 Iran-Contra Hearings

The worst scandal of President Ronald Reagan's career began as a covert operation to fund Nicaragua's contras. Members of the administration oversaw the sale of arms to Iran, then channeled the proceeds to the right-wing group. In addition to paying exorbitant sums for the surplus American weapons, Iran used its influence with terrorists in Lebanon to free seven American hostages. The plan broke numerous laws and flew in the face of Reagan's oft-avowed public refusal to negotiate with terrorists.

A zealous Marine named Oliver North (below) oversaw the daily management of the operation. His misty-eyed patriotism enchanted many people who watched his televised testimony before Congress in 1987. Dressed in full military regalia, North admitted he had lied and willfully destroyed evidence. But he maintained he was just a soldier following orders.

North was convicted for his role in the scandal. That conviction was later overturned on appeal. Reagan, his commander in chief, managed to emerge from Iran-Contra unscathed to the stunned consternation of his critics.

U.S. Bombs Libya

Libyan leader Muammar Qaddafi's adversarial relationship with the U.S. came to a head in 1986.

President Ronald Reagan had long suspected the Libyan leader of initiating acts of terrorism. In April he said he had "irrefutable evidence" that Qaddafi was behind the bombing of a West German nightclub in which one American GI and a Turkish woman were killed. More than 200 people were also injured, among them 50 to 60 U.S. soldiers.

He promptly ordered the largest single air strike since World War II to attack several sites in Libya's most populous cities, Tripoli and Benghazi. About 40 Libyan civilians died, including Qaddafi's adopted baby daughter. The bombs severely damaged military installations, and for awhile, Qaddafi himself was rumored to have been killed. He appeared on television 24 hours later—alive and furious.

The bombing triggered other terrorist attacks in Europe and the Middle East, mainly against U.S. and British citizens; Prime Minister Margaret Thatcher had been one of the few world leaders to support Reagan. While terrorism continued to be in the news, Qaddafi did not. Unable to become a major player in the Arab world, he gradually faded from the headlines.

Challenger Explodes

Most Americans can recall where they were on January 28 when they learned that the space shuttle *Challenger* had exploded (above, right). The spacecraft went down little more than a minute after takeoff while millions watched in horror. All seven people on board were killed.

The 25th shuttle mission garnered much publicity because a civilian had joined the crew. Christa McAuliffe, a high school teacher from Concord, New Hampshire, was selected to be the first

person to teach classes from space. Her students watched the launch on television; and her husband, two children, and parents were among the spectators at Cape Canaveral. The other crewmembers were Commander Francis Scobee, Pilot Michael Smith, Ellison Onizuka, Ronald McNair, Judith Resnik, and Gregory Jarvis.

A small component of the shuttle caused the explosion. The O-rings, or rubbery gaskets that sealed the joints between sections of the rocket boosters, became brittle in the winter weather. Flames spread through the boosters and heated the main fuel tank, which blew up.

In response to the great outcry over the disaster, President Reagan appointed a commission to determine if anyone could be held responsible. Several NASA officials lost their jobs, and shuttle launches were suspended for two years. The remains of the *Challenger*'s crew were buried in Arlington National Cemetery.

Greed Is Good

Arbitrage guru Ivan Boesky told the graduating class of the University of California-Berkeley business school in May, "I urge you to seek wealth, but do it in a

- **JANUARY 25**
The U.S. orders all Americans to leave Libya and freezes Libyan assets in the U.S.

- **FEBRUARY 6**
Haitian President Jean-Claude "Baby Doc" Duvalier is ousted and flees to France.

▶ **FEBRUARY 26**
Corazon Aquino becomes president of the Philippines.

- **FEBRUARY 28**
Swedish Prime Minister Olaf Palme is assassinated while walking home from the theater in Stockholm.

- **MARCH 4**
World Jewish Congress accuses former UN Secretary Gen. Kurt Waldheim of war crimes. He is later elected Austria's president.

- **MARCH 20**
Conservative Jacques Chirac becomes France's prime minister.

338

virtuous and honest way...."

In amassing his multmillion-dollar fortune, Boesky often neglected to practice what he preached. He pleaded guilty in November to using confidential information about pending takeovers to buy and sell stocks, an illegal practice called insider trading. He was fined 100 million dollars, faced up to five years in jail, and was banned from the securities industry.

What worried financiers most about Boesky's plea bargain was his agreement to cooperate with federal investigators in identifying other abusers. On the first business day after the plea was announced, traders began unloading stocks of companies involved in takeovers.

Although greed on Wall Street was not new, the frenzy of mergers, takeovers, and acquisitions that took place in the '80s was phenomenal. More than 25,000 deals worth more than two trillion dollars took place between 1980 and 1988. Concerned about the role Boesky and others like him played in the merger mania, the federal Securities and Exchange Commission joined forces with the U.S. Attorney in New York to stamp out insider trading.

Boesky led the team to its biggest catch, junk bond king Michael Milken, who paid a 500 million dollar fine in 1990 for insider trading and other charges. The men became living examples of what insider trading was and how seriously the government took it.

▶ ICY SUMMIT

President Ronald Reagan's first personal encounter with Soviet General Secretary Mikhail Gorbachev did not end well. During the October summit in Reykjavik, Iceland, in which the leaders met to discuss arms control, Reagan refused to give up his Strategic Defense Initiative, and Gorbachev refused to accept anything less. Each blamed the other for the stalemate.

Gorbachev said he would dismantle his

CHERNOBYL

The most serious nuclear-reactor accident in history occurred in Ukraine when an explosion at a nuclear plant released radiation into the atmosphere. Thirty-one people died from exposure shortly after Chernobyl's No. 4 reactor burst; another 40,000 more would be later diagnosed with cancer (below).

Poor design and human error caused the accident. Workers had been conducting an experiment with the reactor running and its emergency water-cooling system turned off. The reactor's container could not withstand the mounting pressure, and the lid blew off. Flaming particles flew everywhere, touching off dozens of fires on the ground and spreading radiation into Western Europe.

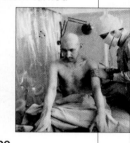

The leak was finally plugged two weeks later, but its harmful effects rippled through the region long afterward.

country's nuclear arsenal if Reagan would put a ten-year moratorium on developing his proposed "missile" shield in outer space. The President refused and the conversations ended abruptly. Gorbachev later said only a "madman" would go forward with arms control if research on SDI continued. Reagan countered that a country willing to abolish nuclear weapons should welcome the development of an antinuclear device.

Relations improved a year later. The two leaders met in Washington, D.C., and signed the Intermediate Range Nuclear Forces Treaty in December, in which both sides agreed to destroy a significant number of nuclear weapons.

■ TRENDS & TRIVIA

Rhode Island is the first state to mandate recycling in households.

Robert Penn Warren is the first U.S. poet laureate.

Richard Ford's *The Sportswriter* is published.

Margaret Atwood's *The Handmaid's Tale* is published.

Jean Harris tells her version of why she killed Dr. Herman Tarnower in her book, *Stranger in Two Worlds.*

Ann Martin's *The Baby-Sitters Club* is published.

Woody Allen directs *Hannah and Her Sisters.*

L.A. Law airs on TV.

Paul Simon releases "Graceland."

The Statue of Liberty turns 100.

Coca-Cola reverts to its original formula after a new one fails.

Hands Across America raises money for the poor.

Clint Eastwood aka "Dirty Harry" is elected mayor of Carmel, California.

Andrew Lloyd Weber's *Phantom of the Opera* opens in London.

Sigourney Weaver stars in *Aliens.*

Singer Co. announces it will stop making sewing machines.

Professional women in America outnumber men for the first time, but they average less pay.

Tom Cruise and Kelly McGillis star in *Top Gun.*

Soviet spacecraft Vega 1 flies within 5,500 miles of Halley's Comet, sending back the first pictures of the comet's icy core.

• **MAY 1**
In South Africa, 1.5 million blacks stay home from work, causing the country's largest labor strike.

• **JUNE 19**
Len Bias, a star basketball player for the University of Maryland, dies of a cocaine overdose at 22.

• **JULY 23**
Britain's Prince Andrew marries Sarah Ferguson in Westminster Abbey.

• **AUGUST 25**
Toxic gas cloud in Cameroon kills 1,200 people.

• **OCTOBER 10**
Federal officials seize a record amount of cocaine—4,620 pounds—in West Palm Beach, Florida.

• **NOVEMBER**
More than 1,000 pounds of toxic chemicals spill into the Rhine River after a warehouse burns in Basel, Switzerland.

• **DECEMBER 10**
Nazi concentration camp survivor and author Elie Wiesel receives the Nobel Peace Prize.

340

When the closing bell rang at the New York Stock Exchange on Monday, October 17, stock prices were down 22.6 percent—almost double the amount dropped in the crash of 1929. A whopping 604.5 million shares had been traded, more than double the previous record. And billions of dollars on paper vanished.

Analysts had many theories about what caused "Black Monday." The U.S. trade deficit, much higher than expected, made foreign investors wary. West German bankers had recently raised their short-term interest rates for the fourth time in three months, which made borrowing less attractive. Stock prices were inflated and out of line with earnings. The market was leveraged out. But no one theory held sway.

The Federal Reserve Board intervened almost immediately. To flood the market with money, the board began buying government securities. Confident with this response, banks resumed lending money to securities firms. Several companies then announced they would buy back their own stocks.

On Wednesday the Dow Jones Industrial average was back up 186.84 points. And two years later, it was back up to precrash levels.

BORK GOES DOWN

Federal Judge Robert Bork's failure to gain Congressional approval to the U.S. Supreme Court was in some part his own doing. The Senate Judiciary Committee amassed enough damaging material from the conservative judge's published opinions to squelch his nomination to the bench in October.

Bork became famous in the previous decade as the solicitor general who fired Watergate Special Prosecutor Archibald Cox in the famous "Saturday Night Massacre." He left the government in 1977 to teach law at Yale University, then returned to Washington five years later when President Ronald Reagan made him a federal judge in the District of Columbia's appellate court. In that capacity and in other writings, he frequently attacked the Supreme Court's record.

Justice Potter Stewart's retirement in 1987 gave Reagan his third opportunity to

ROBERT BORK TESTIFIES AT HIS CONFIRMATION HEARING.

put another conservative in the country's highest court. The President chose Bork, calling him a "prominent and intellectually powerful advocate of judicial restraint." The judge's critics called him a right-wing extremist who would outlaw abortion, overturn civil rights laws, and limit the right to free speech.

After tortuous confirmation hearings, Bork lost in the Senate, 58-42. Republicans, still smarting from the assault, got the chance to grill Democratic nominees for the bench during President Bill

Clinton's Administration several years later. "They wrote the text, and guess what?" said a retired Republican senator who supported Bork. "That's the commando booklet now for the other side."

ARIAS BROKERS CENTRAL AMERICA PEACE

The Arias Peace Plan brought some stability to Central America and a Nobel Peace Prize to its author, Costa Rican President Oscar Arias Sanchez. By signing the treaty, Guatemala, Honduras, El Salvador, Costa Rica, and Nicaragua agreed to cease fighting in one of the world's most troubled regions.

Arias had Nicaragua in mind when he drafted his peace plan early in the year. That country's leftist Sandinista government had been at war with American-backed contra rebels for several years, and the effects of the civil war reverberated throughout Central America.

As the leader of a neutral country, Arias could not support either side. Instead, he crafted a cease-fire and asked the entire region to "take a risk for peace." His plan called for free elections, an end to outside aid to rebels, and amnesty for political freedom. Signed August 7, the treaty went into effect November 7.

The Nobel Committee hailed Arias's initiative as an important work for peace that extended beyond Central America. But U.S. President Ronald Reagan wanted Nicaragua's civil war to end only when the contras were in power. He asked Congress to lend the right-wing rebels an additional $270 million and was turned down.

SEX SCANDALS ABOUND

Respectable newspapers and sensational tabloids alike had a field day with two sex scandals in 1987. One brought down a presidential hopeful, the other, a preacher.

Former Senator Gary Hart was the front-runner for the Democratic

• FEBRUARY
Syrian troops occupy West Beirut and end three years of anarchy.

• FEBRUARY 20
Brazil suspends interest payments on loans from foreign banks.

• FEBRUARY 23
Pop artist Andy Warhol dies after routine gall bladder surgery in New York.

• MAY 17
Iraqi missiles hit the USS Stark in the Persian Gulf; 37 die. Iraqi President Saddam Hussein apologizes to the U.S.

• JUNE 1
Lebanese Prime Minister Rashid Karami is assassinated.

• JULY
Landowners in Brazil begin three-month burning of 80,000 square miles of Amazonian rain forest.

• OCTOBER
President Reagan supports China's crackdown on Tibetans protesting Chinese rule. The Senate votes to condemn China, 98-0.

JIM AND TAMMY FAYE BAKKER

nomination that spring. But his hopes evaporated after the *National Enquirer* ran a story, complete with color photographs, about his extramarital affair with a young model named Donna Rice. There were no photos of Jim Bakker's tryst with church secretary Jessica Hahn, but her allegations were damning enough to end his career. The successful televangelist of the Praise the Lord (PTL) ministry admitted to committing adultery with Hahn in 1980 and using his ministry's money to buy her silence.

Bakker turned the PTL over to Jerry Falwell and was convicted in 1989 of defrauding his followers of 158 million dollars.

▶ LAND PRICES DROP IN THE HEARTLAND
The farm belt's spate of prosperity ended abruptly in the mid-1980s, much as it did in the Depression. The difference between the two lay in the percentage of people directly affected. In the '30s, about 25 percent of America's population were farmers; 50 years later, that figure had dropped to 3 percent.

Before the crash, farmers were enjoying a boom time. Agricultural prices were good. Farmland increased in value as inflation stayed steady. In the Midwest, the average price for an acre of land rose to $725 from $193 during the '70s.

Using their land and produce as collateral, farmers borrowed money to buy new equipment or whatever else they wanted. Many were too young to remember the lessons of the Depression. They felt secure that the land would hold its value, if all else failed.

It did not. As agricultural prices began to fall in the mid-1980s, so did the price of land. Farmers had less money to pay off

GARBAGE!

Nobody wanted the 3,100 tons of putrid garbage Lowell Harrelson had for sale. His scheme turned into an international embarrassment that underscored the thorny issue of waste disposal.

The *Mobro 4000* (below) set sail in March laden with trash from Islip, New York. Harrelson, an Alabama businessman, bought the garbage, with the intent of selling the methane gas it emitted. The crew he hired to tote the fetid cargo never suspected the job would turn into a two-month, 6,000-mile odyssey. "Ours is not to question why," shrugged the tug's mate. "We just go where they tell us."

Six states and three countries refused to accept the cargo. In May, *Mobro*s returned to New York. Islip reluctantly took back its refuse and burned it that fall. The incident forced the town—and many others—to re-examine what they threw away.

their debts and faced even more problems as interest rates rose. Foreclosures became a common occurrence, as they had been in the '30s. Only now, there were fewer farmers working to produce food and other agricultural necessities to supply a much larger population.

The government and charitable organizations stepped in to rescue the farm belt. By 1987 the economy had rebounded somewhat, partially because of the record amounts of government subsidies. But some 240,000 people had given up on agriculture as a way of life.

■ TRENDS & TRIVIA

The Closing of the American Mind, by Allan Bloom, indicts higher education in America for neglecting the classics.

Toni Morrison's *Beloved* is published.

Tom Wolfe's *Bonfire of the Vanities* is published.

Joel Coen directs *Raising Arizona*.

Fox introduces *The Tracy Ullman Show* and *Married...With Children*.

Glenn Close and Michael Douglas star in *Fatal Attraction*.

The Supreme Court orders Rotary clubs to admit women.

Condom commercials are allowed on TV to stop AIDS epidemic.

National Museum of Women in the Arts opens in Washington, D.C.

Burroughs Wellcome's AZT, a drug designed to treat AIDS, wins FDA approval.

FDA approves Merck's Lovastatin (Mevacor) as a treatment for high cholesterol.

Angelica Huston stars in her father John Huston's last film, *The Dead,* based on James Joyce's short story.

The musical *Sarafina!* opens in Johannesburg, written by and starring blacks.

Scott Turow's *Presumed Innocent* is published.

Gabriel Axe releases *Babette's Feast*, the first of several movies whose plots revolve around food.

Texaco files for protection under the U.S. bankruptcy laws, the largest filing in history.

341

• **OCTOBER 4**
Canada and the U.S. agree on a free-trade pact.

• **NOVEMBER**
Vincent Van Gogh's painting "Irises" is sold for 53.9 million dollars at Sotheby's.

• **NOVEMBER**
Congressional committee investigating Iran-Contra releases a report charging President Reagan with failing to obey the Constitution.

• **NOVEMBER 10**
Niger's dictator Seyni Kountche dies after 13 years in power. His chief of staff, Col. Ali Saibou succeeds him.

• **NOVEMBER 28**
Tawana Brawley, 15, claims she was kidnapped and raped by six white men. A grand jury finds that she made up the story.

• **DECEMBER 8**
President Reagan and Soviet Party Leader Gorbachev agree to eliminate intermediate-range nuclear weapons.

• **DECEMBER 16**
In Sicily, a Mafia trial ends with 338 defendants sentenced to jail.

Although neither Iraq nor Iran technically won the bloody war that ended in August 1988, Iraqi President Saddam Hussein felt he had earned the right to dominate the Persian Gulf region.

Hussein invaded Iran in 1980 to settle a territorial dispute over the Shatt al Arab, a crucial waterway into the Persian Gulf, and to stop Iranian Shiite Muslims from influencing their Iraqi counterparts to undermine his Sunni Muslim regime.

Hussein underestimated the power of revolutionary zeal, however. The invasion he expected to be an easy victory became a holy war pitting Muslim against Muslim. Some Arab countries backed Iraq because they feared that Iran's Islamic extremism would destabilize their governments. But others, such as Syria and Libya, supported the Ayatollah.

After numerous attempts to end the war, the UN finally brokered a cease-fire in August 1988. Both countries were devastated. Still, Iraq emerged from the wreckage with a formidable arsenal (above) and great ambition to become a more powerful player on the international stage.

▶ FIRST FEMALE HEAD OF ISLAMIC NATION
At 35, Benazir Bhutto's future looked promising. In December she became the first female prime minister of a Muslim country in Pakistan's first free election since 1977.

Bhutto's father, Zulfikar Ali Bhutto, governed Pakistan between 1973 and 1977. After he was deposed and imprisoned by a military coup, his wife and daughter assumed control of the country's largest political group, the Pakistan People's Party. The two women were imprisoned later, then released in 1984; Zulfikar was hanged in 1979.

Bhutto settled in England until the Pakistani government legalized political parties in 1986. She returned to her homeland, which was then under the control of her father's deposer, Muhammad Zia ul-Haq. He threw her in jail briefly for requesting free elections, then acquiesced. Three months before the elections were held, Zia was killed when his plane exploded. Assassination was suspected, but never proved.

Promising a return to civilian rule, Bhutto and her party swept the elections. Twenty months later, she was ousted on charges of corruption, nepotism, and incompetence. She made a comeback in 1993, but was dismissed again for similar charges in 1996.

▶ TERRORIST BOMB KILLS TRAVELERS
Most of the passengers aboard Pan Am Flight 103 were headed home for the holidays on December 21. The seasonal goodwill vanished in an instant when the jet exploded in midair, six miles above a Scottish village. All 259 people on the plane were killed, and 11 villagers died.

Investigators poured into Lockerbie to discover what caused the tragedy (above, right). They found evidence of plastic explosives in the luggage racks.

Three Middle Eastern terrorist groups

claimed responsibility. The first was made up supposedly of Palestinians unhappy with the PLO's improved relationship with Israel. U.S. officials had warned Pan Am that they had threatened to destroy one of its planes. But because the tip came from an unreliable source, the airline did not inform passengers. Their families filed 500 million dollars in lawsuits against Pan Am, and the company soon folded.

The second group claimed the bombing was to pay the U.S. back for accidentally shooting down an Iranian passenger plane in July. Critics later accused President George Bush of overlooking this claim in order to improve relations with Iran.

The third group got the blame. The U.S. charged two Libyans with planting the explosives in retaliation for the massive American air strike against Libya in 1986. Muammar Qaddafi refused to hand the men over, and extradition struggles dragged into the next decade.

▶ MURDER OF RAIN FOREST ACTIVIST
The murder of Brazilian activist Francisco "Chico" Mendes Filho brought international attention to the plight of the rain forests and those whose lives depended on their existence.

The son of a rubber tapper, or *serenguiero*, Mendes marshaled his colleagues to fight ranchers who wanted to turn the vast rain forests in Brazil's westernmost

● **FEBRUARY**
Members of the Assembly of God remove televangelist Jimmy Swaggert after learning that he has had sex with a prostitute.

● **MARCH**
Romanian President Nicolae Ceausescu announces plans to demolish 8,000-13,000 villages and resettle residents in urban complexes.

● **APRIL 4**
Arizona Governor Evan Mecham is removed from office for diversion of state money and other charges.

● **APRIL 14**
Soviet Union agrees to withdraw troops from Afghanistan, ending nine years of war.

● **APRIL 17**
American sculptor Louise Nevelson dies in New York at 88.

● **MAY 22**
Hungarian Communist Party ousts Janos Kadar after nearly 32 years in power and elevates Karoly Grosz as prime minister.

● **JUNE**
In Rangoon, Burma, police kill 300 students protesting against Gen. Ne Win's military government. He resigns on July 23.

province of Acre into pasture. Worldwide, the number of square miles of tropical woodlands had plummeted to 6 million from 15 million since the 18th century. By the 1980s, rain forest acreage was disappearing on an hourly basis. The serengueiros of Brazil tried to slow that rate as best they could by forming human chains around land scheduled to be cleared or around the crew hired to clear it.

Mendes's organization forged an important bond with Amazonian Indians, who relied on the forests for survival, and international environmental groups. Together, they forced the Brazilian government to set aside extraction reserves where locals could harvest latex and Brazil nuts without damaging the fragile ecosystem. Mendes received the UN's 1987 Global 500 award, thus clinching his status as a hero for environmentalists and human rights activists.

FUNERAL OF CHICO MENDES

Ranchers saw him as public enemy No. 1. On December 22 a rancher and his son killed Mendes as he stepped outside his home near Xapuri. It was the 459th land-related murder in Brazil in 18 months. Darly and Darcy Alves da Silva were convicted in 1990 and sentenced to 19 years in prison.

▶ BUSH ELECTED PRESIDENT

Ronald Reagan's popularity carried over to George Bush in 1988. He became the first sitting Vice President elected to the White House since Martin Van Buren in 1836.

Promising a "kinder, gentler" time, Bush trounced his Democratic opponent,

Massachusetts Governor Michael Dukakis. Most voters did not seem to care about Bush's involvement in Iran-Contra. They liked his aristocratic warmth and conservative values.

In contrast, Dukakis appeared to be a stiff technocrat. But his demeanor was the least of his problems. Republican strategists dug up the case of Willie Horton, a convicted murderer who had raped a woman while on furlough from a Massachusetts jail during Dukakis's tenure. Bush's campaign ads implied that Dukakis personally approved Horton's weekend pass and was also responsible for the state's furlough program. This was not true, as many publications pointed out, but the impact of the ads was overwhelming.

BOOK BURNING

"It was perhaps the strangest valentine one could receive," Salman Rushdie said when he learned that Iran's Ayatollah Khomeini sentenced him to death on February 14. Khomeini denounced Rushdie's novel, *The Satanic Verses*, as a blasphemous attack on Islam, a transgression punishable only by death.

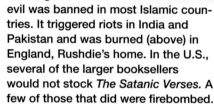

The Indian-born writer's imaginative tale of good versus evil was banned in most Islamic countries. It triggered riots in India and Pakistan and was burned (above) in England, Rushdie's home. In the U.S., several of the larger booksellers would not stock *The Satanic Verses*. A few of those that did were firebombed.

Rushdie disappeared into hiding. Despite Rushdie's denials of intentional blasphemy and Khomeini's death in 1990, Iran did not revoke the sentence, which now had a multimillion-dollar bounty attached.

■ TRENDS & TRIVIA

More than one million fax machines are sold in the U. S.

Prozac comes on the market.

Roseanne debuts on ABC.

Bobby McFerrin's "Don't Worry, Be Happy" turns listeners onto world music.

Gabriel Garcia Marquez's *Love in the Time of Cholera* is published.

Taylor Branch's *Parting the Waters* is published.

Anne Tyler's *Breathing Lessons* is published.

Dustin Hoffman plays an autistic savant in Barry Levinson's *Rain Man*.

Pedro Almodovar directs *Women on the Verge of a Nervous Breakdown*.

Candice Bergen is the irrepressible *Murphy Brown*.

The TV show *The Wonder Years* triggers late '60s nostalgia.

TV viewers join in the fight to locate fugitives with Fox Television's *America's Most Wanted*.

George Bush says "Read my lips —no new taxes."

Neil Sheehan's *A Bright Shining Lie* is published.

Tom Hanks stars in *Big*.

Because of a drought, the U.S. imports grain for the first time in history for domestic needs.

Medical waste washes up on beaches in New York and New Jersey.

Chicago's Wrigley Field installs electric lights to allow nighttime baseball.

• JULY 3
U.S.S. *Vincennes* accidentally shoots down Iranian passenger plane in Persian Gulf, killing 290 people.

• JULY 8
French voters re-elect François Mitterand and reject right-wing candidate Jacques Chirac.

• AUGUST 8
Officials from Angola, Cuba, and South Africa agree to a truce in Angola and Namibia after years of fighting.

• AUGUST 20
Ferocious summer forest fires sweeping Yellowstone National Park fan across 160,000 acres in one day.

• SEPTEMBER 27
Canadian runner Ben Johnson loses his Olympic gold medal for using steroids.

• NOVEMBER
Kohlberg Kravis Roberts buys RJR Nabisco for some 25 billion dollars, the largest corporate takeover in history.

• DECEMBER 7
Earthquake in Armenia kills more than 25,000.

The Soviet Union lost its grip on Eastern Europe in 1989. Their spirits buoyed by Mikhail Gorbachev's pledge to respect their political choices, the people of Hungary, Poland, East Germany, and Romania ripped down the Iron Curtain.

Poland moved first. In August a Solidarity official

became the first non-communist leader since Eastern Europe came under Soviet control. Two months later Hungary abolished the one-party system. In Czechoslovakia protesters triggered a "Velvet Revolution" and elected playwright Vaclav Havel president in December. That month a firing squad in Romania killed President Nicolae Ceausescu and his wife.

In East Germany officials relaxed travel restrictions in response to demonstrations and opened the Berlin Wall (above) on November 9 to jubilant Berliners. The Communist government was swept aside, and Germany moved toward unification. "It was one of those rare times when the tectonic plates of history shift beneath men's feet," *Time* said in 1998, "and nothing after is quite the same."

▶ SPIKE GETS IT RIGHT

Do the Right Thing did not incite riots, as a few experts predicted. Instead, it fired up the imaginations of young black filmmakers who, like Spike Lee, wanted to capture a realistic picture of the African-American experience.

From the moment the movie started in a burst of loud, rebellious rap, it was a winner. Lee, the 32-year-old director, had already cut his teeth on two films, the second of which, *She's Gotta Have It*, won a prize at the 1986 Cannes Film Festival. In his third film, he played Mookie, a pizza delivery boy in Brooklyn who worked for a white man, fathered a child with a Puerto Rican, and moved easily among his black and white neighbors.

Lee's look at black-white relations was significant because it was not idealized. The director chose not to portray all blacks as noble or all whites as clods. They were multidimensional, provocative, and believable.

When a reporter asked Lee what the "right thing" was, he said he did not know. "But I know what the wrong thing is: racism."

▶ DISASTER IN TIANANMEN

Whatever hopes the Chinese had for democratic reform and eliminating government corruption were crushed in June. Soldiers and police killed hundreds of protesters massed in Beijing's Tiananmen

PROTESTERS IN TIANANMEN SQUARE

Square to end the most infamous antigovernment demonstration since the 1949 revolution.

The protest began two months before in April. Students in Beijing flocked to the massive square to honor the late Hu Yaobang, a government official whose crusade against corruption led to his expulsion from the party. Gradually more people joined the students to show their support for Hu's cause, and soon the demonstration had spread into other cities throughout China.

In Beijing, many of the protesters announced they would hold a hunger strike on May 13, timed to take full advantage of the huge number of reporters assembled to cover Soviet leader Mikhail Gorbachev's visit in two days.

Deng Xiaoping imposed martial law on May 20 and dispatched tanks to Tiananmen Square. The protesters, whose ranks had swelled to almost a million, defied the army with human blockades. Deng struck again with a vengeance. A 50-truck convoy rolled into the square in the dark of night on June 3-4, crushing many protesters as they slept in their tents. Ten thousand soldiers armed with assault rifles attacked the crowds. Hundreds, if not thousands, died before the day ended.

▶ VOYAGER PROBES SOLAR SYSTEM'S LIMITS

The Voyager space probes far exceeded NASA's expectations. The two spacecraft had provided scientists with a wealth of information by 1989 when Voyager 2 approached Neptune, one planet shy of the solar system's known limits.

Part of the Mariner series of probes, the Voyagers' mission was to explore the planets of the outer solar system and their satellites. The probes transmitted tantalizing pictures from the worlds beyond—and provocative discoveries. One of Jupiter's moons, Io, had nine active volcanoes—

VOYAGER 2 FLIES PAST MIRANDA, URANUS'S INNERMOST MOON.

a feature no other body in space had besides Earth. Ten moons never before detected orbited Uranus. Saturn had many more rings than astronomers had believed. Winds on Neptune could reach 1,200 miles an hour, which made them the strongest on any planet.

The knowledge gained was invaluable in answering long-standing questions about the solar system, as well as raising new ones.

▶ PANAMANIAN STRONGMAN SURRENDERS Manuel Noriega's double-crossing days were numbered. The Panamanian dictator's ties to Colombian drug lords had negated his usefulness as a CIA informant. In December U.S. troops invaded Panama and forced Noriega to resign. More than 4,000 Panamanian civilians died, and the U.S. was universally condemned for violating international laws.

Noriega rose to power in the military. He became the de facto leader in 1983 when he took control of the country's National Guard. Despite his bad reputation, the general had a good relationship with the U.S. government. He supplied the CIA with information about Cuban leader Fidel Castro and helped President Ronald Reagan aid the Nicaraguan contras.

In the process of doing the latter, Noriega developed a lucrative sideline; the American planes that unloaded weapons destined for the contras in Panama often returned to the U.S. carrying drugs for

OIL SPILL

The wreck of the *Exxon Valdez* was the worst oil spill in U.S. history. About 11 million gallons of crude oil leaked out of the tanker in March. The oil slick contaminated hundreds of miles of Alaska's shoreline and killed thousands of animals.

The ship was cruising through Prince William Sound with a full cargo. Captain Joseph Hazelwood left a third mate not certified to pilot the vessel in charge and retired to his cabin. Shortly after midnight, the ship ran onto sharp rocks.

Exxon's cleanup efforts proved unable to cope with the huge spill. During the year, hundreds of volunteers poured into Alaska to scrub beaches (below) and oil-covered creatures. But nobody could get rid of the oil beneath the surface.

Hazelwood was acquitted of the most serious charges lodged against him. Exxon paid a $100 million fine and $5 billion in punitive damages to Alaskan fishermen.

South American drug lords.

This ruined relations with Noriega's allies in Washington. Several days after U.S. troops had invaded Panama, he sought refuge in Panama City's papal nunciature. After enduring a steady blast of American heavy metal music, Noriega cracked. He was taken to Florida, tried, and convicted in 1992 for drug trafficking, the first time in history that a jury in the U.S. convicted a foreign head of state on criminal charges.

■ TRENDS & TRIVIA

E.L. Doctorow's *Billy Bathgate* is published.

Walt Disney Studios produces *The Little Mermaid*.

Miss Saigon opens in London.

Ivory trading is banned worldwide.

Teenage Mutant Ninja Turtles become popular.

Jessica Tandy and Morgan Freeman star in *Driving Miss Daisy*.

Kenneth Branagh directs and stars in *Henry V*.

Bristol-Meyers merges with Squibb to create the second largest pharmaceutical company in the U.S. (Merck is the largest.)

The *Los Angeles Herald Examiner* folds after 86 years.

I.M. Pei's metal-and-glass pyramid entrance to the Louvre opens, in Paris.

Amy Tan's *The Joy Luck Club* is published.

Cincinnati Reds player-manager Pete Rose is banned from baseball for life for gambling on games.

Virginia governor Douglas Wilder is the first elected black governor since Reconstruction.

New York City elects its first black mayor, David Dinkins.

Romania permits abortion after death of Ceausescu.

The Stealth bomber is developed.

Time, Inc. buys Warner Communications, Inc. to become Time - Warner.

Ford Motor Co. buys Jaguar Motors for 2.5 billion dollars.

• AUGUST 30
Luxury hotel owner Leona Helmsley is convicted of tax evasion and fraud. She is fined 7.1 million dollars and sentenced to four years.

• SEPTEMBER 26
Last Vietnamese troops leave Cambodia, ending nearly 11 years of occupation.

• SEPTEMBER
South Africa's new president F. W. de Klerk releases some political prisoners and meets with members of African National Congress.

◀ OCTOBER 17
An earthquake hits the San Francisco area, killing 63 people and causing partial collapse of the Bay Bridge.

• NOVEMBER
All political candidates supported by right-to-life advocates lose in U.S. elections.

• NOVEMBER 10
Bulgarian President Todor Zhivkov resigns after 35 years in power.

EARTH'S FORCES

by Rick Gore

NATIONAL GEOGRAPHIC SENIOR ASSISTANT EDITOR, SCIENCE

It was April Fools Day, 1984, and in retrospect we might have been behaving foolishly. But we had a story to cover. Mauna Loa, the 13,677-foot-high volcano whose lava flows have built much of the Big Island of Hawaii, had begun a major eruption that was threatening to bury the city of Hilo. A great river of glowing lava 40 feet thick and 250 yards wide was flowing down the mountain toward the city at about two miles an hour. Photographer Jim Sugar and I had diverted to Hawaii the day before from another assignment to report on the eruption. Now we were in a Jet Ranger III helicopter with two National Park Service rangers, headed toward the volcanic vent to interview geologists monitoring the eruption. No one noticed that the chopper, flown in from tourist duty on another island, was not equipped with gas masks. Foolish mistake number one.

Left: Hurricane Elena, Gulf of Mexico   Middle: Kilauea volcano, Hawaii   Right: Northridge earthquake, California

We had also taken lightly what a native Hawaiian had told us earlier that day: "Pele is living here now." Pele is the fire goddess who rules Hawaii's volcanoes, and even geologists sometimes pay Pele some form of respect—tossing out a placatory phrase before heading into the field or leaving her the requisite bottle of gin in the lava. We had shrugged off paying our respects to Pele. Perhaps that was a second foolish mistake.

As soon as the chopper set down, I hurried off down the slope, eager to meet the scientists at the vent several hundred yards away. But as we were landing, Pele's volcano had belched out a cloud of sulfur dioxide, an invisible gas that blocks the exchange of oxygen in human lungs. I quickly felt a burning in my throat and sinuses. Then I saw that the scientists near the vent were wearing gas masks. I began feeling out of breath. Suddenly panicked, I turned to see my companions racing back toward the chopper. One of the rangers was waving wildly at me.

Gasping, I reached the helicopter, and before I could even sit the pilot roared off. He later told me he felt he had only about 30 seconds of consciousness left. We were all coughing violently. I felt tears streaming down my face. My companions all looked ashen. Many slow seconds later, the pilot cleared Pele's cloud, and we started to catch our breaths. In reporting this natural disaster, we had narrowly avoided our own.

Natural hazards have since become one of my beats, and nowhere have I felt closer to the mission of the Society than when covering nature's awesome and destructive powers. Great storms, for instance, have always fascinated the editors of the magazine. The inaugural issue of the magazine in October 1888 ran two articles on a great snowstorm that struck the Atlantic Coast earlier that year. The stories illustrate how far our ability to track and understand destructive weather systems has come in the past century: "Hundreds of reports from masters of vessels enabled us accurately to plot [the storm's] track," the editors note, "a great parabolic curve tangent to St. Thomas, Hatteras, Cape Race, and the northern coast of Norway. Six months later, a report forwarded by the British Meteorological Office, from a vessel homeward bound from the Equator, indicated that it originated far to the eastward off the coast of Africa, and only the other day the log of a ship which arrived at New York, March 30, from Calcutta, supplied data by means of which the storm track can be traced still more accurately, westward of the Cape Verde Islands."

The GEOGRAPHIC's interest in natural hazards broadened to include volcanoes in May 1902 when the volcano Pelée on the Caribbean island of Martinique exploded, killing nearly every resident of the city of St. Pierre in a superheated avalanche of ash and steam. The young Managing Editor of the magazine, Gilbert Hovey Grosvenor, knew upon hearing of the explosion that this was a GEOGRAPHIC subject. He wired the Society's President, Alexander Graham Bell, for approval to send a two-man scientific team to Martinique. "Go yourself to Martinique in interests of Magazine and I will pay your expenses," Bell wired back. "This is the opportunity of a lifetime—seize it."

Much of two issues of the magazine that year were devoted to the scientific team's findings in Martinique. Moreover, Bell's urgent words had set the tone for the GEOGRAPHIC's approach to natural disasters: Be there with cameras and writers as soon as possible. But that mission was not easy in the early years of the century. When the great San Francisco Earthquake of 1906 struck it was impossible to get a team to the scene quickly. The earthquake hit on April 18, and although the magazine got a report into its May issue, the facts had to be gathered at first from a distance. The lead article was written by a geologist at the U.S. Geological Survey in Washington, D.C., Fredrick Leslie Ransome. "In such a stunning disaster," Ransome wrote, "when communication with the outside world is interrupted, when to the heart-shaking terrors of heaving ground and toppling buildings is abided a form of devastation even more appalling, and when the human aspect of the tragedy so overwhelms all other considerations, it is impossible to obtain at once and at a distance from the scene the data necessary for a satisfactory explanation of the initial catastrophe."

During the first two decades of this century the pages of the GEOGRAPHIC were filled with curiosity about real and potential natural disasters. Members read scholarly, but always vividly written, reports of the 1906 eruption of Mount Vesuvius in Italy, a possible awakening of Mount Hood in Oregon, the eruption of Taal volcano in the Philippines, and a severe earthquake in Sicily. The eruption of Katmai volcano in June 1912 inspired the Society's research committee to send a geological team to Alaska to begin a systematic study of its volcanoes. The first result was a 50-page article, filled with photographs and the firsthand tales of geologist George C. Martin. In those days travel to Alaska was painstakingly slow. Martin did not reach Katmai until four weeks after the eruption began.

Coverage of natural disasters slackened during the 1920s and especially during the years of the Depression and World War II. But during the 1950s the future Editor of the magazine Gilbert M. Grosvenor was developing a keen interest in natural disasters while still in college. He became alarmed by catastrophic flooding in Holland after gale-swept seas breached the country's dikes. With fellow students Grosvenor traveled to the Netherlands to help with the rebuilding. Still it was not until the 1960s that modern journalistic coverage of natural disasters emerged in the GEOGRAPHIC. In his 1962 article "Avalanche" Bart McDowell brought poignant details of devastation wrought by an icy landslide that roared off of Peru's tallest mountain, creating a roar "like that of ten thousand wild beasts."

In 1964 the Good Friday earthquake in Alaska sent another future Editor of the magazine, William Graves, to the scene immediately. Fortunately, transportation to Alaska had improved since the Katmai eruption, letting Graves reach Anchorage two days, not four weeks, after the event. His coverage was filled with on-the-scene details and the words of people who had lived through the trauma. "The floor was heaving so badly," one woman told Graves, "that I couldn't stay on my feet. It was like the floors in fun houses, the ones that spin and float up and down. I used to think they were wonderful." Photographers also raced to the scene, and a team of picture editors and art directors in Washington developed visual coverage that would serve as a historical record of this immense tragedy.

The GEOGRAPHIC instantly dispatches its teams to cover major natural disasters, but unlike most of the media, the GEOGRAPHIC stays around, often publishing months later with a more reflective and detailed record of the event. Those articles have filled some of the GEOGRAPHIC's most memorable pages. When Mount St. Helens erupted in 1980, Editor Bill Garrett was determined to provide members with *the* definitive photographic coverage. And from his opening paragraph, staff writer Rowe Findley drew readers powerfully into his personal encounter with the disaster: "First I must tell you that I count it as no small wonder to be alive," he wrote. "Looking back on the fateful events preceding Mount St. Helens' terrible eruption last May 18, I recognize that I—and others—had been drawn into a strange kind of Russian roulette with that volcano in the Cascades.... The very beauty of the mountain helped deceive us. It was a mountain in praise of mountains, towering over lesser peaks, its near-perfect cone glistening white in all seasons."

By the time I flew onto Mauna Loa in 1984 I had been at the magazine nearly ten years, and was steeped in the legacy of writers like Findley, who throughout the 1970s and 1980s brought a compelling and sympathetic personal vision to the tragedies afflicting others. My colleague and former science editor Tom Canby was dispatched to California for both the 1971 San Fernando and 1989 Loma Priéta earthquakes, and roamed the world in 1977 examining the impact of bizarre and violent global weather, producing "The Year the Weather Went Wild."

My own most memorable coverage was Hurricane Andrew in 1992. I shall never forget my first drive through the stricken suburbs south of Miami after the storm. As one who had grown up in the area, I struggled with my own personal sense of loss as I discovered that all my familiar landmarks were gone. Then I began to absorb the anxieties of the victims of the storm. A bereft 11-year-old Haitian girl typified children in the area who regarded the storm as the "monster." "I think it's coming back," she told me. "And I'm gonna cry, cry, cry.... And the windows are gonna pop, pop, pop." A few hours later a woman volunteering at an emergency food distribution center in Homestead told me: "Oh hon, on the day after, people were breaking into stores, stealing and grabbing. And it was so hot! Lord, on the day after, if I could have had anything it would have been an ice cube in my mouth."

Less than two years later, in January 1994, I found myself on a plane to Los Angeles to watch people pick up after the Northridge earthquake. Although the damage was widespread, it rivaled the devastation of Andrew in only a few places, such as the Northridge Meadows apartments, which collapsed, killing 16 people. In covering the Northridge quake, the GEOGRAPHIC took a different tack from its usual approach. The article, "Living with California's Faults," looked ahead at what life on the geological edge might bring to our most populous state.

This eye on the future continues. In the past few years many geologists have become convinced that the Pacific Northwest is struck, on average, every few hundred years by an earthquake on the scale of the 9.2 temblor that hit Alaska in 1964. As a result, a 200-mile-wide and 600-mile-long region that geologists call Cascadia will be severely shaken, its coast ravaged by great tsunamis. Volcanoes and smaller earthquakes also threaten the region, which stretches from about 200 miles north of San Francisco through most of Vancouver Island.

Assigned to cover this disaster that is yet to happen, I spent months in Cascadia. I heard so many worst-case scenarios that it became difficult to take them all seriously. Yet, as I wrote in the May 1998 issue of the magazine, in the article, "Cascadia, Living On Fire," as unlikely as each may seem in any one person's lifetime, they are all going to happen eventually. Again and again. And although I may not be around to cover them all, there's a good chance the NATIONAL GEOGRAPHIC magazine will be on the scene.

1990-

After the Cold War, the Global Society

1990-2000

by Gaddis Smith
LARNED PROFESSOR OF HISTORY, YALE UNIVERSITY

THE COLD WAR WAS OVER. That was the defining characteristic of the 1990s. Mankind was relieved, at least for most of the decade, of the Damoclean threat of nuclear annihilation, and democracy appeared to have triumphed over totalitarianism in a large part of the world. A wave of free-market reforms and a revolution in the technology of communication brought about a surge in the world economy. After decades of paying scant attention, governments said they recognized the necessity of dealing with global environmental problems.

But these beneficent consequences were not evenly distributed. The Cold War thaw was followed in many places by ethnic and nationalistic violence. Economic growth did not occur everywhere, and in fact, toward the end of the decade, growth itself faltered. And despite wide recognition of the problem, man-made threats to the environment and human health continued.

Mikhail Gorbachev, the last Soviet leader and chairman of the Soviet Communist Party, was more responsible for the end of the Cold War than any other individual. Recognizing the paralytic condition of the Soviet bureaucracy and the impossibility of competing with the West in economic development and military power simultaneously, he unilaterally reduced the Soviet armed forces and especially the nuclear components. Winning the trust of the United

Opposite: Nelson Mandela's long struggle for racial equality in South Africa ended with the abolition of apartheid in 1990. Preceding pages: Cable TV technology in the 1990s gave viewers a plethora of choice—500 different channels.

States and the West, he concluded agreements on nuclear arms control, mutual inspection, and East-West cooperation on many fronts. Gorbachev won the 1990 Nobel Peace Prize, but he was a prophet without honor in his own country. His goal had been to save communism with perestroika (restructure) and glasnost (openness). Instead, the fall of the Berlin Wall in November 1989 symbolized the fall of communism throughout Eastern Europe. By 1991 all of reunified Germany belonged to the North Atlantic Treaty Organization (NATO). The Warsaw Pact, Soviet counterpart to NATO, faded into oblivion. On Christmas Day 1991 the Soviet Union itself was dissolved. Gorbachev was replaced by Boris Yeltsin as president of Russia, and the former republics of the Soviet Union were recognized by the rest of the world as independent states. As the decade proceeded, Yeltsin retained a precarious hold on the leadership in spite of his poor health, the deterioration of government services, and military and economic instability. With the bloody failure to suppress armed opposition in Chechnya and the intermingling of criminal and business enterprise, Russia's future course remained an open question.

The death of Diana, Britain's Princess of Wales, in 1997 unleashed a worldwide outpouring of grief.

BENEFITING MOST FROM THE END of the Cold War was the People's Republic of China. Relieved of the need to devote resources to threats from the Soviet Union, China enjoyed an annual economic growth of 10 percent. Major cities such as Shanghai, Guangzhou, and Beijing were transformed by growing participation in world trade. By late in the decade, the world's memory seemed to be fading of the bloody suppression in June 1989 of protests on behalf of democracy in Beijing's Tiananmen Square. China's human rights record was still bad, but the United States and other trade partners reasoned that human rights would be better served by a high volume of trade than by punitive economic sanctions. The Chinese Communist leadership remained firmly in control, undisturbed by outside criticism or the death in February 1997 of longtime leader Deng Xiaoping. On July 1, 1997, China celebrated the return of the British colony of Hong Kong to Chinese sovereignty, symbolizing its rising power and prestige. Meanwhile, China's relations remained tense with Taiwan, the island the Chinese Communists had been unable to seize at the time of their victory over the Nationalists in 1949. A minority of western China watchers saw a strategic threat, but a majority of them believed China's integration into the world economy would ensure a stable, nonaggressive foreign policy.

In the 1990s Russia and the United States no longer encouraged local wars to gain the illusion of victories over the other. By the same token, the two superpowers now lacked the will or means to prevent or suppress conflict. As a result, international peacekeepers were engaged under the blue-and-white flag of the United Nations in the Balkans, Cambodia, Africa, and parts of the Middle East and Latin America.

Keeping the peace was a complex and often futile proposition, however. The 1990s demonstrated the difficulty of applying the principles of the UN Charter. Was the theoretical right of a minority to self-determination superior to state sovereignty—or did a state's right of self-preservation override separatist aspirations of parts of the population? In fact, might self-determination lead to what President George Bush in 1991 called "suicidal nationalism?" The problem was painfully illustrated in the disintegration of the former Yugoslavia into small independent states. The interethnic fighting among Serbs, Croats, and Muslims in Bosnia, one of those states, was suspended by a peace accord signed in November 1995. But the indefinite presence of 60,000 UN forces, including 20,000 Americans, proved necessary to keep an uneasy peace. Meanwhile, in 1998 the Serbian region of Kosovo, 90 percent of whose population was Albanian, became the next site of violence.

There was also tension between the UN's principle of no outside intervention in internal affairs and its call to protect human rights. If a state violated human rights on a lethal scale or was unable to prevent murderous conflict within its borders, should outside intervention be employed? The answer was yes and no. If a government violating human rights was large, well armed, and economically important to the outside world, such as China, the UN held off. If the country was small and chaotic, intervention was more likely, as in Haiti, where a despotic regime was driven from power by the United States and United Nations in 1994.

Handicapped by lack of money and inadequate powers of enforcement, UN troops could do little to prevent the epidemic of lethal violence that erupted on the continent of Africa. In 1990-92, some 350,000 people died in tribal conflict in Somalia. One million Hutu and Tutsi inhabitants were murdered in reciprocal genocide in Rwanda. Civil wars ravaged Liberia and Zaire (renamed the Democratic Republic of the Congo in 1997), and the military government of Nigeria engaged in deadly repression of its opponents. The most hopeful development on the continent occurred in South Africa: the disappearance of the white racist regime based on apartheid (subordination of blacks and strict separation of races). In its place came the government of President Nelson Mandela, released in 1990 after more than a quarter century of political imprisonment as a leader of the African National Congress.

BY MID-1998, THE DECADE'S ONLY INTERNATIONAL WAR involving great powers had come in response to the aggression of Saddam Hussein's Iraq against Kuwait in 1990. A coalition of powers operating under authority of the UN Security Council and led by the United States first blockaded and then rapidly defeated Iraq's armed forces in the winter of 1991. Iraq attacked Israel with Scud intermediate-range ballistic missiles, but did not arm them with nuclear, chemical, or biological weapons. After four weeks of war, the United States and its partners opted for a conditional cease-fire rather than insist on surrender and the ouster of the regime responsible for the aggression. Defiant and unrepentant, Saddam Hussein remained in power, but he had to agree to two conditions. One, the UN would be allowed to verify that Iraq had dismantled its weapons of mass destruction, and two, American planes would be allowed to protect dissident Kurds and Shiite Muslims within Iraq. The decade saw Iraq and the enforcers of UN conditions engaged in a constant struggle, with short bursts of military action and debate over whether economic sanctions against Iraq should be lifted or modified. Meanwhile, Iran abandoned the xenophobic aspects of the 1979 revolution and sought closer ties with the Western world—even the United States, once denounced in Tehran as "the Great Satan."

Around the world, acts of terrorism increasingly replaced traditional warfare. Some were carried out by disturbed individuals acting for poorly understood reasons, such as, in the United States, the mailing of deadly explosives by the so-called Unabomber and the Oklahoma City bombing; or, in Japan, the use of poison gas in the Tokyo subway by a religious cult. Other terrorist acts were committed by groups with an avowed political purpose: to force the British from Northern Ireland, for instance, or to disrupt the peace process between Israel and the Palestinians, or to embarrass the government of Egypt by killing tourists.

IF THE DECADE HAD A BUZZWORD, IT WAS "GLOBALIZATION." The mid-1990s saw accelerating flows of trade, capital, people, and information across previously resistant borders. The virtues of open international markets were proclaimed everywhere and institutionalized through the establishment of the World Trade Organization (1994), the North American Free Trade Agreement linking the United States, Mexico, and Canada (1994), and the continued movement toward full European economic integration with a common currency. The computer-based revolution in communication and data management, gathering steam since the 1960s, enabled capital to be moved instantly around the world. Business transactions linking all parts of the world were concluded in seconds with the swipe of an electronic card or a few keystrokes, practically eliminating the expense of time and space. The Internet and the World Wide Web made it easy for ordinary people to communicate with anyone anywhere in the world who had a direct satellite link or access to a computer and a phone line. Stock market values throughout the world doubled and doubled again, much as they had in the 1920s—an unpopular analogy on Wall Street. Indeed, the faltering in late 1997 of several Asian economies—Indonesia, South Korea, Thailand, even Japan—chilled the world economic outlook.

Although globalization increased the world output of goods and services, it distributed the benefits unequally. On balance, prices fell, but at the expense of the social satisfactions of local, small-scale commerce. Where dozens of small farms once operated now stretched vast expanses of crops cultivated, sprayed, and picked by machines belonging to large agribusiness concerns. In retailing, small family firms were replaced by the outlets of giant multinational operations. If the spread of manufacturing to the developing world meant new jobs at low wages, it also meant the loss of many jobs in older manufacturing regions.

A more global economy stimulated the movement of millions of people from countryside to cities and from poor regions to the more prosperous—accelerating trends a century old. Most of this migration was legal, but the flow of illegal immigrants across borders produced growing resentment. In the United States, illegal immigrants came largely from Mexico, but also from Central America and the Caribbean. In Western Europe, resentment was directed against people from Africa and the Middle East.

In a world of increased migration and burgeoning tourism, human health became a global issue. Although the number of new cases of AIDS leveled off and declined in developed countries, a 1997 World Health Organization report estimated two million AIDS deaths that year, mostly in the developing world. The report also indicated that 30,000,000 people worldwide (one in every 100 adults) was HIV positive. As life expectancy continued to rise for the world as a whole, with local exceptions for the former Soviet Union and parts of Africa, deaths from cancer rose in much of the world, linked with deteriorating environmental quality and cigarette smoking. And even as the campaign against smoking was succeeding in the United States, tobacco use in the developing world increased.

Despite numerous intensive efforts, the international community was unable to bring peace in the region once called Yugoslavia.

Population growth slowed slightly in the 1990s, but demographers predicted that world population would increase from six billion in 2000 to eight billion by 2025, with almost all of the increase occurring in the world's poorest regions. The increasing numbers of people living for two or more decades beyond the date of retirement presented many societies in the developed world with the problem of paying for health and pension benefits for the aged. Meanwhile, dramatic advances in genetic engineering and cloning techniques raised profound questions about the nature of human life and the ethics of tinkering with it at the genetic level.

THE ENVIRONMENT GAINED ITS SHARE OF ATTENTION in the '90s. With the opening of the communist and former communist world to outside observation, the world discovered that environmental damage was hardly a capitalist monopoly. In June 1992 most of the governments of the world and dozens of environmental organizations gathered in Rio de Janeiro, Brazil, for a much publicized Earth Summit, officially a United Nations conference on Environment and Development. The Rio conference embraced the twin ideals of assisting economic growth for the poor nations of the world and taking measures to combat harmful, environmental effects of modern development. Participants looked hard at global warming resulting from the emission of carbon dioxide from the combustion of fossil fuels. Five years later, with evidence mounting that global warming was accelerating, governments met again, in Kyoto, Japan. After round-the-clock negotiations, a treaty was signed pledging the developed nations to reduce greenhouse gas emissions below 1990 levels by the year 2012. The treaty's fate was uncertain, however, as governments and citizens grappled with the challenge of adopting expensive precautions against threats whose impact, if any, was not immediate. At the end of the 20th century, bottom-line economics and next-election politics still failed to confront the deeper human responsibilities for sustaining a livable world into the future.

IN THE UNITED STATES, THE POST COLD WAR DECADE was marked by declining public and Congressional support for expensive and risky foreign policy initiatives, and a political trend away from the liberal faith that government was the best instrument for solving social problems. With the country enjoying falling unemployment, economic growth, and a perhaps momentary federal budget surplus, Democrat Bill Clinton won the Presidency in 1992 and again in 1996. Although he was scrutinized for alleged sexual improprieties, improper financial dealings, and violations of political fundraising laws, his standing in public opinion polls remained high. Republicans, however, won control of both the House and Senate and talked of undoing liberal measures going back to the New Deal. At national and state levels Republicans led a drive to cut taxes, reduce welfare rolls and entitlements, and end government funding of the arts. Affirmative action, as a legally mandated commitment to redress discrimination against African Americans and other minorities in employment and education, was also under attack.

One area of social spending to increase significantly during the decade was the war on crime. Billions of dollars went to build new prisons, and the number of prisoners per 100,000 citizens rose from 139 in 1980, to 292 in 1990, to 427 in 1996. At mid-decade, black males were seven times as likely to be imprisoned as white males. With more money spent on law enforcement, the incidence of violent crime declined in almost every state and city.

For the United States the mid-1990s were seemingly the most prosperous of the century. The stock market's Dow Jones average soared from 2000 in 1987 to 8600 in early 1998. But even as the affluent purchased expensive cars, personal computers, and fancy clothing, the number of those living below the poverty level (income below $13,359 for a family of four in 1990) was 50 percent higher than in the 1970s, while the gap widened between the wealthiest and poorest segments of society.

In short, both the country and the world were poised to enter the 21st century with some problems nearly as intractable as they had been a century earlier. And although the decade had begun with an easing of nuclear tensions, it ended with the nuclear threat again on the rise as longtime rivals India and Pakistan each detonated underground nuclear tests. Finally, if the millennial milestone has no deep moral significance, it does have an expensive economic one: the so-called Year 2000 problem of reprogramming date-based computer systems. ■

In 1997 Great Britain elected its first Labour prime minister, Tony Blair, in more than 20 years.

The GEOGRAPHIC in the 1990s faced financial challenges and major changes.

For the first time in its history, the Society's presidents were not members of the Grosvenor family. The new leadership came from the for-profit world. Financing the changes they wanted to make entailed staff reductions and an overall tightening of the purse strings.

These adjustments were almost imperceptible in the magazine. Changes there reflected a shift in editorial philosophy throughout publishing. Shorter articles often plugged corresponding stories on the Society's Web site, which debuted in 1996. New features were designed to make the magazine more current and self-revealing. "In Focus" gave readers a better grasp of places in the news, such as the Caucasus and Bosnia, through meticulously detailed maps showing the regions' ethnic enclaves. The monthly "Behind the Scenes" outlined Society events, and shared a few amusing anecdotes staff members and freelances came across in the line of duty.

Still the general fare remained the same—exploration, adventure, natural history, and human culture. After more than a century of such coverage, the magazine had a long-standing commitment to fulfill. No amount of change could dislodge that very important legacy.

Dino-mania

Few Americans who had contact with small children would dispute the popularity of dinosaurs in the '90s. The ancient creatures seemed to walk the earth again, led by a big, purple fellow named Barney. The television star wielded a firm, but friendly grip on small-fry everywhere.

To whet the appetites of their elders, the magazine published a series of articles about new discoveries in paleontology. Sometimes the paleontologists themselves became news. Paul Sereno detailed his discovery of one of the world's largest dinosaurs in the June 1996 issue, then found himself a star on an entirely different stage; *People* magazine voted him one of the best looking human beings of the year.

EGGS OF A THERIZINOSAUR FROM THE CRETACEOUS PERIOD

There was no question about who were the stars in "The Great Dinosaur Egg Hunt" (May 1996). Eggs the size of human heads were turning up all over the world, but most came from Asia. Through careful examination of the eggs' interiors, scientists pieced together new information about the dinosaurs that laid them. They then used the fossilized interiors to create models of the embryos. "Such things," wrote Philip Currie, "make my paleontologist's heart beat faster."

Only an embryo can positively establish a dinosaur's species, something that has been done only half a dozen times. "The study of embryos could reveal more about the link between the dinosaurs and their descendants, the birds."

Hubble's-Eye View

Pictures had always been an integral part of storytelling at NATIONAL GEOGRAPHIC. Occasionally, they told the whole story as they did in April 1997's collection of images taken through the Hubble telescope. During the late 1980s and '90s, satellites such as Hubble had taken dozens of spectacular views of outer space, and the GEOGRAPHIC was a natural venue for them.

THE MIRACLE OF STAR BIRTH UNFOLDS IN THE EAGLE NEBULA.

Launched by NASA in 1990, Hubble probably was "the most significant single device to scan the skies" since Galileo invented the telescope three centuries before, said staff writer William R. Newcott. "For the rest of us Hubble is simply the greatest tour guide ever. The Eagle Nebula's towering pillars evoke the same primal awe as Grand Teton. The violence of [the star] Eta Carinae's explosion is as heart stopping as the maw of a roiling volcano. And thanks to Hubble we can begin to register the notion that while earth is our local address, we have an entire universe that we can call home."

Dilemmas of Covering Nature's Wrath

Covering a disaster can pit journalistic ethics against humanitarian inclinations. Magazine staff writer Alan Mairson experienced this firsthand when he covered the Mississippi River's flooding in 1993. After spending weeks with the residents of Hardin, Illinois, as they prepared themselves and their homes for the possibility of flooding, he was torn between his desire for a good story and his fervent hope that his new acquaintances would be spared.

Science editor Rick Gore faced a similar personal dilemma when he was sent to South Florida to write about the aftermath of Hurricane Andrew in 1992. Gore was born and raised near Miami. For him, the huge story was a rude homecoming. His family had survived, but many of the places he knew as a boy were ruined.

SINGLE-COLUMN SUPPORTS GAVE WAY ON KOBE'S HANSHIN EXPRESSWAY

"So many busted up pieces of people's lives," he wrote as he surveyed a trailer park in Homestead. "All that's left of one home is a sofa smashed into the side of a Ford Tempo, a rain-stained piano, and an oven thrust into a refrigerator."

Photographer Karen Kasmauski traveled to Kobe, Japan, several days after an earthquake devastated the city in January 1995, and killed more than 5,000 people. She was deeply moved by the survivors, who for the most part were people like herself—middle class and comfortable.

"It was a lesson in humanity and graciousness under stress to see people just like me respond to disaster," she recalled. "We as journalists can pat ourselves on the back for doing a good job, and we move on. But those people's lives will never be the same. They will always have that emptiness because of the loss; …the only thing you can do as a journalist is empathize with your subjects. Your role is to capture the humanity of the event and bring it back so other people can share it."

"Cry for One Animal..."

Almost a year after the *Exxon Valdez* disgorged 11 million gallons of crude oil into Alaska's Prince William Sound, NATIONAL GEOGRAPHIC looked at the aftermath. It found a host of scientists who could not discuss what they'd found because of ongoing litigation, dozens of volunteers willing to get on their hands and knees to scrub the fouled beaches clean, and Lazarus, an oil-slathered sea otter whom doctors resurrected from the dead. "He showed up as yet one more emergency around 11 p.m…," the January 1990 article reported. "Delivered in a pet carrier, he was barely moving. His breathing stops. So does his heart…. An oxygen mask goes over the otter's muzzle. An intravenous tube goes into his leg. Warm saline solution is injected under his skin, and he is laid in a warm bath. [A veterinarian] holds his jaws open with a bar as a syringe is connected to a tube that carries both an energy booster and an activated charcoal slurry—to counteract the oil's toxicity—into the animal's stomach."

When the otter was out of danger, the team at the Valdez Sea Otter Rescue Center cheered, then spent two hours scrubbing his fur with liquid detergent. A healthy and clean Lazarus was later released into the sound. "Cry for one animal," a volunteer told another, "but work to save the rest."

Making Sense of the Present

As the millennium approached, the GEOGRAPHIC decided not to look into the past or future. Enough could be told about both through a careful examination of the present.

"Making Sense of the Millennium" launched a 20-part series in January 1998. In the introductory essay, assistant editor Joel L. Swerdlow laid out six themes the magazine planned to cover during the next two years: exploration, the physical world, population growth, biodiversity, culture, and science.

"These are stories about the same thing—our relationship to nature and to one another," he wrote. "Some hit close to home, others probe faraway places. Fundamental to all is our need to know more, to explore new worlds."

Most of the subjects were already close to the GEOGRAPHIC's heart. Exploration of the physical world and its cultures were perhaps the most readily identifiable with the Society. Science and biodiversity had become increasingly popular with readers;

A FUSION RESEARCH ACCELERATOR GENERATES POWER.

the magazine therefore devoted many pages to those topics in the 1990s. And population issues had been discussed, albeit infrequently.

"Our goal is to introduce the key issues the world community will face in the coming years, millennium or no," Editor Bill Allen said of the series. "When those goose eggs click into place two years hence, it would help to have an action plan in place."

Operation Desert Cleanup

"Desert Storm may have been a rout," photographer Steve McCurry wrote in the August 1991 issue of NATIONAL GEOGRAPHIC, "but the real battle may well be Desert Cleanup." His photos stood as grim testimonials to his assertion.

Before the Gulf War ended in February, the skies of Kuwait were black with smoke from burning oil wells that had been torched by Iraqi invaders. They dumped almost six million barrels of oil into the Persian Gulf, destroying thousands of creatures above and below the fouled water line. In a slow-flushing system like the gulf, the damage would linger for years.

Author Thomas Canby spent weeks evaluating the war's toll on the land and its creatures. The Iraqi forces left little alive or intact when they retreated. Oil fields were littered with the bodies of horses. Once green oases were now gray. Gutted office buildings stood where businesses had once thrived.

ENVIRONMENTALISTS EXAMINE A FIELD WHERE THE GROUND HAS BEEN ENCRUSTED WITH OIL.

Canby and McCurry met numerous rescue workers from all over the world who came to bring the environment back from the brink. In one of the story's few upbeat moments, Canby visited a bird rehabilitation center in the coastal town of Al Jubayl. There, volunteers often spent up to two hours gently scrubbing oil off a bird's feathers. Of the 1,200 birds brought in, the handlers had saved several hundred.

"Skies gradually will clear over Kuwait and lands downwind...," Canby concluded. "In the shallows along the Saudi coast, plants and animals will recolonize.... Both will remind us that in war the environment is an inevitable casualty."

Understanding AIDS

AIDS and HIV were covered in two articles, one about epidemiology published in January 1991 and another about viruses that ran in the July 1994 issue. Both treated AIDS

A HEALTH WORKER EXPLAINS PROPER USE OF A CONDOM FOR PROTECTION AGAINST AIDS.

as a global problem affecting men and women, unleashed perhaps by commerce, travel, and the gradual clearing of wilderness. Even more ominous was the news that HIV, the virus that causes AIDS, reacted to each new treatment with a new, resistant strain.

"HIV is evolving a hundred million times faster than we are—perhaps as fast as anything on the planet...," said a geneticist interviewed for the virus article. "This is an extraordinarily restless virus. I think we should be prepared for anything."

In keeping with the magazine's traditional reluctance to broach controversial subjects, NATIONAL GEOGRAPHIC's coverage of AIDS and HIV discussed almost every aspect of the disease except for its link to the gay community. Instead, the magazine chose to ignore the issue of sexuality and focus on the disease's scientific aspects.

"Because AIDS is not exclusively a disease of homosexuals, that focus was not critical to the story," an editor wrote Canadian readers who questioned the omission. "Certainly our readers are already aware of the enormous toll AIDS has taken among the gay population in our own country."

The Ice Maiden

Johan Reinhard did not expect to find the mummified remains of a young Inca girl when he climbed Nevado Ampato on September 8, 1995. The anthropologist and a colleague had climbed up a 20,700-foot Peruvian mountain to get a better view of a nearby volcano.

Once they reached the summit, the men spied a cloth bundle on an ice-covered rocky outcrop. Within the fine woolen fabric was the body of a girl who had died about 500 years before. Her frigid grave had preserved her well; much of her skin was still intact, and she had almost a full head of reddish-brown hair. After examining the objects placed around her, Reinhard speculated she had been sacrificed to the mountain god to secure a good harvest.

Juanita or the "Ice Maiden" was perhaps the best preserved pre-Columbian mummy in the Western Hemisphere. "It's a discovery of worldwide importance," one eminent anthropologist told Reinhard. Two other mummies were found near Juanita, less intact but historically useful.

"The intact body tissues and organs...are a storehouse of biological information," Reinhard wrote in the June 1996 issue. "Future studies of the mummy may reveal how she died. Her DNA should enable us to identify not only the region she came from but also who her living relatives are."

The Ice Maiden became an international sensation. Encased in a temperature-controlled glass box, she journeyed to the Society's headquarters in 1996, where long lines of people waited for hours to pay their respects.

AFTER 500 YEARS IN A FROZEN TOMB AN INCA MUMMY WAS FOUND ON A PERUVIAN PEAK.

"In their early death, I cannot help but think, the Ampato maiden and the two other Inca sacrifices have given new life to the memory of their people," Reinhard concluded, "one of ancient history's greatest civilizations."

• Mongol Mogul

Telling the story of the fearsome Mongol leader, Genghis Khan, gave the magazine the chance to explore the steppes and mountains of Central Asia. After spending decades behind the Iron Curtain, the vast region offered the armchair traveler a wealth of new adventures with a little history added to the mix. The two-part biography was published in the December 1996 and February 1997 issues.

The great Genghis's rule stretched from the Yellow Sea to the Mediterranean in the late 13th century. He and his mounted warriors formed what was then the world's most powerful army, made up of their fellow Mongols and a smattering of other ethnic groups they'd conquered.

Author Mike Edwards's ability to weave history with travelogue made him the ideal storyteller. The soft-spoken

Georgian knew Genghis's territory well; he'd traveled through the region on and off for more than 30 years, first as a Peace Corps officer and then as a journalist.

"In Afghanistan even after 750 years people spoke of the Mongol rampage in voices tinged with apoplexy, as if it happened yesterday," Edwards wrote in the first story. " 'Only nine!' exclaimed an old man in the once elegant city of Herat. 'That is all that survived here—nine people!' I almost expected to see corpses in the streets."

To better understand his subject's bloodthirsty image, Edwards placed Genghis in historical context. "The 13th century was one of the most war torn in history, probably exceeded in cruelty only by our own. Crusaders marched in the Holy Land, Chinese dynasties fought one another, and several wars scourged Central Asia before Genghis invaded. Thus Genghis was a man of his time—only more so."

• Creatures of the Canopy

To further the popular and worthy cause of saving the rain forests, the magazine hired an impressive "big gun"—award-winning entomologist Edward O. Wilson. In the December 1991 issue, the famous scientist revealed the abundance of life high above the forest floor in the canopy.

"The canopy is a brilliantly lit, noisy, three-dimensional world," Wilson wrote. "Wind rakes the tree crowns, evaporating moisture away at a rate comparable to that in grasslands....Sunlight bakes the vegetation.... Frequent rainstorms pound the branches and leaves, breaking away the weak ones."

The tall trees and their residents had faced a far more destructive force than any storm, however. Logging, farming, and herding had cleared away about half of the six million square miles on the planet, Wilson said. By 1990 rain and monsoon forests were disappearing annually at a rate of 55,000 square miles, an area larger than Florida.

"Can humanity afford to lose so much of its natural heritage?" Wilson wrote. "The tragedy, as biologists see it, is that large blocks of diversity are being lost before they can be studied.... It is as though the stars began to vanish at the moment astronomers focused their telescopes."

A SCIENTIST EXPLORES A FOREST FRAGMENT BESIDE A CLEAR-CUT.

MANDELA IS FREED

After spending 27 years behind bars, Nelson Mandela (below) was a free man. A jubilant crowd of more than 50,000 people poured into Cape Town on February 11 to greet the crusader for racial equality after he left prison.

"Today the majority of South Africans, black and white, recognize that apartheid has no future," he proclaimed.

Mandela's struggle against apartheid began more than 40 years before when he joined the African National Congress (ANC), a multiracial group that sought democratic reforms. In 1965 he was sentenced to life imprisonment for alleged sabotage, treason, and conspiring to overthrow the government.

His status galvanized the antiapartheid movement around the world. South Africa's white government grappled with internal strife and economic malaise brought on by a battery of international trade sanctions. In 1990 Prime Minister F. W. de Klerk finally capitulated; he legalized the ANC and freed Mandela.

The two leaders then worked together to bring about a "negotiated revolution," for which they shared the Nobel Peace Prize in 1993.

▶ SAVING OLD-GROWTH FORESTS

At the heart of one of the most virulent environmental debates of the decade perched a spotted owl. Perhaps no other creature symbolized so well man's increasing inability to coexist peacefully with nature.

The northern spotted owl (below) lives almost exclusively in the old-growth forests of California and the Pacific Northwest. To thrive, a pair of owls needs a hunting range of about a hundred acres of woodland comprising typically old-growth redwoods, Douglas fir, spruce, or hemlock. These valuable trees were at the top of the most-wanted lists for lumber companies, too. By 1990 loggers were felling about five billion board feet a year from the federally managed forests in the Northwest. As a result, old growth forests—and spotted owls—were disappearing.

To save the owl from extinction, the U.S. Fish and Wildlife Service listed the bird as threatened under the provisions of the Endangered Species Act. This restricted the amount of timber that could be cut in the spotted owl's habitat. Conservationists cheered the government's two-pronged action; it saved the bird and the land.

The timber industry wanted to add something else to the list—itself. Lobbyists and loggers argued that now an entire region was at risk. Thousands of people would be out of work, and the companies

would lose access to valuable wood.

The spotted owl remained on the list. And throughout the Pacific Northwest timberlands, a hostile new bumper sticker surfaced—"Save a logger, eat an owl."

▶ GERMAN REUNIFICATION

At the stroke of midnight on October 3, Germany was reborn. Political demarcation lines vanished as East and West came together again after 45 years apart (below).

The two nations became one with breathtaking speed only months after the Berlin Wall collapsed. Some feared the pace was too swift. But West German Chancellor Helmut Kohl persisted, undaunted by economic and diplomatic obstacles. Most Germans supported his efforts to bring about *Die Wende* (the change) as reunification was called.

The financial hurdles were high. Five decades of communism had left East Germany in bad financial straits, even though it had been a leader within the Warsaw Pact economies. Experts wondered how East German businesses would fare in a competitive, capitalist society.

Kohl began the financial healing process in July by merging the currencies. Most East Germans were allowed to trade up to 4,000 ostmarks for an equal number of more valuable West German deutsche marks; any amount above that could be

---

- **JANUARY 18**
FBI agents arrest Washington, D.C.'s Mayor Marion Barry for smoking crack cocaine. A videotape of the shocking event is televised.

- **JANUARY 25**
Film star Ava Gardner dies of pneumonia at 68 in London.

- **FEBRUARY 26**
Nicaraguans elect Violeta Chamorro president in the country's first free election since the Sandinistas took over in 1979.

- **MARCH 11**
Lithuania declares its independence from the Soviet Union.

- **MARCH 25**
Fire sweeps though a social club in the Bronx and kills 87 people.

- **APRIL 15**
Swedish film star Greta Garbo dies at 84 in New York after years of seclusion.

- **MAY 16**
Muppeteer Jim Henson dies at 53 in New York.

- **MAY 22**
North and South Yemen are reunited after decades of fighting.

exchanged at a two-for-one ratio. Kohl also pumped billions of deutsche marks into the east to jump-start its economy.

The Western powers made NATO membership a prerequisite for reunification. The Soviets opposed this and refused to cede control of East Germany. But Kohl persisted and brokered a deal with Soviet leader Mikhail Gorbachev in July.

Unity came with high costs. The new country had problems with a shortage of housing, strikes, unemployment, and an increase in crime. Taxes went up, and services went down. The East lagged behind the West in living standards and industrial performance. Nonetheless, the reunified Germany boasted one of the world's strongest economies near the century's end.

▶ ARISTIDE'S TUMULTUOUS CAREER
On December 17 a radical priest became Haiti's first freely elected president. Jean-Bertrand Aristide captured more than 60 percent of the vote, coming out far ahead of his ten opponents.

As a young seminarian, Aristide became an adherent of liberation theology, which taught Christians to strive for social and economic justice for all people. Because his outspoken beliefs put him at odds with the repressive rule of Jean-Claude Duvalier, Aristide's superiors sent him outside the country for several years to cool his political activist heels.

He returned to Haiti in 1985 and became pastor of a small parish in one of Port-au-Prince's poorest neighborhoods. The popular priest then led his devoted flock to protest against Duvalier, as well as the proxies who assumed control after his deposition in 1986. Aristide's outspoken radicalism did not endear him to the government or the Catholic hierarchy, which expelled him from his order in 1988. Undaunted by numerous assassination attempts, he campaigned for president

DISABILITIES ACT

The Americans With Disabilities Act recognized the civil rights of an important new political group—the more than 43 million people afflicted with physical or mental disabilities.

President George Bush signed the sweeping civil rights legislation in 1990 (below). It prohibited discrimination against the disabled.

The number of disabled Americans had grown toward the end of the century, partially because medical advances allowed people to live longer. The population increase intensified the need for better accessibility and specific laws designed to assist the disabled. The Americans With Disabilities Act was one of the first steps to recognize those needs. Businesses installed wheelchair ramps and revamped their employment policies. Public transportation stepped up the use of "kneeling" buses. Those who were once considered powerless now emerged as a strong force to be reckoned with—and respected.

two years later. "I have been immunized against fear," he told reporters.

Once elected, he continued to make enemies, particularly in the military. Ten months after the election, Brig. Gen. Raoul Cédras seized control of the government. Aristide and thousands of Haitians sought asylum in the U.S. He returned to office in 1994, escorted into the capital by 20,000 American soldiers.

■ TRENDS & TRIVIA

NBC introduces *Seinfeld*.

A posthumous exhibit of Robert Mapplethorpe's homoerotic photographs raises concerns about public funding for the arts.

M. C. Hammer releases "U Can't Touch This."

Richard Gere and Julia Roberts star in *Pretty Woman*.

Dr. Jack Kevorkian displays his "suicide machine". ▶

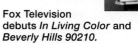

Mel Gibson stars in *Hamlet*.

Fox Television debuts *In Living Color* and *Beverly Hills 90210*.

Martin Scorsese directs *GoodFellas*.

Smoking is banned on all domestic airlines flights.

McDonald's opens in Moscow.

Time-Warner introduces *Entertainment Weekly*, its first new magazine since *People* in 1974.

General Motors introduces the Saturn automobile.

Patrick Swayze and Demi Moore star in *Ghost*.

Washington, D.C.'s National Cathedral is finished after 80 years of construction.

FDA approves Norplant, a birth control device invented by researchers at New York's Rockefeller Institute.

John Updike's *Rabbit at Rest* is published.

Robert Bly's *Iron John* is published and becomes the bible of the men's movement.

365

- **MAY 29**
Boris Yeltsin is elected chairman of the Russian Supreme Soviet.

- **JUNE 22**
An earthquake in northwestern Iran leaves some 40,000 dead and 100,000 wounded.

- **AUGUST 2**
Iraqi forces invade Kuwait.

- **OCTOBER 14**
Conductor Leonard Bernstein dies five days after announcing his retirement.

- **NOVEMBER 9**
Liberal lawyer Mary Robinson becomes Ireland's first female president.

- **NOVEMBER 27**
British Prime Minister Margaret Thatcher leaves her post after 11 years. She is replaced by fellow Tory John Major.

- **DECEMBER 2**
American composer Aaron Copland dies at 90.

1991

In a spectacular reversal of power, the Soviet Union disintegrated in December, leaving in its place 15 republics.

The end began in August when a group of Communist hard-liners tried to depose President Mikhail Gorbachev whose reforms threatened their power. On August 19 they placed the president under house arrest while he vacationed in the Crimea. The coup leaders announced they were in control because Gorbachev was "unwell."

But the putsch could not stop what Gorbachev had begun. In Moscow, Russian Republic President Boris Yeltsin (above) led an angry mob to Parliament where the coup had established headquarters. Within days, the rebels surrendered. Gorbachev was released, shaken but unharmed.

His power, however, was no longer salvageable. The Soviet Union disappeared and Yeltsin was hailed as the architect of the confederation.

Gorbachev was forced to resign on Christmas Day. "The old system," the once powerful leader observed sadly, "fell apart even before the new system began to work."

▶ THE CONFUSING SAGA OF BCCI

The collapse of the Bank of Credit and Commerce International (BCCI) became a major scandal in July when regulators in 69 countries seized the bank's assets on charges that officials had concealed substantial losses from their investors. The regulators estimated losses of about ten billion dollars.

The BCCI scandal was a complex mess that most people had heard of but few really understood. What was clear was that it involved money laundering, extortion, and somehow the silver-haired, ultimate Washington insider, Clark Clifford.

A Pakistani businessman incorporated BCCI as a Luxemborg holding company in 1972. Agha Hasan Abedi's organization soon had a hand in a variety of questionable activities, such as brokering deals for drug lords and peddling military information to Iran. By 1990 it had about 20 billion dollars in assets, including ownership of one of the largest banks in Washington, D.C.

BCCI attempted to hide its ownership of First American Bank shares to get around federal laws. The bank's two top executives, Clifford and his protégé Robert Altman, brokered the deal in 1982 and told regulators the purchasers were a group of Middle Eastern investors. But the government was suspicious, especially after Altman acknowledged that BCCI was one of his numerous legal clients.

When the company collapsed, Altman and Clifford faced charges on the federal and state level. After several years of wrangling, the federal charges were dropped. Altman was acquitted of all charges filed in New York, and the courts there dropped charges against Clifford because he was deemed too ill to stand trial.

As for BCCI, 12 of its officials were convicted of several crimes in Abu Dhabi in 1994. But Abedi, the organization's founder, remained free in Pakistan.

CREMATION OF RAJIV GANDHI

▶ ANOTHER GANDHI ASSASSINATED

Like his mother, Indira, and her close friend, Mohandas K. Gandhi, Rajiv Gandhi was a victim of political zealots. Tamil separatists killed the 46-year-old man on May 21 as he campaigned for reelection in Madras. Seventeen others died when a homemade bomb ripped through the crowd.

To some members of the Liberation Tigers of Tamil Eelam (LTTE), Gandhi's demise was well worth the sacrifice. From their headquarters in the jungles of northwestern Sri Lanka, the Hindu guerrillas had waged a bloody civil war with the island's Buddhist majority since the early 1980s. Indira Gandhi ignored the LTTE's training camps in India's Tamil Nadu district across the Palk Strait from Sri Lanka. But her son did not. In 1987 he dispatched 60,000 troops into Sri Lanka to crush the LTTE; within a year, the guerrillas' ranks had dwindled to less than 1,500 from about 5,000.

When Rajiv announced he would run again to be India's prime minister, the LTTE geared up to stop him. On May 21, 1991, he arrived in Madras, the provincial capital of Tamil Nadu, to speak to voters. As he walked to the podium, he stopped to accept a garland from a young woman. As he bent his head so she could place the flowers around his neck, she detonated a bomb she wore around her waist underneath her clothing. The bomb blew the LTTE agent's head off and crushed her target's skull.

366

- **JANUARY**
Soviet troops crack down on the three rebel republics of Lithuania, Latvia, and Estonia.

- **FEBRUARY 25**
Foreign ministers of Bulgaria, Poland, Hungary, Czechoslovakia, Romania, and the Soviet Union vote to dissolve the Warsaw Pact.

- **MARCH 31**
Iraqi forces seize key Kurdish strongholds in northern Iraq, causing thousands of Kurds to seek refuge in Turkey.

- **APRIL 9**
The Republic of Georgia, birthplace of Joseph Stalin, votes to secede from the Soviet Union.

- **MAY 23**
U.S. Supreme Court rules that counselors at federally funded family planning clinics may not discuss abortion with pregnant women.

- **JUNE 15**
Mount Pinatubo erupts in the Philippines, forcing mass evacuation.

- **JUNE 17**
South Africa's all-white House of Assembly votes to repeal apartheid rules adopted in 1950.

▶ OPERATION DESERT STORM
Liberating Kuwait from its Iraqi invaders in February established the U.S. as the dominant power in the post-Cold War Middle East. Under the rubric "Operation Desert Storm," American troops vanquished the Iraqi army in little more than six weeks.

"We're coming home now proud, confident, heads high," President George Bush proclaimed.

U.S. troops had saved the vast oil fields of Kuwait from falling into the hands of Iraqi President Saddam Hussein. In doing so, the U.S. helped kick the "Vietnam War Syndrome" of intervention and loss. Victory in the Gulf War played well on the home front, too. Bush's approval ratings soared, and he now had an important achievement to tout in his reelection campaign.

The one thing Bush did not do, to the puzzlement of many Americans, was eliminate Saddam Hussein. The Iraqi dictator remained in place despite the fact that he'd lost thousands of troops, his country was devastated, and Kurdish rebels threatened

LIBERATION OF KUWAIT CITY AFTER 42 DAYS OF WAR

his regime. Some experts speculated he'd been left in place to prevent Iranian-backed Shiites in Iraq from turning the country into another center for Islamic extremism. Others said the U.S. did not march on to Baghdad because it was under

ANITA HILL CASE

Clarence Thomas's confirmation hearings for the U.S. Supreme Court lay bare the issue of sexual harassment. A former employee accused the conservative judge (right) of pressuring her for dates and making inappropriate comments.

Anita Hill (below) worked for Thomas when he was head of the Equal Employment Opportunity Commission in the 1980s. In a calm, deliberate manner, she described her former supervisor's behavior to the Senate Judiciary Committee as millions watched the hearings on television.

The judge's demeanor was often in sharp contrast to Hill's. "No job is worth what I've been through—no job." Thomas snapped, "Confirm me if you want…, but let this process end." The Senate confirmed him by a 52-48 vote.

a UN mandate to liberate Kuwait, not remove Hussein.

Gulf War residuals lingered long after the last Americans left the region. Iraqi troops dumped millions of gallons of Kuwaiti oil into the gulf and torched the wells, wreaking havoc on the fragile environment. Gulf War veterans complained of mysterious ailments, which led some physicians to suspect chemical weapons had been used. And the U.S., now responsible for the deaths of thousands of Arab Muslims, realized that it had to jump-start the Middle East peace process once again.

■ TRENDS & TRIVIA

John Grisham's *The Firm* is published.

Susan Faludi's *Backlash: The Undeclared War Against American Women* is published.

Norman Mailer's *Harlot's Ghost* is published.

Oliver Stone directs the movie *JFK.*

Susan Sarandon and Geena Davis star in *Thelma & Louise.*

CNN's Ted Turner marries film star-workout queen Jane Fonda.

Bonnie Raitt releases "Let's Give 'Em Something to Talk About."

Jonathan Demme directs *The Silence of the Lambs.*

International Olympic Committee ends its 21-year boycott of South Africa.

Zhang Yimou directs *Raise the Red Lantern.*

White South African writer Nadine Gordimer becomes the first woman to win the Nobel Prize for literature in 25 years.

Jennie Livingston directs *Paris is Burning.*

The Secret Garden debuts on Broadway.

Keith Carradine stars in *The Will Rogers Follies* on Broadway.

FDA approves ddl, a Bristol-Myers AIDS drug.

Robert Maxwell buys the *New York Daily News* for 40 million dollars.

New York's Grand Central Station becomes strictly a commuter station after 78 years.

American Express celebrates the centennial of its travelers cheques.

367

● JULY 6
Serbian and Croatian leaders tell their people to prepare for war.

● JULY 22
Milwaukee police arrest Jeffrey Dahmer for killing 17 men, some of whom he ate.

● AUGUST
Crowds in Brooklyn riot after a Hasidic Jew hits two black children in a car accident in the Crown Heights neighborhood.

● SEPTEMBER 11
Soviet President Mikhail Gorbachev announces he will withdraw all troops stationed in Cuba.

● SEPTEMBER 24
Writer-cartoonist Theodor Seuss Geisel "Dr. Seuss" dies at 87.

● NOVEMBER 7
Basketball star Earvin "Magic" Johnson announces on television that he has contracted AIDS through heterosexual sex.

● DECEMBER 11
William Kennedy Smith, nephew of the late president John F. Kennedy, is acquitted of raping a woman he met in a Florida nightclub.

The Bosnian civil war became Europe's costliest war in half a century. It began in March when Bosnia became the fourth of Yugoslavia's six republics to declare its independence. But radicals refused to recognize the new multiethnic government in which the largest ethnic groups—Muslims, Roman Catholic Croats, and Eastern Orthodox Serbs—would share power.

Before the war, almost half of Bosnia's 4.3 million people were Muslim, descendants of Slavs who adopted the faith of their Ottoman overlords in the 15th century. About 31 percent were Serbs and 17 percent were Croats. In general, the groups got along. But after independence, Serb and Croat extremists stirred up old

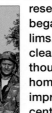

resentments and began killing Muslims. This "ethnic cleansing" left thousands dead, homeless, or imprisoned in concentration camps. Some villages lost their entire population.

By 1996 the U.S. and UN brokered an uneasy cease-fire. "This is a shattered place," a World Bank official told NATIONAL GEOGRAPHIC in 1996. "Every person you meet has a son or daughter, a husband or a wife, maimed or killed."

▶ "CAN WE ALL GET ALONG?"

The riots that ripped Los Angeles apart in the spring reminded the country that racial strife was not a thing of the past.

Hundreds of Los Angelenos were outraged when an all-white jury acquitted four police officers charged with beating an unarmed black man whom they had stopped for speeding in March 1991. The white officers clubbed and kicked Rodney King as he crumpled to the ground beside his car. Unbeknownst to the police, a witness filmed their attack and then publicized the video. The incident triggered a national debate about how police in general treated minorities.

To blacks the April 30 verdict was outrageous. In Los Angeles the frustration of many gave way to rioting. Roving gangs, intent on looting stores and homes, exacerbated the situation. Several black youths dragged a white trucker out of his cab and beat him unconscious as helicopter-borne TV cameramen watched.

The city was ablaze for five days (above) before authorities could bring it under control. More than 50 people were dead, and about one billion dollars worth of property was damaged or destroyed.

Shortly after the verdict came down, the federal government filed civil rights charges against the officers, two of whom were later convicted. But the debacle profoundly disturbed Americans, many of whom had hoped that racism had diminished in the post-civil rights era. Like Rodney King, they surveyed the damage and wondered, "People, can we all get along?"

▶ THE DREAM TEAM

The U.S. Olympic Dream Team was just that—12 of the greatest basketball players ever assembled. Together, they reminded the world that basketball was invented in and dominated by the U.S.

"The only team that can beat us is us," said Coach Chuck Daly as his players trounced team after team in the 1992 Summer Olympics in Barcelona. They outscored their opponents in 14 games by an average of almost 44 points.

Prior to 1992, FIBA, the organization that regulated basketball for the International Olympic Committee, did not allow professional basketball players to compete. In the late 1980s, FIBA members voted overwhelmingly to change that, in part because the Olympic Committee's president wanted to ensure the games showcased the world's best athletes, regardless of whether they were professional or amateur.

The team comprised professionals with the exception of one college player. Sports fans and celebrity hounds crowded the team's hotel in Barcelona to catch a glimpse of Michael Jordan, Earvin "Magic" Johnson (above), Larry Bird, and other star players.

▶ GOOD NIGHT

Johnny Carson's retirement reflected his impeccable sense of timing. The TV legend disappeared behind his striped curtain at the top of his game after sending Americans off to bed with smiles on their

• **JANUARY 1**
Egyptian diplomat Boutros Boutros Ghali becomes Secretary-General of the UN.

• **JANUARY 15**
The European Community recognizes the independent nations of Slovenia and Croatia.

• **FEBRUARY 10**
Writer Alex Haley dies at 70.

• **MARCH 26**
Prize-fighter Mike Tyson is sentenced to ten years in jail after he is convicted of raping a beauty pageant contestant in Indianapolis.

• **APRIL 2**
Mafia Don John Gotti is convicted on five counts of murder in New York.

• **APRIL 9**
Former Panamanian leader Manuel Noriega is convicted on drug trafficking charges in Miami.

• **MAY 6**
Film legend Marlene Dietrich dies at 90 in Paris.

faces for almost 30 years.

The host of NBC's *The Tonight Show* was one of the most influential people in television history. Carson recognized and cultivated the talent of up-and-coming comedians like Flip Wilson, David Letterman, and Jerry Seinfeld. Nothing could escape his wry observations, from current events to his own marital troubles. Sometimes the humor even overwhelmed him, and he'd break out into uncontrollable laughter.

But on May 22 the 66-year-old star could not hold back the tears as Bette Midler saluted his retirement in song. "It's been a helluva lot of fun," Carson told the millions of viewers watching his last show. Then the lights went out, and he left the public eye. He'd garnered numerous awards and was a millionaire many times over; by 1979 *The Tonight Show* alone generated 17 percent of NBC's profits.

▶ RIO SUMMIT

The 1992 UN Conference on Environment and Development held in Rio de Janeiro was the largest gathering of its kind. Representatives from more than a hundred countries met in June to discuss how they could better preserve the Earth.

Two major treaties came out of the Earth Summit. In the first, signers agreed to reduce gas emissions that caused global warming. The second, called the Convention on Biodiversity, required participants to protect endangered species and the habitats they needed for survival.

Five years after the summit not much had been done to fulfill its goals. UN officials reported that animals and plants, as

EARTH SUMMIT DEMONSTRATION IN RIO

well as their habitats, were being obliterated at an "unprecedented rate." Wealthy nations had delivered about half the funds they had pledged to raise to help clean up the planet. And only a handful of developing countries seemed to be on track in capping their emissions at 1990 levels by the year 2000.

"We reached the zenith of our enthusiasm and commitment for sustainable development and the environment in 1992," UN General Assembly President Razali Ismail told the *New York Times* in 1997. "Since then, many other things have come our way. Since then, a sense of parochialism has spread over much of the developed world…."

CLINTON ELECTED

Bill Clinton promised to be a "different kind of Democrat." The presidential nominee pledged to blend old-fashioned Democratic liberal social policies with Republican-style fiscal responsibility.

It was a winning combination. The 46-year-old Arkansas governor (right) catapulted himself into the White House with 43 percent of the popular vote.

Clinton exuded energy and creativity after 12 years of avuncular Republicans. But his charm was a double-edged sword. Rumors of marital infidelities became enough of a problem that he decided to tackle the issue in the most public of forums—TV. With his wife, Hillary, at his side, Clinton told *60 Minutes* that he had "caused some pain" in their marriage. But they'd gotten over it and hoped the American public would, too. Enough people did. "The Comeback Kid" came back again.

369

■ TRENDS & TRIVIA

Cormac McCarthy's *All the Pretty Horses* is published.

Nirvana introduces "grunge" rock.

Congress closes the House of Representatives Bank in the wake of a scandal.

James Ivory directs *Howards End*.

Spike Lee directs *Malcolm X*.

Neil Jordan's film *The Crying Game* shocks audiences with its surprise twist.

Barney and Friends debuts on daytime TV.

The *New Yorker* magazine allows photographs in its stories.

FDA approves Nicoderm, a patch worn on the arm to control the urge to smoke.

Covering 78 acres, Minnesota's Mall of America is the largest shopping mall in the U.S.

R. H. Macy & Co. files for protection under Chapter 11 of the federal bankruptcy code.

Jay Leno replaces Johnny Carson as host of NBC's *The Tonight Show*.

England's Prince Andrew and his wife, Sarah, separate after the paparazzi photograph another man sucking her toes by a pool.

CBS introduces *Northern Exposure*.

American astronauts Mark Lee and Jan Davis become the first married couple to go into space together (aboard the space shuttle *Endeavour*).

The Vatican concedes that Galileo Galilei's theory that Earth orbits the sun was correct and absolves the astronomer posthumously.

- **JUNE 24**
Lloyd's of London, the 300-year-old insurer, announces the worst loss in its history—2.06 billion pounds.

- **JUNE 26**
Secretary of the Navy H. Lawrence Garrett III accepts responsibility for the 1991 "Tailhook" sexual harassment scandal.

- **JULY 1**
African American Willie Williams succeeds Daryl Gates as chief of the beleaguered Los Angeles Police Department.

- **AUGUST**
Hurricane Andrew hits Florida and the Gulf Coast. Almost 60 people die and thousands are made homeless.

- **SEPTEMBER 29**
Brazil's President Fernando Collor de Mello is impeached on charges of taking money from a slush fund and lying to cover it up.

- **OCTOBER**
Liberian rebels kill five American nuns during that country's civil war.

- **DECEMBER 9**
President George Bush sends Marines on humanitarian aid mission to war-torn Somalia.

OSLO ACCORDS

It was a handshake felt around the world. On September 13, PLO leader Yassir Arafat extended his hand to Israeli Prime Minister Yitzhak Rabin, who, after a moment's hesitation, accepted it (below). The men had just taken the first step toward ending the enmity that had plagued their region for almost five decades.

Their historic meeting on the White House lawn was the culmination of two years of top secret negotiations begun in Oslo. Although the peace accord they signed did not address all necessary issues, it mandated significant change in one of the world's most troubled spots.

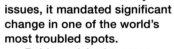

Rabin and Arafat came together partly out of need. A global surge in Islamic extremism had given rise to several new anti-Israeli organizations that made the PLO appear more moderate. There was also some pressure on both sides from ordinary people, fed up with living in a war zone.

But a handshake was not enough to erase years of hatred. Within months, extremists on both sides began working to destroy the fragile peace that Rabin and Arafat so bravely tried to create.

▶ "DON'T ASK, DON'T TELL"
After rancorous debate, President Bill Clinton and the Joint Chiefs of Staff reached a compromise on the issue of homosexuals in the military. The July decision permitted gays to serve in the armed forces as long as they did not reveal their sexual orientation or engage in homosexual activity.

The gay community called the "don't ask, don't tell" policy a cop-out. Before the election, Clinton won the gay vote because he promised to lift the ban. Once in office, he tried to make good, but ran into formidable opposition on Capitol Hill and in the Pentagon. The gay lobby, which had been gaining momentum since the 1960s, did not have enough clout to overthrow the ban after all. Clinton's team tried to spin the new policy as a victory of sorts.

▶ FORMING TRADE BLOCS
International trade issues dominated much of the news in 1993 as two of the world's largest trading blocs struggled to approve treaties designed to strengthen their positions in the global marketplace.

Late in the year, the U.S. Congress ratified the North American Free Trade Agreement (NAFTA), while the European Union had ratified what became known as the Maastricht Treaty.

Representatives from each of the 15 nations in the European Union (known until 1993 as the European Community) approved a plan in 1993 to create a common currency and bank. But high unemployment coupled with overproduction in other countries bedeviled the European bloc. Denmark and England balked at the idea of a common currency. Maastricht looked as though it might not happen.

Across the Atlantic, NAFTA also was in trouble. Signed in 1992 by the leaders of Mexico, Canada, and the U.S., the treaty eliminated trade barriers and tariffs between the three nations during the next 15 years with the intention of creating a free market area and trading bloc better able to compete internationally. In the U.S., however, trade unions and environmentalists howled in protest (right). American businesses would head south, they said, tempted by Mexico's cheap labor market and less stringent antipollution regulations.

Within a few years, NAFTA was in place, and the effects were not as drastic as feared. And the dream of a common currency was closer to becoming a reality.

▶ FEDERAL DISASTER AT WACO
The U.S. government's attempts to raid a religious cult's compound in Waco, Texas, ended in disaster. When the flames that engulfed the building were finally doused, some 80 people were dead, and a federal agency's future looked grim.

The Treasury Department's Bureau of Alcohol, Tobacco, and Firearms (ATF) approached the Branch Davidian compound in February to investigate allegations that members were stockpiling illegal weapons. They had received reports that the group's leader, David Koresh, was physically and mentally abusive.

The Davidians viewed the impending ATF search as the manifestation of cult leader David Koresh's doomsday scenario. They began hoarding food, fuel, and weapons to prepare for the end of the world. When ATF agents came near on February 28, the

• JANUARY 1
Czechoslovakia peacefully splits into the Czech Republic and Slovakia in what Europeans call "the velvet divorce."

• JANUARY 24
Former U.S. Supreme Court Justice Thurgood Marshall dies at 84.

• FEBRUARY 6
Tennis star Arthur Ashe dies of AIDS complications at 49. He was the first black ever to win a Grand Slam event.

▶ FEBRUARY 26
Islamic terrorists bomb New York's World Trade Center, killing five people and wounding hundreds of others.

• MARCH 3
Dr. Albert Sabin, developer of the most widely used polio vaccine, dies at 86.

• MARCH 11
Janet Reno becomes first female attorney general of the U.S.

Davidians opened fire. Four agents and two cult members died.

The siege dragged on for another 50 days. The FBI intervened in April and pumped tear gas into the building to force the occupants out. Instead, the compound caught on fire. Nine cult members escaped, but the rest, including Koresh who shot himself, died while reporters and federal agents watched in horror.

Although the FBI carried out the final raid, the ATF was blamed for the debacle. Militia groups and right-wing extremists cited Waco as the perfect example of an overbearing government. Treasury investigators excoriated ATF agents in a 500-page report, and the little-publicized bureau soon found itself under intense public scrutiny.

▶ THE BRADY BILL

James Brady needed help turning the pages of the speech he'd prepared in honor of the landmark gun control legislation that bore his name. The former presidential press secretary was confined to a wheelchair with the use of one hand only, the victim of a "disturbed young man with a gun."

The road he traveled to see the Brady Bill signed into law was tortuous. Thirteen years before, Brady was shot in the head during an assassination attempt against President Reagan. The partially paralyzed man then began his new life as a poignant fighter in the battle for gun control.

PRESIDENT CLINTON SIGNS THE BRADY BILL AS BRADY LOOKS ON.

SURFIN' THE NET

Before 1993, most Internet surfers worked for the government or in academia. But the surfing population began to take off that year, partially because the National Science Foundation increased the amount of data that could be transmitted between computers in a second.

Within two years, the computer-based worldwide network had revolutionized communications. The Internet was the brainchild of contractors whom the Department of Defense hired in the 1960s to create a decentralized computer network that could withstand destruction of some of its parts. The ARPANET system was launched in 1969 and gradually expanded to include other government agencies, universities, and libraries all over the world.

Personal computers also aided Internet development. More and more users wanted to tap into the wealth of information available through the network. In 1994 about 15 million surfers logged onto the "net" to download documents.

The Brady Bill required gun buyers to wait five days before taking possession. During that time, local authorities checked the buyer's background for prior arrests. Supporters of the bill said this would curb the number of gun-related incidents, but the gun lobby argued such legislation violated the Second Amendment of the Constitution that stated, "A well-regulated militia being necessary to the security of a free State, the right of the people to keep and bear arms, shall not be infringed."

After a seven-year struggle, Congress passed the Brady Bill. President Clinton signed it into law on November 30.

■ TRENDS & TRIVIA

John Le Carré's *The Night Manager* is published.

Larry McMurtry's *Streets of Laredo* is published.

Philip Roth's *Operation Shylock* is published.

The Holocaust Museum opens in Washington, D.C.

Japan's Crown Prince Naruhito marries a young businesswoman named Masako Owada.

Jonathan Demme directs *Philadelphia* with Tom Hanks and Denzel Washington.

Holly Hunter stars in Jane Campion's *The Piano.*

Andrew Lloyd Webber takes *Sunset Boulevard* to the theater.

Harold Prince's play *Kiss of the Spider Woman* debuts.

American novelist Toni Morrison wins the Nobel Prize for literature.

First voice-activated remote control for TV and radio is marketed worldwide.

Robert Waller's *The Bridges of Madison County* is published.

Clint Eastwood wins his first Academy Award for best director of the best film *Unforgiven.*

Computer-generated virtual reality games are a hit.

Stephen Spielberg's *Jurassic Park* rakes in 81.7 million dollars in its first week in theaters.

Harley-Davidson celebrates 90 years of making motorcycles.

Buckingham Palace begins charging admission for tours.

● **MAY 27**
Terrorists bomb Florence's Uffizi Gallery, killing six, and destroying several works of art.

● **JULY 20**
Vincent Foster, Jr., deputy White House counsel, commits suicide in McLean, Virginia.

● **JULY 29**
Israeli Supreme Court overturns the sentence of John Demjanjuk, accused of killing thousands of Jews in a Nazi concentration camp.

● **AUGUST**
Huge amounts of rain cause the Mississippi River to flood. At least 50 people die, and thousands more are homeless.

● **OCTOBER 20**
Benazir Bhutto is sworn in for a second time as Pakistan's prime minister.

● **OCTOBER 25**
Actor Vincent Price, best known for his roles in horror movies, dies at 82.

● **DECEMBER 22**
Australia passes the controversial Native Title Bill, which gives indigenous peoples rights to their native lands.

For the first time in their turbulent history, black South Africans had a say in who would run the country.

In April, 16 million blacks went to the polls, sometimes waiting in lines more than a mile long, for the chance to elect one of their own president.

"Let there be justice for all…," Nelson Mandela proclaimed. "The time for the healing of the wounds has come."

Mandela inherited a monumental challenge. About 50 percent of the black population was illiterate. Most lived in substandard housing, and few owned arable land. There was almost no foreign investment.

The compassionate president had secured a transition that many people thought would never occur. Within four years, access to water and electricity had improved substantially, and the government wisely avoided overspending. Mandela was living proof that the right person in the right place at the right time could indeed make a difference.

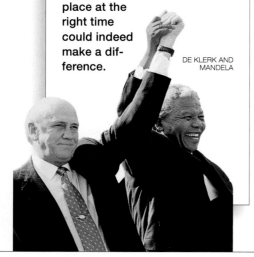
DE KLERK AND MANDELA

▶ IRA LAYS DOWN ITS ARMS

The Irish Republican Army agreed to lay down its arms August 31 after months of internal maneuvering. The announcement was a step, albeit a small one, toward ending the IRA's part in the sectarian violence that had ripped Northern Ireland apart for 25 years and left 3,200 people dead.

Gerry Adams, leader of the IRA's political wing, Sinn Fein (Irish for "we ourselves") had been grappling with the decision since December 1993. The British and Irish governments offered the predominantly Catholic organization a role in the discussions about Northern Ireland's political future if it would refrain from violence. Adams then had the

BELFAST AFTER IRA CEASE-FIRE

formidable task of convincing the various factions of his group that this was acceptable. After wringing several concessions from Protestant Unionists who had their own paramilitaries at work, he received the blessing of several IRA heroes to follow through on the cease-fire.

▶ TROUBLES SOUTH OF THE BORDER

The year 1994 was tumultuous for Mexico from the start. Armed peasants rose up in the south, and two prominent politicians were assassinated. By the year's end, the currency was devalued, deepening the economic crisis and lowering the living standard for most Mexicans.

The uprising, led by the Zapatista

National Liberation Army, was an indication that all was not well south of the border. On January 1 about 2,000 Indians seized seven villages in the southernmost state of Chiapas, one of the country's poorest, and demanded

REBEL AT ZAPATISTA BASE CAMP IN CHIAPAS, MEXICO

greater rights for Mexico's nine million natives. The Zapatistas blamed their poverty on political corruption within the Institutional Revolutionary Party that had ruled Mexico for 65 years.

The Mexican Army drove the Zapatistas underground within the month. The government then faced another crisis in March when Luis Donaldo Colosio, the PRI candidate favored to win the the August presidential election, was assassinated. Seven months later, the party's reform-minded secretary-general was murdered; his brother later accused other party members of the crime.

Colosio's replacement, Ernesto Zedillo Ponce de León, won the election with ease. But he faced massive problems. The economy was poor and foreign investors were abandoning what had been considered a promising market.

▶ CHECHEN WAR

The breakup of the Soviet Union unleashed a torrent of nationalism in Caucasia, the mountainous region straddling Asia and Europe. Nowhere was the outburst more violent than in Chechnya. Russian troops brutally crushed the tiny enclave's independence movement in December.

One of at least 50 ethnic groups packed into an area roughly the size of California, the Chechens were a fiercely independent

372

- **JANUARY 6**
Associates of U.S. figure skater Tonya Harding club Nancy Kerrigan on the knee to prevent her from competing in Olympic games.

- **JANUARY 21**
Lorena Bobbitt is charged with cutting off her husband's penis in retaliation for abuse. She is acquitted by reason of insanity.

- **JANUARY 22**
TV star Telly Savalas, best known as "Kojak," dies of cancer at 70.

- **FEBRUARY 28**
NATO allies launch first air attack in 45 years over Bosnia.

- **MARCH 28**
Eugene Ionesco, foremost playwright in the Theater of the Absurd, dies at 81.

- **APRIL 22**
Former U.S. President Richard M. Nixon dies of complications caused by a stroke at 81 in New Jersey.

- **APRIL 28**
Convicted of spying for Russia's KGB, American Aldrich Ames is sentenced to life in prison.

people. In November Chechnya's regional government tried to secede from the Russian Republic. But because its location, however remote, had military and economic significance, Russian President Boris Yeltsin refused to let the Chechens leave.

Within a year, about 45,000 Chechens were killed, and another 120,000 were refugees. Grozny, the Chechen capital, was decimated. The Chechen rebels continued to wage a guerrilla war from their mountain strongholds, but most of the civilians who survived had given up.

▶ AFRICA'S KILLING FIELDS

More than two million Rwandans fled the country between April and July to escape "ethnic cleansing." It was the fastest growing mass exodus in the latter half of the 20th century. Many wound up in overcrowded, filthy refugee camps in eastern Zaire and died at the rate of one a minute. But the other option, to remain at home, was almost certain death.

Most of the refugees were Hutus, Rwanda's largest ethnic group. In April Hutu extremists killed President Juvenal Habyarimana after he agreed to share power with the Tutsi minority. The assassins claimed the Tutsis were responsible and exhorted Hutus to take revenge on all Tutsis. Within three months, about a million civilians were slaughtered. Thousands of Tutsis escaped across the border

RWANDAN REFUGEES FLEE THEIR COUNTRY.

SIMPSON ARREST

No Hollywood chase scene could have drawn a bigger audience than O. J. Simpson's real-life attempt to avoid arrest on June 17.

Police were about to charge the football hero (below) with murdering his ex-wife, Nicole, and her friend Ronald Goldman, when he took flight. Squadrons of police cars engulfed the L.A. freeway in pursuit and soon many people nation-wide were watching the bizarre scenario unfold on television. Fans of "the Juice" could not believe he was a killer.

After detailed negotiations, Simpson turned himself in. His trial was widely publicized, largely because of the country's fascination with celebrities and the racial element; Simpson is black, his ex-wife and Goldman were white.

Simpson was acquitted of the criminal charges, then convicted in a civil suit. He was free, but no longer a hero.

and settled in refugee camps.

The Tutsi-led Rwandan Patriotic Front overwhelmed the Hutu soldiers and took control of the government in July. By then, thousands of Hutus also had fled to avoid reprisal for the earlier massacres. Their arrival in the camps intensified the hellish situation.

Rwanda's new government urged all refugees to return without fear. During the next two years, they began to trickle in and cobble their lives back together. Precolonial Rwanda had been a remarkable example of tribal cohesion once, and the leaders—Hutu and Tutsi—hoped to achieve the same.

■ TRENDS & TRIVIA

Richard Herrnstein and Charles Murray's controversial book *The Bell Curve* is published.

Benedictine Monks of Santo Domingo release "Chant."

The Rolling Stones release "Voodoo Lounge."

Tom Hanks stars in *Forrest Gump*.

Robert Redford directs *Quiz Show*.

John Travolta stars in *Pulp Fiction*.

U.S. hosts World Cup soccer for the first time.

An all-female team competes in the America's Cup yachting races.

Hubble telescope finds conclusive evidence of black holes.

The first living Vu Quang ox is found in Vietnam (skulls of the species first discovered in 1992).

Walt Disney produces *The Lion King*.

Baseball players' strike cancels the World Series for the first time since 1904.

Fans of '60s music celebrate the 25th anniversary of Woodstock with a concert in Saugerties, N.Y.

The Channel Tunnel, better known as the Chunnel, opens, linking Britain and France.

Edward Albee's play, *Three Tall Women*, debuts.

Alice Munro's *Open Secrets* is published.

U.S. wins more gold medals than at any other Winter Olympics.

Brewpubs become popular with those craving fresh, heartier microbrews.

373

• MAY 19
Former First Lady Jacqueline Kennedy Onassis dies at 64 of lymphatic cancer in New York.

• JULY 8
North Korean President Kim Il Sung dies of a heart attack at 82. His son, Kim Jong Il, succeeds him.

• SEPTEMBER 19
U.S. troops take over Haiti. Junta leader Raoul Cédras steps down. President Jean-Bertrand Aristide returns after three years in exile.

• OCTOBER 18
North Korea agrees to freeze its nuclear program and give international inspectors access to its nuclear sites.

• NOVEMBER 5
Former President Ronald Reagan reveals he is suffering from Alzheimer's disease.

• NOVEMBER 10
Chandrika Kumaratunga is elected prime minister of Sri Lanka. Both her husband and father were killed by political assassins.

• DECEMBER 20
Former U.S. statesman Dean Rusk dies at 85.

The Oklahoma City bombing (below) on April 19 proved that Americans could be terrorists as well as victims. The man behind the destruction of a federal office building in which 168 people died was a war veteran.

Timothy McVeigh and his accomplice, Terry Nichols, believed the government's role

in the destruction of the Branch Davidian compound in Waco was proof that America had become a totalitarian state. They decided to commemorate Waco's second anniversary by blowing up the nine-story Alfred P. Murrah Building in Oklahoma City. Their homemade bomb blew the front of the structure apart.

Rescue teams worked round the clock for days searching the rubble for survivors. Two days after the bombing, McVeigh was arrested; he was sentenced to death in 1997. "What he represents to me is a terrorist...." a juror said after the trial. "He represents a twisted view of the intentions of the government and the principles that this country was founded on." Nichols was eventually convicted on a lesser charge.

STUDENT ASSASSINATES RABIN

When a right-wing law student killed Israeli Prime Minister Yitzhak Rabin on November 4, he threw the ongoing Middle East peace process into a tailspin. Many diplomatic experts feared that the biggest threat to the 1993 Oslo Accords were Jewish extremists, not Islamic radicals.

The 73-year-old prime minister (below) was assassinated as he left a peace rally in Tel Aviv. His assassin, Yigal Amir, said he acted on "God's orders" and did not regret the deed. Israeli extremists like him condemned Rabin for making concessions to the Palestine Liberation Organization in the Oslo Accords. They feared that Rabin would concede more territory in his attempts to improve relations with Lebanon and Syria.

Rabin's efforts to secure peace seemed in remarkable contrast to his military background. The war hero had enough clout to convince many Israelis that PLO leader Yassir Arafat could be trusted. Other world leaders respected Rabin and therefore were willing to work with him toward resolving the troubles that plagued the Middle East. His death left a dangerous void at a critical juncture of the peace process.

"The peace is an open door to economic and social progress," Rabin said minutes before he was murdered. "The peace is not only in prayer but it is the true desire of the Jewish people....Without partners to the peace, there is no peace."

MILLION MAN MARCH

The several hundred thousand black men who flocked to Washington, D.C., to participate in the Million Man March on

October 16 (above) ended the day determined to become better members of society.

"Every one of you must go back home and join some church, synagogue, temple, or mosque," said Rev. Louis Farrakhan, leader of the Nation of Islam and organizer of the march. "Join organizations that are working to uplift black people."

Many of the men gathered before Farrakhan had traveled across the country to take part in the event. The march was intended to be a wake-up call for black men, a reminder to respect black women, denounce drugs and violence, and become active in their communities. It was a message that perhaps only someone like Farrakhan could convey. The controversial yet charismatic leader vocalized the frustrations and anger that many blacks felt they could not articulate.

A year after the march, volunteer agencies in some cities noticed a marked increase in the number of black men signing up, some of whom had not gone to Washington. And those who had continued to speak well of it.

"It was sort of utopian," one participant told a reporter afterward. "If we could just bottle that and make it last."

JUST BEING THERE

On September 6, when Cal Ripken, Jr., (opposite) came to work, 46,272 people showed up to watch. The shortstop for the

---

- **JANUARY 12**
Police in Minneapolis arrest Qubilah Bahiyah Shabazz, one of Malcolm X's daughters, for trying to kill Louis Farrakhan.

- **JANUARY 17**
A massive earthquake rocks the Japanese city of Kobe, leaving thousands dead or homeless.

- **FEBRUARY 20**
U.S. troops land in Somalia to oversee the withdrawal of UN peacekeepers who have tried to intervene in the African nation's civil war.

- **MARCH 16**
Sinn Fein leader Gerry Adams meets with President Clinton, despite the objections of the British government.

- **MARCH 20**
Japanese cult members release a poisonous nerve gas on a Tokyo subway during the morning rush hour.

- **APRIL 2**
Major league baseball team owners accept players' offer to return to work, thus ending a 234-day strike.

- **APRIL 14**
Folk singer and actor Burl Ives dies at 85 in New York.

Baltimore Orioles had not missed one of the 2,130 games his team had played since May 30, 1982. His dedication to attendance paid off; Ripken set the major league record for consecutive games played that day in a game against the California Angels.

Nicknamed "the Iron Man" like Lou Gehrig because of his determined durability, Ripken remains one of the most popular baseball players of the day. He signed on with the Orioles after he finished high school in 1978, then honed his skills in the minors. Three years later, he debuted in the majors, where he soon became known as one of the best shortstops in the sport. The American League named Ripken its most valuable player of 1983 and again in 1991.

When he broke Lou Gehrig's 1939

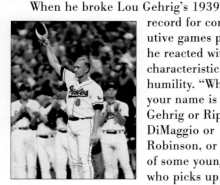

record for consecutive games played he reacted with characteristic humility. "Whether your name is Gehrig or Ripken, DiMaggio or Robinson, or that of some youngster who picks up his bat or puts on his glove, you are challenged by the game of baseball to do your very best day in and day out," he told the crowd at Baltimore's Camden Yards. "And that's all I ever tried to do. Thank you."

▶ U.S. RESUMES RELATIONS WITH VIETNAM
Belatedly turning the page on a troubled chapter of America's past, President Clinton announced on July 11 that the U.S. would resume full diplomatic relations with its former enemy, the Communist government of Vietnam.

"We can now move on to common ground," Clinton said. "Whatever divided us before, let us consign to the past." The President's action was opposed by some

veterans' groups and by activists who charged the Vietnamese were still not cooperating fully in accounting for missing U.S. servicemen. But most Americans appeared willing to accept normalization.

Clinton, whose well-publicized efforts to avoid military service in Vietnam might have given additional ammunition to critics of his decision, avoided either justifying or criticizing U.S. policies during the war but paid tribute in his announcement to those who served. "Whatever we may think about the political decisions of the Vietnam era," he declared, "the brave Americans who fought and died there had noble motives."

REPUBLICANS

For the first time in 40 years, Republicans controlled Congress, and the man credited with the upheaval, Newt Gingrich of Georgia, became Speaker of the House.

The feisty conservative (below) led his adherents to victory in 1994 through his "Contract With America," a program espousing less government that became the GOP's agenda.

During the first 100 days the 104th Congress was in session, Republicans introduced a wide range of bills relating to crime, defense, taxation, and more. The Gingrich faction also was forcing Democrats to make cuts.

But what the GOP had called a "revolution" was really not. Only 3 minor provisions of the 21 outlined in the contract had become law by the year's end; Gingrich's much-vaunted balanced budget amendment collapsed. And the House had appointed an independent counsel to investigate the Speaker for ethics violations.

■ TRENDS & TRIVIA

Tom Hanks stars in *Apollo 13*.

Gray wolves are reintroduced into the Rocky Mountains.

The worst floods since 1945 hit Europe.

O. J. Simpson's *I Want To Tell You* is published.

The *Beatles Anthology* debuts with previously unreleased cuts, such as "Free As a Bird" by the Fab Four.

Chicago Bulls star Michael Jordan comes back to pro basketball after a brief retirement.

Smoking is banned in New York City restaurants.

British film star Hugh Grant is arrested on charges of lewd conduct with a prostitute.

Arnold Palmer plays his last British Open.

French Army Capt. Alfred Dreyfus is officially absolved of treason charges.

Oliver Stone directs *Nixon* with Anthony Hopkins.

The Grateful Dead disband after Jerry Garcia's death.

Shannon Faulkner, the first woman admitted to the Citadel, enrolls after legal battle, then drops out in first week.

Friends star Jennifer Anniston's haircut is widely copied.

Multimillionaire Steve Forbes runs for President and touts the flat tax.

Computer cafes offer espresso and the Internet. ▶

• MAY 10
Doctors in Zaire report an outbreak of the deadly Ebola virus, considered to be more lethal than AIDS.

• MAY 29
Actor Christopher Reeve falls from a horse and is left paralyzed.

• JULY 22
Susan Smith is convicted of murdering her two children. She left her two young boys in her car, then rolled it into a lake.

• AUGUST 1
Disney buys ABC for 19 billion dollars, and Westinghouse Electric Corp. buys CBS for 5.4 billion dollars.

• SEPTEMBER
Senator Robert Packwood resigns after indictment for sexual harassment, financial improprieties, and tampering with evidence.

• OCTOBER 3
A jury acquits O.J. Simpson of killing his ex-wife and her friend.

• DECEMBER 14
World leaders witness the signing of the Bosnia-Herzegovina Peace Accords in Paris.

Three months before he was reelected President, Bill Clinton overhauled the country's welfare system. Public perception of the system, established as part of Franklin D. Roosevelt's New Deal, was negative. Conservatives argued that federal assistance encouraged laziness. But they failed to mention that many welfare recipients lacked the training and intellectual or emotional ability needed to earn a living.

The bill Clinton signed in August gave states basic guidelines for achieving cuts. Most welfare recipients had to find work within two years or risk losing their benefits. Nobody could receive benefits for more than five years in a lifetime.

Clinton's fellow Democrats assailed him for allowing the bill to become law. Three of his top aides resigned in protest. "The premise of this legislation," said Senator Daniel P. Moynihan (D-N.Y.), "is that the behavior of certain adults can be changed by making the lives of their children as wretched as possible."

The President tried to soothe his estranged colleagues by promising to fine-tune the bill during his second term. But the truth was clear; the welfare state concept was no longer acceptable.

▶ TUPAC AMARU'S FAILED COUP

The four-month-long game of chicken that Peruvian revolutionaries played with President Alberto Fujimori ended in disaster for the group. The president, however, emerged as an international hero in the war against terrorism.

The game began on December 17 at a Christmas party in the Japanese Embassy in Lima. Between 20 and 30 guerrillas swept into the event, sealed the exits, and declared the 500 guests were their hostages. The heavily armed crashers were members of Tupac Amaru, a Marxist group that had waged war against the Peruvian government since 1981. They demanded the release of 450 of their comrades from prison.

Fujimori refused. For six years the president had focused on vanquishing terrorists like Tupac and the much larger group, the Shining Path. He'd achieved some success, but not without incurring criticism. In 1992 he dissolved congress, suspended portions of the country's constitution, and gave the military a free hand in its pursuit and prosecution of alleged terrorists. Soon, jails were packed with prisoners, many of whom stood wrongfully accused.

The siege at the Japanese Embassy came to a head on April 22. Peruvian commandos stormed the building, killing all Tupac members inside. Two Peruvian soldiers died in the attack, and one hostage died later. For the moment,

TUPAC AMARU REBELS INSIDE THE JAPANESE AMBASSADOR'S RESIDENCE IN LIMA, PERU

it looked like Fujimori had won the war against terrorism.

▶ TALIBAN TAKES CONTROL IN AFGHANISTAN

By the end of 1996, most of Afghanistan was under the control of rebels who called themselves Islamic fundamentalists. The Taliban's harsh laws virtually banned

TALIBAN FIGHTERS BOW IN PRAYER AT KABUL'S MAIN MOSQUE.

women from public life and further alienated the already remote country from the rest of the world.

Most of the Taliban's members were Pashtuns, who once dominated the region. When the Soviet Union invaded in the late 1970s, many Pashtuns fled into northwestern Pakistan. In 1994 conservative young Pathans formed the Taliban with the intent of restoring their homeland to Islamic rule. As they marched north toward Kabul, their ranks swelled with recruits who were tired of the incessant fighting between the various factions seeking to gain control after the Soviets retreated. The Taliban seized Kabul in October and overthrew the government.

The new regime issued harsh new edicts that particularly affected women. They could no longer work out of their homes or leave unless accompanied by a male relative. They could not attend school. In way of explanation, one Taliban official likened a woman to a rose "you water it and keep it at home for yourself to look at and smell. It is not supposed to be taken out of the house to be smelled."

Iran, a bastion of Islamic fundamentalism, criticized its new neighbor for giving Muslims a bad name. Russian Federation leaders worried that the Taliban's influence would spill across the border into the four predominantly Muslim Central Asian republics. The UN refused to recognize the Taliban, and the U.S. did the same. But saber rattling and condemnations were not enough to dislodge the regime from its tyrannical course.

"This is not Islam that they're imposing," a woman in Kabul told a reporter. "It's Pathan tribal culture, backward and primitive."

▶ THE UNABOMBER

The phalanx of FBI agents assembled outside the crude shack in rural Montana in April wondered about the man inside. Would Ted Kazcynski (below) turn out to be a reclusive genius or the target of one the longest manhunts in agency history?

The disheveled 53-year-old turned out to be both. Kazcynski, a Harvard-educated mathematician, was the Unabomber whose explosive packages had killed three people

and wounded 25 others since 1978. He made bombs from scraps of metal and wood, which he then mailed to his victims across the country.

Kazcynski outlined his gripes with society in a 35,000-word manifesto published in the *Washington Post* on September 19, 1995. The FBI asked the publishers to print the diatribe against modern technology in hopes that someone might recognize the writer's style and argument. It proved to be a brilliant tactic. Kaczynski's younger brother, David, compared the essay

with his brother's letters and, through his lawyer, notified the FBI four months later. After studying the documents, the agents believed they'd finally found their man.

Convicting Kazcynski took another two years. He refused his lawyers' request that he use the insanity defense, then insisted on representing himself. In January 1998 he worked out a deal; in exchange for his guilty plea, he would avoid the death penalty and spend the rest of his life in prison without parole. This satisfied the widow of his last victim. "He will never, ever, kill again," she told reporters.

MARTIAN ROCK

The ancient rock did not look remarkable—a dense gray thing about the size of a large potato. But below its surface, the rock was riddled with microscopic structures (below) that may have been formed by living creatures—on Mars.

NASA scientists announced the stunning discovery in August, but the saga actually began about 3.6 billion years ago when Mars was already a billion years old. The water that covered a portion of the planet's surface may have 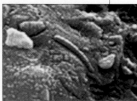 teemed with microbes, which fossilized over time. Some 16 million years ago, an asteroid slammed into Mars, scattering rocks into space. About 13,000 years ago, at least one of those rocks whizzed through the Earth's atmosphere and landed in Antarctica. Scientists pinpointed the rock's origin after comparing the composition of gases trapped inside it with samples taken from the Martian surface in 1976.

Scott Adams's cartoon "Dilbert" focuses on workplace humor.

Michael Johnson of the U.S. becomes the first man to win an Olympic gold medal in the 200- and 400-meter races; he sets the 200-meter record of 19.32 seconds.

Demi Moore stars in *Striptease*.

Nintendo 64 comes out.

Heartthrob with a history John Kennedy, Jr., marries New York socialite Carolyn Bessette.

"Tickle Me Elmo" is the hot Christmas toy.

Cigars become chic for both sexes.

Primary Colors by Anonymous is published; the author is later revealed to be journalist Joe Klein.

Tom Cruise stars in *Mission Impossible*.

The New York Yankees win the World Series for the first time in 18 years.

Kenneth Branagh directs and portrays *Hamlet*.

Leonardo DiCaprio and Claire Danes star in a present-day version of *Romeo and Juliet*.

Akira Kurosawa directs *Ran*.

Earvin "Magic" Johnson briefly returns to pro basketball. The star player retired after he discovered he was HIV positive.

Body piercing becomes popular.

Frank McCourt's *Angela's Ashes* is published.

Orioles' second baseman Roberto Alomar is suspended for the rest of the season after he spits at an umpire.

• JULY 28
Writer-illustrator-naturalist Roger Tory Peterson dies at 87.

▶ AUGUST 29
President Clinton wins nomination for a second term at the Democratic National Convention.

• AUGUST 29
Presidential consultant Dick Morris resigns. He admits to disclosing confidential information to a prostitute.

• NOVEMBER
An Ethiopian jet crashes into the Indian Ocean killing 127 after hijackers refuse to allow pilot to refuel.

• NOVEMBER 12
Saudi passenger plane and Kazakh cargo plane collide in midair over New Delhi.

• DECEMBER 9
Two unmarried American teenagers are charged with killing their newborn baby and leaving the infant's body in a trash heap.

On July 1 Great Britain ceded control of Hong Kong to China, in a dramatic ceremony attended by China's President Jiang Zemin and Britain's Prince Charles.

The ceremony ended 155 years of British rule and returned Hong Kong to its ancestral homeland, though with a promise that the former colony would be able to keep its own separate political, legal, and economic system for 50 years.

To the Chinese, reversion wiped out a historical insult.

To many in the West, it represented the potential loss of personal, political, and economic freedoms for 6.3 million Hong Kong citizens who became subject to China's authoritarian system (above).

There was wariness on both sides as the July 1 reversion date passed. Chinese authorities realized a delicate balancing act would be needed to integrate Hong Kong into China without damaging its successful economy. Hong Kong residents, for their part, waited cautiously to see whether Communist officials would respect their supremely capitalist way of life.

▶ BELOVED BENEFACTRESSES DIE

Two of the world's most admired women died within a week of each other in 1997. Britain's Princess Diana was killed in a car crash on August 31. Mother Teresa died in her bed three days later.

The difference in age and lifestyle was substantial; Diana was the glamorous 36-year-old ex-wife of Prince Charles who dated an Egyptian playboy; Mother Teresa was an 87-year-old bride of Christ who had devoted her life to the poor.

Yet they were bound together as women whom the public adored. Diana tried to reach out to those far beyond the glittering world of British royalty. She campaigned for the eradication of land mines and raised money for AIDS research. She challenged her royal in-laws to shed their stiff formality for more warmth. Her subsequent alienation from them became a badge of honor.

Mother Teresa's tireless work with the world's forgotten souls attracted much praise. World leaders and celebrities flocked to her side to see and be seen with her—not unlike Diana. Both women used their stature to help others. And the loss of the two was a major blow to the world.

▶ TORY IN LABOUR'S CLOTHING

In seizing control of the British Parliament for the first time in 23 years, Labour Leader Tony Blair followed the old chestnut "if you can't beat 'em, join 'em." He tacked the most popular of the conservative Tory party's policies onto Labour's platform, ripped away his party's old socialist facade, and thereby laid the foundations for a landslide in May.

"Margaret Thatcher's emphasis on free enterprise was right," Blair said, tipping his hat to the grande dame of the opposition. He expropriated her legacy by pledging to keep his hands off taxes, government spending, and any businesses his conservative predecessors had privatized. Blair pushed his party to the center, thereby making himself the candidate wavering conservatives could feel comfortable with. His "new Labour" would be a respectable, middle-class party that knew when to say no.

The 43-year-old lawyer became England's youngest prime minister since 1812. "Blair's historic achievement was to exorcise the voters' fear of Labour...," British historian Paul Johnson wrote in Time. "This was, in essence, a constitutional vote by the people to keep the two-party system alive, to insist that the other fellow be given a chance."

▶ DIALING FOR DOLLARS

Vice President Al Gore's fund-raising efforts came into question off and on throughout 1997, not unlike the predictions about his political future.

Republicans accused Gore of soliciting campaign contributions over the telephone from his office, which was a misuse of federal property, and accepting money from foreigners, another fund-raising violation. The latter allegation came to light after the Vice President attended a fund-raiser at a Buddhist temple in Los Angeles before the 1996 election. Gore first said he thought he was attending some sort of "community outreach" event. But after some reflection—and new evidence—his staff said he believed he was dispatched to the temple for "donor maintenance."

Gore's dialing for dollars evolved into a thornier issue. Raising soft money—funds for the Democratic National Committee—on federal property was not illegal. However, raising hard money—funds used by a specific candidate—was, and such was the case with some of the funds Gore raised. In a vacuum, the technicality might have passed off as a

---

• JANUARY 22
Madeleine Albright is confirmed as the first female Secretary of State.

• MARCH 26
39 members of the Heaven's Gate cult commit suicide in hopes of boarding a spaceship they believed was following Comet Hale-Bopp.

▶ JUNE 25
Jacques-Yves Cousteau dies.

• JUNE 28
Prize-fighter Mike Tyson bites off a piece of Evander Holyfield's ear during a championship bout.

• JULY 1
Actor Robert Mitchum dies.

• JULY 2
Actor Jimmy Stewart dies.

bookkeeping mistake. But, in conjunction with the Buddhist nuns' testimony and accusations that the Clinton Administration operated on a favors-for-funds policy, it looked bad. Presidential hopefuls who once thought Gore would be unbeatable competition in the 2000 election began to reconsider.

▶ THE NANNY NIGHTMARE

The case of a 19-year-old British au pair convicted of killing her 8-month-old charge was every parent's nightmare come true—those they trusted with their children would hurt them.

Louise Woodward (below) denied allegations that she violently shook Matthew Eappen out of frustration, on February 4 in Newton, Massachusetts. The infant died that day, and police filed murder charges against Woodward. Nine months later, after

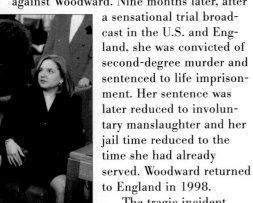

a sensational trial broadcast in the U.S. and England, she was convicted of second-degree murder and sentenced to life imprisonment. Her sentence was later reduced to involuntary manslaughter and her jail time reduced to the time she had already served. Woodward returned to England in 1998.

The tragic incident brought the controversial topic of child care in America once again into tight focus. According to one study, two-thirds of American mothers with children under six years of age work full time. Finding good child care providers was difficult, especially for middle- and lower-income parents.

In a surprising twist, many observers blamed the Eappens for the tragedy, especially Deborah Eappens for choosing to work part-time instead of staying at home

CLONED

Science fiction and science took a giant step closer to each other in 1997 when Dr. Ian Wilmut (below) of Scotland's Roslin Institute announced that he and his team of researchers had cloned a sheep.

The technique they used was deceptively simple. First, they took a cell from a Finn Dorset ewe and removed its nucleus, which contains the cell's DNA. Then, they removed the nucleus from an unfertilized egg of a Scottish Blackface ewe. They fused together the adult nucleus and the denucleated egg.

After the patchwork egg was implanted into the womb of a third ewe, it developed into an exact copy of the Finn Dorset that donated the nucleus since the egg contained her DNA only. Reporters were quick to point out that it took a spark of electricity to trigger the fusion, not unlike Dr. Frankenstein's use of lightning to animate his creation.

Dolly the clone was blissfully unaware of the controversy brewing around her. Immediately after Wilmut's announcement, speculation turned to the possibility of cloning humans. With visions of clones raised solely to perform menial labor or provide donor organs, many governments moved to ban research toward the cloning of humans.

to raise two boys. The backlash revealed that despite the progress women had made in the 20th century, a large number of people still maintained that a woman's place was in the home.

■ TRENDS & TRIVIA

Ellen DeGeneres becomes first gay star of a sitcom, on ABC's *Ellen.*

Seymour Hersh's *The Dark Side of Camelot* is published.

Beanie babies become collector's items.

379

Stiletto heels are in fashion again.

Country music singers like Shania Twain and LeAnn Rimes are hot.

Representative Susan Molinari (R-N.Y.) quits Congress to become a network anchor.

Elton John releases new version of "Candle in the Wind" in honor of Princess Diana.

George Lucas's classic *Star Wars* film trilogy is updated and re-released.

Charles Frazier's *Cold Mountain* is published.

Burt Reynolds stars in *Boogie Nights.*

Roma Downey and Della Reese star in CBS's *Touched by An Angel.*

Tommy Lee Jones and Will Smith are *Men in Black.*

IBM supercomputer Deep Blue defeats Gary Kasparov in chess tournament.

Twenty-one-year-old golfer Tiger Woods wins the Masters by a record 12 strokes.

Comet Hale-Bopp, detected in 1995 by Alan Hale and Thomas Bopp, is the brightest comet to pass near Earth since the 16th century. ▶

◀ JULY 5
NASA's Sojourner beams back images of Mars taken as it scoots across the planet's surface.

▶ JULY 15
Fashion designer Gianni Versace is killed outside his house in Miami, Florida, by serial killer Andrew Cunanan, who later kills himself.

● OCTOBER 12
Pop country singer John Denver dies in a plane crash in California.

● OCTOBER 27
The Dow Jones industrial average drops 554.26 points as a result of the unstable Asian market, then rebounds later.

● NOVEMBER 19
Kenny and Bobbi McCaughey of Carlisle, Iowa, become the parents of the first known set of septuplets to survive after birth.

380

At 1:25 p.m on December 19, for only the second time in U.S. history, an American President was impeached by the House of Representatives, setting the stage for a Senate trial and possible removal from office. By a vote of 228-206, the House accused President Bill Clinton of giving "perjurious, false, and misleading" grand jury testimony concerning his affair with White House intern Monica Lewinsky.

Minutes later, the House voted 221-212 for a second impeachment article, charging the President had obstructed justice in the White House probe and in the case of Paula Jones, a former Arkansas state employee suing Clinton over an alleged sexual advance in 1991. The House relied mainly on evidence collected by independent counsel Kenneth Starr, originally appointed to investigate the Clintons' role in an Arkansas land deal.

Just hours before the impeachment vote, House Speaker-designate Bob Livingston of Louisiana told stunned colleagues that he would resign after acknowledging extramarital affairs.

Livingston urged Clinton to do likewise, but the President vowed to serve "until the last hour of the last day of my term."

▶ COLD WAR REDUX

India and Pakistan tested nuclear weapons in May, touching off a South Asian nuclear arms race. Their actions underscored the futility of international efforts to halt the spread of nuclear weapons.

India entered the fray first when it tested nuclear weapons near the Pakistani border on May 11 and 13. Pakistan responded with its own nuclear tests. Both countries said the weapons were developed for self-defense.

The showdown stemmed from long-standing conflicts over Kashmir, the mountainous territory wedged between India, China, Pakistan, Afghanistan, and Tajikistan. At the time of partition in 1947 India absorbed most of Kashmir; Pakistan administered a portion of the northwest. Kashmir's predominantly Muslim population clashed with the Hindu-dominated Indian government, while Islamic Pakistan supported the Kashmiris. Despite the frequent outbursts of violence, India refused to give up Kashmir.

The nuclear tests were the latest developments in the Kashmir conflict. In response to international sanctions, India and Pakistan promised to halt further testing. But both had joined the group of countries with the demonstrated capability of making nuclear weapons.

The Washington Post

Clinton Impeached

House Approves Articles Charging Perjury, Obstruction

Livingston Quits As Designated House Speaker

Mostly Partisan Vote Shifts Drama to Senate

Clinton Vows to Finish Out Term

▶ BILL GATES AND UNCLE SAM

In what many experts called the most important antitrust suit in decades, the U.S. government and 20 state attorneys general charged Microsoft, Inc., with unfair business practices in May.

The suit accused the computer software giant of using its position as the primary supplier of computer operating

systems to dominate the Internet access market. Because Microsoft's Windows operating system is essentially the brains in more than 90 percent of all computers, Microsoft had been accused of unfair use of its market power in placing conditions on PC makers that effectively stop competitors in the Internet browsing software market.

Federal lawyers also contended that Microsoft exacted other requirements from PC makers. These practices flew in the face of the Sherman Antitrust Act, the 19th-century law that was used to break up oil, railroad, and telephone monopolies in the past.

Microsoft's multibillionaire owner Bill Gates (above) denied the government's allegations and vowed that his company would defend itself vigorously. Lawyers on both sides buckled down to prepare for a lengthy legal battle.

▶ ASIA'S ECONOMIC CRISIS

Stock markets tumbled across East Asia amid a speculative sell-off of national currencies as the region suffered its greatest economic crisis since World War II. A combination of bad loans, lower exports, and weakening currencies led to a crisis of investor confidence.

Asia's most critical currency, the Japanese yen, slumped badly as a result of Japan's extended economic malaise, dampening export opportunities for developing countries in the region. As global

---

• **FEBRUARY 3**
A U.S. Marine Corps jet in Italy accidentally cuts a cable-car wire and sends 20 skiers to their deaths.

• **APRIL 15**
Former Khmer Rouge leader Pol Pot, responsible for the deaths of more than a million Cambodians, dies at 73 of a heart attack.

• **MAY 14**
Legendary crooner Frank Sinatra dies of a heart attack at 82, in California.

• **MAY 29**
Former Republican senator and presidential candidate Barry Goldwater dies at 89, in Arizona.

• **JULY 6**
Cowboy movie star and fast-food entrepreneur Roy Rogers dies at 86.

• **JULY 13**
Japanese voters deliver a crushing defeat to the ruling Liberal Democratic Party and Prime Minister Hashimoto resigns.

• **JULY 13**
A gunman enters the U.S. Capitol. Two Capitol policemen are killed and the gunman and a tourist are wounded.

markets awoke to the crushing losses of Japanese financial institutions, they shunned new investments in previously successful Asian economies such as Indonesia, where President Suharto left office after 32 years in the face of popular discontent and a plummeting currency. The forced departure of a seemingly entrenched leader demonstrated the power the troubled economy now wielded over the region's future.

In nearby countries such as Thailand, whose collapsing economy sparked a crisis in the fall of 1997, national reform measures and IMF loans began to show results. But emergency IMF support in Indonesia and Korea could not halt widespread suffering and discontent. Asia's economic interdependence, so critical to its previous history of burgeoning growth, was perceived now as a weakness as the "contagion" of investor fears spread from country to country.

▶ AT LONG LAST, AN IRISH PEACE
The war-weary folk of Ireland voted overwhelmingly for peace on May 22 in the first island-wide election since 1918. The vote ended decades of "the Troubles," the sectarian violence between the Catholic majority and Protestant minority.

The first step forward took place in April when leaders from Ireland and Great Britain Bertie Ahern and Tony Blair, (below), met with eight local political parties, including the Irish Republican Army. Under the agreement's provisions, Northern Ireland would remain part of Great Britain unless majorities north and south of the border voted for reunification. Ireland would withdraw its claim to the entire island, and Northern Ireland would be governed by a locally

elected assembly.

Other provisions were more problematic. Within two years, all convicted terrorists would be released, and all militias were to relinquish their weapons. Some observers worried the country would once again plunge into chaos.

In spite of such concerns, 71 percent of the Irish population supported the accords. "There are no issues that are impossible to resolve," one politician said.

EL NIÑO

Meteorologists attributed the problematic weather that began in late 1997 and lasted well into 1998 to El Niño. It became a scapegoat for any bad weather. It was named El Niño (Spanish for "Christ Child") because South Americans first noticed currents of warm water just off the west coast around Christmas. During an El Niño, the warm water characteristic of the western Pacific flows east toward South America. The combination of higher temperatures (shown in red in the image below of El Niño-induced change in sea surface topography) and low nutrients can kill fish that thrive in the eastern Pacific's cooler waters.

Torrential rains caused landslides in South and North America. Parts of the U.S. had a mild winter and cool, wet spring. Scientists had varying opinions about the cause of El Niño. "Weather is always abnormal," said one. "Perhaps the only thing more complex is human behavior itself."

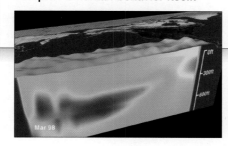

Mar 98

■ TRENDS & TRIVIA

After a guest on her program says beef is unsafe, beef producers in Texas unsuccessfully sue TV host Oprah Winfrey for damages.

St. Louis Cardinal Mark McGwire and Chicago Cub Sammy Sosa both top the MLB record of 61 home runs per season set by Roger Maris in 1961—McGwire with 70, and Sosa with 66.

Pfizer introduces Viagra to combat impotence.

Still Me by former Superman hero Christopher Reeve, paralyzed in a riding accident, is published.

James Cameron's film *Titanic* grosses close to a billion dollars worldwide. ▶

Jim Carrey stars in *The Truman Show*.

The euro debuts as a currency.

NBC's *Seinfeld* goes off the air.

In *Here But Not Here: My Life with William Shawn and the New Yorker*, Lillian Ross reveals her 35-year romance with her editor.

The herb St. John's Wort is a natural alternative to Prozac.

After playing in a record 2,632 consecutive baseball games, Cal Ripken of the Baltimore Orioles finally sits out a game.

The Hubble Space Telescope takes pictures of what scientists believe is the first recorded planet outside the solar system.

Basketball great Michael Jordan's Chicago Bulls win their sixth championship in a decade.

A $295.7 million Powerball jackpot is paid out in Indiana, the largest lottery payoff to date in the world.

381

• **AUGUST 20**
U.S. cruise missiles strike terrorist-linked sites in Afghanistan and Sudan in retaliation for twin bombings at U.S. embassies in Africa.

• **OCTOBER**
Hurricane Mitch devastates Central America, killing up to 15 thousand people and leaving more than a million homeless.

• **OCTOBER 16**
Augusto Pinochet, charged by Spain with murdering Spanish citizens while dictator of Chile, is arrested in London.

▶ **OCTOBER 29**
John Glenn goes back into space aboard the shuttle to conduct experiments on the effects of space travel on aging adults.

• **NOVEMBER 6**
Newt Gingrich resigns as Speaker of the House after Republicans lose ground to Democrats in mid-term elections the day before.

• **NOVEMBER 16**
U.S. bombing campaign begins in Iraq after Saddam Hussein reneges on prior agreements to cooperate fully with UN arms inspectors.

1999

382

The Balkan tinderbox ignited again in 1999, sending NATO to war for the first time in the alliance's 50-year history. The crisis flared in the Serbian province of Kosovo, where Slobodan Milosevic's Yugoslavian government inflicted increasing terror on the province's ethnic Albanian majority. As killings and expulsions mounted, the United States and its NATO partners launched an 11-week bombing campaign that forced Milosevic to pull out his forces. Shortly before the bombing ended, a U.N. tribunal indicted the Yugoslav leader for war crimes.

Under the protection of NATO peacekeepers, hundreds of thousands of refugees returned home, but much of Kosovo was in ruins and its political status remained in dispute. Violence continued as Albanians terrorized the few Serbs who had not fled. In Serbia, meanwhile, Milosevic's time finally ran out. After losing to opposition leader Vojislav Kostunica in a national election on September 24, 2000, Milosevic first tried to override the vote and cling to power, but a popular uprising in Belgrade forced him to resign. On October 7, Kostunica took office, promising a new era of democracy.

▶ CLINTON ACQUITTED

"Senators, how say you? Is the respondent, William Jefferson Clinton, guilty or not guilty?"

With those words, shortly after noon on February 12, Chief Justice William H. Rehnquist opened the very last act of the five-week impeachment trial. In the roll calls that followed, all 45 Democratic senators voted to acquit the President on both charges. The perjury count failed by 45-55, with 10 Republicans joining the Democrats in declaring Clinton not guilty. On obstruction of justice, with 5 Republicans voting for acquittal, the vote was 50-50—meaning that House prosecutors had not even secured a simple majority on either count, let alone the two-thirds vote needed to remove Clinton from office.

Though the Senate votes saved his Presidency, few were willing to declare Clinton exonerated. History, said Democratic Senator Bob Graham of Florida, would judge that Clinton "dishonored himself and the highest office in our American democracy." And Tom Daschle of South Dakota, the Democratic leader, declared that even though it ended in acquittal, the impeachment process represented a form of punishment "commensurate with the failure of the President to act appropriately."

▶ THE WORLD GROWS OLDER

One of the most profound changes in human society at the close of the 20th century lay in the simple arithmetic of the world's population.

Declining birth rates and a dramatic rise in life expectancy created a worldwide "aging explosion." A United Nations study forecast that the Earth's over-65 population would grow by more than a billion in the next 50 years. In the United States, demographers estimated that by 2021, the entire country would resemble Florida in the 1990s, with nearly one-fifth of the population over 65. The "old-

est old," those 85 and older, will explode even more quickly, doubling by 2020 and again by 2040.

Some consequences were obvious, such as huge new burdens on pension and health-care systems. But other issues loomed, too. Would older employees stay on the job longer, and if so, would younger workers find themselves stuck in lower-paid, less satisfying jobs? Would support for schools diminish with more and more voters past child-rearing age? How will people well into their own 60s cope with the emotional and financial demands of caring for aging parents? The age boom, an event without precedent in human history, seemed certain to affect every area of economic, political, community, and family life. "We are going," said one population expert, "where we've never been."

▶ COLONIAL FADEOUT

In the last days of 1999, two of the last vestiges of the colonial era passed peacefully into history. The United States relinquished the Panama Canal, which had been under U.S. control since its construction. "It's yours," former President Jimmy Carter, representing the U.S. gov-

ernment, told Panama's President Mireya Moscoso after signing the official transfer documents in a ceremony December 14. Five days later, on the opposite side of the Earth, China regained sovereignty over the tiny enclave of Macau, ending 442 years of Portuguese rule. Like the former British colony of Hong Kong, which reverted to Chinese rule in 1997, Macau was designated a "special administrative region" where the capitalist system and local laws would remain in force for 50 years.

When the Portuguese flag was hauled down a few minutes before midnight and replaced by the five-starred red and gold Chinese flag, Europeans no longer ruled anywhere in Asia. From the colonial empires that had dominated vast areas of the globe when the century began, only a few Caribbean islands and some remote specks of land in the Pacific and South Atlantic now remained.

▶ JORDAN RETIRES; DIMAGGIO DIES

Two of the century's most celebrated sports heroes left the scene in 1999. Superstar Michael Jordan of the Chicago Bulls retired from basketball and Joe DiMaggio, the "Yankee Clipper" of baseball's Golden Age, died at 84.

Almost everything about the two men was a study in contrasts. The immensely dignified DiMaggio represented a kind of old-fashioned aristocracy of talent. He played and lived with a majestic elegance, awing fans with his skill and grace but remaining reserved, even aloof, as a personality. Jordan embodied the celebrity culture of modern America—and the bound-

less commercialization of fame. "Ads infinitum," one magazine recalled in reporting on Jordan's retirement, which was almost as big a story in the business section as on the sports pages.

For all their differences, though, Jordan and DiMaggio had this much in common: talent, extraordinary determination, and an almost mystical presence that would remain, for anyone who saw them play, the definition of greatness in sport.

DEATH AT SCHOOL

"They were anti-everything," another student said about Dylan Klebold and Eric Harris after the two teenagers walked into their school and shot to death 12 students and a teacher, then killed themselves. The bloodbath at Columbine High School in Jefferson County, Colorado, capped a horrifying series of school shootings that had already taken 12 lives in seemingly safe, stable communities.

The Columbine massacre touched off a national soul-searching, as Americans pondered whether their culture of guns, violent entertainment, and fragmented family and community life had contributed to the tragedy. Stiffer gun-control laws were proposed in Congress and many state legislatures, and political leaders from President Clinton on down exhorted the entertainment industry to tone down violent images. Yet no one seemed sure how to end the youthful alienation that brought the threat of inexplicable death to even the most typical and orderly American towns.

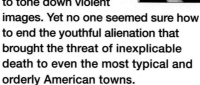

■ TRENDS & TRIVIA

Amid unprecedented hype, *Star Wars: Episode I, The Phantom Menace* is released.

Jack Kevorkian ("Dr. Death"), who gave lethal drugs to a 52-year-old man to assist in his suicide, is convicted of second-degree murder.

Three decades after they first came into use, birth control pills are finally legalized in Japan.

Internet stock trading spawns a new breed of "day traders" who seek to profit on minute-by-minute share price fluctuations.

Morse code is dropped as official means of communication at sea.

Megamerger mania: Mobil marries Exxon; Bell Atlantic merges with GTE; Pfizer joins Warner-Lambert and Viacom swallows CBS.

Pluto's status as the ninth planet is saved when the International Astronomical Union turns down a proposal to reclassify it as one of 10,000 "minor planets."

Ralph Ellison's second novel, *Juneteenth*, is posthumously published, 47 years after his classic *Invisible Man*.

DVDs (Digital Video Disks) are described by industry boosters as "the fastest growing consumer electronics product in history."

Britain's Queen Elizabeth II remains the sovereign in Australia as 55 percent of Aussie voters reject a proposal to declare a republic.

The Kansas State Board of Education adopts new rules that no longer require teaching evolution in public schools. Creationists hail the action; many science teachers are dismayed.

The reputation of the Olympics is tarnished as reports emerge that several local organizing committees bribed International Committee members in their efforts to win selection as host sites.

◀ **MARCH 20**
After 20 days aloft, balloonists Bertrand Piccard and Brian Jones complete the first round-the-world balloon flight.

• **MARCH 29**
The Dow Jones industrial average closes above 10,000 for the first time.

• **JUNE 2**
In South Africa's second democratic election, Thabo Mbeki is elected to succeed retiring President Nelson Mandela.

• **JUNE 16**
John F. Kennedy Jr., his wife, and his sister-in-law are killed when their private plane crashes off Martha's Vineyard, Massachusetts.

• **NOVEMBER 18**
12 present and former students are killed at Texas A&M when a huge logpile built for the traditional Thanksgiving bonfire collapses.

• **NOVEMBER 30**
Protesters launch three days of street disorders to disrupt the World Trade Organization meeting in Seattle.

I t was the closest presidential election in U.S. history, and the first in the modern era to be disputed after the votes were in. For five weeks after Election Day, Americans waited to learn whether Democrat Al Gore or Republican George W. Bush would be their next president. The result hinged on the outcome in Florida, since the electoral votes in the other 49 states were so evenly split that neither candidate had a majority (though Gore won the popular vote nationwide). Florida's initial count gave Bush an infinitesimal lead of fewer than 2,000 votes, out of six million cast in the state. Democrats desperately pushed for court-ordered recounts in several pro-Democratic counties that might tip the majority and Florida's 25 electoral votes to Gore; Republicans just as desperately tried to freeze the count. After a seesaw legal fight in state courts, the dispute went to the U.S. Supreme Court, which on December 12 ruled against further recounts and gave the presidency to Bush. The justices' vote was 5-4, symbolically dividing the court as closely as the country itself. When the Florida count ended, Bush's lead—in effect, the margin of decision in the national election—was only 537 votes.

▶ CRACKING THE GENETIC CODE

"The book of life," one scientist called it: the human genome, or the threadlike strands of DNA that contain the entire set of encoded instructions for creating a living person and all the traits that distinguish him or her from every other being. On June 26, in  a White House ceremony, scientists from the federal Human Genome Project and private researchers announced that they had created a "working draft" of the genome, enabling researchers to read 90 percent of the genetic text.

Deciphering the genetic code—widely compared to such historic feats as development of the periodic table of elements—opened the way for potential stunning breakthroughs in medicine, with the possibility of working with a person's genetic material to fight or prevent a wide array of diseases, or of erasing genetic flaws that carry illnesses from one generation to the next. It also promised major new insights into the study of human evolution.

The genome program raised social, ethical, and policy questions as well: some specific, such as how to regulate commercial use of genetic data and how to prevent possible discrimination by employers or insurers; and others as broad and basic as, in the words of one project document, dealing with the "impacts of genetic advances on the concepts of humanity and personal responsibility."

▶ TECH BUBBLE BURSTS

The deafening whoosh that millions of investors heard in 2000 was the air rushing out of the technology stock bubble.

By year's end, the tech-stock mania, with its spinoffs of day traders, instant dot-com billionaires, and a frenzied enthusiasm that could not imagine any direction except up-up-up forever, seemed a distant memory. The NASDAQ index, charting the exchange that is home to most tech issues, had risen for eight straight years, adding an astounding 86 percent in 1999. But after reaching its peak of 5,048.62 on March 10, 2000, the index sank all the way down to 2,470.52 on the year's last trading day, the largest yearly loss for a major index since 1931. Yesterday's legendary gainers were now big-time losers. Yahoo stock was down 86 percent for the year, Dell Computer down 66 percent. Amazon.com began the year at $89 and ended it at $15.56; America Online slid from $83.88 to $34.80. Lesser dot-com names disappeared from the stock tables altogether, and large and small tech firms began laying off workers.

Most analysts agreed—at least in hindsight—that irrational demand for tech stocks had driven prices far too high, and a drop was inevitable. But it remained to be seen whether the sector would bounce back, or if investors who had been burned in 2000 would stay away for a long time.

▶ NEW LEADERSHIP IN RUSSIA

Russia began the year with a new president. An exhausted and ailing Boris Yeltsin unexpectedly resigned on the last day of 1999, naming Vladimir Putin to succeed him. The 47-year-old Putin, a judo expert and a professional KGB officer for most of his career, had served as premier since August, but was still barely known to the Russian public when he became acting president.

- **MAY 14**
Anti-gun moms march in Washington.

- **MAY 24**
Israeli forces pull out of southern Lebanon, ending more than two decades of occupation.

- **JUNE 10**
Syrian President Hafez Assad dies at 69 and is succeeded by his son, Bashar, a 35-year-old ophthalmologist.

- **JUNE 14**
Presidents of North and South Korea begin first-ever summit between leaders of the divided nation.

- **JUNE 28**
Six-year-old Cuban castaway Elian Gonzalez returns home after a seven-month tug-of-war.

- **JULY 8**
An antimissile missile fails to intercept a mock incoming rocket, making two failures in three tests of the proposed missile defense system.

- **JULY 14**
A Florida jury orders cigarette makers to pay $144.8 billion in damages to sick smokers or their survivors.

In part because they knew so little about him, Russians across a wide spectrum of political views saw their ideas and hopes reflected in their new leader, and his popularity rating soared. Russian liberals, however, remembering Putin's KGB past, worried about his commitment to democratic rule. Putin himself did not sound like a fan of electoral politics. Anyone seeking to win office through elections, he had once observed disparagingly, "has to be insincere and promise something which you cannot fulfill, so you have to be a fool who does not understand what you are promising or deliberately be lying."

After taking office, Putin was blunt and unsparing in acknowledging the country's deep crisis. His goals were equally plain: to restore order and stability, and to regain Russia's place as a great power. Some of Putin's policies, particularly his pursuit of the bloody war against separatist rebels in Chechnya and a series of crackdowns on the independent news media, raised fears about Russian democracy. But many Russians appeared pleased by their new president's brand of leadership. On March 26, Putin won election as president in his own right, capturing 52 percent of the vote.

▶ MIDEAST BLOODSHED

For two weeks in July, Israeli Prime Minister Ehud Barak and Palestinian leader Yassir Arafat met at Camp David, Maryland. With a hovering President Clinton as mediator, they came closer than ever before, but in the end they could not bridge their historic differences and ended the summit without a peace agreement. Barely two months later, whatever hope of peace remained was battered in a new wave of violence, the bloodiest in years.

FAT NATION

Americans were getting fatter as the new century dawned. The craze for fitness and the billions spent on diet foods and advice might suggest otherwise, but according to the U.S. Centers for Disease Control, the number of seriously fat Americans rose by 60 percent in the 1990s alone. By the end of the decade, one in five adults was obese, defined as 30 percent over ideal body weight. Among children, 11 percent were estimated to be seriously overweight. "Don't look now," wrote one journalist, "but Generation X is on its way to becoming Generation XL."

The reasons were obvious: eating too much, eating the wrong things, and not exercising enough. All these reasons seemed imbedded in the

national lifestyle: huge restaurant portions, for example, or modern suburbs with no sidewalks and shopping concentrated in vast malls, making it difficult or even dangerous for anyone to walk to the store or for children to walk or ride a bike to school.

The spark was a provocative visit by the hawkish Israeli politician Ariel Sharon to a sanctuary revered by Muslims atop Jerusalem's Temple Mount. Violent disorders began almost immediately, and in the next two days, at least 17 Palestinians were killed—the first of hundreds who would die, along with dozens of Israelis, in the continuing violence. Barak's political career was a casualty, too. Four months after the outbreak began, he would lose his office to Ariel Sharon.

■ TRENDS & TRIVIA

Despite panicky predictions, the Y2K bug doesn't sting; the new century starts without widespread computer breakdowns.

Vermont is the first state to legalize gay "civil unions."

Census-takers count 281,421,906 Americans.

Pope John Paul II apologizes to the world for the Catholic church's past sins, including injustice toward Jews, women, and indigenous peoples.

"Who Wants to Marry a Millionaire" and "Survivor" hit TV.

Bridgestone/Firestone recalls 6.5 million tires for possible safety hazards.

Gasoline prices skyrocket, hitting $2 a gallon in some states.

Yankees meet Mets in the first "subway series" since 1956.

Federal Trade Commission denounces Hollywood for marketing violent entertainment to kids.

Superstar shortstop Alex Rodriguez gets $252 million contract from the Texas Rangers.

"I love you" virus attacks computers.

Two of the world's most durable ruling parties fall: Mexican voters throw out the Institutional Revolutionary Party after 71 years, and the Nationalist Party is voted out in Taiwan after governing for 52 years.

Harry Potter captivates kids, adult readers, and the best-seller lists.

385

◀ JULY 25
A Concorde crashes near Paris, killing 113 people—the first fatal crash in the supersonic jet's 25-year history of commercial service.

● AUGUST 4
Britain's Queen Mum turns 100.

● AUGUST 7
Picked as Al Gore's running mate, Connecticut Senator Joseph Lieberman becomes the first Jew on a national ticket.

● AUGUST 12
A Russian nuclear missile submarine, the *Kursk*, explodes and sinks in the Barents Sea, killing 117 sailors and a civilian passenger.

● SEPTEMBER 28
The U.S. Food and Drug Administration approves the RU-486 abortion pill for sale in the United States.

● OCTOBER 12
17 U.S. sailors die in the Yemeni port of Aden when a suicide-bomb attack badly damages the U.S.S. *Cole*.

THE CENTURY AT A GLANCE

▶ 1 9 0 0 - 1 9 0 9

• ARTS & ENTERTAINMENT
Pablo Picasso's "blue period" (1901)
The Great Train Robbery (film) (1903)
Nickelodeon movie theaters (1905)
"Mutt and Jeff" is first daily cartoon (1907)
Picasso introduces Cubism (1907)
"Ashcan School" of art debuts (1908)
Frank Lloyd Wright designs the Robie House (1909)

• BUILDING AND TRANSPORTATION
Mombasa-Victoria-Uganda Railway built (1901)
Aswan Dam completed (1902)
First airplane flight (1903)
New York City subway opens (1904)
Trans-Siberian Railway completed (1904)
Model-T introduced (1908)

• BUSINESS & LABOR
Rise of Big Business in America
International Ladies Garment Workers Union forms (1900)
King Gillette markets the first disposable razor (1903)
The Protestant Ethic and the Spirit of Capitalism (Weber) (1904)
Labor unrest in Russia leads to "Bloody Sunday" (1905)
Labour Party formed in Great Britain (1906)

• CONSERVATION
First national wildlife refuge (1903)
National Conservation Commission (1908)

• DISASTERS
San Francisco earthquake (1906)

• EDUCATION
Alfred Binet devises a system to measure aptitude (1905)

• GLOBAL AFFAIRS
All-India Muslim League (1906)
Triple Entente (1907)

• IMMIGRATION
Immigration to U.S. peaks at 1.2 million (1907)
U.S. denies immigration to Japanese (1908)

• LEADERS & RULERS
Queen Victoria dies (1901)
Empress Dowager Cixi dies (1908)

• LITERATURE
Heart of Darkness (Conrad) (1902)
The Virginian (Wister) (1902)
The Hound of the Baskervilles (Doyle) (1902)

• MEDICINE & HEALTH
Discovery of antigens (1900)
The Interpretation of Dreams (Freud) (1900)
Mosquitoes proven to carry yellow fever (1900)
Discovery of hormones (1902)
Cause of tuberculosis discovered (1905)
"Typhoid Mary" is first known typhoid carrier in U.S. (1906)
Gene theory of inheritance established (1909)
Syphilis treated with new drug Salvarsan (1909)

• PEOPLE
Helen Keller graduates from college (1904)
Frenchman Alfred Dreyfus vindicated of treason charges (1906)

• POPULAR CULTURE
Carry Nation begins rampage against alcohol (1901)
World's Fair opens in St. Louis (1904)
Stanford White murder trial (1907)
Boy Scouts founded in England (1908)

• RELIGION
Pope Pius X issues encyclical rejecting modernism (1907)

• SCIENCE & TECHNOLOGY
Quantum theory (1900)

Brownie camera (1900)
A wireless telegraph invented (1901)
Curies discover radium (1903)
Radio diode invented (1904)
Einstein introduces the special theory of relativity (1905)
Ammonia manufacturing process (1909)
Bakelite plastic (1909)

• SPORTS
First World Series (1903)

• WARS & CONFLICTS
Boer War (1899-1902)
Boxer Rebellion (1900-1901)
Russo-Japanese War (1904-1905)

• WOMEN'S ISSUES
International Ladies Garment Workers Union forms (1900)

▶ 1 9 1 0 - 1 9 1 9

• ARTS & ENTERTAINMENT
"Alexander's Ragtime Band" (Berlin) (1911)
International Exhibition of Modern Art (1913)
Birth of a Nation (film) (1915)
Monet begins water lily paintings (1916)
United Artists movie studio founded (1919)
Bauhaus school of architecture opens (1919)

• BUILDING & TRANSPORTATION
Panama Canal completed (1914)

• BUSINESS & LABOR
Carnegie Corporation formed (1911)
Assembly line instituted by Henry Ford (1913)
Federal Reserve Act (1913)
The tractor revolutionizes agriculture (1915)

• CONSERVATION
Gifford Pinchot fired by Taft (1910)
Organic Act (1916) creates the National Park Service

• DISASTERS
New York City Triangle factory fire (1911)
Titanic hits an iceberg and sinks (1912)
Lusitania is torpedoed and sinks (1915)

• GLOBAL AFFAIRS
Revolutionaries seize control in China (1911)
African National Congress formed (1912)
Bolsheviks overthrow Russian government (1917)
League of Nations proposed by Wilson (1918)
Paris Peace Conference (1919)
Treaty of Versailles (1919)

• LEADERS & RULERS
Porfirio Diaz unseated (1910)
Emperor Puyi forced to relinquish throne (1911)
Archduke Franz Ferdinand and wife assassinated (1914)
Tsar Nicholas II abdicates throne (1917)
Nicholas II and royal family executed (1918)
Kaiser Wilhelm II flees Germany (1918)
President Wilson suffers stroke (1919)

• LITERATURE
Tarzan of the Apes (Burroughs) (1914)
Eminent Victorians (Strachey) (1918)

• MEDICINE & HEALTH
Albert Schweitzer opens clinic in Africa (1913)
"Spanish Flu" pandemic (1918)

• PEOPLE
Grigory Rasputin murdered (1916)

• POPULAR CULTURE
Vernon and Irene Castle popularize dancing
Appearance of Halley's comet incites hysteria (1910)
Modern brassiere invented (1913)

• RACE, ETHNICITY, DISCRIMINATION
NAACP protests racism in *Birth of a Nation* (1915)
"Red Summer" race riots (1919)

• SCIENCE & TECHNOLOGY
Tank and submarine are wartime innovations
Rutherford's atomic structure theory (1911)
"Superconductivity" (1911)
A "continental drift" theory (1912)
Bohr's atomic structure theory (1913)
Method of flash-freezing food perfected (1917)

• SPORTS
Jim Thorpe wins gold at Olympic Games (1912)

• U.S. GOVERNMENT & POLITICS
White Slave Traffic Act (1910)
Progressive ("Bull Moose") Party formed (1912)
Wilson declares war against Germany (1917)
Espionage Act (1917)
Sedition Act (1918)
18th Amendment establishes Prohibition (1919)

• WARS & CONFLICTS
World War I (1914-1918)
Mexico plunges into Civil War
Korea annexed by Japan (1910)
Central Powers surrender (1918)

• WOMEN'S ISSUES
Woman suffrage march on Washington (1913)

▶ 1 9 2 0 - 1 9 2 9

• ARTS & ENTERTAINMENT
Rudolph Valentino in *The Sheik* (film) (1921)
Cotton Club opens (1921)
"Rhapsody in Blue" (Gershwin) (1924)
Art Deco movement (1925)
The Jazz Singer (film) (1927)
Amos 'n' Andy radio serial debuts (1928)
Museum of Modern Art opens in N.Y. (1929)

• BUSINESS & LABOR
British labor unions strike (1926)
Florida real estate boom goes bust (1926)
Stock market crash (1929)

• DISASTERS
Tokyo earthquake and fires level city (1923)

• EDUCATION
Scopes trial (1925)

• EXPLORATION & DISCOVERY
King Tutankhamen's tomb discovered (1922)
Lindbergh flies solo across Atlantic (1927)

• GLOBAL AFFAIRS
League of Nations convenes (1920)
Lenin declares New Economic Policy (NEP) (1921)
Washington disarmament conference (1921)
Irish Free State created (1921)
Mussolini's Blackshirts seize control in Italy (1922)
End of Ottoman rule in Turkey (1922)
Hitler leads attempt to overthrow German government (1923)
Chiang Kai-shek leads Chinese Nationalist revolution (1927)
Kellogg-Briand Pact (1928)

• IMMIGRATION
Congress adopts restrictive immigration laws (1924)

• LEADERS & RULERS
Warren G. Harding dies (1923)
Vladimir Ilich Lenin dies (1924)
Trotsky expelled from Soviet Union (1929)

• LITERATURE
Main Street (Lewis) (1920)
Mein Kampf (Hitler) (1925)

The Great Gatsby (Fitzgerald) (1925)
Book-of-the-Month Club launched (1926)
Winnie-the-Pooh (Milne) (1926)
Coming of Age in Samoa (Mead) (1928)
Lady Chatterley's Lover (Lawrence) (1928)
All Quiet on the Western Front (Remarque) (1929)
A Farewell to Arms (Hemingway) (1929)
Goodbye to All That (Graves) (1929)

•MEDICINE & HEALTH
Insulin is new treatment for diabetes (1922)
Iron lung invented (1927)

•POPULAR CULTURE
First commercial radio broadcast (1920)
Emily Post's etiquette book debuts (1922)
The Charleston (1923)
Leopold-Loeb murder case (1924)
New Yorker magazine debuts (1925)
First TV broadcast (1927)
Walt Disney introduces Mickey Mouse (1928)
St. Valentine's Day Massacre (1929)

•RACE, ETHNICITY, DISCRIMINATION
Marcus Garvey leads African American mass movement
Shuffle Along is the first big all-black Broadway hit
Harlem Renaissance
NAACP champions anti-lynching legislation (1922)
Ku Klux Klan swells to four million members (1923)

•RELIGION
Aimee Semple McPherson turns religion into show business (1926)
Anti-Catholic prejudice in the U.S. Presidential election (1928)

•SPORTS
"Black" Sox baseball scandal (1920)
Gertrude Ederle swims English Channel (1926)
Babe Ruth leads the N.Y. Yankees to winning season (1927)

•U.S. GOVERNMENT & POLITICS
Senate rejects Treaty of Versailles and League of Nations (1920)
Teapot Dome scandal (1923)
Federal Bureau of Investigation (FBI) established (1924)

•WOMEN'S ISSUES
American Birth Control League founded (1921)
Virginia Woolf explores gender issues in *A Room of One's Own* (1929)

▶ 1930-1939

•ARTS & ENTERTAINMENT
Works Progress Administration (WPA) supports artists during Depression
"American Gothic" (Wood) (1930)
"Brother, Can You Spare a Dime" (song) (1932)
Tarzan, the Ape Man (film) (1932)
King Kong (film) (1933)
Marx brothers' *Duck Soup* (film) (1933)
Hollywood begins enforcing morality in films (1934)
Benny Goodman swing concert in Carnegie Hall (1938)
Gone With the Wind (film) (1939)
The Wizard of Oz (film) (1939)
Marian Anderson concert at Lincoln Memorial (1939)

•BUILDING & TRANSPORTATION
Empire State Building opens (1931)
DC-3 revolutionizes air travel (1935)

•BUSINESS & LABOR
The Great Depression
Growth of labor unions
Unemployed war veterans rally in Washington (1932)
Securities Exchange Act (1934)
National Labor Relations Act (1934)
Committee for Industrial Organization (CIO) founded (1935)
Fair Labor Standards Act (1938)

•DISASTERS
Dust storms devastate Midwest farmland (mid-1930s)
Hindenburg explodes (1937)

•EDUCATION
Institute for Advanced Study opens (1930)

•EXPLORATION & DISCOVERY
Amelia Earhart flies solo across the Atlantic (1932)
Amelia Earhart disappears on around-the-world flight (1937)

•GLOBAL AFFAIRS
Mohandas K. Gandhi leads salt tax protest (1930)
Smoot-Hawley Act (1930)
Soviet collectivization results in famine (1932-1933)
German voters support Nazi party (1932)
United States and U.S.S.R. resume diplomatic relations (1933)
U.S. occupation ends in Haiti (1934)
Mao Zedong rises to power during the Long March (1934)
Military seizes control in Japan (1936)

•LEADERS & RULERS
King Edward VII abdicates throne (1936)

•LITERATURE
The Maltese Falcon (Hammett) (1930)
The Story of Babar (de Brunhoff) (1931)
Brave New World (Huxley) (1932)
Launch of Pocket Books (1939)

•POPULAR CULTURE
The Joy of Cooking (Rombauer) (1931)
Lindbergh baby kidnapping (1932)
Roosevelt's first "fireside chat" (1933)
Dionne quintuplets born (1934)
War of the Worlds radio broadcast (1938)

•RACE, ETHNICITY, DISCRIMINATION
Alabama rape trials spotlight Jim Crow justice (1931)
Joe Louis is first black American superstar (1937)

•RELIGION
First issue of *Catholic Worker* (newspaper) (1933)
Jews deprived of German citizenship (1935)
Nazis murder Jews during "Kristallnacht" (1938)

•SCIENCE & TECHNOLOGY
Development of commercial fiberglass production (1938)
Nuclear fission discovered (1938)
America's atom-bomb project is conceived (1939)

•SPORTS
First World Cup soccer tournament (1930)
Jesse Owens wins Olympic gold in Berlin (1930)
Lou Gehrig retires due to illness (1939)

•U.S. GOVERNMENT & POLITICS
Roosevelt's New Deal
The press wins in First Amendment ruling (1931)
Roosevelt's "Hundred Days" (1933)
Amendment repeals prohibition (1933)
Social Security Act (1935)
Rural Electrification Agency made permanent (1936)
Presidential judge appointment law fails (1937)

•WARS & CONFLICTS
Japan seizes Manchuria (1931)
Italy invades Ethiopia (1935)
Spanish Civil War (1936-1939)
Japan invades China (1937)
German troops seize Austria and Sudetenland (1938)
World War II begins (1939)

▶ 1940-1949

•ARTS & ENTERTAINMENT
Citizen Kane (film) (1941)
Jackson Pollock exhibit opens (1948)
Death of a Salesman opens at the Morosco Theatre (1949)

•BUILDING & TRANSPORTATION
Fair Employment Practices Commission formed (1941)
Truman's Employment Act (1946)
"Levittown" (1947)
Taft-Hartley Act (1947)

•EDUCATION
G.I. Bill offers educational opportunities (1946)

•EXPLORATION & DISCOVERY
Thor Heyerdahl sets sail on the *Kon-Tiki* (1947)

•GLOBAL AFFAIRS
Stalin brings down Iron Curtain (1946)
Hindustan splits into Pakistan and India (1947)
Truman signs Marshall Plan (1948)
State of Israel proclaimed (1948)
Berlin Airlift (1948-1949)
People's Republic of China established (1949)
Soviet Union detonates atomic bomb (1949)
North Atlantic Treaty Organization (NATO) established (1949)

•LEADERS & RULERS
Franklin D. Roosevelt dies (1945)
Mohandas K. "Mahatma" Gandhi assassinated (1948)
Hitler commits suicide (1945)
Mussolini executed (1945)

•LITERATURE
Native Son (Wright) (1940)
1984 (Orwell) (1949)

•MEDICINE & HEALTH
The Common Sense Book of Baby and Child Care (Spock) (1946)
Kinsey report on American sexuality (1948)

•PEOPLE
Anne Frank dies at Belson (1945)

•POPULAR CULTURE
Birth of commercial TV (1941)
War rationing begins (1942)

•RACE, ETHNICITY, DISCRIMINATION
Mandate against discrimination in defense industries (1941)
Jackie Robinson is first major league Black American baseball player (1947)
Truman ends segregation in Armed Services (1948)

•RELIGION
Jews persecuted in Europe
Hindus and Muslims clash on Indian subcontinent (1947)

•SCIENCE & TECHNOLOGY
Manhattan Project launched (1942)
Penicillin mass produced (1943)
First computer (ENIAC) built (1946)
Radiocarbon dating developed (1947)

•U.S. GOVERNMENT
Selective Training and Service Act (1940)
Lend-Lease bill approved (1941)
U.S. begins internment of Japanese (1942)
Truman Doctrine (1947)
Truman outlines his "Fair Deal" program (1949)

•WOMEN'S ISSUES
Women's Army Auxiliary Corps is created (1942)

•WORLD WAR II (1939-1945)
British soldiers evacuated from Dunkirk (1940)
German army enters Paris (1940)
Air superiority wins Battle of Britain (1940)
Ethiopia liberated by British (1941)
Pearl Harbor (1941)
U.S. declares war on Japan (1941)
Germany invades Russia (1941)
Battle of Midway (1942)
Battle of El Alamein (1942)
Battle of Stalingrad (1942-1943)
Allies land in Sicily (1943)
Battle of Kursk (1943)

Warsaw ghetto uprising (1943)
Operation Overlord (1944)
Allies begin Berlin air raids (1944)
D-Day invasion (1944)
Battle of the Bulge (1944)
Liberation of Paris (1944)
V-E Day (1945)
U.S. drops atomic bombs on Japan (1945)
Yalta Conference (1945)
U.S. assaults at Iwo Jima and Okinawa (1945)
Holocaust horrors emerge (1945)
Philippines freed from Japanese occupation (1946)
Nuremberg trials (1945-1946)

▶ 1 9 5 0 - 1 9 5 9

• ARTS & ENTERTAINMENT
Elvis Presley
Rock 'n' roll
Motown
French new wave cinema
"Peanuts" cartoon introduced (1950)
I Love Lucy debuts (1951)
High Noon (film) (1952)

• BUILDING & TRANSPORTATION
Highway Act (1956)
First transatlantic passenger jet (1958)

• BUSINESS & LABOR
AFL and CIO merge (1955)

• DISASTERS
Andrea Doria sinks (1956)

• EDUCATION
National Defense Education Act advocates science in schools

• GLOBAL AFFAIRS
East German pro-democracy riot quashed (1953)
Warsaw Pact (1955)
Hungarian rebellion (1956)
Suez Canal nationalized (1956)
Ghana gains independence (1957)
China's Great Leap Forward (1958)
St. Lawrence Seaway opens (1959)
Antarctic Treaty (1959)
"Kitchen debate" between Nixon and Khrushchev (1959)

• LEADERS & RULERS
Elizabeth II ascends British throne (1952)
Eisenhower elected U.S. President (1952)
Joseph Stalin dies (1953)
Guatemalan President Guzman overthrown (1954)
Prince Rainier III of Monaco marries Grace Kelly (1956)
François "Papa Doc" Duvalier becomes Haitian president (1957)
Fidel Castro assumes leadership of Cuba (1959)

• LITERATURE
Beat Generation
The Lonely Crowd (1950)
The Catcher in the Rye (Salinger) (1951)
Invisible Man (1952)
Peyton Place (1956)
The Cat in the Hat (Seuss) (1957)

• MEDICINE & HEALTH
DNA structure discovered (1953)
Polio vaccine (1955)
Thalidomide scare (late 1950s)

• POPULAR CULTURE
McDonalds restaurants gain popularity
"Baby boomers"
Playboy magazine debuts (1953)

• RACE, ETHNICITY, DISCRIMINATION
Brown v. Board of Education outlaws segregation in schools (1954)
Rosa Parks inspires bus boycott (1955)
Segregated busing outlawed in U.S. (1956)

• SCIENCE & TECHNOLOGY
Hydrogen bomb developed
First electronic digital computer (1951)
First nuclear power reactor (1951)
Sputnik (1957)

• SPORTS
Roger Bannister runs mile in under four minutes (1954)

• U.S. GOVERNMENT & POLITICS
McCarthy hearings investigate suspected communists
National Security Council urges increase in defense spending (1950)
Truman fires MacArthur (1951)
U.S. Congress sets presidential term limits (1951)
Nixon gives "Checkers" speech (1952)
Rosenbergs executed for spying (1953)

• WARS & CONFLICTS
China invades Tibet (1950)
Korean War (1950-1953)
Mau Mau rebellion (1952)

▶ 1 9 6 0 - 1 9 6 9

• ARTS & ENTERTAINMENT
"The Twist"
Pop art
James Bond debuts on screen in *Dr. No* (1962)
The Beatles tour America (1964)
Florence flood threatens Renaissance art treasures (1966)
The Graduate (film) (1967)
Woodstock rock concert (1969)

• BUSINESS & LABOR
Cesar Chavez farm workers' march (1966)

• CONSERVATION
Silent Spring (Carson)

• GLOBAL AFFAIRS
American spy Francis Gary Powers captured by Soviets (1960)
Communist soldiers begin building Berlin wall (1961)
Cuban missile crisis (1962)
Mao Zedong launches China's cultural revolution (1966)
Tribal warfare leads to starvation in Africa (1967)

• LEADERS & RULERS
John F. Kennedy elected U.S. President (1960)
South Vietnamese Premier Ngo Dinh Diem assassinated (1963)
John F. Kennedy assassinated (1963)
Indira Gandhi becomes Prime Minister of India (1966)

• MEDICINE & HEALTH
Report issued outlining dangers of cigarette smoking (1964)
Masters and Johnson report on sex (1966)
First successful human heart transplant (1967)

• PEOPLE
Edward Kennedy involved in drowning on Chappaquiddick Island (1969)

• POPULAR CULTURE
Anti-war protests
Psychotropic drugs
"Summer of Love" (1967)
Manson "family" murders (1969)

• RACE, ETHNICITY, DISCRIMINATION
Lunch counter sit-ins (1960)
Freedom riders (1961)
Martin Luther King, Jr.'s speech in Washington, D.C. (1963)
Civil Rights Act (1964)
Malcolm X assassinated (1965)
Race riots ravage Watts area of Los Angeles (1965)
Voting Rights Act guarantees blacks right to vote (1965)
Black Panther organization founded (1966)
Thurgood Marshall is first black American on Supreme Court (1967)
Martin Luther King, Jr. assassinated (1968)

• RELIGION
Prayer in schools illegal (1962)
Second Vatican Council convenes (1962)

• SCIENCE & TECHNOLOGY
First operational laser pulse (1960)
Soviet Yuri Gagarin is first man in space (1961)
America lands first man on moon (1969)

• SPORTS
Cassius Marcellus Clay knocks out Sonny Liston (1964)
Joe Namath leads New York Jets to Superbowl win (1969)

• U.S. GOVERNMENT & POLITICS
Alliance for Progress encourages democracy in Latin America
Peace Corps established (1961)
Lyndon Johnson promises "Great Society" (1964)
Gulf of Tonkin Resolution (1964)
Miranda v. Arizona results in protection for accused criminals (1966)

• VIETNAM WAR (1964-1973)
Johnson dispatches Marine battalions to Danang (1965)
TET Offensive (1968)
My Lai massacre (1968)

• WARS & CONFLICTS
Bay of Pigs (1961)
Six Day War (1967)
"Prague Spring" (1968)
Catholics and Protestants begin bitter battle in Northern Ireland (1969)

• WOMEN'S ISSUES
Birth control pills introduced (1960)
The Feminine Mystique (Friedan) (1963)
National Organization for Women (NOW) founded (1963)

▶ 1 9 7 0 - 1 9 7 9

• ARTS & ENTERTAINMENT
"Doonesbury" cartoon debuts (1970)
All in the Family debuts (1971)
Saturday Night Live debuts (1975)
Roots (1977)
Saturday Night Fever (1978)

• BUSINESS & LABOR
Grape boycott ends (1970)

• CONSERVATION
First Earth Day (1970)

• DISASTERS
Malfunction at Three Mile Island nuclear reactor (1979)

• GLOBAL AFFAIRS
Chile elects Marxist president (1970)
Nixon attends summit in Beijing (1972)
SALT I treaty signed in Moscow (1972)
Ireland's "Bloody Sunday" (1972)
Palestinian terrorist assault at Olympic Games (1972)
Arab oil embargo (1973)
Democracy restored in Greece (1974)
Syria-Israeli truce (1974)
Helsinki Accords (1975)
Khmer Rouge begins campaign of terror (1975)
Raid at Entebbe (1976)
China's second revolution (1976)
Anwar Sadat makes peace overture to Israel (1977)
Camp David Accords (1978)
Iran becomes first Islamic republic (1979)
"Thatcher Revolution" begins in Britain (1979)

• LEADERS & RULERS
Idi Amin installed as Uganda's Prime Minister (1972)
Ferdinand Marcos regains control in Philippines (1973)
Ethiopian Emperor Haile Selassie overthrown (1974)
Richard Nixon is first U.S. President to resign (1974)
Juan Carlos assumes Spanish throne (1975)

MEDICINE & HEALTH
Computerized axial tomography (CAT) (1971)
Karen Ann Quinlan "right-to-die" case (1976)
First test-tube baby born (1978)

POPULAR CULTURE
College students killed during antiwar protests (1970)
Patty Hearst kidnapping (1974)
Serial killer "Son of Sam" caught (1977)

RACE, ETHNICITY, DISCRIMINATION
Start of school busing to combat segregation (1971)
American Indian protest at Wounded Knee (1973)
Soweto students killed protesting apartheid policies (1976)
Race cannot be a decisive factor for school admission (1978)

RELIGION
Karol Wojtyla becomes Pope John Paul II (1978)
Cult members commit mass suicide in Jonestown (1978)
Jerry Falwell founds Moral Majority (1979)

SCIENCE & TECHNOLOGY
Mariner 9 begins mapping surface of Mars (1971)
Silicon microprocessor (1971)

SPORTS
Secretariat wins racing's Triple Crown (1973)
Hank Aaron breaks home run record (1974)

U.S. GOVERNMENT & POLITICS
Pentagon Papers (1971)
George Wallace shot by would-be assassin (1972)
Nixon Administration on trial over Watergate scandal (1973)

VIETNAM (1964-1973)
Christmas bombings of Hanoi and Haiphong (1972)
U.S. evacuates Saigon as it falls to the Viet Cong (1975)

WARS & CONFLICTS
Thousands "disappear" in Argentina's "dirty war" (1976)
Soviets invade Afghanistan (1979)

WOMEN'S ISSUES
Roe v. *Wade* legalizes abortion (1973)

▶ 1 9 8 0 - 1 9 8 9

ARTS & ENTERTAINMENT
First 24-hour TV news channel (1980)
MTV debuts on cable television (1981)
Band Aid rock concert raises money for famine victims (1984)

BUSINESS & LABOR
Breakup of AT&T (1982)
Stock prices plunge on "Black Monday" (1987)

CONSERVATION
Fish kills raise awareness of acid rain (1982)
Greenpeace ship sunk by French agents (1985)
Activist Francisco "Chico" Mendes Filho is murdered (1988)
Exxon Valdez oil spill contaminates Alaska shoreline (1989)

DISASTERS
Soviet missile brings down Korean Air Lines jet (1983)
Leak in Bhopal chemical plant kills thousands (1984)
Space shuttle *Challenger* explodes (1986)
Nuclear reactor explosion at Chernobyl (1986)
Pan Am Flight 103 blown up over Lockerbie, Scotland (1988)

GLOBAL AFFAIRS
Cubans refugees flood U.S. (1980)
Poland's Solidarity movement driven underground (1981)
Benigno Aquino assassinated in Philippines (1983)
Terrorists blow up U.S. Marine barracks in Beirut (1983)
Strategic Defense Initiative ("Star Wars") (1983)
U.S. Congress outlaws aid to Nicaraguan contras (1984)
Mikhail Gorbachev begins sweeping reforms (1985)
Terrorists seize cruise ship *Achille Lauro* (1985)
U.S. bombs Libya (1986)
Arms control summit in Reykjavik (1986)
Arias Peace Plan (1987)
Iron curtain ripped down across Eastern Europe (1989)
Demonstrators killed in China's Tiananmen Square (1989)

LEADERS & RULERS
The Prince of Wales marries Diana Spencer (1981)
Indira Gandhi assassinated (1984)
Vice President George Bush elected President (1988)
Benazir Bhutto elected Prime Minister of Pakistan (1988)

LITERATURE
The Satanic Verses (Rushdie) (1988)

MEDICINE & HEALTH
Smallpox vanquished (1980)
New epidemic named AIDS (1981)

POPULAR CULTURE
Crack cocaine breeds crime wave (1983)
John Lennon killed by crazed fan (1980)
Vietnam Veterans Memorial dedicated (1982)
Bernhard Goetz's vigilante shooting on N.Y. subway (1984)
Police bomb Philadelphia headquarters of MOVE (1985)
Gary Hart loses Democratic nomination over sex scandal (1987)

RACE, ETHNICITY, DISCRIMINATION
Film *Do the Right Thing* looks at race relations (1989)

RELIGION
Televangelist Jim Bakker admits to adulterous affair (1987)

SCIENCE & TECHNOLOGY
First generation of personal computers introduced (1981)
Scientists confirm hole in ozone layer (1985)
Voyager 2 explores solar system (1989)

SPORTS
Australia II wins America's Cup (1983)

U.S. GOVERNMENT & POLITICS
Gramm-Rudman-Hollings Act (1985)
Oliver North testifies at Iran-Contra hearings (1986)
Robert Bork's nomination to the Supreme Court rejected (1987)

WARS & CONFLICTS
Civil War in El Salvador
Israel invades Lebanon (1982)
Falklands War (1982)
Cease-fire brokered in Iraq-Iran war (1988)
U.S. invades Panama (1989)

WOMEN'S ISSUES
First woman on Supreme Court (1981)
Phyllis Schlafly leads protest against ERA (1982)
First woman nominated for U.S. vice president (1984)
First female head of Islamic nation (1988)

▶ 1 9 9 0 - 2 0 0 0

ARTS & ENTERTAINMENT
Johnny Carson retires as host of *The Tonight Show* (1992)

BUSINESS & LABOR
Collapse of Bank of Credit and Commerce International (BCCI) (1991)
North American Free Trade Agreement (NAFTA) (1993)
Maastricht Treaty (1993)
Antitrust suit brought against Microsoft, Inc. (1998)
Stock markets tumble across East Asia (1998)
The NASDAQ index sinks along with tech stocks (2000)

CONSERVATION
Logging in Pacific Northwest threatens spotted owl (1990)
UN Conference on Environment and Development (1992)

DISASTERS
El Niño causes floods and landslides (1997-1998)

GLOBAL AFFAIRS
East and West Germany are reunified (1990)
Soviet Union crumbles into 15 separate republics (1991)
Yassir Arafat and Yitzhak Rabin sign peace accord (1993)
IRA agrees to lay down its arms (1994)
Zapatista rebel uprising in Mexico (1994)
U.S. resumes relations with Vietnam (1995)
Tupac Amaru revolutionaries take hostages in Lima (1996)
Taliban gains control in Afghanistan (1996)
Great Britain cedes control of Hong Kong to China (1997)
India and Pakistan clash over nuclear testing (1998)
Ireland votes for peace (1998)
Control of Panama Canal returned to Panama (1999)

LEADERS & RULERS
Jean-Bertrand Aristide elected president of Haiti (1990)
Rajiv Gandhi assassinated (1991)
Bill Clinton elected U.S. President (1992)
Nelson Mandela elected president of South Africa (1994)
Yitzhak Rabin assassinated (1995)
Princess Diana killed in car crash (1997)
Labour Leader Tony Blair elected British Prime Minister (1997)
Vladimir Putin elected Russian President (2000)

POPULAR CULTURE
Anita Hill accuses Supreme Court nominee Clarence Thomas of sexual harassment (1991)
O.J. Simpson on trial for murder (1994)
Bomb blows up the Murrah Building in Oklahoma City (1995)
Ted Kazcynski (the Unabomber) caught in Montana (1996)
Au pair Louise Woodward on trial for murder (1997)
World-wide "aging explosion" predicted (1999)
Massacre at Columbine High School, Colorado (1999)
U.S. Centers for Disease Control says more Americans are overweight (2000)

RACE, ETHNICITY, DISCRIMINATION
Americans With Disabilities Act (1990)
Nelson Mandela freed from prison in South Africa (1990)
Million Man March in Washington (1995)

RELIGION
Branch Davidian raid in Waco, Texas, ends in disaster (1993)
Mother Teresa dies (1997)

SCIENCE & TECHNOLOGY
Surfing the Internet becomes popular (1993)
Cloning produces a sheep called Dolly (1997)
A working draft of the human genome is completed (2000)

SPORTS
U.S. basketball Dream Team wins gold at Olympic Games (1992)
Cal Ripken, Jr. sets record for consecutive games played (1995)
Michael Jordan retires from basketball (1999)
Baseball legend Joe DiMaggio dies (1999)

U.S. GOVERNMENT & POLITICS
"Don't Ask, Don't Tell" policy in military (1993)
Brady Bill (1993)
Newt Gingrich becomes Speaker of the House (1995)
Clinton overhauls welfare system (1996)
Fund-raising practices by Vice President Gore questioned (1997)
President Clinton is impeached (1998), then acquitted (1999) on charges related to a sex scandal
Democrats call for a recount in the 2000 Presidential election

WARS & CONFLICTS
Operation Desert Storm (1991)
Bosnian civil war begins (1992)
Chechnya rises up against Russian troops (1994)
Rwandan civil war (1994)
Ethnic Albanians are slaughtered in Kosovo (1999)
Middle East violence flares in Jerusalem (2000)

Boldface indicates illustrations

393

Library, London/New York. 230, Burt Glinn/Magnum Photos, Inc. 232 (left), Victor R. Boswell, Jr. 232 (ct), B. Anthony Stewart. 232 (rt), Joseph D. Lavenberg.

1960-1969: 236-237, Dennis Brack/Black Star. 238, Donald J. Crump. 240, 252 (both), 258 (left), 259 (up), 260 (up), 265 (up), 266, Hulton Getty/Tony Stone Images. 243, 269 (up), Image Works/Tom Miner/Sipa Press. 245, Charles Bonnay/Black Star. 246, Joe Munroe. 247 (left), Des Bartlett/Armand Denis Productions. 247 (rt), Holly LaPratt. 248, Robin Lee Graham. 249 (up), Daniel Tomasi. 249 (low), Hugo Van Lawick. 250 (both), 251 (up), 255 (rt), 258 (rt), 259 (low), 260 (low), 263 (both), 265 (ct), 267 (left), UPI/Corbis. 251 (low), Corbis. 253 (left), Steve Shapiro/Black Star. 253 (rt), Deutsche Presse Agentur/Archive Photos. 254 (up), Alinari/Giraudon. 254 (low), 255 (left), 257 (both), 264 (up), 265 (low), 268 (rt), 269 (low), Archive Photos. 255 (ct), Erich Hartmann/Magnum Photos, Inc. 256 (up), James P. Blair. 256 (low), Charles Moore/Black Star. 261 (left), Lou Jacobs, Jr./Black Star. 261 (rt), 262 (rt), Express Newspapers/Archive Photos. 262 (left), AFP/Archive Photos. 264 (low), LDE/Archive Photos. 267 (rt), Joseph Louw/LIFE Magazine © Time, Inc. 268 (left), 270 (rt), NASA. 270 (left), Stephanie Maze. 270 (ct), Bruce Dale.

1970-1979: 274-275, 283, 296 (left), 298 (rt), 299 (up), 300 (left), 300 (up), 301 (low), 302 (up), 303 (ct), 304 (up), 304 (ct), 305 (low), 306 (left), Corbis. 276, 294 (both), 295 (ct), 295 (low), 299 (low), 301 (up), 307 (both), UPI/Corbis. 278, Owen Franken/Corbis. 281, Alain Mingam/The Gamma Liaison Network. 284 (left), Jeff Foott. 284 (rt), James P. Blair. 285 (both), Bruce Dale. 286 (left), Leroy Woodson. 286 (rt), Pierre Mion. 287 (left), Rick Smolan. 287 (rt), Albert Moldvay. 288 (left), John Filo/Archive Photos. 288 (rt), Todd Gipstein/NGS Image Collection. 289 (up), Russell Reif/Archive Photos. 289 (low), 292 (left), 293 (up), 295 (up), 296 (low), 297, 298 (left), 302 (low), 304 (low), 306 (rt), Hulton Getty/Tony Stone Images. 290 (left), 305 (up), Archive Photos. 290 (rt), CBS/Archive Photos. 291 (left), Frederick Lewis/Archive Photos. 291 (rt), Alfred Pasieha/Science Photo Library/Photo Researchers, Inc. 292 (right), Camera Press/Archive Photos. 293 (low), C.J. Zimmerman/FPG International. 296 (up), Villard/Sipa Press. 300 (low), The Bassford Collection. 303 (up), Fotos International/Archive Photos. 303 (low), Jason Weisfeld, M.D. 306 (ct), From *Afghanistan: Soviet Vietnam* © 1992 by Vladislav Tamarov. Published by Mercury House, San Francisco, CA, and reprinted by permission. 308 (left), Dewitt Jones. 308 (ct), Carol Hughes. 308 (rt), Jim Richardson.

1980-1989: 312-313, Anthony Suau/The Gamma Liaison Network. 314, 326 (left), 328 (rt), 332-333 (all), 334 (left), 335 (both), 336 (left), 341 (low), UPI/Corbis. 316, Novosti Press/FPG International. 319, Eric Bouvet/The

Gamma Liaison Network. 321, Reuters/Archive Photos. 322 (left), Jon Schneeberger, Ted Johnson, Jr., NGS & Anthony Peritore, NGS. 322 (rt), Bill Curtsinger. 323 (left), Ralph Perry/Black Star. 323 (rt), Peter G. Veit. 324, Ken Duncan. 325 (up), Emory Kristof. 325 (low), Flip Nicklin. 326 (up), John Hoagland/The Gamma Liaison Network. 326 (rt), Michel Abramson/The Gamma Liaison Network. 326 (low), David Weintraub/Photo Researchers, Inc. 327, Cynthia Johnson/The Gamma Liaison Network. 328 (left), 330 (up), Hulton Getty/Tony Stone Images. 329 (up), Express Newspapers/Archive Photos. 329 (low), Sutton/The Gamma Liaison Network. 330 (low), Archive Photos. 331 (up), Reuters/Win Mcnamee/Archive Photos. 331 (low), Ricardo Watson/Archive Photos. 334 (rt), Reuters/Rob Taggart/Archive Photos. 336 (rt), Steven Falk/The Gamma Liaison Network. 337 (up), T. Seigmann/The Gamma Liaison Network. 337 (ct), Reuters/Khaled Abu Seif/Archive Photos. 337 (low), V. DeWal/P.N.S./The Gamma Liaison Network. 338 (up), Mike Brown/The Gamma Liaison Network. 338 (ct), Markel/The Gamma Liaison Network. 338 (low) Corbis. 339, Vladimir Vyatkin/Russian Information Agency "Novosti". 340, Mark Reinstein/FPG International. 341 (up), John Barr/The Gamma Liaison Network. 342 (left), F. Lochon/The Gamma Liaison Network. 342 (rt), Reuters/Corbis. 343 (left), The Gamma Liaison Network. 343 (rt), Bradford Telegraph/FSP/The Gamma Liaison Network. 344 (left), Priit J. Vesilind/NGS Image Collection. 344 (rt), Moyer/The Gamma Liaison Network. 345 (up), NASA/Science Photo Library/Photo Researchers, Inc. 345 (ct), Natalie Fobes/Tony Stone Images. 345 (low), Mark Downey/The Gamma Liaison Network. 346 (left), Original NASA photograph printed from digital image © 1996 Corbis. 346 (ct), Robin T. Holcomb. 346 (rt), Bill Nation/Sygma.

1990-2000: 350-351, 360 (left), Louie Psihoyos. 352, K. Bernstein/The Gamma Liaison Network. 354, FSP/The Gamma Liaison Network. 357, Jasmin Krpan/The Gamma Liaison Network. 359, Reuters/Ahmed Jadallah/Archive Photos. 360 (rt), NASA. 361 (up), The Sankei Shimbun. 361 (low), George Steinmetz. 362 (left), Steve McCurry. 362 (rt), Karen Kasmauski. 363 (left), Stephen L. Alvarez. 363 (rt), Mark W. Moffett. 364 (left), Mike Persson/The Gamma Liaison Network. 364 (ct), Laguna Photo/The Gamma Liaison Network. 364 (rt), Chip Hires/The Gamma Liaison Network. 365 (left), Diana Walker/The Gamma Liaison Network. 365 (rt), Amy E. Powers/The Gamma Liaison Network. 366 (left), Georges Meril-

lon/The Gamma Liaison Network. 366 (rt), Deville-Bartholomew/The Gamma Liaison Network. 367 (left), G. Bassignac/G. Saussier/L. Van Der Stockt/The Gamma Liaison Network. 367 (ct), 367 (rt), 369 (up), Brad Markel/The Gamma Liaison Network. 368 (left), Shone/The Gamma Liaison Network. 368 (ct), Douglas Burrows/The Gamma Liaison Network. 368 (rt), Pool J.O Barcelone/The Gamma Liaison Network. 369 (low), Antonio Ribeiro/The Gamma Liaison Network. 370 (left), 375 (left), Reuters/Gary Hershorn/Archive Photos. 370 (up), Robert E. Daemmrich/Tony Stone Images. 370 (low), Gifford/The Gamma Liaison Network. 371, Reuters/Corbis. 372 (left), 376 (up), Corbis. 372 (ct), Kelvin Boyes/The Gamma Liaison Network. 372 (up), Alyx Kellington/The Gamma Liaison Network. 373 (up), The Gamma Liaison Network. 373 (low), Scott Daniel Peterson/The Gamma Liaison Network. 374 (left), Reuters/Rick Wilking/Archive Photos. 374 (up), Cynthia Johnson/The Gamma Liaison Network. 374 (low), Andres Hernandez/The Gamma Liaison Network. 375 (ct), Reuters/Gary Cameron/Archive Photos. 375 (rt) Jonathan Elderfield/The Gamma Liaison Network. 376 (low), Reuters/Zoraida Diaz/Archive Photos. 377 (up), NASA. 377 (ct), Derek Pruitt/The Gamma Liaison Network. 377 (low), Robert Kusel/Tony Stone Images. 378 (up), Jeffrey Aaronson/Network Aspen. 378 (low), Yousuf Karsh/Woodfin Camp & Associates. 379 (left), Reuters/Ian Waldie/Archive Photos. 379 (low left), NASA/Jet Propulsion Laboratory. 379 (low ct), Reuters/Gareth Watkins/Archive Photos. 379 (low rt), Bob Yen/The Gamma Liaison Network. 380 (left), The Washington Post. 380 (rt), Reuters/Jim Bourg/Archive Photos. 381 (left), Reuters/Russell Boyce/Archive Photos. 381 (up ct), NASA. 381 (low ct), Joe McNally. 381 (rt), Fotos International/Archive Photos. 382 (up left), Antonella Nusca/The Gamma Liaison Network. 382 (low left), M. Deville/N. Quidu/J.M. Turpin/The Gamma Liaison Network. 382 (rt) Lambermont/Photonews/The Gamma Liaison Network. 383 (up left), Joe Traver/The Gamma Liaison Network. 383 (low left), AP Photo/Keystone/Fabrice Coffrini. 383 (rt), Kevin Moloney/The Gamma Liaison Network. 384 (up), Digital Art/Corbis. 384 (low), Mark Wilson/Newsmakers/The Gamma Liaison Network. 385 (up), Laski Diffusion/The Gamma Liaison Network. 385 (ct), Donna Day/Stone. 385 (low left), Buzz Pictures/Sygma/Corbis. 385 (low rt), Reuters NewMedia, Inc./Corbis.

Printed and bound by Quad/Graphics, West Allis, WI.
Color separations by CMI Color Graphix, Inc., Huntingdon Valley, Pennsylvania.
Dust jacket printed by Miken Companies, Inc., Cheektowaga, New York.
Visit the Society's Web site at www.nationalgeographic.com.

Library of Congress Cataloging-in-Publication Data
National geographic eyewitness to the 20th century / prepared by the Book Division, National Geographic Society.
    p. cm.
    Includes index.
    ISBN 0-7922-7049-5 (reg.). −ISBN 0-7922-7025-8 (dlx.).
    1. History, Modern−20th century. 2. History, Modern−20th century−Chronology. 3. Twentieth century. I. National Geographic Society (U.S.). Book Division. II. National geographic.
D421.N37 1998
909.82−dc21
                           98-22756

Published by
The National Geographic Society

John M. Fahey, Jr. *President and Chief Executive Officer*
Gilbert M. Grosvenor *Chairman of the Board*
Nina D. Hoffman *Executive Vice President*

Prepared by
The Book Division
Kevin Mulroy *Vice President and Editor-in-Chief*
Charles Kogod *Illustrations Director*
Barbara A. Payne *Editorial Director*
Marianne R. Koszorus *Design Director*

STAFF FOR THIS BOOK
John G. Agnone *Project Editor and Illustrations Editor*
Rebecca Lescaze *Text Editor and Research Editor*
Marianne R. Koszorus *Art Director*
Susan K. White *Designer*
Patti H. Cass *Illustrations Researcher*
Roberta R. Conlan *Text Editor*
Cynthia M. Barry, Mark A. Galan,
Arnold R. Isaacs, Robin T. Reid *Contributing Writers*
Victoria Garrett Jones *Researcher*
Dale-Marie Herring *Assistant Editor*
Thomas B. Blabey, Kristin M. Edmonds, Mary E. Jennings, Lawrence M. Porges
Assistant Researchers
R. Gary Colbert *Production Director*
Lewis R. Bassford *Production Project Manager*
Richard S. Wain *Production*
Meredith C. Wilcox *Illustrations Assistant*
Melissa Farris, David M. Seager *Design Assistants*
Peggy J. Candore, Kevin G. Craig *Staff Assistants*

MANUFACTURING AND QUALITY CONTROL
George V. White *Director*
John T. Dunn *Associate Director*
Vincent P. Ryan *Manager*

Anne Marie Houppert *Indexer*

ACKNOWLEDGMENTS

The Book Division wishes to thank the individuals and organizations
mentioned or quoted in this publication for their guidance and help.
We are particularly grateful to our chief consultant Robert D. Johnston, assistant professor and director of undergraduate studies in the
history department at Yale University. Dr. Johnston is currently finishing his first book, *The Radical Middle Class: Populist Democracy and
the Question of Capitalism in Progressive Era Portland, Oregon.*

In addition, we are grateful to the following individuals: Alice Beck-
with, Ph.D.; Robert Bee, Ph.D.; Thomas Berger, Ph.D.; Mal Bochner;
Mark Borthwick, Ph.D.; Christine Brennan; Steve Broening; David
Brown, Ph.D.; Roger Buckley, Ph.D.; Tim and Jennifer Cohen; Liz
Connell; Alejandro Corbacho; Marius Deeb, Ph.D.; Paul Edwards;
Louis Galambos, Ph.D.; Norman Gauthier, Ph.D.; Louis Giannetti,
Ph.D.; Benjamin Ginsberg, Ph.D.; Domenic Grasso, Ph.D.; Joel B.
Grossman, Ph.D.; Cheryl Brown Henderson; Davis H. Howes III,
Ph.D.; George E. Killian; Hugh LaFollette, Ph.D.; Roger Launius; Jef-
frey Lefebvre, Ph.D.; Stuart Leslie, Ph.D.; Ellen Luchinsky; Elizabeth
Mahan, Ph.D.; Alice Mering; Luis Mocete; Alan Ogden; Bob Phillips,
Ph.D.; Peter Piot, Ph.D.; Louise Pistell; Gene Rasmussen; Tony Reid;
Leslie Rice; Chris Scaptura; Joe Schiesl; Stephen Schlesinger, Ph.D.;
Tim Sellers, Ph.D.; Elliot Sperling, Ph.D.; Ronald L. Taylor, Ph.D.;
David Timberman; Rudolph Tokes, Ph.D.; Tim Waples, Ph.D.; Sue
Whitmore; Nicholas Wolfson, Ph.D.; I. William Zartman, Ph.D.

ADDITIONAL READING

The reader may wish to consult the *National Geographic Index* for
related articles and books. The following sources may also be of interest: Frederick Lewis Allen, *Only Yesterday*; Stephen E. Ambrose,
Nixon: Ruin and Recovery; Terry H. Anderson, *The Movement and the
Sixties*; Roger Angell, *Five Seasons*; Michael Barone, *Our Country*;
John Morton Blum, *Years of Discord*; Raymond Bonner, *Waltzing With
a Dictator*; Tim Brooks and Marsh Earle, *The Complete Directory to
Prime Time Network TV Shows*; C. D. B. Bryan, *The National Geo-
graphic Society: 100 Years of Adventure and Discovery*; Peter N. Car-
roll, *It Seemed Like Nothing Happened at All*; Gorton Carruth,
American Facts and Dates; William H. Chafe, *The Unfinished Journey*;
Clifton Daniel, ed., *Chronicle of the 20th Century*; E. J. Dionne, Jr.,
Why Americans Hate Politics; Fred W. Friendly and Martha J. H.
Elliott, *The Constitution: That Delicate Balance*; G. S. P. Freeman-
Grenville, *Chronology of World History*; Sir Martin Gilbert, *A History
of the Twentieth Century, Volume One 1900-1933*; Lorraine Glennon,
ed., *Our Times: The Illustrated History of the 20th Century*; David Hal-
berstam, *The Fifties*; Edmund H. Harvey, Jr., ed., *Our Glorious Cen-
tury*; Alexander Hellemans and Bryan Bunch, *The Timetables of
Science*; Arnold R. Isaacs, *Without Honor*; A. H. Janson, *History of
Art*; Haynes Johnson, *Sleepwalking Through History*; Ephraim Katz,
The Film Encyclopedia; Burton I. Kaufman, *The Presidency of James
Earl Carter*; William Manchester, *The Glory and the Dream*; Tom
McGrath, *MTV: the Making of a Revolution*; Richard B. Morris and
Jeffrey B. Morris, eds., *Encyclopedia of American History*; Kirsten
Olsen, *Chronology of Women's History*; Michael E. Parrish, *Anxious
Decades*; Geoffrey Perrett, *America in the Twenties*; Ronald Reagan,
An American Life; Arthur M. Schlesinger, Jr, ed., *The Almanac of
American History*; Jane and Michael Stern, *The Encyclopedia of Bad
Taste*; Irwin Stambler, *The Encyclopedia of Pop, Rock, and Soul*;
James L. Stokesbury, *A Short History of World War I*; Michael Tam-
bini, *The Look of the 20th Century*; David Wallechinsky, ed., *The Peo-
ple's Almanac Presents the 20th Century*; T. H. Watkins, *The Great
Depression*; Bruce Wetterau, *The New York Public Library Book of
Chronologies*; Neville Williams, *Chronology of the Modern World*.